ANTHROPOLOGY
EXPLORED *Second Edition*

Edited by
Ruth Osterweis Selig,
Marilyn R. London,
and P. Ann Kaupp

Illustrated by
Robert L. Humphrey

With a foreword by
David W. McCurdy

SMITHSONIAN BOOKS

Washington

ANTHROPOLOGY
EXPLORED *Second Edition*

The Best of Smithsonian *AnthroNotes*

Copy editor: Susan Warga
Production editor: Robert A. Poarch
Designer: Kathleen Sims

Library of Congress Cataloging-in-Publication Data

Anthropology explored : the best of Smithsonian AnthroNotes.—2nd ed. / edited by Ruth Osterweis Selig, Marilyn R. London, and P. Ann Kaupp ; illustrated by Robert L. Humphrey ; with a foreword by David W. McCurdy.
   p.   cm.
   Includes bibliographical references and index.
   ISBN 1-58834-093-7 (alk. paper)
   1. Anthropology. I. Osterweis Selig, Ruth. II. London, Marilyn R. III. Kaupp, P. Ann. IV. Anthro notes.
   GN31.2.A57 2004
   301'.071—dc21
                                                2003045640

British Library Cataloguing-in-Publication Data available

Manufactured in the United States of America

10 09 08 07 06 05 04   5 4 3 2 1

∞ The paper used in this publication meets the minimum requirements of the American National Standard for Information Sciences—Permanence of Paper for Printed Library Materials ANSI Z39.48-1984.

Maps for chapters 13, 16, 26, and 32 drawn by Marcia Bakry. Chapter 32, figure 2 drawing by Marcia Bakry; figures 3–6 drawings adapted by Marcia Bakry.

All chapters included from the first edition of *Anthropology Explored*, some with new titles, are newly revised or have new update sections in this second edition. The chapters in this edition are based on the following issues of *AnthroNotes: The National Museum of Natural History Publication for Teachers* (editors: Alison S. Brooks, P. Ann Kaupp, JoAnne Lanouette, Ruth O. Selig; guest editor, Marilyn R. London, 1994–97; illustrator, Robert L. Humphrey). **Bold entries indicate chapters entirely new to the second edition.**

1. vol. 8, no. 3, 1986
2. vol. 19, no. 3, 1997
3. vol. 22, no. 1, 1999
4. vol. 24, no. 1, 2003
5. vol. 14, no. 3, 1992
6. vol. 17, no. 3, 1995
7. vol. 11, no. 2, 1989
8. vol. 18, no. 3, 1996
9. vol. 12, no. 1, 1990
10. vol. 20, no. 1, 1998
11. vol. 18, no. 1, 1996
12. vol. 15, no. 3, 1993

13. vol. 16, no. 2, 1994
14. vol. 14, no. 1, 1992
15. vol. 9, no. 3, 1987
16. vol. 22, no. 1, 2000
17. vol. 14, no. 2, 1992
18. vol. 5, no. 1, 1983
19. vol. 12, no. 3, 1990
20. vol. 22, no. 3, 2001
21. vol. 15, no. 2, 1993
22. vol. 19, no. 1, 1997
23. vol. 12, no. 2, 1990
24. vol. 20, no. 2, 1998

25. vol. 6, no. 1, 1984
26. vol. 19 no. 2, 1997
27. vol. 7, no. 3, 1985
28. vol. 18, no. 3, 1996
29. vol. 23, no. 1, 2002
30. vol. 23, no. 2, 2002
31. vol. 12, no. 1, 1990
32. vol. 22, no. 2, 2001
33. vol. 10, no. 2, 1988
34. vol. 17, nos. 1–2, 1995
35. vol. 23, no. 2, 2002
36. vol. 13, no. 3, 1991

To the memory of Robert L. Humphrey

"As an anthropologist, I particularly enjoy drawing for AnthroNotes *because
I am able to work as an artist and an anthropologist simultaneously."*

CONTENTS

EXAMINING OUR ARCHAEOLOGICAL PAST

EXPLORING OUR MANY CULTURES

FOREWORD

David W. McCurdy

nthropology provides a unique and powerful way to look at the
human experience. Unlike other social scientists, such as psychologists
or sociologists, economists or political scientists, anthropologists use
the broadest possible framework to study human physical and cultural development and variation. The field is holistic and comprehensive and its subdisciplines interdependent—as is reflected in many of this volume's essays,
which defy easy classification into one subfield or another and, therefore,
could easily be placed in more than one of the book's three major sections.

Culture is the central concept of anthropology; not surprisingly, culture
is explored throughout this volume. Culture is the knowledge that humans
acquire and share with other people and use to interpret experience and to
generate behavior. It is the patterns, rules, and customs of acting, thinking,
feeling, and communicating. We only come to understand our common capacity for culture as we see it expressed with unique identity in a specific culture. While all cultures attempt to satisfy basic human needs, cultures express
differences in such areas as food, shelter, and clothing; language; subsistence;
religion and world view; political organization; technology; kinship; and gender relationships.

The anthropological perspective infusing the contributions to this volume
reveals that our own culture is one of many created by the human species.
Anthropology's comparative approach helps us understand other cultures
and other peoples within our own community, as well as ourselves. It is in
this context that the chapters in this volume speak forcefully, illuminating,
first, our primate ancestry, evolutionary development, and physical variation;

second, the emergence of various ancient societies, documented by archaeologists using increasingly sophisticated methodologies, technology, and dating techniques; and, third, the diversity of human languages and cultures
around the globe.

ANTHRONOTES

For twenty-five years the Smithsonian Institution's Department of Anthropology has published *AnthroNotes,* a publication dedicated to bringing anthropology—its subject matter, concepts, and theory—to as broad an audience as possible. As past president of the General Anthropology Division of
the American Anthropological Association and coeditor of the division's publication, *General Anthropology,* I have highly recommended *AnthroNotes*
through the years. I am pleased to see this revised, expanded edition of *Anthropology Explored,* which brings even more *AnthroNotes* selections to a
wide audience of students, teachers, anthropologists, and members of the
general public.

The book spans the entire field of anthropology and offers an alternative
or supplement to the traditional introductory textbook. Its chapters, all based
on material from *AnthroNotes,* provide concise and excellent syntheses of
topics of broad interest. Almost all include updates detailing research developments since the selections first appeared in *AnthroNotes* and since the first
edition of this volume appeared. These updates inform the reader of current
discoveries and also shed light on the process of research and discovery itself. The book has an excellent introduction, which summarizes the selections and highlights the major questions, concepts, methodologies, and contemporary relevance of the field. This edition also includes brief chapter
abstracts, helpful to general readers as well as teachers and students.

AnthroNotes editors believe that research-based articles convey their information best through nontechnical language, and that even the most sophisticated concepts can be communicated through clear analysis and concise narrative. The authors include several Smithsonian scholars as well as
other distinguished specialists in the field. The late Robert L. Humphrey,
artist and anthropologist from George Washington University's Department
of Anthropology, provided the illustrations, each one inspired by a specific
chapter.

Anthropology Explored: The Best of Smithsonian AnthroNotes will take
you into the world of anthropology and anthropologists. The chapters illuminate not only the world around you but also much about yourself as a
member of the human family. I invite you to enjoy this anthropological journey through time and space.

PREFACE

Ruth Osterweis Selig

We live in a rapidly changing society, in a time of global transformation, clashing cultures, and increasing cultural diversity. Anthropology provides us with concepts, perspectives, and a general framework for understanding ourselves and others in this changing world of the twenty-first century.

This collection of case studies traces the emergence of humans through millions of years, describes archaeologists' understanding of early and more recent settlements, and explores the diversity of cultures around the globe. The reader will discover not only societies undergoing transformation today but also recent changes in anthropologists' methods and perspectives. Individual chapters include updates that summarize the latest discoveries in the subjects discussed, while the original cartoon illustrations by the late artist and anthropologist Robert L. Humphrey provide additional insights and amusing commentary.

The essays are culled from our award-winning Smithsonian publication, *AnthroNotes*. Since 1979 the Smithsonian Institution's Department of Anthropology has published *AnthroNotes* as a major vehicle of public outreach, bringing readers the latest in anthropological and archaeological research, focusing on cutting-edge topics presented in depth but in a lively, engaging, and accessible style. Dedicated to the wider dissemination of new discoveries in anthropology, *AnthroNotes* brings the best of the field to a broad audience.

ORGANIZATION

Anthropology Explored consists of three main sections. "Investigating Our Origins and Variation" focuses on primates, human origins, and human variation; "Examining Our Archaeological Past" highlights archaeologists' understanding of the past in the Old and New Worlds; and "Exploring Our Many Cultures" includes case studies of many different societies in many different countries, including the United States.

Essays in each of the three major sections include both an introductory abstract and references for further reading. Almost every chapter except those prepared within the last two years includes an update, specifically written for the second edition. These updates, designed to demonstrate the process by which new knowledge accumulates through research and discovery, emphasize new technologies, current events (such as the U.S. 2000 Census), and new perspectives, illuminating not only the chapter's topic but also changes in anthropology as a discipline. In the four chapters that focus on the contributions of a particular anthropologist (Selig's chapters on Potts, Stanford, and Smith; Kaupp's chapter on Shuy), the scholar whose work is profiled provides the update. Along with the new abstracts and references for further reading, these updates make this volume a clear demonstration that in science knowledge can only be the best information we have at any one time. Essay authors are leading specialists in their fields, and the volume concludes with short biographies of these distinguished contributors.

WHAT'S NEW IN THE SECOND EDITION?

Thirteen new chapters; twenty-three new essay updates

Thirty-six new abstracts; thirty-six chapters have new suggestions for further reading

New topical essays on forensic anthropology, refugees, repatriation, race, cultural relativism and universal human rights, Vikings, human aggression, and body art

Emphasis on new discoveries and new technologies; incorporation of DNA studies and the data from the U.S. 2000 Census

More chapters on cultural anthropology; additional societies outside the Americas; more maps

Many new features strengthen this second edition of *Anthropology Explored,* including twenty-three update sections, an expanded table of contents, abstracts, and new recommendations for further reading for all chapters. There are thirteen completely new chapters. Two on human evolution, one on human aggression, and another on race are included in the first section. New archaeology chapters on the Vikings and the ancient Maya are included in the second section. The third section contains new cultural chapters on issues of current concern such as refugees, cultural relativism and universal human rights, linguistic survival, and repatriation.

The book's introduction has been expanded to provide a discussion of basic concepts, issues, and methodologies in anthropology. It also includes definitions of anthropology's five subfields (physical, archaeology, cultural, linguistics, and applied). After an initial general discussion, the introduction divides into three parts, each focusing on the essays from one of the volume's three sections. The introduction can be read all at once, but it also can be read in these three parts. As a whole, the introduction highlights the major concepts and methods used in physical anthropology, archaeology, and cultural anthropology (including linguistics and applied anthropology) and provides summaries of various chapters, including major questions raised and answered.

The introduction makes clear that anthropology is best understood as both a science and one of the humanities, and that its holistic framework gives it a unique perspective through which one can celebrate humanity's diversity and commonality.

ACKNOWLEDGMENTS FOR THE SECOND EDITION

Since the first edition was published, two undergraduate interns, Alyssa Fisher and Natalie How, worked diligently during the summer of 2002 checking bibliographic references and preparing analyses of each chapter. Their work and the insightful questions they prepared for each essay are reflected in the volume, particularly in the new abstracts and references for further reading.

In the fall of 2002 a group of educators provided guidance on ways to make this second edition more useful for teachers as well as the general public. Although we were not able to incorporate all their suggestions, several new aspects of this edition reflect their advice. An Instructor's Guide to the second edition, written by Mount Holyoke College senior Anna Peterson and Ruth O. Selig, owes much to this talented group, including Mary Boteler, John Campbell, Gloria Chernay, Jessie Diffley, Mary Fran Doyle, and David Whitacre.

We also want to thank Scot Mahler, acquisitions editor for Smithsonian Books, who encouraged the project and made helpful suggestions, as well as Emily Sollie, Robert A. Poarch, and Janice Wheeler, also from Smithsonian

Books. We also thank our supervisors, particularly William Fitzhugh, Douglas Erwin, Cristián Samper K., and the late Carolyn L. Rose, for their support of this project and the time we devoted to it.

AnthroNotes began as a newsletter for graduates of the National Science Foundation–funded George Washington University/Smithsonian Institution Anthropology for Teachers Program. The editorial team of *AnthroNotes* (P. Ann Kaupp, Ruth O. Selig, Alison S. Brooks, and JoAnne Lanouette) was the original staff of that program and represents over fifty years of teaching, from middle school through graduate school, including workshops and courses for teachers. The late artist and anthropologist Robert L. Humphrey provided cartoon illustrations for our teacher training brochures and continued illustrating *AnthroNotes* until his untimely death in late 2002. Marilyn R. London was an *AnthroNotes* editor from 1994 to 1997 and served as one of the editors for the first and second editions of *Anthropology Explored*. Today, more than nine thousand people receive *AnthroNotes*, with an increasing number in this country and abroad being general readers interested in anthropology, archaeology, and museums. To our readers, we say a grateful thank you.

FOR CLASSROOM USE

To obtain an examination copy of this volume, write to Smithsonian Books, Marketing Department, Smithsonian Institution, PO Box 37012, MRC 950, Washington, D.C. 20013-7012. Note the course name, number, frequency, and projected enrollment. The Press will send an examination copy along with an invoice payable within sixty days. The invoice will be cancelled if the book is adopted. Otherwise the copy may be returned in saleable condition or purchased at a 20% discount.

This second edition of *Anthropology Explored* has an Instructor's Guide, which contains chapter summaries, discussion and examination questions, a glossary, and further teaching resources. This guide is available from the Anthropology Outreach Office, as are other materials relevant to the classroom, such as the Teacher's Packet in Anthropology. Write to: Anthropology Outreach Office, Smithsonian Institution, PO Box 37012, NHB MRC 112, Washington, D.C. 20013-7012; anthroutreach@nmnh.si.edu.

THE ART OF ANTHROPOLOGY

A Note from the Artist

Robert L. Humphrey

Why use cartoons to illustrate serious articles in an anthropological publication?

One of the most important attributes that differentiates our species from the rest of the animal kingdom is our ability to laugh, and even more important, to laugh at ourselves. The enormous variety of human behaviors observed and recorded by anthropologists should teach us, if nothing else, the infinite capacity for human folly. The ability to make and understand cartoons represents some of the most complex symbolic thought, expression, and self-reflection of which we humans are capable.

Admittedly, it is sometimes difficult to find the humor in some of the articles in *AnthroNotes*. Not all cartoons are meant to be funny, but they *are* intended to combine visual elements in such a way as to startle—to capture our attention and focus it momentarily on a new idea, or on a familiar idea seen from a new perspective. By synthesizing multiple elements into a single focus, cartoon art causes us to see an event or phenomenon through new eyes, making us laugh, or even think!

The first cartoons appeared on the walls of Upper Paleolithic caves in France and Spain more than thirty thousand years ago, and the artists who created those images worked much as cartoonists do today. A good cartoon simplifies, distills, and refines an event until it instantly communicates a moment in time that the artist has singled out as being different from the preceding moment or the next one. Immediacy is the essence of a successful cartoon.

Simplicity underlies all cartoons, but the process of creating that simplicity is highly complex. First comes the development of a single idea through its

visual representation in the mind; only then can drawing begin. I often make twenty or thirty sketches of the same face just to perfect an expression, and the caption is so critical to the timing of the humor that it may take days and multiple revisions to complete. Researching the setting, costumes, and props; eliminating every detail not absolutely necessary to the final impression; developing the expressions and words—these are all hidden from the viewer, who may think the cartoon was completed in a moment's time. If the cartoon is successful, the hard work of the cartoonist should be completely concealed from the viewer.

As an anthropologist, I particularly enjoy drawing for *AnthroNotes* because I am able to work as an artist and an anthropologist simultaneously. Every drawing is an ethnography or archaeological site of its own—a specific time and place, a complete environment peopled by thinking, behaving, interactive beings. Further, I suspect there is no better guide to the morality, politics, religions, and social issues—in short, the culture—of our times than our cartoons. Each idea in a good cartoon may be every bit as complex as the theoretical research on which a paper for an academic journal is based and may take just as long to emerge. In fact, writing an academic paper bears similarities to cartooning: the activity consists of focusing on a single idea worth exploring in detail and then developing the right language, verbal or visual, to express it.

As an anthropologist, I realize it is important to symbolize without stereotyping, to lampoon a serious topic without being tasteless, since the cartoonist's goal is to communicate ideas, not just to amuse the reader. The most amazing part of this experience is what others read into my cartoons; they find humor in things I did not anticipate or, worse, they miss what I meant to be most obvious. Unlike my academic papers, my cartoons often do distort ordinary perceptions by violating some kind of cliché and looking at something familiar in an off-kilter way. To do this while remaining sensitive to an extraordinarily eclectic and critical readership can be quite a challenge.

Nevertheless, cartooning is well worth the challenge. If we can learn to laugh at ourselves, it becomes very easy to see through racism, sexism, fundamentalism, and all the other nasty isms that our species is too often prey to. One of the favorite quotations of cartoonists is a comment on the cartoons of Thomas Nast by the corrupt political leader of old Manhattan, Boss Tweed: "Stop them Damn pictures," Tweed said. "I don't care so much what they write about me . . . my constituents can't read—but damn it, they can see pictures!"

INTRODUCTION

Human Origins, Diversity, and Cultures

Ruth Osterweis Selig

Who are we and where did we come from?

How and where did the human species develop over time?

How can we best explain and understand human diversity?

Creation stories, widespread throughout human societies, attest to the universal human passion for understanding ourselves and the world around us. Where did we come from and where are we going, as individuals, as a society, as a species that developed on earth? How did the incredible variety of human beings—differing physically, culturally, linguistically—develop through time? How have human societies adapted to a wide range of changing environments, cultural contacts, and technological innovations?

The search for the answers to these fundamental questions lies at the heart of the field of study called anthropology. *Anthropology* means "the study of people." Anthropologists study the physical and cultural development of people, and their diversity. The chapters in this volume present specific case studies that take you alongside anthropologists as they investigate the origins, nature, and cultures of humankind. Although each chapter focuses on a specific topic, issue, or subject, the volume as a whole provides a view of the entire field of anthropology, a field of increasing relevance to the modern world.

Human diversity, whether physical, cultural, or political, is among the most pressing issues in our shrinking world. Anthropology seeks to explain

1

that diversity—its origins, manifestations, and implications. Anthropology provides an important lens for examining the dynamic complexity, diverse cultures, and global changes in our world today.

THE ANTHROPOLOGICAL PERSPECTIVE

As David McCurdy explains in his foreword, anthropology looks at peoples and cultures from a broad perspective, seeking to understand the nature and development of human beings—through all human history and in all cultures around the globe. Whether specialized in biological, cultural, or applied anthropology, linguistics, or archaeology, most anthropologists have a deep and abiding interest in understanding their fellow human beings—their past, present, and future, their physical development and variation, and their diverse cultures around the globe.

All human beings face a common set of problems: obtaining food, shelter, and clothing; maintaining social order; securing good health; reproducing themselves and their societies; and understanding their place in the world, including outsiders and the supernatural. The dilemmas and opportunities created by these issues constitute our common human condition. Human culture is the principal means through which communities solve these challenges, shaping the expression of their identity in unique ways adapted to their specific environments.

Sometimes when we come into contact with practices and beliefs different from our own, we express amusement or even ridicule, condescension and even disgust. When we take an attitude of superiority to the practices or beliefs of other cultures, we are being ethnocentric because we are judging others' cultural behaviors or beliefs by our own. Anthropologists long have held that our own culture can best be viewed as one of many, neither superior nor inferior to others. This comparative approach helps us understand other cultures and other peoples within our own community, but it also helps us see ourselves with new perspective and understanding. By coming to understand other people from their own cultural perspective, we can better compare our culture to others, not by placing one above another but by placing all within the broad range of human experience.

This anthropological perspective, called cultural relativism, has undergone examination and revision in recent years, particularly in the light of universal human rights and the violation of those rights [see Fluehr-Lobban, "Cultural Relativism and Universal Human Rights," in this volume]. Nonetheless, the concept of cultural relativism remains at the heart of the anthropological enterprise and of the broad perspective the subject brings to the study of cultures around the world (Selig 1993:4, 15–16).

ANTHROPOLOGY EXPLORED

This volume consists of three main sections. The first, "Investigating Our Origins and Variation," focuses on primates, human origins, and human variation. This section's essays address a series of questions: Who are we and where did we come from? How did our ancestors change and develop through millions of years? Why do we come in so many different shapes, sizes, and colors? How do scientists study our origins and our diversity? The second section, "Examining Our Archaeological Past," highlights archaeologists' understanding of the past, in both the Old and New Worlds. Chapters in this section answer such questions as: What do we know about the earliest humans? How do we learn about our ancient past? How does archaeology differ from history? How is archaeology relevant today? The third section, "Exploring Our Many Cultures," focuses on cultural diversity and how anthropologists study varied societies in many different countries, including the United States. The authors address such questions as: Why do we live in such diverse cultures? How have cultures changed over time? How do anthropologists study other cultures? How does culture help us adapt and survive?

The essays in this volume provide an introduction to the subject matter and methodologies of the entire field of anthropology, including physical anthropology, cultural anthropology, archaeology, applied anthropology, and linguistics. These five subfields of anthropology can be defined as follows:

Physical anthropology, sometimes called biological anthropology, is the subfield specializing in human variation in time and space, including evolution and genetics.

Cultural anthropology is the subfield emphasizing the study of cultures, including the similarities and differences between societies.

Archaeology is the subfield that studies culture history through the systematic examination of cultural and material remains.

Anthropological linguistics is the subfield that studies language forms across time and space, and their relation to culture and social behaviors.

Applied anthropology is the subfield that uses anthropological knowledge, theory, perspectives, and methods to address contemporary social or cultural problems.

SECTION 1: INVESTIGATING OUR ORIGINS AND VARIATION

Few of us ever stop to think about the most fundamental questions regarding the human species: Who are we and where did we come from? Over millions of years, how did our earliest ancestors change? Why are we such a diverse species? In what ways are we truly different from one another? What methods do scientists use to answer these puzzling questions?

The anthropologists who seek answers to these questions are called physical or biological anthropologists. Like all biologists, they have trained for many years to carry out research on the physical characteristics of animal organisms, past and present, and the interaction of those organisms with their environment. In this case, the animal species under examination is *Homo sapiens*. Some physical anthropologists study fossil remains to understand human evolution. Others study our closest cousins in nature, the primates, and how they live in their natural habitats—their group size, feeding habits, care of infants, social organization, tool use, and communication skills. Still other physical anthropologists study skeletal differences, disease patterns, blood types, and relationships to various environments.

Like other scientific disciplines, physical anthropology has undergone revolutionary changes in recent years. New technologies developed in molecular biology are now used to explore the DNA structure of once living tissue, and other advanced technologies—scanning electron microscopes, high-speed computers, and sophisticated X-ray machines—have expanded our knowledge immeasurably. Such innovations have also aided forensic anthropologists, who are trained to assist medico-legal agencies—medical examiners, police, and the FBI—in the identification of human remains. Such specialists use their training in anatomy, forensic pathology, dentistry, and radiology to ascertain biological age at death, time elapsed since death, sex, race, stature, and method of death.

The first six chapters in this section focus on primates and human evolution. This is followed by chapter 7, "Stories Bones Tell," by physical anthropologist Kathleen Gordon, which provides an excellent overview of the work of physical and forensic anthropologists, detailing not only the range of their work but also the variety of fascinating stories and information they have uncovered. Whether discussing diet, disease, demography, the Japanese Ainu, or African American history, Gordon demonstrates that "the study of modern, historic, and prehistoric skeletons has made it possible for anthropologists to contribute an enormous and diverse array of information about human behavior and morphology, past and present." In her 2003 update Gordon details the exciting discovery that scientists can extract DNA not only from soft tissue but also from ancient bone, demonstrating the enormous impact that molecular biology, genetics, and DNA studies have had on physical anthropology in recent years.

In chapter 1 Gordon introduces the reader to the field of primatology and the story of humans teaching primates to communicate through human language, using visual symbols. In the process of discovering that speech and language are not synonymous (apes seem utterly incapable of the first but quite capable of rudimentary forms of the second), researchers have learned a great deal not only about chimpanzees' capacity for understanding and communicating through symbolic language but also about our possible early preadaptation to a cultural way of life.

Since the 1960s, when Louis Leakey first urged Jane Goodall to study chimpanzees in Africa, primatologists have undertaken long-term studies of chimpanzees, gorillas, and orangutans in their natural habitats, detailing their social relationships, tool use, parental behavior, and intergroup rivalries. Primatologist Robert Sussman looks at some of this research in the light of some scholars' assertions regarding ape and human tendencies toward conflict and violence. Sussman's chapter asks whether humans are inherently violent, but its author also investigates other fascinating questions, such as how genetics and learning help explain human behavior, the role aggression plays in chimpanzee and human society, and whether humans and chimpanzees share certain fixed behaviors.

The search for understanding human origins has long fascinated students and the general public. Studying anthropology in the ninth grade, Rick Potts determined to become a paleoanthropologist and devote his life to understanding human evolution. Potts' story is one of dedication and determination, reflected today in his directing the Smithsonian's Human Origins Program with its large-scale National Science Foundation-funded field expeditions to both Africa and China. Chapter 3, about Potts' career (the original article written by Selig), includes a new update (written by Potts) describing this recent research in Africa and China. This is followed by a chapter Potts coauthored with Alison Brooks, detailing the most recent information scientists have discovered about the earliest period of human evolution, 7 million to 1 million years ago. The more recent period of human evolution, just the last 200,000 years, is detailed in chapter 5, by Brooks, "The Emergence of Modern Humans," which has been completely revised for the second edition of *Anthropology Explored*.

One of the most difficult challenges for scientists is to understand the physical characteristics of our earliest ancestors; even more challenging is drawing inferences about early human behavior. Such inferences are subject to interpretation, not only by scientists but also by artists whose representations shape how we view our early ancestors. In chapter 6, "The Real Flintstones: Artists' Depictions of Human Ancestors," archaeologist Diane Gifford-Gonzalez offers an analysis of depictions of early humans in popular books, describing some misleading and speculative reconstructions. This chapter argues for closer collaboration between scientists and artists to create images for museums and popular books that will accurately reflect our ancestors.

Chapter 8 discusses a topic of abiding interest to all physical anthropologists: disease. Taking a broad synthetic view, the chapter's authors detail three epidemiological revolutions in human history. The first occurred with the emergence of agriculture and urban centers, and the second with the industrial revolution and modern technology; the third, which is under way today, is marked by the growing resistance to antibiotics among human populations. As the authors explain, "The emergence of infectious disease has been one of the most interesting evolutionary stories of the last few decades and has captured the interest of scientists, the general public, and the media."

The essay on disease is one of several chapters that could have been placed in any one of the volume's three sections, underscoring the point made about the interdependency of anthropology's subfields by David McCurdy in his foreword. Chapter 9, "The Moche: An Ancient Peruvian People," also could have been placed in any one of the book's three sections. Its author, John Verano, is a physical anthropologist who has been reconstructing Moche health, disease, and demography by analyzing the skeletal remains from Moche sites in Peru, excavated by the Peruvian archaeologist Walter Alva. Numbering as many as fifty thousand people, the little-known Moche were an agricultural people living along the northern coast of Peru about twelve hundred years before the more famous Inca. Verano's 2003 update provides a fascinating look at the darker side of the Moche: the practice of ritual human sacrifice.

"American's MIAs: Forensic Anthropology in Action" describes the work to recover, repatriate, and establish definite identifications for American service members (POWs/MIAs) lost in past wars. The authors, forensic scientists Robert Mann and Thomas Holland, describe the difficult work of finding, recovering, and identifying American POWs/MIAs by the only laboratory of its kind—the U.S. Army Central Identification Laboratory, Hawai'i (CILHI).

The final two chapters of this section focus on race, a topic of enduring interest to anthropologists and the general public alike. The first article, authored by former *Washington Post* science writer Boyce Rensberger, offers a clear discussion of race, concluding that "the great lesson of anthropology, biology, and genetics is that all people are the same in all essentials but are highly diverse in a few things." The article is informed by recent discussions among physical anthropologists, as is the final chapter, "Race and Ethnicity," written by two physical anthropologists, Alison Brooks and Fatimah Jackson, and cultural anthropologist Roy Richard Grinker. Using new data from the 2000 census, Brooks revised and updated the chapter for this volume, bringing to bear recent comparative DNA studies that today shed light on relationships between populations. The chapter traces the long history of racial classification, as well as the increasing use of ethnicity to define identity. Like Rensberger's chapter, "Race and Ethnicity" raises serious doubts about the possibility of using clear biological characteristics to classify peoples into separate races.

As a unit, section 1 traces the emergence of the human species through millions of years, detailing current methods and techniques that scientists use to study our origins and variability. Except for chapter 6, all the contributions either have 2003 update sections, are completely revised for this second edition, or were written since the first edition appeared (see copyright page for details). Most importantly, all the chapters tell fascinating stories, are consistently well written, and together help us understand the mysteries of our past evolution and our present variation.

SECTION 2: EXAMINING OUR ARCHAEOLOGICAL PAST

Despite the glamour of archaeology in the popular press as well as in films such as *Raiders of the Lost Ark,* it is because of the scientific methods of archaeology that we know so much about human history, particularly before we had written records. It is, after all, only in the last 5,000 years that we have had written records, but our human ancestry began more than 4 million years ago! We are indeed indebted to archaeology.

The chapters in the second section reflect this debt and convey much of the richness and excitement of the field. Because of the importance of dating and chronology in archaeology, the essays are arranged in rough chronological order. Several chapters consider the question of origins: of the Vikings, the earliest Americans, agriculture in the New World, the earliest South Americans, the Maya, and the Eskimo/Inuit culture. The discussions of African American archaeology and ethnoarchaeology bring a contemporary view to the question of how archaeologists help us understand the past through each new generation's perspectives.

Chapters 13 and 14, by Melinda Zeder and Mark Cohen, respectively, focus on the earliest evidence of domestication and its consequences for the human species. The development of agriculture and animal domestication may be the most significant turning point in human history, eventually leading to human specialists and urban centers. Zeder's chapter demonstrates the enormous changes that new technologies and DNA analysis have brought to archaeological analysis and the painstaking work involved in such investigations. Cohen's chapter presents a somewhat controversial hypothesis: that human nutrition has declined throughout human history while the variety and types of diseases have increased. His update includes a discussion of the debate his original ideas engendered, and how he has responded to his critics.

Chapter 15 turns to the Old World and to Africa. John Fisher details his ethnoarchaeological research among the Efe peoples living in the Ituri Forest in the Democratic Republic of the Congo. He compares his findings with similar ethnoarchaeological research among the Ju/'hoansi (!Kung or San peoples) of the Kalahari desert in Botswana. Ethnoarchaeology combines the study of modern-day hunters and gatherers with traditional archaeology of ancient sites, and the author explains how this research can help fill in the inevitable gaps in the archaeological record.

The !Kung, described in the volume's final chapter on aging, are a people made famous among anthropologists by Elizabeth Marshall Thomas' publication *The Harmless People* and the film *The Hunters,* made by her brother John Marshall. Fisher was part of the Ituri Project, codirected by Irven De-Vore, who also ran the Harvard Kalahari study of the !Kung. Fisher worked in the Democratic Republic of the Congo, about 100 kilometers from where Colin Turnbull studied the Efe, as detailed in his book *The Forest People.* These two hunting-gathering peoples (the Efe and the !Kung), studied in great detail during the 1960s, have undergone much change in recent decades, change described in the update sections of Fisher's chapter on the Efe and Brooks and Draper's final chapter on aging.

Many of the archaeology essays in the second section deal with the Americas, since that is where American archaeology had its beginnings and was nourished for over 150 years. In "The Vikings: Old Views and New Findings," Arctic specialist William Fitzhugh reviews new archaeological and historical evidence that is changing our view of these early seamen, craftsmen, tradesmen, and farmers. His essay also explains how popular misconceptions of the "barbarous Vikings" have perpetuated stereotypes and affected our views of history. In chapter 17, "Who Got to America First? Fact and Fiction," Stephen Williams, emeritus professor, Harvard University, takes on one of the more contentious issues in his field, detailing the evidence and lack of evidence for the earliest contacts with the Americas, some believed to be even before the Vikings. I leave it to our readers to find out Williams' conclusions.

Evidence of the earliest inhabitants of North and South America continues to be of great interest for New World archaeologists. Two of the country's leading specialists in the field, Dennis Stanford for North America and Tom Dillehay for South America, report on their investigations in chapters 18 and 19. In chapter 18, Selig tells the story of one man's lifetime search to answer the questions of when, where, and how the first humans arrived in the Americas. The subject of her story, Dennis Stanford, writes the chapter's update section, detailing his latest theory that waves of migrating peoples came to the New World, including some in boats from across the Atlantic Ocean. Tom Dillehay's chapter and recent update describe his work at Monte Verde, a 12,500-year-old site in southern Chile. Like Stanford, Dillehay believes that people ancestral to Clovis may have lived in what is today Chile, as far back as 15,000 to 18,000 years ago. The section's next chapter, "Who Were the Ancient Maya?" by leading specialist Jeremy Sabloff, reveals how new research is illuminating the development and accomplishments of the Maya over a 2,000-year period and how these new insights are changing traditional views of Maya history.

My discussion in chapter 21 moves north again and details the dramatic story of Bruce D. Smith's groundbreaking research to document the eastern United States as an independent center of the discovery of agriculture. Smith's update details recent refinements in this research area since my essay first appeared. Moving still farther north, chapter 22, by William W. Fitzhugh, focuses on the origins and development of Eskimo culture, and more generally on new circumpolar perspectives. Fitzhugh's update focuses on global warming, demonstrating how research in the Arctic helps tell the story of environmental change while also developing powerful new tools for investigating the past and predicting the future.

Chapter 23, the last one in the archaeology section, looks at a subject of increasing interest to historians and anthropologists: the daily lives of enslaved African Americans, as reflected in their material remains. A relatively new field of study when Theresa Singleton first wrote this essay, her 2003 update details significant developments in both research directions and theoretical frameworks that have occurred since the 1990s.

Although the general public often associates archaeology with romantic images of fieldwork, the search for hidden treasures, and the recovery of lost civilizations, section 2 demonstrates the realities of archaeology as a subfield of anthropology, with rigorous field study, painstaking laboratory analysis, and careful scholarship. The result of all this effort is the unfolding of an ever more complex story of human cultural development through time.

SECTION 3: EXPLORING OUR MANY CULTURES

Many chapters in the first two sections reflect broad synthetic approaches to specific topics in physical anthropology and archaeology. The chapters make clear that physical anthropologists and archaeologists use methods resembling those of natural scientists. The methods of cultural or social anthropology are different, and set anthropology as a discipline apart from all others. It is these same methods that make the chapters in section 3 quite different in approach and topic from sections 1 and 2. Cultural anthropologists, although interested in broad questions of adaptation and cross-cultural comparisons, often write about specific cultures at specific times and places, concentrating on one or two aspects of a society.

The ways that cultural anthropologists study other societies is designed to help them understand specific cultures and to understand human behavior within a cultural context. There are four major methods used by cultural anthropologists reflected in section 3 (Selig 1993). The first is *participant observation,* a method referring to an anthropologist living among the people being studied, participating as an "insider" in the culture, observing and learning to behave appropriately, using the language, knowledge, and perspective of the culture. The second method is *fieldwork using informants and collaborators,* a method referring to the close relationships an anthropologist often forms with key members of a society, depending on them to give information about and entry into the society. In the early days of anthropology, fieldwork occurred mostly in remote areas of the world, among small-scale societies whose language and cultures were little known to the Western world. Today anthropologists are as likely to conduct fieldwork in an American urban setting, a British university, an African port city, or an Asian factory. In these settings, key informants still play a role in the fieldwork site.

The third method, *ethnohistorical research,* is conducted in libraries and archives, town and tribal record depositories, or wherever relevant documentary evidence can be found. Such research enables anthropologists to add a time dimension to their research, tracing back in time the development of particular societies. The final method or approach, *cross-cultural comparison,* is central to anthropology's comparative approach. The study of cultures other than our own not only helps us understand others in our communities and the world but also helps us see ourselves in a new light. For example, when the term *family* occurs in an anthropology textbook, its definition reflects all the familylike groups in the world, including nuclear, single-parent, and extended families in the United States; extended families and polygamous families in Asia and Africa; and female-headed families in the Caribbean. Hence the term *family* is based on the broadest possible comparison of human living and kinship arrangements (Selig 1993:23).

Anthropologists are keenly aware today that it is difficult to truly understand another culture, and that their own culture will necessarily influence their perceptions of other people. Furthermore, indigenous peoples throughout the world have made it clear that any representation they consider valid must come, at least in part, from people raised in the culture itself. Representation has become a major issue for anthropologists in the twenty-first century and is reflected in several of the chapters in the third section.

The section begins with chapter 24, highlighting cultural relativism, a core concept in anthropology, and the controversy it can engender in the light of universal human rights violations, particularly under totalitarian regimes. Carolyn Fluehr-Lobban's article defines the issues, details illustrative cases using her own fieldwork, and suggests how anthropologists might be helpful in societies that sanction abuse in various forms, but particularly as it affects women. An emphasis on female rights and power also is reflected in the next chapter, which describes changing women's roles in a traditional highland Peruvian society that Catherine Allen visited in 1975, 1995, and 2000. The dual organization of men and women and the changes taking place in gender roles and relationships continue to raise the central question of the chapter: How can women be so influential and powerful if they are almost invisible in the political arena?

The next two chapters (26 and 27) focus on ethnohistory, a methodology that combines fieldwork with the study of written records, in this case the ethnohistory of northern Mexico and Plains Indian cultures. Changes affecting these societies as well as cultural anthropology as a discipline will become evident to readers. These chapters are followed by a bit of Smithsonian Institution history, offered within the context of collaboration with Native Americans. JoAllyn Archambault and William Sturtevant's "Native Americans and Smithsonian Research" also reflects the Institution's long involvement with anthropology, which emerged largely within a Smithsonian context in the nineteenth century, well before there were any university departments devoted to the field.

The enormous variety of human societies and cultures stands out clearly in these chapters, which will take readers around the globe to Sonqo, a Quechua-speaking community in the highlands of southern Peru (chapter 25); Native American communities in Wyoming, Montana, and Oklahoma, (chapter 27); and Chiapas, Mexico (chapter 31), where projects in linguistic survival bring anthropologists and native speakers together to work in new and innovative ways. From the New World, readers can spread across the continents of the Old World, traveling along the Silk Road with Richard Kurin (chapter 29), who details the history and cultural traditions of this ancient complex of trade routes. In section 3, one also travels to areas of global conflict, for example, in the Middle East and Africa, to places of great tragedy where refugees present one of the world's most pressing ethical dilemmas today. Anthropologist Stephen Lubkemann details how anthropologists are contributing to our understanding of the causes and effects of massive forced displacement of huge numbers of people to escape war, persecution, and natural disasters (chapter 30), while Carolyn Fluehr-Lobban, in her article on universal human rights (chapter 24), confronts some of the most difficult issues facing anthropologists.

Section 3 is filled with fascinating anthropologists as well as fascinating cultures. Robert Laughlin, longtime Smithsonian researcher among the modern descendants of the Maya in Chiapas, Mexico, recounts his inspiring story of bringing Maya literacy to modern-day Indians in Mexico. "Linguistic Survival Among the Maya" details Laughlin's career, first working on a massive dictionary that took more than a decade to complete, and then helping his collaborators in Chiapas develop a writers cooperative, a puppet theater, and a bilingual publications program. Today Laughlin and his Maya collaborators have helped create a live-performance theater, a full-scale literacy program, and a multilingual website.

Section 3 also sheds light on contemporary issues, conflicts, and customs, and is designed to stir both debate and serious discussion. Chapters focus on repatriation (34 and 35), cultural and linguistic extinction (28 and 31), human rights abuses (24 and 30), and discrimination (24, 26, and 30), as well as unusual cultural customs such as tattoo and piercing (described in chapter 32, on body art).

The transformation of both societies and the discipline of anthropology in the twenty-first century becomes clear through reading this section's essays. For example, in recent years anthropological perspectives and methods have found many useful applications in the professional world, as reflected in chapter 33, by P. Ann Kaupp and Roger Shuy. This case study demonstrates how linguists have helped doctors, lawyers, and teachers better understand their communication with patients, courtroom witnesses, and students, respectively. Applied anthropology is a flourishing and growing subfield of the discipline today, with, for example, medical and educational anthropologists, as well as applied linguists, working in many different professional settings.

The third section also explains how cultural anthropologists go about doing their work. Several essays elucidate methodology, including the ethnohistorical analysis of documents (chapters 26 and 27); ethnographic interviewing (chapters 25, 27, 30, and 36); new work in applied linguistics (chapters 31 and 33); and collaboration with Native peoples (chapters 27, 28, 31, 34, and 35). Many of these same essays reflect changes in anthropology over the past few decades, particularly the shift in emphasis from objectivity and facts to subjectivity and the Native point of view. As will also be clear from a careful reading of these essays, anthropologists also have shifted their goals, from publishing "objective" accounts of others' societies to increased collegial collaboration with indigenous peoples. This section and the volume close with "Aging: An Anthropological Perspective," a chapter describing aging in five different societies, reminding us again of the inseparability of our biological and cultural heritage, one of the motifs of the entire volume.

The third section focuses on cultural anthropology and emphasizes the value of traditional anthropological methods—participant observation, informants and collaborators, fieldwork, and cross-cultural comparison. These methods provide anthropologists with a special perspective and a set of highly useful professional skills. These are skills that other professionals can easily use, in particular teachers in school settings or students if they undertake ethnographic or simple interviewing projects in their own communi-

ties (Selig 1997). These skills offer a unique way to gather and analyze information and can be developed, practiced, and applied by all those who have the opportunity to live and work among other cultures.

CONCLUSION

As our world becomes increasingly diverse, and as more and more people from varied cultural backgrounds live and work side by side, anthropological perspectives, concepts, and methods can be highly useful in many different settings. This volume documents the tremendous challenges that face those who seek to understand our physical and cultural heritage as well as our many varied cultures, but it also demonstrates the enormous enrichment that comes as a result of such efforts.

REFERENCES

Selig, Ruth O., ed. 1993. *Anthropology and Culture, Central Themes and Teaching Resources*, pp. 1–28. American Anthropological Association Task Force on the Teaching of Anthropology, Co-chairs, Lawrence B. Breitborde and Jane J. White. Editorial Committee: David Givens, Patricia J. Higgins, Conrad Kottak, David McCurdy, and William C. Sturtevant. This unpublished manuscript, developed for students and teachers, serves as the basis for the section "The Anthropological Perspective."

Selig, Ruth O. 1997. "The Challenge of Exclusion: Anthropology, Teachers and Schools." In Conrad P. Kottak, Jane J. White, Richard H. Furlow, and Patricia C. Rice, eds., *The Teaching of Anthropology: Problems, Issues, and Decisions*, pp. 299–307. Mayfield.

Thomas, Elizabeth Marshall. 1959. *The Harmless People*. Alfred A. Knopf.

Turnbull, Colin. 1961. *The Forest People*. Simon and Schuster.

INVESTIGATING OUR ORIGINS AND VARIATION

Who are we and where did we come from?

How did our ancestors change and develop through millions of years?

Why do we come in so many different shapes, sizes, and colors?

How do scientists study our origins and our diversity?

1 "APE-ING" LANGUAGE

Communicating with Our Closest Relatives

Kathleen D. Gordon

What have experiments teaching chimpanzees and bonobos taught us about primate communication and possibly about the evolution of human language? Physical anthropologist Kathleen Gordon's article answers many of our questions about how researchers have developed methodologies to demonstrate that our primate cousins can come to understand symbolic or spoken English, its grammar or syntax, and even its abstract meaning.

What would other animals tell us about themselves if only they could speak? What could a close relative such as the chimpanzee tell us about ourselves and our history? Like Dr. Doolittle, researchers have long dreamed of communicating with other species. Over the past years numerous experiments have shown that a capacity for symbolic language is not necessarily the sole preserve of *Homo sapiens* and that it may indeed be possible to have meaningful communication across species boundaries.

It has become increasingly clear to anthropologists in the past decade that although there are dramatic differences between the overall behavior and life-ways of humans and the great apes, many of the characteristics once thought to be unique to humankind are being discovered, albeit in a very limited form, in the behavioral repertoires of the chimpanzee, gorilla, and orangutan.

For instance, it used to be thought that only humans used tools. Then Jane Goodall at the Gombe Stream Reserve in Tanzania electrified the world with the news that chimpanzees used rudimentary tools in the wild, to fish for termites and to sponge up water. Others have observed chimpanzees elsewhere using rocks as hammers and anvils to crack open palm nuts. Some anthropologists countered that only humans actually made tools, but, once again, chimpanzees were found to prepare their termite sticks with considerable care and foresight. One captive orangutan was even taught to chip stone tools. Clearly, no other animal species depends on tools for survival to the extent that the human species does (and has done probably for millions of years), but it is nonetheless true that at least our closest relatives are capable of tool-using and tool-making behavior that foreshadows that of human beings.

In the same way, it now appears that the ability to think about and refer to things in the abstract, or by means of symbols, may be due in part to a common substrate of intelligence that we share with the chimpanzee, gorilla, and orangutan. Although it is not yet clear whether any of the great apes make use of this capacity in the wild, recent experiments in laboratories and primate colonies have shown that all apes are able to learn symbolic systems of communication modeled after human language. Further, apes can communicate with humans and other apes about objects, persons, places, and activities using these "artificial" languages. For those who believed that language and the ability to communicate about something other than one's immediate emotions were the sole province of human beings, these experiments have provided a fascinating glimpse into the minds of apes and perhaps have given us clues to the communicative potentials of our last common ancestor.

TEACHING CHIMPANZEES LANGUAGE

The first attempts to teach chimpanzees how to speak took place in the 1940s. The method used mimicked the way human infants learn language. Baby chimpanzees were raised in human homes, by human caretakers, and were treated as if they were human. One such chimpanzee, Viki, was eventually able to use pictures to ask for objects or activities. On tests of conceptual discrimination, she was as accurate as similarly aged human children. But Viki was never able to pronounce more than three words, even after years of training and constant exposure to human speech. Her surrogate mother summed up the experiment in the 1951 book *The Ape in Our House:* "We said that if an ape had proper upbringing, it might learn to speak spontaneously. But we were wrong. You can dress an ape in the finest of finery, buy it a tricycle, and kiss it to death—but it will not learn to talk."

Viki's inability to master spoken language was not a training problem, we now know. It has since been demonstrated that in addition to some differences in their vocal tracts, apes simply lack the special brain connections that make human speech possible. In the 1960s psychologists began to realize that

language had to be distinguished from speech when thinking about primate communication abilities. Because human language is expressed through speech, we tend to equate one with the other, but any formal communication system is a language.

If chimps cannot speak, perhaps they can use a different form of language. As a result of further fieldwork among chimpanzees in their natural habitat, some observers noticed that chimpanzees use hand signals in their natural communications with one another. Suggesting that chimpanzees might be more successful at learning methods of communication that used the chimpanzee's native gestural abilities, Allen and Beatrice Gardner, working at the University of Nevada in the 1960s, taught their chimp infant, Washoe, to make hand signals in American Sign Language (ASL). The success the Gardners were able to achieve excited anthropologists, psychologists, and linguists everywhere. During her four years of training Washoe learned 150 signs, used them in combinations (though never in such a constant order as to resemble a real sense of syntax), and, apparently by imitation and observation, learned some signs that were never taught to her (such as "smoke"). She also invented some signs on her own and adapted others.

Washoe's success with sign language was not unique. Over the past fifteen years similar experiments have been conducted with other common chimpanzees and with the bonobo (pygmy chimpanzee), the gorilla, and the orangutan. Most of the experiments have focused on sign language, but such studies are difficult to control scientifically, and utterances must be filmed to be preserved. Hoping to avoid these methodological problems, some experimenters devised artificial languages, based on plastic tokens or keyboard symbols, in order to better control and record the animals' actual utterances.

Sarah, a common chimpanzee, was taught by David and Ann Premack to manipulate plastic discs of various shapes and colors to name and ask for objects and to make simple sentences. Another chimpanzee, Lana, at the Yerkes Primate Center in Atlanta, Georgia, was taught Yerkish, an artificial language using lexigrams (graphic symbols) on a keyboard connected to a computer. This system had the advantage of eliminating the human trainer and with it the possibility that humans were unconsciously cuing the animals to make appropriate responses, a criticism that continues to cloud some of the results of the sign language studies.

The artificial language systems have had their share of critics too. With such narrow training, some say, the animals have little opportunity to use language in the important ways in which humans use it, namely, to construct a world, to obtain desirables, and to regulate the behavior of others. "Language" it may be, but it is divorced from the open social context that makes language a meaningful phenomenon instead of a trivial game.

Although the sign language experiments are difficult to conduct, to maintain, and to verify by objective means, they still provide us with the most compelling evidence of the apes' capacity for symbolic language. Because these studies are relatively open, they also document the ability of trained animals to use symbolic communication in innovative and productive ways, such as to convey spontaneous or novel thoughts and desires. Koko, a lowland gorilla who was raised from infancy and taught ASL by Dr. Francine Patterson, now has a sign vocabulary of some five hundred words and recognizes five hundred more. This is the largest vocabulary of any of the signing apes. Most important, Koko uses her abilities to joke with, lie to, and insult her human and animal companions as well as to perform more mundane vocabulary exercises and comprehension tests, which are administered to obtain objective information about her language skills. Koko has used sign language to protest to trainers about boring vocabulary drills, to ask for a kitten as a pet (which she got), and to insult her young male gorilla companion Michael ("Michael stupid toilet devil").

To be sure, not all authorities have been willing to accept that the behavior being taught and used is truly "language." Before these studies were first undertaken, it was assumed by many prominent linguists that human language was so distinct and qualitatively different from all other forms of communication that it could not be explained as an evolutionary development from any more primitive communication system. But the language studies showed that ape language did share some of the important components of human communication. Apes could use a symbolic system of arbitrary referents, could generalize (that is, transfer meaning from one context to another appropriate one, as in the use of the word *Coke* to mean all sweet dark drinks), and could use signs or symbols to create new words or combinations

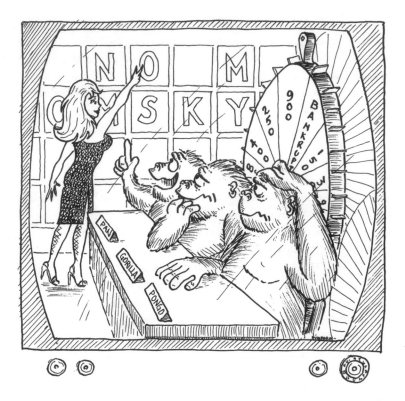

of words spontaneously in response to unfamiliar objects. As a result, some linguists began to draw ever stricter definitions of what constitutes "real" language and claimed the apes were merely "aping" their trainers and not producing intentional, patterned, or grammatical language at all. One experimenter, Herbert Terrace, who had worked with the chimpanzee Nim, concluded that his experiments showed only that Nim was mimicking his trainers and at best could use signs as simple demands.

Workers who had experience with raising infant apes countered that Nim, in particular, had an unstable environment, with so many changes in personnel that his language training may have been compromised. Problems with objectively verifying tests of any ape's language comprehension and usage also occur when the animals are bored or when the tester is a stranger to the animal. Motivation and emotional state contribute to ape testing performance just as they do to that of human children.

OVERCOMING METHODOLOGICAL OBSTACLES

Fortunately, the researchers at the Yerkes Center have found ways around these various methodological impasses. The latest results of the work of Sue

Savage-Rumbaugh and her colleagues are the most impressive yet. Dr. Savage-Rumbaugh worked for many years training two common chimpanzees, Sherman and Austin, to use Yerkish. Their training was considered successful, but nonetheless the two chimpanzees required intensive conditioning first to acquire symbols and then to progress from a simple stage of symbol association to the more abstract representational use of symbols. In sum, although common chimpanzees clearly can deal with symbolic usage on a conceptual level, they still do not learn language in the same way, at the same pace, or with anywhere near the same facility as do human children, even with the kind of intensive conditioning that children never undergo.

More recently the Yerkes group has worked with the bonobo, or pygmy chimpanzee, a little-known ape that until not long ago was considered to be merely a smaller version of the common chimp. Startling behavioral differences between the two closely related species have been found, both in field studies and in laboratory colonies, and the bonobo's language abilities are remarkably advanced in comparison with those of the common chimpanzee. Kanzi, a young male being raised by his mother, showed spontaneous use of the Yerkish keyboard and recognition of symbols without any training or conditioning behavior. His sole experience with language came by observing his mother, who was actively trained during his infancy. When it became clear that Kanzi was able to learn the Yerkish lexigrams independently, the research project was altered so that Kanzi would never be trained in the same manner as previous study subjects. Instead, he was given full access to the keyboard, both inside the laboratory and outside as he roamed the fifty-five-acre enclosure. Kanzi requests all food, activities, and personal contact with his human and ape companions by means of the keyboard. Because of this research design, the criticism of past studies, that the apparent linguistic behavior is only a conditioned response, has been avoided.

Kanzi's language use differs from that of Austin and Sherman. Unlike them, Kanzi will name objects he does not want immediately, so his responses are not reward-dependent. He frequently uses gestures and vocalizations in conjunction with lexigrams, and his gestures are more controlled and precise. Most fascinating is the fact that Kanzi understands spoken English. Although it seemed that Austin and Sherman did also, it was not until their English comprehension was tested (in the absence of the usual contextual and gestural cues) that their performance on identification tests dropped to slightly better than chance. Using lexigrams improved their scores once more, to almost 100 percent. Kanzi's performance shows no drop with the switch to English, and in fact he seems to use the spoken English as an additional cue to the meaning of lexigrams. More recent studies of Kanzi's younger sister, Mulika, indicate that Kanzi's abilities are not unique, leading Savage-Rumbaugh to conclude that the bonobo has some innate language abilities not shared with the common chimp, abilities that seem more like those of humans.

What do these results tell us about how animals communicate naturally among themselves? Very little is known about how wild chimpanzees communicate with each other, or about the complexity of their messages. These studies would seem to indicate that chimpanzees very likely use several types of cues simultaneously, such as vocalizations, gestures, and eye contact. No study in the wild has yet documented the range of chimpanzees' natural communications, but that may simply be a question of the human observers not knowing what to look for.

Some surprising results have been obtained from studies of monkey calls. Recording both vocalizations and behavior of wild vervet monkeys, Robert Seyfarth and Dorothy Cheney have shown that these monkeys have different alarm calls for each of their four major predators and different vocalizations for different types of social interactions. The calls seem to be a simple kind of representational signaling. Interestingly, while some of these calls are acoustically distinguishable to the human ear, others are not. If wild monkeys are capable of such unsuspected behavior, it seems likely that apes may also be able to communicate some types of information to each other, some of which we may not be able to hear.

Do these experiments provide any clues about how language might have begun in the human past? From these studies, and from observations of human infants, it seems clear that the ability to conceptualize and to hear complex vocalized messages can exist before the ability to produce actual speech is present. The ape experiments also show that once started, language use and learning can continue, even without further human training. For instance, Washoe, now living in a colony with other signing apes, has learned a few signals from her companions. They have also invented or modified signs on their own. Washoe has even taught signs to her adopted son, Louis, who continues to pick up additional vocabulary by imitating the other apes. Roger Fouts, the researcher in charge of the colony, reports that Jane Goodall has remarked on the low levels of aggression among the signing chimps, compared with chimps in other situations. This is an especially telling observation, since one of the theories about why language evolved in humans suggests that language became necessary to regulate social behavior. Whatever its origin, language, even among apes, may be an important diffuser of the tensions of group living. These experiments make it seem likely that the ability to symbolize might well have been present in the last ancestor we share with all the living great apes (that is, about 11 to 12 million years ago). It is now possible to see human language not as a trait without a past, unique to human beings, but rather as one extreme development of primitive communicative abilities and potential shared with our nearest relatives, the great apes.

UPDATE

Do apes have language? The answer to this question, of course, is that they don't. But what would we say of a one-year-old human infant? Does she have language? A two-year-old? A five-year-old? Language emerges as the infant matures, and so it seemed reasonable for us to take a developmental approach in our study. . . . We need to look for parallels between ape language and human language in the earliest stage of development and, having established these, see how far the apes can travel down the path toward human language. (Savage-Rumbaugh and Lewin 1994:157)

Sue Savage-Rumbaugh's ongoing language studies with the bonobo Kanzi continue to challenge previous results and assumptions. Kanzi's precocious success with the Yerkish lexigram language shows that at least some apes can learn language systems spontaneously, without training, conditioning, or rewarding. The critical factors—as with human children—seem to be early exposure to language and an environment that is both highly social and language-rich.

Much of the scholarly world continues to reject the notion that animals are capable of any kind of "language," and attempts to publish the work with Kanzi have frequently been rejected by major scientific journals. Undaunted, Savage-Rumbaugh and her collaborators have continued to uncover fascinating aspects of Kanzi's language abilities. With linguist Patricia Greenfield, Savage-Rumbaugh learned that Kanzi's multiword utterances began to follow some formal syntactic or grammatical rules. In addition to following an English grammatical rule of word order (first action, then object, e.g., "hide peanut," not "peanut hide"), presumably picked up from his human companions, he has also invented some unique grammatical rules himself. For instance, when he wants to engage someone in an action, he first specifies the action ("tickle") by choosing a lexigram on the keyboard and then specifies with a gesture the agent who is to do the tickling. Not only does he follow this pattern (action via lexigram, then agent via gesture) even when he has to travel across the room to get to the keyboard and the agent is sitting next to him, but it is also a rule that runs counter to the word order of the English spoken around him. These observations, that Kanzi's language use follows some arbitrary grammatical rules and that he is capable of making up some of these rules, satisfy some of the most important requirements for deeming language behavior truly grammatical.

Even more astounding is the discovery that Kanzi also shows substantial comprehension of spoken English. This has been tested exhaustively with sophisticated methods designed to avoid the problems of bias and unintentional cuing noted in other ape-language experiments. During testing, only Kanzi hears the test sentence through headphones, so the tester noting his responses does not know what question he was asked. In this situation, the tester does not know what the correct response is and cannot inadvertently cue Kanzi to select the right answer. His understanding of spoken English (72 percent correct responses) compared favorably with that of a 2½-year-old girl tested in the same way (66 percent correct).

Kanzi's latest exploits have been in the realm of toolmaking and archaeology. Some theories of human evolution have held that the development of language and the development of stone toolmaking may have gone hand in hand, both of them results of a unique human capacity for conceptual thought. Archaeologist Nick Toth had long wondered whether the earliest human toolmakers were doing something cognitively beyond the conceptual abilities of apes or were merely applying an apelike intelligence to non-apelike problems and activities. The continuities between apes and humans that Savage-Rumbaugh has uncovered in language ability inevitably led to questions about other supposedly unique human behaviors requiring conceptual ability. Could Kanzi learn to make stone tools as the earliest hominids did?

Toth and Savage-Rumbaugh devised an experiment with three components: motivation to make stone tools (in the form of a food treat in a transparent plastic box tied up with string); the materials to make sharp stone flakes capable of cutting the string (a mound of rocks and cobbles in his compound), and instruction in producing stone flakes (stone-knapping demonstrations by Toth). However, Kanzi was never trained or coached in this new activity; he was merely provided with the opportunity to participate if he wished.

Kanzi learned to appreciate the usefulness of flakes quickly and also to discriminate between sharp and dull ones. However, producing flakes himself took much longer—after two months, he was regularly producing small flakes up to one inch long. To maintain his motivation to make better flakes, the string securing the treat box was made thicker and thicker, requiring larger flakes to cut through it. But Kanzi confounded the researchers when, instead of improving his stone-knapping technique to get better and larger flakes, he innovated and started throwing the cobble down on the hard tile floor, where it would shatter into a number of usable flakes.

Toth the archaeologist was frustrated by this innovation. While from a psychologist's point of view Kanzi got high marks for problem solving, this new production method was never going to result in an Oldowan-type tool. Carpeting was installed on the floor. Once again Kanzi found a way around the research design—he simply pulled back the carpeting at a seam and hurled the cobbles on the exposed floor. Finally, however, when the weather improved and tool experiments were moved outside, Kanzi was forced to abandon the throwing technique and produced ever better flakes. But he eventually reverted to his original solution when he figured out how to throw one rock at another one he placed on the ground. Again he produced flakes, but in his own way and on his own terms.

Despite his proficiency at solving the problem at hand, Kanzi has not yet produced flakes that are the technical equals of real Oldowan stone tools. If nothing else, this experiment has given anthropologists a new respect for the complexity of this earliest human stone tool culture. And it has inspired Toth to wonder what kind of tools preceded the Oldowan—and whether we would even be able to identify them. Kanzi's primitive cores and flakes, which look more like naturally fractured rock than like human artifacts, have opened a window on this earlier horizon.

Recently anthropologists have turned the tables on this research by identifying and excavating chimpanzee nut-cracking sites in Taï National Park, Côte d'Ivoire, where chimps have been observed cracking open nuts of various tropical trees using stone hammers and anvils (Mercader, Panger, and Boesch 2002). This behavior has been reported since the 1600s. The researchers reasoned that the "archaeological" signature of this behavior might be recoverable, given the fact that chimps frequently use the same sites over and over and leave behind not only nut shells but also the hammers and broken pieces of stone that they use and reuse to gain access to the calorie-rich nutmeats inside. While these assemblages differ in most ways from even the earliest identifiable hominid archaeological localities, the authors report some similarities in stone breakage and conclude that additional study of these sites might help paleoanthropologists detect sites dating from even earlier stages in human toolmaking than the Oldowan.

Meanwhile, Savage-Rumbaugh, Shanker, and Taylor (1998) have published a fuller account of Kanzi's life at Yerkes and his linguistic abilities. In their book they also discuss the various forces and intellectual mind-sets that continue to make such behavior difficult for many scientists to accept as evidence of real language acquisition. One of these is the reluctance of many cognitive scientists to grant that animals other than *Homo sapiens* may possess what is known as a "theory of mind." This is the ability to grasp that others may see and think about the world differently than oneself. Beyond demonstrating that at least some apes are capable of using a language system to communicate across species lines, Savage-Rumbaugh presents evidence that Kanzi does, in fact, have a "theory of mind." His communicative abilities have made it possible for him to show that he attributes intentions and feeling to others, that he can empathize with others about feelings that he does not at that moment experience himself, and that he feels the need to communicate things about his own mental state to the individuals around him. If the point of language is to tell others things we assume they do not know, then Kanzi has spontaneously discovered and capitalized on this useful quality in his daily life, as he purposefully attempts to shape his surroundings and the behavior of others around him to better satisfy his personal preferences.

Kanzi the communicating bonobo is no longer unique. His younger sister Panbanisha has also become an adept and active communicator using the same lexigram system and also understands spoken English. For a while it seemed possible that bonobos might have more innate facility with language training than the common chimpanzees Savage-Rumbaugh had worked with earlier at Yerkes. But Panzee, a common chimp who was co-reared with Panbanisha, also learned the lexigram system and responded to spoken English, indicating that the critical variables in language acquisition may reside more in the animal's age and social context than in innate species-specific capacity.

Moreover, the kind of training researchers are now implementing has branched out into other realms and modes. In other research centers, common chimpanzees have been taught to count with Arabic numerals and even to read English words. Ai is a 25-year-old chimpanzee in the Primate Research Institute at Kyoto University, Japan. Originally trained by Tetsuro Matsuzawa (1985) to discriminate and name different objects, colors, and numbers up to six, using symbols on a keyboard (Matsuzawa 1985), Ai has also been taught to read several dozen characters in kanji, a written form of Japanese, and is now able to count from zero to nine, and can also order the numerals 0 to 9 in sequence (Kawai and Matsuzawa 2000). She is able to memorize and recall strings of up to five numbers, which compares rather favorably with the human "magic number seven" effect. Humans can easily remember seven-number strings but have a harder time processing strings containing anything more than seven items. Five seems to be the chimpanzee's "magic number" capacity. Researchers at Kyoto have recently been surprised to discover that Ai's young son, ten-month-old Ayuma, appears to be spontaneously teaching himself to read the kanji characters as well. As with Kanzi, Ayuma has never been coached directly but has spent much time observing his mother's training.

Sally Boysen, a psychologist at Ohio State University, has also worked with counting chimpanzees, but her most recent project involves teaching two very young chimps how to read the names of over a dozen objects, tools needed to acquire treats, and their own printed names, all in alphabetic English (Boysen and Berntson 1989). While Keeli and Ivy were initially started out with traditional letter recognition and building words by spelling them out, Boysen found that their progress was much faster once she switched to whole-word recognition (*cat, key,* [soda] *pop,* etc.). The two young chimps now have to request foods, or the tools needed to obtain the foods, by using the correct English words. The researchers are not, however, teaching any kind of word order or syntax; they want to see if the chimps will spontaneously impose a regular word order on their own utterances.

Nonetheless, there is still no general consensus among language-study skeptics that all this mounting evidence—anecdotal as well as the rigorously tested results—amounts to "real" language acquisition on the part of non-human primates. As Shanker points out (Savage-Rumbaugh, Shanker, and Taylor 1998), it seems as if the increased success of research with ape language experiments have, instead of creating a climate of greater acceptance of the capacity of other species for linguistic, abstract communication, merely caused the skeptics to become more defensive and to relocate the Rubicon of discontinuity between humans and all others further out of reach. As Matt Cartmill trenchantly sums up, "The skeptics will always be able to find reasons for insisting that 'language' is something peculiar to our species. If the fortress of syntax falls, they can retreat to passive verbs or compound sentences as the true markers of human uniqueness. . . . No matter how we raise them, chimpanzees are never going to speak English or read this book. . . . The arresting fact here is . . . that speechless animals have any linguistic abilities at all. That they do strengthens the case for thinking that our minds, like our bodies, are largely something we have inherited from our animal ancestors and share with our close animal relatives" (Cartmill 1995:76–77). Savage-Rumbaugh, Shanker, and Taylor (1998) further suggest that some of the resistance to seeing this connectedness may stem from its logical implication, that is, that chimpanzees and other apes are intellectually sophisticated organisms with mental capabilities very similar to young *Homo sapiens* and therefore deserve the same rights of freedom and existence that we (ideally) grant to our own kind.

FURTHER READING

Boysen, Sally, and G. G. Berntson. 1989. "Numerical Competence in a Chimpanzee (*Pan troglodytes*)." *Journal of Comparative Psychology* 103:23–31.

Cartmill, Matt. 1995. "Significant Others." *Natural History* 104(6):74–77.

Cheney, Dorothy L., and Robert M. Seyfarth. 1990. *How Monkeys See the World.* University of Chicago Press.

Gardner, R. A., and B. T. Gardner. 1969. "Teaching Sign Language to a Chimpanzee." *Science* 165:664–72.

Hayes, Cathy. 1951. *The Ape in Our House.* Harper.

Kawai, Nobuyuki, and Tetsuro Matsuzawa. 2000. "Numerical Memory Span in a Chimpanzee." *Nature* 403:39–40.

Linden, Eugene. 1981. *Apes, Men and Language.* Penguin. (A survey of the sign language studies with apes.)

Matsuzawa, Tetsuro. 1985. "Use of Numbers by a Chimpanzee." *Nature* 315:57–59.

Mercader, Julio, Melissa Panger, and Christophe Boesch. 2002. "Excavation of a Chimpanzee Stone Tool Site in the African Rainforest." *Science* 296:1452–5.

Patterson, Francine G., and Eugene Linden. 1981. *The Education of Koko*. Holt, Rinehart, and Winston. (Describes the training of Koko the gorilla and the controversies about language experiments.)

Savage-Rumbaugh, E. Sue, and Roger Lewin. 1994. *Kanzi: The Ape at the Brink of the Human Mind*. John Wiley and Sons.

Savage-Rumbaugh, E. Sue, Stuart G. Shanker, and Talbot J. Taylor. 1998. *Apes, Language, and the Human Mind*. Oxford University Press.

2 ARE HUMANS INHERENTLY VIOLENT?

Robert W. Sussman

By challenging the authors of the book Demonic Males, *primatologist Robert Sussman asks us to look at our basic human nature and ask what we can learn about ourselves from other primates. The chapter poses other questions, such as how genetics and learning help explain human behavior, what role aggression plays in chimpanzee and human society, and whether humans and chimpanzees share certain biologically fixed behaviors.*

Are human beings forever doomed to be violent? Is aggression fixed within our genetic code, an inborn action pattern that threatens to destroy us? Or, as asked by Richard Wrangham and Dale Peterson in their recent book, *Demonic Males: Apes and the Origins of Human Violence,* can we get beyond our genes, beyond our essential "human nature"?

Wrangham and Peterson's belief in the importance of violence in the evolution and nature of humans is based on new primate research that they assert demonstrates the continuity of aggression from our great ape ancestors. The authors argue that twenty to twenty-five years ago most scholars believed human aggression was unique. Research at that time had shown great apes to be basically nonaggressive, gentle creatures. Furthermore, the separation of humans from our ape ancestors was thought to have occurred 15–20 million years ago (mya). Although Raymond Dart, Sherwood Washburn, Robert Ardrey, E. O. Wilson, and others had argued through much of the twentieth century that hunting, killing, and extreme aggressive behaviors were biological traits inherited from our earliest hominid hunting ancestors, many anthropologists still believed that patterns of aggression were environmentally determined and culturally learned behaviors, not inherited— *receive* characteristics.

Demonic Males discusses new evidence that killer instincts are not unique to humans but rather are shared with our nearest relative, the common chimpanzee. The authors argue that it is this inherited propensity for killing that allows hominids and chimps to be such good hunters. *An inclination/natural tendency to behave in a particular way*

According to Wrangham and Peterson, the split between humans and the common chimpanzee was only 6–8 mya. Furthermore, humans may have split from the chimpanzee-bonobo line after gorillas, with bonobos (pygmy chimps) separating from chimps only 2.5 mya. Because chimpanzees may be the modern ancestor of all these forms, and because the earliest australopithecines were quite chimpanzee-like, Wrangham speculates (in a separate article) that "chimpanzees are a conservative species and an amazingly good model for the ancestor of hominids" (1995, reprinted in Sussman 1997:106). If modern chimpanzees and modern humans share certain behavioral traits, these traits have "long evolutionary roots" and are likely to be fixed, biologically inherited parts of our basic human nature and not culturally determined.

Wrangham argues that chimpanzees are almost on the brink of humanness:

> Nut-smashing, root-eating, savannah-using chimpanzees, resembling our ancestors, and capable by the way of extensive bipedalism. Using ant-wands, and sandals, and bowls, meat-sharing, hunting cooperatively. Strange paradox . . . a species trembling on the verge of hominization, but so conservative that it has stayed on that edge. (Sussman 1997:107)

Wrangham and Peterson (1996:24) claim that only two animal species, chimpanzees and humans, live in patrilineal, male-bonded communities with "intense, male-initiated territorial aggression, including lethal raiding into neighboring communities in search of vulnerable enemies to attack and kill." Wrangham asks:

> Does this mean chimpanzees are naturally violent? Ten years ago it wasn't clear. . . . In this cultural species, it may turn out that one of the least variable of all chimpanzee behaviors is the intense competition between males, the violent aggression they use against strangers, and their willingness to maim and kill those that frustrate their goals. . . . As the picture of chimpanzee society settles into focus, it now includes infanticide, rape, and regular battering of females by males. (Sussman 1997:108) *A person who kill a child infant especially their own*

Since humans and chimpanzees share these violent urges, the implication is that human violence has long evolutionary roots. "We are apes of nature, cursed over six million years or more with a rare inheritance, a Dostoyevskyan demon. . . . The coincidence of demonic aggression in ourselves and our closest kin bespeaks its antiquity" (Sussman 1997:108–9).

A good way to describe a book/story thats similar in style

INTELLECTUAL ANTECEDENTS

From the beginning of Western thought, the theme of human depravity runs deep, related to the idea of humankind's fall from grace and the emergence of original sin. This view continues to pervade modern "scientific" interpretations of the evolution of human behavior. Recognition of the close evolutionary relationship between humans and apes, from the time of Darwin's *Descent of Man* (1874) on, has encouraged theories that look to modern apes for evidence of parallel behaviors reflecting this relationship.

By the early 1950s large numbers of australopithecine fossils and the discovery that the large-brained "fossil" ancestor from Piltdown, in England, was a fraud led to the realization that our earliest ancestors were more like apes than like modern humans. Accordingly, our earliest ancestors must have behaved much like other nonhuman primates. This, in turn, led to a great interest in using primate behavior to understand human evolution and the evolutionary basis of human nature. The subdiscipline of primatology was born.

Raymond Dart, discoverer of the first australopithecine fossil some thirty years earlier, was also developing a different view of our earliest ancestors. At first Dart believed that australopithecines were scavengers barely eking out an existence in the harsh savanna environment. But from the fragmented and damaged bones found with the australopithecines, together with dents and holes in these early hominid skulls, Dart eventually concluded that this species had used bone, tooth, and antler tools to kill, butcher, and eat their prey, as well as to kill one another. This hunting hypothesis "was linked from the beginning with a bleak, pessimistic view of human beings and their ancestors as instinctively bloodthirsty and savage" (Cartmill 1997:511). To Dart, the australopithecines were

> confirmed killers: carnivorous creatures that seized living quarries by violence, battered them to death, tore apart their broken bodies, dismembered them limb from limb, slaking their ravenous thirst with the hot blood of victims and greedily devouring livid writhing flesh. (1953:209)

Cartmill, in a 1993 book, shows that this interpretation of early human morality is reminiscent of earlier Greek and Christian views. Dart's own 1953 treatise begins with a seventeenth-century quote from the Calvinist writer R. Baxter: "of all the beasts, the man-beast is the worst / to others and himself the cruellest foe."

Between 1961 and 1976 Dart's view was picked up and extensively popularized by the playwright Robert Ardrey (*The Territorial Imperative, African Genesis*). Ardrey believed it was the human competitive and killer instinct, acted out in warfare, that made humans what they are today: "It is war and the instinct for territory that has led to the great accomplishments of Western Man. Dreams may have inspired our love of freedom, but only war and weapons have made it ours" (1961:324).

MAN THE HUNTER

In the 1968 volume *Man the Hunter*, Sherwood Washburn and Chet Lancaster presented a theory of the evolution of hunting, emphasizing that it is this behavior that shaped human nature and separated early humans from their primate relatives.

> To assert the biological unity of mankind is to affirm the importance of the hunting way of life. . . . However much conditions and customs may have varied locally, the main selection pressures that forged the species were the same. The biology, psychology and customs that separate us from the apes . . . we owe to the hunters of time past . . . for those who would understand the origins and nature of human behavior there is no choice but to try to understand "Man the Hunter." (1968:303)

Rather than amassing evidence from modern hunters and gatherers to prove their theory, Washburn and Lancaster use the nineteenth-century concept of cultural "survivals": behaviors that persist as evidence of an earlier time but are no longer useful in society.

> Men enjoy hunting and killing, and these activities are continued in sports even when they are no longer economically necessary. If a behavior is important to the survival of a species . . . then it must be both easily learned and pleasurable. (1968:299)

MAN THE DANCER

Using a similar logic for the survival of ancient "learned and pleasurable" behaviors, perhaps it could easily have been our propensity for dancing rather than our desire to hunt that can explain much of human behavior. After all, men and women love to dance; it is a behavior found in all cultures but has even less obvious function today than hunting. Our love of movement and dance might explain, for example, our propensity for face-to-face sex, and even the evolution of bipedalism and the movement of humans out of trees and onto the ground.

Could the first tool have been a stick to beat a dance drum, and the ancient Laetoli footprints evidence of two individuals going out to dance the "Afarensis shuffle"? Although it takes only two to tango, a variety of social interactions and systems might have been encouraged by the complex social dances known in human societies around the globe. I am joking, of course, but the evidence for man the dancer is just as good (or lacking) as is that for man the hunter or man the killer.

SOCIOBIOLOGY AND E. O. WILSON

In the mid-1970s E. O. Wilson and others described a number of traits as genetically based and therefore human universals, including territoriality, male-female bonds, male dominance over females, and extended maternal care leading to matrilineality. Wilson argued that the genetic basis of these traits was indicated by their relative constancy among our primate relatives and by their persistence throughout human evolution and in human societies. Elsewhere I have shown that these characteristics are neither general primate traits nor human universals (Sussman 1995). Wilson, however, argued that these were a product of our evolutionary hunting past.

> For at least a million years—probably more—Man engaged in a hunting way of life, giving up the practice a mere 10,000 years ago. . . . Our innate social responses have been fashioned through this life style. With caution, we can compare the most widespread hunter-gatherer qualities with similar behavior displayed by some of the non-human primates that are closely related to Man. Where the same pattern of traits occurs in . . . most or all of those primates— we can conclude that it has been subject to little evolution. (Wilson 1976, in Sussman 1997:65–66)

Wilson's theory of sociobiology, the evolution of social behavior, argued that (1) the goal of living organisms is to pass on one's genes at the expense of all others, and that (2) an organism should cooperate with others only if (a) they carry some of his/her own genes (kin selection) or (b) if at some later date the others might offer aid to the organism (reciprocal altruism).

To sociobiologists, evolutionary morality is based on an unconscious need to multiply our own genes, to build group cohesion in order to win wars. We should not look down on our warlike, cruel nature but rather understand its success when coupled with "making nice" with some other individuals or groups. The genetically driven "making nice" is the basis of human ethics and morality.

> Throughout recorded history the conduct of war has been common . . . some of the noblest traits of mankind, including team play, altruism, patriotism, bravery . . . and so forth are the genetic product of warfare. (Wilson 1975:572–3)

The evidence for any of these universals or for the tenets of sociobiology is as weak as was the evidence for Dart's, Ardrey's, and Washburn and Lancaster's theories of innate aggression. Not only are modern gatherer-hunters and most apes remarkably nonaggressive, but in the 1970s and 1980s studies of fossil bones and artifacts showed that early humans were not hunters and that weapons were a later addition to the human repertoire. In fact, C. K. Brain (1981) showed that the holes and dents in Dart's australopithecine skulls matched perfectly with fangs of leopards or with impressions of rocks pressing against the buried fossils. Australopithecines apparently were the hunted, not the hunters (Cartmill 1993, 1997).

BEYOND OUR GENES

Wrangham and Peterson's book *Demonic Males* goes beyond the assertion of human inborn aggression and propensity toward violence. The authors ask a critical question: Are we doomed to be violent forever because this pattern is fixed within our genetic code, or can we go beyond our past—get out of our genes, so to speak? The authors believe that we can look to the bonobo or pygmy chimpanzee as one potential savior, metaphorically speaking.

Bonobos, although even more closely related to the common chimpanzee than humans, have become a peace-loving, lovemaking alternative to chimpanzee-human violence. How did this happen? In chimpanzees and humans, females of the species select partners that are violent: "[W]hile men have evolved to be demonic males, it seems likely that women have evolved to prefer demonic males . . . as long as demonic males are the most successful reproducers, any female who mates with them is provided with sons who themselves will likely be good reproducers" (Wrangham and Peterson 1996:239). However, among pygmy chimpanzees females form alliances and have chosen to mate with less aggressive males. So, after all, it is not violent males that have caused humans and chimpanzees to be their inborn, immoral, dehumanized selves; it is, rather, poor choices by human and chimpanzee females.

Like Dart, Washburn, and Wilson before them, Wrangham and Peterson believe that tendencies to killing and violence are inherited from our ancient relatives of the past. However, unlike these earlier theorists, Wrangham and Peterson argue this is not a trait unique to hominids, nor is it a by-product of hunting. In fact, it is just this violent nature and a natural "blood lust" that makes both humans and chimpanzees such good hunters. It is the bonobos that help the authors come to this conclusion. Because bonobos have lost the desire to kill, they also have lost the desire to hunt.

> [B]onobos tell us that the suppression of personal violence carried with it the suppression of predatory aggression. The strongest hypothesis at the moment is that bonobos came from a chimpanzee-like ancestor that hunted monkeys

HIGHER PRIMATES

and hunted one another. As they evolved into bonobos, males lost their de-
monism, becoming less aggressive to each other. In so doing they lost their
lust for hunting monkeys, too. . . . Murder and hunting may be more closely
tied together than we are used to thinking. (Wrangham and Peterson
1996:219)

THE SELFISH GENE THEORY

Like Ardrey, Wrangham and Peterson believe that blood lust ties killing and
hunting tightly together, but in the latter's argument it is killing that drives
hunting. This lust to kill is based upon the sociobiological tenet of the selfish gene. "The general principle that behavior evolves to serve selfish ends
has been widely accepted; and the idea that humans might have been favored
by natural selection to hate and to kill their enemies has become entirely, if
tragically, reasonable" (Wrangham and Peterson 1996:23).

The authors make two arguments that humans and chimpanzees share biologically fixed behaviors: (1) they are more closely related to each other than
chimpanzees are to gorillas, and (2) chimpanzees are a good model for our
earliest ancestor and retain conservative traits that should be shared by both.

The first of these statements is still hotly debated and, using various genetic evidence, the chimp-gorilla-human triage is so close that it is difficult

to tell exact divergence time or pattern among the three. The second statement is just not true. Chimpanzees have been evolving for as long as humans and gorillas, and there is no reason to believe ancestral chimps were similar to present-day chimps. The fossil evidence for the last 5–8 million years is extremely sparse, and it is likely that many forms of apes have become extinct, just as have many hominids.

Furthermore, even if the chimpanzee were a good model for the ancestral hominid, this would not mean that humans would necessarily share specific behavioral traits. As even Wrangham and Peterson emphasize, chimps, gorillas, and bonobos all behave very differently in their social behavior and in their willingness to kill conspecifics.

EVIDENCE AGAINST "DEMONIC MALES"

The proof of the "demonic male" theory must rest solely on the evidence that violence and killing in chimpanzees and in humans are behaviors that are similar in pattern; have ancient, shared evolutionary roots; and are inherited. Besides killing of conspecifics, Wrangham "includes infanticide, rape, and regular battering of females by males" as a part of this inherited legacy of violent behaviors shared by humans and chimpanzees (Sussman 1997:108).

Wrangham and Peterson state: "That chimpanzees and humans kill members of neighboring groups of their own species is . . . a startling exception to the normal rule for animals" (1996:63). "Fighting adults of almost all species normally stop at winning: They don't go on to kill" (1996:155). However, as Wrangham points out, there are exceptions, such as lions, wolves, and spotted hyenas, and I would add a number of other predators. In fact, most species do not have the weapons to kill one another as adults.

Just how common is conspecific killing in chimpanzees? This is where the real controversy may lie. Jane Goodall described the chimpanzee as a peaceful, nonaggressive species during the first twenty-four years of study at Gombe (1950–1974). During one year of concentrated study, Goodall observed 284 agonistic encounters; of these, 66 percent were due to competition for introduced bananas, and only 34 percent "could be regarded as attacks occurring in 'normal' aggressive contexts" (1968:278). Only 10 percent of the 284 attacks were classified as "violent," and "even attacks that appeared punishing to me often resulted in no discernable injury. . . . Other attacks consisted merely of brief pounding, hitting or rolling of the individual, after which the aggressor often touched or embraced the other immediately" (Goodall 1968:277).

Chimpanzee aggression before 1974 was considered no different from patterns of aggression seen in many other primate species. In fact, Goodall explains in her 1986 monograph *The Chimpanzees of Gombe* that she uses data mainly from after 1975 because the earlier years present a "very different picture of the Gombe chimpanzees" as being "far more peaceable than humans" (1986:3). Other early naturalists' descriptions of chimpanzee behavior were consistent with those of Goodall and confirmed her observations. Even different communities were observed to come together with peaceful, ritualized displays of greeting (Reynolds and Reynolds 1965; Suguyama 1972; Goodall 1968).

Then, between 1974 and 1977, five adult males from one subgroup were attacked and disappeared from the area, presumably dead. Why after twenty-four years did the patterns of aggression change? Was it because the stronger group saw the weakness of the other and decided to improve their genetic fitness? But surely there were stronger and weaker animals and subgroups before this time. Perhaps we can look to Goodall's own perturbations for an answer. In 1965 Goodall began to provide "restrictive human-controlled" feeding. A few years later she realized that

> the constant feeding was having a marked effect on the behavior of the chimps. They were beginning to move about in large groups more often than they had ever done in the old days. Worst of all, the adult males were becoming increasingly aggressive. When we first offered the chimps bananas the males seldom fought over their food; . . . now . . . there was a great deal more fighting than ever before. (1971:143)

The possibility that human interference was a main cause of the unusual behavior of the Gombe chimps was the subject of an excellent but generally ignored book by Margaret Power (1991). Wrangham and Peterson (1996:19) cite this book in a footnote, but as with many other controversies, they essentially ignore its findings, stating that chimpanzee violence might have been considered unnatural behavior if it weren't for the evidence of similar behavior occurring since 1977 and "elsewhere in Africa" (Wrangham and Peterson 1996:19).

FURTHER EVIDENCE

What is this evidence from elsewhere in Africa? Wrangham and Peterson provide only four brief examples, none of which is very convincing:

1. Between 1979 and 1982, the Gombe group extended its range to the south, and conflict with a southern group, Kalande, was suspected. In 1982 a "raiding" party of males reached Goodall's camp. The authors state: "Some of these raids may have been lethal" (Wrangham and Peterson 1996:19). However, Goodall describes this "raid" as

follows: One female "was chased by a Kalande male and mildly attacked. . . . Her four-year-old son . . . encountered a second male—but was only sniffed" (Goodall 1986:516). Although Wrangham and Peterson imply that these encounters were similar to those between 1974 and 1977, no violence was actually witnessed. The authors also refer to the discovery of the dead body of Humphrey; what they do not mention is Humphrey's age, thirty-five, and that wild chimps rarely live past thirty-three years.

2. Six adult males from one community in the Japanese study site of Mahale disappeared one by one over the twelve-year period from 1970 to 1982. None of the animals was observed being attacked or killed, and one was sighted later roaming as a solitary male (Nishida, Hiraiwa-Hasegawa, and Takahtat 1985:287–89).

3. In another site in West Africa, Wrangham and Peterson report that Boesch and Boesch believe "that violent aggression among the chimpanzees is as important as it is in Gombe" (Wrangham and Peterson 1986:20). However, in the paper referred to, the Boesches simply state that encounters by neighboring chimpanzee communities are more common in their site than in Gombe (one per month versus one every four months). There is no mention of violence during these encounters.

4. At a site that Wrangham began studying in 1984, an adult male was found dead in 1991. Wrangham states: "In the second week of August, Ruizoni was killed. No human saw the big fight" (Wrangham and Peterson 1996:20). Wrangham gives us no indication of what has occurred at this site since 1991.

In fact, this is the total amount of evidence of warfare and male-male killing among chimpanzees after thirty-seven years of research. The data for infanticide and rape among chimpanzees are even less impressive. In fact, data are so sparse for these behaviors among chimps that Wrangham and Peterson are forced to use examples from the other great apes, gorillas and orangutans. However, just as for killing among chimpanzees, both the evidence and the interpretations are suspect and controversial.

CAN WE ESCAPE OUR GENES?

What if Wrangham and Peterson are correct and we and our chimp cousins are inherently sinners? Are we doomed to be violent forever because this pattern is fixed within our genetic code? After 5 million years of human evolution and 120,000 or so years of *Homo sapiens* existence, is there a way to rid ourselves of our inborn evils?

What does it do for us, then, to know the behavior of our closest relatives. Chimpanzees and bonobos are an extraordinary pair. One, I suggest shows us some of the worst aspects of our past and our present; the other shows an escape from it. . . . Denial of our demons won't make them go away. But even if we're driven to accepting the evidence of a grisly past, we're not forced into thinking it condemns us to an unchanged future. (Wrangham 1995, in Sussman 1997:110)

In other words, we can learn how to behave by watching bonobos. But if we can change our inherited behavior so simply, why haven't we been able to do this before *Demonic Males* enlightened us? Surely there are variations in the amounts of violence in different human cultures and individuals. If we have the capacity and plasticity to change by learning from example, then our behavior is determined by socialization practices and by our cultural histories and not by our nature. This is true whether the examples come from benevolent bonobos or conscientious objectors.

CONCLUSION

The theory presented by Wrangham and Peterson, although it also includes chimpanzees as our murdering cousins, is very similar to "man the hunter" theories proposed in the past. It also does not differ greatly from earlier European and Christian beliefs about human ethics and morality. We are forced to ask: Are these theories generated by good scientific fact, or are they just "good to think" because they reflect, reinforce, and reiterate our traditional cultural beliefs, our morality, and our ethics? Is the theory generated by the data, or are the data manipulated to fit preconceived notions of human morality and ethics?

Since the data in support of these theories have been weak, and yet the stories created have been extremely similar, I am forced to believe that "man the hunter" is a myth, that humans are not necessarily prone to violence and aggression, but that this belief will continue to reappear in future writings on human nature. Meanwhile, primatologists must continue their field research, marshaling the actual evidence needed to answer many of the questions raised in Wrangham and Peterson's volume.

UPDATE

Since I wrote my original article in 1998, Richard Wrangham (1999) has attempted to address some of the questions about and criticisms of the theories concerning innate aggression in humans and chimpanzees that he proposed in his earlier publication, *Demonic Males*. He now cites ten chimpanzee kills recorded on the basis of direct observations or fresh bodies and up to ten more suspicious disappearances. These occur at four different research sites that have been studied for a total of ninety years. He also reports that in four other sites, where chimpanzees have been studied for an additional eighty years, lethal violence has not been observed. More importantly, Wrangham further develops his theoretical argument, in particular using three major concepts to support his hypothesis that violent behavior is basic to both humans and chimpanzees. These three concepts are coalitionary killing, the imbalance-of-power hypothesis, and a dominance drive.

Wrangham believes that warfare in humans and violent, deadly attacks in chimpanzees are examples of a phenomenon he labels "coalitionary killing." Adult males in these species collaborate to kill or brutally wound other adults. Coalitionary killing generally is rare among animal species but is found in social insects and some social carnivores. Among primates it occurs only in chimpanzees and humans. "The ancient origin of warfare is supported by the rarity of coalitionary lethal violence toward adult conspecifics in other primates, and by evidence that . . . chimpanzees and humans share a common ancestor around 5–6 mya" (1999:3).

Second, Wrangham believes that the principal adaptive explanation linking coalitionary killing in chimpanzees and humans is what he refers to as the "imbalance-of-power hypothesis." This "states that coalitionary kills occur because of two factors: intergroup hostility, and large power asymmetries between rival parties" (1999:3). Thus, chimpanzee males will attack other conspecifics if they outnumber them and have a low risk of injury to themselves. "By wounding or killing members of the neighboring community, males from one community increase their relative dominance over the neighbors . . . this tends to lead to increased fitness of the killers" (1999:11–12). Because of the complexity of modern warfare, these types of lethal raids can be seen more readily in humans in "primitive" warfare among "pre-state" societies (1999:5). Wrangham believes that the imbalance-of-power hypothesis is also relevant to dominance interactions among members of the same community, and some of the coalitionary kills he cites occurred within chimpanzee communities.

Third and finally, Wrangham believes that the long-term evolutionary explanation of coalitionary killing is attributed to a "dominance drive" that favors unprovoked aggression. Such aggression is brought about by the opportunity to attack at times of low personal risk, thus substantially reducing competition from neighboring communities. The dominance drive is related to increased fitness, allowing the killers to leave more of their dominant-killer genes to the next generation.

Although there are a number of problems with each of these points, I will concentrate only on what I consider to be the most serious flaw of each argument. Other criticisms of Wrangham's approach can be found in the following readings listed at the end of this chapter: Sussman 1999, 2000; Tang-Martinez 2000; Marks 2002.

Regarding coalitionary killing, Wrangham assumes that certain behaviors resulting in conspecific killing among ants, wolves, chimpanzees, and humans (especially those in primitive, pre-state societies) are similar phenomena. Presumably they have the same biological bases and motivations and therefore are driven by the same underlying natural causes. Thus he gives these behaviors a label, "coalitionary killing," and in creating a name, he creates a phenomenon. Yet the extremely vague similarities between the behaviors observed do not necessarily indicate that the behaviors have any biological similarity whatsoever.

When comparisons are made between human and animal behavior and it is assumed that behaviors that are similar in appearance have similar functions and evolutionary histories, a basic principle of biology is violated. Form alone does not provide information about function or shared genetic or evolutionary history. Referring to "rape" in dragonflies, "slavery" in ants, or "coalitionary killing" in chimpanzees and humans may sound like science but is, as Marks states, "a science of metaphorical, not of biological, connections" (2002:104).

With regard to the imbalance-of-power argument, are we to believe that whenever a group of chimpanzees or humans perceives weakness in another individual or group, that group will attack and kill? Does this depend upon a genetic relationship? If not, why not? In what precise circumstances do we actually see coalitionary killing, and when does it not occur? One would expect that if violence occurred every time there was a potential imbalance of power in chimpanzee group meetings and in within-group dominance interactions, surely coalitionary killing would be much more common than the ten to twenty incidents recorded in 170 years of observation. In fact, killing is exceedingly rare given the potential for these conditions. Furthermore, do all humans or human groups attempt, or at least wish, to kill individuals in weaker, nonrelated groups? Given the drive for dominance and the imbalance-of-power hypothesis, why not? Do humans normally desire to do so but are restrained by laws and regulations and the fear of punishment? Is this why it is easier to compare primitive, pre-state human societies with chimpanzees, since such societies are less constrained by laws and regulations because they are closer to "nature"? As Wrangham states, "[M]ales are expected by this hypothesis to take advantage of power over neighbors, especially when unfettered by social or cultural constraints" (1999:22).

In fact, neither chimpanzees nor humans attack in all circumstances of imbalance of power, and coalitionary killing is extremely rare in both species. Wrangham agrees that it is the context that is critical for understanding violent behavior, and it is the context that is not explained by (or relevant to) the proposed hypotheses. "Whether or not an individual employs violence is expected to depend on the proximate stimuli, about which we still know little. . . . Such questions are critical for understanding who becomes violent, and when" (1999:22). It seems necessary to have a good understanding of the circumstances and proximate causes of a behavior before developing evolutionary explanations for that behavior.

Finally, with regard to the dominance drive argument, Robert Hinde, one of the most respected animal behaviorists of our time, has considered the concept of psychological and behavioral "drives" at length. He emphasizes that the word *drive* is problematic because it has been used in so many different ways. The term may refer to hypothesized entities that are believed to exist but that have not yet been identified, or to stimuli or responses, or to physiological or psychological states, or to neurological or non-neurological states. The term can also refer to biogenic states, in which changes in behavior are related directly to changes in the internal state of the organism, or psychogenic states, in which they are not. Hinde warns:

> Even within one usage, however, there is a tendency to use drive as a blanket variable—drive concepts are used to provide unitary explanations of a variety of characteristics of behavior which may depend, in fact, on diverse mechanisms. . . . A unitary concept of drive can be taken to imply that these diverse characteristics of behavior depend on the same features of the underlying mechanism. There is no a priori reason why this should be so, and some reasons for thinking to the contrary. (1970:199–200)

Where measures of behavior can be directly correlated, such as drinking leading to a cessation of thirst, the proposition of an intervening drive variable may be a valuable tool for research. However, when correlation between behaviors is not perfect, "such a concept is misleading and can be a positive hindrance" (1970:196). The use of the concept of drive in relation to the extremely complex set of behavioral and contextual phenomena related to dominance seems to me to be entirely inappropriate.

Wrangham argues that those who criticize his theory do not appreciate the relevance of biological arguments for understanding warfare or the importance of the comparative method in biology. I disagree. Rather, I believe his critics are simply not convinced that the concepts of "coalitionary killing," the "imbalance-of-power hypothesis," and a "dominance drive" are sufficient to explain violent behavior in chimpanzees or humans.

FURTHER READING

Ardrey, Robert. 1961. *African Genesis: A Personal Investigation into Animal Origins and Nature of Man*. Atheneum.

Ardrey, Robert. 1966. *The Territorial Imperative*. Atheneum.

Bock, Kenneth. 1980. *Human Nature and History: A Response to Sociobiology.* Columbia University Press.

Brain, C. K. 1981. *The Hunted or the Hunter? An Introduction to African Cave Taphonomy.* University of Chicago Press.

Cartmill, Matt. 1993. *A View to a Death in the Morning: Hunting and Nature Through History.* Harvard University Press.

Cartmill, Matt. 1997. "Hunting Hypothesis of Human Origins." In F. Spencer, ed., *History of Physical Anthropology: An Encyclopedia,* pp. 508–12. Garland.

Dart, Raymond. 1953. "The Predatory Transition from Ape to Man." *International Anthropological and Linguistic Review* 1:201–17.

Darwin, Charles. 1874. *The Descent of Man and Selection in Relation to Sex.* 2nd ed. Henneberry.

Ehrlich, P. 2000. *Human Natures: Genes, Cultures, and the Human Prospect.* Island.

Goodall, Jane. 1968. "The Behavior of Free-Living Chimpanzees in the Gombe Stream Reserve." *Animal Behavior Monographs* 1:165–311.

Goodall, Jane. 1971. *In the Shadow of Man.* Houghton Mifflin.

Goodall, Jane. 1986. *The Chimpanzees of Gombe: Patterns of Behavior.* Belknap.

Gould, Stephen J. 1996. *The Mismeasure of Man.* W. W. Norton.

Hinde, R. A. 1970. *Animal Behavior: A Synthesis of Ethology and Comparative Psychology.* 2nd ed. McGraw-Hill.

Marks, J. 2002. *What It Means to Be 98% Chimpanzee: Apes, People, and Their Genes.* University of California Press.

Nishida, T., M. Hiraiwa-Hasegawa, and Y. Takahtat. 1985. "Group Extinction and Female Transfer in Wild Chimpanzees in the Mahali Nation Park, Tanzania." *Zeitschrift für Tierpsychologie* 67:281–301.

Power, Margaret. 1991. *The Egalitarians, Human and Chimpanzee: An Anthropological View of Social Organization.* Cambridge University Press.

Reynolds, V., and F. Reynolds. 1965. "Chimpanzees of Budongo Forest." In I. DeVore, ed., *Primate Behavior: Field Studies of Monkeys and Apes,* pp. 368–424. Holt, Rinehart, and Winston.

Suguyama, Y. 1972. "Social Characteristics and Socialization of Wild Chimpanzees." In F. E. Poirier, ed., *Primate Socialization,* pp. 145–63. Random House.

Sussman, R. W. 1995. "The Nature of Human Universals." *Reviews in Anthropology* 24:1–11.

Sussman, R. W., ed. 1997. *The Biological Basis of Human Behavior.* Simon and Schuster.

Sussman, R. W., ed. 1999. *The Biological Basis of Human Behavior: A Critical Review.* 2nd ed. Prentice Hall.

Sussman, R. W. 2000. "Piltdown Man: The Father of American Field Primatology." In S. C. Strum and L. M. Fedigan, eds., *Primate Encounters: Models of Science, Gender, and Society,* pp. 85–103. University of Chicago Press.

Tang-Martinez, Z. 2000. "Paradigms and Primates: Bateman's Principle, Passive Females, and Perspectives from Other Taxa." In Shirley C. Strum and Linda M. Fedigan, eds., *Primate Encounters: Models of Science, Gender, and Society,* pp. 261–74. University of Chicago Press.

Washburn, S. L., and C. K. Lancaster. 1968. "The Evolution of Hunting." In R. B. Lee and I. DeVore, eds., *Man the Hunter,* pp. 293–303. Aldine.

Wilson, E. O. 1975. *Sociobiology: The New Synthesis.* Harvard University Press.

Wilson, E. O. 1976. "Sociobiology: A New Approach to Understanding the Basis of Human Nature." *New Scientist* 70:342–45. (Reprinted in Sussman 1997.)

Wrangham, R. W. 1995. "Ape, Culture, and Missing Links." *Symbols,* spring:2–9, 20. (Reprinted in Sussman 1997.)

Wrangham, Richard, and Dale Peterson. 1996. *Demonic Males: Apes and the Origins of Human Violence.* Houghton Mifflin.

Wrangham, R. W. 1999. "Evolution of Coalitionary Killing." *Yearbook of Physical Anthropology* 42:1–30.

3 ONE MAN'S SEARCH FOR HUMAN ORIGINS

Ruth Osterweis Selig

In the ninth grade Rick Potts dreamed of becoming a paleoanthropologist. Today he is the director of the Smithsonian's Human Origins Program and is known for his pioneering approach to landscape-scale excavations and his variability selection theory of human evolution. This chapter includes Selig's original article describing Potts' research career, along with a new update by Potts detailing his most recent work in East Africa and China and his hypothesis regarding how adaptability evolved in the human species.

Alan Walker once said to me, "It does not matter how much you can convince yourself; it only matters how much you can convince your skeptics"—that is science in a nutshell.

—Rick Potts, April 2, 1999

Of all the animal species on earth, only humans ask from where they came. Paleoanthropologists strive to answer the what, why, and how of that remarkable journey. In a recent article, "Why Are We Human?" Rick Potts, director of the Smithsonian's Human Origins Program, summarized the state of current knowledge:

Due to the rapid pace of discovery, scientists now have fossils from more than 5,000 individuals as far back as 5 million years. That record offers strong evidence that we evolved from apelike species in Africa, and genetic evidence confirms that our closest biological cousins are the African chimpanzees. Scientists from many different fields agree that humans and chimpanzees evolved from a common ancestor that lived between 5 million and 8 million years ago. (1999a:1)

Today we know that as many as twelve to fifteen different humanlike species evolved in the past. Why did some continue and change while most died out? It is this question that has consumed Rick Potts' life, beginning when he was a ninth grader in suburban Philadelphia's Abington High School. The story of Potts' determination to answer this question reveals much about human evolution and paleoanthropology, but it also offers insight into one scientist's single-minded passion and the development of a new theory—"variability selection"—to explain the why and the how of human origins. This article presents three intertwined stories: (1) the development of one paleoanthropologist's career, (2) the development of the human species through time, and (3) the development of a new theory of human evolution: variability selection.

These three stories illuminate the inextricable nature of scientific advances, human knowledge, and the individual scientist. In addition, the story of Rick Potts underscores the interplay between inherent disposition and environmental influence, no small irony for a scientist whose theory of human evolution focuses on the interplay between the environment and the human lineage's evolving predisposition toward adaptability, diversity, and versatility. The necessity to understand time both as personal time during which an individual life unfolds and as geologic time within which the human lineage evolved is another theme running through the three stories.

THE EARLY YEARS

In a recent interview Potts traced his earliest interest in origins to playground discussions with his older brother, today a mathematician. Potts' awareness of a passion for human origins became evident during a ninth-grade world civilization class: "When I left ninth grade, I knew I would become an anthropologist and that I would spend my life studying human origins in East Africa. I went to sleep at night dreaming of doing just that." That ninth-grade year Potts asked his parents, neither of whom had gone to college, to buy him two books: Desmond Morris' *The Naked Ape* and Robert Ardrey's *African Genesis*. He still remembers devouring the sections on animal behavior.

"By the end of ninth grade I was completely hooked; then, in the eleventh grade, I took a half-year anthropology course." His brother was studying anthropology at college, and they shared books and ideas. A history and a biology teacher supported Potts' ambitions. "My history teacher shared my passion for understanding time, and we talked many times about the differences between individual and geological time." She invited Potts to take the

RICK'S PASSION FOR THE STUDY OF
HUMAN ORIGINS BEGAN IN NINTH
GRADE....

AP exam even though his parents could not afford the cost (she paid for the exam), and he was not even in the AP history class. That experience and the encouragement of his biology teacher made a deep impression on Potts. By the end of twelfth grade, in 1971, Potts chose to attend a local university, Temple, where he could study anthropology and pursue his goal of researching human origins in East Africa.

Karl Butzer had published his groundbreaking *Environment and Archaeology: An Ecological Approach to Prehistory* that same year. Potts' first anthropology professor at Temple believed the study of the human past could not be separated from the study of ancient ecology and assigned all his students to read Butzer. In his first two years Potts immersed himself in biological studies, focusing on natural selection and adaptation. He took courses in cognitive sciences and physiology, fascinated by the connection between brain physiology and behavior, realizing there was no way to separate the study of physical evolution from cultural evolution. His senior thesis, on stone tools, argued that tools carry information not only about the human capacity for technology but also about general human behavior. Comparing stone tools of successive hominid species meant comparing cultural and behavioral differences among species. All this seems familiar today, but in the early 1970s studies of stone tools usually meant statistical studies describing various types of technologies, with no reference to such larger issues of behavior or culture.

Potts went straight into graduate school, choosing Harvard primarily because several of its professors called him for interviews ("I felt as if I was a sports team's recruit; I had not heard much about Harvard given my humble roots, but I was impressed by their interest in me"). Neanderthal specialist Erik Trinkaus, then a young assistant professor, read Potts' application, commenting that "he seemed all over the place." A year later Trinkaus remembered his comment and told him: "Now I understand: You want to focus on only one thing, but you want to take everything into account to do it."

Paleoanthropologist Alan Walker, then also teaching at Harvard, became a mentor. Most importantly, he arranged for Potts to do his Ph.D. research on Olduvai Gorge, gaining Mary Leakey's blessing for the work. Thus began the last phase in Potts' journey to become a paleoanthropologist—working in the field. First he was to travel to France to gain experience at several archaeological excavations, then to East Africa to work both at Olduvai Gorge in Tanzania and at the Kenya National Museum in Nairobi to work on the materials previously excavated by Mary and Louis Leakey at Olduvai Gorge. Rick Potts was twenty-three years old, it was 1976, and he was about to live out his boyhood dream.

Potts explained that in the 1960s and even the 1970s, the study of human origins was still about finding fossil bones and analyzing stone tools, particularly for the early Plio-Pleistocene period of 1.5 to 2.5 mya. Researchers were not yet really concerned about behavior or landscapes. "It was a wonderful time for me to be starting out, with my growing interests in ecology, behavior and natural selection."

THE EVOLUTION OF EARLY HUMANS

The context for understanding Potts' research activities over the next two decades is the story of human evolution, a story he has recounted in several popular accounts of the process that transformed a 5-million-year-old tropical ape into a human species of worldwide influence (1999a). Distinctively human qualities emerged over a period of about 5 million years rather than all at once.

As Potts explains the dramatic story, walking regularly on two legs (bipedalism) was the first big step, forever altering the way our ancestors interacted with their environment. By 4 mya apelike individuals (the australopithecines) had evolved who were bipedal but retained an ability to climb trees. Their brains were about one-third the size of a modern human's, they weighed between 60 and 108 pounds, and their height ranged from 3.5 to 5 feet tall.

Among either the australopithecines or the earliest members of our own genus *Homo*, stone toolmaking began to be common by about 2.5 mya. The earliest fossils of *Homo* are at least 2.3 to 2.5 million years old, a time period that also sees an increase in cranial or brain capacity. By 1.9 mya the species *H. erectus* had reached modern human size and body proportions and was fully committed to bipedal walking. *H. erectus* was the first hominid to leave Africa, spreading to Asia by about 1.6 million years ago. *H. erectus'* brain size, however, was not fully human, on average only about two-thirds to three-fourths that of fossil modern humans. The relationship of *H. erectus* to the various species before it is still hotly debated. How later fossil humans with modern brain size are related to ourselves is also controversial, particularly in the case of the Neanderthals [see Brooks, "The Emergence of Modern Humans," in this volume].

Only after the brain had reached modern size do we see the complex behaviors we associate with being human: art, clothing, complex stone technology, symbolic representation, and religious behaviors such as burial. These emerged only within the past 100,000 years. Although there is no complete agreement among scientists to explain the emergence of fully modern humans, it is agreed that our species, modern *H. sapiens,* has been the only human species on Earth for at least the last 25,000 years. It is only within the past 10,000 years that farming and herding, cities, writing, trade, and warfare arose.

As should be clear from this brief synopsis, humanity's features emerged over time; there was no single threshold or step when humans originated.

OLDUVAI GORGE

It was to examine early stone tool development that Potts traveled to East Africa to do the research for his Ph.D. In 1977 he arrived in Nairobi to reanalyze the fossil bones and stone tools discovered and described by the Leakeys, as well as to analyze other data from Bed I of Olduvai Gorge. It was Mary and Louis Leakey's work at Olduvai Gorge (1936–1985) that had helped shape scientific and popular ideas about the earliest origins of human behavior. It was they who tried to identify the maker of the early "Oldowan stone tools" and to clarify early hominid technology and activity at Olduvai Gorge, then considered the world's oldest archaeological site. Today, the Oldowan industry has been dated to at least 2.5 mya at older East African sites, and it lasted with little change for about 1 million years. To some specialists such as Glynn Isaac, the pivotal question in the archaeology of early humans was to explain "how high density clusters of stone artifacts and animal bones were found together" (1994:8).

New taphonomic studies had begun to document the processes by which fossil bones and associated stone artifacts were deposited, damaged, and buried over time. Processes such as water transport or feeding by carnivores could alter what archaeologists found millions of years later and, therefore, could influence archaeological inferences about hominid activity. Potts and his colleague Pat Shipman conducted a groundbreaking study on bones from Olduvai Gorge using a scanning electron microscope, comparing marks on fossil bones with marks produced by known causes (such as carnivore activity or damage from excavation) on modern bones. In the journal *Nature* Potts published his first major scientific paper, describing how stone tool marks could be distinguished from damage to bones made by carnivores and other taphonomic processes. With a clearer understanding of human and carnivore tooth marks, Potts now had a way of seeing how early human toolmakers and carnivores had overlapped or interacted (Potts and Shipman 1981). He concentrated on the hominids' ability to make and transport tools over long distances, freeing them from the apes' "eat-as-you-go" survival strategy. The hominids' transporting tools and food to a single place was a critical transition to creating single places of rest, later known as "home base campsites."

Potts' first book, *Early Hominid Activities at Olduvai* (1988), summarizes his detailed reanalysis of Olduvai hominid behavior that explained site formation. Four levels of analysis are detailed: How did the site form? What did humans do there? How did the different sites at Olduvai reflect different activity patterns in space? How did the hominids' activities change through time?

In the late 1970s, while Potts was preparing his dissertation, Glynn Isaac published his influential articles describing home base sites, places where hominids apparently gathered together over 1 mya to share food and tools (1978). Other anthropologists had been studying home base behavior among modern hunters and gatherers, and Isaac proposed an analogy between these societies and the early hominid ancestors. In his dissertation, Potts used studies of taphonomy, water transport, and landscape analysis to challenge Isaac's view. Contrary to Isaac, Potts concluded that the Olduvai sites did not represent home bases; instead, the earliest hominid sites at Olduvai came before home base development. Based on his reevaluation of the Oldowan material, Potts asserted that hominids collected stone materials and parts of animal carcasses, obtained through scavenging and hunting, and left them at specified locations, so-called stone caches, for future processing. In fact, carnivores such as leopards and hyenas, attracted to the carcass remains, would have prevented the use of these sites by hominids as the places of primary social activity implied by the home base theory. Potts called his hypothesis "resource transport" (1984, 1991). It was a major theoretical breakthrough, made before he had his Ph.D. in hand, and it was well received by older colleagues in the field, including Isaac.

In 1983 Potts, then an assistant professor of anthropology at Yale University, returned to Africa, this time to direct paleontological/archaeological excavations at Lainyamok, Kenya. Mary Leakey traveled down to visit Potts' excavation and, impressed with his work, suggested he turn his attention to the much larger area of Olorgesailie. The following year Potts gained permission from Richard Leakey, director of the National Museums in Kenya, to work long-term at Olorgesailie. By 1985 the Smithsonian's National Museum of Natural History had hired Potts to start a new Human Origins Program at the Institution. Within a year he had written the first of many grant proposals to fund large-scale excavations at Olorgesailie. Potts' career was launched.

OLORGESAILIE

For an aspiring paleoanthropologist, Olduvai Gorge was a dream come true, but it was Olorgesailie that changed Potts' life. In the beginning he was after bones and tools and the opportunity to test some ideas regarding home bases by enlarging the context of hominid behavior. To do this work, Potts began to develop a landscape-scale approach to the excavation and study of hominid tools, animals bones, and the overall environment. At a single level, 990,000 years old, Potts' team excavated many sites, including a huge elephant butchery site. For several summers Potts' team worked to reconstruct the lifeways and environmental context of *H. erectus*, 1 million to 600,000 years ago. Potts differentiated his approach from fossil collecting; he was searching to understand the ecological niche of early humans by focusing on excavating an entire landscape, not just surface collecting across the land or putting another fossil onto the family tree.

Soon, however, Potts began to ask new questions regarding space and time. What was the ecology of the region through time? What habitats did the various hominids living there have to cope with over a million years? With the new dates available at Olorgesailie, Potts realized he could document an entire sequence from 1.2 million up to 49,000 years ago. It was, he said, "an archive of environments, a textbook of hominid behavior . . . the Rift Valley writ large through time." To analyze and assess this remarkable "archive through time," Potts again assembled an international team to excavate and synthesize the complex data. Potts has always stressed a team approach, working with "geologists, archaeologists, paleontologists, environmental scientists, and a great group of well-trained Kenyan excavators."

ENVIRONMENTAL OSCILLATION

By the early 1990s environmental issues had come to the forefront of public attention and scientific concern, resulting in new research and multiple techniques to measure environments. Potts adapted these techniques to understanding past climates, environments, soils, and vegetation—applying many of these new techniques to his amazing "slice through time" (1998a:96–104). What he found was startling. The dating and stratigraphic analysis at Olorgesailie uncovered a widening variability through time. Furthermore, Olorgesailie was the tantalizing lead-in to an examination of the larger global picture of environmental change. Looking at the incontrovertible evidence from soils, vegetation, and lake sediments worldwide, Potts could no longer avoid the key idea: oscillation.

By 1992 Potts had become committed to understanding the impact of environmental change on early hominids. Much of that year Potts spent walking up and down the hillsides of the site. "I could walk up a hillside and see the bands of the blinding white sediments of the lake replaced by gray and brown soils followed by the thin salt layer indicating the lake had dried up. But then a little further forward in time, the lake would be back. You walk up and down and the oscillation of the environment becomes unmistakable, and you realize that that was the challenge to the hominids, the oscillation of the environment." But how did that challenge operate?

EAST AFRICAN MAMMAL STUDY

In 1992 Potts thought constantly about the extreme environmental variability he saw as the channel through which the human lineage had passed. He kept asking himself where all our human versatility and diversity had come from, and if and why humans had evolved differently from other animals, whose evolution he had studied for years. "If natural selection is going to hone an organism's characteristics to the specific environment in which it lives, then how do you transform a small population of apelike hominids into a species of worldwide influence, diverse and extremely flexible in their behavior? That is the critical ecological question of human evolution."

Understanding the adaptive challenges for other East African mammals might be a key. As Potts explains, with humans we have the unique situation of human evolution, and our only comparison is with earlier hominids who did not survive. So Potts turned to a study of large mammals in Africa, reanalyzing the fossil animals from Lainyamok, a large and diverse sample ideal for such a study. Together Olorgesailie and Lainyamok span the period during which modern human brain size developed—a critical time for human evolution. Potts and colleague Alan Deino published their analysis documenting the extinction of an entire group of mammals during this period, around 400,000 years ago (1995). They hypothesized that large numbers of mammals became extinct as a response to rapid climatic fluctuations and extreme dietary specialization. As the mammals eating coarse, low-lying vegetation became extinct, smaller, more versatile, and more generalized eaters emerged; these are the large mammal species still with us today. Potts wondered if the human lineage had gone through a similar pattern of extinction and adaptation as a response to extreme environmental change.

A NEW BOOK

In 1990 Potts had signed a contract with the publisher William Morrow and Co. to write a book dealing with Olorgesailie and environmental change. He wrote half the book and then in 1992 realized his entire thinking was shifting. "I had a series of brainstorms at night, wondering if and how environmental oscillation had been the major influence on the developing human lineage. I realized I had to start the book over again. I called my editors and told them I was throwing out everything I had written, but I promised to start over. I knew I was on to something big and that it would take time to work out the details. All the training I had in college and graduate school, all the early conversations I had with my brother, all my reading of Charles Darwin flooded back. I knew I had to deal with the question of environmental variability and its impact as a major selective factor explaining human evolution."

Potts realized immediately he would have to challenge one of the major theories and assumptions of human evolution: the transition in Africa from widespread forests to widespread savanna grasslands as the major explanatory factor for the emergence of bipedal, tool-using human beings. In his book *Humanity's Descent* (1996a) he proposed instead a new theory of environmental variability as the key selective factor explaining the emergence of the human species.

THE SAVANNA HYPOTHESIS

According to conventional wisdom, our earliest ancestors were forced to adapt to a new, drier savanna environment that replaced a once heavily forested landscape. Bipedal walking developed as a favored adaptation to the ground, with hominids using their newly freed hands to make and use tools, especially for hunting. This led to increased eating of meat and other sources

WHY ARE WE HUMAN ?

of protein that fueled a larger brain. Eventually food sharing, home base living, social interaction, and division of labor by sex emerged. The savanna hypothesis, which Potts was originally taught, had made a lot of sense, but it didn't fit the environmental fluctuations that he had documented. Over the short run some hominids may have adapted to specific environments including the savanna, but over millennia the human lineage had to accommodate to and cope with huge oscillations or swings in the environment that were manifested all over the world (1998a:109–12).

VARIABILITY SELECTION

It was this variability that Potts identified as the key to the three distinctive breakthroughs of human evolution: bipedal walking (4–1.9 mya), stone tool making (2.5–1.5 mya), and increased brain size (700,000–150,000 years ago)—each coinciding with increased environmental oscillation. There was a larger amount of savanna in certain areas of the world, but increased fluctuation was just as much a hallmark of global climate and much more influential on the course of human evolution. Potts called his new theory "variability selection," a process that links adaptive change to large degrees of environmental variability. The theory refers to variability as a selection agency, not to the variability or versatility that developed in the human population.

As Potts explains, variability selection "is, in essence, a hypothesis about how hominid evolution has been a response to environments and environmental change." After years of reconstructing environmental variability, as well as the evolution and extinction of mammal species, Potts realized that the survival of a versatile species capable of adjusting to novel surroundings was the story of human evolution. As environmental conditions drastically fluctuated, the evolutionary winners were populations that evolved a capacity to respond in new ways to diverse habitats. This process—variability selection—favors genes that improve an organism's adaptability, and the theory explains why our particular pattern of human evolution occurred. As Potts says, " it is not the whole explanation, but I believe it is a critical piece."

Variability selection is also a theory that Potts knows modifies one of the tenets of Darwinian evolution: long-term directional consistency in selection over time, consistency implied, for example, in the savanna hypothesis. In a 1996 article in *Science* Potts explains the significance of his theory to understanding human evolution: "Hardly just noise, long-term fluctuation was a signal of potentially major evolutionary consequence. I have proposed the term *variability selection* to describe the effects of repeated, dramatic shifting in Darwinian selection over time. This inconsistency over many generations may have had an important impact on hominid evolution" (1996b:922).

NATURAL SELECTION

As Potts explains in a recent article: "Natural selection is the process by which adaptive structures are evolved and maintained. As a result of this century's union of population biology, genetics, and paleontology (the neo-Darwinian synthesis), natural selection is regarded as the main cause of change in organisms in relation to their surroundings" (1998b:81). Traditionally this meant consistency of adaptation over time. "Selective consistency, or long-term uniform selection pressure, is largely assumed to be the way by which adaptive complexity evolves" (1998b:81). But the adaptive conditions of hominid evolution over time, according to Potts' research, were highly inconsistent on a local to global scale.

Potts' theory posits that inconsistency of environmental conditions had critical implications for hominid evolution. There are several ways organisms can respond to habitat fluctuation (1998b:84–85). The first is simply to follow the preferred environment, an adaptive pattern that works for a while but can lead to extinction when large environmental fluctuations occur. The second is to broaden the range of conditions under which an organism can live. This can be achieved by both genetic polymorphism (several different genetic potentials existing within the same population) or by phenotypic plasticity, when organisms can respond differently at any given time with the same genotypic inheritance.

A third avenue of flexibility is variability selection, or the evolution of adaptive mechanisms within a population that "assist an organism's sophisticated intake of and responsiveness to environmental data" (1998b:85). Examples of such adaptive mechanisms might be new locomotor systems (such as bipedalism) and an enlarged brain to process and generate complex cognitive responses. In light of Potts' theory, the evolution of the brain takes on new meaning, as it is our brain that enables us to adapt to changing conditions, novel problems, and multiple solutions. Climatic oscillation becomes more intense after 700,000 years ago, and it is from this time to about 150,000 years ago that the human brain reaches modern size. Potts has stated that his theory requires that we may have to "significantly revise the way natural selection is construed to have operated—not merely as *selection pressure* or as *adaptation to* a model environment, but as a response to habitat and resource variability from place to place and over time" (1994:23).

Potts points out that in each epoch of human evolution there were species that evolved as specialists, that adapted to a specific environment and lived alongside more versatile forms that survived after the more specialized forms became extinct. Two examples he cites are the robust australopithecines and the cold-weather-adapted Neanderthals, both highly specialized hominids that became extinct. The eventual ability of a single versatile lineage, extraordinarily diverse in its behavior, to survive and spread worldwide may well have evolved as the result of adaptation to our planet's variable environment.

NATURE AND HUMANKIND

The relationship of nature and humankind is one of the recurring and most thought-provoking themes of Potts' popular and extremely well-written volume *Humanity's Descent* (1996a). "It is important to get the relationship between Nature and humankind right, both in its long-term development and in its present possibility" (1996a:44). Potts explains that humans' penchant for setting themselves apart from nature stems from an illusory divide into natural and human domains—a divide that has "never existed over the long course of human presence on Earth" (1996a:267). The implications of this key insight have profound public policy ramifications, for, as Potts says, "the world now rests . . . on the legacy left by a single species" (1996a:44). The fact that our essential human qualities emerged as the result of our ecological

relationship to nature contrasts with the ironic observation that our resulting dominion today could disrupt forever the ecological balance on earth.

CONCLUSION

Science moves forward by the process of hypothesis testing, development of
new theories, unearthing new data, and proposing alternative explanations.
In science, the development of a major new hypothesis or theory is always
extraordinary in its originality. It is, nonetheless, also a beginning because
colleagues will test such new ideas with their own data and their own understanding. For Potts, Olorgesailie was the inspiration, environmental
change the key to the development of a major new theory to explain human
evolution. Variability selection is a dramatic insight and a theory that others now must take into account in their attempt to explain the human past.
Potts and his fellow paleoanthropologists will develop other insights, and
modifications of Potts' theory of variability selection will inevitably be made
over time. But the importance of this new and provocative theory will stand
as a major contribution to the ongoing study of human origins.

What Potts' journey demonstrates is that one scientist's approach to understanding the world around him can grow from many seeds: a sharp, fertile mind with a penchant for the big picture; a lifelong passion to find out
where humans came from; and a determination to look at the whole puzzle,
not just a single piece. Teachers, mentors, colleagues, and the scientists who
came before all influenced Potts. Just as his theory connects the development
of the human lineage to the millennia of challenging environments, so one
can see Potts' life developing from the interaction of his unique mind and
driving passion with the influences of his family, teachers, colleagues, and experiences—his environment through time.

POSTSCRIPT

As this *AnthroNotes* article was being written, Potts flew to London to present his theory of variability selection at the invitation of the Linnean Society.
Potts must have been aware that in July 1858 Charles Darwin and Alfred
Wallace, at the urging of the geologist Charles Lyell and the botanist Sir
Joseph Hooker, presented simultaneously their papers on evolution through
natural selection also to the Linnean Society. On May 24, 1859, Thomas Bell,
president of the society reported in his presidential address, "The year which
has passed . . . has not . . . been marked by any of those striking discoveries

which at once revolutionize, so to speak, the department of science on which they bear" (1860:viii). For the impact of variability selection, as with the theory of natural selection, only time will tell.

UPDATE

Rick Potts

Written by Ruth Selig in 1999, the first part of this chapter focuses on the idea of variability selection and how I began to develop it with intensive field-work at a single site, Olorgesailie. Olorgesailie was the first inspiration for the variability selection idea, but I knew at the time that no one field site could yield all the answers. I would have to go to new sites to test the hypothesis and also try to build a more comprehensive theory to explain new observations, especially as others considered the theory and debated its merits.

It has been a fruitful four years since I was first interviewed for this chapter, in April 1999, and our work has progressed in three major directions: (1) my research team has started a comparative study of human evolution in China and East Africa, looking at the archaeological and fossil record in an environmental context; (2) our landscape-scale approach to early archaeological sites in East Africa has been described in a series of publications, lending a more diachronic perspective to our work; and (3) the variability selection hypothesis of human evolution is now reframed to focus more sharply on the question of how adaptability evolved in the human species.

Comparing South China and East Africa

A National Science Foundation grant awarded in 2002 will allow our international team of scientists to undertake the first in-depth comparative study of East African and East Asian early human evolution within an environmental context—a study that will take place over five years. This is a particularly exciting prospect since these are the two areas of the world with the longest documented record of human origins. Our research also will reconsider an older view, that hominid evolution in China was isolated from developments in other parts of the world.

Back in 1991 when I traveled to China to deliver a lecture, I was invited by Chinese colleagues to lead new excavations in the Bose Basin, which had been known to Chinese archaeologists for several decades but never carefully studied. I was interested in South China because the ancient environment there was thought to be very stable, showing little change over time, in contrast to the highly variable environments apparent at Olorgesailie. It seemed to me that East Asia and East Africa represented two distinct "natural laboratories" in which humans had evolved, with their own unique environmental histories and responses by early humans. I wanted to know whether environmental change challenged the adaptability of early human populations equally in both regions or in completely different ways, affecting their ability to endure across different kinds of environments. The Bose Basin of China is a big place, around 300 square miles in area, allowing us to apply our landscape approach to excavation. I also could reconsider the whole question of "Pleistocene stability" and whether human evolution in China was truly isolated from other places.

In 1995 my Chinese colleagues and I applied this landscape approach by setting up multiple small excavations over a wide area rather than the traditional approach of digging one large site rich in stone tools. We found that the Bose Basin environment was far more variable than previously thought and that the archaeological assemblages show evidence of flaking capabilities, strategies of stone flaking, and distributions of tools across the region that are quite similar to those of Acheulean handaxe makers of East Africa, such as the early humans who lived at Olorgesailie. Our findings contrasted with the static portrait of Chinese archaeology and environments normally considered. The early humans of Bose, for instance, were able to adapt and colonize a landscape laid bare by a meteorite impact in Southeast Asia around 800,000 years ago. Over a longer time period, the region's environment appears to have been unstable, with strong parallels to the dynamic mid-Pleistocene environments of Europe and East Africa. The Bose stone technology, dated to around the time of the meteorite impact, is more compatible with that of western Eurasia and Africa than usually thought. This finding implies similar technical, cultural, and cognitive capabilities in both China and western Eurasia and Africa. We are hopeful that the next few years will yield further insights into the matter of how early humans adapted and evolved in the face of changing landscapes in these two distinct regions, offering our first comparative look at human evolutionary history in East Asia and East Africa.

Olorgesailie

Publications over the last several years have described the larger paleolandscape of the Olorgesailie region. This work involves taking individual excavation sites and connecting them into a single paleolandscape at one point in time, and then seeing how a series of paleolandscapes—including places visited by early humans—changed over time. By applying this approach to several levels at Olorgesailie and even older sites in northern Kenya and Tanzania, we can begin to ask how early human behavior changed and varied from one slice of time to another over the past 2.3 million years. This approach allows us a new way of trying to answer the question of what early humans were doing and why they were doing it.

One study we are currently undertaking is an initial test of how the record of early human fossils and archaeological remains correlates with environmental shifts and climate variability in Africa, where the longest record of human ancestry is known. Our analysis focuses on four intervals (two each of high and low climate variability) between 1.96 and 1.51 mya in the fossil-rich Turkana Basin of northern Kenya, and four more intervals between 1.0 and 0.83 mya and between 0.73 and 0.46 mya in the Olorgesailie basin, the periods where we find the greatest abundance of archaeological and faunal remains. So far it seems that some important changes in human and faunal evolution occurred, especially in eras of higher environmental instability, but much more testing and reexamination of our findings are necessary before we can draw any firm conclusions.

Reframing the Variability Selection Theory

When Selig's article about our work first appeared in *AnthroNotes*, my book (1996a) on the variability selection theory was already published, and scientific articles that elaborated the theory had just come out (1998a, b). In the years since, there have been many reactions to the theory, many positive and some, of course, less positive. Reactions have been helpful and constructive for the most part, encouraging me to focus even more strongly on the thesis that adaptability may have evolved in response to escalating environmental change and inconsistent conditions of natural selection.

Any new theory attracts responses, and the process of dialogue helps refine the initial formulation. In my case, comments have come from climatologists, geologists, physical anthropologists, archaeologists, geneticists, and evolutionary theorists. Specialists in geology and climate change have been overwhelmingly positive; evolutionary theorists who focus on the specific mechanics of how evolution works have been more critical. Since we have yet to do computer simulations or mathematical testing, some of the criticisms have come from scientists with particular interest in these types of modeling. New ideas of evolutionary theory take years to work out, and I am, of course, eager to see the variability selection theory tested through such modeling and computer simulations; I am gearing up to start this work in the next year.

What has become increasingly clear to me is that human evolution has been characterized by two different ecological themes—habitat-specific adaptation and increased adaptability. Most early hominid lineages were ecologically and geographically constrained. But some later lineages, such as the one including *Homo erectus,* were able to break out of these constraints because of increased capacity to adjust to many different kinds of habitats. The question posed, then, is how significant increases in adaptability came about. What I suggest is that adaptability may evolve as an unanticipated consequence of individuals living, dying, and reproducing under specific environmental conditions. Over time conditions change. And as a genetic population or lineage faces increasingly variable environments over time, the dynamic pattern of selection (variability selection) may favor the ability of the descendents to survive other kinds of environmental change. This can happen, I hypothesize, even though any one individual may live in a much narrower range of conditions than encountered by its many ancestors over a much longer time frame.

Traditional biology focuses primarily on the environment as a consistent entity, asking about the constant features in the environment to which organisms adapt and how the resulting adaptation helps the organism evolve in a single "directional mode." What the variability selection theory asks us to do is to focus not on the consistent properties of the environment to which organisms adapt, but instead on the dynamic, inconsistent qualities (for example, periodic droughts over long time spans, alternating with periods of high rainfall). These inconsistent or unstable qualities then act as a filter for genes that, over time, help build up an organism's ability to buffer environmental change. This new focus on environmental dynamics leads us, in the end, to consider a process of evolution that serves to decouple the organism from any single ancestral environment, and instead gives the organism tremendous leverage in adapting to many different environments.

Human evolution took place in an era of exceptional environmental complexity, and we know that humans are exceptional in using technology and information (language, for example) to buffer themselves, individually and socially, from environmental disturbances. This points to a capacity that distinguishes the human species from almost all others: its ability to adapt to many different environments. Some process of genetic and behavioral change enabled certain lineages of our ancestors to become decoupled from any one ancestral environment. Much of the comparative work I am now engaged in—which brings together studies of early humans and environments from China to Kenya, and even includes genetic research—is designed to illuminate this process further.

FURTHER READING

Ardrey, Robert. 1977. *African Genesis*. Bantam Books.

Bell, Thomas. 1860. "The Year Which Has Passed." Presidential address to the Linnean Society on the anniversary of Linnaeus' birth, May 24, 1859. *Proceedings of the Linnean Society of London*, viii–xx. Bound in *Journal of the Proceedings of The Linnean Society: Botany 4*.

Butzer, Karl. 1971. *Environment and Archeology: An Ecological Approach to Pre-history*. 2nd ed. Aldine-Atherton.

Isaac, Glynn. 1978. "The Food-Sharing Behavior of Proto-human Hominids." *Scientific American* 238:90–108.

Morris, Desmond. 1967. *The Naked Ape: A Zoologist's Study of the Human Animal*. McGraw-Hill.

Potts, Rick. 1984. "Home Bases and Early Hominids." *American Scientist* 72:338–47.

Potts, Rick. 1988. *Early Hominid Activities at Olduvai*. Aldine de Gruyter.

Potts, Rick. 1991. "Why the Oldowan? Plio-Pleistocene Toolmaking and the Transport of Resources." *Journal of Anthropological Research* 47(2):153–76.

Potts, Rick. 1994. "Variables versus Models of Early Pleistocene Hominid Land Use." *Journal of Human Evolution* 27: 7–24.

Potts, Rick. 1996a. *Humanity's Descent: The Consequences of Ecological Instability*. William Morrow and Co.

Potts, Rick. 1996b. "Evolution and Climate Variability." *Science* 273:922–23.

Potts, Rick. 1998a. "Environmental Hypotheses of Hominid Evolution." *Yearbook of Physical Anthropology* 41: 93–136.

Potts, Rick. 1998b. "Variability Selection in Hominid Evolution." *Evolutionary Anthropology* 7:81–96.

Potts, Rick. 1999a. "Why Are We Human?" *Washington Post*, April 14, "Horizon" section, 1, 4–5.

Potts, Rick. 1999b "Human Evolution." In *Encarta Encyclopedia*, "Prehistory." Microsoft Corp. Online Encyclopedia. Aldine-Atherton.

Potts, Rick, and Alan Deino. 1995. "Mid-Pleistocene Change in Large Mammal Faunas of East Africa." *Quaternary Research* 43:106–13.

Potts, Rick, and Pat Shipman. 1981. "Cutmarks Made by Stone Tools on Bones from Olduvai Gorge, Tanzania." *Nature* 291: 577–80.

4 NEW RESEARCH IN EARLY HUMAN ORIGINS 7 TO 1 MILLION YEARS AGO

Alison S. Brooks and Rick Potts

The earliest period of human evolution, 7 million to 1 million years ago, presents a very complex story of our beginnings and has changed fundamentally our view of the past from just a decade ago. Brooks and Potts' article reports on the flood of new evidence, accumulating at an increasing rate, which suggests new answers to old questions: Where and when did our genus, Homo, *originate? How many related species existed prior to 1 million years ago? What enabled our early ancestors to expand out of their African homeland, and when did this migration first occur?*

The last decade has witnessed a dramatic increase in the pace of new discoveries about human beginnings. Many aspects of the human story as we knew it a decade ago have changed, and we continue to be surprised by the variety, adaptations, and sophistication of our earliest ancestors.

The number of new finds is truly extraordinary. In the twenty-six years between 1964 and 1990, for example, only four new species (two species in the genus *Australopithecus* and two in the genus *Homo*) were added to our hominin family tree, and no new genera were proposed. In only eleven years between 1991 and 2002, eight new hominid species were proposed, four of them so distinctive that they were placed in new genera, implying they were at least as different from previous finds as chimpanzees are from us or from gorillas.

Why this sudden increase in the rate of discovery? In part it is due to an increasing number of workers in the field and to the opening or reopening of new areas to researchers. For example, Ethiopia, home to two of the new species, was largely closed to international researchers for ten years before 1991. The desolate region of Chad, where two other new species were found, had hardly been explored before 1994. Another factor is the expanded funding available to an increasingly multinational research effort; it is not unusual for today's exploration teams to consist of scientists from a dozen different nations, including African, Asian, South American, and Pacific ones. The diversity of new finds has been accompanied by advances in the reconstruction of ancient environments and how humans adapted to them, and by new ways of studying and understanding physical differences among fossils. This review will discuss the impact of these new finds, as well as the new analytical methods for studying them.

THE FAMILY TREE IN 1990

Have these new finds really changed anything about how we view our earliest beginnings? The answer is yes. As recently as 1990 the family tree itself seemed rather simple and straightforward; the most common model was a tree with only seven or perhaps eight species in all, and only one or two side branches. Most of the time the hominid niche was filled by only one species, except between about 2.6 and 1.3 million years ago (mya), when related species occupied a side branch. First, or so we thought, there was "Lucy" (*Australopithecus afarensis*), from about 3.6 to 2.9 mya. *A. afarensis* was small but walked bipedally—an adaptation, we thought, to life in the open savanna as Africa became drier and its forests shrank. Then there were more "evolved" australopithecines who came in two varieties: the gracile type (*Australopithecus africanus*) and the robust type with huge teeth and a bony crest on top of the skull (*Australopithecus robustus, A. boisei,* and *A. aethiopicus*). The former group was thought to have evolved into an early form of our own species, *Homo,* while the latter side branch became more and more specialized, lived alongside early *Homo* for a while (for perhaps as much as a million years), and then died out. Early *Homo,* in turn, supposedly went through a direct progression from *H. habilis* to *H. erectus* to *H. sapiens,* marked by increasing brain size and decreasing tooth size. Neanderthals might have been another, late, side branch. Until about 1.3–1.4 mya, Africa, specifically eastern and southern Africa, was considered the only home of our ancestors. And the first migrants out of Africa, *H. erectus,* went not to Europe but to Asia, arriving in China and Java only about 1 mya, or so it was thought. No firm evidence existed in 1990 for the occupation of Europe prior to 500,000 years ago—and as of 1990 the earliest known occupants of that continent did not fit into *H. erectus* but were more advanced toward *H. sapiens,* with larger brains, rounder skulls, smaller teeth, or other more specialized features.

BEFORE LUCY

To call a new fossil a hominin, or a member of the human lineage, palaeontologists look for evidence of our most unusual features: bipedalism, thick dental enamel and large flat molars for chewing tougher foods, and differences in the canine teeth—male apes have big sharp ones used to threaten other males, and humans all have small blunt ones. If leg and pelvic bones are missing, bipedalism can be inferred indirectly because it changes the shape of the vertebrae and ribs. Bipedalism also changes the place where the spine enters the braincase—the entry hole (foramen magnum) is further forward under the skull rather than toward the back. Australopithecines who lived until ca. 1.3 mya had small brains not much larger than chimpanzees, very large chewing teeth, and a large projecting, almost concave or dish-shaped face, together with bony ridges and even crests on the skull where the large chewing muscles attached. Fossils classed in our own genus, *Homo,* which first appears around 2.3 mya, have larger brains, smaller molar teeth, and a nose that projects from the plane of the face—they are also often associated with clear evidence of technology such as chipped stone artifacts and bones cut with stone tools.

But what came before *Australopithecus afarensis,* who already had reduced canines and large molar teeth and also walked bipedally and may have climbed trees to feed or sleep at night? Only a couple of indeterminate teeth and scraps of bone filled the gap between the presumed split with the chimpanzee lineage, estimated at ca. 5–9 mya on genetic grounds, and *A. afarensis. A. afarensis* was the only example of what a hominin from 3.5 mya might look like, and there are no diagnostic fossils of chimpanzee or gorilla ancestors after about 8 mya. (There are at least two fossil species just before this time that may be related to the lineage of the African great apes and humans: a gorilla-like upper jaw from the Samburu Hills of Kenya [*Samburupithecus*] dated to 9.5 mya, and several fossils from Greece dating to 9.5–8.5 mya [*Graecopithecus*] with large canines and apelike browridges.) Now six new species, provisionally classed with the hominins and dated to between 7 mya and 3 mya, suggest considerable diversity among our earliest ancestors.

The newest find and the oldest fossil of these is also the most unexpected: a beautifully preserved skull complete with a face, published in 2002 and given a new genus and species name, *Sahelanthropus tchadensis.* First, it does *not* come from East Africa, but from the site of Toros-Menalla in the flat desert margin of the Sahara (the Sahel) in the west-central African country of Chad. Second, the fossil mammals found with it include not only species such as saber-toothed cats, three-toed horses, and elephants with upper and lower tusks that lived about 6–5 mya in Africa, but also very primitive animals, called anthracotheres, that lived in Libya and other places until around 7 mya but died out shortly afterward, placing this new hominin between 6 mya and 7 mya. The cranium and teeth do not look at all like what we might have expected in a "missing link" between *Australopithecus* and a chimpanzee ancestor. *Sahelanthropus* had a very small brain no larger than that of a chimpanzee, massive brows larger than those of a gorilla, and thin dental enamel (though thicker than a chimpanzee's). But it also possessed rather small canine teeth and a surprisingly small and vertical (nonprojecting) lower face, closer to *Homo* than to *Australopithecus*. The spinal column entered the base of the skull relatively far forward suggesting bipedal posture, but definitive determination of this awaits the discovery of diagnostic pieces of the lower limb or pelvis. And while there were many fossil animals at the site whose teeth suggest that they ate grass, the immediate environment of *Sahelanthropus* was more like a swampy gallery forest (along a river or flood plain) than a savanna, judging by the hippos, crocodiles, otters, fish, and monkeys found along with the fossil.

Back in Kenya, a 6-million-year-old hominin, *Orrorin tugenensis*, also known as "millennium man," was found in the Baringo basin of central Kenya in the fall of 2000 and published in 2001. The geological layer in which the fossils were found is dated to between 5.6 and 6.2 mya by the relatively accurate argon-argon dating technique, which measures the regular decay of radioactive potassium atoms into argon gas in volcanic sediments. The thirteen skeletal fragments from possibly five individuals (more bones have reportedly been discovered since) included teeth and jaw fragments, a left thigh bone, a finger bone, and bones from the arm. While not yet well studied or published, the fossils show a mix of primitive and advanced traits. The canines are large and the premolar is described as "apelike," but the molars are small, with thick enamel. Similarly, the arm and finger bones are curved for climbing in the trees, but the femur (thigh bone) is very large and robust, and its shape and large hip joint suggest bipedalism to its discoverers, if not to many skeptics. *Orrorin* lived alongside hippos, rhinos, and antelopes.

ARDIPITHECUS AND EARLY AUSTRALOPITHECUS

In northern Ethiopia's Middle Awash Valley south of Hadar (where Lucy was found), two new sites dating to 5.8–5.2 and 4.4 mya, respectively, have yielded remains of yet another ancestral hominin species: *Ardipithecus ramidus* (from *ardi-*, meaning "ground" or "floor," and *ramid-*, meaning "root" in the local Afar language). Fossils of the earlier subspecies (*Ardipithecus ramidus kadabba*) included a toe bone described as similar to a bipedal one. Both this subspecies and the later one (*Ardipithecus ramidus ramidus*) have teeth and jaws that combine a different mosaic of traits than *Orrorin* or *Sahelanthropus*. *Ardipithecus* had relatively large canines compared to *Australopithecus,* but blunter and smaller than those of apes; the premolars are similarly intermediate in their asymmetry; the molars are smaller and more elongated than in *Australopithecus,* and the dental enamel is thinner. The ear opening is small, as in apes, rather than large, as in hominins. Other fossils of *Ardipithecus* await the tedious and painstaking task of restoration, which the bones' fragile and fragmentary condition requires, before any scientific comparisons can be made. *Ardipithecus* was also not a savanna animal—the most common other fossils at the later site belonged to kudus and colobus monkeys, along with bats, a primitive bear, and a number of small mammals.

By 4.2–3.9 mya the first species of *Australopithecus* appears in northern Kenya's Lake Turkana region, but in a different, more primitive form than *A. afarensis* (Lucy). The new species is called *Australopithecus anamensis* (for *anam,* "lake" in the Turkana language). It was definitely bipedal, judging from the large size of the tibia (shin bone) and the asymmetry and elongated shape of its upper end that forms part of the knee joint. The hand, nonetheless, was large and strong, for climbing in the trees. Like other species of *Australopithecus,* this one had larger, square-shaped molars with thick enamel, but the canine and first lower premolar were intermediate in size and shape between those of Lucy and *Ardipithecus,* and the ear opening was small, as in apes and *Ardipithecus.* This first *Australopithecus* didn't live in a savanna either, although the environment may have been more open than that of *Ardipithecus.* At one site (Kanapoi) *A. anamensis* shared the environment with fish, hippos, kudu, and impala, suggesting a bushy woodland, while at another site (Alia Bay) the environment was more likely a riverine gallery forest.

LUCY'S COUSINS

New finds and species of the last eleven years are not limited to the period before 4 mya. Many new finds have expanded our knowledge of *A. afarensis* itself, suggesting a very large degree of sexual dimorphism and further evidence that this species both walked bipedally and retained considerable ability to climb trees. *Afarensis* has been joined in the 4–3-million-year range by new fossils of *A. africanus* in South Africa, and by two new species in western and eastern Africa, respectively. The new early South African fossils include a set of foot bones (nicknamed "Little Foot") dating to at least 2.9–3.1 mya at the cave of Sterkfontein (Member 2). While similar to the feet of later bipeds, this one may have retained some ability to grasp tree limbs, although the reconstruction is controversial. In 1998 much of the rest of the skeleton was found embedded in the cave floor where it fell, millions of years ago, but will require years of painstaking work to excavate from the solid limestone conglomerate or breccia that formed around and over it. New paleobotanical studies at Sterkfontein from the main australopithecine level (Member 4) recovered fossilized vines that today occur only well inside the tropical forest far to the north. No open savannas here either!

Another new find in this time range is remarkable for its location—1,500 miles west of Lake Turkana in another region of Chad called Bahr el Ghazal. *Australopithecus bahrelghazali* is dated to around 3.0–3.4 mya based on rough ages of the primitive fossil elephants, horses, pigs and rhinos found with it. These are interpreted as inhabiting a mixed forest-woodland, rather than an open savanna. The fossil, a mandible, is similar to *A. afarensis* but with thinner tooth enamel and other distinctive traits. The second new species, from the fossil-rich region of Lake Turkana, is so different from *Australopithecus* that it has been placed in a different genus entirely: *Kenyanthropus platyops* (flat-faced Kenya man). This fossil, an almost complete skull, lacks the browridges, concave or "dished" face, large molar teeth, and other features of *Australopithecus* and has a more rounded braincase and smaller teeth. In some ways it most resembles later fossils attributed to our own genus, *Homo*, including the famous fossil KNM-ER 1470, attributed to *H. rudolfensis*.

NEW VIEWS OF HUMAN ANCESTRY

Does this new species push Lucy and all the australopithecines off the direct line to humans onto a side branch? In some ways, not only *Kenyanthropus* but even the ancient *Sahelanthropus* shared some advanced features with later *Homo* that are missing in *Australopithecus*. The new evidence makes it difficult to describe human ancestry in such a linear way. The period leading up to and including Lucy is now represented by a confusing diversity of not-quite-human forms: at least four species before *A. afarensis,* and three *A. afarensis* contemporaries. Most or all may represent experiments with some form of bipedalism, almost always combined with an ability to grasp tree limbs. The evidence for bipedalism is strongest where the leg bones are represented—definite in the australopithecines, including *A. anamensis,* likely for *Ardipithecus,* and more debated for *Orrorin* and *Sahelanthropus.* Some species, such as the australopithecines, have flat projecting faces, large thick-enameled molars, and small canines. Others have large molars and thinner enamel (*A. bahrelghazali*) or larger canines and thinner enamel (*Sahelanthropus, Ardipithecus*), or smaller canines, smaller molars, and thick enamel (*Orrorin*). Faces were variously vertical or projecting, with or without large browridges. In short, it is as if there were a large basket of possible dental, facial, and cranial traits, and each species pulled out a few different traits almost at random. What is implied is a long period of experimentation within a new ape niche, part arboreal, part terrestrial. Efforts to compress this into a tree, with definite ancestor and descendant relationships or even groupings, will depend entirely on which traits the paleoanthropologist chooses to emphasize. But which traits did evolution emphasize?

We cannot understand the large amount of variation among early hominins by just listing and comparing all the traits. Instead we need to understand how traits are linked functionally, how they develop during growth, and how they are related to genetic changes. A very small genetic change in the pattern of growth, speeding up or slowing the growth of one body part relative to another, could fundamentally alter the resulting body shape. The fact that we share 95–98 percent of our genes with chimpanzees, and even 80 percent with a laboratory mouse, means that genetic control of how the face or limbs grow, for example, may be very similar across all the mammals. Some genes just turn on earlier and allow longer or faster growth of certain body parts in chimpanzees, other parts in humans. And one genetic change may have multiple effects on the resultant body. Since bodies also respond to function and usage during growth, anthropologists are conducting laboratory experiments on many different species other than primates to help them understand how the interplay of function and genetics can explain differences in the fossil record. In the past five years George Washington University scientists have studied how lower limbs respond to walking stress by observing sheep on treadmills, and how jaws and cranial bones respond to chewing stress by feeding hyraxes different diets. Modeling techniques derived from engineering studies of design stresses help to interpret the data, and CT scans of the animals help scientists see the changes as they develop.

For the moment, the best strategy is simply to divide the most archaic forms from the australopithecines, and to recognize that experimentation and diversity continued, even during the apparent dominance of *Australopithecus* between 3.5 and 2 mya. Exploration of new regions in Africa may continue to provide radical challenges to our models of human ancestry. For example, while these early bipedal experimenters inhabited different environments, none of them seemed to have lived in the savanna, and all of them retained an ability for tree climbing.

THE EMERGENCE OF *HOMO*

The 3–2 mya period is perhaps the most critical for the emergence of our own genus, but new finds of five different species have questioned the direct ancestry or even the definition of *Homo*. *A. africanus* continues in South Africa, but in East Africa *A. afarensis* disappears early in this time range, and two developments follow. The first is the appearance of robust australopithecines (or *Paranthropus*) by 2.6 mya, with extra-large molar teeth and sagittal crests along the top of the skull (in *A. aethiopicus* and *A. boisei*). This is followed around 2.3 mya by the appearance of *Homo* (including *H. rudolfensis*), with a slightly larger brain and/or smaller molar teeth.

Explorations at Bouri in the Middle Awash region of Ethiopia at 2.6 mya have revealed a new species, *Australopithecus garhi* (*garhi* means "surprise" in the Afar language), contemporary with the earliest robust australopithecine from Lake Turkana (*A. aethiopicus*). *A. garhi*'s big molars and thick enamel recall the robust australopithecines, but it lacks their reduced incisors and dished face. In addition, arm and leg bones of a single individual found within 300 meters of the skull may or may not belong to the same species. But the bones are unique for their time period—arms as long as Lucy's for climbing, but much longer legs for walking. This suggests that habitual bipedal walking may have become well established before humans gave up the trees altogether.

The oldest known stone tools also come from 2.6–2.5 mya in Ethiopia, but about 100 kilometers to the north at Gona, near Hadar. Other stone tools from Hadar, from Lokalelei on Lake Turkana, and from Kanjera on the east side of Lake Victoria date to around 2.1 to 2.3 mya. How did stone tool making originate? Chimpanzees use many kinds of simple tools, fashioned from sticks, leaves, and stones, and their hands are well adapted to manipulating objects. In Côte d'Ivoire chimpanzees use stones to crack nuts, transporting the stones several hundred meters to anvils near nut-bearing trees, and occasionally detaching stone chips and flakes as an unintentional byproduct of nut cracking. The potential for transporting stone and manipulating it to make stone tools may have been present in our most distant common ancestor. The early stone tools at Lokalelei, Gona, and Hadar, however, are surprisingly elaborate, involving the removal of as many as thirty flakes from a single core. Many of the flakes were quite thin and/or regularly shaped. Attempts to teach orangutans, chimpanzees, and bonobos to flake stone show that the early tools from East Africa required a degree of spatial cognition and manual dexterity (including the ability to use the fourth and fifth fingers to stabilize the stone being struck) that may be beyond the apparent abilities of chimpanzees. It is likely, then, that human stone technology

is older than 2.5 mya, although the concentration in space and intensity of stone-tool use and manufacture that resulted in the formation of archaeological sites may not predate the Gona finds.

The first fossils attributed to *Homo,* especially new finds from Hadar, date to 2.3 mya, implying that the initiation of stone-tool making may precede the development of a larger brain and smaller teeth. No stone tools were found in direct association with *A. garhi,* but there was indirect evidence of their use. In the area that yielded the limb bones there were a number of bones of extinct horses and antelopes that showed signs of butchery. Deep scratches with the characteristic sharp edges of stone tool cut marks indicate where meat and sinews had been sliced from the bone, and hammerstone impact fractures made while the bones were fresh show how they had been broken open for marrow. If this behavior can be attributed to *A. garhi,* then this hominid clearly shares behavioral features with later humans, even though its brain was still small and the teeth still large. It may be an early indicator of what we now recognize as a common pattern of *Homo,* in which new behaviors drive and select for changes in morphology—tools before brains.

In South Africa, *Homo* and stone tools appear together around 2 mya at Sterkfontein, followed soon thereafter by the first robust australopithecines, perhaps suggesting a spread of both ideas and species from the north. New South African data come from the lab as well as the field, as in, for example, a study of stable isotopes in robust australopithecine teeth. Most of the carbon in our bones and teeth is the common form, carbon-12, but a tiny amount is a stable isotope with an extra neutron: carbon-13. In tropical environments the amount of carbon-13 is higher in grasses than in trees, so grazers have higher amounts than browsers or fruit eaters. The study indicated that the amounts in robust australopithecine teeth were high. Since members of the human family are unlikely to have eaten grass, the study's authors concluded that the australopithecines were occasional carnivores who preyed on grazing animals. But another possibility is that robust australopithecines ate the underground tubers of grassy plants or sedges high in carbon-13. Dating from tools, cut-marked bones, and stable isotopes combine to suggest major changes in diet in the course of early human evolution.

HOW HUMAN ARE *H. HABILIS* AND *H. RUDOLFENSIS*?

The earliest members of the genus *Homo* are *Homo habilis,* defined in 1964 on the basis of specimens found at Olduvai Gorge, and *Homo rudolfensis,* defined in 1986 on the basis of specimens found east of Lake Turkana. Since 1985 accumulating evidence has demonstrated that at least one of these species still maintained a number of specializations for life in the trees, like long arms, short legs, and curved fingers. In addition, these hominids exhibit very little of the marked reduction in tooth size that characterizes our genus and leads to our smaller faces. *Homo* was supposedly characterized by large brains, language, tool dependence, and manual dexterity. New data have shown that the brains of these fossils are not large compared to their body mass, and we cannot determine whether or not they had language abilities to a greater extent than the apes. Tools now appear before the first fossil attributed to *Homo* and occur with *Australopithecus* and *Paranthropus* as well. New studies of hand function show that the hand of *H. habilis* was not as fully modern as we had supposed. In a major review of these issues, Wood and Collard suggest that *H. habilis* and *H. rudolfensis* do not share the adaptations characteristic of later members of the genus *Homo* and should be grouped instead with *Australopithecus*. The first member of our own genus would then be *H. erectus* (or the early African variant *H. ergaster*), dating to not more than 1.9 mya.

OUT OF AFRICA?

For many years it was thought that the first humans to leave Africa were *H. erectus*. The date of their expansion out of Africa supposedly was not earlier than 1.4 mya, based on an early site of this age at 'Ubeidiya in Israel. Lack of sites suggested that Europe was unoccupied until half a million years ago.

But the last eleven years have changed these views as well. Old (but controversial) dates of ca. 1.8 mya have been proposed for both Southeast Asia and China, although there are questions about both the dates themselves and the human nature of some of the items being dated, for example, hominins and stone tools in South China. Perhaps the most exciting new finds come from the site of Dmanisi in the Caucasus Mountains of Georgia, at the gates of Europe. Here on a small promontory in sediments of an ancient lake and river margin, levels dating to just after 1.8 mya have yielded an unusual array of fossils. At least six individuals have come to light so far, some with very large jaws, others with small brains, thin browridges, and relatively large canine teeth for a member of the genus *Homo*. The associated faunal remains include other African migrants that spread easily across different habitats (e.g., ostriches and hyenas). The artifacts are simple flakes and cores, not the symmetrical handaxes of later *H. erectus*. The variability within the small number of fossils from this site is hard to understand, but the implications for an early exit from Africa are clear. Even if the Dmanisi dates are somewhat later, humans left Africa before they became large, before they had developed the more complex technologies and larger brains of later *H. erectus*, and possibly before they had fully abandoned the trees.

But where did they go? Evidence is accumulating for the early occupation of East Asia, as least as early as 1.3 mya. But solid European evidence beyond Dmanisi is lacking until around 800,000 years ago. At the Gran Dolina cave, near Atapuerca, Spain, a new species, *Homo antecessor,* is based on fragments from the TD6 level. Its approximate date of 800,000 years ago comes from the fact that the fossils lie below a magnetic change point. The sediments above have a magnetism similar to that of today, but the sediments at the fossil layer and below it have a reversed magnetism, that is, the "north" recorded by the sediments is actually "south" today. Evidence of magnetic reversals occurs in sediments all over the world, and the most recent shift from "reversed" back to "normal" has been dated by argon laser techniques to 780,000–791,000 years. The fragments include the lower face of a child with several teeth, a fragment of frontal bone (forehead region), a small piece of a jaw, and several long bone fragments. At least six individuals are represented, and some of the bones show cut marks made while the bone was fresh, a possible sign of cannibalism. As at Dmanisi, stone tools at Gran Dolina also consist of very simple cores and flakes, rather than large bifacial handaxes.

The discoverers of *H. antecessor,* Bermudez de Castro and colleagues (1997), argue that the shape of the nose region is not that of *H. erectus* but instead resembles some features of *H. sapiens* and Neanderthals (hence the name *antecessor*). They argue that it is the ancestor of both Neanderthals and modern humans before the two lines diverged. Others suggest that it may be the ancestor of a Neanderthal lineage that split off from the modern human lineage before *H. antecessor*. Without more pieces from Gran Dolina or other European fossils from the same time period, however, it is difficult to say whether its separate status will continue. It could also prove to be just an early form of a European species known as *H. heidelbergensis*, which lived in Europe from about 500,000 to about 200,000 years ago. The dating is also only approximate since we do not know how much time elapsed between the burial of the fossil and the magnetic shift at about 790,000 years ago.

The interesting question raised by the naming of a new European species at an early date is the antiquity of the separation between a European human lineage leading to Neanderthals and an African human lineage leading to modern humans. Were Neanderthals, who do not appear until around 200,000 years ago, the final branch of a large European tree, all adapted to colder and more seasonal conditions than elsewhere in the Old World? Did the split between the two lineages occur after or before *H. antecessor?* In either case, if the split is ancient, how do we explain the later development of behavioral similarities between Neanderthals and their African and Near Eastern cousins? Could this be a case of parallel evolution? Or is this new member of the family tree just a temporary offshoot that died out without descendants?

Other new evidence for hominin presence in southern Europe at an early date includes several sites from Italy that may be almost as old as Gran Dolina. The site of Ceprano includes human fossil material—the crushed skullcap with a relatively large cranial capacity of ca. 1050 cc may be comparable to *H. antecessor,* to late *H. erectus,* or to another human type more advanced than *H. erectus*. Dates at most of these sites are based on volcanic horizons that are correlated to nearby levels dated by argon-argon. Ceprano thus may be more than 700,000 years old, while the oldest levels at Notarchirico, which contain several bifaces, are more than 650,000 years old. Another Italian site, Isernia, with a simple flake-tool industry, may be of comparable age or up to 100,000 years younger. Like many early African sites and Dmanisi, these early sites appear to represent concentrations of human activity on lake shores, along with the cut and possibly scavenged bones of very large mammals such as elephants and rhinos. The oldest evidence from middle or northern latitudes of Europe, however, is much later, ca. 500,000 years ago. Only Notarchirico contains early bifaces, while all of the European sites older than 700,000 years ago contain only simple flake tools.

What enabled our early ancestors to expand out of their African homeland? Was it their use of underground food resources that allowed them to exploit dry and open habitats? (This might explain why the occupation of Europe was later, since most tubers don't survive if the ground freezes—the high-altitude-adapted potato is the great exception). Were they simply following large mammals into the open grasslands of Asia, hunting and/or scavenging as they went? Did they control fire, or had they invented cooking or effective hunting techniques? How did they meet the competition from new carnivore species, like wolves and saber-tooth cats, as they moved into new territories? What did their simple technology allow them to do? How did their increasing technological competence enable the growth of human populations? Why do bifaces and large cutting tools appear to be common in some areas and environments and not in others? We hope that new research now under way in South China, Central Asia, Turkey, and southeastern Europe may provide new and exciting data bearing on these questions.

FURTHER READING

Asfaw, B., T. D. White, O. Lovejoy, B. Latimer, S. Simpson, and G. Suwa. 1999. "*Australopithecus garhi*: A New Species of Hominid from Ethiopia." *Science* 284:629–35.

Bahn, Paul G. 1996. "Treasure of the Sierra Atapuerca." *Archaeology* 49(1):45–48.

Balter, Michael, and Ann Gibbons. 2002. "Were 'Little People' the First to Venture out of Africa?" *Science* 297:26–27.

Bermudez de Castro, J. M., J. L. Arsuaga, E. Carbonell, A. Rosas, L. Martinez, and M. Mosqueria. 1997. "A Hominid from the Lower Pleistocene of Atapuerca, Spain: Possible Ancestor to Neandertals and Modern Humans." *Science* 276:1392–5.

Brunet, M., A. Beauvilain, Y. Coppens, E. Heintz, A. H. Moutaye, and D. Pilbeam. 1995. "The First Australopithecine 2,500 Kilometres West of the Rift Valley (Chad)." *Nature* 378:273–75. (Comment by Bernard Wood on p. 239.)

Brunet, Michel, F. Guy, D. Pilbeam, H. T. Mackaye, A. Likius, D. Ahounta, A. Beauvilain, C. Blondel, H. Bocherens, J.-R. Boisserie, L. de Bonis, Y. Coppens, J. Dejax, C. Denys, P. Duringer, V. Eisenmann, G. Fanone, P. Fronty, D. Geraads, T. Lehmann, F. Lihoreau, A. Louchart, A. Mahamat, G. Merceron, G. Mouchelin, O. Otero, P.P. Campomanes, M. Ponce de Leon, J.-C. Rage, M. Sapanet, M. Schuster, J. Sudre, P. Tassy, X. Valentin, P. Vignaud, L. Viriot, A. Zazzo, and C. Zollikofer. 2002. "A New Hominid from the Upper Miocene of Chad, Central Africa." *Nature* 418:145–51.

Carbonell, E., J. M. Bermudez de Castro, J. L. Arsuaga, J. C. Diez, A. Rosas, G. Cuenca-Bescos, R. Sala, M. Mosquera, and X. P. Rodriguez. 1995. "Lower Pleistocene Hominids and Artifacts from Atapuerca-TD6 (Spain)." *Science* 269:826–30. (Comment by J. Gutin on pp. 754–55.)

Clarke, Ronald J. 1998. "First Ever Discovery of a Well-Preserved Skull and Associated Skeleton of *Australopithecus*." *South African Journal of Science* 94: 460–63.

Clarke, Ronald J., and Philip V. Tobias. 1995. "Sterkfontein Member 2 Foot Bones of the Oldest South African Hominid." *Science* 269:521–24. (See also story at www.discoveringarchaeology.com.)

De Heinzelin J., J. D. Clark, T. D. White, W. Hart, P. Renne, G. WoldeGabriel, Y. Beyene, and E. Vrba. 1999. "Environment and Behavior of 2.5-million-year-old Bouri Hominids." *Science* 284:625–29.

Delson, Eric, Ian Tattersall, John A. Van Couvering, and Alison S. Brooks, eds. 2000. *Encyclopedia of Human Evolution and Prehistory*. Garland. (See especially articles on *Australopithecus anamensis* [by Fred Grine], pp. 123–24, *Australopithecus bahrelghazali* and *Australopithecus garhi* [by E. Delson], pp. 124–25, Ceprano [by E. Delson], pp. 163–64, Isernia [by A. Brooks], p. 351, and Venosa sites [by A. Brooks], p. 723.)

Gabunia, L., and A. Vekua. 1995. "A Plio-Pleistocene Hominid from Dmanisi, East Georgia, Caucasus." *Nature* 373:509–12.

Gabunia, Leo, Absalom Vekua, David Lordkipanidze, Carl C. Swisher III, Reid Ferring, Antje Justus, Medea Nioradze, Merab Tvalchrelidze, Susan C. Anton, Gerhard Bosinski, Olaf Jöris, Marie-Antoinette de Lumley, Givi Majsuradze, and Aleksander Mouskhelishvili. 2000. "Earliest Pleistocene Hominid Cranial Remains from Dmanisi, Republic of Georgia: Taxonomy, Geological Setting, and Age." *Science* 288:1019–25.

Gore, Rick, 2002. "National Geographic Research and Exploration: New Find." *National Geographic* 202(2):n.p.

Haile-Selassie, Yohannes. 2001. "Late Miocene Hominids from the Middle Awash, Ethiopia." *Nature* 412:178–81.

Kimbel, William H., Donald C. Johanson, and Yoel Rak. 1994. "The First Skull and Other New Discoveries of *Australopithecus afarensis* at Hadar, Ethiopia." *Nature* 368:449–51. (Comment by L. Aiello on pp. 399–400.)

Kimbel, W. H., R. C. Walter, D. C. Johanson, K. F. Reed, J. L. Aronson, Z. Assefa, C. W. Marean, G. G. Eck, R. Bobe, E. Hovers, Y. Rak, C. Vondra, T. Yemane, D. York, Y. Chen, N. M. Evensen, and P.E. Smith. 1996. "Late Pliocene *Homo* and Oldowan Tools from the Hadar Formation (Kada Hadar Member), Ethiopia." *Journal of Human Evolution* 31:549–61.

Kuman, Kathleen. 1994. "The Archaeology of Sterkfontein—Past and Present." *Journal of Human Evolution* 27(6):471–95.

Leakey, Meave G., C. S. Feibel, I. McDougall, and A. Walker. 1995. "New Four-Million-Year-Old Hominid Species from Kanapoi and Allia Bay, Kenya." *Nature* 376:565–71.

Leakey, Meave, Fred Spoor, Frank H. Brown, Patrick N. Gathogo, Christopher Kiarie, Louise Leakey, and Ian McDougall. 2001. "New Hominin Genus from Eastern Africa Shows Diverse Middle Pliocene Lineages." *Nature* 410:433–40.

Locke, R. 1999. "The First Human?" *Discovering Archaeology* 1(4):32–39.

Mercader, Julio, Melissa Panger, and Christophe Boesch. 2002. "Excavation of a Chimpanzee Stone Tool Site in the African Rainforest." *Science* 296:1452–5.

Morwood, M. J., P. B. O'Sullivan, F. Aziz, and A. Raza. 1998. "Fission-Track Ages of Stone Tools and Fossils in the East Indonesian Island of Flores." *Nature* 392:173–76. (Also commentary by A. Gibbons [1998], "Ancient Island Tools Suggest *Homo erectus* was a Seafarer," *Science* 279:1635–7.)

Panger, Melissa, Alison S. Brooks, Brian G. Richmond, and Bernard Wood. 2002. "Older than the Oldowan? Rethinking the Emergence of Hominid Tool Use." *Evolutionary Anthropology* 11(6):235–45.

Pickford, Martin, Brigitte Senut, Dominique Gommery, and Jacques Treil. 2002. "Bipedalism in *Orrorin tugenensis* Revealed by Its Femora." *Comptes Rendus Palevol* 1:1–13.

Plummer, Tom, Laura Bishop, Peter Ditchfield, and Jason Hicks. 1999. "Research on Late Pliocene Oldowan Sites at Kanjera South, Kenya." *Journal of Human Evolution* 36:151–70.

Richmond, Brian G., and William L. Jungers. 1995. "Size Variation and Sexual Dimorphism in *Australopithecus afarensis* and Living Hominoids." *Journal of Human Evolution* 29(3):229–45.

Richmond, B. G., and D. S. Strait. 2000. "Evidence that Humans Evolved From a Knuckle-Walking Ancestor." *Nature* 404:382–85. ("News and Views" comment by M. Collard and L. C. Aiello [2000], "From Forelimbs to Two Legs," *Nature* 404:339–40.)

Roche, H., A. Delagnes, J. P. Brugal, C. Feibel, M. Kibunjia, V. Mourre, and P. J. Texier. 1999. "Early Hominid Stone Tool Production and Technical Skill 2.34 Myr Ago in West Turkana, Kenya." *Nature* 399:57–60.

Rowlett, R., M. G. Davis, and R. B. Graber. 1999. "Friendly Fire: The First Campfires Helped Hominids Survive the Night." *Discovering Archaeology* 1(5):82–89.

Ruff, C. B., Eric Trinkaus, and T. W. Holliday. 1997. "Body Mass and Encephalization in Pleistocene *Homo*." *Nature* 387:173–76.

Semaw, S., P. Renne, J. W. K. Harris, C. S. Feibel, R. L. Bernor, N. Fessaha, and K. Mowbray. 1997. "2–5 Million-Year-Old Stone Tools from Gona, Ethiopia." *Nature* 385:333–36.

Senut, Brigitte, Martin Pickford, Dominique Gommery, P. Mein, K. Cheboi, and Yves Coppens, 2001. "First Hominid from the Miocene (Lukeino Formation, Kenya)." *Comptes Rendus de l'Académie des Sciences de Paris, Série IIa* 332:137–44.

Sponheimer, Matthew, and Julia A. Lee-Thorp. 1999. "Isotopic Evidence for the Diet of an Early Hominid, *Australopithecus africanus*." *Science* 283(5400):368–70.

Swisher III, Carl C., G. H. Curtis, T. Jacob, A. G. Getty, A. Suprijo, and Widiasmoro. 1994. "Age of the Earliest Known Hominids in Java, Indonesia." *Science* 263:1118–21.

Vekua, Abesalom, David Lordkipanidze, G. Philip Rightmire, Jordi Agusti, Reid Ferring, Givi Maisuradze, Alexander Mouskhelishvili, Medea Nioradze, Marcia Ponce de Leon, Martha Tappen, Merab Tvalchrelidze, Christoph Zollikofer. 2002. "A New Skull of Early *Homo* from Dmaniusi, Georgia." *Science* 297: 85–89.

Vignaud, P., P. Duringer, H. T. Mackaye, A. Likius, C. Blondel, J.-R. Boisserie, L. de Bonis, V. Eisenmann, M.-E. Etienne, D. Geraads, F. Guy, T. Lehmann, F. Lihoreau, N. Lopez-Martinez, C. Mourer-Chauviré, O. Otero, J.-C. Rage, M. Schuster, L. Viriot, A. Zazzo, and M. Brunet. 2002. "Geology and Palaeontology of the Upper Miocene Toros-Menalla Hominid Locality, Chad." *Nature* 418:152–55.

White, Tim D., G. Suwa, and B. Asfaw. 1994. "*Australopithecus ramidus,* a New Species of Early Hominid from Aramis, Ethiopia." *Nature* 371:306–12. (Comment by Bernard Wood on pp. 280–81.)

Wood, Bernard. 2002. "Hominid Revelations from Chad." *Nature* 418:133–35.

Wood, B., and M. Collard. 1999. "The Changing Face of Genus *Homo*." *Evolutionary Anthropology* 8(6):195–207.

Wrangham, R. W., J. H. Jones, G. Laden, D. Pilbeam, and B. Conklin-Brittain. 1999. "The Raw and the Stolen: Cooking and the Ecology of Human Origins." *Current Anthropology* 40(5):567–94.

5 THE EMERGENCE OF MODERN HUMANS

Alison S. Brooks

In this newly revised and updated chapter, paleoanthropologist Alison Brooks summarizes the often controversial story of where, when, and why modern humans like ourselves first appeared on earth. The enormous impact of new fossil and archaeological discoveries, new dates, and the genetics revolution on our views of human origins is evident, particularly in Brooks' analyses of various DNA studies of the last decade.

One of the most controversial and least understood events in human evolution occurs toward the end of the story. Where, when, and why did modern humans like ourselves first appear, and how did they come to occupy most of the earth? Study of this stage of evolution is not new; in fact, it began more than 170 years ago with the discovery of Neanderthal fossils in Belgium in 1830. In 1868 the coexistence of extinct animals such as mammoths with anatomically modern but very robust humans was documented at the site of Cro-Magnon, in southern France.

After all this time, why do we still not know more about an event so close to our own era? And why are the arguments over this event so bitter?

WHAT'S SO MODERN ABOUT MODERN HUMANS?

Anatomically, modern humans are distinguished from their predecessors by their relatively gracile (less robust or less muscular) skeletons and smaller teeth. Although the size of the brain itself did not increase in moderns from the preceding archaic stage, the braincase became taller, less elongated from front to back, and more sharply flexed at its base, where it joins the face. In essence, the face became almost completely situated under the braincase, rather than sticking out in front of it, as in earlier human ancestors and other primates. Smaller teeth also left the chin sticking out in front, and browridges became reduced. Archaic *Homo* species, with modern-size brains but big browridges, large faces, and large teeth, occupied Europe, Asia, and Africa before the appearance of modern *Homo sapiens*. The term *Neanderthals* refers to one relatively isolated, cold-adapted population of these archaics who lived in western Eurasia between about 200,000 and 35,000 years ago.

CANDELABRAS AND HATRACKS

Throughout the twentieth century, two basic variants of the story vied for acceptance in the scientific community. The "candelabra" view recognizes only one major branching of the human line. After the initial dispersal of humans to the three major Old World continents, beginning as early as 1.7 million years ago with the species *Homo erectus,* the populations of each region evolved in parallel fashion into modern humans. Some migration or gene flow between the regions ensured that new characteristics appearing in one region would eventually spread to all. In this theory, most of the immediate ancestors of the modern humans of Africa are found in Africa, while the immediate ancestors of the Chinese are found in China, and so forth.

Also according to this view, the immediate ancestors of Europeans are their predecessors on that continent—namely, the Neanderthals. The current version of the candelabra theory is referred to as "multiregional evolution" (MRE), because it allows more migration from region to region than earlier versions.

In a contrasting view, known as the "hatrack" theory, a single main stem or center pole leads to modern humans, with branches at intervals through time representing evolutionary dead ends. According to this theory, the Neanderthals of western Europe are one such dead end; the "Peking Man" or *Homo erectus* fossils of East Asia are another. Until recently, the central stem was always given a European or Near Eastern identity, through such fossils as "Piltdown" (a now-discredited forgery), Swanscombe (a large English skullcap without a face, dating to a period just before the earliest Neanderthals), or the Skhūl fossils from Israel. The central role of Europe in human evolution was attributed by some to the influence of a colder climate, a limited growing season, and more reliance on both hunting and food storage, all of which were once thought to have promoted intelligence and growth of the brain.

THE "CANDELABRA" VS. THE "HATRACK" THEORY

In the current version of the hatrack theory, however, the central stem is African, and all the earlier fossils of other continents constitute the dead ends of human evolution. Since, in this view, all anatomically modern humans derive from recent African ancestors, the modern theory is called the "out-of-Africa" hypothesis.

How can two such disparate views continue to coexist? Why do the data not exclusively support one or the other? And why has the hatrack school shifted its focus from Europe to Africa? Three new D's—new dates, new data (fossil and archaeological), and new DNA studies—have combined to heighten the debate surrounding modern human origins.

DATING THE DATA

By 35,000 years ago the shift to modern humans was virtually complete throughout Europe, Asia, Africa, and even Australia. The most accurate dating technique for the later periods of archaeology, radiocarbon dating, gives good results back to about 35,000 years ago, but not much older. Some dates of 38,000 to 40,000 years ago are acceptable, but dates in the range of 40,000 or older are decidedly dubious. Most of the story of modern human origins lies beyond 40,000 years ago. Until the 1980s there were no reliable ways to determine the age of anything between 40,000 and 200,000 years ago.

A range of new techniques has come into general use for exactly the period when modern humans must have emerged, between 200,000 and 40,000 years ago. These techniques include (1) measuring the accumulation of radiation damage from soil radiation in buried crystalline materials such as flints or quartz sands (thermoluminescence); (2) measuring the decay of uranium that soaks into buried bones and teeth from groundwater (uranium series), or uranium-caused radiation damage in the crystals of tooth enamel (electron spin resonance); and (3) studying the decay of the proteins encapsulated in hard tissues of fossil animals, such as mollusc shells, bones, teeth, and ostrich eggshells (amino acid racemization).

Unlike radiocarbon, none of these techniques is entirely independent of the burial environment. Thermoluminescence and electron spin resonance dates can be thrown off by inaccurate measurement of the soil radiation or by heating or reexposure of the sample before the archaeologist finds it. Protein decay rates are dependent on temperature, which is difficult to estimate for 40,000 to 200,000 years ago. And no one yet understands how fast uranium soaks into bones and teeth. Uranium and its decay products can also wash out again, causing inaccuracies in the dating results. Using two different techniques to date the same site can help avoid these problems, at least when the two sets of results agree.

The effect of the new dating techniques has been to make many sites and fossils in Africa earlier than was previously thought. The European dates did not change quite as much, because the ebb and flow of ice ages had provided a chronology that tied most of the sites together, even in the absence of exact numbers.

Once the chronology of Africa was worked out on the basis of its own internal sequence of dates, comparative faunal extinctions, and climate changes, it became obvious that the earliest fossils in Africa with projecting chins and small teeth were much older than the Cro-Magnons of Europe. In a 1992 discussion of ostrich eggshell dates, I and my colleagues suggested that several of the most important early African sites with modern humans (Klasies River Mouth and Border Cave) date as far back as 105,000 years ago or older. Modern human teeth at Mumba shelter in Tanzania were dated to about 130,000 years by uranium series. In 2003 Tim White and others announced three new fossil skulls from the Middle Awash region of Ethiopia attributed to *Homo sapiens* and dated to between 154,000 and 160,000 years ago. While they are more primitive than younger *Homo sapiens* fossils in some respects, such as the browridges and back of the skull, they have no typical Neanderthal features. The skulls demonstrate the great antiquity of modern humans in Africa and argue for the absence of Neanderthal ancestry in modern humans (White et al. 2003; Clark et al. 2003).

Meanwhile, new dates for Zhoukoudian (Peking Man sites) and other sites from China and Java suggest that East Asia was occupied exclusively by the more primitive species *Homo erectus* until after 300,000 years ago. The new Chinese fossils announced in 1992, which supposedly represent a transition between H. *erectus* and H. *sapiens,* do *not* show that this transition happened in China *first,* as several newspaper reports seemed to suggest. Some disputed dates for *H. erectus* in Java imply survival of this archaic species until as late as 40,000 years ago. That the earliest modern humans were African seems quite well established, although very few sites have been dated thus far.

In Europe, the new dates have had two principal impacts. First, they demonstrate the great antiquity in Europe of the Neanderthal-type long face, large nose, and flattened bulge at the back of the head. The oldest fossil now referred to as Neanderthal (Le Biache, France) was discovered in 1976 and is about 190,000 years old, while older fossils (e.g., Arago in the Pyrenees) with some Neanderthal characteristics date to 300,000 years ago or older. Second, newer and more precise radiocarbon dates from the end of Neanderthal times show that, in particular areas, the transition from Neanderthal to Cro-Magnon was quite abrupt. A Neanderthal from Saint-Césaire in France, found in 1979, is about 35,000 years old, while the Cro-Magnon fossils probably date to as early as 34,000 years ago, on the basis of comparisons with the Pataud site next door. Such an abrupt transition does not leave enough time for evolution to have occurred in place. In addition, the oldest modern human fossils and archaeological sites of the Aurignacian culture of Cro-Magnon are found in eastern Europe just before 40,000 years ago, while Neanderthals still lived in the West, which is just what one would expect if modern humans invaded Europe from Africa via the Near East. And in the Near East itself, modern humans from Qafzeh, in Israel, excavated in the 1960s, have been dated to about 92,000 years ago by thermoluminescence on burned flints, and a similar antiquity was suggested for at least some of these fossils by our work on ostrich eggshells. Still unclear in the Near East is the chronological relationship of the Qafzeh modern humans to Neanderthals. What might explain Neanderthal dominance of this region *after* a brief period of modern human occupation at 92,000 years? One possible answer lies in the tiny bones of birds, rodents, and insectivores found with the human fossils. Earlier modern humans are accompanied by tropical African birds, mice, voles, and so on, while later Neanderthals are accompanied by cold-adapted animals from Eurasia.

If Neanderthals were the cold-adapted archaics and the earliest modern humans were tropical, this shifting pattern implies that the distribution of the two populations was originally limited by ecological considerations, and that the Near East represented a boundary zone that shifted as the world's climate changed. When modern humans returned to dominate the region by 40,000 years ago, they seem to have invented a way to get around this ecological limitation. The animals found at Near Eastern modern human sites dating later than 40,000 years ago remain primarily cold-adapted.

THE "AFRICAN EVE" HYPOTHESIS

That humans were modern in appearance in the tropics long before these characteristics appear in Europe seems confirmed by the new dates and data. But what is the relationship of the first modern humans in Africa to the later ones who occupied Europe after 35,000 years ago? This relationship is the hottest part of the current controversy.

In 1987 geneticist Rebecca Cann and her colleagues proposed that a recent migration out of Africa within the last 200,000 years had completely replaced all other human populations. None of the archaic East Asians or the Neanderthals of Europe had left any descendants at all. All modern humans share a recent African ancestor. The data used to support this hypothesis came not from the fossil record or from the dating lab, but from analysis of genetic differences among people living today.

The most common and abundant genetic material (DNA), which occurs in the nucleus of a cell, changes too slowly to measure recently evolved differences—even comparing humans to chimpanzees reveals a difference of 1 to 5 percent between the two species, depending on the DNA differences (repetitions, deletions, etc.) used in the comparison. But mitochondria, small organelles within cells that are important in converting food to energy, contain a more rapidly changing form of DNA. Since the few mitochondria in sperm are not transmitted to the egg, an individual's mitochondria derive entirely from the mother via the ovum. A family tree of human genetic similarities, based on mitochondrial DNA (mtDNA), reflects only female ancestry, hence the "Eve" in the hypothesis.

This last common ancestor of all humans is thought to have been African because Africans are more variable in their mtDNA than the peoples of other continents, which suggests that they have been in place the longest. Furthermore, some genetic variants are unique to Africa, while all the variants on other continents have roots in Africa. If Neanderthals from Europe or *Homo erectus* from China contributed to our ancestry, where is their unique mtDNA?

What about "Adam"? The Y chromosome appears to determine maleness but very few other characteristics. Family trees based on similarities in the genetic makeup of the Y chromosome reflect only male ancestry, since women do not have one. In several studies of global Y chromosome genetic variation, the same pattern was observed as in the mitochondrial genome:

greater divergence and unique patterns in African populations, but all patterns outside that continent derived from basic African models. The most variable DNA in both studies belonged to the small, isolated populations of hunter-gatherers in the Kalahari Desert (e.g., !Kung), the forest basin of the Democratic Republic of the Congo (Mbuti, Aka, Efe), and the click-language hunter-gatherers of northern Tanzania (Hadza and Sandawe).

At first the major debate was over possible errors or omissions in the sample (use of African Americans instead of Africans, assuming little admixture in the maternal line) and the timing of the dispersal from Africa. Using as a guide the degree of differentiation developed within Australia and New Guinea (first colonized about 60,000 years ago) or among the populations of the Americas, it was estimated that human mtDNA diversifies from a common ancestor at a rate of 2 to 4 percent per million years. Since the total amount of difference observed in modern populations was only about 0.57 percent, this implies a time scale of 140,000 to 290,000 years since all humans last shared a common ancestor.

The family tree itself was questioned initially on statistical grounds. Given enough time and tries, the computer program used to generate the published family tree can also generate alternative trees in which Africa plays a diminished role. Yet repeated studies continue to conclude that Africa was our species' genetic homeland. Recent decoding of the entire human genome also allows step-by-step reconstruction of the exact mutation sequence by which two individuals came to differ at particular places in their DNA and can show which one has the more "ancestral" form.

ANCIENT AFRICANS: WHOSE ANCESTORS?

What was the relationship between the Neanderthals or other archaics of regions outside Africa and their successors? Is there any evidence of population movement from Africa to Europe or East Asia? Did invaders interbreed with the older populations of these areas, or did they simply wipe them out? Much of the argument hinges on current analyses of the fossils themselves. Three issues are central: (1) Who were the Neanderthals (and what explains their robust body form)? (2) Are there any intermediate fossils between Neanderthals (or archaics) and modern humans? (3) Are there regional continuities in facial shape or teeth that continue across the transition from archaic/Neanderthal to modern?

Up through the early 1970s, it was widely suggested that if you gave a Neanderthal a shave and a haircut (and a shopping trip to J. C. Penney), you would not recognize him on the New York subway. In the 1970s Erik Trinkaus began a lengthy study of Neanderthals from a new perspective—

below the neck. His analysis strongly suggested that *all* Neanderthals, including those from the Near East but *not* the archaics from tropical environments and East Asia, shared a common and very unusual postcranial form. Their bones, even in the fingers and toes, were extremely thick and bore heavy markings for muscle attachments that could not be found in modern samples of skeletons. The joint surfaces were sometimes twice as large as the modern human average. Discovery of a pelvis from Kebara, Israel, suggested that the way the body was carried was quite different, as the spinal column was more deeply indented into the back than in ourselves. Yet from the same site a hyoid bone, which attaches to the voice box, suggested that the movement of the throat, tongue, and voice box in producing speech was similar to ours, despite the greater distance in Neanderthals between the tongue and the back of the throat. The debate over Neanderthal language continues. One study by Kay and colleagues (Kay, Cartmill, and Balow 1998) suggests that the bony canal containing the nerve for the tongue muscle used in speech was as large in Neanderthals as in ourselves and shows that they spent a lot of time in oral communication.

More and more Neanderthal sites show evidence of cannibalism—human bones smashed and cut and treated like other faunal remains. This may go along with an analysis of the bone chemistry of Neanderthals published in 1992 that indicates they were almost exclusively carnivorous. In addition, Neanderthals, like other cold-adapted animals, had very large, deep chests and short lower arms and legs, to better conserve body heat (but see Aiello and Wheeler 2003 for a contrary view). New studies of the face suggest that the very long, projecting face and huge, broad nose were distinctive; other large-faced archaics from Africa or East Asia had shorter, flatter faces, with more angulated cheekbones. The distinctions between Neanderthals and other archaics appeared quite striking and led most scholars to exclude African and East Asian archaic fossils from the Neanderthal category. Neanderthal morphology was peculiar: you would definitely notice it even on the New York subway!

Perhaps the defining aspect of modern human morphology was the repositioning of the face beneath the braincase instead of out in front, creating a new relationship between the tongue and the back of the throat that facilitated speech. This new relationship, as discussed by Lieberman, can be most clearly seen in the morphology of the sphenoid, the bone that divides the braincase from the face and cradles the pituitary gland just behind the nose. Since most of this morphology is *inside* the skull, studying it requires CT scans of the fossils, a new application of this technology. Most hospitals have down times late at night when they are willing to allow use of their machines by paleontologists. The Smithsonian's division of physical anthropology has its own CT scanner. Some CT scans of important fossils are even available on the Web (http://www.anthropology.at/basis.html?virtanth/virtanth.html).

CHEWING STRESS AND BROWRIDGES

Are there any transitional fossils? In Africa, several fossils such as a skull from Florisbad dated to ca. 260,000 years ago may represent an intermediate category. According to Trinkaus, even the early moderns themselves at Klasies River Mouth, for example, are more robust in their limbs than the Cro-Magnons of Europe. In Europe the argument is very heated. Those who argue for interbreeding between Cro-Magnons and Neanderthals (such as M. Wolpoff, G. Bräuer, F. H. Smith, and E. Trinkaus), or even for an indigenous evolution from Neanderthals to Cro-Magnons (C. L. Brace), point to the less extreme characteristics of some later Neanderthals or to the presence of significant browridges and large, rugged faces along with definite chins at modern human sites in central Europe. From 25,000 years ago in Portugal, long after the Neanderthals are thought to have disappeared from Europe, a new fossil child is said to display some Neanderthal features in its skeleton. In a heated exchange in the pages of the *Proceedings of the National Academy of Sciences*, Erik Trinkaus, the senior morphologist in the study, suggested it was an example of hybridization between Neanderthals and modern humans, while Ian Tattersall, another authority on Neanderthals, argued that this is not demonstrated.

The genetics revolution has also had an impact on views of the Neanderthals as well as on other developments in human history. Five recent studies of mitochondrial DNA (passed only through the female line) extracted from the original Neanderthal fossil and others from Croatia and Siberia show that Neanderthals were *very* different genetically from ourselves. The differences are so great that geneticists estimate that our ancestors split off from them at least 600,000 years ago. Transitional or even archaic *Homo sapiens* fossils from Asia are quite rare; most of the best specimens from China have not been documented in an accessible form. Regional continuities in Asia, however, are striking to proponents of the multiregional evolution theory (M. Wolpoff, Wu Xinzhi, A. G. Thorne, and G. G. Pope). If the earliest modern Asians came from Africa, why do the earliest ones we find already have the flat upper faces and dental characteristics of Asians today? Why are the earlier archaic Asians also flat-faced? Out-of-Africa theorists (such as Christopher Stringer) argue that the flat faces and other features are either primitive features retained in that population or simply adaptations to the cold, dry Asian climate that are favored each time a new human population reaches the area.

REVOLUTION OR EVOLUTION?

In their 2002 book *The Dawn of Human Culture,* Richard Klein and Blake Edgar argue that modern humans became fully modern in their behavior rather suddenly about 40,000 years ago. They suggest that this "human revolution" was due to a genetic mutation that greatly facilitated human language. Their theory is bolstered by new evidence that single genes can have a dramatic effect on people's ability to form sentences and speak. In Europe, major changes in technology (blade and bone tools), economic strategies (ambush hunting, fishing), size of social networks, and symbolic activities (art) occurred over a few thousand years as the Cro-Magnons replaced the Neanderthals between ca. 38,000 and 35,000 years ago.

But is this also true in Africa, where humans appear modern in physical shape more than 100,000 years ago? Even with much more limited exploration than in Europe to date, some of the modern behaviors associated with the "human revolution" appear well before 40,000 years ago in Africa. While the later Neanderthals ran down their prey and stabbed them with sharpened sticks or an occasional stone-tipped spear, Africans hafted small, delicate stone points onto spear or even arrow shafts; made stone blades, backed triangles, or crescents, barbed bone points, and other bone tools; engaged in regular fishing and ambush hunting; ground their food (and some pigments) with grindstones; scratched designs on ostrich eggshell fragments and ocher plaques; and traded precious raw materials such as obsidian over more than 500 miles. The early modern humans who made a brief foray from Africa into the Near East ca. 90,000 years ago also buried their dead with grave goods, unlike most Neanderthals.

New data show that by 50,000 years ago Africans wore beads of ostrich eggshell and engaged in organized mining of precious raw materials. Elsewhere, modern humans had used boats perhaps as early as 60,000 years ago to reach Australia, New Guinea, and New Caledonia, where rock art has been dated to 32,000 years ago. Outside Europe, the "great leap forward" began much earlier and was more like a slow jog, with occasional detours and backward movements.

BUT WERE THE CRO-MAGNONS AFRICAN?

The earliest modern Europeans, called Cro-Magnons after the site in France where their remains were first discovered, had the long limbs and linear bodies of heat-adapted Africans. Only after about 20,000 years in Europe did their bodies take on the shorter limbs and larger torsos of cold-adapted populations. But the archaeological picture is more ambiguous. According to recent dates on archaeological sites, the Aurignacian culture of the Cro-Magnons appears *first* in central and southeastern Europe, just before 40,000 years ago, spreading to an area near Barcelona, Spain, by about 38,000 years ago and finally to France and Germany by 34,000 years ago. Southern Spain, near the Straits of Gibraltar, is one of the *last* areas to make the transition from the Mousterian culture of Neanderthals—archaeology does not suggest an invasion via this route. The big blades, thick scrapers, and bone points of the Aurignacian are quite unlike anything from the preceding Mousterian culture of Neanderthals, so it was assumed that it came into Europe from outside. Yet there is nothing outside in this time range, either in the Near East or in North Africa, from which the Aurignacian can be derived. In much of Africa and the Near East at about 40,000 years ago, the stone industries were characterized by finely made small blades, many with narrow points created by blunting or battering the sides, or by small points with a tang or projection for hafting. The Aurignacian does show up in the Near East, but recent dates suggest that this is only *after* it was well established in Europe, at about 34,000 years ago. The Near East may have been a migration corridor, but it was open in both directions.

CAN THIS CONTROVERSY BE RESOLVED?

The controversy over modern human origins is particularly heated because it concerns ourselves and our most recent history. The argument has been widely featured in the public media: *Time, Newsweek*, the *New York Times*, and several television specials. Unlike the controversy over earlier phases of human evolution, many of the voices expressed in these pieces are the voices of nonscientists, who argue that up to now Eurocentric bias has suppressed recognition of our true heritage. While the discoveries of the past two decades have gone far toward demonstrating the priority of continents other than Europe in the evolution of modern humans, the data also suggest that this was not a simple event of evolution followed by migration in one direction.

Replacement of earlier populations may not have been total. More and better dates and data, particularly from regions such as western Asia, Turkey, and the Balkans, as well as Africa, may help clarify the complex interactions involved in this transition.

FURTHER READING

Aiello, Leslie L., and Peter Wheeler. 2004. "Hominid Physiology and the Glacial Climate." In T. H. van Andel and W. Davies, eds., *Neanderthal and Modern Humans in the European Landscape of the Last Glaciation: Archaeological Results of the Stage 3 Project*. McDonald Institute Monographs. Cambridge: McDonald Institute for Archaeological Research.

Arsuaga, Juan Luis. 2002. *The Neanderthal's Necklace: In Search of the First Thinkers*. Translated by Andy Klatt. New York: Four Walls Eight Windows.

Clark, J. Desmond, Yonas Beyene, Giday WoldeGabriel, William K. Hart, Paul R. Renne, Henry Gilbert, Alban Defleu, Gen Suwa, Shigehiro Katoh, Kenneth R. Ludwig, Jean Renaud Boisserie, Berhane Asfaw, and Tim D. White. 2003. "Stratigraphic, Chronological and Behavioural Contexts of Pleistocene *Homo sapiens* from Middle Awash, Ethiopia." *Nature* 423:742–47.

Defleur, A., T. White, P. Valensi, L. Slimak, and E. Crégut-Bonnoure. 1999. "Neanderthal Cannibalism at Moula-Guercy, Ardèche, France." *Science* 286:128–31. (Also commentary by E. Culotta, "Neanderthals Were Cannibals, Bones Show," 18b–19b.)

Delson, Eric, Ian Tattersall, John A. Van Couvering, and Alison S. Brooks, eds. 2000. *Encyclopedia of Human Evolution and Prehistory*. New York: Garland. (See especially articles on *Homo sapiens*, by C. B. Stringer, 334–39, and on modern human origins, "Multiregional Evolution," by A. Thorne, 425–29; "Out of Africa," by C. B. Stringer, 429–32; "The Genetic Perspective," by J. Marks, 432–34; and "Archaeology and Behavior," by A. S. Brooks, 434–43.)

Duarte, C., J. Mauricio, P. B. Petitt, P. Souto, E. Trinkaus, H. van der Plicht, and J. Zilhao. 1999. "The Early Upper Paleolithic Human Skeleton from the Abrigo do Lagar Velho (Portugal) and Modern Human Emergence in Iberia." *Proceedings of the National Academy of Sciences* 96:7604–9.

Henshilwood, C., and J. Sealey. 1997. "Bone Artifacts from the Middle Stone Age at Blombos Cave, Southern Cape, South Africa." *Current Anthropology* 38:890–95.

Kay, R. F., M. Cartmill, and M. Balow. 1998. "The Hypoglossal Canal and the Origin of Human Vocal Behavior." *Proceedings of the National Academy of Sciences USA* 95:5417–9. (Rebuttal by D. DeGusta, W. H. Gilbert, and S. P. Turner, 1999, "Hypoglossal Canal Size and Hominid Speech," *Proceedings of the National Academy of Sciences USA* 96:1800–4.)

Klein, Richard G. 2000. "Archaeology and the Evolution of Human Behavior." *Evolutionary Anthropology* 9(1):17–36.

Klein, Richard G., and Blake Edgar. 2002. *The Dawn of Human Culture*. John Wiley.

Krings, M., H. Geisert, R. W. Schmitz, H. Krainitzki, and S. Pääbo. 1999. "DNA Sequence of the Mitochondrial Hypervariable Region II from the Neanderthal Type Specimen." *Proceedings of the National Academy of Sciences USA* 96:5581–5.

Krings, M., A. Stone, R. W. Schmitz, H. Krainitzki, M. Stoneking, and S. Pääbo. 1997. "Neandertal DNA Sequences and the Origin of Modern Humans." *Cell* 90:19–30.

Lieberman, D. E. 1998. "Sphenoid Shortening and the Evolution of Modern Human Cranial Shape." *Nature* 393:158–62.

McBrearty, Sally, and Alison S. Brooks. 2001. "The Revolution That Wasn't: A New Interpretation of the Origin of Modern Human Behavior." *Journal of Human Evolution* 39(5):453–563.

Spoor, F., M. C. Dean, P. O'Higgins, and D. E. Lieberman. 1999. "Anterior Sphenoid in Modern Humans." *Nature* 397:572.

Stringer, Christopher B., and Clive Gamble. 1993. *In Search of the Neanderthals*. London: Thames and Hudson.

Tattersall, Ian. 2000. "Paleoanthropology: The Last Half-Century." *Evolutionary Anthropology* 9(1):2–16.

Tattersall, I., and J. H. Schwartz. 1999. "Hominids and Hybrids: The Place of Neanderthals in Human Evolution." *Proceedings of the National Academy of Sciences* 96:7117–9.

Trinkaus, Erik, and Pat Shipman. 1993. *The Neandertals: Changing the Image of Mankind*. New York: Knopf.

White, Tim D., Berhane Asfaw, David DeGusta, Henry Gilbert, Gary D. Richards, Gen Suwa, and F. Clark Howell. 2003. "Pleistocene *Homo sapiens* from Middle Awash, Ethiopia." *Nature* 423:737–41.

Wong, Katy. 2000. "Who Were the Neanderthals?" with contributions by Erik Trinkaus, Cidalia Duarte, Joao Zilhao, Francesco d'Errico, and Fred H. Smith. *Scientific American* 282(4):98–107.

6 THE REAL FLINTSTONES

Artists' Depictions of Human Ancestors

Diane Gifford-Gonzalez

In this amusing and thought-provoking essay, archaeologist Diane Gifford-Gonzalez challenges the reader to question the objectivity and validity of many artistic renderings of prehistoric human life. Based on an analysis of 136 pictures of early modern humans in popular books, the author details several misleading speculative reconstructions, calling for closer collaboration between scientific experts and illustrators, in order to more accurately represent our past.

THE DRUDGE

You have probably seen her, frequenting the diorama scene at your local museum or in that coffee table book on human evolution. It is likely that you have not given her a second glance, she is so much a part of the scenery. She is the Drudge on the Hide: the woman on her hands and knees scraping away at the skin of a large animal, on the margins of the home camp scene. The men are usually center stage foreground, doing something interesting, while she's over there, hiding out. You usually cannot see her face; she is looking down, and the artist may not have bothered to sketch in her brows or mouth. She is not talking to anyone; no one is talking to her. Even in the high-tech Upper Paleolithic, she never manages to get that skin up on a stretching frame and to work it sitting or standing, as do documented hide workers. The men may be down in the cave, trancing, dancing, and doing art, but she's scraping away on all fours, same as back in *Homo erectus* times (Eugène Dubois was obviously not thinking of her when he named the species).

THE ASCENT OF THE DRUDGE

Conventionalized representations such as the Drudge repeat themselves through the works of various artists, their postures and actions suggesting that artists have drawn from their own fine-arts traditions, rather than from ethnographically informed suggestions from their scientist collaborators. The Drudge on a Hide, for example, mimics the scullery maid scrubbing the floor in the background of eighteenth-century evocations of bourgeois success.

THE GUY WITH A ROCK

Another common motif, the Guy with a Rock about to hurl a huge rock into a pit containing a large and unhappy beast (mammoth, mastodon, woolly rhino, or cave bear), suggests herculean figures in portrayals of classical myths. Though his hunting mates sport the latest ballistic weapons, this stone-age conservative has a hefty rock as his weapon of choice from 2 million B.C. to Holocene bison hunts in Dakota. One can imagine the dialogue: "Dammit, Og, we told you to leave the rock at home and bring a spearthrower!" "Right, Og, remember last time, when the mammoth threw the rock back and broke Morg's leg?" "Hey! This rock has been in my family for a million years!"

THE DEER ON A STICK

The homecoming from a successful hunt incorporates the Deer on a Stick motif. The massive prey portrayed in most hunt scenes shrinks to a readily transported package, hefted on a pole between two extraordinarily tidy hunters. They are never shown bringing home dismembered animal parts, nor besmirched with gore. If anyone is portrayed close to such nastiness, it is the woman crouched over a bloody hide. Faced with the lack of fit between ethnographic data on animal butchery and these scenes, one's mind readily wanders down Freudian, rather than archaeological, corridors.

MAN THE TOOLMAKER

Man the Toolmaker, the most common stereotypic portrayal of men at work, pounds stone on stone in a technique more suitable to smithing than to stone percussion, echoing mythical and quotidian blacksmiths in classic oil paintings. Depending upon where his anvil lies, the Toolmaker risks either blinding or genital mutilation, in which art he often appears jovially inclined to instruct the young.

MADONNA WITH CHILD

The other common female motif besides the abject Drudge is the Madonna with Child, a youthful woman standing with a baby in her arms and doing absolutely nothing. Cumulatively, illustrations of paleolithic women present a contrast to the busy lives of ethnographically documented mothers in hunter-gatherer societies. A stone-age woman's life seems to have begun with placid but immobile young motherhood, in which she was rooted decoratively to the spot as camp life swirled about her, followed by dull and dumpy middle age, with her hiding out on the margins of the fun stuff (still not a whit of social interaction), followed by aged and inactive sitting and watching as she waits for the paleolithic version of the Grim Reaper to work his way up the valley. It is a wonder women learned to talk at all.

Once you really consider them, paleolithic figures such as the Drudge and her companions do seem hackneyed and ethnographically uninformed. Anyone with experience of rural life nearly anywhere on the planet can see that they portray the Stone Age through a Western—suburban—lens, two steps from the Flintstones.

Archaeologists can readily testify to the difficulties of assigning gender or maturational stage to most of the activities portrayed, in view of humanity's global diversity in cultural practices. Yet the graphic story reaching out from the museum halls and the pages of the book on the coffee table treats men's and women's—and youngsters' and oldsters'—estates as foregone conclusions. When viewed cumulatively, as we would see them in our lifetimes of museum-going and reading, the vast majority of existing portrayals give us a narrow and repetitious view of prehistoric human life.

THE VISUAL/INFORMATION GAP

Given this repetitiveness, it is easy to fault the artists for a lack of imagination in their mechanical reproduction of earlier motifs. However, the fault is really in the shared vision of artists and experts, archaeologists and paleoanthropologists such as myself. Our vision in the literal sense has been faulty because we have not seen these stereotypes for what they are and challenged their perpetuation. In the more abstract sense, our vision has failed, because we experts have not offered artists who seek our expertise better-informed and more imaginative alternatives. Ironically, the texts accompanying such illustrations, usually drafted by science writers, often offer up-to-date, ethnographically informed perspectives. This emphasizes the great information gap between many of the artists and the text-based workers, a gap not bridged by scientific experts.

Many scientific experts may literally overlook visual depictions in museums or popular books simply because they are for the general public. Experts are trained to think of scientific communication as written text, and graphics such as illustrations of specimens, maps, and graphs as subsidiary material. Speculative reconstructions of prehistoric life are dismissed by many as "museum stuff" for the general public, and unsuitable for real scientists to use or even to help create.

This is a profoundly mistaken and potentially dangerous perspective. Portrayals of human ancestors present a parallel, visually based narrative of the human past. This visual narrative, because of its pervasiveness and communicative potency, must be taken seriously. Widely used in museums and popular literature, it represents much of the knowledge that laypersons have of the prehistoric past. In the face of Barney Rubble and other enduring icons of pop prehistoricity, museums and educational books strive to impress and convince the viewer of "the real facts" through the power of visual arts. The style in which these portrayals are executed is central to their plausibility and power and merits a closer look.

For Western viewers, naturalistic representation is read as objective reporting, and rigorous naturalism characterizes science illustration. Historian of science Barbara Stafford (1991) argues that this stylistic convention developed over the seventeenth and eighteenth centuries as scientists and explorers strove to present convincing images of newly discovered worlds within the human body and around the globe. Given our cultural conditioning, the realistic graphic style itself advances claims for the plausibility of what it depicts. It is therefore the style of choice for science fiction graphics and Disneyland, as well as for prehistoric representations in your local museum or coffee table book.

As portrayed in artists' representations, the prehistoric past is enticingly "real" and accessible. The natural details of landscape, vegetation, and animal life and the painstakingly reconstructed hominid bodies themselves render the scenes plausible. These people, or near-people, have hands, eyes, and facial expressions, and they draw us in toward them. Yet the "naturalness" of the human bodies, their expressions, and gestures serves to subtly support another argument for plausibility that we overlook at our peril: that their social world as depicted was also real. These bodies are gendered, they display the marks of age, and they exist in the scenes as socially identified actors. If their realistic style and context are arguments for their credibility, then what primordial human conditions are conveyed so powerfully and plausibly?

GENDER/AGE DISCRIMINATION IN VISUAL REPRESENTATIONS

To further explore this question, I analyzed 136 pictures of early modern humans (Cro-Magnons) of the last Ice Age [see Brooks, "The Emergence of Modern Humans," in this volume] in books readily available to lay readers in North America, Great Britain, and France (Gifford-Gonzalez 1993). I documented the types of persons and activities portrayed and commonly repeated motifs, such as the Drudge, looking for the cumulative pattern of artistic choices in portraying different ages and genders. As a whole, the portrayals consistently exclude children and older people from active, useful roles. They represent women's work in patronizing ways, if at all, implying that the real early human story consisted of a suite of male activities, which are themselves really rather limited too.

Who and what most often fills the frame of these portraits of the past reveals the assumptions of both makers and viewers. Of the 136 pictures, about 85 percent include young to middle-aged men, while only half include women; children appear in slightly more than 40 percent of the scenes, and elders in less than a fifth. Although scenes depicting men exclusively are common, only 3 of 136 portray women only, and no pictures show only elders or only children, or any combination of women, elders, and children without men. Of the 1,076 individual human figures in these pictures, about 49 percent are men, 22 percent are women, 23 percent are children, and about 6 percent are older persons.

Critics of Western art and advertisements have shown that men's and women's bodies are differentially represented in dynamic motion, with women's bodies being placed in lower positions and shown in more static poses than those of men, and that active, "important" activities are in the hands of men (e.g., Berger 1972; Goffman 1979). It should come as no surprise that these portrayals of Cro-Magnon men show upright walking and running more frequently than would be predicted from their proportion in the sample, while the opposite is true of women. Males are also disproportionately depicted with arms in dynamic motion, as when making and wielding tools or lifting loads. Women are less often shown in such dynamic poses, and children never. Elders are almost never represented upright, much less in motion or doing anything active. Only men of a certain age participate in hunts, carry game home, and conduct rituals. It is mostly men who construct, create art, make tools. Only women scrape hides, hold babies, or touch children.

THE QUESTION OF RACE

This discussion does not permit an extended treatment of the equally important question of which racial groups are recruited to visually depict stages of hominid evolution. I invite the reader to engage in a brief examination of magazine covers concerning human evolution, to see which gender and which racial features "sell." Most often U.S. magazine representations (e.g., "The Way We Were," 1986) show "our" ancestral modern human as white, male, and in his prime. Discussions of the "African Eve" hypothesis for modern human origins in *Time* and *U.S. News & World Report* offered a diluted Africanity in the faces they presented, and "Eve" naturally required a male companion for inclusion on a cover.

Ruth Mathis, a graduate student in archaeology at the University of Massachusetts, Amherst, wrote a compelling indictment of traditional visual narratives of human evolution from an African American viewpoint (1991). Specifically, she pointed to the common practice of presenting *dark-skinned* australopithecines and *light-skinned* modern humans as opposite ends of the evolutionary spectrum. One can make biologically based arguments for portraying the earliest African hominids with heavily pigmented skin, but Mathis notes there is no compelling scientific basis for consistently choosing white people to represent the most advanced species, since non-European varieties of modern humans populated all continents by the end of the Ice Age. She stresses the alienating impacts of these visual narratives on the children of color who visit museums to learn more about human history and view these narratives with their own consciousness of racial stereotypes.

TOWARD MORE EQUITABLE AND
REALISTIC REPRESENTATION

The challenge for illustrators and experts really is not to fashion politically correct portrayals of human ancestors (drawing a Guy on a Hide or a Gal with a Rock), nor to produce accurate but pedestrian ones (daily trips to the waterhole, perhaps). Nor should we throw up our hands and say real scientists should not use such inevitably speculative illustrations anyway. Exciting exceptions to the stereotypic rules of illustration do exist. French illustrator Véronique Ageorges (Saint-Blanquat and Ageorges 1989) and former Smithsonian artist John Gurche (e.g., in Waters 1990) have created scenes that reflect a deep appreciation for the rich archaeological and ethnographic resources available. Their human ancestors engage in a range of technically believable activities and include strong older persons and capable women and children, interacting with one another in good and ill temper. Women, children, and older persons break the confines of their occupational strait-jackets, making art, dancing, fabricating tools, and foraging away from camp. Men wear ornaments, smile, and are idle. Significantly, these artists have built on their own expert knowledge, rather than relying on the testimony of other experts, who for the most part have seemed little concerned with the social content of these dioramic scenes.

As a scientist, I see these artists' representations as science fictions—visually mediating the often complex research tactics of specialists for an interested, educable public. When I call these reconstructions science fictions, I mean no slur. In fact, strong philosophical parallels exist between what "real scientists" trying to understand unseeable ancient events do and what a careful artist does in these representations. We each link together points of scientific fact—things we think we know for sure—into narratives of educated guesses and arguments of plausibility. From this perspective, the work of the most thoughtful of my artist colleagues in portraying ancient humans exactly parallels my own struggles to make sense of the evidence actually left behind by them.

Once each acknowledges the social power of the visual assertions about our ancestors that populate our museums and popular books, rich possibilities for collaboration between scientists and artists emerge. As an archaeologist trained in an anthropological view of the past and a citizen of an ethnically and racially diverse nation, I believe we can serve the greater public by expanding the range of possible pasts represented in depictions of prehistoric people. I am not arguing for revising past worlds as they have conventionally been represented using a representational quota system, by which various ages, genders, and races get their fair share of prestige as defined in these works—where women hunt, men scrape hides, old folks run and dance,

though all probably did a good deal of these activities. Rather, why not combine scientific rigor and creativity to offer viewers social arrangements different from any known today, or hominid species with truly different adaptations and behaviors? By picturing unexpected past worlds—inhabited not by mimicries or parodies of ourselves but by those who may have been strong, successful, yet very unlike us—we might succeed in actually drawing more viewers into the real problems, possibilities, and pleasures of research on the past.

FURTHER READING

Berger, John. 1972. *Ways of Seeing*. Viking Press.

Gifford-Gonzalez, Diane. 1993. "You Can Hide, but You Can't Run: Representation of Women's Work in Illustrations of Palaeolithic Life." *Visual Anthropology Review* 9:3–21.

Goffman, Erving. 1979. *Gender Advertisements*. Harper and Row.

Mathis, Ruth. 1991. "Race and Human Origins Narratives: Whose Past?" Unpublished manuscript.

Moser, Stephanie. 1996. "Visual Representation in Archaeology: Depicting the Missing-Link in Human Origins." In B. S. Baigrie, ed., *Picturing Knowledge: Historical and Philosophical Problems Concerning the Use of Art in Science*, pp. 184–214. University of Toronto Press.

Moser, Stephanie, and Clive Gamble. 1997. "Revolutionary Images: The Iconic Vocabulary for Representing Human Antiquity." In B. L. Molyneaux, ed., *The Cultural Life of Images: Visual Representation in Archaeology*, pp. 185–212. Routledge.

Rudwick, Martin J. S. 1992. *Scenes from Deep Time: Early Pictorial Representations of the Prehistoric World*. University of Chicago Press.

Saint-Blanquat, Henri de, and Véronique Ageorges. 1989. *Lascaux et Son Temps*. Casterman.

Stafford, Barbara M. 1991. *Body Criticism: Imaging the Unseen in Enlightenment Art and Medicine*. MIT Press.

Waters, Tom. 1990. "Almost Human." *Discover* 11(May):42–44, 53.

"The Way We Were. Our Ice Age Heritage: Language, Art, Fashion, and the Family." 1986. *Newsweek* (November 10).

7   STORIES BONES TELL

Kathleen D. Gordon

What types of information can physical and forensic anthropologists learn from human skeletal remains, and how is the information used? Whether discussing diet, disease, or demography, the Japanese Ainu or African American history, Gordon underscores the significant contributions physical anthropologists have made to our understanding of human behavior and history. The author's update details the enormous impact that molecular biology, genetics, and ancient DNA studies have had on physical anthropology in recent years.

Collecting and studying human skeletons in museums and scientific laboratories is at present a complex, controversial activity. The purpose of this chapter is to explore the kinds of information scientists obtain by studying human skeletons, and how that information is used.

A physical anthropologist is trained to determine many facts about an individual from bones alone. For instance, sex identification often can be determined by the differences in the pelvis and skull. Even bone fragments may be sexed; some chemical components of bone differ between men and women. Age at the time of death can be estimated very closely by looking at the teeth and at the fusion between different parts of the same bone, especially for children and young adults. For older people, the estimates are less exact and rely more on changes in joint surfaces, fusion between skull bones, and microscopic details of internal bone structure. Height is estimated by the length of the long bones, especially the leg bones. Ancestry can often be determined by looking at characteristics of the facial skeleton. Statistical studies of tooth, skull, and face shape can even distinguish closely related groups within the same major population.

The skeleton reveals information about lifestyle as well. Well-developed muscles leave their mark on bone and tell of heavy physical activity during life. Habits (such as pipe smoking) and handedness may leave traces on teeth or in asymmetric bone and muscle development. Health, injuries, and many diseases, such as syphilis, tuberculosis, arthritis, and leprosy, may leave traces on bone. A subfield of physical anthropology, paleopathology, is devoted to the study and diagnosis of diseases in ancient human remains.

From these studies, paleopathologists are often able to provide medical insights into the history and ecology of modern human diseases. For instance, childhood illness or malnutrition can be detected by abnormalities in tooth enamel and bone mineralization. By noting the position of these abnormalities, physical anthropologists, with their knowledge of normal growth patterns of bones and teeth, can often pinpoint at exactly what age the illness or growth disturbances occurred. From this it can be determined whether a child's health problems were caused by a sick or poorly nourished mother, by early weaning, or by later periods of food shortage.

VICTIM IDENTIFICATION

Because of their skill at piecing together an individual's life history from skeletal clues, physical anthropologists are constantly in demand to help identify humans who have been the victims of accidents or foul play. The forensic anthropologist can tell authorities whether bones are human and, if the bones are disarticulated, whether they all come from the same individual. Physical anthropologists have helped authorities in Argentina locate and identify skeletons of people kidnapped and murdered by political extremists during the country's earlier period of upheaval. Anthropologists helped confirm the identification of a skeleton thought to be that of Nazi war criminal Josef Mengele. Other scientists use information learned from studying museum skeletons to help provide facial reconstructions of what missing children might look like several years after their disappearance. Still others are using their knowledge of skeletal biology to help identify victims of mass disasters.

BURIAL REMAINS

Why do scientists collect and study more than one skeleton from the same site or cemetery? Isn't one enough? The answer depends on what questions

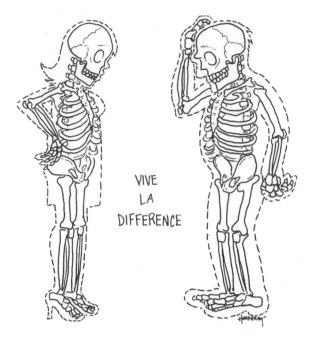

VIVE
LA
DIFFERENCE

the scientist wants to answer. Although a single skeleton can tell us much about an individual, that person is known only in isolation, and people do not live in isolation. To the anthropologist, much more important information about whole social groups, their history, their relationships with neighboring and past cultures, their diet and health, and their social customs and relationships can be obtained only by studying large numbers of skeletons from the same culture or living site. Such population-wide studies require many specialized analytic techniques that depend on having large numbers of observations in order to be valid.

The Case of the Ainu

Many of these population studies have provided information about past human migrations, declines, and relationships that were unrecorded even in traditional stories and myths. For instance, research by anthropologists on the Ainu of Japan has resolved some long-standing questions about their origins. Traditionally many Japanese have considered the Ainu to be an ethnic minority of low status whose physical features are somewhat different from the majority population. Although Japanese tradition holds that modern Japanese are descended from the prehistoric Jomon culture found throughout Japan, two studies now show that the Ainu are the true descendants of the Jomon people. According to studies of minute variations in the teeth and skulls of the modern inhabitants of Japan, and of various prehistoric cultures from Japan and other parts of Asia, the modern Japanese are most likely the descendants of invaders from northern China called the Yayoi, who conquered the islands a little over 2,000 years ago. An interesting twist to the story is that many of the medieval Japanese warrior class, the samurai, show physical features that suggest that they were descendants of Jomon mercenary armies recruited by the Yayoi during their military conquest. As the samurai gained power and status, they eventually intermarried with the Yayoi ruling classes and passed on some of their typically "Ainu" facial traits into the modern upper classes of Japan. Today's Ainu are the descendants of unabsorbed Jomon populations who were pushed into increasingly marginal areas by the Yayoi-Japanese and their Jomon-derived samurai.

Similar kinds of studies have been used to provide answers to questions as diverse as how many waves of prehistoric immigrants populated Australia, how much white admixture there is in various American Indian groups, and how much intermarrying there was between Pueblo groups in the Southwest and Europeans during the contact period. Other researchers using the same techniques have been able to chart the progressive distinctiveness of American Indian groups from other Asian and Pacific island populations to estimate when American Indian migrants first entered the Western Hemisphere and when the various tribes became separate.

Mohenjodaro Revisited

Scientists utilizing new techniques have even been helpful in resolving questions about classical civilizations. The city of Mohenjodaro, the center of Harappan civilization in the Indus Valley, was thought to have been sacked by Aryan warriors invading in 1500 B.C. After studying the human remains from Mohenjodaro, anthropologists have now concluded that no massacre ever occurred because they found no battle injuries on the bones. They also found no evidence of genetic differences between populations before, during, and after the decline of Mohenjodaro, which makes an invasion of foreigners very unlikely. However, the skeletons did show high levels of disease and parasites, which might have been a more important cause of the Harappan decline than any invasion or conquest.

DISEASE, DIET, AND DEMOGRAPHY

Studies of cemeteries show scientists how human groups interact with their environment, and how they in turn are affected by changes in the physical world they occupy. Reconstructions of demography, diet, and growth and

disease patterns help physical anthropologists understand the ecology of prehistoric groups and make some surprising discoveries about human adaptations, such as the health costs of agriculture and the origins of some modern human diseases.

Many diseases can be diagnosed from skeletons, and it is sometimes possible to recover fossilized bacteria, and occasionally amino acids for blood
typing, directly from bone. One extensive study of Grecian cemeteries from
ancient to modern times traced the increase in malaria-resistant anemia (tha-
lassemia, similar to sickle cell anemia in Africa) in Grecian populations and
showed the effects of changes in ecology and social and economic patterns
on the health and life span of ancient and recent Greeks. By looking at groupings of skeletons in cemeteries, the scientist was also able to reconstruct families or clans, and to show that anemic groups were more fertile than others.

Studies of skeletons can also tell what people ate, even without having any
cultural information. Some techniques measure certain chemical isotopes and
trace elements in ground bone. These amounts will differ depending on the
proportion of meat to vegetables in the diet and on the type of plant foods
eaten. Results have shown that in some prehistoric groups men and women
had different diets, with men sometimes consuming more meat and women
eating more plant foods. Other studies have shown that different diets leave
different microscopic scratch patterns on tooth surfaces, and several kinds
of prehistoric diets can be distinguished in this way.

Changes in diet often cause changes in health, which can be seen in the
skeleton. The shift to a reliance on maize in the prehistoric Southwest diet
coincided with an increase in porous bone in skeletons, a sign of iron deficiency anemia. In maize farmers from Dickson Mounds, Illinois, defects in
tooth enamel, which are caused by stress during childhood, are more numerous. Infant mortality was also higher and adult age at death lower than
in preagricultural groups. Similar studies of Hopewell mounds concluded
that the agricultural Hopewell had more chronic health problems, dietary
deficiencies, and tuberculosis than preagricultural groups. Agriculture is usually thought to bring an improvement in quality of life, but the surprising
conclusion that prehistoric agriculture marked a decline in general health in
the New World has been confirmed by many other studies [see Cohen,
"Progress? The Facts of Ancient Life," in this volume].

Recent Population Studies

Studies of human skeletons can be useful even for recent populations, when
written records are limited or have been lost. Several studies have reconstructed the living conditions of African Americans both during slavery and
after its end. Skeletons recovered from an eighteenth-century New Orleans

cemetery showed many differences in nutrition and physical stress between urban and rural slaves. Skeletons from a late-nineteenth- to early-twentieth-century cemetery in Arkansas open a window on this period, which is not well documented by other historical sources. Researchers concluded that men commonly left the community (there were few male burials), and that some of the community intermarried with the local Indian population. On the whole, the population was poorly nourished and had low resistance to disease. Many infants died at birth of widespread bacterial infections. Children's skeletons show dietary deficiencies and chronic infections, with many dying at eighteen months, the weaning age. Iron deficiency anemias were common, probably because of corn-based diets; high levels of arthritis indicate heavy physical labor; and many signs of injuries on male skeletons may be evidence of high levels of interpersonal violence. Even without written records, the skeletons in this post-Reconstruction community tell us of continual malnutrition, poor health, and levels of physical stress that even exceeded those found in some communities during slavery [see Singleton, "The Archaeology of African American Life," in this volume].

Ancient Diseases in Contemporary Populations

Physical anthropologists find many contemporary diseases in earlier human populations. Some show peculiar distributions in the United States today, which can sometimes be tied to disease prevalence in the past. One of these is osteoporosis, a weakening of bone due to a calcium-poor diet and low bone mass resulting from low levels of exercise during life. This condition afflicts primarily elderly white females, leading to spontaneous fractures and spinal deformities. Surprisingly, anthropologists have discovered that osteoporosis is common in living and prehistoric Eskimos of both sexes, and appears at an earlier age when compared to American whites. However, fractures and spinal problems have not been common in Eskimo populations. In spite of the traditional calcium-poor Eskimo diet, vigorous exercise results in heavier bones that protect the individual in old age. Now, however, increased life span and alterations in lifestyle may contribute to a rise in osteoporotic bone disorders in Arctic populations in the future.

Evidence of a disease in prehistory is sometimes useful in understanding its cause. Osteoarthritis is often found in prehistoric skeletons. Changes in the locations and numbers of joints affected, and in the proportions of men and women afflicted, have suggested that systemic factors affecting only one sex or the other may be involved in the severity of modern arthritis, an insight that may help focus further research efforts. Studies of prehistoric skeletons have shown that high levels of tooth decay are typical only of agricultural populations. This has led to the observation that sticky carbohydrates common to most agricultural diets have something to do with the epidemic of tooth decay modern populations are experiencing. But mineral deficiencies may also be involved, as some high levels of cavities and periodontal disease have been found in nonagricultural prehistoric Illinois Indians. Since the mineral content of groundwater would affect the disease resistance of tooth enamel, such studies have pointed to mineral supplementation of drinking water as a means of combating tooth decay. Tuberculosis has been found in skeletons as early as 5,000 years ago in the Old World and by at least A.D. 1000 in the New World. It is associated with keeping livestock and living in sedentary or urban centers. Cemetery studies in Europe have shown a curious relationship between tuberculosis and leprosy, also a very ancient disease. Skeletons rarely show signs of both diseases, and as tuberculosis became more common in Europe in the late Middle Ages, signs of leprosy in European skeletons declined. Medical researchers now speculate that exposure to tuberculosis provides individuals with some immunity to leprosy.

Some health problems are more common in Native Americans than in the general population. One of these is rheumatoid arthritis, which had been thought to be a recent disease possibly caused by an infection. The discovery of rheumatoid-like lesions in prehistoric American Indians has changed the focus of medical research on this disease. Another condition more common than expected in some Native American tribes is the cleft palate/cleft lip complex of congenital bone defects. Clefting of the face has been found in prehistoric skeletons from the same region, though it is not as common as in the modern population. It is not known whether this shows a real increase in the problem, or if burials of prehistoric babies who died from their condition are simply not recovered as often as adults. Some researchers speculate that the increase, if real, might be the result of more inbreeding in tribal populations than would have occurred in the past, after groups were confined on reservations, and traditional migration and marriage patterns were disrupted.

PATTERNS OF SOCIAL ORGANIZATION

It might seem surprising that we can learn much about the patterns of political and social organization of past cultures from a study of bones, but in fact physical anthropologists and archaeologists can discover a great deal about social customs in prehistory through studies of cemeteries. This is only possible, however, with data about age and sex of each burial.

Evidence of status and marriage patterns is often visible in cemetery populations. Anthropologists studying skeletons from the prehistoric North American site of Moundville, Alabama, reconstructed three different status groups in Moundville society. These included individuals whose remains ei-

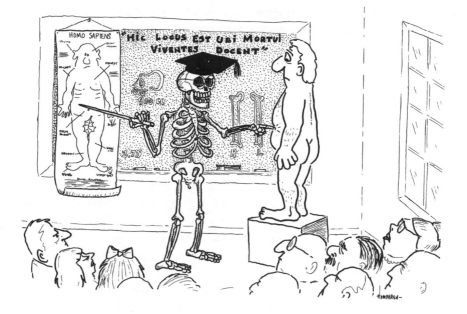

ther were used as trophies or were possibly sacrifices sanctifying the mound-building process, an intermediate group containing both men and women, and a high-status group composed entirely of adult men. By analyzing genetic differences among men and women in the same cemetery, it is often possible to reconstruct marriage and residence patterns. For instance, in one study of prehistoric and historic Pueblo cemeteries, women in each cemetery had very similar genetic markers, while the men in each group were quite variable for those same traits. This indicates that women lived and were buried with their kin groups, while men lived and were buried with unrelated groups. The ancient Pueblo people were matrilocal, just as the modern tribes are today. Some studies have revealed a relationship between an individual's status during life and his or her physical characteristics, such as height. Taller people tend to have higher-status markers in their graves in several prehistoric cultures. This is more often true for men, but in some groups taller women also had higher status. By studying skeletons for indications of growth disturbances and disease, scientists can sometimes tell whether the greater height of high-status people was due to better diet and more resources, or whether they were just genetically predisposed to be taller.

CONCLUSION

The above examples show how anthropologists can learn about many facets of the lives of individuals and communities of past cultures by studying their skeletal materials. The study of modern, historic, and prehistoric skeletons has made it possible for anthropologists to uncover an enormous and diverse array of information about human behavior and morphology past and present. None of these studies could have been accomplished without the thorough study of human skeletons. To obtain this information, scientists commonly use techniques that were unheard of and unanticipated even a generation ago. It is certain that many more new approaches to reconstructing past lives from bones will be discovered in the future. Many collections may be studied and restudied, in the quest for new answers to old questions, or for answers to new questions altogether.

Prehistoric populations left us little of their history and experience from which to learn. By careful study of their skeletons, we gain an understanding of ancient humans that would not otherwise be possible. The late J. Lawrence Angel, a noted Smithsonian physical anthropologist and forensic expert, always kept a sign in his laboratory: *Hic locus est ubi mortui viventes docent* (In this place, the dead teach the living). They teach us about the past, and if we listen carefully, about the future as well.

UPDATE

It is perhaps ironic that just at the time when many human skeletal collections in museums are threatened or shrinking because of claims filed under the Native American Graves Protection and Repatriation Act (NAGPRA)— which requires federal institutions and museums to inventory their collections of Native American human remains and funerary objects and repatriate them to culturally affiliated tribes upon request—new advances in molecular biology are providing us with innovative and exciting techniques to learn about the genetics of past human populations directly from bones themselves [see Bray, "The Repatriation Mandate," in this volume].

Researchers first discovered that DNA could be recovered from soft tissues of some ancient species in 1984, when mitochondrial DNA (mtDNA) sequences were cloned from an old museum skin of the quagga, an extinct zebra-like animal. The following year Svante Pääbo, then a Swedish graduate student in molecular biology, managed to clone DNA from ancient Egyptian mummies in several museum collections. In the next decade DNA was extracted from a variety of fossilized remains: wheat seeds, insects trapped in amber (featured as the source of dinosaur DNA in the movie *Jurassic Park*), 18-million-year-old magnolia leaves, and human brains preserved in bodies buried in a Florida peat bog more than 7,000 years ago.

But the most exciting result came when it was discovered that DNA could be recovered not just from unusually preserved soft tissues but from ancient bone itself. Since bone is by far the most prevalent kind of fossil, this has opened up a new arena of research possibilities. One study using this approach was an analysis of the relationships of the moas of New Zealand, an extinct group of flightless birds that disappeared shortly after humans colonized the islands around 1,000 years ago. Researchers were able to determine that the extinct moas were not closely related to the kiwis, the other flightless birds of New Zealand, and that they must have colonized the region before the kiwis, which probably migrated from Australia where their cousins, the emus and cassowaries, still survive. More spectacularly, Brigham Young University researchers claimed in 1995 to have isolated DNA from fossil dinosaur bones some 80 million years old, but so far the sequences recovered have been too short to convince most other researchers that the DNA really derives from dinosaurs. More studies of this material are under way, but the difficulties the Brigham Young researchers have encountered are typical of problems that the field of ancient DNA research has yet to resolve.

The earliest ancient DNA studies relied on the technique of molecular cloning to produce a large enough amount of DNA to analyze. In this method, the extracted ancient DNA is fused to a carrier DNA molecule and introduced into bacteria to multiply the original strand, hopefully into thousands of copies. But molecular cloning is severely hampered by the damage all ancient DNA has undergone, most of which occurs in the first few hours after death. The bacteria often fail to make copies when the sequence is damaged, or the copies they make may reproduce errors caused by degradation of the original fragment. Because the clones resulting from this procedure are so few, it was often hard to reproduce results and sometimes impossible to perform particular experiments at all.

The prospects for ancient DNA studies improved dramatically in the late 1980s with the invention of polymerase chain reaction (PCR) This is a test-tube cloning technique that produces many more copies of the target DNA fragment than does molecular cloning and is not nearly as affected by any underlying damage in the original. Because of its high rate of multiplication, or amplification, of the original DNA fragment, PCR can be successful even when a sample has only one or a few intact molecules of DNA.

Nonetheless, even when PCR reproduces billions of copies to work with, complete sections of genes are seldom recovered from ancient DNA. Most ancient sequences range from 100 to 500 base pairs of nucleotides in length, whereas intact genes range from 75 base pairs to over 2 million, depending on the complexity of the gene involved. Bone, interestingly enough, seems to provide a more stable environment for the preservation of DNA than soft tissues, because sequences retrieved from bone are longer on average than those that have been derived from soft tissue.

The most difficult challenge in the study of ancient DNA is how to avoid contamination. Scientists may be able to amplify minute amounts of DNA, but sometimes the results show that it must have come from the researchers or excavators themselves. Stringent procedures to reduce contamination from the first moment of fossil recovery through the entire laboratory protocol are being developed by researchers in order to improve success. Contamination during fossilization by microbes and fungi is also a problem, though selecting particular target genes such as those on mitochondria or in hemoglobin and collagen may eliminate the problem, since plants and fungi do not carry these. Although the Brigham Young researchers have convinced others that they indeed have extracted DNA from 80-million-year-old bones, the question remains, whose DNA? While the bones are within the size range of dinosaurs typical of the strata from which they were recovered, DNA results showed a closer similarity to whales than to the reptile or bird sequences expected in this comparison. Whether this is an anomaly, a result of contamination, or an indication of more variability within dinosaurs than anticipated cannot yet be determined. So while fossil bone may be plentiful, methodological issues will probably prevent an immediate bonanza of ancient DNA results.

Some human applications have already shown their worth. DNA studies of the Tyrolean "Iceman," a mummified human body found eroding out of a melting Alpine glacier in 1991, were instrumental in ruling out the possibility that the body was planted as a hoax. Early skeptics had wondered if the mummy was not really Egyptian or Peruvian instead of European. Mitochondrial DNA analysis clearly showed that the 5,000-year-old man was most likely part of the local central-northern European population and not at all similar genetically to either African or American groups. But in the long-running case of Kennewick Man, whose 9,300-year-old skeleton was found eroding out of a bank of the Columbia River a few years ago, DNA analysis has not proven helpful in determining his closest relationships. Three expert laboratories were given bone samples to analyze, but none was able to extract uncontaminated DNA suitable for testing. Highly mineralized bone simply may not preserve enough collagen to extract, and burial or deposition in a wet environment with fluctuating temperatures will further degrade or contaminate the DNA. Such a disappointing outcome is not uncommon, and researchers in the field have proposed "criteria of authenticity" to which studies should adhere in order for their results to be credible. However, ensuring this high standard of authenticity is cumbersome and expensive, and, regrettably, not all published results yet satisfy these standards (Cooper and Poinar 2000).

DNA and other biological markers from ancient bone are also shedding light on the history of human disease. Researchers at the University of Newcastle upon Tyne have isolated a substance in old bone (mycolic acid) that indicates the mycobacteria that cause tuberculosis, and which is detectable even when there is no macroscopic evidence of disease on the bone surface. Gene sequences for sickle cell anemia have been isolated from dried bone, sufficient to permit a differential diagnosis (Faerman et al. 2000). DNA evidence has also been obtained from skeletons in fifth-century-A.D. Roman cemeteries that confirms the hypothesis that widespread outbreaks of falciparum malaria probably contributed directly to the decline of the Roman Empire (Sallares and Gomzi 2001).

Analyses of modern DNA in contemporary New World populations have provided several competing scenarios reconstructing early migrations into North America. While the traditional archaeological benchmark for the earliest occupations is tied to the Clovis culture (now calibrated to about 13,350 radiocarbon years ago), some scientists analyzing evolutionary rates of mtDNA change have concluded that the migrations into the New World must have occurred much earlier, by at least 20,000 years and possibly as early as 40,000 years ago (Schurr 2000). Also at issue is the number of waves of migration: linguistic and earlier genetic studies had suggested that colonization from Asia occurred in two or three waves, and that Amerind, Na-Dene, and Aleut-Eskimo groups may have migrated at separate times. However, newer studies of more genetic markers from both contemporary and several prehistoric skeletal populations show that there are four distinct mitochondrial "lineages" in the New World (haplogroups A, B, C, and D) and that most tribal groups studied so far show at least two of these and often all four. This implies that there was more likely a single migration, not separate waves, with all four lineages represented among the initial migrants. Even more recently, a fifth lineage has been identified, the X haplogroup, which occurs in low percentages in several widespread North American native groups. The X haplogroup also has been tentatively identified in some prehistoric North American skeletons as well (Norris Farms, Illinois, and Windover, Florida), and intriguingly, unlike the other four, it cannot be found in any Asian population thus far studied. Instead, the X haplogroup is found in several European and western Eurasian groups. Its occurrence in prehistoric populations in North America eliminates the possibility that the X lineage is a result of post-Columbian intermixing with European colonists.

These genetic data, coupled with suggestions from some archaeologists that cultural horizons earlier than Clovis exist in North America and that the closest cultural resemblance to Clovis-style fluted points comes not from Asia but from the Solutrean culture of western Europe, paint a picture of the peopling of the New World that is suddenly quite complex and highly controversial [see Selig and Stanford, "Researching the First Americans," in this volume]. And when the earliest Paleoindian skeletal remains, such as Kennewick and Spirit Cave, show morphologies not very similar to modern Asians and contemporary Native Americans, the mix of competing hypotheses (and the political agendas sometimes imputed to them) becomes practically incendiary. Further studies of prehistoric DNA—both in the New World and the Old—will have a vital role to play in sorting out this complexity.

Ancient population movements in the Old World also may benefit from studies of recent and prehistoric DNA. Linguistic and blood group studies had been thought to show that modern European populations date from a relatively recent migration of Neolithic farming peoples from the Middle East, around 10,000 years ago. More recent mtDNA analysis has turned up evidence suggesting instead that 80 percent of modern Europeans show lineages that predate this Neolithic influx, back to at least 30,000 to perhaps 45,000 years ago (Richards et al. 2000).

Researchers hope that ancient DNA studies will eventually help sort out the transition to modern *Homo sapiens* and our enigmatic relationship to the Neanderthals [see Brooks, "The Emergence of Modern Humans," in this volume]. Indeed, mtDNA has now been successfully extracted from three different Neanderthal fossils (Relethford 2001), and while they all showed close similarities and evidence of being part of the same gene pool, all are quite different from mitochondrial DNA of modern humans from any part of the world. Those who subscribe to the "out-of-Africa" or replacement model of modern human origins found this to be the most convincing evidence to date to support the species-level distinction between Neanderthals and modern humans. Those who favor the multiregional model point out that mitochondrial lineages could be easily lost through various demographic processes; that mitochondrial separation does not say anything about how much Neanderthal contribution there might have been to the nuclear DNA of modern people; and that until there is comparable genetic material from similarly old anatomically modern fossils, the Neanderthal DNA cannot be meaningfully interpreted. After all, it might be that early modern people also looked quite genetically dissimilar from modern humans.

The newest analysis to roil these waters reported on extracted mtDNA from an ancient but anatomically modern skeleton from Lake Mungo, Australia, dated at around 60,000 years old, and from several younger individuals from Kow Swamp. These individuals are considered to be fully modern but show skeletal morphologies more robust and archaic-looking than do contemporary indigenous Australians. Remarkably, the oldest but most modern-appearing skeleton yielded an mtDNA sequence that is not represented at all in any of the modern groups known. It is now clear that at least some early modern mitochondrial lineages have been completely lost as well and show no close relationships with modern human DNA. Further, there is a disconnect between skeletal appearance and genetic modernity, just as there may well be between nuclear and mitochondrial genomes. The fact that the three Neanderthals are mitochondrial outliers relative to today's humans is now matched by the fact that some early modern fossils are outliers as well. As with so many controversies in paleoanthropology, only more data points will clarify this picture.

FURTHER READING

Bass, William M. 1996. *Human Osteology: A Laboratory and Field Manual*. 4th ed. Missouri Archaeological Society.

Brothwell, D. R. 1981. *Digging Up Bones*. 3rd ed. Cornell University Press.

Brown, T. A., and K. A. Brown. 1992. "Ancient DNA and the Archaeologist." *Antiquity* 66:10–23.

Cooper, Alan, and Hendrik N. Poinar. 2000. "Ancient DNA: Do It Right or Not at All." *Science* 289(5482):1139.

Faerman, Marina, A. Nebel, D. Filon, M. G. Thomas, N. Bradman, B. D. Ragsdale, M. Schultz, and A. Oppenheim. 2000. "From a Dry Bone to a Genetic Portrait: A Case Study of Sickle Cell Anemia." *American Journal of Physical Anthropology* 111(2):153–63.

Hagelberg, Erika. 1993/1994. "Ancient DNA Studies." *Evolutionary Anthropology* 2(6):199–207.

Pääbo, Svante. 1993. "Ancient DNA." *Scientific American* 269 (November):86–92.

Relethford, John. 2001. "Ancient DNA and the Origin of Modern Humans." *Proceedings of the National Academy of Science* 98(2):390–91.

Richards, M., V. Macaulay, E. Hickey, E. Vega, B. Sykes, V. Guida, C. Rengo, D. Sellitto, F. Cruciani, T. Kivisild, R. Villems, M. Thomas, S. Rychkov, O. Rychkov, Y. Rychkov, M. Golge, D. Dimitrov, E. Hill, D. Bradley, V. Romano, F. Cali, G. Vona, A. Demaine, S. Papiha, C. Triantaphyllidis, G. Stefanescu, J. Hatina, M. Belledi, A. Di Rienzo, A. Novelletto, A. Oppenheim, S. Norby, N. Al-Zaheri, S. Santachiara-Benerecetti, R. Scozari, A. Torroni, and H. J. Bandelt. 2000. "Tracing European Founder Lineages in the Near Eastern mtDNA Pool." *American Journal of Human Genetics* 67(5):1251–76.

Sallares, Robert, and Susan Gomzi. 2001. "Biomolecular Archaeology of Malaria." *Ancient Biomolecules* 3(3):195–213.

Schurr, Theodore G. 2000. "The Story in the Genes." *Scientific American Discovering Archaeology* 2(1):59–60.

Ubelaker, Douglas H. 1999. *Human Skeletal Remains: Excavation, Analysis, and Interpretation*. 3rd ed. Taraxacum.

8 DISEASE IN HUMAN EVOLUTION

George J. Armelagos, Kathleen C. Barnes, and James Lin

This chapter describes three periods of major change in the human way of life, with each transition marked by the emergence of new diseases. The chapter addresses the question of why diseases changed as humans moved from being gatherer-hunters to agriculturalists to urban dwellers in the midst of industrialization. The author also discusses the history of syphilis and today's health crisis with the reemergence of infectious diseases with antibiotic resistance.

For millions of years, humans and their ancestors have suffered from diseases—both the kind caused by infectious pathogens (e.g., bacteria, viruses, parasites) and the kind caused by our own bodies as they age and degenerate. Over this long period, humans have constantly created new ways of living and eating. From the point of view of a bacterium or virus, however, any shift in the physical makeup or behavior of its human host represents a challenge to be overcome. As a result, new diseases emerged with each major change in the human way of life.

For nearly four million years, humans lived in widely dispersed, nomadic, small populations that minimized the effect of infectious diseases. With the agricultural revolution about 10,000 years ago, increasing sedentism and larger population groupings resulted in the first epidemiological transition in which infectious and nutritional diseases increased (Barrett et al. 1998). Within the last century, with the advent of public health measures, improved nutrition, and medicine, some populations in developed nations underwent a second epidemiological transition. During this transition, infectious diseases declined and noninfectious, chronic diseases and degenerative conditions increased. Today we are facing a third epidemiological transition, with a reemergence of infectious diseases that were thought to be under control and the emergence of "new" pathogens; many of these pathogens are resistant to multiple antibiotics and have the potential to be transmitted on a global scale. Populations that experienced the second epidemiological transition and those that never experienced it are both increasingly exposed to antibiotic-resistant pathogens.

Emerging pathogens are seen as new diseases, discovered when they have an impact on our adaptation or survival. Even when we take a more holistic ecological perspective, it is often limited to a position that considers emerging disease as the result of environmental changes that are relevant only to the present situation as it affects humans here and now. We often fail to consider the economic and political factors that bring humans in contact with pathogens (Farmer 1999). This article argues that the emergence of new diseases has been the human pattern since the origin of the hominids and accelerated with the shift to agriculture 10,000 years ago (Armelagos 1998).

PALEOLITHIC BASELINE

The cultural period of the stone age that began 2.5 to 2 million years ago. Mark by the earliest use of tools made of chip stone

For most of their 4 million years of evolutionary history, human populations lived in small, sparsely settled groups. Population size and density remained low throughout the Paleolithic. Fertility and mortality rates in small gathering-hunting populations would have to have been balanced for the population size to remain small.

Demographic factors creating this stability are still a matter of discussion. Some demographers argue that gatherer-hunters were at their maximum natural fertility, balanced by high mortality. However, gatherer-hunters maintained a stable population with controlled moderate fertility balanced by moderate mortality (Armelagos et al. 1991).

The demographic changes following the Neolithic may provide insights into the case for population stability controlled by moderate fertility and mortality during the Paleolithic. Following the Neolithic revolution, a dramatic increase in population size and density occurred. It was thought that the Neolithic economy generated food surpluses that led to a better-nourished and healthier population with a reduced rate of mortality. Since populations were at their natural maximum fertility, there would have been a rapid increase in population size.

The empirical evidence suggests an alternative scenario in the shift from gathering and hunting to agriculture. The picture suggests a much bleaker picture of health. Instead of experiencing improved health, there is evidence of a substantial increase in infectious and nutritional disease (Cohen and Armelagos 1984). A paradox emerges if the traditionally accepted models of Paleolithic fertility and mortality are correct. How can a population experiencing maximum fertility during the Paleolithic respond with exponential growth in population when people's health is deteriorating? The only model that could explain this paradox is one in which Paleolithic populations were controlling fertility and infectious disease was not a problem.

A consideration of the disease ecology of contemporary gatherer-hunters provides insights into the types of disease that probably affected our gatherer-hunter ancestors. Gatherer-hunters had two types of disease to contend with in their adaptation to their environment (Barrett et al. 1998). One class of disease would be those organisms that had adapted to prehominid ancestors and persisted with them as they evolved into hominids. Head and body lice (*Pediculus humanus*), pinworms, and possibly malaria would be included in this group. Add to this list most of the internal protozoa found in modern humans and such bacteria as salmonella, typhi, and staphylococci (Cockburn 1971) .

The second class of diseases is the zoonotic, which have nonhuman animals as their primary host and only incidentally infect humans. Humans can be infected by zoonoses through insect bites, by preparation and consumption of contaminated flesh, and from wounds inflicted by animals. Sleeping sickness, tetanus, scrub typhus, relapsing fever, trichinosis, tularemia, avian or ichthyic tuberculosis, leptospirosis, and schistosomiasis are among the zoonotic diseases that could have afflicted earlier hunter-gatherers (Cockburn 1971).

Although early human populations were too small to support endemic (constantly present) pathogens, they maintained some kind of relationships with the vectors that would later serve to perpetuate such human host-specific diseases as yellow fever and louse-borne relapsing fever. Certain lice were ectoparasites as early as the Oligocene, and the prehumans of the early Pliocene probably suffered from malaria, since the mosquito necessary for transmission of the disease (genus *Anopheles*) evolved by the Miocene era. However, Frank Livingstone (1958), an anthropological epidemiologist, dismisses the potential of malaria in early hominids except in isolated incidences because of the small population size and an adaptation to the savanna, an environment that would not have included the mosquitoes that carry the malaria plasmodium. Recent genomic analyses of human genetic response (G6PD deficiency) to malaria support this position.

The range of the earliest hominids was probably restricted to the tropical savanna. This would have limited the pathogens that were potential disease agents. During the course of human evolution, the habitat expanded gradually into the temperate zones and eventually the tundra. Hominids would have avoided large areas of the African landscape because of tsetse flies and thus avoided the trypanosomes they carried. Frank Lambrecht (1985) argues that the evolution of the human species and its expansion into new ecological niches would have led to a change in the pattern of trypanosome infection. While this list of diseases that may have plagued our gathering-hunting ancestors is informative, those diseases that would have been absent are of greater interest. The contagious community diseases such as influenza, measles, mumps, and smallpox would have been missing. There probably would have been few viruses infecting these early hominids, although Cockburn (1967) disagrees and suggests that the viral diseases found in nonhuman primates would have been easily transmitted to hominids.

THE FIRST EPIDEMIOLOGICAL TRANSITION: DISEASE IN AGRICULTURAL POPULATIONS

The reliance on primary food production (agriculture) increased the incidence and the impact of disease. Sedentism, an important feature of agricultural adaptation, conceivably increased parasitic disease spread by contact with human waste. In gathering-hunting groups, the frequent movement of the base camp and frequent forays away from the base camp by men and women would decrease their contact with human wastes. In sedentary [stationary] populations, the proximity of habitation area and waste deposit sites to the water supply is a source of contamination. While sedentism did occur prior to the Neolithic period in those areas with abundant resources, once there was the shift to agriculture, sedentary living was necessary.

The domestication of animals provided a steady supply of vectors and greater exposure to zoonotic diseases. The zoonotic infections most likely increased because of domesticated animals, such as goats, sheep, cattle, pigs, and fowl, as well as unwanted domestic animals such as rodents and sparrows, which developed permanent habitats in and around human dwellings. Products of domesticated animals such as milk, hair, and skin, as well as the dust raised by the animals, could transmit anthrax, Q fever, brucellosis, and tuberculosis. Breaking the sod during cultivation exposed workers to insect bites and diseases such as scrub typhus (Barrett et al. 1998). Frank Livingstone showed that slash-and-burn agriculture in West Africa exposed populations to *Anopheles gambiae*, a mosquito that is the vector for *Plasmodium falciparum*, which causes malaria. Agricultural practices also create pools of water, expanding the potential breeding sites for mosquitoes. The combination of disruptive environmental farming practices and the presence of domestic animals also increased human contact with arthropod (insect) vectors carrying yellow fever, trypanosomiasis, and filariasis, which then developed a preference for human blood. Some disease vectors developed dependent relationships with human habitats, the best example of which is *Aedes aegypti* (the vector for yellow fever and dengue), a mosquito that breeds in stagnant pools of water in open containers. Various agricultural practices increased contact with nonvector parasites. Irrigation brought contact with schistosomal cercariae, and the use of feces as fertilizer caused infection from intestinal flukes (Cockburn 1971).

The shift to agriculture led to a change in ecology; this resulted in diseases not frequently encountered by forager populations. The shift from a varied, well-balanced diet to one that contained fewer types of food sometimes resulted in dietary deficiencies. Food was stored in large quantities and widely distributed, probably resulting in outbreaks of food poisoning. Intensive agricultural practices among the prehistoric Nubians resulted in iron deficiency anemia, as did the reliance on cereal grains; weaning practices and parasitic infestation were also factors. The combination of a complex society, increasing divisions of class, epidemic disease, and dietary insufficiencies no doubt added mental stress to the list of illnesses.

DISEASE IN URBAN POPULATIONS

The development of urban centers is a recent phenomenon in human history. In the Near East, cities as large as 50,000 people were established by 3000 B.C. In the New World, large urban settlements were in existence by A.D. 600. Settlements of this size increased the already difficult problem of removing human wastes and delivering uncontaminated water to the people. Cholera, which is transmitted by contaminated water, was a potential problem. Diseases such as typhus (carried by lice) and the plague bacillus (transmitted by fleas or by the respiratory route) could be spread from person to person. Viral diseases such as measles, mumps, chicken pox, and smallpox could be spread in a similar fashion. Due to urbanization, populations for the first time were large enough to maintain disease in an endemic form. It is estimated that populations of 1 million would be necessary to maintain measles as an endemic disease. What was an endemic disease in one population could be the source of a serious epidemic (affecting a large number of people at the same time) disease in another group. Cross-continental trade and travel resulted in intense epidemics (McNeill 1976). The Black Death, resulting from a new pathogen, took its toll in Europe in the 1300s; this epidemic eliminated at least a quarter of the European population (approximately 25 million people).

The period of urban development can also be characterized by the exploration and expansion of populations into new areas that resulted in the introduction of novel diseases to groups that had little resistance to them (Mc-

Neill 1976). For example, the exploration of the New World may have been the source of the treponemal infection (syphilis) that was transmitted to the Old World. This New World infection was endemic and not sexually transmitted. When it was introduced into the Old World, a different mode of disease transmission occurred. The sexual transmission of the treponeme created a different environment for the pathogen, and it resulted in a more severe and acute infection. Furthermore, crowding in the urban centers, changes in sexual practices such as prostitution, and an increase in sexual promiscuity may have been factors in the venereal transmission of the pathogen.

The process of industrialization, which began a little over 200 years ago, led to an even greater environmental and social transformation. City dwellers were forced to contend with industrial wastes and polluted water and air. Slums that arose in industrial cities became focal points for poverty and the spread of disease. Epidemics of smallpox, typhus, typhoid, diphtheria, measles, and yellow fever in urban settings were well documented. Tuberculosis and respiratory diseases such as pneumonia and bronchitis were even more serious problems, with harsh working situations and crowded living conditions. Urban population centers, with their extremely high mortality, were not able to maintain their population bases by the reproductive capacity of those living in the city. Mortality outstripped fertility, requiring immigration to maintain the size of the population.

THE SECOND EPIDEMIOLOGICAL TRANSITION: THE RISE OF CHRONIC AND DEGENERATIVE DISEASE

The second epidemiological transition refers to the shift from acute infectious diseases to chronic noninfectious, degenerative diseases. The increasing prevalence of these chronic diseases is related to an increase in longevity. Cultural advances result in a larger percentage of individuals reaching the oldest age segment of the population. In addition, the technological advances that characterize the second epidemiological transition resulted in an increase in environmental degradation. An interesting characteristic of many of the chronic diseases is their particular prevalence and epidemic-like occurrence in transitional societies—those populations undergoing the shift from developing to developed modes of production. In developing countries, many of the chronic diseases associated with the epidemiological transition appear first in members of the upper socioeconomic strata, because of their access to Western products and practices.

With increasing developments in technology, medicine, and science, the germ theory of disease causation developed. While there is some controversy about the role that medicine has played in the decline of some of the infectious diseases, a better understanding of the source of infectious disease exists, and this admittedly has resulted in increasing control over many infectious diseases. The development of immunization resulted in the control of many infections and recently was the primary factor in the eradication of smallpox. In the developed nations, a number of other communicable diseases have diminished in importance. The decrease in infectious disease and the subsequent reduction in infant mortality has resulted in greater life expectancy at birth. In addition, there has been an increase in longevity for adults, and this has resulted in an increase in chronic and degenerative diseases (McKeown 1976).

Many of the diseases of the second epidemiological transition share common etiological factors related to human adaptation, including diet, activity level, mental stress, behavioral practices, and environmental pollution. For example, the industrialization and commercialization of food often results in malnutrition, especially for those societies in transition from subsistence forms of food provision to agribusiness. The economic capacity to purchase food that meets nutritional requirements is often not possible. Obesity and a high intake of refined carbohydrates are related to the increasing incidence of heart disease and diabetes. Obesity is considered to be a common form of malnutrition in developed countries and is a direct result of an increasingly sedentary lifestyle in conjunction with steady or increasing caloric intake.

A unique characteristic of the chronic diseases is their relatively recent appearance in human history as a major cause of morbidity. This is indicative of a strong environmental factor in disease etiology. While biological factors such as genetics are no doubt important in determining who is most likely to succumb to which disease, genetics alone cannot explain the rapid increase in chronic disease. While some of our current chronic diseases such as osteoarthritis were prevalent in early human populations, other, more serious degenerative conditions such as cardiovascular disease and carcinoma were much rarer.

THE THIRD EPIDEMIOLOGICAL TRANSITION

Today human populations are moving into the third epidemiological transition. There is a reemergence of infectious diseases with multiple antibiotic resistance. Furthermore, this emergence of diseases has a potential for global impact. In a sense, the contemporary transition does not eliminate the possible coexistence of infectious diseases typical of the first epidemiological transition (some 10,000 years ago). In the year 2000, the World Health Organization (WHO) reports that of the 55 million deaths each year, 14 million were the result of infectious, parasitic disease and respiratory disease.

WHO calculates that 2 billion people in the world are infected with the hepatitis B virus, 2 billion are infected with tuberculosis, and 40 million people have HIV/AIDS.

The emergence of infectious disease has been one of the most interesting evolutionary stories of the last decade, capturing the interest of scientists and the public (Garrett 2001). With the publication of books such as *The Hot Zone* (Preston 1995) and the release of movies such as *Outbreak,* the popular media have captured the public's fascination with emerging diseases as threats to human survival. There is genuine scientific concern about the problem. David Satcher, former director of the Centers for Disease Control and Prevention in Atlanta, Georgia, noted twenty-two diseases that have emerged in the last twenty-two years, including those caused by rotavirus, Ebola virus, *Legionella pneumophila* (Legionnaire's disease), Hantaan virus (Korean hemorrhagic fever), HTLV I and HTLV II, staphylococcus toxin, *Escherichia coli* 0157:h7, HIV, human herpesvirus 6, the hepatitis C virus, and hantavirus isolates.

The emergence of disease is the result of an interaction of social, demographic, and environmental changes in the global ecology and in the adaptation and genetics of the microbe, influenced by international commerce and travel, technological change, breakdown of public health measures, and microbial adaptation. Ecological changes such as agricultural development projects, dams, deforestation, floods, droughts, and climatic changes have resulted in the emergence of diseases such as Argentine hemorrhagic fever,

Korean hemorrhagic fever (Hantaan), and hantavirus pulmonary syndrome. Human demographic behavior has been a factor in the spread of dengue fever and the source for the introduction and spread of HIV and other sexually transmitted diseases.

The engine that is driving the reemergence of many of the diseases is ecological change that brings humans into contact with pathogens. Except for Brazilian purpuric fever, which may represent a new strain of *Haemophilus influenzae,* biotype *aegyptius,* most of the emerging diseases are of cultural origin. The development of antibiotic resistance in any pathogen is the result of medical and agricultural practices. The indiscriminate and inappropriate use of antibiotics in medicine has resulted in hospitals that are the source of multi-drug-resistant strains of bacteria that infect a large number of patients. Agricultural practices in which animal feed is supplemented with subtherapeutic doses of antibiotics have risen dramatically in the last half century. In 1954 500,000 pounds of antibiotics for both human and animal use were produced in the United States; today 40 million pounds are produced annually.

CONCLUSION

Recently much attention has focused on the detrimental effects of industrialization on the international environment, including water, land, and atmosphere. Massive industrial production of commodities has caused pollution. Increasingly there is concern over the health implications of contaminated water supplies, overuse of pesticides in commercialized agriculture, atmospheric chemicals, and the future effects of a depleted ozone layer on human health and food production. At no other time in human history have the changes in the environment been more rapid or so extreme. The increasing incidence of cancer among young people and the increase in respiratory disease have been associated with these environmental changes.

Anthropogenic impact from technology has been the pattern since Neolithic times. Within the last 300 years transportation has played a major role in disease patterns by bringing larger segments of humans into contact with the pathogens at an accelerated rate. The emergence of disease in the New World upon contact with Europeans was a consequence of large sailing ships that became a major mode of transportation. Now it is possible for a pathogen to move between continents within a matter of hours. We live in a time where there exists a virtual viral superhighway, bringing people into contact with pathogens that affect our adaptation. The present pattern reflects an evolutionary trend that can be traced to the beginning of primary food production. The scale has changed. The rates of emerging disease and their impact can now affect large segments of the world population at an ever-increasing rate, and we need to be increasingly aware of the implications for today's human populations around the globe.

UPDATE

The reconstruction of human disease ecology requires data from a number of sources. Bioarchaeology provides direct evidence of disease patterns of morbidity and mortality in prehistory. Another tool has emerged that may help to clarify the evolution of disease: the genomic diversity of pathogens and parasites provides clues to the phylogenetic relationships and patterns of adaptation to their hosts. Applying a molecular clock allows scientists to determine when the pathogen began to parasitize the host. For example, molecular analysis of the three modern taenid tapeworms that parasitize humans and were assumed to have become a problem during the Neolithic are now thought to have originated as human parasites in the Paleolithic (Hoberg, Jones, et al. 2000; Hoberg, Alkire, et al. 2001). These tapeworms appear to have begun to diversify 160,000 years ago. After the domestication of sheep, pigs, goats, and cows, humans became infected with tapeworms.

We can apply this method of genomic analysis to measure human genetic response to disease. Recent analysis of the genetic structure of variants of glucose-6-phosphate dehydrogenase (G6PD) deficiency confirms that malaria has only recently had a major impact on human populations (Tishkoff et al. 2001). The independent A and Med mutations in glucose-6-phosphate dehydrogenase suggest that this polymorphism originated no longer than 10,000 years ago. This suggests that while malaria has been present since the Miocene, it was not a selective force in human population until after the agricultural revolution.

FURTHER READING

Armelagos, George J. 1998. "The Viral Superhighway." *The Sciences* 38(1):24–30.

Armelagos, George J., Alan H. Goodman, and Kenneth H. Jacobs. 1991. "The Origins of Agriculture: Population Growth During a Period of Declining Health." *Population and Environment* 13(1):9–22.

Barrett, Ronald, Christopher W. Kuzawa, Thomas McDade, and George J. Armelagos. 1998. "Emerging Infectious Disease and the Third Epidemiological Transition." In W. Durham, ed., *Annual Review Anthropology* 27: 247–71.

Cockburn, T. A. 1967. "Infections of the Order Primates." In T. A. Cockburn, ed., *Infectious Diseases: Their Evolution and Eradication.* Charles C. Thomas.

Cockburn, T. A. 1971. "Infectious Disease in Ancient Populations." *Current Anthropology* 12(1):45–62.

Cohen, M. N., and G. J. Armelagos, eds. 1984. *Paleopathology at the Origins of Agriculture*. Academic.

Farmer, Paul. 1999. *Infections and Inequalities: The Modern Plagues*. University of California Press.

Garrett, Laurie. 2001. *Betrayal of Trust: The Collapse of Global Public Health*. Oxford University Press.

Hoberg, E. P., N. L. Alkire, A. de Queiroz, and A. Jones. 2001."Out of Africa: Origins of the Taenia Tapeworms in Humans." Proceedings of the Royal Society of London—Series B. *Biological Sciences* 268(1469):781–87.

Hoberg, E. P., A. Jones, R. L. Rausch, K. S. Eom, and S. L. Gardner. 2000. "A Phylogenetic Hypothesis for Species of the Genus *Taenia* (Eucestoda: Taeniidae)." *Journal of Parasitology* 86(1):89–98.

Lambrecht, Frank L. 1985. "Trypanosomes and Hominid Evolution." *Bioscience* 35(10):640–46.

Livingstone, Frank B. 1958. "Anthropological Implications of Sickle Cell Gene Distribution in West Africa." *American Anthropologist* 60:533–62.

McKeown, T. 1976. *The Modern Rise of Population*. Academic.

McNeill, W. H. 1976. *Plagues and People*. Anchor.

Preston, Richard. 1995. *The Hot Zone*. Doubleday.

Swedlund, Alan, and George J. Armelagos. 1990. *Disease in Populations in Transition: Anthropological and Epidemiological Perspectives*. Bergin and Garvey.

Tishkoff, Sarah A., Robert Varkonyi, Nelie Cahinhinan, Salem Abbes, George Argyropoulos, Giovanni Destro-Bisol, Anthi Drousiotou, Bruce Dangerfield, Gerard Lefranc, Jacques Loiselet, Anna Piro, Mark Stoneking, Antonio Tagarelli, Giuseppe Tagarelli, Elias H. Touma, Scott M. Williams, and Andrew G. Clark. 2001. "Haplotype Diversity and Linkage Disequilibrium at Human G6PD: Recent Origin of Alleles That Confer Malarial Resistance." *Science* 293(5529):455–62.

9 THE MOCHE

An Ancient Peruvian People

John W. Verano

An ancient but little known Peruvian culture, the Moche, numbering as many as 50,000 people, lived 1,200 years before the more famous Inca. Physical anthropologist John Verano has spent many years analyzing the skeletal remains from Moche sites, helping to answer questions regarding this fascinating people, including their physical characteristics and life expectancy. Verano's update focuses on recent evidence of the "dark side" of the Moche world—the practice of ritual human sacrifice, apparently a long-standing practice of the Moche.

A discovery of a royal tomb at Sipán focused public attention on the Moche, an ancient but little-known Peruvian culture (see Alva 1988, 1990; Donnan 1988, 1990). Numbering as many as 50,000, the Moche were an agricultural people who resided along the northern coast of Peru as early as 1,200 years before the Inca. In one of the world's driest deserts, they diverted streams from the adjacent Andes into a large network of irrigation canals to grow corn, beans, squash, peanuts, peppers, potatoes, and manioc, as well as avocados and other fruit. They kept guinea pigs and ducks, herded llamas for wool and meat, raised crawfish in the irrigation canals, and fished and hunted sea lions from boats. Their territory stretched over 220 miles along the coast and included towns of up to 10,000 inhabitants: warriors, priests, nobles, artisans, traders, servants, farmers, and fishermen. To house their dead they built platforms topped with pyramids, today called *huacas*. Moche art and technology were comparable in sophistication to that of the Maya, their contemporaries. Beautiful gold and copper metalwork, inlays and beads of turquoise, shell, and coral, woven materials, and richly decorated ceramics depicting everyday scenes, warfare, and ritual have been uncovered in the tombs. Unlike the Maya, however, the Moche did not develop a writing or glyph system.

Ongoing excavations at the site of Sipán, directed by Peruvian archaeologist Walter Alva, are revealing a wealth of new information about the ancient Moche civilization. Over several years I had the good fortune to be able to work with him in Peru, helping to analyze the skeletal remains from the Sipán tombs and other sites.

ANCIENT PEOPLES OF THE COAST

The Moche are one of several ancient civilizations that developed in the coastal valleys of northern Peru. The Moche kingdom dominated the north coast from about A.D. 100 to A.D. 750. Their culture disappeared some 700 years before the Inca empire began expanding out of the southern highlands. Best known for their beautiful ceramics and expressive art style, the Moche also left evidence of their relatively brief florescence in the form of numerous mud-brick pyramids, which still dot the river valleys of the north coast today.

Human occupation of the coast of Peru goes back many thousands of years. Survival in the otherwise inhospitable coastal desert of Peru is made possible by a series of seasonal rivers and streams that carry water down from the western slopes of the Andes Mountains. These rivers turn the narrow coastal valley floors into green oases, a stark contrast to the surrounding barren desert. Ancient peoples of the coast learned several thousand years ago to draw water off these rivers into irrigation canals, turning desert into productive agricultural land. Over the centuries many technological advances were made in canal building, eventually leading to complex irrigation networks, which linked several valleys of the north coast and provided productive agricultural land for thousands of coastal inhabitants.

When the Spanish conquistadors first passed through the northern coastal valleys in the 1530s, they marveled at the size and sophistication of the irrigation networks. Strangely, however, these first European visitors found many valleys only sparsely populated and numerous agricultural fields abandoned. What the Spanish did not know at the time was that a devastating disease, probably smallpox, had spread through the Inca Empire some 10 years earlier, taking thousands of victims with it. Smallpox, which had swept like wildfire through the Caribbean, Mexico, Central America, and then down through Ecuador and Peru, was one of the most deadly of the many infectious diseases brought from Europe to the New World in the sixteenth century. New World peoples, who had no immunity to the disease, died by the thousands. The epidemic that swept through Peru in the 1520s killed the Inca emperor and his legitimate heir and led to a bitter civil war between contenders for the throne. It was this divided and traumatized empire that Francisco Pizarro and his soldiers boldly conquered in 1532.

CONQUISTADORS AND *HUAQUEROS*

By the end of the sixteenth century, disease, conquest, and social disruption had forever changed the face of the north coast of Peru. The last of its great civilizations had collapsed, and much of its rich past was lost before it could be recorded by historians. Conquistadors who had sacked the last of the gold and silver from the storehouses and temples of the Inca then turned to the pyramids and burial places of the Inca's ancestors. Hoping to find the buried treasure of former kings, they plundered pyramids and ancient burial grounds up and down the coast of Peru. Historians have recently found early colonial documents requesting formal permits from the Spanish crown to "mine" pyramids for gold. And mine them they did—teams of hundreds of forced laborers were used to tunnel into these structures. The scars of sixteenth- and seventeenth-century looting can still be seen at many coastal sites today. In the Moche Valley on the north coast of Peru, a particularly determined group of "miners" in search of gold even diverted a river to cut into the center of a large pyramid.

The tradition of grave robbing, which began during the early colonial period, unfortunately has continued for centuries in Peru. *Huaqueros,* as they are commonly known today, are professional grave robbers, many of whom make a lifetime career of digging up ancient graves and selling the artifacts. Although the looting and destruction of archaeological sites is strictly prohibited by law in Peru, the limited resources of police and local government officials are simply not sufficient to control the activity. Realizing the importance of preserving and studying its rich pre-Columbian heritage, the Peruvian government actively supports archaeological research by both Peruvian and foreign scholars. Such research is gradually bringing to light a long and fascinating sequence of pre-Columbian cultural development.

RECONSTRUCTING THE PAST

Peruvian archaeology traces its roots to the late nineteenth century, when archaeologists began making the first systematic attempts to reconstruct the prehistory of the region. Many of these early excavations focused on coastal Peruvian sites because of the exceptional preservation of perishable materials. The coast of Peru is one of the driest deserts in the world, receiving meas-

urable rainfall only on rare occasions. Such dry conditions make for excellent preservation of plant remains, textiles, and wooden objects—things rarely encountered by archaeologists working in other areas of the world. Bodies buried in the hot, dry sand become naturally mummified, providing physical anthropologists with rare glimpses of details such as ancient hairstyles and body decoration (a number of tattooed mummies are known from coastal Peru). I will never forget a naturally mummified dog I helped excavate at an archaeological site on the north coast several years ago. Sometime around A.D. 1300, the dog's owner had carefully wrapped the pet in a cloth shroud and buried it outside the wall of a desert city. Seven hundred years later when we unwrapped the shroud, the dog was perfectly preserved, with ears standing straight up and lips drawn back in a permanent snarl.

Despite the destruction of many pre-Columbian cemeteries by artifact hunters, physical anthropologists have been able to make some important discoveries about the physical characteristics of ancient Peruvians, both by studying skeletal material left behind by grave robbers and, increasingly in recent years, by working side by side with archaeologists conducting scientific excavations. Over a period of seven years, I was fortunate to participate in the excavation of several important Moche sites along Peru's north coast. Previous skeletal studies have characteristically focused on only a few isolated sites. Through my study of the skeletal remains, it has been possible to acquire large collections that permit us for the first time to make observations of Moche health, diseases, and demography on a population level.

PHYSICAL ANTHROPOLOGY OF THE MOCHE

Until recently the physical characteristics of the Moche people were known to us primarily through the way they depicted themselves in ceramic sculpture and painted murals. Their physical remains had received surprisingly little attention by physical anthropologists. Part of my recent research has concentrated on the study of Moche skeletal remains recovered over the past five years from excavations and surface collections at the site of Pacatnamú, a major pre-Columbian ceremonial center. These collections, which are now housed in a research facility in Trujillo, Peru, constitute the largest sample of well-documented human skeletal remains ever recovered from the Peruvian north coast and are, therefore, a valuable resource both for the study of physical variation among prehistoric coastal populations and for understanding patterns of health and disease among ancient Andean peoples.

THE PACATNAMÚ SKELETONS

Most of the Moche skeletal collections from Pacatnamú pertain to the final phase of the Moche kingdom (Moche V) and date to approximately A.D. 500–750. The skeletal sample we have recovered comprises 65 burials excavated from a single cemetery, 26 burials encountered in other parts of the site, and surface collections (approximately 590 specimens) made from three large Moche cemeteries recently damaged by looters.

Life Expectancy in Moche Times

In both the large surface-collected sample and the smaller number of individuals recovered from Moche tombs at Pacatnamú, males and females were present in about equal numbers. Although individuals of all ages, from children to people over 50, were represented, skeletal remains of infants and young children were rare in the surface collections, and infants were underrepresented in the excavated burials. Remains of children are more fragile and preserve less well than bones of adults, although it is possible that not all infants and children were buried in cemetery areas.

In the cemetery, which we excavated completely, the remains of 67 individuals were recovered. Almost a third of these (20) were under 5 years old, while only 4 individuals were represented in the child and adolescent age range (ages 5–19). This age distribution is consistent with the U-shaped mortality curve commonly observed in living human populations, where probability of death is highest during the first year of life, declines during early childhood and adolescence, and climbs sharply again in the adult years. Of the individuals who died after childhood, about one-third lived to a mature middle age, dying between 35 and 49 years. But a significantly larger proportion of males (12 out of 23) died as adolescents (15–19 years) and young adults (20–34 years), while the majority of females (12 out of 23) fall into the old adult age class (50+). If this sample is representative of the Moche population at Pacatnamú as a whole, these differences suggest that Moche women had a substantially greater probability of reaching old age than did men. Was this due to greater violence or more hazardous activities among men or to greater susceptibility of males to disease? We do know that the Moche frequently depicted scenes of warfare and the capture and sacrifice of prisoners. However, we have found very little skeletal evidence of fractures or other injuries in the Moche sample from Pacatnamú, which makes it difficult to attribute earlier mortality in males to warfare.

Physical Characteristics of the Moche People

Based on his early studies of ancient Peruvian skeletons, Aleš Hrdlička (1911) of the United States National Museum (at present the National Museum of Natural History) described prehistoric peoples of the Peruvian coast as broad-headed (brachycephalic) and of relatively short stature. The Moche population at Pacatnamú conforms well to this description. Living stature calculated from Moche skeletons for both males (average 5′3″) and females (average 4′11″) is very similar to that of present-day north coast people of Indian origin. The Moche had wide faces and prominent, relatively narrow noses. Approximately half of the Moche skulls we studied show artificial cranial modification. This modification varies from mild to pronounced flattening of the back of the skull, with flattening of the forehead region occasionally visible as well. Broadening of the cranial vault and slight broadening of the cheeks are noticeable in most modified skulls, although I believe the modification we see was probably the unintentional result of infant cradle-boarding rather than a conscious attempt by the Moche to alter the shape of the head. No depictions of infants in cradle boards are known from Moche art, nor have physical remains of cradle boards been found in a Moche context, perhaps because of poor organic preservation. However, well-preserved cradles and cloth bands that were used to fix an infant's head to the cradle board have been recovered from later coastal cemeteries, along with skulls showing the same form of modification or reshaping observed among the Moche at Pacatnamú.

Family Cemeteries

One preliminary but intriguing finding on Moche mortuary practices has come out of my study of skeletons at Pacatnamú. Here I expected to find one large cemetery where the local population buried their dead, as I had found at other sites in this area. I found instead numerous small cemeteries throughout the site and began to investigate why so many cemeteries were in use during a single time period.

Variation in the morphology of the facial skeleton is known to be a sensitive indicator of population differences and has been used successfully by physical anthropologists to differentiate ancient populations as well as to identify the population affiliation of recent forensic cases. By applying some of these techniques to Moche skulls at Pacatnamú, I was able to determine that individuals buried in the same cemetery resembled one another (in their facial morphology) more closely than they did individuals buried in other cemeteries of the same time period. Since greater resemblance implies closer genetic relationship, I interpreted the results as suggesting that the Moche buried their dead by family group. This conforms with the findings of the sixteenth-century Spanish chronicler Cieza de Leon, who on his travels in 1547 through the valley where Pacatnamú is located learned that native people buried their dead by kinship group in the hills and bluffs above the valley floor. This, along with the results of my research at Pacatnamú, suggests that burial by family group was a very ancient practice in the valley.

Health and Disease

All the Moche skeletal material excavated or surface-collected at Pacatnamú was examined for evidence of disease or nutritional deficiency. Infants and children showed little sign of nutritional stresses due to low protein or insufficient calories (something that I found in some later burials at the site), and adults were relatively robust. All the older individuals and several younger adults had some degree of arthritis in the joints, particularly in the hips, knees, shoulders, and elbows. In the older adults, arthritis of the temporomandibular (jaw) joint was also common. The Moche also suffered from tooth decay and loss; middle-aged adults (35–49) had lost an average of 4.9 teeth and had cavities in an average of 3.6 of the remaining teeth, while old adults over 50 had lost an average of 17.2 teeth. Remaining teeth were frequently affected by periodontal disease. This is consistent with a growing body of data on dental disease among prehistoric agriculturalists, indicating that people who eat diets rich in soft foods and carbohydrates frequently have a high incidence of cavities and other dental disease, even in the absence of refined sugars.

UNDERSTANDING THE MOCHE: ONGOING RESEARCH AND FUTURE PROSPECTS

Recent archaeological excavations at sites such as Sipán are rapidly increasing our knowledge about ancient Moche culture. The study of their skeletal remains is providing additional information about their physical characteristics, health, and mortality patterns. The high-status tombs found at Sipán pose some new research questions, which we are currently working to answer. For example: Are there differences in the health, stature, or other physical characteristics of the Moche elite that might reflect a lifestyle and diet different from that of Moche commoners? Do the skeletons of the elite show any rare or unusual skeletal traits that might suggest a lineage of hereditary Moche rulers? Do the skeletons that surround the central occupants of elaborate tombs at Sipán represent retainers or relatives of the deceased?

Ongoing research may provide answers to these and other questions about the population responsible for this remarkable prehistoric South American culture. It may well be that the next generation of schoolchildren will be as familiar with the Moche as with the Inca, who dominated the coast of Peru 1,200 years later.

UPDATE

Since the publication of the foregoing discussion on the Moche, many new and exciting discoveries have come to light at Moche archaeological sites. More elite tombs have been found at Sipán, along with other discoveries, such as rooms filled with dedicatory offerings of ceramics, metal objects, and human and animal bones. In 1993 objects from the Sipán tombs began a tour of the United States in the exhibition *Royal Tombs of Sipán*, which opened at the Fowler Museum of Cultural History at the University of California, Los Angeles. The exhibition made its final appearance at the Smithsonian's National Museum of Natural History in June 1995 before returning to Peru to be permanently installed in the newly renovated and expanded Brüning Archaeological Museum, located in the town of Lambayeque, just outside the bustling city of Chiclayo.

The discoveries at Sipán have been joined by important finds at other Moche sites. A mortuary complex similar to Sipán, called San José de Moro, located in the Jequetepeque Valley near Pacatnamú, has been the focus of excavations since 1990 by Christopher Donnan and more recently by Luis Jaime Castillo of Catholic University in Lima. The site is unique in that it has yielded the first tombs of high-status Moche women ever found by archaeologists. Based on the elaborate funerary masks and other grave goods buried with them, Donnan and Castillo believe that these women served as priestesses in religious ceremonies involving human sacrifice. San José de Moro also is important because it dates to the final phase of the Moche culture and provides a last glimpse of this civilization before it disappeared.

Other important Moche discoveries in the last few years have been made in two river valleys further south. Huge polychrome painted murals of

Moche deities, warriors, and prisoners have been found at two major Moche ceremonial centers: at the Pyramid of the Moon in the Moche River Valley, and at the El Brujo complex in the neighboring Chicama River Valley. These murals are some of the finest examples of Moche polychrome mural painting ever found. Two major Peruvian archaeological projects have been conducting excavations at these two sites for over 10 years now and have produced a great deal of new information on the architecture of Moche ceremonial centers and their associated habitation sites and craft production areas.

Among the most interesting discoveries to come out of this recent work is new evidence of the "dark side" of the Moche world: the practice of human sacrifice. Breakthroughs in the study of Moche art from Sipán and San José de Moro, as well as archaeological excavation from the Pyramid of the Moon, provide convincing evidence that the Moche sacrificed war prisoners at their major ceremonial centers in elaborate rituals directed by priests dressed as Moche deities. Until 1995 the evidence was indirect, derived from new interpretations of Moche art based on the contents of the elite tombs at Sipán and San José de Moro. In 1995, however, actual physical evidence of prisoner sacrifice was found for the first time at the Pyramid of the Moon by Canadian archaeologist Steve Bourget. Bourget (Bourget and Millaire 2000) discovered a sacrificial site in a walled plaza behind the pyramid that would eventually produce the skeletal remains of more than 70 victims.

During the summers of 1995–1997 I was able to study these skeletal remains to determine the sex and physical characteristics of the victims and their age at death, as well as to identify injuries and possible cause of death. The results of my analysis confirmed that the victims (all adolescent or young adult males) were probably war captives, and that the manner in which they were sacrificed matched what is depicted in Moche art. In 1996, when a small test pit was excavated by archaeologists in an adjacent plaza, more human sacrifices were found. In the summers of 2000 and 2001, I directed the excavation of this second plaza, with funding from the National Geographic Society. This excavation produced dozens more sacrificial victims similar to those found by Bourget, but dating several hundred years earlier, based on radiocarbon dates we obtained from rope and other material found with the victims' bones. We now can confirm that Bourget's discovery was not an anomaly: human sacrifice was a long-standing practice of the Moche. Moreover, the scenes of human sacrifice the Moche depicted on their ceramic vessels and on wall murals at their temples—long assumed to be mythical depictions of a supernatural world—we now realize are realistic portrayals of rituals that actually were performed by the Moche.

The field of Moche studies has seen dramatic advances over the past decade. The pace of research is accelerating, with new scholars entering the field and new archaeological projects being organized. Several international colloquia have been organized in recent years to bring together Moche specialists to present their latest findings and interpretations (Pillsbury 2001; Uceda and Mujica 1994). The Moche have also become popular subjects for television documentaries. At last count I have been interviewed for five of these films, and more are currently in the production pipeline.

It will be interesting to see how far our knowledge of this fascinating culture will be expanded over the next decade, but one thing is clear: the final chapter on the Moche is far from written.

FURTHER READING

Alva, Walter. 1988. "Discovering the New World's Richest Unlooted Tomb." *National Geographic* 174(10):510–48.

Alva, Walter. 1990. "New Tomb of Royal Splendor." *National Geographic* 177(6):2–15.

Alva, Walter, and Christopher B. Donnan. 1994. *Royal Tombs of Sipán*. 2nd ed. Fowler Museum of Cultural History, University of California, Los Angeles.

Bourget, Steve, and Jean-François Millaire. 2000. "Excavaciones en la Plaza 3A y Plataforma II de la Huaca de la Luna." In Santiago Uceda, Elias Mujica, and Ricardo Morales, eds., *Investigaciones en la Huaca de la Luna 1997*, pp. 47–60. Universidad Nacional de Trujillo, Facultad de Ciencias Sociales.

Donnan, Christopher B. 1988. "Iconography of the Moche: Unraveling the Mystery of the Warrior-Priest." *National Geographic* 174(10):550–55.

Donnan, Christopher B. 1990. "Masterworks of Art Reveal a Remarkable Pre-Inca World." *National Geographic* 177(6):16–33.

Donnan, Christopher B., and Luis Jaime Castillo. 1992. "Finding the Tomb of a Moche Priestess." *Archaeology* 45(6):38–42.

Hrdlička, Aleš. 1911. "Some Results of Recent Anthropological Exploration in Peru." *Smithsonian Miscellaneous Collections* 56(16). Smithsonian Institution.

Pillsbury, Joanne, ed. 2001. *Moche Art and Archaeology in Ancient Peru*. National Gallery of Art.

Uceda, Santiago, and Elias Mujica, eds. 1994. *Moche: Propuestas y Perspectivas: Actas del Primer Coloquio sobre la Cultura Moche, Trujillo, 12 al. 16 abril de 1993*. Travaux de l'Institut Français d'Etudes Andines, t. 79. Universidad Nacional de la Libertad, Instituto Frances de Estudio Andinos, Asociacion Peruana para el Fomento de las Ciencias Sociales.

Verano, John. 1997a. "Physical Characteristics and Skeletal Biology of the Moche Population at Pacatnamú." In Christopher B. Donnan and Guillermo A. Cock, eds., *The Pacatnamú Papers*, vol. 2: *The Moche Occupation*, pp. 189–214. Fowler Museum of Cultural History, University of California, Los Angeles.

Verano, John. 1997b. "Human Skeletal Remains from Tomb 1, Sipán (Lambayeque River Valley, Peru) and Their Social Implications." *Antiquity* 71(273):670–82.

Verano, John W. 2001a. "The Physical Evidence of Human Sacrifice in Ancient Peru." In Elizabeth Benson and Anita Cook, eds., *Ritual Sacrifice in Ancient Peru*, pp. 165–84. University of Texas Press.

Verano, John W. 2001b. "War and Death in the Moche World: Osteological Evidence and Visual Discourse." In Joanne Pillsbury, ed., *Moche Art and Archaeology in Ancient Peru,* pp. 111–25. National Gallery of Art.

Television Documentaries on the Moche

1993   *Secrets of the Moche,* The Learning Channel, Discovery Communications
1996   *Blood and Treasure in Peru,* Ancient Mysteries series, Arts and Entertainment Network
1999   *Pyramid of Doom,* The Learning Channel
2002   *Ancient Clues,* Episode 2B, "Huaca," Discovery Channel, Canada
2002   *Moche Murder Mysteries,* National Geographic Explorer/MSNBC

10 AMERICA'S MIAs

Forensic Anthropology in Action

Robert W. Mann and Thomas D. Holland

In this article, two forensic physical anthropologists describe the work that goes on, year in and year out, in a largely unknown facility to recover, repatriate, and establish definite identifications for American service members (POWs/MIAs) lost in past wars. Readers will learn why the identification of these remains is both sensitive and difficult, and why the context in which these remains are found is so important for accurate identification.

What do Jeffrey Dahmer, the Branch Davidian standoff, the crash of Korean Airlines Flight 801, the War of 1812, Operation Desert Storm, the terrorist attacks of September 11, 2001, and thousands of American soldiers listed as prisoners of war (POWs) or missing in action (MIAs) share in common?

Few people are aware that forensic anthropologists assisted with each of these cases and continue to serve in many emergency response and mass disaster teams as well as acting as consultants to a variety of medical and legal agencies in the United States and abroad. Forensic anthropologists apply their skills to some unusual and difficult cases, including the location, recovery, and identification of the remains of American POWs/MIAs by the only laboratory of its kind—the U.S. Army Central Identification Laboratory, Hawai'i (CILHI). It is in this laboratory that physical anthropologists and teams of specialists work to establish definite identifications for American service members lost in all past wars.

The role of forensic anthropology historically has been to assist medico-legal agencies—medical examiners, police, and the FBI—in the identification of recent homicides. From an examination of skeletonized remains, forensic anthropologists first distinguish whether they are animal or human. If the latter, they then ascertain biological age at death, time elapsed since death, sex, race, stature, and method of death. Forensic anthropologists must have specialized training in radiology, anatomy, dentistry, and forensic pathology in order to complete their objectives. The awareness of unique skeletal and dental features also helps them establish a positive personal identification [see Gordon, "Stories Bones Tell," in this volume].

BACKGROUND

Although most forensic anthropologists are affiliated either with a university or research facility (e.g., Smithsonian Institution), fifteen are employed by the Department of the Army at the CILHI. Located adjacent to Pearl Harbor on Hickam Air Force Base, Oahu, the laboratory has, in addition to its anthropologists, four forensic dentists and more than two hundred soldiers and civilian support staff. The CILHI grew out of the Vietnam War and CIL-THAI (Thailand); it moved to its present location in Hawai'i in 1991. This world-class laboratory has the largest staff of forensic anthropologists in the United States and is responsible for the worldwide recovery, repatriation, and identification of the remains of American service members from all past wars. At present there are nearly 80,000 American MIAs from World War II, 8,100 from the Korean War, and 1,900 from the Vietnam War. Since 1973, the laboratory has been responsible for the identification of 800 previously unaccounted-for service members.

The search for POWs/MIAs is a very sensitive issue among many Americans who have lost children, spouses, and friends as part of the tragedies of war. Although these soldiers, sailors, airmen, and civilians were "lost" at war, they have not and never will be forgotten. In fact, the slogan of the American POW/MIA effort is "You are not forgotten."

Just as Americans long for the return of their loved ones, so do the people of other countries who also have missing friends and family members. The Vietnamese people, for example, have exceptionally strong, close family ties that are strained by the loss of a loved one. There are over 333,000 Vietnamese MIAs, most of whom will never be identified, even if found, because of the lack of Vietnamese medical and dental records from which to base a comparison and subsequently an identification. In addition, most Vietnamese soldiers were buried in large open fields or dense mountain jungles in unmarked or poorly marked graves, all signs of which will disappear with time.

IN THE FIELD

The CILHI has a dual role. First, it deploys 12-person teams of experts throughout the world to find and excavate graves and aircraft crash sites. Second, it provides for the laboratory analysis and identification of American MIAs. A typical recovery team consists of an anthropologist, a military officer, a noncommissioned officer-in-charge (the foreman), an explosive ordnance disposal technician for disarming or removing bombs, a medic, an interpreter, a radio operator, a photographer, and a mortuary affairs specialist.

While most of the world's forensic anthropologists work from the relative comfort of a laboratory, those at the CILHI must travel to distant and often remote areas of the world in order to excavate and recover POW/MIA remains. One recent year alone, for example, the laboratory sent teams to Vietnam, Laos, China, North Korea, South America, the Pacific Islands, Russia, and Armenia. The terrain in these countries varies from ice-laden landscapes to tropical rain forests, and the hazards include malaria, snakes, scorpions, spiders, unexploded ordnance (bombs and mines), and precarious mountains. Housing conditions in the field also vary from hotels and guest houses in the larger cities to sharing an eight-person tent in the jungles of such inhospitable places as Laos and Cambodia for up to forty-five days. The team must carry everything necessary to be self-sufficient throughout the mission, including excavation equipment, electrical generators, fuel, tents, food, cooking supplies, medicine, and bottled water—all trucked in or flown in by helicopters. It is a physically and mentally demanding job that requires dedication, professionalism, and stamina.

Although the teams excavate isolated graves, the majority of excavations currently undertaken by the CILHI are air crashes in Southeast Asia. Many of these aircraft were lost over the infamous Ho Chi Minh Trail, which actually consists of a vast network of footpaths, tunnels, and dirt roads that served as a clandestine supply and personnel pipeline connecting North and South Vietnam during the war. The difficulty for the excavation/recovery teams, however, is that by the time they reach a crash site there is little remaining of the aircraft. Over a period of twenty or thirty years, human intervention and environmental variables have resulted in the decay and loss of remains, personal effects, and aircraft wreckage.

A Recovery Example

One such case is an F-4 Phantom jet that crashed in Quang Binh, central Vietnam, in 1969. During the search for the site, a witness told one of the authors that as soon as the airplane stopped burning, he and many other villagers rushed to the crash site and scavenged the wreckage for useable parts.

Using only their bare hands, they bent and snapped aluminum from the fuselage, cut electrical wiring with machetes, and used a blowtorch to cut thick metal rods into useable lengths. Everything that could be scavenged from the site was either carried back to the village and used around the home or sold to the nearest scrap dealer. This and other crash sites serve as a sort of "hardware store" where villagers living in remote areas obtain items and materials otherwise unavailable. Examples of the creative use of wreckage include rice-house rat guards and boats made from fuselage aluminum, smoking pipes made from hydraulic fittings, knives and machetes formed from propeller blades, rubber Ho Chi Minh sandals cut from aircraft tires, and fence posts, flower pots, and pig troughs worked from aerial-dispensed cluster bomb units that resemble four-foot-long canoes.

In forensic anthropology, the physical relationship of one item to another (i.e., its context) and whether the objects are on the ground or buried are important in reconstructing what amounts to a police crime scene. Legally, forensic anthropologists and dentists deal in evidence. Unfortunately, villagers who remove aircraft wreckage from a site remove the very evidence that U.S. recovery teams need to identify the aircraft. For example, aircraft engines and many electronic components have serialized data plates unique to each aircraft. Finding one serialized data plate or identification tag (dog tag) can turn an otherwise unidentifiable jumble of wreckage into an identifiable aircraft. Incredibly, excavation teams working in Southeast Asia often recover only 100 to 150 pounds of twisted wreckage from a 28,000-pound jet. The rest either disintegrated on impact or was destroyed as a result of secondary explosions, burning, or scavenging.

During the act of scavenging aircraft wreckage, villagers sometimes find personal effects such as dog tags, wristwatches, wedding bands, and religious medallions. If found, these items are taken from a crash site and either used or worn by villagers or sold, traded, or subsequently lost. What must be borne in mind is that a wedding band or medallion to a villager living high up in the mountains does not bear the same sentimental value or significance as it does to Westerners. To villagers, an identifying dog tag can be fashioned into a useful implement such as a small knife or tweezers for removing facial hair, one Vietnamese form of shaving.

The basic excavation strategy at a crash site is to let the evidence speak for itself. Only when there is no more wreckage coming out of the ground does the team cease working at a crash or grave site.

By searching for life-support-related equipment (parachutes, oxygen bottles and hoses, flight helmets, flight suits), the anthropologist and life-support technician may be able to account for the aircraft's occupants. Determining the number of occupants on board an aircraft when it crashed can be done based on duplicated or multiple life-support related gear. For example, a parachute harness has only two metallic D-rings. If the aircraft that crashed was an F-4, it carries a maximum of two occupants. If three parachute D-rings are recovered from among the wreckage, it is safe to say that two people were on board at the time of impact.

Even with the presence of three D-rings, could one of the occupants have survived this F-4 crash? This question can be answered only after reviewing all of the evidence and carefully considering the preponderance of the evidence. The items recovered from the crash site must provide substantial and wholly consistent evidence that the occupants were on board at the time of impact and that the crash was not survivable. In the case of this F-4 jet, portions of the cockpit were found near engine components; pieces of a flight suit, helmet, and wristwatch were recovered among cockpit debris; and two parachute D-rings, a religious medallion, one tooth, and two bone fragments were found near the flight suit material. This strongly suggests that one person was in the aircraft when it crashed and that the crash was not survivable. (In this scenario we knew that the second individual parachuted from the aircraft and was rescued within hours.)

IN THE LABORATORY

At the end of each recovery mission in Vietnam, all bones, teeth, and personal effects that were turned over by Vietnamese citizens or excavated by the six U.S. recovery teams are received at the Vietnamese Institute of Forensic Medicine in Hanoi. Each set of remains—sometimes no more than a few dime-sized bone fragments—is hand-carried to the institute in locked and sealed hard plastic cases by a Vietnamese official. Once at the Institute, the cases are opened during one of the regularly scheduled Joint Field Reviews, which are attended by Vietnamese forensic specialists and a CILHI forensic anthropologist and forensic dentist. The task of the joint team is to conduct a preliminary examination to determine which of the remains may be American. All suspected American remains are repatriated to the CILHI for detailed forensic analysis. (Vietnamese remains are retained by Vietnamese officials for burial.) The remains are flown in a military C-141 airplane to the CILHI in American-flag-draped containers for the identification phase.

At the CILHI, the remains are laid out in anatomical order on a foam-covered table, and a forensic dentist and anthropologist are assigned to the case. The two scientists work independently of each other in order not to bias their conclusions. The dentist focuses on the teeth and the anthropologist on the skeletal remains. The remains are inventoried and photographed and the teeth are X-rayed and compared to antemortem (before death) records, charts, and X-rays. Dental X-rays provide the vast majority of identifications, as the dental fillings and morphology provide unique individualizing features for basing a positive identification. Other methods of identification include mitochondrial DNA derived from bones and teeth, unique skeletal features such as a healed broken bone, and video superimposition made by overlaying an image of the skull on a facial photograph.

When the dentist and anthropologist have completed their work, their conclusions are put in writing and compared. The skeletal attributes derived by the anthropologist must be consistent with those of the individual identified by the dentist. In other words, if the suggested identity provided by the dentist is a twenty-two-year-old white male with a living stature of 5'11", then the anthropological indicators must be in agreement. If the anthropologist determines that the bones are those of a black male age thirty to thirty-five with a height of 5'5", there is a problem. One possibility for the conflicting data is that the bones are from one person and the teeth from another (i.e., commingled remains). Once this portion of the examination process is completed, the reports are compiled and submitted for inside peer review by other CILHI scientists.

The next step is to submit the recommended identification to the CILHI laboratory director, the CILHI commander, and three laboratory consultants for outside review of scientific integrity and accuracy of interpretation. The reports then are sent to the Casualty and Memorial Affairs Office in Alexandria, Virginia, the appropriate service's Office of Mortuary Affairs in Washington, D.C. (who assigns a representative to present the case to the family), and finally to the Armed Forces Identification Review Board. If the family disagrees with the suggested identification, they have the right to hire their own consultant, who will review the laboratory's findings, examine the remains, and draw his/her own conclusions. If the family's consultant disagrees with the recommended identification, the entire case may be sent back to the original anthropologist and dentist for a second go-round. In all, the process is quite difficult, and there are many checks and balances to ensure that each case is handled accurately and in accordance with strict scientific procedures. Once the family agrees to the recommended identification, which most commonly happens, the remains are forwarded to them for burial at the government's expense.

While finding, recovering, and identifying American POWs/MIAs is a costly as well as physically and mentally demanding job, the POW/MIA issue deserves our fullest attention and unwavering efforts. America's POWs/MIAs truly are not forgotten.

UPDATE

The Central Identification Laboratory (CILHI) has grown by leaps and bounds since 1998 and has experienced several significant events, including the identification of 107 missing service members in 2000. Included in this group were nineteen Marine Raiders killed on a raid on Makin Island in the South Pacific in 1942. The Raiders, made famous in the movie *Gung Ho!*, were part of a tactic to divert Japanese forces from Guadalcanal. They hit the beach at night in rubber boats launched from two U.S. submarines waiting off the coast. Their presence on the island was made known when one of the American soldiers accidentally discharged his rifle. When the fighting was over, thirty U.S. Marines were missing.

Half a century later, a Makin Islander who helped bury the Americans led the excavation team to the general location where the nineteen marines were allegedly buried. The mass grave yielded not only bones and teeth but helmets, grenades, a pipe (tobacco), Boy Scout knives (issued to the marines when other knives were out of stock), and several dog tags. Once identified at the CILHI, the nineteen Raiders were buried either in their hometowns or in a mass grave in Arlington National Cemetery. It was the largest number of identifications in a single case.

The following year, however, brought the single most crushing blow to the Central Identification Laboratory and its sister organization, the Joint Task Force–Full Accounting: a tragic helicopter accident in central Vietnam in April 2001. This crash took the lives of nine Vietnamese and seven Americans, members of an investigative team that was on its way to survey an American airplane shot down during the Vietnam War. These soldiers, like those who have gone before them, made the ultimate sacrifice. Although their deaths were a terrible loss, the job of finding and returning our MIAs to families must and will continue.

FURTHER READING

Bass, W. M. 1996. *Human Osteology: A Laboratory and Field Manual*. 4th ed. Special Publication No. 2, Missouri Archaeological Society.

Holland, T. D., B. E. Anderson, and R. W. Mann. 1997. "Human Variables in the Postmortem Alteration of Human Bone: Examples from U.S. War Casualties." In W. D. Haglund and M. H. Sorg, eds., *Forensic Taphonomy: The Postmortem Fate of Human Remains*, pp. 263–74. CRC Press.

Holland, T. D., and R. W. Mann. 1996. "Forensic Aviation Archaeology: Finding and Recovering American MIA Remains." *Cultural Resources Management* 10:29–31.

Iserson, K. V. 2001. *Death to Dust: What Happens to Dead Bodies?* 2nd ed. Galen.

Krogman, W. M., and M. Y. Iscan. 1986. *The Human Skeleton in Forensic Medicine*. 2nd ed. Charles C. Thomas.

Mann, R. W., T. D. Holland, A. D. Webster, and W. E. Grant. 1996. "The Search for American MIAs: Forensic Anthropology in the Field." *The Director* 64(12):34–38.

Maples, W. R., and M. Browning. 2002. *Dead Men Do Tell Tales: The Strange and Fascinating Cases of a Forensic Anthropologist.* Arrow.

Owsley, D. W., and R. L. Jantz, eds. 1994. *Skeletal Biology in the Great Plains: Migration, Warfare, Health, and Subsistence.* Smithsonian Institution Press.

Rathbun, T. A., and J. E. Buikstra. 1984. *Human Identification: Case Studies in Forensic Anthropology.* Charles C. Thomas.

Reichs, K. J. 1998. *Forensic Osteology: Advances in the Identification of Human Remains.* 2nd ed. Charles C. Thomas.

Rhine, Stanley. 1998. *Bone Voyage: A Journey in Forensic Anthropology.* University of New Mexico Press.

Shipman, Pat, Alan Walker, and David Bichell. 1985. *The Human Skeleton.* Harvard University Press.

Stewart, T. Dale. 1979. *Essentials of Forensic Anthropology.* Charles C. Thomas.

Ubelaker, D. H. 1999. *Human Skeletal Remains: Excavation, Analysis, Interpretation.* 3rd ed. Taraxacum.

Ubelaker, D. H., and H. Scammell. 2000. *Bones: A Forensic Detective's Casebook.* HarperPaperbacks.

11 A NEW WAY TO LOOK AT RACE

Boyce Rensberger

Although often controversial, the topic of race is of enduring interest to anthropologists and the general public. In an article first published in the Washington Post, science writer Boyce Rensberger presents a clear discussion of race, concluding that "the great lesson of anthropology, biology, and genetics is that all people are the same in all essentials but are highly diverse in a few things. These differences have arisen not because there are fundamentally different kinds of people but simply because we are a restless, curious, hopeful migratory species whose intelligence has allowed us to make a good living in almost every environment on earth."

You're not a racist. You know that deep down inside, all people are pretty much the same, no matter what color their skin or what shape their eyelids.

But you are curious about differences among these groups that we call races. Everybody is.

Why do most people from Europe have pale skin? Why is the hair of Africans tightly curled? Why do most Africans and most Europeans—and their descendants in this country—have eyes that are shaped alike but are so different from an Asian's eyes? Or maybe you wonder why people come in so many colors and facial forms in the first place. And many people wonder whether the differences are more than skin deep.

These are honest, scientifically worthy questions. In fact, scientists have tried for centuries to answer them. After discarding many mistakes in their interpretations, today's researchers generally agree on three major discoveries.

1. There are many more differences among people than the obvious ones such as skin color and facial form. Dozens of other variations have been found that are more than skin deep. We'll look at some of them shortly.

2. These differences have been good for the human species. If we were not so diverse, we would not be such an evolutionary success. For example, without the protection of dark skin, our ancestors in Africa could not have survived the strong tropical sun. And when some of those ancestors migrated to the climate of northern Europe, where there is less sunlight, they could not have survived unless they lost most of their skin color. We'll get back to this too.

3. The third conclusion is probably the hardest to understand: that races don't really exist, at least not outside our imaginations. We all use the word *race* as if it meant something specific and clear-cut. We talk and act as if blacks, whites, and others belong to different groups that developed naturally long ago. But, according to most anthropologists today, that isn't true. They say races are mostly arbitrary categories invented by people to fit a misunderstanding about how human beings evolved. A few centuries ago, European scientists claimed that races were natural divisions of the human species. Some even argued that races represented a series of evolutionary stages, some more "advanced" than others. The old-time researchers knew of very few differences among various peoples and did not fully understand how evolution works. In fact, the concept of race was developed long before 1859, when Charles Darwin, the English naturalist, published his discoveries about evolution.

In 1735 Carl von Linne, the Swedish naturalist better known as Linnaeus, said there were four races. Over the years dozens of other classifications have been proposed, some arguing that there are as many as thirty-one or even thirty-seven races.

Today, anthropologists are aware of many differences that were never noticed before and that don't correspond to racial categories. More important, the more that researchers study people worldwide, the more they realize that if they take into account all the hidden differences, they get a very different picture of what is similar or dissimilar among groups. If you consider each feature by itself, you see that a person of one supposed race can be more like a person of another supposed race than like someone of his or her own race.

Take blood, for example. African blacks may be any of the four major blood types: A, B, O, and AB. The same is true of European whites and of

Asiatic peoples. If you are a type O, your blood is more closely related to that of any other type O person—regardless of race—than it is to a type B or type A of your own race. If you need a blood transfusion, you shouldn't care whether the donor's skin color is like yours; you want someone with blood like yours. The same is true of organ transplants. Your closest genetic match for a donated kidney, for example, could easily be somebody of another race.

The same race-blind relationships are true of many physical factors, from the critical to the trivial. Take earwax, which comes in two kinds. One is wet and sticky; the other is dry and crumbly. The vast majority of Africans and Europeans have the same kind—wet and sticky—while the vast majority of Asians have the dry kind.

We can also look at racial differences from another angle. Lots of people think that skin color is a major factor in pigeonholing people in racial groups. Yes, it is true that most Africans and their descendants have skin that is darker than that of most Europeans and their descendants. But millions of people in India, classified by some anthropologists as members of the "Caucasoid," or "white," race, have darker skin than most Americans who call themselves black. Does their black skin mean that they should be grouped with black Africans? Or does their straight hair mean they should be grouped with Europeans?

Also, many "Negroid" people living in sub-Saharan Africa today (such as the !Kung San, or Bushmen) have skin no darker than that of many

Mediterranean peoples, such as the Spaniards, Italians, and Greeks. And there are people in New Guinea who have skin color and hair type similar to many Africans but have no known ancestral links to Africa.

And here's another angle to think about. If you want to classify all black Africans in one group, how do you deal with the fact that within Africa live several kinds of people with much more dramatic differences than skin color? There are the world's smallest people, the Mbuti pygmies of Zaire who average 4'7" and whose size is very similar to that of a dark-skinned group in the Philippines called the Negritos [see Fisher, "Ethnoarchaeology Among the Efe: African Hunter-Gatherers," in this volume]. And there are the world's tallest, the Tutsi of Rwanda, who average 6'1"—close to the average for the very pale-skinned Scandinavian peoples. The two African ethnic groups live just a few hundred miles apart but have remained separate. In size, they more closely resemble other ethnic groups who live very far away.

Now that human genetic profiles are becoming better known, it is clear that within black Africa there are groups with much larger genetic differences than exist between any African group and either Europeans or Asians. A modern racial classification would have to posit several races just for black Africans.

Among Africans are still other kinds of diversity that are more than skin deep. Such differences within the usual broad racial groups have led most anthropologists to say that it makes no sense to think of races as biological categories. You can classify specific traits but not people, who are bundles of different combinations of traits.

The late Sherwood L. Washburn, who was an anthropologist at the University of California at Berkeley, has long questioned the usefulness of racial classification. "Since races are open systems which are integrating, the number of races will depend on the purpose of the classification," he says. "I think we should require people who propose a classification of races to state in the first place why they wish to divide the human species."

The overwhelming conclusion of anthropologists, in short, is that no physical feature distinguishes any race. Not even a combination of traits will do the job.

SO HOW COME PEOPLE ARE DIFFERENT?

Biologists say that most racial differences arose as a result of a process called natural selection. This is the phenomenon that Darwin discovered in the nineteenth century, and it explains a lot about how evolution happens. In a nutshell, it means that if a mutation—a change in a person's genes—produces a useful feature, the person with that change is more likely to be healthier, live longer and, most important for evolution, have more children. Since the change is in the genes, the children inherit it. Because the change gives each person an advantage in survival, eventually those with it will outnumber those without it.

Skin color provides an excellent example. People whose ancestors have lived a long time in the tropics have dark skin. And the farther people lived from the equator, the lighter their skin. Even southern Europeans usually are darker than northern Europeans. In Africa, the darkest skins are near the equator, but at the north and south ends of the continent, the skins are lighter. In southern India, many people are as dark as the blackest Africans, while northern Indians are about as light as southern Europeans. Whatever the skin color, it is all due to different amounts of a dark brown substance called melanin.

This tropics-to-poles spectrum has evolved in response to the sun's intensity in local regions. Too much sun causes sunburn and skin cancer. Too little deprives the body of vitamin D. Without this vitamin, bones grow crooked, resulting in a disease called rickets. In the tropics, the sun is so strong that enough gets through dark skin to make all the vitamin D a person needs.

When dark-skinned people first migrated out of Africa and into northern climates, they may well have suffered rickets, which also can deform the pelvis, making childbirth dangerous or impossible. But because skin color can vary slightly even within a family, lighter-skinned children would be less affected. As a result, they would probably grow up to have more children than their darker relatives. And those children would be even more likely to have lighter-skinned children of their own.

After many generations, the natural effect of the combination of dark skin and low sunlight would select for people who had lost more and more of their original color. This is Darwin's natural selection at work.

Only a few external differences other than color appear to provide a survival advantage. The strongest case can be made for nose shape. People native to colder or drier climates tend to have longer, more beak-shaped noses than those living in hot and humid regions. This is because the nose's job is to warm and humidify air before it reaches the sensitive lungs. The longer the air's path to the lungs, the warmer and more humid the air.

Migration is a key player in the evolutionary drama. Geneticists know that if all members of a species stay in one breeding population, all will stay the same or change in the same ways. But if some members move away and become isolated from the rest of the species, the two groups evolve in different ways. Any mutation in one group eventually can change it forever but can have no effect on the other group—as long as the two don't interbreed.

Human beings are very mobile. They like to pull up stakes and move long distances before settling down. Many times the migratory group loses all contact with the old folks at home. This is why hundreds of different languages have developed. If our ancestors had stayed in touch over thousands of years, we'd probably all speak the same language today. Another result of losing touch is reproductive isolation, which means that any changes in the genes cannot be transmitted to another group.

The fact that people of so many different physical types do exist is proof of long periods of reproductive isolation.

SEXUAL SELECTION PLAYS A ROLE

Aside from the examples above, there is little evidence that any other visible differences among people have any practical advantage. For example, nobody knows why Asiatic people have that special form of upper eyelid or flatter facial profiles.

The thin lips of northern Europeans and many Asians have no known advantage over the full lips of many Africans and Middle Eastern peoples. Why do middle-aged white men go bald so much more often than men of other backgrounds? Why does the skin of the !Kung San, or Bushmen, wrinkle so heavily in middle age when that of most other Africans resists wrinkling far better than that of Europeans?

One possible explanation is another evolutionary process that Darwin also discovered—sexual selection. This differs from natural selection, in which the environment chooses who will survive. In sexual selection, the choice is up to the prospective mate.

In simple terms, ugly persons will be less likely to find mates and pass on their genes than will beautiful people. And of course the definition of beauty varies from culture to culture. Consider the fact that white Europeans and their descendants are usually so much hairier than Africans or Asians. Some anthropologists have suggested that this evolved because white women, like female lions, preferred males with imposing facial fur.

There is a third way that differences can appear in isolated groups—especially traits that are neither good nor bad for a person. Imagine a family with straight ridges in their fingerprints. If the children marry people with curved fingerprints, their new genes (offering no advantage) might never become common, or might even disappear. But if this one family strikes out on its own and founds a new settlement in some remote region, straight-ridged fingerprints eventually might be the rule among all the family's descendants. This kind of evolution is called genetic drift.

Although reproductive isolation is essential to produce differences, there is plenty of evidence that no group of humans has stayed isolated for more than a few thousand years. For one thing, a very long separation between two groups allows their genes to become so different that the groups no longer can interbreed. The fact that all peoples can intermarry and have healthy children proves that we all remain members of the same species. Our differences are trivial in a biological sense. In fact, geneticists have estimated that the variations in genetic makeup that account for racial differences occupy only about 0.01 percent of our genes.

SO, WERE THERE EVER PURE RACES?

Until the mid-twentieth century, most researchers assumed that so-called pure races once existed. Those early thinkers had great trouble figuring out who belonged in which race, and eventually they decided that it was simply because migrations and intermarriage had mixed up, or blended, the once-distinct traits. Today most anthropologists hold that pure races never existed. They think that human beings have always been migrating and intermarrying, spreading new genes worldwide. So while a few populations remained isolated long enough for genetic drift to produce a few distinctive physical characteristics, the isolation was broken often enough for broadly advantageous genes to flow in and out.

Genes useful in all parts of the world would spread quickly—those, for example, that might improve the immune system. Surely the fastest to spread were the genes that improved the brain. In fact, anthropologists who study the earliest human beings agree that a fully modern brain evolved long before any of today's races came into existence.

Genes useful only in some areas would tend not to become common when they were carried to other places. Dark skin, for example, is not an advantage in cold climates. Light skin is a serious disadvantage in tropical climates. So skin color genes could not flow far and persist, at least not until the age of milk fortified with vitamin D, large hats, and long sleeves.

Still, many genes that had no significant good or bad effects—such as those of blood type or earwax, can spread far, and did. But few have come to 100 percent prevalence anywhere. In fact, the varying degrees of prevalence of certain traits provides a clue to the kind of race mixing and genetic blending that has always been part of human history. For example, if you plot the Old World distribution of three major genetically controlled features, type A blood, hair form, and skin color, you will see that the traits are largely independent of one another. No combination of traits can be offered as defining any race.

The bottom line, anthropologists agree, is that the science does not support the idea of races as natural units, now or in the past. You cannot pick just one or even a few traits and claim that they define a biological category.

People have tried to do this using the most visible features, such as skin color and facial form, but have ignored all unseen genetic variability.

Perhaps if humans were blind to everything but earwax, we would say there are two races. If all that mattered was ABO blood type, we would argue that there are four races.

SO WHAT?

After the many misunderstandings of the past, the great lesson of anthropology, biology, and genetics is that all people are the same in the essentials but are highly diverse in a few things. These differences have arisen not because there are fundamentally different kinds of people but simply because we are a restless, curious, hopeful migratory species whose intelligence has allowed us to make a good living in almost every environment on earth.

Human beings are more mobile than ever, and genes are flowing farther and more widely than ever. In many parts of the world this is blending once-diverse features. But if the past is a guide, no amount of blending is likely to take away the diversity that has made the human species so successful and that surely will prove useful as the environment on earth changes in centuries ahead.

SET UP YOUR OWN RACIAL CLASSIFICATION

If there really are races, shouldn't you be able to see them when you plot the distribution of genetic traits such as skin color, hair form, and blood type? The fact is that these and all other variable traits are distributed independently. In other words, just because you have one trait, it has nothing to do with whether you have another one. Consider the Aborigines of Australia. Their hair form (wavy-straight) is like that of European whites. Their skin color is like that of African blacks. And their prevalence of blood type A resembles that of a huge swath of the world from Europe to southern Asia.

You might think it would help to consider additional features such as the shapes of noses, lips, and eyes. But it doesn't. They too are independently distributed, and maps showing their distribution would be even more confusing.

RACE AND INTELLIGENCE

Arguments that one human population is intellectually superior to another are fairly new in human history, dating mainly from the time of massive enslavement of Africans. The idea of using Africans in the New World, however, grew out of the racist assumption that they were superior to American Indians. Bartolomé de Las Casas, a Spanish priest of the 1500s, argued that Indians being enslaved by the Spanish conquerors were not up to the "civilized" work demanded of them in farming, mining, and industry. He argued that the colonial rulers should import more advanced peoples such as Africans.

Much later, when some people challenged the morality of slavery, defenders claimed that Africans were not fully human, especially in intellect.

In modern times, researchers have made many tests of the mental powers of all groups of people and repeatedly found that if they test people of equivalent social and educational background, they find no significant differences. As far back as 1961, the council of the American Anthropological Association ruled unanimously that it knew of no evidence that any population was less capable than any other of participating fully in modern, complex society. Further studies have reinforced that conclusion.

FURTHER READING

American Anthropological Association. 1998. "AAA Statement on Race." *Anthropology Newsletter*, September, p. 3. Available at www.aaanet.org/committees/minority/index.htm#statements.

American Association of Physical Anthropologists. 1996. "AAPA Statement on Biological Aspects of Race." *American Journal of Physical Anthropology* 101:569–70.

Brace, C. Loring. "Does Race Exist? An Antagonist's Perspective." Available at www.pbs.org/wgbh/nova/first/brace.html.

Brace, C. Loring. "A Four-Letter Word Called 'Race.'" Available at www.multiracial.com/abolitionist/word/brace.html.

Brace, C. Loring, and Kevin D. Hunt. 1990. "A Non-Racial Craniofacial Perspective on Human Variation: A(ustralia) to Z(uni)." *American Journal of Physical Anthropology* 88:341–60.

Brown, Ryan A., and George J. Armelagos. 2001. "Apportionment of Racial Diversity: A review." *Evolutionary Anthropology* 10(1):34–40.

Gill, George W. "Does Race Exist? A Proponent's Perspective." Available at www.pbs.org/wgbh/nova/first/GILL.html.

Gould, Stephen Jay. 1996. *The Mismeasure of Man*. Rev. and expanded edition. W. W. Norton.

Molnar, Stephen, ed. 2001. *Human Variation: Races, Types and Ethnic Groups*. 5th ed. Prentice Hall.

Mukhopadhyay, Carol, and Rosemary C. Henze. 2003. "Using Anthropology to Make Sense of Human Diversity." *Phi Delta Kappan* 84(9):669–78.

Olson, Steve. 2002. *Mapping Human History: Discovering the Past Through Our Genes*. Houghton Mifflin.

Rensberger, Boyce. 1994. "A New Way to Look at Race." *Washington Post*, November 16, "Horizon" section. (This chapter of *Anthropology Explored* was excerpted from this longer, heavily illustrated article, with permission from the *Washington Post.*)

Reynolds, Larry T., and Leonard Lieberman. 1996. *Race and Other Misadventures: Essays in Honor of Ashley Montagu in His Ninetieth Year.* General Hall.

Shipman, Pat. 1994. *The Evolution of Racism.* Simon & Schuster.

12 RACE AND ETHNICITY

Alison S. Brooks, Fatimah L. C. Jackson, and
Roy Richard Grinker

This chapter, thoroughly revised in 2003, traces the centuries-long history of race categorization, answering the question of why race has been important to scientists and American society at large. The recent impact of the decoding of the human genome is highlighted, reflecting current studies of human variation that often use direct comparison of DNA segments. The increasing use of ethnicity as a way for people to define their identity is explored, with the authors concluding that "a conception of identity as mutable and contingent on circumstance may offer some optimism for the future."

[Varieties of *Homo sapiens:*] **Africanus negreus (black), Americanus rubescens (red), Asiaticus fuscus (tawny), and Europaeus albescens (white).** (Linnaeus 1758)

In my opinion, to dismember mankind into races . . . requires such a distortion of the facts that any usefulness disappears. (Hiernaux 1964:43)

Race and subrace do represent a truth about the natural world, which cannot be adequately described without consideration of them. (Baker 1974:4)

Race is a term originally applied to populations who shared close common ancestry and certain unique traits, but it has been so overworked and its applications so broad and general that race is nearly useless and is often replaced by *ethnic group.* (Molnar 1992:36)

It is important . . . to have a clear . . . understanding of the difference between race and racism, on the one hand, and ethnicity and ethnocentrism on the other. (Smedley 1993:29)

Shortly after birth, each American baby is placed in a box—not a physical box, just a box on a piece of paper. This process, which counts the child as belonging to one and only one "race" or "ethnic group," will be repeated over and over throughout an individual's lifetime. Current American "boxes" include: (1) White, (2) Black (African American), (3) Hispanic, (4) American Indian or Alaska native (Eskimo or Aleut), (5) Asian (multiple categories), or (6) Pacific Islander (multiple categories). Anthropology departments sometimes receive desperate calls from parents: "I am from Pakistan—should I check 'White' or 'Asian'?" "My wife and I belong to different groups—how do we classify our baby?"

As a child grows, the box often will be designated by others, without the person's knowledge or input, as though a simple set of rules could generate a "correct" classification. But is there such a set of rules? Such classification implies that pure races and cultures existed with little intermixture in the recent past. But did such a time ever exist? Before air travel? Before Columbus? Before Marco Polo?

As the initial quotations suggest, anthropologists disagree about the subject of race and ethnicity, and opinions have radically changed over time. Far from reflecting biological and cultural "reality," race and ethnicity are increasingly seen as arbitrary constructs fulfilling a social need, with content and limits negotiated among members of each society. How else can we explain why university affirmative action offices in the United States group people from the Indian subcontinent with "whites," whereas in the U.S. 2000 Census and in South Africa under apartheid, they were officially "Asians"? Japanese visitors to South Africa, however, were classified as "whites," while 3.5 million non-Asian South Africans were classified as "coloured," neither "black" nor "white."

In the 1990 U.S. census, every non–Native American who was *not* of Asian descent had to check either "Black" or "White." By 2000, the issue of ancestry consumed three separate questions on the short form answered by everyone and four questions on the long form. People were asked first to specify if they were Hispanic/Spanish/Latino or not. (Those answering yes were asked to specify further whether they were Cuban, Mexican, Puerto Rican or "Other—please specify group.") Then, the census asked, what is the person's race: White, Black (or African American or Negro), American Indian/Alaska Native (specify tribe), Asian Indian, Chinese, Filipino, Japanese, Korean, Vietnamese, Native Hawaiian, Guamanian/Chamorro, Samoan, Other Pacific Islander (specify), or Other (specify)? Both the expanded list

and the new rule allowing respondents to check more than one box reflect fundamental confusion between race and national origin or ethnic group. A later question on both forms asked the person to specify his/her ancestry or ethnic origin and gave as examples many of the same terms (African American, Korean, Mexican) also used to specify race or Hispanic status on the previous page.

For over a hundred years, science—particularly its biological and anthropological branches—has been asked three questions: Do races exist? If so, why? What is the most accurate racial classification, whether absolute or relative to geography and history? Larger questions, most recently addressed by the scientists themselves, are: Why do we care? Why is the race issue important to scholars, and, even more so, to American society at large?

EARLY CLASSIFICATIONS: EIGHTEENTH CENTURY

Anthropology is the field of knowledge most closely connected to the study of human differences, although attempts to recognize and describe such differences are more ancient than the formal study of anthropology. The French naturalist Georges Buffon, writing in the mid-eighteenth century, may have been the first scholar to use the word *race* to describe the varieties within a single species, whether humans or dogs, and to attribute these differences to local alterations of a single ancestral group. Like more modern biologists, he saw these physical differences as responses to different climates, diets, and even patterns of behavior or cultural practices. We now know that agriculture, for example, resulted in decreasing tooth size in modern humans.

In the eighteenth century, following Linnaeus' classification of the varieties of *Homo,* the German scholar and physician Johann Friedrich Blumenbach developed the concept of human races. He drew up lists of physical and behavioral differences among five major races: Caucasian (Linnaeus' white or *Europaeus albescens*), Mongolian (*Asiaticus fuscus* L.), Ethiopian (*Africanus negreus*), American (*Americanus rubescens* L.), and Malay—the latter not distinguished in Linnaeus' classification but added in later editions of Blumenbach's work to encompass the peoples of Southeast Asia and the Pacific. Like Buffon, Blumenbach argued for a single origin of humankind but thought that some races had "degenerated" from their original state.

RACE AND RACISM: NINETEENTH CENTURY

From Blumenbach on, physicians dominated the study of human physical differences, emphasizing human anatomy rather than a broad natural-history viewpoint. Early-nineteenth-century scholars, such as the American physician Samuel Morton, used flawed statistics to show that Caucasians had the largest brains, Negroes the smallest (Gould 1996). Morton attributed these differences to separate creation (polygenism), rather than to adaptation or degeneration, and saw them as immutable. Gould, Smedley (1993), and others have argued that this shift reflects the emergence of a world view in which physical differences or race dominated all other kinds of differences, such as class or nationality, and were used to justify the oppression of Africans in particular by peoples of European descent.

Smedley's chapter "Growth of the English Ideology of Race in America" argues that the English, isolated from the more cosmopolitan Mediterranean world, were particularly unprepared to assimilate people with cultural and physical differences. The English colonized Ireland and America at the same time and grouped both Irish and American natives as "heathen," "idolatrous," "wild," and "savage," characteristics used to justify the appropriation of native lands by the more "civilized" English and the removal or enslavement of the natives themselves.

Anthropologists, though clearly enmeshed in a racist and ethnocentric European and American culture of nineteenth-century scholarship, saw themselves as countering the prevailing theories of the day by asserting human unity. In 1871 Edward B. Tylor, an English founder of anthropology, defined the discipline as the study of "man and the races of man." Although Tylor was careful to separate race and culture, physical anthropologists, many of whom continued to support polygenism, tended to confuse race and culture

as well as to regard psychological traits and cognitive abilities as inborn, like skin color and hair form.

BIOLOGY AND CULTURE: SEPARATE BUT CONFUSED

The confusion of biology and culture continued into the functionalist era of the 1920s and 1930s with the application of organic models and adaptationist explanations to social phenomena. For example, it was asserted that just as dark skin evolved to protect humans from excessive ultraviolet radiation, so "joking relationships" with the mother's brother evolved to balance a strict avoidance relationship with the father and his relatives. Many so-called functional explanations of biological traits, in particular, were based on untested assumptions. Black boxes are perfect radiators of heat, so it was assumed that dark bodies would perform better in hot weather. In a series of tests conducted by the French army in North Africa, however, performance differences between whites and blacks under extreme heat conditions failed to materialize. The confusion of biological and cultural or ethnic differences, together with an extreme view of racial and ethnic separation derived from the polygenists, was incorporated into Nazi ideas of racial hierarchy and purity.

HOW MANY RACES?

With more than two hundred years of scholarship on the topic of human variation, do we know how many races or how many ethnic groups there are? Biologists define races as populations of a species that differ genetically from one another. The emphasis on genetic differences is important, since two unrelated populations that inhabit the same area can come to resemble one another physically, as both respond to the same selective forces. Since gene pools change over time in response to natural selection, mutation, random events, and migration or hybridization, biological races are also limited in time. Can the human species be divided into populations that differ genetically from one another?

Many anthropologists today would argue that such a division is impossible due to extensive migration and hybridization among human groups throughout human history. In a reaction to the discredited studies of the early twentieth century, many anthropologists have pointed to the continuous or clinal nature of human variation, arguing that biological races do not in fact exist. There is no line across the middle of the Sahara or the Mediterranean that divides people into white and black, nor is there a north-south line in Eurasia dividing whites from Mongoloids or Asians. Even the New World remained in genetic contact with the Old through the intermingling of seafaring peoples from both sides of the Bering Sea, as well as of Inuit and Norse in Greenland. Nor is there a set of physical criteria that will reliably differentiate members of these large racial groups. The use of skin color will group Africans with native peoples of Australia and south Indians, while the use of hair form and hair color will group the latter two with Europeans. Skin color is strongly correlated with UV radiation and responds relatively rapidly to new selective pressures as populations move from one UV zone to another. New research suggests that average skin color in a population represents an adaptive balance between allowing sufficient UV penetration to synthesize vitamin D and blocking the UV-induced destruction of folate; both vitamin D and folate are necessary substances for human reproduction.

What about genetics? Should not a comparison of the genetics of different populations allow us to define differences and reconstruct historical relationships? Yes, argues L. L. Cavalli-Sforza of Stanford University, who has used genetic traits determined from blood samples to construct trees of relatedness for large numbers of human groups worldwide. Genetic traits unrelated to surface differences were once considered to reflect a deeper genetic relationship between peoples, unaffected by natural selection. We now know, however, that even such supposedly neutral features as blood group (A, B, AB, or O) are often subject to natural selection in a way that creates similarities in groups that are otherwise unrelated. For example, both the Irish and the Blackfoot Indians have similar frequencies of type A blood; this is more likely to reflect a common disease history than any migration event of the past. People with type A blood appear to have been more susceptible to smallpox, while people with O blood were more frequently felled by bubonic plague.

With the decoding of the human genome, studies of population relationships today are more likely to be carried out through the direct comparison of segments of DNA. Different DNA segments from a human body provide a range of information about population history. For example, a comparison of DNA regions on the Y chromosome, found only in males, tells us about the history of a population's male lineage, while comparisons of the DNA found in our mitochondria (small organelles that produce the energy to power each of our cells) show only our female lineage, as the few mitochondria in sperm do not normally survive in the fertilized egg. DNA from the autosomes (chromosomes other than the X or the Y) changes more slowly than mitochondrial DNA (mtDNA) but can still provide interesting data about human origins. Even the DNA of our parasites and viruses is being studied for information about population relationships of their human hosts. A typical study will derive the sequence of bases in each sample of DNA from a particular region of someone's mitochondria or chromosome and compare this individual's sequence to that of all the other individuals. Often the series of random changes (mutations) that turned one sequence of bases into another can be determined, as well as which sequence is the ancestral one. Within each type of DNA, sequences that share a common set of mutations or changes are called a "haplogroup." Each population has different frequencies of haplogroups, and similarity in the patterning of haplogroups implies that two populations are closely related. In addition, geneticists use an estimate of the number of mutations per year to suggest how long ago two haplogroups and/or two populations shared a common ancestor.

All types of DNA confirm that human diversity is greatest in Africa and that all of today's humans originated from that continent within the last 200,000 years. The mitochondrial genome also shows that Asians and Pacific Islanders are the next most diverse, and Europeans the least diverse. Europeans share many of the Asian haplogroups, suggesting to some that the first modern Europeans did not come directly from Africa but passed first through central Asia. Most Native American haplogroups appear to derive from Siberia, although one North American haplogroup (X) is almost unknown in Asia but common in Europe. This haplogroup reflects ancient contact rather than recent admixture, as it has also been found in pre-Columbians through new techniques of recovering ancient DNA. Whether it reflects an early sea migration from Europe or an old common ancestor of Asians and Europeans who left few Asian descendants remains to be determined. Mitochondrial DNA and Y chromosomes provide different perspectives on population history—in Finland, for example, Y chromosome variants distinctive to Finland reflect both Finnish isolation and male lineage ancestry in Central Asia, like the Finnish language. Finnish women, however, share the maternal lineage of other Europeans, according to their mtDNA.

At the individual level, is it possible to study a person's DNA and to suggest the populations to which he or she is most closely related? At the basic level, genetic analysis constructs clusters or trees based on the overall similarity of the genomes in *individuals* of different populations. But these trees often cluster individuals from different populations, particularly in very diverse regions such as Africa. In genetics publications, the diversity of a population sample is usually summarized by a pie chart showing the frequency of the different haplogroups in each population being studied. By chance, any individual could harbor DNA segments that are less common in the population of his/her ethnic ancestors, and more common in some other population. Jonathan Marks (1995, 2002), among others, cautions against the too rapid acceptance of population relationships based on DNA similarities. To sample a population's genes, the geneticist must first define the population limits. In so doing, he or she may artificially limit the genetic variation of the population's DNA by eliminating people who live close to another ethnic group or "look different." For example, should Africa be represented by four or five populations, defined by the observer, from different areas of the continent, or by random samples from a few people every few miles across the continent? The latter may be preferable but is very hard to achieve in practice. In addition, different techniques of statistical analysis may yield different results.

How do we define a local population of humans for the purpose of sampling it and comparing it to others? On a local level, geographers have demonstrated the existence of breeding populations in humans, reflected in the statistical tendency to select one's mate from within a certain radius. Even in industrialized societies of the twentieth century, this radius may be surprisingly small: a mile or two in mid-twentieth-century England (Molnar 1992:195).

In each situation, however, the breeding population of suitable or even actual mates is always culturally circumscribed or expanded in ways that defy geographical proximity. Immigrants may be required to take a mate from their home population or encouraged to marry into the new one. Cultural rules may prescribe marriage to a cousin (Bedouin) or to the most geographically distant person available (Ju/wasi).

Mates taken from outside the geographer's radius may bring changes to the genetic frequencies of the local population or even create new populations. African American populations exhibit different genetic frequencies from those of their presumed parent populations in West and Central Africa, owing to the American pattern of exogamy (mating outside one's group) among once separate African ethnic groups, as well as gene flow with non-African populations in the Americas (primarily western Europeans and eastern Native Americans). In addition, African Americans were exposed to a different set of natural selection factors in America—climatic, nutritional, and disease differences. For example, the Duffy blood group gene Fy- protects against a particularly deadly form of malaria called vivax malaria. Virtually 100 percent of contemporary West and Central Africans carry the Fy- gene and are protected against vivax malaria. European, Asian, and Native American populations, on the other hand, maintain low frequencies of the Fy- gene and are susceptible to this infectious disease. Approximately 89–93 percent of African Americans carry the Fy- gene, reflecting the reduced natural selection pressure of vivax malaria in America as well as genetic change in non-African groups. Similarly, the gene frequencies of individuals classed as white in America frequently reflect substantial percentages of genes that are more common in nonwhites. This pattern strongly suggests that in the American environment, the flow of genes between formerly geographically distinct peoples has been multidirectional, influencing the subsequent composition of each group.

Restrictions on interbreeding within the geographer's average radius, due to caste or religious differences, for example, may create genetically differentiated groups that occupy the same local area. This has been the case in Ireland, where Catholics and Protestants rarely intermarry, or in India, where marriages usually take place within defined caste groups. (Women are always more mobile than men in India, as reflected in the mtDNA.) As a result, differences within populations are often as great as differences between populations, making it almost impossible to assign individuals to particular groups based on physical or genetic traits alone. Even in a case where some anthropologists argue for major racial differences—for example, Khoisan versus Negroid—in actuality it is impossible to assign every individual to one or the other of these groups on physical grounds alone, just as it is impossible to assign individuals in America to the categories of the census on physical grounds alone. Within the African continent, for example, there is more physical, physiological, and genetic diversity than there is between Africans and any other group, or between Europeans and East Asians. At no time in the past did totally pure or isolated races exist.

A glance at most introductory texts of physical anthropology, however, shows that efforts to list a few major geographical subdivisions are still current, although always qualified by noting that not all individuals or populations can be put into the categories. Most of these lists closely approximate the original five races of Blumenbach, although some also elevate the Khoisan-speaking peoples of southern Africa to that level of distinctiveness—for example, *Homo sapiens hottentotus,* also called Sanids (Baker 1974:303–24, 624) or Capoids. Interestingly, the greatest variation in these lists is in the treatment of what the U.S. Census Bureau calls "Asian and Pacific Islanders." Where Blumenbach recognized only Mongolians and Malays, others, using 1950s studies by Stanley Garn, may divide the latter into Australians, Melanesians, Micronesians, and Polynesians. In addition, some taxonomies classify peoples of the Indian subcontinent as a separate race. Groups that are assumed to lie outside these large categories, or geographical races, from African Americans to the Ainu of Japan, are either subsumed, ignored, or treated as curiosities, isolates, or "hybrids."

ETHNICITY INSTEAD OF RACE

As noted by Molnar, the term *race* is increasingly replaced in public documents and folk taxonomies by the term *ethnic group* or *ethnicity*. Ethnicity is a more recent concept in anthropology than race, although the underlying concept of ethnos or ethnology, denoting a people distinguished by cultural traits is older, dating back to at least the mid-nineteenth century. According to the *Oxford English Dictionary*, the term *ethnicity* was first used in 1953 by the sociologist David Riesman to explain how individuals and groups in multicultural settings shape their identities and their political and economic goals in terms of their interactions with one another.

How do groups (or the scholars who study them) construct or define the boundaries of an ethnic group? As in the case of race, two contrasting views of ethnicity exist. The "primordialists" hold that ethnicity arises from similarities between individuals of the group in physical features and language. These features have the power to impart a sense of group and individual identity, of belonging to the community. Ethnicity in this view is "natural" and is based on biological (skin color, body shape) or linguistic affinities that are distinct from and prior to particular social or historic conditions. In contrast, instrumentalist models hold that groups create ethnicity for political and economic interests. In this view, ethnicity is rationally oriented toward the fulfillment of specific goals, such as access to economic power, nationalism, or freedom from colonial rule.

Most scholars today reject these simplistic alternatives and hold the position that neither is sufficient to explain ethnic group structure and sentiment. Primordialism overlooks the fact that ethnic identity is not a natural feeling that simply emerges mysteriously in all human communities but a complex and dynamic set of symbolic meanings patterned in history. Instrumentalists are so concerned with political and economic motivations that they sometimes ignore the question of how the particular elements or symbols of an ethnic identity are chosen. Ethnic consciousness may depend on perceived biological similarities, on a common language or linguistic structure, or on numerous cultural factors and learned behaviors ranging from religion to styles of speech and interaction.

Some ethnicities have been determined in large part by recent historical events such as colonization, nationalism, or urbanism. In Ethiopia, the Falasha Jews were named by Amharic leaders (*falasha* means "exile" in Amharic), while in Europe, the Bosnian Muslims identified themselves as Muslims both as a way to further their political power in previous Islamic states, and, more recently, as a form of resistance to Yugoslavian nationalism.

Other ethnicities have long histories. For example, in Africa, the Hutu and Tutsi of Rwanda and the Tswana and Sarwa of Botswana predate the onslaught of European colonialism. Nor can the ethnic composition of nations in Europe (e.g., Basques, Flemish) or northern Africa be explained as a correlate of modernity. This is not to imply that ethnic sentiments are "traditional" and unchanging, only that what people believe about their past has a direct relationship to what they are doing in the present. People may *believe* their ethnic ties are ancient, but the meaning and definition of these changes over time and differs according to historical circumstance. Ethnicity among Hutu and Tutsi, for example, while embedded in a long precolonial history, underwent drastic changes in just two years, 1959–61, when the states of Rwanda, Burundi, and Zaire were created. The Muslims of Bosnia, mobilized by ancestry and modern nationalism, do not fit neatly into either the primordialist or instrumentalist conceptions.

ETHNICITY AND STEREOTYPES

Like racial categories, ethnic categories have a static quality that can perpetuate stereotypes of cultural homogeneity and mask within-group variation. Categories such as "European Americans," "African Americans," "Hispanic Americans," and "Asian Americans" comprise many smaller, culturally diverse groups. When we fail to recognize this internal variation, we perpetuate stereotypes that often do great disservice, and assume that all members of each category are alike.

One benefit of an ethnic focus in anthropology is that it requires us to search for ways in which people, not nature, create their identities. Unfortunately, this emphasis has yet to broaden into public usage.

In the U.S. census of 1970 and 1980, the clearest example of a race with little or no biological component was the category "Hispanic." This grouping originally was designed to encompass Spanish-speaking migrants from Latin America, who also were categorized as "brown" owing to various admixtures of Africans, native South Americans, and peoples from Spain, Portugal, and other European (and Asian) countries. But if the purpose was to define a biological entity, why should Europeans recently arrived from Spain or non-Latin individuals who have acquired a Spanish surname through marriage be included? Why should Spanish-speaking immigrants from Latin America with German surnames be excluded? How should Latin Americans of primarily African descent be categorized? In the 1990 census, the category "Hispanic" was redefined as an ethnic group so that an individual can also classify him- or herself by race as "White," "Black," or "American Indian." But what ethnic group combines Portuguese from Brazil and Argentineans of Welsh or Syrian descent, except with reference to the Anglo culture of the United States?

In the United States, on the other hand, African Americans or blacks and European Americans or whites remain overemphasized. This practice leads to increasing polarization between these groups and creates false notions of biological and cultural homogeneity within them. Such practices rooted in the political, economic, and historical circumstances of this nation continue to obscure the very real commonalities shared by members of the same sex, class, community, or job category, as well as the common values and beliefs of a uniquely American culture that the two groups have jointly created.

If identities, whether racial or ethnic, are indeed cultural and historical constructs, then they are also changeable. At a time when ethnicity is so often associated with violent conflict throughout the world, a conception of identity as mutable and contingent on circumstance may offer some optimism for the future.

FURTHER READING

Baker, J. R. 1974. *Race.* Oxford University Press.

Crews, D. E., and J. R. Bindon. 1991. "Ethnicity as a Taxonomic Tool in Biomedical and Biosocial Research." *Ethnicity and Disease* 1:42–49.

Gould, Stephen J. 1996. *The Mismeasure of Man.* Rev. and expanded edition. W. W. Norton.

Hiernaux, Jean. 1964. "The Concept of Race and the Taxonomy of Mankind." In Ashley Montagu, ed., *The Concept of Race,* pp. 29–45. Free Press of Glencoe.

Jackson, F. L. C. 1992. "Race and Ethnicity as Biological Constructs." *Ethnicity and Disease* 2:120–25.

Linnaeus, Carolus. 1758. *Systema Naturae.* 10th ed. Laurentius Salvius.

Marks, Jonathan. 1995. *Human Biodiversity: Genes, Race, and History.* Aldine de Gruyter.

Marks, Jonathan. 2002. *What It Means to Be 98% Chimpanzee: Apes, People and Their Genes.* University of California Press.

Molnar, Stephen. 1992. *Human Variation: Races, Types, and Ethnic Groups.* 3d ed. Prentice-Hall. (5th ed., 2002.)

Olsen, Steve. 2002. *Mapping Human History: Discovering the Past Through Our Genes.* Houghton Mifflin.

Semino, Ornella, Giuseppe Passarino, Peter J. Oefner, Alice A. Lin, Svetlana Arbuzova, Lars E. Beckman, Giovanna De Benedictis, Paolo Francalacci, Anastasia Kouvatsi, Svetlana Limborska, Mladen Marcikiæ, Anna Mika, Barbara Mika, Draga Primorac, A. Silvana Santachiara-Benerecetti, L. Luca Cavalli-Sforza, and Peter A. Underhill. 2000. "The Genetic Legacy of Paleolithic *Homo sapiens sapiens* in Extant Europeans: A Y Chromosome Perspective." *Science* 290:1155–9.

Smedley, Audrey. 1993. *Race in North America: Origin and Evolution of a Worldview.* Westview. (2nd ed., 1999.)

Tylor, Edward B. 1871. *Primitive Culture.* J. Murray.

Wallace, Douglas C., Michael D. Brown, and Marie T. Lott. 1999. "Mitochondrial DNA Variation in Human Evolution and Disease." *Gene* 238:211–30.

Wolf, Eric R. 1982. *Europe and the People Without History.* University of California Press.

MITOMAP (human mitochondrial genome database): www.mitomap.org

EXAMINING OUR ARCHAEOLOGICAL PAST

What do we know about the earliest humans?

How do we learn about our ancient past?

How does archaeology differ from history?

How is archaeology relevant today?

13   AGRICULTURAL ORIGINS IN THE ANCIENT WORLD

Melinda A. Zeder

The evolutionary development of agriculture and animal domestication may be the most significant turning point in human history, eventually leading to specialization and urban centers. This chapter explores the origins, gradual development, and consequences of the Neolithic Revolution. Zeder makes clear in her update the complex number of factors that might explain the emergence of agriculture, as well as the importance of new technologies and dating techniques to trace its origins.

How can a heap of long-buried, extremely fragmented animal bones help us better understand the origins of agriculture, perhaps the most significant turning point in the course of human history?

Agriculture, which anthropologists define as the domestication of both plants and animals, changed forever the evolution of human societies. While agriculture brought about unparalleled productivity and ever-improving standards of living, it also led to swelling populations, widespread hunger, and irreversible environmental change. It should be no surprise, then, that the causes and consequences of the origins of agriculture, often called the Neolithic Revolution, are recurring topics of lively debate within the field of archaeology.

What were the preconditions that gave rise to the domestication of plants and animals? Why did people nearly 10,000 years ago begin to experiment with crops and the rearing of livestock? When and why did these practices replace gathering wild resources and hunting game as the primary means of feeding people?

EARLY-TWENTIETH-CENTURY VIEWS

Theories explaining the causes and consequences of agriculture are not only varied but frequently contradictory. In the late nineteenth through the mid-twentieth centuries, many researchers viewed agriculture as a technological breakthrough, forever freeing humankind from a life on the margins: a mean, brutish existence that relied on wits and luck for survival. Agriculture, in this view, brought an era of bounty, with rich harvests of predictable and nutritious plants and animals. The ability to reap these harvests expanded with each new technological refinement—the plow, draft animals, irrigation. Farmers' labor was seasonal, affording people leisure time to invent labor-saving technologies as well as cultural elaborations in the arts and sciences. Early agriculture was the first major watershed, setting the stage for the subsequent grand threshold of human achievement—the development of civilization.

MID-TWENTIETH-CENTURY VIEWS

During the 1960s and 1970s the world became increasingly concerned about scarcities of primary resources and overpopulation, and people began demanding limits to growth. Within this context a very different picture emerged of the origins of agriculture. The life of the hunter-gatherer, past and present, was no longer described as one of hardship, privation, and ceaseless toil. Rather, anthropologists saw hunter-gatherers as the original "affluent society"—people with modest needs met by occasional hunting forays and sporadic collecting. Agriculture was viewed as a kind of expulsion from Eden, brought about by the inevitable expansion of population beyond the capacity of hunter-gatherer strategies to satisfy basic needs. The price of the pre-Neolithic baby boom, the punishment for taking the first bite of the domesticated apple, was the farmer's life of hardship and toil.

In this view, growing crops and raising animals provided more food, but the food was less nutritious and less palatable than people had previously enjoyed. Agriculture accelerated the rate of population increase, giving rise to more widespread hunger than the world had ever seen. The reduction in biological diversity accompanying the spread of agriculture undermined the stability of natural resources, paving the way for periodic, devastating ecological crises.

These two alternative visions of the origins of agriculture, as blessing or blight, serve as opposite poles of the debate. Researchers are discovering, however, that the story of the development of plant and animal domestication and the resultant food-producing economies is far richer and more complex than either of these two views indicates.

EXPULSION FROM EDEN ?

Earlier interpretations, for example, posited that all peoples throughout the Near East adopted food-producing technologies quickly and completely, never looking back to earlier days of hunting and gathering. The wide array of suitable plant and animal domesticates, favorable local environmental conditions, and human population dynamics may well explain a generally rapid embrace of food production as a more reliable subsistence strategy than hunting and gathering. But within the Near East, the domesticates and the timing of their adoption varied, with each region emphasizing different combinations of cereals and animals in varying rates and sequences. The Khabur Basin provides one case study illustrating the variation in human adaptation to the development of farming and herding.

THE KHABUR BASIN OF ANCIENT MESOPOTAMIA

The Khabur Basin is nestled in the far northeastern corner of modern-day Syria, bordered by Turkey to the north and Iraq to the south and east (see map). The northern Khabur Basin is dissected by the Khabur River and a number of streams (or wadis, as they are called in the Near East) fanning out across the basin. These wadis are often dry in the searing summer months. From the late fall through the spring, they carry seasonal rains and runoff from northern upland areas. These seasonal streams converge where the Khabur River begins its journey southward, eventually joining the Euphrates River. There is a steep north-south gradient of rainfall in the Khabur Basin. Precipitation in the far north is more than enough to support rain-fed, non-irrigation agriculture, but rainfall levels decrease precipitously southward, where rain-fed farming becomes an increasingly risky business.

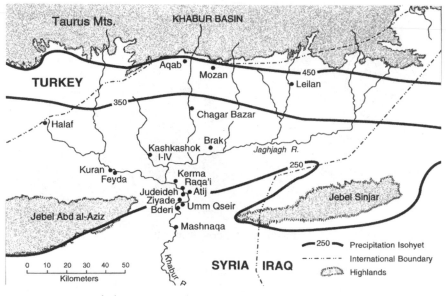

Khabur Basin Settlements (courtesy Marcia Bakry)

Early Settlement in the Khabur Basin

Settlement in the Khabur Basin was sparse until about 6000 B.C. No known sites in the region date to before 14,000 B.C., and only two sites date to between 14,000 and 10,000 B.C. The eighth millennium B.C. (8000 to 7000 B.C.) saw the introduction of farming and herding into the basin. For almost 2,000 years a few small communities, located exclusively in the better-watered northern region, relied primarily on domestic resources: cereal grains, lentils, and pulses (pod-bearing plants such as peas and beans), as well as sheep and goats, and later pigs and cattle. Then the northern steppe witnessed a substantial increase in settlement. A number of farming communities arose in the upper Khabur Basin, all of which produced a distinctive pottery, linking them to the Halafian cultural tradition, which spread widely across northern Mesopotamia.

The Halafian Period, named after Tell Halaf in the northern Khabur Basin, is believed to have experienced a remarkable proliferation of rain-fed farm communities, an expansion of far-flung trading networks, and possibly the development of more complex social organization. Plant and animal remains recovered from Halafian sites in well-watered areas suggest that these communities relied heavily on domestic crops and livestock, although wild plants and animals were also gathered and hunted in small amounts.

UMM QSEIR

The first indication of population movement out of the northern steppe into the arid southern steppe comes from Halafian levels at the small site of Umm Qseir, situated just below the 10-inch (250-millimeter) rainfall boundary. Umm Qseir is located about 19 miles (30 kilometers) away from the nearest contemporary site and is very small: no more than a quarter of an acre (110 hectares) in size. Excavators from Yale University found only ephemeral traces of architecture at Umm Qseir and essentially no tools used in grain harvesting and processing. The entire Halafian occupation of Umm Qseir seems to have lasted no more than 200 years, between 6000 and 5000 b.c., and the site was probably never occupied by more than two or three families. We originally thought this tiny Halafian outpost was a seasonal encampment, used by small groups who traveled with their flocks from established villages in the north to take advantage of the abundant southern spring grasses.

Animal Bone Analysis

Through extensive analysis of the plant and animal remains from Umm Qseir, we tested our first hypothesis: that the site was a seasonal encampment of mobile herders or pastoralists. Our analysis demonstrated this hypothesis to be dead wrong.

Through the painstaking, sometimes frightfully dull study of thousands of broken bones and fragments of charred seeds, we uncovered clues to help us reconstruct the daily subsistence of the people living in this tiny community in Mesopotamia between 6000 and 5000 b.c. The clues told us much about the complexity of these people's yearly strategies to survive.

An average season of archaeological excavation in the Near East can yield upward of 50,000 bones, each of which is of interest to the zooarchaeologist, who specializes in studying animal bones. The bone analysis requires an incredible amount of patience and a sharp eye for seeing patterns after thousands of observations have been recorded. Bones first have to be washed and dried, sorted, labeled, and coded for a variety of information: animal species, skeletal element, side, type of breakage, and so on. The zooarchaeologist makes these observations, often using skeletons of modern animals to help identify bone fragments.

The bones and teeth of an animal carry hidden clues to the age and season in which that animal was killed. Long bones (such as the femur or radius) fuse at certain known ages. If you find an unfused distal end of a sheep humerus, you know that sheep was killed before it reached its first birthday. Like human children, mammals lose their baby teeth, and their adult teeth erupt at known ages. The rate at which teeth wear with use over time also is known for some animals, as are the peak birth months.

Zooarchaeologists use this knowledge when analyzing bones to calculate the age at which an animal was killed, and in some cases the season. With a large enough sample of bones, they can construct an age profile of the flock and the primary seasons in which the animals were slaughtered. From this profile, they can draw a range of conclusions about the relationship of humans to the animals with which they lived—both domestic and wild.

The central question that now began to take shape was whether Umm Qseir was a seasonal settlement for pastoral herders coming down from the north or a year-round settlement.

Pigs Offer the First Clues

Domestic species of the residents of Umm Qseir in the sixth millennium (6000–5000 B.C.) included sheep, goat, and pig, but no domestic cattle. The absence of the full range of Neolithic domesticates (sheep or goat, pig, and domestic cattle) at first supported the hypothesis that Umm Qseir was a site for pastoralists taking seasonal advantage of the lush, late winter/early spring pasturage in the region. However, pigs did not fit easily into this scenario. Pigs have neither the legs nor the temperament for long-distance migration, and though there are some instances of pig drives in the past, swine are not customarily associated with pastoralists in the Near East. In fact, pigs are usually taken as markers of a sedentary lifestyle. It was possible, however, that Halafian Umm Qseirians drove a pig or two down to the area each spring along with their domestic sheep and goats. Information on both the age and, especially, the season of death of the pigs consumed at Umm Qseir was necessary to resolve this question. An examination of pig teeth from Umm Qseir indicated that the slaughter of swine at the site focused on animals 6 to 18 months of age. This is a common culling (slaughter) pattern for *domestic* swine. Yet, although there is an emphasis on young pigs, the kill-off of swine at Umm Qseir was not confined to piglets. There were also older animals, in the range of 3 to 4+ years, which is indicative of the presence of quite elderly swine at Umm Qseir. Not just one or two pigs were brought to the site each season; rather, a viable breeding herd must have been present.

The kill-off of pigs at Halafian Umm Qseir also reflected a strong seasonal pattern. Slaughter of swine seems to have been most common from May to October, particularly from August through October. This period includes the arid summer months and the early rainy season—the period of leanest resources in the region. Intensity of swine slaughter slackens in the months between November and April, the period of greatest bounty of plant and animal resources in the middle Khabur Basin.

Sheep and Goats Offer Additional Clues

We tentatively concluded that pigs were present at Umm Qseir throughout the year and that at least some Umm Qseir residents lived here on a permanent basis. But did all the residents live here all year long? Perhaps just a few people resided here year round, eating pigs in the hard times, to be joined by pastoralists in the late winter and early spring, pasturing their sheep and goats. To find the answer, we needed to look carefully at the sheep and goat age and seasonality data.

Sheep and goat age distributions indicate that culling focused on animals in the 1- to 2.5-year range. Once again, the bones told us that both young lambs and kids and older sheep and goats were eaten at the site. Seasonality data indicate relatively low kill-off in the first six months after birth (from February to July), and a peak in slaughter of lambs and kids in the second six months (between August and January). In the following six-month periods, mortality consistently slackens in the late winter and early spring and increases in the summer and fall. Once again, it is these months of the hot, dry summer and the sodden, unproductive early rainy season that are the hardest on herds in the region today. This is most likely season for kill-off of domestic sheep and goats from resident herds. It is, however, the least likely season for pastoralists to be here, since these are the hardest months in this region.

If these animal bones had been the result of nomadic pastoralist culling, they would have reflected a kill-off in the late winter and early spring, when flocks would have been brought to the southern region to feed on the luxuriant spring grasses of the steppe. In addition, there would be a virtual absence of animals in the more stressful dry summer and early winter months, when pastoralists with their herds would have headed north.

Wild Animal Clues

The biggest surprise from this collection of bones did not come from domestic animals, however, but from wild ones. Unlike contemporary and earlier sites on the northern steppe—where domesticated animals are overwhelmingly the most commonly eaten in early farming villages— at Halafian Umm Qseir, bones of domestic animals comprise less that half of the bone sample. Wild species dominate. People were eating gazelle, wild ass, wild cattle, deer, hare, turtles, fish, birds, and freshwater clams—all local wild resources in the area.

Seasonality data for the Umm Qseir gazelle add to our understanding of the subsistence economy. Many gazelles showed an advanced state of wear on the lower deciduous third molar, a tooth that is shed at about 14 months of age. Hence these animals were hunted and killed around the time of their first birthday. Since gazelle in the region give birth in March and April, this means there was special emphasis on spring gazelle hunting. Wild game attracted to the region to feed on the tasty spring grasses would have been easy prey during this time of year.

Final Clues from Plant Remains

Plant remains from Umm Qseir reinforce the picture painted by the faunal (animal) data; the site must have been occupied year-round. Contrary to our initial hypothesis, Halafian occupants of Umm Qseir were not pastoralists, but rather pioneering farmsteaders. People came to this previously uninhabited region, bringing with them their domestic sheep, goats, and pigs, as well as domestic crops—in effect carrying with them the basic elements of the Neolithic Revolution. In this relatively untouched environment with its plentiful wild resources, these early settlers did not march in lockstep to the drum of the Neolithic Revolution. They did not settle down to a traditional village life dependent on domestic resources. Nor did they use the area only as a seasonal feedlot for their domestic flocks. Instead, Halafian Umm Qseirians took full advantage of the natural (wild) riches of this new environment in its seasons of plenty, while relying on their domestic resources to tide them over the lean times. Spring was the most bountiful season at Umm Qseir—a time when crops of emmer, barley, and pulses were harvested, and when wild game feeding on the abundant spring growth of the steppe was easy prey. During the hotter summer months and into the unproductive winter season, when game was in all likelihood more dispersed across the steppe, Umm Qseirians could rely on stored grain, fall-fruiting wild shrubs and trees, and their domestic stock of sheep, goat, and pig.

NORTH AND SOUTH KHABUR BASIN COMPARED

Subsequent and ongoing analysis of animal and plant remains from seventeen sites in the Khabur Basin demonstrates that Umm Qseir is not unique, but rather is part of an increasingly interesting and unexpected picture of post-Neolithic subsistence in the region. These sites date from the first introduction of domesticated plants and animals into the region (8000–7000 B.C.) through the rise of the first state-level societies (3000–2000 B.C.). Village communities in the better-watered, more densely populated north (today a highly productive dry farming zone) followed the expected post-Neolithic subsistence pattern, with increasingly exclusive reliance on domestic crops and herd animals. Even so, there is evidence that wild animals remained relatively plentiful in the area up through about 3000 B.C. In contrast, for more than 2,000 years small, isolated communities on the drier southern steppe developed highly localized subsistence practices. Residents of the southern steppe mixed and matched selected domesticates with a heavy dependence on a variety of wild resources. People of the more arid, marginal, sparsely populated area apparently compensated for the unpredictability of a high-risk environment by expanding their resource base to include both domestic and wild resources. Significantly, the greatest dietary eclecticism seems to be found not in the fertile heartland but in the more arid frontier. In the more difficult environment, people met the challenge by combining their earlier reliance on wild game with newer domesticated resources.

CONCLUSION

There are no more herds of wild animals on today's treeless steppe. The rich diversity of wild plants that once supported these herds has been replaced by monocrop irrigated fields and by highly degraded pasture in outlying areas. The long-term environmental impact of intensive agropastoral economies on wild resources in this region is inarguable.

Our information indicates, however, that the onset of environmental degradation did not immediately follow the introduction of farming and herding. Early inhabitants of this region mixed agriculture and hunting/collecting without significant ill effects on indigenous wild species of plants or animals. Significant ecological change accompanied the urban-based, agricultural economy several thousand years after the establishment of the first farming communities in the region. The small sample of plant remains from sites on the southern steppe dating to the third millennium B.C. indicates that by this time hardwoods had been replaced by fast-growing shrubby plants, and animal dung had become the primary fuel source.

What does this case study of subsistence in the Khabur Basin tell us about the consequences of beginning agriculture in the Near East? Judging from this example, it would seem that the impact of the Neolithic Revolution was not nearly as uniform nor as irreversible as it is often portrayed. Once people became farmers and herders, many still continued to practice hunting and gathering, mixing old and new strategies. The times after the "revolution" do not conform to theories that see the origin of agriculture as either a technological blessing or an environmental blight that locked people into an economy based solely on domesticated resources. The story of post-Neolithic societies in northern Mesopotamia is far more nuanced than any of these broad-brush models would have it. There is, instead, a complex interplay between the environmental conditions that set the general parameters of pos-

sible subsistence strategies in a region, and a web of social and economic factors that shape the subsistence choices people make at different places and different times. A technology, once discovered, need not shackle people into its
exclusive practice; a social organization or an economy, once established, need
not be an immutable obstacle to cultural flexibility or human ingenuity.

UPDATE

It seems impossible that more than a decade has passed since I wrote the article "New Perspectives on Agricultural Origins in the Ancient Near East"
for *AnthroNotes*. A whole generation of secondary-school students has
grown and is now pursuing advanced studies or careers (some, I hope, as anthropologists). And yet when I reflect on the accomplishments that have been
made in understanding agricultural origins and impact over this time, I am
similarly impressed by how much we have done.

In particular, many strides have been made in identifying initial stages of
domestication in the archaeological record, providing a tight temporal
framework for these initial baby steps toward agriculture, and piecing together the great puzzle of how and why agriculture arose in the Near East.
Archaeologists are using new technologies, such as atomic mass spectrometry (AMS) radiocarbon dating, that allow us to precisely date small fragments
of early domesticates, giving us a much more refined and accurate picture
of the timing of initial domestication. They are collaborating with molecular
biologists, examining DNA of both modern ancestors of early domesticates
and ancient DNA from archaeological animal bones and plant remains to
trace the genetic shifts involved in the transition from wild to domestic.

In addition, we have been able to sharpen more traditional analytical techniques for identification of initial domesticates in the archaeological record.
Israeli botanist Mordechai Kislev's work with modern populations of wild
barley has shown us that seed types that we used to automatically accept as
domestic also occur in low numbers in the wild. We now know that we need
more than the presence of just one or two of these seeds to signal domestication. Instead, it is their prevalence in a sample of archaeological plant remains that is the leading indicator of domestication. Sue Colledge and Gordon Hilman, working in Syria, have done breakthrough work looking at the
weed complexes that coincide with deliberate cultivation, and they use the
presence of these weeds in archaeobotanical samples as an effective new
marker of cereal domestication.

My own work with modern wild and domestic goats has led to the development of a new and more sensitive way of detecting the shifts in the ages
and sexes of animals killed in the past that allows us to distinguish between

the animal harvest strategies used by hunters from those of herders. By reconstructing profiles of the ages and sexes of animals killed by ancient people, we can detect the earliest stages of human management of animals, which result in their domestication. For goats, human management first occurred in the heartland natural habitat zone of wild goats long before we see any alterations in physical skeletal features used in the past to identify early domestication. Molecular biologists have been working with the DNA of both modern plants and animals and ancient DNA to help pinpoint the location of the origin or, in many cases, origins of initial domestication of these now ubiquitous crops (wheat, barley, rye, oats, lentils, peas) and livestock animals (sheep, goats, pigs, cattle, horses).

The picture of agricultural origins that now emerges from all this work is one of a long transitional period during which people across the arc of the Fertile Crescent responded to the post–Ice Age recovery of wild cereals, pulses such as lentils and peas, nut trees, and the wild animals that depended upon them. The combination of plant and animal resources utilized by post–Ice Age peoples varied in different parts of this large territory. But in each place, we can use our new archaeological tools of AMS dating, DNA analysis, and more refined methods of identifying initial domestication to get a better picture of how and when people of the past settled down and became increasingly dependent on collecting wild cereals and hunting local game.

We also now know there was a sudden reversal in improving climates and a return to Ice Age conditions in a period called the Younger Dryas (11,000–10,000 years ago), followed by the beginning of climatic conditions similar to those found in the region today. It is at this point, across the whole Fertile Crescent that we begin to see clear signs of the domestication of different cereals and livestock animals. These climatic shifts, while not necessarily the sole cause of domestication, may then have helped both pull and push people into moving from intensive utilization of wild plant and animal resources to their deliberate cultivation and management through domestication. What all this work has shown us is that explanations of agricultural origins that rely on only one or two factors—climate change, technological innovation, over population, social competition—do not do justice to the complexities of the past. The origins of agriculture probably involved all these factors coming together in unique and complex ways that varied with each instance of domestication and agricultural emergence. Now, with the new tools for identifying and dating initial domestication at our disposal, we are in a fine position to work on these complex, but fascinating regional puzzles in a way never before possible.

The second area of advance over the past ten years has been the study of the social and environmental impact of agricultural origins and intensification. In my own work in the Khabur Basin, which I discussed in my original chapter, we have since analyzed many more bones from a large number of sites across this region, spanning a 5,000-year period from about 7500 to 2500 B.C. This work has largely confirmed the earlier picture gained from our first work at the tiny site of Umm Qseir. What we now see is that over the course of the first four and a half thousand years of occupation (from 7500 to about 3000 B.C.), people in different parts of the region followed a number of highly localized subsistence strategies. Small village communities in the better-watered northern part of the Khabur concentrated primarily on domesticated livestock and crops, with wild resources playing a relatively minor supporting role. However, several occupational layers at one of these northern communities contain an extraordinarily high proportion of wild game—gazelle, auroch, and onager—suggesting that a variety of game species were still available in some quantity in the northern steppe. In contrast, wild species were much more heavily utilized by settlements established in the more arid and more sparsely occupied southern portion of the region prior to the third millennium B.C. Wild animals, in fact, often predominate in southern settlements, with each site having its own distinctive signature mixture of wild and domestic resources.

Then in a brief period of about 500 years, beginning about 3000 B.C., people in the south abandoned these more localized strategies that focused so heavily on the unique combination of wild and domestic foods and began instead to concentrate almost exclusively on raising sheep and goats and growing fodder crops. At the same time people in the north were similarly eliminating wild resources from their diet in favor of domestic animals and crops plants. We also see a number of large cities and towns begin to emerge in the better-watered northern steppe. For a variety of reasons, I suspect that the abandonment of wild resources in the Khabur did not result from harmful human impact on the environment, at least not initially. Instead, it is likely that the shift toward a more uniform domestic subsistence economy had more to do with the need to produce large enough quantities of agricultural products—grain, meat, and perhaps most importantly wool—to feed and clothe urban-based potters, smiths, weavers, and bureaucrats living in cities. The environmental impact of the growth of a large, coordinated, urban-centered agropastoral economy in the region is inarguable. There are no herds of wild gazelle or onager today, nor are there many trees, native wild plants, or nondegraded pasture areas. But our work has continued to highlight the fact that environmental degradation is not an immediate automatic outcome of agriculture. Instead, this work shows that serious environmental impact may be a much delayed outgrowth of the emergence of cities, with the associated increase in scale of an agricultural economy and the growing need to feed large numbers of people not actively engaged in producing food for themselves.

Today, the study of the origins and the impact of ancient agriculture stands on an exciting threshold. Drawing from earlier work and utilizing an ever-expanding array of new scientific methods and tools for discovering the past, we are on the brink of remarkable discoveries and insights into how our ancestors became farmers and herders, leading us along the path to agriculture and city life that dominates our world today.

FURTHER READING

Bar-Yosef, O., and R. Meadow. 1995. "The Origins of Agriculture in the Near East." In D. Price and A. B. Gebauer, eds., *Last Hunters, First Farmers: New Perspectives on the Transition to Agriculture*, pp. 39–94. School of American Research Advanced Seminar Series. Santa Fe: School of American Research Press.

Clutton-Brock, Juliet. 1989. *The Walking Larder: Patterns of Domestication, Pastoralism, and Predation.* Unwin Hyman.

Cowan, C. W., and P. J. Watson. 1992. *The Origins of Agriculture: An International Perspective.* Smithsonian Institution Press.

Legge, Tony. 1996. "The Beginning of Caprine Domestication in Southwest Asia." In David R. Harris, ed., *The Origins and Spread of Agriculture and Pastoralism in Eurasia*, pp. 238–62. Smithsonian Institution Press.

Smith, Bruce D. 1998. *The Emergence of Agriculture.* W. H. Freeman.

Zeder, Melinda A. 1991. *Feeding Cities: Specialized Animal Economy in the Ancient Near East.* Smithsonian Institution Press.

Zeder, Melinda A. 1994. "After the Revolution: Post-Neolithic Subsistence in Northern Mesopotamia." *American Anthropologist* 96(1):97–126.

Zeder, Melinda A. 1998a. "Pigs and Emergent Complexity in the Ancient Near East. In Sarah Nelson, ed., *Ancestors for the Pigs*, pp. 109–22. MASCA Research Papers in Science and Archaeology. MASCA, University Museum, University of Pennsylvania.

Zeder, Melinda A. 1998b. "Environment, Economy, and Subsistence on the Threshold of Urban Emergence in Northern Mesopotamia." In Michel Fortin and Olivier Aurence, eds., *Espace Naturel, Espace Habité en Syrie Nord (10ᵉ–2ᵉ millénaire av. J.-C.)*, pp. 55–67. Bulletin of the Canadian Society for Mesopotamian Studies 33. The Canadian Society for Mesopotamian Studies.

Zeder, Melinda A. 1999. "Animal Domestication in the Zagros: A Review of Past and Current Research." *Paléorient* 25:11–25.

Zeder, M.A. 2001. "A Metrical Analysis of a Collection of Modern Goats (*Capra hircus aegargus* and *Capra hircus hircus*) from Iran and Iraq: Implications for the Study of Caprine Domestication." *Journal of Archaeological Science* 28:61–79.

Zeder, Melinda A. 2003. "Food Provisioning in Urban Societies: A View from Northern Mesopotamia." In Monica Smith, ed., *The Social Construction of Ancient Cities*, pp. 156–83. Smithsonian Institution Press.

Zeder, Melinda A., and Brian Hesse. 2000. "The Initial Domestication of Goats (*Capra hircus*) in the Zagros Mountains 10,000 Years Ago." *Science* 287: 2254–7.

14 PROGRESS? THE FACTS OF ANCIENT LIFE

Mark N. Cohen

Most people assume that history is the story of progress, and that human health, nutrition, and economic well-being have improved through time. The author uses three lines of evidence to demonstrate his opposing hypothesis that human nutrition has declined through human history, while the variety and types of diseases have increased. Cohen's update includes a discussion of the debate his original ideas engendered, and how he responded to his critics.

How many of us consciously or unconsciously assume that human history is largely a tale of progress through time? Can anyone dispute that the development of modern medicine, sanitation facilities, and almost universal education have brought us today to an era of great benefits for all? If we look far back into human history, did it not all begin with the "Neolithic Revolution," the domestication of plants and animals that ushered in sedentary farming, earliest cities, trade networks, large-scale governments, and craft specialization? Did not these, in turn, bring humankind to a new level of well-being from which progress could continue steadily up to today? [See Zeder, "Agricultural Origins in the Ancient World," in this volume.]

Most of our elementary, secondary, and college texts still reflect a deep human belief in the progress wrought by "civilized" life, by the developments growing out of ancient cities. Unfortunately, our sense of human history as steady progress in human well-being does not accord with the actual data at hand. Instead, the facts provide innumerable clues that "civilized" living has been accomplished only at considerable cost to most of the players. We

THREE METHODS OF RECONSTRUCTING PATTERNS OF HEALTH & NUTRITION

need to revise our thinking, our teaching, and our textbooks to reflect this information.

RECONSTRUCTING THE PAST

Scientists use three main means of reconstructing patterns of health and nutrition in ancient societies. The first method focuses on small groups (hunter-gatherers) in the modern world to offer clues about our prehistoric ancestors. The !Kung San of the Kalahari (sometimes known as the Bushmen) come to mind most readily, but there are dozens of such groups (among whom the vaunted "affluent" San actually appear somewhat impoverished) scattered across the various continents [see Fisher, "Ethnoarchaeology Among the Efe: African Hunter-Gatherers," in this volume].

The second method relies on what geologists call "uniformitarian" reasoning to argue that natural processes—in this case the processes of nutrition and disease—must have operated in the past much as they do today and can therefore be reliably reconstructed. The third and most recently exploited method analyzes the skeletons of prehistoric populations to measure health and disease. Although many skeletons are now being reburied, there were once many thousands available for study. Many prehistoric communities were each represented by several hundred skeletons. There are, for example, six hundred representing one Maya town in my own small college laboratory—a fairly good sample from which conclusions could be drawn about health and disease in an ancient community.

None of these three methods—looking at modern hunters and gatherers, studying modern disease processes, or analyzing ancient skeletal remains—

is wholly satisfactory. Contemporary hunting and gathering populations do live in the modern world, after all, so they are not exact prototypes of prehistoric groups. Disease processes involve living organisms that can evolve; thus they may not adhere to uniformitarian principles as reliably as do rocks. And prehistoric skeletons document only a limited sample of human ills. But the three methods taken together gain strength, often supporting one another in the manner of the legs of a tripod.

In any case, these three types of evidence are the only information that we have ever had concerning prehistoric health, or that was available to Hobbes or Rousseau or any of the more recent philosophers, historians, and educators who write the textbooks and the history books we use with our students. Taken together, the three types of evidence paint a picture very different from the one we were shown as children, and it is important to correct the erroneous old images of progress still found in many of our "authoritative" texts.

EVIDENCE ON NUTRITION

The evidence suggests, first, that the quality of human nutrition—the balance of vitamins, fats, minerals, and protein—has for the most part declined through human history except, of course, among the ruling classes. We talk of twentieth-century increases in stature (humans getting taller) as proof of improving nutrition, yet prehistoric hunting and gathering populations were often as tall as, if not taller than, the populations that replaced them, and the predominant trend in human stature since early prehistory has been downward. (The people of Europe of the seventeenth and eighteenth centuries to whom we usually compare ourselves with pride are, in fact, among the shortest people who ever lived.) Eclectic diets of fresh vegetable foods with some meat apparently ensure hunting and gathering populations a good balance of vitamins and minerals, and in fact such groups generally have access to relatively large amounts of meat and protein, rivaling consumption in the affluent United States and exceeding modern Third World averages by a large margin.

Modern hunter-gatherers rarely display clinical manifestations of protein deficiency, iron deficiency anemia, or deficiencies of any other vitamin or mineral even when more "sophisticated" farmers nearby are deficient. To the initial surprise of health teams, infantile and childhood malnutrition, marasmus and kwashiorkor, are also quite rare among hunter-gatherers. These diseases are more common among sharecroppers or other modern populations forced by poverty to rely on a single food such as rice or maize. The most poorly nourished people turn out to be the poor or lower classes of historic and modern "civilized" states from which modern trade systems withhold or actively withdraw various nutrients.

The most common shortage among modern hunter-gatherers is one of calories. Paradoxically to any American who has ever gone on a diet, modern hunter-gatherers tend to be chronically lean while otherwise well nourished, probably as a result of exercising and eating lean animal products and high-roughage vegetable foods. They get no "free" processed calories. In addition, modern hunter-gatherers are making a living in some of the poorest environments on earth, the only environments still left to them after the expansion of modern states.

The skeletons of prehistoric hunter-gatherers generally confirm this sense of good nutrition. They commonly show fewer signs of porotic hyperostosis (the skeletal manifestation of a type of anemia) than the skeletons of later populations. Rickets (bending of bones), a disease of vitamin D deficiency reflecting poor diet and/or lack of exposure to sunlight, is primarily a disease of modern cities and is extremely rare either in modern hunter-gatherers or in ancient skeletons. Teeth of early archaeological populations display relatively little enamel hypoplasia, the scars of infantile illnesses, or periods of malnutrition, which are permanently recorded in the teeth.

Whether the reliability of human food supplies has improved with time is one of the most controversial and most important issues that needs to be resolved in assessing the "march of human progress" through time. There are many anecdotes about hunger or starvation among historic and modern hunter-gatherers. However, these typically occur in the Arctic or in extreme deserts, where more advanced civilizations do not even try to compete, or they occur in contexts where modern states restrict the movement of hunters or limit their activities. To judge by the relative efficiency with which different kinds of wild foods can be obtained, prehistoric hunter-gatherers would have been particularly well off when they lived in environments of their own choosing and before large game animals (one of the richest food sources) were depleted, as appears to have been the case on every continent occupied by early people. We like to think that modern transportation and storage capabilities have alleviated hunger, and they can; nevertheless, farmed fields may be inherently less stable than naturally selected wild resources. Being mobile may be safer in the face of famine than being sedentary.

Moreover, storage and transportation can fail; governments can and do refuse to help the needy; and in a world of economic specialists and private property, people may be unable to command the price of food even when food is plentiful. We have to remember that any government, the institution that can protect its people, is double-edged, since it is almost always in some way protecting a privileged class. Modern trade networks inevitably move food (both calories and quality nutrients) away from some populations in favor of others.

The archaeological record of skeletons reflects no steady record of improvement. In fact, if the clues in our teeth are used as the measure, one could argue that the frequency of stressful episodes to which the average individual has been exposed generally increases through time in most parts of the world. The historical record of famine in Europe, Russia, or China over the past several centuries also suggests no improvement until perhaps the last 150 years—and, of course, people in the Third World are still not protected from starvation.

DISEASES THROUGH TIME

In addition to the decline in the quality of human nutrition, the second point confirmed by all three types of evidence is that the variety and intensity of human infections and infectious diseases have generally increased through human history. Epidemiological theory predicts that diseases will not be transmitted as readily among small groups of people who change their base camp periodically as they are when people live in large permanent human settlements.

Diseases transmitted directly from person to person via the air or by touch, such as influenza, operate most efficiently when population density is high and large crowds are gathered (that is one reason why schools and other similar institutions commonly help disease to spread). Diseases that spread through human feces (including cholera, most other diarrhea, and hookworm) will obviously be most dangerous for large permanent populations where feces accumulate. Historic outbreaks of cholera in London occurred amid high-density populations whose wells had been contaminated by latrines. Such conditions also facilitate the spread of diseases such as bubonic plague, which are carried by rats or other parasites on accumulations of human garbage. And as the experiences of American Indians after the arrival of Columbus demonstrate, long-distance travel and large-scale trade can spread diseases with devastating effect (it has been estimated that 90 percent of the Native American population was destroyed by disease). The history of bubonic plague in France, which decimated large port cities but left villages in the interior unharmed, is a good example of the dangers of urban living and, conversely, the ability of small size and isolated population patterns to provide protection against infectious diseases.

It is, in fact, a fairly commonplace observation that hunting and gathering bands are relatively infection-free and that the rates of many diseases increase when mobile hunters are settled in larger permanent camps. The skeletal record again provides confirmation. Signs of infection in the skeleton become more common as people settle in large-scale cities in essentially every region of the ancient world where the appropriate study has been done. In addition, the low incidence of anemia among ancient hunter-gatherers is thought by many scholars to reflect low rates of parasitic infestation as much or more than diet. Tuberculosis, one of the specific diseases that can often be detected in skeletons, is conspicuously absent or quite scarce in the archaeological record until relatively recent times.

Moreover, many "epidemic" diseases appear to require a critical threshold of population size (either in one place or connected by rapid transport) in order to spread. Measles, mumps, smallpox, influenza, and German measles all appear to need large and rapidly reproducing human populations to survive. The implication is that these diseases did not spread until the recent growth of cities and transportation networks. However, once many Europeans were immunized by constant childhood exposure, these diseases became major vehicles of conquest in the spread of European hegemony. These diseases not only killed many Native Americans but also appeared to provide evidence that Europeans were divinely favored.

Many other diseases that plague modern populations are also rare or absent in modern hunter-gatherers. High blood pressure is generally not found in hunter-gatherers regardless of age, "racial type," or location. Diets naturally low in sodium may be one reason; another may be the lack of the fatty buildup in blood vessels that contributes to widespread high blood pressure, strokes, and heart attacks. Diabetes also seldom occurs among hunter-gatherers, although the same individuals may be prone to diabetes when fed a modern diet. Bowel and breast cancer are relatively rare in populations who do not live a modern lifestyle. While this is sometimes attributed to a lower life expectancy, in fact the proportion of adults over age sixty in hunting and gathering societies can be comparable to that of our own.

LIFE EXPECTANCY

The history of human life expectancy is difficult to reconstruct. Life expectancy, the number of years an individual can expect to live, refers to a rough average of age at death in a population, not to how long the oldest individuals live. (A group will have a life expectancy of forty if half the group lives to eighty and half the group dies at birth.) We can observe modern hunter-gatherers and measure their individual life spans, but in most cases the cause of death will be something that was not part of ancient life, such as a tuberculosis epidemic. Most observed deaths are from infectious diseases, and most of those are diseases we consider modern. We can determine the ages of skeletal populations, but they may not be complete. Moreover, while it is relatively easy to establish the age of children from their teeth and unfused bones, determining the age of adults is difficult and inexact. Nevertheless, the combined data suggest that our early ancestors had a life expectancy at birth of about twenty-five years, a low figure but one that again compares favorably with figures from much of urban Europe as late as the eighteenth or nineteenth century, and from India well into the twentieth.

In particular, hunters and gatherers seem to have been fairly successful in rearing their young. A survey of all of the known modern hunter-gatherer populations suggests that they lose an average of 20 percent of their children as infants and about 45 percent before adulthood, figures that accord reasonably well with the evidence of ancient skeletons. These figures, terrible as they are, compare favorably with most of Europe prior to about 1850 and with many major American cities as late as the turn of the last century.

CONCLUSION

The point of the foregoing remarks is that our models of history—the models that consciously or unconsciously shape our planning for the future—are misleading. They are based too much on the experience of the privileged classes, which mistake their privilege for progress. In the seventeenth century, Thomas Hobbes characterized primitive life as "nasty, brutish, and short" at a time when life for most of his compatriots was apparently shorter and was certainly nastier, at least for all those outside the ruling classes, than it was in earlier populations.

We do not simply progress. Many aspects of so-called civilization—the adoption of sedentary farming, cities, trade, social class distinctions—are mixed blessings for the participants. It is more accurate to see history as simple population growth and the endless competition between ever larger political units in which some societies lose and some societies win, without necessarily generating benefits for all of their citizens.

It is particularly important to be aware of our own biases and our often unconscious desire to believe in progress, as well as our tendency to forget the larger frames of reference through which human history develops. The facts of ancient human life not only inform the understanding of our past but also help us plan more carefully for the future.

UPDATE

Knowledge has grown on many fronts in the last decade, particularly those concerned with individual diseases and individual historical situations. Articles in the *Annual Review of Anthropology* in 1992 and 1993 reviewed new knowledge of nutritional adaptation, prehistoric arthritis, and the transfer of diseases from Europe to the Americas after Columbus (Dobyns 1993). The latter subject also is the focus of two books, by Larsen and Milner (1994) and Verano and Ubelaker (1992). The causes and effects of the adoption of agriculture were debated in several articles in *Current Anthropology* and *American Anthropologist* for the same years. A book by Stuart-Macadam and Kent (1992) debates and refines the meaning of the skeletal pathology known as porotic hyperostosis, caused by anemia.

A major challenge prevails concerning the interpretation of data from skeletal pathology, which contributed significantly to this chapter, and to the books on which it was based. Cohen (1991, and this chapter) used the relative frequency of visible pathology in prehistoric skeletons to represent or at least approximate the relative frequency of disease in the once-living populations—a common practice among skeletal pathologists. Critics writing in *Current Anthropology* (Wood et al. 1992) argued that while this interpretation may be correct, other interpretations are possible. For example, since responses to disease are slow to develop in the skeleton, an increase in skeletal pathology might not mean more disease but an increase in the proportion of individuals who survived the diseases long enough to develop skeletal scars. Increased visible skeletal pathology, they argue, *could* paradoxically be a sign of relatively good health or at least greater longevity.

In response, Cohen (1992) noted that epidemiological and ethnographic studies of living people independently suggest that the various pathological conditions (and diseases) discussed should be expected to have increased during the economic transitions in question—so Cohen's argument is supported by two other lines of evidence. What we know about the history of infection and nutrition suggests that hunter-gatherers were better nourished and freer of background infections than later populations. Since background nutrition and preexisting infections are major determinants in the outcome of disease, later populations were probably not more likely to survive episodes of disease. Furthermore, alternate explanations that might explain changes in pathology in individual populations are not able to explain the worldwide trends in visible pathology described. For example, improved survivorship cannot explain the visible worldwide trend toward increased skeletal pathology after the adoption of farming. Population growth rates before and after the adoption of farming (the change in the average rate is extremely small) indicate there cannot possibly have been a large enough increase in survivorship on a world scale to account for the large increases in visible skeletal pathology. In fact, since there is some evidence that human fertility went up after the adoption of farming (Cohen 1991; Wood et al. 1992)—which could easily account for the very slight acceleration in population growth—

it is unlikely that survivorship increased at all. In fact, it may well have declined. The debate continues.

It is also important to point out that the overall conclusions about the rise of civilization—and the very meaning of civilization—presented in this chapter have not been challenged. There seems to be a broad sense within anthropology, medicine, and nutrition that the data and recent conclusions in the field as a whole are well represented in the chapter and in Cohen's book (originally published in 1989), even though the conclusions come as a surprise to nonprofessionals.

Since the first edition of *Anthropology Explored* was published, a number of new studies have been added to the available evidence representing a wider range of areas of the world including South and Southeast Asia and Japan, Mesoamerica, and South America (see partial summaries in Larsen 1995, 2000; Steckel and Rose 2002). The new samples largely but not universally conform to the expectations described in this chapter. *Digging for Pathogens* (Greenblatt 1998) and the forthcoming expanded edition of that book provide an introduction to the exciting new techniques for determining prehistoric patterns of disease based on DNA research and the study of antibodies. With these new research techniques, prehistoric tuberculosis, leprosy, and syphilis now can be identified in skeletons whether or not the skeletons show gross pathology. This is a field that is rapidly expanding.

FURTHER READING

Aufderheide, Arthur C., and Conrado Rodriguez-Martin, eds. 1998. *The Cambridge Encyclopedia of Human Paleopathology*. Cambridge University Press.

Cohen, Mark Nathan. 1991. *Health and the Rise of Civilization*. Yale University Press.

Cohen, Mark Nathan. 1992. "The Osteological Paradox Reconsidered." *Current Anthropology* 33:358–59.

Cohen, Mark Nathan. 1998. *Culture of Intolerance: Chauvinism, Class, and Racism in the United States*. Yale University Press.

Dobyns, Henry F. 1993. "Disease Transfer at Contact." *Annual Review of Anthropology* 22:273–91.

Greenblatt, Charles L., ed. 1998. *Digging for Pathogens: Ancient Emerging Diseases—Their Evolutionary, Anthropological, and Archaeological Context*. Balaban Press. (Forthcoming expanded volume from Oxford University Press.)

Kiple, Kenneth, and Kriemhild Conee Ornelas. 2000. *The Cambridge World History of Food*. Cambridge University Press.

Larsen, Clark Spencer. 1995. "Biological Changes in Human Populations with Agriculture." *Annual Review of Anthropology* 24:185–213.

Larsen, Clark Spencer. 2000. *Skeletons in Our Closet: Revealing Our Past Through Bioarchaeology*. Princeton University Press.

Larsen, Clark Spencer, and George R. Milner, eds. 1994. *In the Wake of Contact: Biological Responses to Conquest.* Wiley-Liss.

Steckle, Richard, and Jerry Rose, eds. 2002. *The Backbone of History.* Cambridge University Press.

Stuart-Macadam, Patricia, and Susan Kent, eds. 1992. *Diet, Demography and Disease: Changing Perspectives on Anemia.* Aldine de Gruyter.

Verano, John W., and Douglas H. Ubelaker, eds. 1992. *Disease and Demography in the Americas.* Smithsonian Institution Press.

Wood, James W., George R. Milner, Henry C. Harpending, and Kenneth M. Weiss. 1992. "The Osteological Paradox." *Current Anthropology* 33: 343–58.

15 ETHNOARCHAEOLOGY AMONG THE EFE

African Hunter-Gatherers

John W. Fisher Jr.

Jack Fisher and his wife, Helen Strickland, have lived in two of the most remote and isolated areas of the world: the Ituri Forest of the Democratic Republic of the Congo and the Kalahari Desert in northeastern Namibia. In both locations, they conducted ethnoarchaeological research, seeking clues to human adaptation to extreme environments as well as trying to better understand the archaeological sites of our prehistoric ancestors. This article and its recent update explain many similarities between the Efe of the Ituri Forest and the Ju/'hoansi (!Kung San or Bushmen) of the Kalahari Desert, documenting the changes in the lifeways and values of present-day hunter-gatherers as they give up their traditional nomadic way of life and become progressively sedentary, often as a consequence of external forces such as development and globalization.

The tall, dark green forest canopy on each side of the dirt road pressed closer and closer together overhead with each passing mile of westward travel. As the emerald-green grasslands of the former Zaire-Uganda border country dwindled behind us, I sat high in the back of our Toyota Hilux pickup on a pile of food, gasoline containers, Toyota spare parts, camp supplies, and shovels and hoes that we always carried to dig the pickup out of deep mud. Our destination: the Ituri Forest Project's field station in a remote area of the Ituri Forest inhabited by the Efe Pygmies. This station—where Helen Strickland, my wife, and I would live for a year—lies along an almost impenetrable narrow track, one and one-half days' journey and more than 120 kilometers from the eastern edge of the forest. Here, the villages of the sedentary horticulturists and their wide swaths of cleared and cultivated land are fewer and more widely separated than in the forest margins or on its main roads.

INDEPENDENT HUNTER-GATHERERS OR SERFS?

The various groups of Ituri Forest Pygmies, collectively called Mbuti by their village neighbors (or BaMbuti, meaning "Mbuti people"), are well known to anthropologists through studies by English, Japanese, American, and German scholars. Although they have been cited as a classic example of tropical forest hunter-gatherers, their economic independence from village agriculturists has been much disputed. In the 1920s and 1930s, Paul Schebesta, a German anthropologist, noted in the first comprehensive study of the Mbuti their strong reliance on cultivated foods from the gardens of villagers, to whom Mbuti were bound in a type of master-serf relationship. He expressed doubt that the Pygmies he saw could have survived without such foods. Perhaps the best-known studies, however, are those of the English anthropologist Colin Turnbull (1961), who worked with a group of Mbuti net hunters about 110 kilometers southwest of our research area. Turnbull argued that the Mbuti were not dependent on their sedentary horticulturist neighbors for basic staples but could live off the wild foods of the forest for extended periods. Although the Mbuti often chose to participate in a symbiotic relationship with the villagers, in which each group provided the other with certain foods (bananas, manioc, game meat) and services (field labor, initiation and funeral rites), Turnbull described Mbuti culture as an independent entity, based on identity with a dependence on the forest.

THE ITURI PROJECT

The Efe are one of the most isolated Pygmy groups and hunt almost entirely with bows and arrows rather than with nets. One of the goals of the Ituri Project, which began in 1980, was to document the subsistence practices of the Efe, as part of a broad study of their adaptation to a forest environment. During the 1960s and early 1970s the project codirector, Irven DeVore, had helped direct the Harvard Kalahari Project, an ecologically oriented study of the Ju/'hoansi (!Kung San or Bushmen) of the Kalahari Desert in Botswana. The Ituri Project, one of the first comprehensive studies of human ecology, demography, and health and nutrition among tropical forest hunter-gatherers (and horticulturists), was designed to build on and further explore some of the results of the Kalahari study. In particular, the Kalahari project had demonstrated a major reliance on vegetable foods, long birth spacing, low fertility, and a high degree of personal and group mobility among desert hunter-gatherers. These conclusions were further corroborated by other studies of desert hunter-gatherers in Australia. Would these adaptations persist in the more stable environment of the tropical forest? Did the cyclical fluctuation of wet and dry seasons in the forest affect group structure and mobility in the same way as the seasonal changes of the desert? What were the major resource limitations for humans in this environment, where most mammals are small and many dwell in the forest canopy? How independent were the Efe of their village horticulturist neighbors, the Lese?

Since 1980 more than a dozen anthropologists and other researchers have come to the Ituri field station to gain a relatively long-term perspective on the cyclical fluctuations in the forest environment and on the ways in which the Efe and the Lese have adapted to this environment (Bailey and DeVore 1989). These researchers have observed a symbiotic relationship between the Efe and the Lese. For instance, two-thirds of the calories the Efe consume come from cultivated foods—bananas, manioc, rice, peanuts, sweet potatoes, and other plants—grown mostly in Lese gardens. Efe women, in return for these foods, assist the Lese in planting, caring for, and harvesting the gardens. Efe men help the Lese by clearing patches of forest for gardens and by providing honey, meat, and other forest products. In exchange, the Lese provide the Efe with such items as metal tools and clothing. Efe sometimes plant small gardens, but their mobile lifestyle, moving to a new camp every two or three weeks, is not compatible with the constant care that gardens require in the tropical forest.

Forest foods make up one-third of the calories in the Efe diet. These foods include wild plants such as yams and the olive-sized fruit of the African canarium tree, honey, fish, and meat. Several species of duiker (small antelope) and monkey are their primary prey. Less frequently, they hunt animals up to the size of buffalo and elephant. Men, armed with metal-tipped arrows, hunt duiker using a variety of strategies. One method involves a man and dogs working together to flush out game while other men, carefully and quietly positioned, wait for duiker to come within arrow range. On other occasions, a solitary man waits in quiet ambush on a platform built in a tree of ripe fruit. In the early morning and late afternoon duiker will feed on fruit that have dropped to the ground, and, if lucky, the hunter will get a shot at an animal.

Monkeys are hunted with poison-tipped arrows, their wooden shaft carved to an extremely fine point. Poison, made from several forest plants, is applied to the tip and dried over the coals of a fire. To hunt monkeys in the forest trees, solitary hunters stalk their prey quietly and when within range of the animal shoot several arrows.

Despite the hunting skill of the Efe, we and other researchers find it diffi-cult to imagine that the Efe could live in the forest in the absence of culti-vated foods, on which they seem to rely quite heavily. Forest ecologists work-ing elsewhere in the Ituri Forest were not able to identify among the wild plants gathered by the Efe year-round abundant sources of carbohydrates comparable to the mongongo nuts and roots collected by the Ju/'hoansi. If cultivated carbohydrate-rich staples are essential to human existence in the tropical forest, then human occupation of the deep forest may be limited to the last 2,000 to 3,000 years, since the domestication of food crops in Africa.

THE ARCHAEOLOGY OF PRESENT-DAY EFE LIFE

As archaeologists, Helen and I were to document the material remains of Efe life, just as the Harvard Kalahari Project had done for the Ju/'hoansi (Yellen 1977). My interest in hunter-gatherers came from my work with the mate-rial remains of prehistoric hunter-gatherers of the Great Plains, such as I found at sites in Colorado with bones of bison and mammoth, as well as stone spear tips and other artifacts left by people long ago. The interpreta-tion of these ancient sites, however, requires some insight into hunter-gatherer ecology and behavior. Was this the kind of debris normally deposited near or in the family dwelling, or were these the kinds of bones and stone tools normally left at a kill location? How much and what parts of the skeleton were usually left behind when a mammoth (or elephant) or other animal was butchered? How many people did a mammoth feed, and how often would one have been killed? What kinds of debris did other food-procurement prac-tices generate? Can group size and organization be reconstructed from an-cient debris patterning? How is domestic space organized and used? By care-fully observing the Efe as they carried out routine activities at their campsites, we hoped to learn how to make sense out of the ancient pieces of bone and stone and other clues at archaeological sites, to reconstruct what life was like in the past.

A central question concerns the degree to which the camp design, activity patterns, and disposal practices of hunter-gatherers are universal among all hunter-gatherer groups or are affected by different environments or cultural rules. Archaeologists had often assumed that tools and bones found together related to a single activity, spatially segregated from other activities. The Kalahari research, however, suggested that hunter-gatherer camps were small, closely spaced circles of ephemeral huts. Since most in-camp activities were conducted around the family hearth in front of the hut, debris from many distinct but spatially overlapping activities tended to be concentrated in a ring surrounding an open public space. Only messy activities were carried out in special activity areas on the outskirts of Ju/'hoansi camps. Since the size of the debris ring was proportional to the number of huts, it could be used to estimate the number of families and hence the population of a Ju/'hoansi camp. If these patterns and others were also present among tropical and Arctic hunter-gatherers, then perhaps the patterning could be used to understand the hunter-gatherer sites on the Great Plains 11,000 years ago.

The research that Helen and I carried out benefited considerably from the work of other researchers on the project. Their studies give a detailed picture of Efe subsistence practices and of other aspects of their adaptations to the forest environment. Thus we had a strong foundation from which to focus on material aspects of Efe life, in particular the spatial organization of their camps. We found that although each campsite is unique in the details of camp layout, all camps conform to a single general pattern (Fisher and Strickland 1989).

The first step in setting up an Efe camp is to clear away smaller trees and undergrowth. The size of these clearings ranges from 40 square meters to about 550 square meters, depending on the camp population. The number of people living at a camp ranges from three to about thirty-five or forty. Each nuclear family inhabits a dome-shaped hut made of a frame of saplings covered with broad leaves. Huts are situated near the perimeter of the camp in an oval layout. Each hut has one or more fires inside for warmth at night and a fire outside the hut near the door.

Trash heaps, located beside and behind the huts, are a feature of all camps. Initially composed of cleared brush, the Efe trash heaps continue to grow through the life of the camp as its inhabitants discard food remains, ashes from fires, and worn-out or broken implements.

The placement of huts within a camp is strongly influenced by interpersonal relationships and kinship ties. Families that get along particularly well will situate their huts close together, whereas those that are feuding will place themselves a good distance apart.

The location of day-to-day campsite activities—preparing food, eating, making and repairing implements, socializing, and relaxing—conforms to a pattern. Almost all such activities are performed inside the camp perimeter. For safety reasons, applying poison to arrows is usually done outside of camp. Children's play takes place inside the camp and in some cases in a separate area cleared nearby.

The fireplace situated outside the doorway of each hut serves as the focus for many activities. Women sit beside the fire to prepare and to cook food. Men relax and socialize by the fire, and here they also get ready for the hunt, carving new arrow shafts, sharpening metal arrowheads, or strengthening their bow stave over the hot coals. During a rainstorm, these activities are conducted inside the hut. Most of the debris generated by these activities eventually ends up on the trash heaps.

Efe huts vary considerably in size. Floor area ranges from about 1.3 square meters to 13.6 square meters (the average is 5.1 square meters). To our surprise, we discovered that the size of a hut does not correlate with the number of people who live in it. Some large huts had only two or three occupants; conversely, some small huts were the home of five or six people. A partial explanation might be that sleeping arrangements, especially among children, are fairly loose at Efe camps. One night the children may sleep in their parents' hut and the next night in that of their grandparents. Even adults sometimes move around. And if one family moves away to another camp, an incoming family might inhabit the empty hut rather than build its own. This loose fit between hut size and number of occupants is distressing archaeologically; it means that archaeologists cannot estimate accurately the population of a camp on the basis of the floor area of individual huts. However, this loose fit might not be characteristic of other hunter-gatherer societies; further studies might be illuminating in this regard.

The makeup of Efe camps is rather fluid. Families and individuals move in and move away during the life span of a camp. This flexibility seems to be characteristic of most or all hunter-gatherer societies. Sometimes, during the life span of a campsite, one (or more) of the families will abandon their hut and build a new one at the same camp. This behavior could confuse archaeologists into thinking that more families had lived at the camp than was the case, because there would be little archaeological evidence for recognizing that the same family had lived sequentially in two huts. Hence, the archaeologist probably would overestimate the number of families that had lived at the camp.

Efe reoccupation of a recently abandoned camp is another fairly common behavior that could lead archaeologists into overestimating camp population.

Some families might reinhabit the hut they had previously lived in. Often, however, one or more families will build a new hut and leave their previous one unoccupied. The reason for returning to an abandoned camp goes back, at least in part, to Efe ties with the Lese. Although Efe move from one camp to another rather frequently, they usually do not move very far. Lese villages and gardens are a fixed point on the landscape where Efe obtain material sustenance and social interaction. As a consequence, Efe rarely move more than a day's journey away from their affiliate village.

We discovered that when the Efe move camp, they sometimes leave behind a wide variety of possessions such as clay pots, glass bottles, baskets, and sharpening stones. They do this, we think, because of the restricted mobility that is characteristic of their settlement pattern. Clay pots, for example, are heavy and breakable compared with their aluminum pots. During the honey season, when they move deeper into the forest, the Efe might leave clay pots behind, knowing that they eventually will return to the vicinity of their previous camp and retrieve these belongings. It seems unlikely that other hunter-gatherer societies that have a more wide-ranging and less "tethered" settlement pattern would practice this kind of storage to the same extent as the Efe do.

COMPARING THE EFE TO OTHER HUNTER-GATHERERS

The knowledge gained during our year studying the Efe has considerable potential for assisting archaeologists in interpreting prehistoric archaeological sites with respect to questions such as the possible size range of the population that lived at the site, the length of time the site was occupied, the nature of activities carried out at the site, and the practice of storing implements. However, we must recognize that the patterns of the Efe cannot be casually generalized as a model for all prehistoric hunter-gatherer societies.

A comparison of Efe and other present-day hunter-gatherers, including the Ju/'hoansi and various groups in Australia, reveals that despite many similarities with these peoples, some important differences set the Efe apart. Similarities exist, for example, in the general layout of Efe and Ju/'hoansi camp-sites. A Ju/'hoansi camp consists of a circular arrangement of closely spaced brush huts, each hut the home of a nuclear family. As with the Efe and other Mbuti Pygmy groups, the distance separating huts in a Ju/'hoansi camp is swayed, in part, by kinship ties and interpersonal relationships. A family fire is situated in front of the hut at a Ju/'hoansi camp, and a wide variety of domestic tasks is carried out around the fire.

Differences between Efe and Ju/'hoansi camps emerge in some details of layout and use. Trash heaps are not a feature of all Ju/'hoansi camps; those occupied for less than two weeks might lack them altogether. Ju/'hoansi campsites tend to cover a larger area than Efe sites, and the amount of camp space per person is greater among the Ju/'hoansi. Habitation sites of Western Desert Aborigines in Australia far exceed the Efe and Ju/'hoansi in both these attributes. And when Ju/'hoansi move out of a camp, they leave behind few or no possessions for future reuse other than nut-cracking stones.

One of the great challenges facing archaeologists today is to explain the similarities and the differences among hunter-gatherer groups. Recent studies have suggested that Australian Aborigine campsites are much larger than those of the Ju/'hoansi because there is little fear of natural predators in Australia. The Kalahari Desert, on the other hand, is home to several dangerous animals, notably lions, leopards, and hyenas. However, this explanation probably does not account for the small size of Efe campsites. We never heard Efe express anxiety about predators—in fact, the greatest danger comes from the falling branches of trees. More likely, they build compact camps to keep within sight and sound of each other, thus maintaining a physical and emotional cohesiveness in the dense forest.

If we could spend another year in the Ituri, what questions would we address? We would like to explore the way material goods move between the Lese and the Efe and among neighboring Efe bands. Which objects are owned individually and which are treated as communal property? What factors influence the size of huts and of domestic space if not the number of occupants? These and other questions will continue to draw archaeologists such as ourselves to the Ituri, the Kalahari, the Arctic, the Australian deserts, Malaysia, and other areas to study living hunter-gatherers.

UPDATE

The spatial organization of hunter-gatherer residential campsites can be studied from an almost limitless variety of research directions. Careful analysis of our maps of Efe campsites reveals, for example, that one can reconstruct the location of dwellings at a campsite by studying the spatial relationships between fireplaces and trash heaps (Fisher and Strickland 1991). This has considerable importance for archaeologists investigating prehistoric campsites, for although actual dwellings are unlikely to be preserved at most sites, there is a stronger chance of uncovering fireplaces and nonperishable debris discarded onto trash heaps. Reconstruction of the location and number of dwellings at ancient sites provides archaeologists with powerful information for making inferences about the size of those communities and the use of space for living and social arrangements.

In an ethnoarchaeological study of Alyawara campsites in Australia, James

O'Connell (1987) made a number of interesting and archaeologically important discoveries. For one thing, the distribution within a site of discarded debris is strongly influenced by the size of the discarded item. Larger items tend to be tossed directly onto a nearby trash pile, whereas small items are often dropped right at the activity area where they are used. Moreover, additional sorting by size occurs when activity areas are swept during camp cleanup; smaller items often inadvertently remain behind at the activity area rather than being relocated onto a trash heap. The archaeological significance of size sorting is that items that are used separately and that have no functional relationship to one another could end up lying side by side simply because they have a similar size. At Alyawara camps, small items such as razor blades and soda can pop-tops often lie in close proximity to one another even though these items were not connected by the same activity. Conversely, soda cans and pop-tops, which are used and discarded as part of a single activity (drinking a can of soda), did not occur together on the ground. The difference in size between cans and lids caused them to become separated at and after discard. This finding reinforces an important lesson: archaeologists investigating ancient sites need to give up the long-cherished belief that close spatial proximity of excavated objects constitutes sufficient evidence, by itself, to signify that those items had been used together in a particular activity.

Changes in the lifeways and values of present-day hunter-gatherers as they give up a nomadic way of life and become progressively sedentary, often as a consequence of external forces, have a substantial effect on the spatial organization of their residential sites. The camps of traditional Ju/'hoansi (!Kung) in the Kalahari, as discussed earlier in the chapter, were arranged in a compact circle, and hut doorways usually faced into the camp center. Privacy was not an overriding concern, and residents could see into one another's huts. As the Ju/'hoansi in Botswana became more sedentary, their camps lost this intimacy. The arrangement of huts became more linear, with greater space separating adjacent huts. In this changing way of life, the increased accumulation of personally owned items, denoting wealth, exacerbated the desire for greater privacy. These changes, examined by John Yellen (1990) among Ju/'hoansi in Botswana, reflect profound shifts in the economy and value system of these people.

Additional changes in site structure resulting from the effects of increased sedentism have been reported among peoples elsewhere in the Kalahari Desert (Hitchcock 1987). Trash dumps are larger at the sites of sedentary groups, and the distance from hearths and houses (working and living areas) to the trash dumps is much greater at these sites than at the camps of more nomadic groups.

In 1996 and 1998 Helen Strickland and I, accompanied by our son, Philip, traveled to the Kalahari Desert in northeastern Namibia to conduct ethnoarchaeological research among Ju/'hoansi. These people are of the same ethnic group as the Ju/'hoansi (!Kung) living across the border in Botswana studied by John Yellen (1977, 1990). Ju/'hoansi is the name these people apply to themselves, and anthropologists increasingly use it in place of the term !Kung. We were very interested in seeing for ourselves the Ju/'hoansi and their villages (residential campsites) because of the profound contrast between the semiarid environment of the Kalahari Desert and the lush tropical rain forest where the Efe live. [See also Brooks and Draper, "Aging: An Anthropological Perspective," in this volume.]

The Ju/'hoansi we visited live in some two dozen villages situated within a radius of about 25 kilometers around the town of Tsumkwe. Their lives have changed considerably and in important ways from traditional conditions. For example, most villages now have a borehole (well) that provides a permanent supply of drinking water, and the people receive food subsidies. Although people still gather wild plants and hunt wild animals to an extent, some people also raise domestic plants and/or animals. Consequently, the Ju/'hoansi no longer follow their traditional nomadic, mobile settlement pattern over the landscape. They have become more sedentary, inhabiting a village for up to several years.

Despite these changes in Ju/'hoansi lifeways, we discovered opportunities for fascinating research into the spatial organization of their villages. Strong linkages still exist to their traditional way of life. The Ju/'hoansi construct fairly simple dwellings. Some older people still build a traditional, dome-shaped dwelling consisting of a framework of poles covered with grass (supplemented occasionally with a partial covering of blanket or of plastic sheeting). Others have abandoned this traditional style in favor of a wattle-and-daub dwelling modeled after those of other peoples living in northern Namibia. The Ju/'hoansi arrange the dwellings at a village in a pattern of their own choice. They cook over simple open fires and dispose of refuse in and around the village. Fireplaces are the focus not only for cooking but for other campsite activities, such as making or maintaining implements, and socializing. Shady spots under trees also are important activity areas. These villages, when compared to traditional campsites of nomadic Ju/'hoansi of several decades ago, offer a valuable opportunity to examine the effects of increasing sedentism on the spatial organization of settlements.

The arrangement of dwellings at Ju/'hoansi villages we visited in 1996 and 1998 generally had an oval shape, although a small number of villages were laid out in a more linear pattern. In this attribute, the villages are similar to their traditional counterparts. The average distance from each dwelling to its closest neighboring dwelling (measured from dwelling center) is 9.2 meters, which greatly exceeds the spacing at camps of traditional, mobile Ju/'hoansi and at Efe camps. The distance from the doorway of a dwelling to the associated exterior fireplace averages 3.68 meters, which also is greater than the corresponding distance at camps of traditional Ju/'hoansi and of Efe. The arrangement of dwellings at villages of sedentary Ju/'hoansi encompasses an area of some 875 square meters, which greatly exceeds the size of campsites of mobile Ju/'hoansi and of Efe. The villages of sedentary Ju/'hoansi are even larger if one includes the area outside of the arrangement of dwellings where refuse is discarded and ashes from fireplaces accumulate in dumps. Indeed, large ash dumps are a prominent and distinctive feature at these villages.

The ultimate goal of ethnoarchaeological research into the spatial organization of residential sites is to apply this knowledge to the analysis and interpretation of ancient, archaeologically investigated sites. An interesting and productive example of the application of ethnoarchaeological insights to the interpretation of an ancient site is the Orbit Inn site, located in Utah (Simms and Heath 1990). More recently, the Boar's Tusk site, located in southwestern Wyoming, provided an opportunity to apply ethnoarchaeological models to the interpretation of an archaeological site (Fisher and Frison 2000).

The Boar's Tusk site consists of eleven features (each a concentration of heat-altered rocks, animal bones, charcoal, and artifacts), each seemingly the remains of a dwelling or shelter. The absence of ash dumps and trash heaps at this site suggests a relatively brief duration of occupation. The features are arranged in an oval configuration. If these eleven features were dwellings that had been inhabited contemporaneously, then they created a campsite that was substantially larger than even the villages described above of sedentary Ju/'hoansi. The arrangement of features at Boar's Tusk encompasses an area of about 3,080 square meters, and the distance between each feature and its closest neighbor averages 14.0 meters. What accounts for this greater site size at Boar's Tusk? We don't know for sure, but the strong ethic of sharing that exists among Efe and traditional Ju/'hoansi might give us at least part of the answer. During our year among the Efe, Helen and I saw the Efe routinely share cooking implements, smoking pipes, firewood, drinking water, and other items between households at their camps. It struck us that this high level of sharing between households was facilitated by living in a small campsite. Sharing also was integral to the lives of traditional Ju/'hoansi. We aren't sure of the extent of sharing between households at the Ju/'hoansi villages we visited in 1996 and 1998 in Namibia, but among the Ju/'hoansi in Botswana, sharing declined as their traditional lifeways became altered (Yellen 1990). At the Boar's Tusk site, it seems possible that sharing between households as a fundamental adaptive strategy was less significant than sharing is to the Efe and the traditional Ju/'hoansi, and that this difference is reflected in the greater spacing between dwellings and in the large size of the Boar's Tusk site.

The Boar's Tusk and Orbit Inn archaeological investigations, and the valuable ethnoarchaeological insights resulting from research conducted among many different peoples during the past four decades, hint at the great wealth of archaeologically important methodological and theoretical advances that can be obtained through ethnoarchaeological research among peoples living today.

FURTHER READING

Bailey, Robert C. 1989. "The Efe: Archers of the African Rain Forest." *National Geographic* 176(5):664–86.

Bailey, Robert C., and Irven DeVore. 1989. "Research on the Efe and Lese Populations of the Ituri Forest, Zaire." *American Journal of Physical Anthropology* 78(4):459–71.

Binford, Lewis R. 1983. *In Pursuit of the Past: Decoding the Archaeological Record.* Thames and Hudson.

Fisher, John W. Jr., and George C. Frison. 2000. "Site Structure and Zooarchaeology at the Boar's Tusk Site, Wyoming." *Plains Anthropologist* 45(174), *Memoir* 32:89–108.

Fisher, John W. Jr., and Helen C. Strickland. 1989. "Ethnoarchaeology Among the Efe Pygmies, Zaire: Spatial Organization of Campsites." *American Journal of Physical Anthropology* 78(4):473–84.

Fisher, John W. Jr., and Helen C. Strickland. 1991. "Dwellings and Fireplaces: Keys to Efe Pygmy Campsite Structure." In C. S. Gamble and W. A. Boismier, eds., *Ethnoarchaeological Approaches to Mobile Campsites: Hunter-gatherer and Pastoralist Case Studies,* pp. 215–36. Ethnoarchaeological Series 1, International Monographs in Prehistory.

Hitchcock, Robert K. 1987. "Sedentism and Site Structure: Organizational Changes in Kalahari Basarwa Residential Locations." In Susan Kent, ed., *Method and Theory for Activity Area Research: An Ethnoarchaeological Approach,* pp. 374–423. Columbia University Press.

Kroll, E. M., and T. D. Price, eds. 1991. *The Interpretation of Archaeological Spatial Patterning.* Plenum.

O'Connell, James F. 1987. "Alyawara Site Structure and Its Archaeological Implications." *American Antiquity* 52(1):74–108.

Simms, Steven R., and Kathleen M. Heath. 1990. "Site Structure of the Orbit Inn: An Application of Ethnoarchaeology." *American Antiquity* 55(4):797–813.

Turnbull, Colin M. 1961. *The Forest People.* Simon and Schuster.

Yellen, John. 1977. *Archaeological Approaches to the Present: Models for Reconstructing the Past.* Academic.

Yellen, John. 1990. "The Transformation of the Kalahari !Kung." *Scientific American* 262(4):96–105.

16   THE VIKINGS

Old Views and New Findings

William W. Fitzhugh

Popular misconceptions about the "barbarous Vikings" abound, but new archaeological and historical evidence is changing our view of these early seamen, craftsmen, tradesmen, and farmers. Fitzhugh's article teaches us much not only about the Vikings, but also about how stereotypes affect our views of history, and why we know so little about Leif Eriksson compared to Christopher Columbus.

The year 2000—give or take a year or two—is the thousandth anniversary of the Viking discovery of North America, of Leif Eriksson's touchdown on land he called Vinland, five hundred years before Christopher Columbus. Leif Eriksson's epic voyage, which brought the first Europeans to the New World, culminated two hundred years of Norse exploration and settlement in the North Atlantic. Although his accomplishment did not lead to permanent settlement in the Americas, Leif's voyage achieved an important and highly symbolic circling for humankind, connecting our species into a single global system, completing humanity's million-year journey out of Africa and to the farthest reaches of the earth.

In 1992 schoolchildren across America celebrated the Quincentenary—the five hundredth anniversary of Christopher Columbus' voyage to the New World—yet few teachers or their students probably took note of the earlier episode of European contact in the New World. An exhibition at the National Museum of Natural History, *Vikings: The North Atlantic Saga*, focused attention on this earlier "discovery of America" and the wider contributions of the Vikings and their Norse descendants, who continue to inhabit North Atlantic regions into the modern day.

The exhibition provided the first comprehensive treatment of Norse exploration and settlement of the North Atlantic region between A.D. 860 and 1500, illuminating new research in archaeology, history, and the natural sciences that is transforming our understanding of the Vikings and their impact on history. *Vikings: The North Atlantic Saga* told the story of West-Vikings, the hardy Norse who settled the Faeroes, Iceland, and Greenland, and from there traveled west to the North American lands they called Helluland (Baffin Island), Markland (Labrador), and Vinland (Newfoundland). The dramatic story of the Viking expansion across the North Atlantic is a chapter of North American history that deserves to be more widely known.

Images of the Vikings have radically changed through the centuries. These images began in negative European monastery accounts of marauding Vikings pillaging and plundering; appear in thirteenth-century Icelandic saga tales of the daring voyages of Erik the Red and Leif Eriksson; were transformed to romanticized descriptions of Viking valor by nineteenth-century historians and poets; were reinterpreted in twentieth-century archaeological descriptions of settlements, ships, and cemeteries; and today are being reanalyzed by natural scientists examining pollen and ice cores. The stories of the Vikings unfold through time, creating their own version of how history is written and images and stereotypes emerge. These stories are often shrouded in mystery, misunderstandings, and popular imagery, only to be transformed at a later date into some quite different conception.

The Vikings thus present a rich case study for those interested in learning about the past and about the many ways we learn about that past, since our knowledge of the Vikings has changed so radically over time as new evidence and analytical tools have emerged.

THE NORTH ATLANTIC STORY

Vikings: The North Atlantic Saga exhibition focused on the Vikings' little-known North Atlantic story, the inspiring tale of Viking seafaring farmers who made the North Atlantic a Norse "lake" for one thousand years. The story included those who settled down and maintained a vibrant Christian Norse society in Greenland for five hundred years, and those who explored and settled briefly in northeastern North America and maintained contacts with Native American Indians and Inuit for four hundred years before Columbus arrived in the Caribbean. None of this history is well known to North Americans or to Europeans because the historical and scientific

evidence documenting this West-Viking story has only just begun to be published. New studies, including literary research into the Viking sagas,
archaeological excavations of Norse and Native sites, and historical and environmental research, bring to life an exciting new picture of a western Atlantic portion of the Viking world that has until recently been neglected and
unknown.

The exhibition began with a presentation of Viking history and culture in
Scandinavia and its expansion into Europe and the British Isles. The visitor
could follow the early Viking pioneers who explored and settled Iceland in
the mid-ninth century, then learn about their ships, their navigation techniques, and the various reasons why the West-Viking expansion took place,
including the need to find new lands for an expanding population and stock-
raising economy. One of the lures for the Vikings was walrus ivory, which by
this time had become more precious than gold in the high courts and church
chambers of Europe.

The Icelandic portion of the exhibition featured the social and environmental changes that occurred when Vikings arrived and set up a new society
in this land of fire and ice. The rapid peopling of the landscape, the removal
of its fledgling forests, and the installation of large stocks of animals permanently transformed the island into what it is today: an agrarian-industrial nation whose economic interests and environmental resources must be carefully
managed to avoid ecological catastrophe. Here archaeological and natural
science illuminate the causes of the failed Norse colonies in Greenland and
the changes Vikings brought to the Icelandic landscape, which caused great
population loss and economic hardship even in that more temperate land.
These serve as a reminder of the past, of overexploitation in a part of the
world where climatic cooling can have devastating effects. Iceland also presents a case study of ethnic merging, with a new nation arising out of Celtic
and Norse immigrants, a society that adapted a system of Nordic self-
government based on community assemblies that has been a model of modern democracy, dating back to the first general assembly at Thingvellir in
930. But perhaps the greatest contribution to emerge from Iceland was the
recording and preservation of the sagas, and particularly the sagas relating
to the discovery of America.

Iceland was the staging point for the final series of West-Viking expansions
that led to Erik the Red's discovery and settlement of Greenland and the extension of that effort further west into North Greenland, then beyond into
North America. Recent archaeological work not only offers a window into
the four-hundred-year span of Norse Greenland (985–1450), but also gives
us exciting new information about Viking voyages to Vinland. Evidence for
the latter is presented from cartography and archaeology and includes a reconstruction of the Viking site discovered at L'Anse aux Meadows in north-

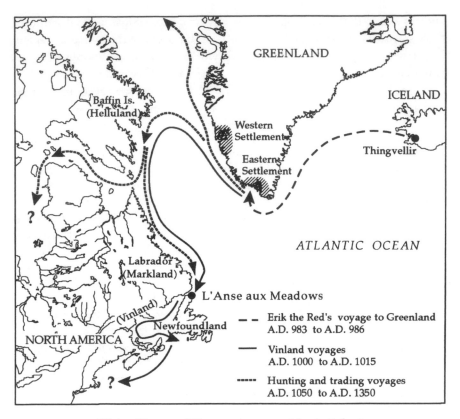

Viking Westward Voyages (courtesy Marcia Bakry)

ern Newfoundland. This portion of the exhibition also includes new information about contacts between the Norse and various Native American
groups (Indian, Dorset, and Thule culture). These contacts suggest that the
Norse may have been trading for ivory as well as gathering timber from
Markland (Labrador), that their voyages to America continued for several
hundred years after the Vinland voyages ceased in the early eleventh century,
and that Norse-Native contacts were confined largely to the Arctic regions
of northeastern North America. Recent archaeological research now shows
that Norse activities in North America were much more extensive than previously believed and may have included purposeful trade and exchange.

Scholars continue to debate answers to the controversial question of where
Vinland was, and there are many claims and counterclaims made about
Viking landings in America. Even today Leif Eriksson remains at best a shad-
owy figure, mentioned only in passing in textbook accounts of the early history of North America. Fortunately, his exploits were passed down as oral
literature for more than two hundred years, then were written down in the
thirteenth century by Viking descendants in Iceland, in the *Saga of the Green-*

landers and *Erik the Red's Saga*. For generations, most historians discounted these sagas as valid sources, but in 1960 the discovery of the Norse settlement in northern Newfoundland changed the world's view of the Vikings in North America. A 1986 *AnthroNotes* article, "Vinland Revisited: 986–1986," by Alison S. Brooks, offered a detailed description of these saga accounts and the archaeological evidence supporting Norse settlement in the New World:

> For years, archaeologists searched for the original location of the Vinland settlement from Nantucket to Labrador. Finally, in 1960, at L'Anse aux Meadows on the northern tip of Newfoundland, a Norwegian archaeologist, Helge Ingstad, discovered remains of three long sod houses on a sheltered harbor, on land visited both by ancestral Eskimos before the Norse era, and by Indians. Greenland Norse houses had stone foundations. But these New World houses lacked such foundations and so could be explained as temporary dwellings. Furthermore, one of five small outbuildings contained a small amount of slag from an iron smithing operation. Radiocarbon determinations of charcoal associated with the slag suggest an age of around A.D. 1000. Over 100 objects of European manufacture were unearthed; a spindle whorl attests to the weaving of wool and to the presence of women. A cloak pin of bronze, a material unknown to Native Americans, was similar in style to those found in Viking settlements of the British Isles. Finally, some wooden floorboards from a boat indicate directly the presence of Norse ships. The authentication of the L'Anse aux Meadows site as a Norse settlement of brief duration has been widely accepted by archaeologists. (1986:4)

Since Brooks wrote her summary account in 1986, even more Viking objects have been found in archaeological sites from northern Maine to the high Arctic, indicating a wide zone of Norse activity and revealing a pattern of Norse exploration and native contacts that lasted for nearly five hundred years.

"VIKINGS" AND "NORSE"

By the latter part of the eighth century, the Norse had largely mastered the challenges of making a living in their Scandinavian homelands and had developed a remarkable ship that gave them the ability to seek adventure, profit, and new lands beyond the coastal farms of western Norway. In doing so, the early Norse earned a new identity—Vikings—in the eyes of their European neighbors, an identity that followed them far across the North Atlantic and down to modern times.

To many, the term *Viking* has become indelibly associated with seafaring warriors, explorers, and entrepreneurs, despite the fact that this word was only sporadically applied directly to the Nordic peoples; the British used it to refer to the "curse of the north," the marauding sailors who regularly despoiled the British coastal settlements after the famous Viking raid on Lindisfarne monastery in A.D. 793. That date is generally taken as the beginning of the Viking Age, which lasted 250 years until the Normans, descendants of the Vikings, crossed the channel from Normandy, France, to invade England in 1066. The term *Viking* is thought to have originated from a place in southern Norway called Vik, which became an early center of Viking raiding fleets. The name soon came to refer to Norse-speakers, called Northmen by their southern adversaries, who sallied forth from *viks* ("bays" or "harbors" in Old Norse, or "refuges" in Old English) seeking adventure and profit. Those "bay men" who went off raiding were said to go "a-viking" or were simply called "vikings."

The term *Viking* did not refer to the Nordic peoples who stayed home. Those who shared a similar language (Old Norse) and cultural traditions that distinguished them from other linguistic or ethnic groups were known by various ethnic names, such as Goths, Norwegians, or Danes. The pioneering Norse who discovered and settled lands in Iceland and Greenland during the Viking Age were not technically Vikings. Collectively these ninth- and tenth-century Norse are sometimes called West-Vikings, although their traditions and history are primarily those of Nordic seafaring farmers rather than the Viking marauders who terrorized Europe.

Thus the term *Norse* is preferred and is especially appropriate for medieval Nordic peoples of the North Atlantic who were predominantly Christian after A.D. 1000 and culturally derived primarily from Norway. However, the long history of the search for the "Vikings" in North America and its modern popular use has made it the only term recognizable to a general North American audience. Hence the term Viking is used in this article to characterize the Northmen during the entire period from A.D. 793 until A.D. 1066, when William the Conqueror of Normandy invaded England and defeated King Harold, effectively ending the Viking Age. Following this period raids ceased and the political and economic integration of Scandinavia, Europe, and the North Atlantic settlements moved forward rapidly. After this time Nordic peoples of northern Europe, Iceland, and Greenland should more correctly be called Norse, as befitting the Christian medieval society that they had become, rather than Vikings, which unfortunately is North American customary usage for all Viking Age and medieval Nordic contacts in North America.

VIKINGS AT HOME

Most Norse lived as farmers on small plots of land or served as retainers to kings or locally powerful chiefs and their supporters. Despite their reputation as shipbuilders, sailors, and warriors, the Norse identified themselves as farmers rather than as fishermen, hunters, trappers, or traders, even though individuals might spend considerable periods of the year engaged in these tasks. Carpentry and especially boat building were not trades; they were skills known to all Viking men, just as spinning, weaving, and clothes making were known to all Viking women. However, there were no activities more central to Norse identity than stock farming—the raising of cattle, sheep, goats, and pigs.

The technological element upon which Viking expansion and influence depended was boat building and maritime skill. Little was known about Viking ships until the late 1800s when Norwegian burial mounds were excavated, revealing well-preserved ships; more recent excavations have further documented Viking ship types and their development from the eighth to the twelfth centuries. Tree-ring dating of the wooden ships has provided a precise chronology for their construction and repair. Viking boats were designed to be dragged across long portages as well as to withstand fierce ocean storms. Such ships gave Vikings the ability to trade, make war, carry animals, and cross open oceans.

The magic ingredients that made Viking ships possible were iron, carpentry skills, abundant timber, and a large labor force. The Viking technique of smelting produced iron that could withstand salty waters. The availability of iron for tools and fastenings meant that even moderately well-off farmers could muster the materials and manpower to build a ship. Before the Viking Age, owning a ship was a mark of status for the powerful chieftains. During the Viking Age ships became a necessity for even lesser chieftains and successful farmers. Swarms of Viking boats could be produced, and during the long midwinter farming break, the Baltic and North Seas came alive with Viking crews out for valor and profit.

THE VIKING AGE

The territorial expansion of the Vikings from their Scandinavian homelands that began in the last decades of the eighth century was the fundamental historical reality that created the Viking Age. This expansion started as seasonal raids on the northern and western British Isles by Norwegian Vikings, who first invaded the Shetlands and Orkneys and then used these as bases for staging raids on northern Scotland, Ireland, and the west coast of England. Danish Vikings struck along England's eastern coast and along the northwestern shores of the mainland south of Denmark. Viking chiefs had already become familiar with these lands through trading activities, and within a few decades after the strikes began, the purpose of the raids became more economic and political. Soon, Vikings were trading and extorting money (called Danegeld) more than they were raiding and stealing, although the raids continued sporadically throughout the British Isles and western Europe for the next two centuries, and even extended to Spain, the Mediterranean, and North Africa.

Over time Vikings who went raiding returned to regions they had first visited as marauders and took wives and land and settled there permanently, leaving younger and more boisterous generations to go "a-viking" elsewhere. In this way Viking population and lands expanded rapidly during the ninth and tenth centuries, and soon farming, trading, and diplomacy became as common as raiding and pillaging for Vikings living abroad. Danish Vikings expanded settlements along the eastern coast of Britain, and towns soon grew up in Dublin and York, while Normandy became a Nordic territory and later a duchy of France.

At the same time as Viking raids and settlements were transforming western Europe, Vikings from Sweden were exploring, raiding, and building economic relationships to the east through European and Russian river systems leading to the Black Sea, the Caspian Sea, and the eastern Mediterranean. Swedish Vikings became powerful traders, politicians, and mercenaries in these regions, and founded a dynasty that ruled Novgorod in what is today Russia and Kiev in modern Ukraine. During the Byzantine Empire, they sold their services as protectors of the ruling caliphs. These eastern Vikings brought back immense wealth to Scandinavia in the form of Eastern silver and artifact treasures from as far away as the Caspian Sea, Baghdad, and even India.

Vikings who ventured west, primarily Norwegians and those who had re-settled in the British Isles, embarked on a different course, settling the islands of the North Atlantic as farmers and hunters who supplied medieval Europe with such exotic goods as ivory, falcons, and precious fur, in addition to wool. These hardy Norse farmers reached the Faeroes by A.D. 825 and Iceland by 870. By 930 a population of 30,000 Norse had become established in Iceland, and all its arable lands were occupied. Thereafter, communication between Iceland and Norway and the British Isles was maintained on a regular basis. By 930 the Icelandic parliament was founded, and in 982 Erik the Red, outlawed from Iceland, set off to explore Greenland, returning to Iceland in 985 to lead a colonizing effort that founded Greenland's Eastern and Western Settlements.

In or about A.D. 1000 Leif Eriksson set out to explore lands west and south of Greenland, which he called Helluland (Baffin Island), Markland (Labrador), and Vinland (Newfoundland). During the next decade or so other Vinland voyages were made by other members of his family. Thereafter Vinland explorations ceased and during the following 350 years, until the

Greenland colonies were abandoned about 1450, the Norse in this distant settlement remained oriented primarily to Iceland, Norway, and the British Isles. However, historical records and finds of Norse artifacts in Native American archaeological sites show that throughout this period, Greenlandic or Icelandic Norse occasionally visited Markland for timber and made sporadic contacts with native peoples in northwest Greenland and the Canadian arctic.

The West-Viking story may be likened to a ninth-century Nordic wave that surged out of Scandinavia and the northern British Isles at the peak of the Viking Age and raced across the North Atlantic to Iceland, Greenland, and northeastern North America during a period of unusually warm, stable climatic conditions. Many theories have been advanced to explain the events that propelled the Vikings outward from their northern homelands: developments in ship construction and seafaring skills, internal stress from population growth and scarce land, loss of personal freedom as political and economic centralization progressed, and the rise of state-sponsored Christianity over traditional pagan belief. Probably all are correct to some degree, but the overriding factor was the awareness of the opportunities for advancement abroad that lured Norsemen from their home farms. By taking on lives as soldiers of fortune, Vikings, who faced declining opportunities at home, could dramatically alter their prospects by becoming wealthy, reaping glory and fame in battle, and achieving high status as leaders and heroes based on their own abilities and deeds. With success abroad, one could advance rapidly to positions of prestige and power in the relatively open structure of Viking society.

THE GREENLAND COLONIES

The final chapter of the Norse story in the North American region concerns the history of the two colonies established by Erik the Red in Greenland. Much is known of life in Norse Greenland from the sagas and from nearly two hundred years of archaeological investigations. In recent decades important new sites have yielded rich information about the Greenland Norse, including the Farm Beneath the Sand site. Here a farm that was occupied for three hundred years was preserved in permafrost and yielded many spectacular artifacts, including an entire door, a loom, and whole animal carcasses. Studies of such sites enable scholars to ask how the Greenland colonies functioned and whether they died out as the result of a little ice age, overpopulation and depletion of natural resources, isolation from Europe, raids by pirates, Inuit (Eskimo) attack or territorial infringement, immigration to America, or simply gradual population loss.

A NEW IMAGE FOR THE VIKINGS (?)

VIKING AMERICA THROUGH TIME

After the disappearance of the medieval Norse from Greenland and the integration of the Icelandic Norse into the broader European economic and political scene, little was heard of Vikings in North America until the early nineteenth century. Before the 1830s North Americans knew the Vikings only as the Europeans saw them—as raiders and pillagers of Europe. These views changed rapidly after 1837, when the saga texts became available in English translations. These sagas indicated that Leif Eriksson and others had explored and settled in as-yet-unknown areas of northeastern North America. The discovery of literature describing Viking explorations that may have reached southern New England struck American antiquarians like a thunderclap. Information about mysterious rock engravings, a conspicuous old stone tower in Newport, Rhode Island, and a pagan burial containing "plate armor" all became grist for a new nineteenth-century Viking craze in North America. This early American obsession with Vikings was sealed when Henry Wadsworth Longfellow published his epic poem, *The Skeleton in Armor*. This tale of a love-struck Viking warrior who sailed to America, built the Newport Tower for his lost love, and came to an unhappy end buried in his armor in an unmarked grave in nearby southeastern Massachusetts became an indelible part of nineteenth century American literary romanticism. Scholars later discovered that the inscriptions and burial were Native American and dated to the colonial period and that the tower was built in the mid-seventeenth century by Governor Benedict Arnold. However, by then the popular Viking imagery was indelibly imprinted in the American imagination.

In the 1890s Ebenezer N. Horsford of Boston lectured and published scores of books on his theories of Viking contacts in New England. Although his and many other claims of Viking cities such as Norumbega and artifact finds have been dismissed by scholars, the allure of a "Viking America" lives on and continues to motivate a small circle of advocates whose steadfastness in promoting evidence of Viking and earlier European Neolithic or Bronze Age finds in America have been termed "fantastic archaeology." Most of these finds are the results of innocent mistakes, but a considerable number are pranks or hoaxes based on finds of real Viking artifacts that came to America in the late nineteenth and early twentieth centuries as heirlooms with Scandinavian immigrants.

Understanding the history of this phenomenon and its broader roots in popular attitudes about Vikings in European and American society helps explain the enduring nature of the American public's romance with things Viking. North Americans today associate the term *Nordic* with winter sports events or episodes from the public radio show *A Prairie Home Companion*. The term *Viking* connotes a brawny, battle-crazed berserker from comic books or the Monty Python movies, but its only sure recall is the Minnesota Vikings football team. All Vikings in popular culture renditions wear helmets with horns, despite the fact that Vikings never had horns on their helmets; this persistent image seems to have originated as a nineteenth-century Wagnerian opera costume based on archaeological finds of Danish Bronze Age horned helmets. Clearly America's romance with the Vikings is based on more than historical fact!

CONCLUSION

The new millennium presents us with the opportunity to explore a little known chapter in the history of North America that has been emerging with evidence from the L'Anse aux Meadows site and finds of Norse artifacts in Native American sites in northeastern North America. These finds confirm information related in the Vinland sagas and extend the range of Norse contacts or influence in North America from Greenland to Maine. The fact that these finds date from 1000 to 1400 corroborates historical evidence that the Iceland and Greenland Norse continued to visit North America long after Leif Eriksson's initial Vinland voyages ceased about 1015. Even though the

Norse did not establish permanent settlements in North America, their continuing visits ensured that a tradition of knowledge about these lands, resources, and peoples remained alive in Greenland until about 1450 and in Iceland down to the present day.

Perhaps the most important outcome of contact gained was Native American familiarity with European habits, behavior, and materials that helped them take best advantage of future European interactions. This information must have been passed down through time within Native societies, for when later Europeans arrived (for example, Martin Frobisher in Labrador in 1576–78), Inuit groups were already familiar with people they called *kablunat* (white men) who came in big ships with interesting things to trade.

Finally, investigation of the Norse North Atlantic saga teaches us much about the Vikings and later Norse societies who opened this early northern bridge to North America. To date, the Scandinavian component in the history of the Americas is absent from the popular tradition and educational base of American history. It is useful, therefore, to consider how this tradition—a northern European Nordic tradition—played a crucial role in the early American contacts, maintained itself through the Middle Ages, and passed information on to others, perhaps even to Columbus himself. In fact, it is believed that Christopher Columbus visited Iceland shortly before his voyages to North America. Surely, Columbus would have heard about the saga lands to the west from sailors or scholars he met. After a quiescent period between 1400 and 1800, Nordic influence reemerged as a wave of immigrants to North America in the eighteenth and nineteenth centuries began making major new contributions to North American society.

To a great extent, our next millennium will be shaped by the very same values that motivated the Vikings in their western push across the Atlantic—the need to explore new horizons, to test the human spirit, to seek opportunities wherever they exist. Such is the historical message of the Viking story.

FURTHER READING

Begley, Sharon. 2000. "The Ancient Mariners." *Newsweek,* April 3, pp. 48–49, 52–54.

Brooks, Alison. 1986. "'Vinland' Revisited: 986–1986." *AnthroNotes* 8(1):1–4, 14.

Byock, Jesse. 2001. *Viking Age Iceland*. Penguin.

Fitzhugh, William W. 2000. "Vikings Arrive in America." *Scandinavian Review* 87(3):50–56.

Fitzhugh, William W., and Elisabeth I. Ward, eds. 2000. *Vikings: The North Atlantic Saga*. Smithsonian Institution Press. (This chapter of *Anthropology Explored* is a much shorter and much revised version of the introduction to this publication.)

Graham-Campbell, James, and Colleen Batey, eds. 1994. *Cultural Atlas of the Viking World*. Facts on File.

Ingstad, Anne Stine. 1977. *The Discovery of a Norse Settlement in America: Excavations at L'Anse aux Meadows, Newfoundland, 1961–1968*. Translated by Elizabeth Seeberg. Oslo: Universitetsfolaget.

Roesdahl, Else. 1998. *The Vikings*. Rev. ed. Penguin.

The Sagas of Icelanders: A Selection. 2000. Preface by Jane Smiley; introduction by Robert Kellogg. Allen Lane.

Sawyer, Peter, ed. 1997. *The Oxford Illustrated History of the Vikings*. Oxford University Press.

Vesilind, Priit. 2000. "In Search of Vikings." *National Geographic Magazine* 197:2–27.

The Vinland Sagas: The Norse Discovery of America. 1966. Translated with an introduction by Magnus Magnusson and Hermann Pálsson. New York University Press.

Ward, Elisabeth. 2000. "Vikings in America." *Muse* 4(5):30–36.

Viking and Norse Bibliography for Teachers and Students:
http://www.mnh.si.edu/vikings/learning/bibliography.html

17   WHO GOT TO AMERICA FIRST?

Fact and Fiction

Stephen Williams

Who got to America first and how did they get there are two of the oldest questions in American archaeology. Williams' article details various factual and fictional explanations and the evidence for them. The article raises such fascinating questions as: What types of inquiry and evidence are important to consider? What is unusual about inscriptions on rocks in North America as one source of evidence? Why has it been so difficult to prove or disprove various theories? Finally, why has there been such controversy over issues related to human migrations to the New World?

A s most of us know, 1992 was the 500th anniversary of Christopher Columbus' famous voyage to the New World. In recent years, the assertion that Columbus "discovered" America when his trio of ships made landfall in the Bahamas has been questioned by a number of concerned individuals. Native Americans are understandably disturbed at the suggestion that their status as the "first" Americans is somehow being challenged. Most scholars now insist that the first human settlers of this continent were indeed the ancestors of the contemporary Indian tribes. Their first migration (from Asia via the Bering Strait area) probably occurred more than 15,000 years ago, with several more waves of migrants arriving some thousands of years later.

But if that is the widely held explanation, what is all the argument about? Most of the debate surrounds hypothetical later arrivals in the New World, especially during the past 3,000 years, and purportedly mainly from locations to the east, across the Atlantic. A smaller number of proponents look

"AT THIS RATE IT'LL PROBABLY TAKE THEM 500 YEARS TO SORT IT OUT..."

to trans-Pacific connections during this same period of time. What sort of evidence and how we evaluate it is the subject of concern for many anthropological scholars today. As this review will indicate, these are not new questions, nor are they ones that can be settled for all time—the same ones keep reappearing over the centuries.

The century following Columbus' well-documented voyages, none of which actually reached North America, was one of questioning, too. Had Columbus reached Asia or the West Indies? Who were these inhabitants that met him as he stepped ashore? We still refer to them as "Indians" because of the mistaken view that the islands, and later the mainland, were part of the Asian continent, not the New World at all. Magellan's circumnavigation of the world in the 1520s would establish the Western Hemisphere as a separate land mass, but then the question arose as to the origin of the inhabitants. Here speculations ran wild. By the end of the century (1590), a Spanish church scholar, Joseph de Acosta, would publish a marvelously well-constructed answer: the inhabitants of the New World came from Asia across a land bridge, arriving as hunters, then developing agriculture and later high civilizations such as he had seen in Peru and Mexico. He specifically discounted possible trans-Atlantic connections to the Lost Tribes of Israel or the mythical sunken continent of Atlantis.

Modern scholars would agree with Acosta's scenario, but just about a decade later another Spanish cleric, Gregorio Garcia, wrote a two-volume work that would open the gates of migration to the Lost Tribes, refugees from Atlantis, Carthaginians from North Africa, and many more. He refused to be partial to any on his long list, but they were almost all trans-Atlanteans, bringing seeds of civilization with them. Thus in 1607 the battle was joined: the New World native cultures were either derived from land-based Asian migrants (Acosta) or transplanted from the Old World by trans-Atlantic seafarers (Garcia). The argument has lasted until today.

METHODS OF INQUIRY

The origin of the earth's inhabitants is a central question in anthropology. The answer is also one that requires careful evaluation of all the information available to us each time the question is asked. Acosta and Garcia were limited in the facts they had at hand, although both had lived in several parts of the New World before addressing the problem—no armchair scholars here. But what kinds of evidence do anthropologists bring to bear on such questions today?

First, we consider the people themselves: What do they look like? Whom do they resemble? Simple questions in the 1600s: outward appearances were all they had. In today's world of biological anthropology, we turn to sophisticated analysis of genetics and DNA to try to see way back in time as human populations spread across the globe. We can clearly tie Native American origins back to Asia, although we may quibble about exactly at what time and with which Asian groups they are most closely linked genetically.

Second, we consider the cultures of the Native Americans, especially those aspects of culture that will allow a long look back in time. In this case, linguistics, the study of languages, is an important information source. Native American languages represent enormous diversity, much more so than in comparable areas in the Old World, where diversity has decreased over time. This pattern of diversity suggests both internal diversification and repeated migrations from North Asia. According to some scholars, the degree of linguistic diversity in the New World points to a history of tens of millennia.

Third, when we look at the artifactual content of New World cultures, we conclude that most of these myriad artifacts, covering thousands of years, are definitely of New World origin, although certain aspects of some material cultures do show north Asian connections, especially in the Paleo-Indian period, 7,000 to 10,000 years ago [see Selig and Stanford, "Researching the First Americans: One Archaeologist's Journey," in this volume].

Finally, we turn to a rather different category, that of the plants and animals associated with New World cultures. Here too, just a few specific Asian connections exist: dogs are clearly longtime associates of humankind and quite surely accompanied some of the very first Americans from Siberia. Plants are quite another matter, and here we are discussing agricultural items only. All the major food plants, such as corn, potatoes, and beans, are derived with the help of human intervention from plants domesticated by Native Americans. Only a few questionable items await further study concerning a possible outside origin; these are the bottle gourd and cotton. The sweet potato, another enigma, seems to have gone from South America to Polynesia, just to confuse the issue.

With those basics in place, we can enter the fray of evaluating other sources of evidence for transoceanic connections with one certain understanding: if a hypothesis is bolstered by strong emotional concerns, almost everything can and will be believable to some supporters. Recognizing that each of us has a personal bias that influences our own view of the world does not make us immune to its force, but at least we can consciously try to make our evaluations as bias-free as possible.

MOUNDBUILDERS

Archaeological evidence concerning the question of who got here first would necessarily have to await the development of the discipline of archaeology in North America. Thomas Jefferson is very often cited as the father of American archaeology, and he certainly attempted one of the first archaeological explanations of the question when he wrote in his famous *Notes on the State of Virginia* (1787) about an Indian mound that he had excavated many years before. However, his strongest evidence to support his belief in an Asian origin (via the Bering Strait) of the Native Americans was from his study of Indian languages. He cited the diversity of these languages as proof that they had been here a long time.

Other scholars joined Jefferson in this well-thought-out view. Yet in the early nineteenth century the westward expansion of settlement into the Ohio Valley produced a great deal more archaeological evidence from Indian mounds. As interpreted by some new voices, the accumulating data supported the supposition that these mounds and the rather elaborate artifacts found in them were made by the exotic "Moundbuilders," purportedly an advanced and extinct culture not connected to native peoples. The hypothesis spawned some very popular books, such as that by Josiah Priest (1833), that were fanciful in their interpretations and careless in their evaluation of the data.

The voice of reason came from Samuel Haven in a Smithsonian-sponsored volume (1856) that supported the Bering Strait hypothesis and called some of the wilder notions "vagaries." We now know that much of the Moundbuilder hypothesis was based on fraudulent documents, such as the Grave Creek and Davenport inscriptions, which tried to give support for literate trans-Atlantean cultures making inroads on the prehistory of the Ohio and

Mississippi valleys. It just was not so, and again thanks to the Smithsonian's major research project on mound exploration under John Wesley Powell, the Moundbuilder myth was laid to rest by 1900. The mounds, the earthworks, and the artifacts were the handiwork of American Indians, not that of trans-Atlantean invaders.

VIKINGS IN AMERICA

There was much more than just mounds and Native Americans to argue about. By 1891 a volume entitled *America Not Discovered by Columbus,* by Rasmus B. Anderson, would contain a lengthy bibliography with some 350 sources on the topic. It listed claims of America's discovery by Chinese, Arabs, Welsh, Venetians, Portuguese, and Poles. However, the majority of these references supported the notion of Vikings as the ones who got here first in the race across the Atlantic. This hypothesis came into being more than 150 years ago and really had only the literary evidence from the Norse sagas to support it.

Not that it was not a worthwhile idea. Few doubted that Vikings in North America could or did happen. There just was no archaeological evidence to prove it. Again frauds came to the rescue; if you cannot discover the data you need, just manufacture it! Thus was born the fake Kensington Rune Stone in the 1890s and the "salting" of the Beardmore site in Canada with real Norse artifacts to be used to support a pre-Columbian Norse presence in North America. But good archaeology by Helge Ingstad would finally come to the fore in 1960 with the right answer: Norse ruins at L'Anse aux Meadows on the northern tip of Newfoundland, complete with sod huts and artifacts such as a brass pin, a soapstone spindle whorl, and iron nails, all dated to about A.D. 1000. Was it the home of Leif Eriksson? Archaeologists are not sure, but we do know that the Vikings certainly made it to the New World long before Columbus [see Fitzhugh, "The Vikings: Old Views and New Findings," in this volume].

OTHER SOURCES OF NEW WORLD INFLUENCES

With an affirmative reply to the Viking presence, one might think that much else might logically follow. What about Chinese voyagers in junks across the Pacific, Lost Tribes from Israel still looking for a homeland, Phoenicians from the Mediterranean, Celts from Ireland or Wales, or West Africans in Mexico? Well, all of the above and more have been suggested by various writers in the twentieth century alone. Some of the best-known authors among recent long-range diffusionists are Harold Gladwin, Barry Fell, and Ivan Van Sertima.

First, let us consider whether or not such voyages were possible during the past 3,000 years. The answer is a very strong yes. The maritime exploits of the Polynesians during this period are well known and documented by excellent archaeology in the Pacific. They colonized the entire eastern Pacific. Much earlier (50,000 years ago), migrants from Southeast Asia made their way to New Guinea and Australia; part of that trek quite probably included water crossings.

Some of the proposed trans-Atlantic crossings were supposedly made by cultures known to have had maritime skills. Indeed, the fact that Atlantic crossings (especially in summer) in small boats, even solo attempts, have been successfully made is well known. The Pacific, too, has been conquered in recent times by rafts and small boats, but with a fair number of casualties, although the latter fact is not as well advertised. So we may accept that it could have been done with the maritime expertise available from 1000 B.C. on, although the modern successes have benefited from navigational and safety aids not available to all would-be travelers in earlier times.

But what is the basic evidence for this multitude of ocean crossings to the New World that some chroniclers now insist took place in the past? There is certainly no biological evidence that can be used to support any such trips. One would have to admit that additions to the New World gene pool by these shiploads of mariners might be hard to detect. Nor have modern studies of prehistoric human skeletal remains in the New World shown any identifiable evidence to support the presence of such overseas visitors.

Save for the Norse finds discussed above, no important archaeological discoveries have been made, if one means intrusive sites with buildings, artifacts, and trash heaps attributable to such voyagers. The evidence that has been used to support these hyperdiffusionist claims falls into two major categories: (1) inscriptions found on cliffs, rocks, artifacts, or crude stone structures where no other pertinent artifacts are found (e.g., Dighton Rock in Massachusetts); and (2) stone sculptures and other figurative pieces of art that are thought to depict foreign visitors or to resemble the artistic work of non–New World cultures, such as the colossal Olmec head (Grove 1992).

The inscriptions in a wide variety of purported Old World scripts have been found from one coast to the other, from the Rocky Mountains to the suburbs of Tucson, Arizona; from the Maine coast to the Great Basin of Nevada and Utah. Many of the inscriptions contain mixed texts with symbols of different times and origins. These finds also share another unusual characteristic: none have produced any nearby artifacts or associated living areas. They stand alone as sentinels of the past with no archaeological context—a very strange situation. Who left them? How did the ancient voyagers travel so far without leaving a single trace other than these inscriptions? Why did they do it? One set of inscriptions *with* accompanying artifacts are the Michigan relics, or Soper frauds, manufactured by James A. Scotford between 1890 and 1920. Although debunked for decades, these pseudo-cuneiform messages are still being deciphered today by some enthusiasts. The study of stone and ceramic sculptures to prove foreign connections has flourished in Mesoamerica, the area of high culture in Central America. Here these works of art are thought to demonstrate bearded voyagers from abroad, and in the case of the great stone heads from Vera Cruz, Mexico (some are eight to ten feet in diameter), they are thought to confirm trans-Atlantic travel from Africa to Mesoamerica and the Olmec ca. 700 B.C. This hypothesis of African origins has been supported for several decades by Ivan Van Sertima of Rutgers University and is, in my opinion, based on a mixture of ethnic pride and personal bias. The facial features of these heads, in particular, were thought to represent Africans; however, they are also similar to the features of many Native Americans from the Olmec area. Any resemblance between the peoples of West Africa and Mesoamerica is more likely due to common adaptation to tropical conditions than a closely shared ancestry.

The hypothesis that important cultural transfer from West Africa to Mesoamerica occurred was first put forward by Leo Wiener of Harvard University in several books published between 1920 and 1926. A professor of Slavic languages, Wiener thought that he had discovered important linkages based on "sound-alike" resemblances between the languages of the two areas. He also found what he considered to be other important comparative resemblances in materials as varied as women's hairstyles and tobacco pipes.

Wiener's researches were the impetus for Van Sertima's own involvement with this topic, and they now form an important bit of data for Afrocentrist historical arguments. Unfortunately, current archaeological research in Mesoamerica fails to support any of the claims of Wiener and Van Sertima for direct connections between the two areas. Where were the African landfalls in Mesoamerica, and why are there no African cultural artifacts observable in the well-excavated sites of the Olmec of the Mexican coast? (Furthermore, the new chronology for the development of Olmec culture places its beginnings considerably before 700 B.C.)

Until we have solid archaeological evidence to support other hypotheses, it can be said quite clearly that Columbus was not the first to find America, nor were the Vikings, although they beat Columbus by about 500 years. Instead, it was small bands of Native Americans who first "discovered" the New World via the Bering Strait many thousands of years earlier. Although this is certainly not an impossible hypothesis, at present there is no credible evidence that links any of the oft-cited trans-Atlanteans with any archaeological discoveries in North America. As far as is now known, the Native

"WELL, I DON'T THINK IT'S SO DANG MYSTERIOUS."

Americans were the masters of their own fate. They produced their myriad diverse cultures throughout the New World independent of foreign intervention.

UPDATE

One might hope that the question of who got to America first would remain within the scope of well-known groups capable of coming from across the Atlantic or Pacific (Kennewick Man, for example), but that, unfortunately, still is not the case. Some recent writers have even suggested that Atlantis was in Lake Titicaca in Bolivia—surely a long reach. Even the arguments about the authenticity of the Kensington Stone are still hot. However, there have been recent updates on Viking matters (Fitzhugh and Ward 2000) and the Mormon tablets (Larson 1996). My own recent writings deal with both the history of the putative Asian Bering Strait crossings and the intellectual history of that pathway to America (Williams 2002a, 2002b).

My research activities now have turned to other aspects of the history of archaeology beyond *Fantastic Archaeology* (1991). One of my recent publications debunks the myth of the Moundbuilders (2002c). Despite much literature to the contrary (and my own previous view), I now realize that the non-Indian Moundbuilder was a very small minority view. Most nineteenth-century scholars really did believe that the American Indians were indeed the creators of these great earthen monuments.

My coedited volume with David Browman (2002) grew out of the Second Gordon R. Willey Biennial Symposium on the History of Archaeology and covers a wide range of topics, including the putative Bering Strait crossings and the intellectual history of that pathway to America (Williams 2002a, 2002b). Browman and I now are researching the history of the development of archaeology at Harvard University, relying considerably on archival documentation, covering the seven decades from 1860 to 1930.

FURTHER READING

Anderson, Rasmus B. 1891. *America Not Discovered by Columbus*. S. C. Griggs. (Reprinted 1930, Leif Eriksson Memorial Association.)

Browman, David, and Stephen Williams, eds. 2002. *New Perspectives on the Origins of Americanist Archaeology*. University of Alabama Press.

Fagan, Brian M. 1995. *Ancient North America: The Archaeology of a Continent*. Rev. ed. Thames and Hudson.

Feder, Kenneth L. 1990. *Frauds, Myths, and Mysteries: Science and Pseudoscience in Archaeology*. Mayfield.

Fitzhugh, William W., and Elisabeth I. Ward, eds. 2000. *Vikings: The North Atlantic Saga*. Smithsonian Institution Press.

Grove, David. 1992. "Updating Olmec Prehistory." *AnthroNotes* 14(2):9–12, 14–15.

Haven, Samuel F. 1856. *Archaeology of the United States*. Smithsonian Institution Press. (Reprinted 1973, AMS Press for Peabody Museum of Archaeology and Ethnology, Harvard University.)

Jefferson, Thomas. 1787. *Notes on the State of Virginia*. John Stockdale. (Reprinted 1999, Penguin.)

Larson, Stan. 1996. *Quest for the Gold Plates: Thomas Stuart Ferguson's Archaeological Search for the Book of Mormon*. Freethinker Press.

Priest, Josiah. 1833. *American Antiquities, and Discoveries in the West*. Hoffman and White.

Williams, Stephen. 1991. *Fantastic Archaeology: The Wild Side of North American Prehistory*. University of Pennsylvania Press.

Williams, Stephen. 2002a. "The Strait of Anian: A Pathway to the New World." In Browman and Williams 2002, pp. 10–29.

Williams, Stephen. 2002b. "From Whence Came Those Aboriginal Inhabitants of America." In Browman and Williams 2002, pp. 30–59.

Williams, Stephen. 2002c. "Reviewing Some Late 19th Century Archaeological Studies: Exploding the Myth of the 'Myth.'" In Andrew Bachner, comp. and ed., *Proceedings of the 21st Mid-South Archaeological Conference: Ethnicity in Archaeology*. Memphis.

18 RESEARCHING THE FIRST AMERICANS

One Archaeologist's Journey

Ruth Osterweis Selig

This chapter clearly demonstrates that the story of when, where, and how the first humans arrived in the Americas is always changing as new archaeological evidence is found. The first half of the chapter, written by Selig, focuses on archaeologist Dennis Stanford. He, in turn, provides the update, which details his theory that various waves of migrating peoples came to the New World, including perhaps some from across the Atlantic Ocean.

If I could find one clearly stratified site with some busted mammoth bones, a couple of crude flake tools, and a single human bone, all in unquestionable association with a charcoal hearth dated 19,500 years ago—I'd have my dream.
—Dennis Stanford, February 1983

What keeps a man looking a lifetime for evidence he knows he may never find? What keeps him excavating sites that turn out to be dead ends, hiring research associates to disprove his latest theory, or traveling to South America and China to find a single tantalizing clue? A dream or maybe just a hunch that he might turn out to be right after all. If Dennis Stanford finds the evidence he has been searching for since 1971, he will unravel one of the major mysteries in North American archaeology: when did the first human beings arrive in the Western Hemisphere? [See Williams, "Who Got to America First? Fact and Fiction," in this volume.]

No serious archaeologist today questions that Native American populations originated from a generalized Mongoloid people that developed in eastern Asia and Siberia during the late Pleistocene. Sometime after 50,000 years ago, hunting bands entered the New World following the herds of mammoths and mastodons, camels and horses teeming across the 1,000-mile-wide grassy plain exposed in the Bering Sea when Ice Age glaciers caused a drastic reduction in sea level. But when did the great crossing first take place?

Recent history is clear. As of 11,000 years ago, human hunters inhabited virtually all of the Americas. Sophisticated Clovis spear points from more than 40 sites in North and South America serve as unmistakable evidence that humans were hunting mainly, or exclusively, mammoths and perhaps bison. But the sudden appearance and rapid spread of Clovis culture remains an archaeological mystery. One thousand years after the first appearance of Clovis spear points, the fluted-point technology had spread across two continents, and most of the huge animals that were once hunted had become extinct. Were the Clovis hunters the first Americans? If they were, why have no Clovis points been found in eastern Asia or northern Siberia? If the Clovis technology was invented in America or, as the late Robert L. Humphrey has suggested, en route to America, where it spread among preexisting populations (Humphrey 1966), when did these earlier migrants first enter the continent? If humans were here before 11,000 years ago—and Dennis Stanford firmly believes that they were—how can archaeologists prove it?

PRE-CLOVIS BONE TECHNOLOGY?

The Yukon Territory's Old Crow Basin yielded a clue in the late 1960s when a caribou bone that had been worked by human hands into a scraping tool was found to be 27,000 years old. The date led archaeologists to propose that pre-Clovis people made use of a bone technology for many tools. Stone was scarce, and bone tools were readily available from butchered carcasses.

In the mid-1970s, Dennis Stanford painstakingly excavated large deposits of broken mammoth bone at two Colorado sites called Dutton and Selby. The animals had died before 11,000 years ago, and their disarticulated broken bones seemed to bear evidence of human activity. "At Dutton in the summer of '76, looking down at a pile of busted camel bone in a 12-foot-deep excavation, with a stone tool found at a level below 16,000 years old, I thought I had found it." Stanford and his colleagues hypothesized that the bones were broken for marrow by humans smashing heavy stone boulders onto them. Today, the stone tool has been mapped as lying at the bottom of a gopher hole and the "busted" bones have been more carefully analyzed. Stanford is no longer sure that Dutton is the dream site he had once thought.

Proposing that pre-Clovis people depended on a bone technology was risky, because broken and polished bones, unlike stone Clovis points, can

be produced by natural forces. Though willing to go out on a limb and willing to risk an innovative hypothesis, Stanford was not willing to close his mind to this possibility—even if it meant disproving the bone technology theory. For this attitude, and for his painstakingly meticulous excavation and analysis, he is esteemed among his colleagues, who watched with interest as Stanford entered a second, highly innovative phase of investigation through experimental archaeology.

ELEPHANT EXPERIMENTS

In order to eliminate nonhuman explanatory factors, Stanford and his associates sought to find out what other natural agencies could produce similar results on bone. At the same time, in order to see if humans could indeed produce and use bone tools, he began to butcher dead elephants and make tools from the bones of Ginsberg, Maggie, and Tulsa.

These large elephants were dead when Dennis arrived on the scene ready to simulate Pleistocene mammoth butchering. The early, carefully documented results were encouraging: bones broken over stone anvils resembled broken bones at Dutton and Selby; the resulting bone tools worked extremely well in carving up skin and meat; and the wear, polish, and striation matched those on ancient bones. In fact, Stanford remembers, "one flaked bone from Ginsberg looked identical to the 27,000-year-old bone tool from Old Crow."

But many archaeologists remained skeptical, and Stanford was eager to face the skeptics head on. In the mid-1970s Gary Haynes, a graduate student at Catholic University, saw Stanford's evidence for pre-Clovis bone technology and expressed serious skepticism. Stanford encouraged Haynes to try disproving the bone technology theory and supported his plan to feed fresh bones to the Kodiak bears and African lions at the National Zoo. This research, along with studies of captive wolf colonies that were fed whole carcasses of deer and moose, produced for Haynes his first clear evidence that the Ice Age "tools" might instead be the results of gnawing by carnivores that polished and broke the bones.

From those first zoo experiments there evolved a remarkable professional relationship: Stanford developed hypotheses and Haynes sought to disprove them. Both of them published papers advancing the science of archaeology and taphonomy—the study of what happens to bones after an animal dies in the wild, a subject of increasing importance to archaeologists. For several years, Haynes traveled to the Canadian Northwest Territories to watch bison herds preyed on by wolves in order to document what happens to carcasses in the wild. Then Haynes traveled to Africa to record the behavior of elephant herds and to describe modern elephant bone accumulations.

What Haynes discovered was exactly what Stanford thought he might find: evidence that natural agencies could produce the spiral fractures, the polish, the wear patterns, and the striations on bone that archaeologists once thought reflected human activity. Wolves chewing on big-game carcasses produce polish as well as tooth marks; bison wallowing in the dust actually fragment and polish previously deposited bone; carnivores break bones to get at marrow just as humans do; and gravel produces the scratches once thought to be clear-cut evidence of human tool use. Broken mammoth bones, previously thought too massive to be broken by natural causes, are explained by Haynes' research, documenting that elephants walk over and break the bones of dead elephants. The resulting broken bones look very much like the broken bones in Dennis Stanford's office that were taken from the Dutton and Selby sites. Even the flaked tusk "tools" have been found in the wild, the result of elephants knocking into one another as they struggle to get to water in the dry season.

At times, Stanford says, he feels "like just walking out, leaving the bones and stones behind, and going to herd sheep." He and Haynes agree that humans and carnivores can produce closely similar evidence for future archaeologists to excavate, and it may be impossible in many cases to differentiate the exact circumstances of bone breakage in the past. But by 1982 Stanford had concluded that the bones at Dutton and Selby did not show *unmistakable* evidence of human activity. Herding sheep, however, was not going to solve the problems.

Instead, Stanford decided to embark on a joint effort that would include research in the High Plains of North America and Northeast Asia, the hypothesized homeland of the Paleo-Indian precursors. With funding provided through the National Geographic Society and Wenner-Gren Foundation, Chinese and American archaeologists worked together during the summer of 1981 at the Lamb Spring site in Colorado excavating a large pile of mammoth bones, many of which had been broken before burial over 1,000 years ago. Lying in the same deposit was a 33-pound boulder that could have been used by pre-Clovis people to break the long bones. Once again Stanford felt he might be on the trail of pre-Clovis hunters, for why would 90 percent of the large long bones be broken while the majority of fragile bones (such as ribs) remain intact?

Haynes' research results on wallowing African elephants cannot neatly explain the modified bones at Lamb Spring. So in the summer of 1983 Haynes went to excavate modern "elephant graveyards" in Africa: these are the waterhole sites where elephant skeletons have accumulated for many decades.

Stanford, meanwhile, went off to another well-stratified site, Blackwater Draw, New Mexico. This site was excavated originally between 1932 and 1937. "Then no one thought there was even a Clovis people, and so no one dug below the Clovis level. Local legend has it that pre-Clovis material has been found there and we hope to find it."

CLUES IN CHINA

After Blackwater Draw, Stanford returned to China, where he spent the fall of 1982. There he did not find any evidence of Clovis technology or even tools that look like Clovis antecedents. But he was able to examine all the Pleistocene collections in the museums, and he traveled to most of the Paleolithic archaeological sites. What he discovered was broken bones, flaked bone, and crude stone artifacts, all very similar to what is found at the sites in North America such as Lamb Spring. Evidence for a highly evolved lithic technology does not appear in China until perhaps as late as about 14,000 years ago, when a microlithic (small tool) technology developed that bears close resemblance to that of the early Eskimo peoples, who are later arrivals on the North American continent.

If the earliest American cultures did not originate in eastern China, where is their source? A new idea tantalizes Stanford. Perhaps the roots of Paleo-Indian culture developed in north-central China. No archaeologist since before World War II has examined the sites west of Manchuria, the first stop on Stanford's planned trip to China in 1984.

He must, therefore, continue his search in America, tracking down the bones and the stones that might give him the unmistakably clear association of human tools with extinct animal remains that he is sure exists somewhere, if only he knew exactly where to look.

UPDATE

Dennis J. Stanford

In the twenty years since this publication (originally titled "Bones and Stones or Sheep"), ideas about the early peopling of the Americas have changed radically, demonstrating that current knowledge is only the best we have at any one time. This 2003 update to Selig's article outlines some of the newest and most exciting discoveries and how they have led to new thinking about the ever emerging story of the First Americans.

The great mystery in North American archaeology remains the same as in 1983: when, where, and how did the first human beings arrive in the Western Hemisphere? We have much stronger evidence today—linguistic and physical anthropological evidence—to support multiple migrations from various areas of Asia, including northeastern Siberia but also probably Southeastern Asia and Eastern Europe. Even more exciting, we have some new thinking about the earliest migration routes, with early migrants perhaps even coming into the southeastern United States from a totally different place than previously thought possible: Western Europe by way of maritime travel over the Atlantic Ocean!

In addition to some of these new lines of argument, we also have evidence now to show that the Clovis people were not the sole early inhabitants of North America. We now believe there were other groups of peoples here, some using Clovis technology and some not, and we have increasing evidence for their existence in South America as well. Hence we no longer believe the earliest inhabitants were simply of Siberian origin or even that they should be called Paleo-Indians. Twenty years ago I predicted there were earlier occupations of North America before Clovis, and in that I was correct, but where I was wrong was in the unilinear model of finding a single early Paleo-Indian people predating Clovis. Instead, we probably are dealing with waves of many migrations, some back and forth across the Bering land bridge, of peoples originating in Eastern Europe and Siberia, and others from Southeast Asia. Only some of these peoples developed Clovis technology, probably as a response to an increasingly arid environment. We also may well be dealing

with people who crossed the Atlantic Ocean, moving from lands that today belong to France and Spain into what is the Eastern United States.

To put all this in personal perspective, a bit of history may be helpful. In 1966, I accompanied the late Bob Humphrey, anthropological cartoonist and illustrator of *AnthroNotes* and *Anthropology Explored,* to the North Slope of Alaska in the search for evidence of the first Americans. As fellow archaeology graduate students at the University of New Mexico, we were both quite sure that Clovis people, the makers of fluted spear points and hunters of mighty mammoths, colonized the Americas some 12,000 years ago and that they were indeed the first people of the New World. We presumed that Clovis ancestors crossed the Ice Age land bridge that connected Asia to the Americas. When the ice-free corridor opened up as a result of the melting of the great continental glaciers, these ancestors moved southward, populating the Americas within a few centuries. It seemed perfectly clear that since Native Americans are physically related to Asians, they had to have a common ancestry. Thus, discovering evidence for the peopling of the Americas seemed a simple matter. All we had to do was to find related pre-Clovis artifacts in Alaska or northeast Asia.

And that's exactly what we did. On the banks of the Utokok River in remote northwest Alaska, we found fluted points. They were not identical to Clovis, but their technology of manufacture demonstrated a positive link. After all, we shouldn't expect an earlier model to be identical to the final model—only related. A radiocarbon-dated mammoth bone found nearby suggested a possible age of 17,000 years old, a bit early, but we didn't know how long Clovis people waited for the door to the ice-free corridor to open. Bob wrote his dissertation and eventually published a paper in *Current Anthropology* (Humphrey 1966). End of story? No!

We expected that when it became possible to see the archaeology of Siberia, we would find yet more distant ancestors of Clovis people. By the

1980s a changing relationship with the Soviet Union allowed for the exchange of scholars. This presented an opportunity to examine firsthand the archaeology of northeast Asia and drive the final nail home to seal the case of the missing ancestors. But alas, the late Paleolithic stone technology of Siberia was based on wedge-shaped cores for the production of microblades, which were then inset into the side of antler, bone, or ivory projectile points. This is a totally different weaponry system than that of the Clovis fluted biface projectile points. But, we thought, Siberia is a large place, and perhaps future finds would include bifaces and a large macroblade technology, similar to those made by Clovis flintknappers.

Unfortunately, as of the summer of 2002 the known late Paleolithic stone technology of Siberia still remains centered on the production of microblades. Furthermore, a reinvestigation of the radiocarbon dates for the oldest late Paleolithic sites in Northeastern Asia has given us another surprise. All these sites are either the same age or slightly younger than Clovis. In fact, at present there are no radiocarbon-dated sites within approximately 3,000 miles of the Bering Straits that are much older than 11,000 years. This is a major problem. After all, if people had come from Siberia to the New World, the sites in the Old World have to be older than the sites in the New World.

What about the fluted points that Bob Humphrey and I found on the North Slope? If these artifacts were pre-Clovis, and if the ice-free corridor model is correct, additional fluted points that are older than Clovis should be found in Alaska as well as in the ice-free corridor. Indeed, a few fluted points have been found. But a reassessment of these sites in Alaska strongly suggests that these artifacts date to less than 10,000 years old. While the only fluted point found in a datable context in the corridor was at Charlie Creek Cave, British Columbia, its radiocarbon age is a mere 9,500 years old—much too late for pre-Clovis. This date poses another major problem for the Clovis-first model, but it makes sense, particularly because recent geological work in the ice-free corridor suggests that it was uninhabitable until around 11,000 years ago. The logical implication of these dates is that the people who made the northern fluted points are likely descendants of Clovis peoples, not ancestors. This was a real surprise in the light of my thinking back in 1983, when this article first appeared in *AnthroNotes*.

In the original article there is mention of a caribou bone tool from Old Crow, as well as broken mammoth bones from the Dutton and Selby sites. The hypothesis of a pre-Clovis culture bone and stone technology is no longer considered tenable; with new radiocarbon dating techniques, the Old Crow Basin bone tool was shown to be only about 6,000 years old. The bone tool theory was a popular one in the early 1980s, but Gary Haynes, a graduate student working with me, set out to disprove the theory and managed to show the complexities of the issues and disprove many of the bone tools.

What we now are learning is that bone tools are still important evidence, but they have to be in association with lithic materials as well. Otherwise, there are just too many other possible explanations for their existence. Gary Haynes has continued to do important work, including studies of elephant bones in Zimbabwe, Africa. Today he is chairman of the Anthropology Department at the University of Nevada at Reno.

Blackwater Draw remains an important site. We found a Clovis level and, more importantly, a water well that Clovis people dug at a time when the surface springs were drying up. Unfortunately for the Clovis inhabitants, the well proved to be a dry hole. This find is certainly tantalizing, as it raises the whole question of environmental impact and the possibility that an increasingly dry environment severely affected the Clovis lifestyle. The Lamb Spring site, also described in the original article, was taken over by the Archaeological Conservancy, which, working with the Denver Museum of Science and Technology, the University of Colorado, and Douglas County, is planning on building an on-site museum, for which I am serving as consultant.

During the 1990s I began to look at sites in the southeastern United States, including Tennessee and Kentucky, where there is early dated Clovis material, evidence that perhaps Clovis technology developed in the east and then moved westward. It now appears that the Clovis complex, marked by distinctive projectile points, was an interesting but short-lived archaeological phenomenon. The technology was apparently highly adaptive to diverse, mosaic environments. It arose first, I think, in the American Southeast out of earlier unfluted biface traditions and spread within a relatively short time span, from about 11,500 to 10,900 years ago, into the Southwest and Plains. After this period, apparently the pluvial lakes rose and again watered the countryside. In addition, the rangelands improved, and the bison populations probably increased dramatically. As in the east, Clovis hunters adapted to new environmental conditions and adjusted their weaponry and settlement pattern accordingly. In the Rocky Mountains and adjacent Plains, Clovis became what we know today as the Folsom bison hunting culture.

So we can return to our original question: Where did Clovis ancestors come from and how did they get to North America? Unless they arrived before the last great ice age, they would have had to do so by sea. By boat? Were the mammoth hunters descendants of mariners?

Before you cry, "No way!" let me briefly point out that sometime between 60,000 and 50,000 years ago, ancient mariners arrived on the shores of Australia. In so doing they were out of sight of land for some 80 kilometers. Maybe the first ocean crossing was accidental, but eventually enough folks arrived on the island continent to create a sustainable population. After some 30,000 years of research and development of marine technology, sailors from Japan (then part of the Asian continent) navigated to and returned from islands located some 100 kilometers offshore. These voyages can be documented because the early mariners collected obsidian for the manufacture of stone tools and the obsidian could have come only from specific sources that are unique to certain islands. To achieve this task, they first had to know the obsidian source was on these islands, perhaps indicating exploring voyages. To get to the islands and return home implies some form of navigation, and to have done so, they likely sailed windward or at least across the current on one leg or more of the voyage.

In all of Northeast Asia there is as yet no known late Paleolithic technology based on the production of bifaces and macroblades similar to the technology we find in North American sometime after 11,000 years ago. The only other place in the world where such a technological combination occurs is in the Solutrean culture of what is today northern Spain and southwestern France.

Dating between 20,000 and 16,500 years ago, the Solutrean culture flourished on the Ice Age Atlantic coast and presumably the now inundated continental shelf. A number of scholars in the past have pointed out the similarities between Clovis and Solutrean technologies, but several seemingly irresolvable obstacles prevented them from postulating a historic connection. Chief among these problems is the age difference of some 5,500 years and the belief that these Paleolithic peoples could not have navigated the Atlantic Ocean. Since we now believe that early navigation of the sea was possible and even probable, especially for folks who for generations had lived by the sea, we will turn our attention to the time gap.

The oldest dates for Clovis are in the southeastern area of the United States, where there are more Clovis sites and artifacts than are found in any other region of the country. I believed, as do others, that this implies a longer and more concentrated occupation of Clovis people in this area. As early as 1991, I published a paper suggesting that the distinctive Clovis technology evolved from a southeastern unfluted point and macroblade complex known as Suwannee. As yet undated, Suwannee has long been thought by mainstream archaeologists to be late Clovis. Why late Clovis? Simply because we all know that Clovis was the earliest, hence every other culture comes later!

A number of years ago a site was found in southwestern Pennsylvania known as Meadowcroft Rockshelter. The earliest occupation levels of this site boast artifacts dated to a very early time period, between 12,000 and 14,000 years old. The validity of this site has long been in contention because of possible contamination of the charcoal, presumably causing the dates to be very old. However, recent geological research has strongly argued that there is no problem with contamination and the early dates are likely valid.

In the last several years, another discovery was made at a site called Cactus Hill in southeastern Virginia. The earliest occupation level at this site produced artifacts similar to those from Meadowcroft. The Cactus Hill occupation has a hearth feature that dates to around 16,000 years ago. The technology present at both sites includes bifacial projectile points and blades.

These artifacts could easily be lost in either a Solutrean or a Clovis collection. Not that they are identical, but the technologies are clearly similar and would be considered by an analyst to be within the outside norms of either group. Thus it would appear that Cactus Hill and Meadowcroft fill the time gap between Solutrean and Clovis.

Given this information, one could easily argue that the Clovis technology developed out of the Cactus Hill/Meadowcroft technology, which in turn had its roots in Solutrean. Recently Bruce Bradley, an excellent lithic technologist and expert in both Clovis and the Old World Paleolithic, and I decided that we should together reevaluate the hypothesis of a Solutrean connection to Clovis. Is this similarity an issue of direct historical connection and cultural development, or is it simply a matter of independent invention by people solving similar problems with similar raw material resources?

To answer this question we examined as many Solutrean and Clovis assemblages as possible and compared the assemblages on a number of levels, ranging from simple presence or absence of tool types down to the minutiae of manufacturing steps. We are currently working on a book manuscript that describes in detail the results of these studies. It is clear to us that there are so many traits in common among the three groups (Solutrean, Clovis, and Cactus Hill/Meadowcroft) that it is difficult to imagine that their similarities resulted by chance. Furthermore, a cluster analysis groups these technologies together and separates them from other European Paleolithic technologies and from the trans-Siberian/Alaskan lithic technologies.

Clearly if there is final proof, it will reside in paleobiology studies such as morphometric analysis of human remains, DNA studies, and the like. These studies, along with Paleolithic archaeology and interdisciplinary research, suggest that the peopling of the Americas is a complicated issue with no single answer. Even if people were crossing the Atlantic, others were also crossing from Asia over the Bering Strait, perhaps in several different episodes. Additionally, without a doubt we know people crossed from Northeast Asia into what is today Alaska after 11,000 years ago and from there moved southward through Alberta and eastern British Columbia. I now believe, however, that these folks were not the ancestors of the Clovis people, a belief I have held firmly for most of my professional life.

FURTHER READING

Bonnichsen, R., Dennis Stanford, and J. L. Fastook. 1987. "Environmental Change and Developmental History of Human Adaptive Patterns: The Paleo-Indian

Case." In W. F. Ruddiman and H. E. Wright Jr., eds., *North America and Adjacent Oceans During the Last Deglaciation: The Geology of North America,* vol. K-3, pp. 403–24. Geological Society of America.

Bonnichsen, Robson, and Karen L. Turnmire, eds. 1999. *Ice Age Peoples of North America: Environment, Origins, and Adaptations of the First Americans.* Oregon State University Press for the Center for the Study of the First Americans.

Dillehay, Thomas D. 2000. *The Settlement of the Americas: A New Prehistory.* Basic Books.

Dixon, E. James. 1993. *Quest for the Origins of the First Americans.* University of New Mexico Press.

Dixon, E. James. 1999. *Bones, Boats, and Bison and the First Colonization of Western North America.* University of New Mexico Press.

Frison, George C., ed. 1996. *The Mill Iron Site.* University of New Mexico Press.

Haynes, Gary. 2002. *The Early Settlement of North America: The Clovis Era.* Cambridge University Press.

Humphrey, Robert L. 1966. "The Prehistory of the Utokok River Region in Arctic Alaska: Early Fluted Point Tradition with Old Relationships." *Current Anthropology* 7(5):586–88.

Jablonsky, Nina G., ed. 2002. "The First Americans: The Pleistocene Colonization of the New World." *Memoirs of the California Academy of Sciences,* No. 27. California Academy of Sciences.

Martin, P. S. 1984. "Prehistoric Overkill: The Global Model." In P. S. Martin and R. G. Klein, eds., *Quaternary Extinctions: A Prehistoric Revolution,* pp. 354–404. University of Arizona Press.

Meltzer, David J. 1995. "Clocking the First Americans." *Annual Review of Anthropology* 24:21–45.

Stanford, Dennis. 1991. "Clovis Origins and Adaptations: An Introductory Perspective." In Robson Bonnichsen and Karen L. Turnmire, eds., *Clovis: Origins and Adaptations,* pp. 1–13. Center for the Study of the First Americans, Oregon State University.

Stanford, Dennis, and Bruce Bradley. 2002. "Ocean Trails and Prairie Paths? Thoughts About Clovis Origins." In Jablonsky 2002, pp. 255–71.

19 THE FIRST SOUTH AMERICANS

Archaeology at Monte Verde

Tom D. Dillehay

The 12,500-year-old Monte Verde site, in southern Chile, has helped shift thinking about the earliest human migrations into the Americas. Like Dennis Stanford, Dillehay believes that groups of hunters and gatherers possibly ancestral to the Clovis people may have lived in what is today Chile as far back as 16,000–13,000 B.C. Although no human bones have been found thus far, there has been other evidence to suggest human occupation.

When did human beings first set foot in the New World? How did they get here? What lifeways did they follow? How did they adapt to and affect the ancient American ecosystem? These questions have been hotly debated for over a hundred years. Scientists now agree only that big-game hunters were in North America by 11,000 years ago [see Williams, "Who Got to American First? Fact and Fiction," and Selig and Stanford, "Researching the First Americans: One Archaeologist's Journey," in this volume].

The earliest possible date for the initial arrival of early humans and other aspects of their culture are disputed, although fieldwork over the last twenty-five years has yielded more evidence about their economy, technology, and social organization. The biggest surprises have come from South America, where recent work suggests that this continent was occupied by at least 12,000 years ago, and possibly much earlier, by people with very diverse subsistence strategies.

In recent years, the most significant advances in the study of the first Americans have come from innovative data recovery and analysis techniques

that have yielded vastly more accurate reconstructions of ancient environments and subsistence strategies. For example, the soil from a house floor
at Monte Verde, in Chile, contained amino acids specific to collagen, a protein found in bone, cartilage, and skin. Microscopic analysis of the material
suggested that a thick skin, possibly a mastodon hide, had been used in the
construction of the shelter. We now know that the earliest peoples—such as
the Clovis and Folsom—were not just specialized big-game hunters armed
with large bifacially chipped projectile points. Reliable evidence from the
Meadowcroft Rockshelter site in Pennsylvania, the Monte Verde site in
southern Chile, and others scattered throughout the hemisphere suggests the
widespread presence of people who not only hunted large and small game
but also collected wild plant food and fished in streams and lakes.

In the early 1970s, evidence about the first South Americans was limited
to a small series of stone tools and animal bones, mostly from caves and rock
shelters. Dates for these sites were often questionable, and many of the tools
were not clearly made by human hands. A significant new body of evidence,
mainly retrieved by Latin American archaeologists—including Gonzalo Cor-
real, Gerardo Ardila, José Cruxent, Augusto Cardich, Lautaro Núñez, Gus-
tavo Politis, Nora Flegenheimer, Niède Guidon, and Pedro Schmitz—has
been reported from early radiocarbon-dated stratigraphic contexts in many
parts of South America. The Tequendama, Tibíto, and El Abra sites in
Colombia, the Monte Verde and Quereo sites in Chile, the Los Toldos site in
Argentina, and several sites in Uruguay and north-central Brazil, including
Pedra Furada, all yielded radiocarbon dates of about 11,500 years ago or
earlier. As a result of archaeological investigations at these sites, we can now
place the minimum time for the first occupation of South America at approximately 12,000 years ago, possibly even 20,000 years ago.

MONTE VERDE DISCOVERED

The Maullin River flows through the cool forested country west of the Andes
in south-central Chile. In 1976, when I was directing the anthropology program at the Southern University of Chile, in Valdivia, a number of Chilean
and Argentinean colleagues and I were surveying the river. Buried in the
banks of a small tributary creek, we discovered the unusual open-air wetland
site of Monte Verde. Layers of peat bog, which form only in cool, wet climates where organic materials are waterlogged before they have a chance
to decay, had preserved organic remains to an extraordinary degree. There
we found not only chipped stone tools and the bones of extinct animals but
also well-preserved wooden artifacts, dwelling foundations of both earth and
wood, and the remains of edible and possibly medicinal plants. What makes

Monte Verde especially interesting is the form and arrangement of the architecture and activity areas, which reveal a social and economic organization much more complex and generalized than previously suspected for a late Ice Age culture of the New World. A long sequence of radiocarbon dates on stratigraphic noncultural and cultural deposits places this cultural episode at between 12,000 and 13,000 years ago. In another area of the site, deeper deposits contain stone tools and possibly cultural features that may date to an even older culture.

The majority of late Pleistocene sites so far excavated in the Americas contain stone tools, animal bones, and some plant material. The finds rarely consist of organic remains such as wooden implements, and thus may represent a small portion of the cultural evidence. The preservation, diversity, and complexity of organic and inorganic remains at Monte Verde have been studied by an interdisciplinary research team in an effort to reconstruct the paleoecology of the site area and to evaluate critically the evidence for human intervention in the site. These specialists include more than sixty scientists from such disciplines as geology, palynology, botany, entomology, animal pathology, paleontology, ecology, forestry engineering, malacology, diatomology, and microbiology.

Collectively, these studies have shown that the area around Monte Verde today has moderately warm, dry summers and cold, rainy winters, with a mean annual temperature fluctuating between 12 and 15 degrees centigrade. The climate that prevailed in the late Pleistocene after the ice sheets receded resembled this setting, although it was probably slightly cooler and more humid. A forest made up of a mixture of deciduous and coniferous trees covers the region today; it supplies numerous varieties of edible tubers, nuts, berries, fruits, and soft and leafy plants abundantly throughout the year. There are also small game, freshwater mollusks, and fish. In late Pleistocene times, mastodons, saber-toothed tigers, ground sloths, and probably paleo-camelids roamed the area. The nearest point on the Pacific coast lies about 55 kilometers west and 20 kilometers south of the site and offers many edible species of marine organisms. All of these sources of food were available to the early inhabitants of Monte Verde.

LATE PLEISTOCENE SETTLEMENT STRUCTURE

The Monte Verde site is divided into east and west sides. On the east side of the site the remains of ten or eleven foundations of residential huts have been recovered. The foundations are formed by small timbers, limbs, and roughly shaped planks usually held in place by wooden stakes. Fallen branches and

THE ARCHAEOLOGISTS FOUND EVIDENCE OF
SKIN HOUSES, WOODEN TOOLS, FOOTPRINTS
AND COPROLITES AT THE SITE....

vertical post stubs reveal that the hut frames were made primarily of hardwoods. The side walls were placed about 1 meter apart against a wall foundation and then apparently draped with animal skins, as suggested by the presence of a few small fragments of skin still clinging to the fallen side poles. Preliminary results of microscopic and other studies by microbiologists and pathologists suggest that the skins are most likely from a large animal, probably the mastodon.

A wide variety of plant remains, stone tools, food stains, and small braziers (shallow pits for holding burning coals) was found on the living surface inside each hut. The braziers, which contained ash, specks of charcoal, and the remains of numerous plant foods, were probably used to heat each hut and warm the food. Cooking was evidently a communal effort, as shown by the discovery of two large clay and charcoal hearths centrally located outside the huts. The recovery of three roughly shaped wooden mortars and several grinding stones near the hearths suggest that the preparation of plant food took place next to the hearths.

Who were these ancient South Americans? No human bones have yet been recovered from the excavations at Monte Verde, but there are two indirect indicators of information about the site's inhabitants. One is the imprint of a foot preserved in stored clay around one of the large hearths. The other indirect source of information consists of possible coprolites (fossil excrement) that appear to be of human origin. These were recovered from small pits dug in the ground, also near a hearth.

The west side of the site is characterized by a nonresidential structure and activity area. The central feature is a roughly ovoid-shaped artificial rise of sand and a few gravels. Resting on this rise is an architectural foundation made of sand and gravel compacted to form a peculiar wishbone shape, with a rectangular platform protruding from its exterior base. Fragments of upright wooden stubs were present approximately every few centimeters along both arms of the structure. Presumably these are the remains of a pole frame draped with hides. The same type and size of braziers recorded on the east side of the site were found on the occupation surface both inside and outside the structure. Of particular interest is the association of the hearths with preserved bits of apparent animal hide, burned seeds and stalks of bulrush reed, and masticated leaves of plants found in warmer environments and used by the present-day Mapuche for medicinal purposes. The shape, the location, and the artifactual content of the wishbone feature suggest that the structure and this end of the site served a special purpose, rather than being living quarters.

STONES AND BONES AT MONTE VERDE

The stone tools from Monte Verde are similar to those from other sites in the Americas, although the use of naturally fractured stones, common at Monte Verde, has not been widely reported from other sites. The Monte Verdeans utilized three different methods for making stone tools: flaking, pecking-grounding, and modification through use on some unflaked stones. The organic remains are more unusual. More than four hundred bones, including those of extinct camelids, mastodons, and small game, were recovered from the site. Most of the bone remains are rib fragments of at least seven individual mastodons. Several bones were modified as possible digging sticks, gouging tools, or other implements.

Besides the wooden architecture foundations, several types of artifacts made of wood were excavated, including a sharply pointed lancelike implement, three crude wooden mortars, two tool hafts or handles, five digging sticks, and more than three hundred pieces of wood exhibiting cut or planed facets, burned areas, cut marks, and/or smoothed and thinned surfaces. Several bones were sharpened and burned. Their association with underground plant parts (tubers) and with grooved wooden slats with horizontal grooves suggest that they might have been used as digging sticks and gouging tools.

INTERPRETATIONS

What did the ancient Monte Verdeans capture with their assortment of stone, bone, and wooden tools? From the array of inorganic and organic remains, we can determine that they were exploiting resources from distant reaches of the Maullin Valley. Most of the differing environmental zones were aquatic areas: swamps, bogs, river bottoms, marshes, estuaries, and lagoons. How many people lived at the site? Ten or eleven residential structures and one unique structure have been excavated. Among the modern Mapuche, similar huts are occupied by two or three individuals. By analogy, we estimate that at least twenty-five to thirty-five individuals lived at Monte Verde during the Late Pleistocene.

If wood had not been preserved, we would have recovered only stone tools, postholes, stains, and perhaps bones and mollusk shells. Evidence of plant foods and most of the residential characteristics that tell us this was a village would have been lost. In fact, the site might well have been interpreted as a kill site with a temporary residential component, like most of the North American Paleo-Indian sites.

CONCLUSION

The preservation of the perishable materials at Monte Verde and the diversity of the social, technological, and economic activities represented there make this site exceedingly important and scientifically unique at this time. Monte Verde cautions us to keep an open mind toward the possible diversity of lifestyles of the first Americans and of the various ways these lifeways might be expressed and preserved in a local archaeological record.

This very early dated occupation site comes from the southern end of South America and hence reminds us that we will probably discover and verify yet earlier sites in North America in the future.

As was the case in the past twenty-five years, the next few years will certainly produce more information on these problems and on other types of sites and will provide additional evidence about the entry date of the first Americans and about their environment, technology, and life ways. I doubt, however, that the most emotionally charged question of when people first arrived on this continent will ever be settled to everyone's satisfaction. The first human site in the New World may never be found, and even if it were, we probably would never recognize it as such.

UPDATE

Much rethinking has taken place in recent years as a result of new discoveries in archaeology and in historical linguistics and genetics. Several archaeological sites in North America have great potential to document earlier signs of human occupation. The eastern United States in particular has yielded more convincing evidence of cultures ancestral to Clovis—in addition to Meadowcroft Rockshelter, Cactus Hill in Virginia, and the Topper Site in South Carolina—suggesting that groups of hunters and gatherers possibly ancestral to the Clovis people may have lived in those areas as far back as 13,000 to 16,000 years ago. These possibilities are supportive of the 12,500-year occupation at Monte Verde, because if people first came to the Americas across the Bering land bridge, we would expect earlier dates in North America. It also is likely that multiple early migrations took place and that people migrated along the edge of the ice sheets from northern Europe into eastern North America, a theory recently developed by Dennis Stanford and Bruce Bradley.

There also is discussion of possible influences from Africa and even Australia. Walter Neves of the University of São Paulo believes that the oldest skeletal material from Brazil more strongly relates to ancient Africans and Australians than to modern Asians and Native Americans. This suggests the presence of non-Mongoloid as well as Mongoloid populations in the Americans. He believes that these migrants did not come directly from Africa or Australia but rather splintered off from an earlier group that moved through Asia and eventually arrived in Australia.

Linguists and geneticists also postulate earlier migrations. Johanna Nichols of the University of California at Berkeley believes that a high diversity of languages among Native Americans could only have developed from an earlier human presence in the New World, perhaps as old as 20,000 to 30,000 years ago. Several geneticists present the same argument derived from genetic diversity. Based on comparisons between certain genetic signatures shared by modern Native Americans and modern Siberians, it has been estimated that people from Siberia entered the New World at least 25,000 years ago.

These new discoveries and ideas are not without their critics, of course. Staunch Clovis proponents who have spent their entire careers defending the old Clovis theory still hold to the notion that the first Americans were mainly big-game hunters who entered the Americas from Siberia no earlier than 12,000 to 11,500 years ago. These proponents believe that notions of a pre-Clovis presence are based on dubious radiocarbon dates, site stratigraphy, and interpretations of the evidence. Although these criticisms are frequently constructive and encourage a more rigorous approach to the study of the first Americans, they are often based on anecdotal tales and little, if any, scientific evidence. Despite the continuing debate over the first peopling of the Americas and the ambiguity of some interdisciplinary evidence, two issues are becoming clear. Although the Clovis theory accounts for a portion of the first chapter of human history in North America, it fails to explain the earliest cultural and biological diversity in the Western Hemisphere, especially in South America. Regardless of the ambiguity of evidence, the first American populations were a melting pot for a very long time, with genetic and cultural roots from many different areas.

FURTHER READING

Bryan, A. L., ed. 1986. *New Evidence for the Pleistocene Peopling of the Americas.* Center for the Study of Early Man, University of Maine.

Chatters, James C. 2001. *Ancient Encounters: Kennewick Man and the First Americans.* Simon and Schuster.

Dillehay, Tom D. 1989. *Monte Verde: A Late Pleistocene Settlement in Chile,* vol. 1: *A Palaeoenvironment and Site Context.* Smithsonian Institution Press.

Dillehay, Tom D. 1997. *Monte Verde: A Late Pleistocene Settlement in Chile,* vol. 2: *The Archaeological Context and Interpretation.* Smithsonian Institution Press.

Dillehay, Tom D. 2000. *The Settlement of the Americas: A New Prehistory.* Basic Books.

Fagan, Brian M. 1987. *The Great Journey: The Peopling of Ancient America.* Thames and Hudson.

Meltzer, David J. 1993. *Search for the First Americans.* Smithsonian Books.

Thomas, David Hurst. 2000. *Skull Wars: Kennewick Man, Archaeology, and the Battle for Native American Identity.* Basic Books.

20 WHO WERE THE ANCIENT MAYA?

Jeremy A. Sabloff

The Maya have long fascinated both scholars and the general public, because of their intellectual and artistic achievements and the large urban centers they built, which we can still visit today. Sabloff's chapter reveals how new research is illuminating the development and accomplishments of the Maya over a 2,000-year period and how these new insights are changing traditional views of Maya history.

Ancient Maya civilization flourished for more than 2,000 years, lasting from approximately 500 B.C. until the A.D. 1540s, the time of the Spanish Conquest. The ancient Maya are renowned for their achievements in art, architecture, writing, science, and urban planning in the varied and challenging environment of the greater Yucatán peninsula and neighboring areas. Today the ancient Maya civilization's cultural heirs, who number in the millions, continue to thrive in modern-day Mexico and Central America.

In recent years pathbreaking archaeological, epigraphical, and ethnohistorical research is providing significant new insights into the development and accomplishments of the ancient Maya. Scholars now understand that the Maya territory was an integral part of a wider cultural area known as Mesoamerica, which includes the Maya area and most of Mexico to the north. The ancient Maya were not an isolated culture but had numerous economic, political, and ideological interactions with peoples in other parts of Mexico such as the Gulf Coast lowlands, the Valley of Oaxaca, and the Basin of Mexico.

THREE GEOGRAPHIC ZONES

The Maya area covers over 300,000 square kilometers that today includes southern Mexico, Guatemala, Belize, and parts of Honduras and El Salvador. This huge area can be divided into three geographic zones: the lowlands, the highlands, and the Pacific coastal plain and piedmont. Today, a wide variety of environments can be found in these zones, which do not differ significantly from those of more than 2,000 years ago. The Maya successfully exploited these differing and challenging environments but also had to cope with their fragility and the impact of short-term changes such as drought and natural disasters such as volcanic eruptions. Ancient Maya civilization reached its zenith in the lowlands, especially in the south, but all of the geographic zones played key roles in the growth and flowering of this fascinating, complex pre-Columbian culture. Through time, the demographic, economic, and political focus of ancient Maya civilization shifted across the landscape of this vast and varied homeland area.

The beginnings of complexity emerged in the Pacific coastal and piedmont zone. This productive zone, which runs along the entire southern margin of the Maya area, has relatively high rainfall and a variety of fertile agricultural regions. The coastal plain is crosscut by a large number of small rivers that flow south from the adjacent highlands. The shoreline and widespread rivers offered numerous trade routes, which the ancient Maya exploited throughout their history. The low foothills of the highlands to the north also supported intensive cultivation of such key crops as cacao.

Shortly after the beginnings of complexity emerged along the coastal plain, both the highlands and the lowlands began to develop rapidly, with writing flourishing first in the highlands and large monumental architecture flourishing first in the lowlands. The lowlands ultimately emerged as the center of Maya civilization, first in the south and later in the north. The highland, Pacific coastal, and piedmont zones also witnessed important developments throughout the later history of Maya civilization. Although the Spanish conquered the whole area, beginning in the early sixteenth century A.D., the timing and intensity of the Conquest differed significantly within and among the geographic zones.

EARLY HISTORY

What became the Maya area was initially occupied soon after the close of the last ice age, more than ten thousand years ago. Over the following millennia, small groups of nomadic hunters and gatherers utilized the area's varied animal and plant resources, leaving occasional traces of their short-term occupations in the form of stone tool fragments. The beginnings of the domestication of the crucially important maize plant currently can be traced as early as the middle of the fourth millennium B.C. (3500 B.C.), with later settled village life—based on the productivity and storage of cultivated plants— emerging by the second millennium. It is at this time that the roots of ancient Maya civilization emerged.

The chronology of ancient Maya civilization has traditionally been divided into three parts—Preclassic, Classic, and Postclassic—each with its own subdivisions. These chronological periods were originally formulated to mark significant changes in Maya history, especially what was seen as the peak of Maya civilization, namely, the Classic period in the southern lowlands.

Recent research has shown that the hallmarks of the Classic period—writing, monumental art and architecture, the corbeled vault, and polychrome pottery—were all present during Preclassic times. New research also demonstrates that the Postclassic period was *not* a time of Maya decline after the end of the Classic; other zones besides the southern lowlands witnessed significant cultural developments as well. Nevertheless, the traditional periodization of Maya history remains well entrenched in both scholarly and popular usage, and to avoid confusion, I will continue to use it in this article.

However, as I maintained more than a decade ago, it is useful to group these traditional periods into three longer phases without internal subdivisions: the Early Phase (2000 B.C.–300 B.C.), the Middle Phase (300 B.C.–A.D. 1200), and the Late Phase (A.D. 1200–1540s). These period names use more neutral terms than the word *classic* and, I believe, better correspond to the general developmental trends in the ancient Maya world than does the traditional period scheme. In this paper I will refer to both the traditional periods and the longer phases.

THE EARLY PHASE (2000 B.C.–300 B.C.)

This phase includes the Early and Middle Preclassic periods, the time when scholars can trace the beginnings of Maya civilization to settled agricultural villages, which cultivated a number of productive crops, including maize. The earliest villages were in the Pacific coastal and piedmont zone, but the highlands and southern lowlands soon followed. The rise of complex technological, economic, political, artistic, and religious developments also can be traced to this time period. Thereafter, growing populations throughout the Maya area moved into previously unoccupied zones, and the size of individual farming villages expanded.

MAYA HISTORY

Between 1000 and 500 B.C., increasing population, together with de-creasing land available for settlement and agricultural production, led to larger population aggregations. This in turn brought with it administrative developments, more intensive forms of agriculture to support the growing populations, and ultimately the emergence of competition and conflict over scarcer lands and resources.

The first highly visible signs of change began to appear by 500 B.C., if not earlier, as several population centers began to increase relatively rapidly in size, and large public buildings burst upon the scene at population centers such as Nakbé, El Mirador, and Tikal in the southern lowlands, and Kami-naljuyú and El Portón in the highlands. Monumental carved stones with de-pictions of local rulers also first appeared in the highland and coastal zones during the Early Phase. It is evident that rulers were able to mobilize con-siderable labor forces to construct large public buildings and use monumen-tal sculpture to glorify and consolidate their economic, political, and reli-gious powers.

Moreover, even in these early times, the Maya already were interacting with groups in neighboring areas, such as the Olmecs from the Gulf Coast and the Zapotecs from Oaxaca. These interactions led to trade, as well as the introduction of new ideas and ideologies. For example, hieroglyphic writing and calendrics were invented north of the Maya area in places such as the Valley of Oaxaca. The Maya built on these early innovations to produce their own sophisticated writing system before the end of the Early Phase. Clearly, what archaeologists generally call "chiefdoms" emerged at this time, as many Maya settlements grew in cultural complexity, and the roots of Maya cities and states were planted.

THE MIDDLE PHASE (300 B.C.–A.D. 1200)

This Middle Phase includes the Late Preclassic, the Classic, the Terminal Classic, and the Early Postclassic periods in the older classification. It is during this long and critical phase that Maya civilization is widely perceived to have reached its height. Cities attained their largest size; rulers had their greatest powers, and artistic, architectural, and scientific achievements were extraordinary. The locus of widespread cultural developments during the first period of the Middle Phase was in the highlands and Pacific coastal and piedmont zones, and most particularly in the southern highlands. However, in the southern lowlands, sites such as El Mirador and Tikal soon rose to prominence.

In recent years, scholars have recognized that many of the hallmarks of Classic Maya civilization were present by the Late Preclassic period, if not earlier. In particular, the growth of urban centers, political states, and dynastic rulership can be traced to this time in both the highlands and the lowlands. Hieroglyphic inscriptions with calendric and historical information became more widespread in the highland and Pacific coastal and piedmont zones but soon spread into the lowlands. By the middle of Late Preclassic times, the people had also begun to utilize the uniquely Maya calendric system—the Long Count—which was based on a linear calendar that reckoned time from a start date of 3114 B.C. However, use of Long Count dating did not become common in the lowlands until Classic times. Rulers at El Mirador constructed some of the largest structures ever built in the Maya area, consisting of immense stone platforms supporting huge elite buildings.

Toward the end of the Late Preclassic period, the highland and Pacific coastal centers suffered a major decline, as did some of the lowland centers such as El Mirador, which had close ties to the highlands. The reasons for this decline remain unclear. It is at this time that the political and economic locus of Maya civilization shifted from the highlands to the lowlands. The idea of dynastic rule, which had been present in the highlands, took root in the lowlands and both older sites such as Tikal and relatively newer ones such as Copán, near the southern frontier of the lowlands, grew in size and importance under dynastic political leadership. Although some highland sites recovered from their decline at the close of the Late Preclassic period, they lost their preeminence to the lowlands.

The Classic Period (A.D. 300–800)

During the Classic period Maya civilization burgeoned in all geographic zones. Populations at older centers increased, while many new cities were founded as the growing numbers of peoples filled in the landscape. Although there is great scholarly debate about the population figures, by the beginning of the Late Classic period the overall lowland population alone may have exceeded 5 million and the larger cities such as Tikal had populations in the many tens of thousands. The arts and architecture thrived, significant achievements in astronomy and mathematics were made, and an intricate ideological system involving numerous deities with multiple personae evolved. Social divisions became exacerbated, with a small elite class growing in wealth and power and a large peasant class supplying the food and labor that supported the expanding cities. There is considerable scholarly debate about whether the non-elite class was further divided into a series of subclasses as well.

The Maya area was an important player in the larger Mesoamerican cultural system during the Classic period. Cities such as Tikal, Copán, and Kaminaljuyú had ties to Teotihuacán—the great city in the Basin of Mexico—and elite goods and peoples moved over relatively large distances. Archaeological and epigraphic data indicate that Teotihuacán played an important role in the political and economic development of Maya civilization, although the exact nature of this role remains unclear and controversial.

Recent dramatic advances in the decipherment of Maya hieroglyphic texts now allow scholars to appreciate the very complicated political landscape during Classic times in the lowlands and the waxing and waning of political fortunes of individual cities and ruling dynasties. Important archaeological research at the great urban centers of Tikal and Calakmul, for instance, along with new historical understandings from the texts, have illuminated the rivalries between these two cities. Tikal and then Calakmul and then Tikal again gained the upper hand with either direct or indirect influence over a number of other lowland centers.

In addition, significant ongoing research at Copán has been able to tie together dynastic rule, architectural growth, urban and rural settlement, and the ecology of the Copán Valley in a much clearer picture of the city's rise and fall throughout the Classic period. As similar knowledge is gained at other Maya cities, scholarly understanding of this key time period clearly will be significantly strengthened.

Terminal Classic (A.D. 800–1000) and Early Postclassic (A.D. 100–1200) Periods

Toward the close of the eighth century A.D., after a lengthy flourishing, many of the principal cities in the southern lowlands declined rapidly in population and power. From this time on, the southern lowlands remained relatively lightly populated and drastically less important both politically and economically. The causes of this demise were systemic and multiple, with demographic stress, a possible drought, trade disruptions, and intercity conflicts all implicated in this downturn.

Scholars used to believe that Maya civilization collapsed in the ninth century A.D., but recent research indicates that this was not the case. First, some southern lowland cities, especially those located near water trade routes and rich cacao- and cotton-growing areas, continued to thrive while other cities were declining. Second, cities in the northern lowlands, especially Chichén Itzá and others such as Uxmal, began to thrive just as many southern cities were collapsing. Third, the Chontal, a mercantile, water-oriented Maya group from the Gulf Coast lowlands who had close economic contacts with many areas of ancient Mesoamerica, began to spread their influence at this time in both the highlands and the lowlands. Ultimately they focused their attention on the northern lowlands.

Thus, just as the demographic, political, and economic focus of Maya civilization had shifted from the southern highlands to the southern lowlands in the first part of the Middle Phase, so did the focus shift again in the latter part of the phase, from the southern lowlands to the northern lowlands. Contrary to previous understandings, Maya civilization did not collapse, but continued to prosper, albeit in a different and more restricted area.

This new northern florescence can be seen in such zones as the hilly Puuc region, where densely packed cities such as Uxmal, Kabah, Sayil, and Labná thrived at the end of the Classic period and the first half of the Terminal Classic. The indigenous Maya population of the region grew rapidly at this time, exploiting the best agricultural lands in the northern lowlands. The reasons for the rise of the Puuc region sites and their relatively brief heyday have yet to be established. Recent research has shown that a few Puuc sites developed much earlier in the Classic, while the research my colleagues and I carried out at Sayil does not indicate any influx of population from the south at the end of the Classic. So the connections between the southern decline and northern florescence were not demographic but were probably at least in part economic. The causes of decline of the Puuc sites also are unclear. Drought and overpopulation are two of the factors often mentioned in this regard.

However, new research at the great site of Chichén Itzá and elsewhere in the north is beginning to shed new light on this hitherto enigmatic city and

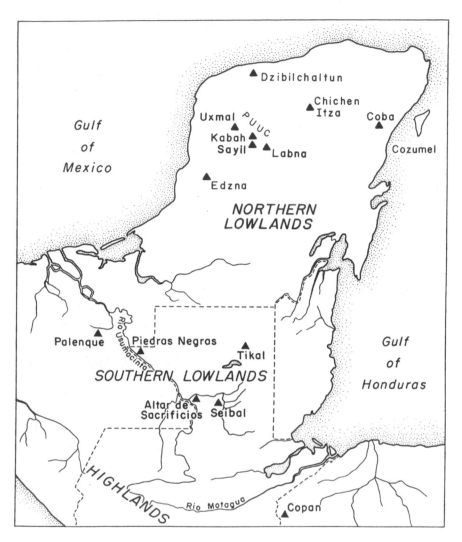

Urban Centers in the Northern and Southern Lowlands (courtesy Jeremy Sabloff)

its relations with the Puuc region. This research indicates that Chichén Itzá had widespread political (including military conquest) and economic influence throughout the northern lowlands during the Terminal Classic and into the Early Postclassic period. It may have defeated the cities in the Puuc region, causing their decline, and appears to have had no rivals by the early tenth century A.D. Chichén Itzá had tremendous religious importance, and its sacred well, or *cenote,* was a key pilgrimage destination. Its ruler, perhaps Chontal Maya, had close relationships with groups elsewhere in Mesoamerica, especially Central Mexico.

Most scholars now believe that this major political capital was not conquered by the Toltecs of Central Mexico. The similarities between Toltec Tula and Maya Chichén Itzá likely resulted from common cultural ties. Sometime toward the close of the Early Postclassic period, Chichén Itzá declined for reasons that still are not fully understood, and the northern lowlands split into a number of small political entities.

THE LATE PHASE (A.D. 1200–1540s)

The Late Phase witnessed some important cultural shifts in ancient Maya civilization. These included new emphasis on mercantile activities, changing urban designs, significantly diminished investments by the ruling elite in large, labor-intensive architectural projects to glorify themselves and their cities, and innovative forms of political control. The latter is best illustrated by the emergence of an extensive political confederacy led by the northern lowland center of Mayapán, which was a walled city with a dense population of about 12,000 people within its boundaries. Long-distance, waterborne trade around the Yucatán peninsula gained greater importance, with several trading centers becoming key nodes in the exchange of bulk goods such as cotton, honey, and salt. In the highlands, a series of regional centers that had first emerged toward the end of the Middle Phase gained additional power and prominence. These cities were still thriving at the time of the sixteenth-century Spanish Conquest. However, Mayapán had declined by the middle of the fifteenth century, and the political scene throughout the lowlands when the Spanish arrived was one of small, decentralized polities.

The Spanish Conquest

The Spanish Conquest of the Maya area began with the early voyages of Grijalva, Hernández de Córdoba, and Cortés from 1517 to 1519 and was essentially complete by the 1540s. Parts of the area remained unconquered, and some Maya remained resistant to Spanish and then to Mexican control even up to modern times. The Spanish Conquest destroyed much of the Maya elite and their cultural practices, and it decimated a significant part of Maya population through introduced diseases such as measles and smallpox. Military conquest, disease, and Spanish political control effectively brought an end to Maya civilization after more than two thousand years.

FURTHER READING

Culbert, T. Patrick. 1996. *Maya Civilization*. Exploring the Ancient World Series, edited by Jeremy A. Sabloff. St. Remy Books and Smithsonian Books.

Foster, Lynn V. 2002. *Handbook to Life in the Ancient Maya World*. Facts on File.

Marcus, Joyce. 1995. "Where is Lowland Maya Archaeology Heading?" *Journal of Archaeological Research* 3(1):3–53.

Martin, Simon, and Nikolai Grube. 1995. "Maya Superstates." *Archaeology* 48(6):41–46.

Pohl, Mary D., Kevin O. Pope, John G. Jones, John S. Jacob, Dolores R. Piperno, Susan deFrance, David L. Lentz, John A. Gifford, Marie E. Danforth, and J. Kathryn Josserand. 1996. "Early Agriculture in the Maya Lowlands." *Latin American Antiquity* 7(4):355–72.

Sabloff, Jeremy A. 1985. "Ancient Maya Civilization." In C. Galenkamp and R. E. Johnson, eds., *Maya: Treasures of an Ancient Civilization*, pp. 34–36. Harry N. Abrams.

Sabloff, Jeremy A. 1990. *The New Archaeology and the Ancient Maya*. W. H. Freeman.

Sabloff, Jeremy A. 1998. "Ancient Maya Civilization in Space and Time." In Peter Schmidt, Mercedes de la Garza, and Enrique Nalda, eds., *Maya*, pp. 52–71. Bompiani. (This chapter of *Anthropology Explored* is a much shorter and much revised version of this heavily illustrated chapter.)

Schele, Linda, and David Freidel. 1992. *A Forest of Kings: The Untold Story of the Ancient Maya*. William Morrow.

Schmidt, Peter, Mercedes de la Garza, and Enrique Nalda, eds. 1998. *Maya*. Bompiani.

Sharer, Robert J. 1994. *The Ancient Maya*. 5th ed. Stanford University Press.

Webster, David. 2002. *The Fall of the Ancient Maya: Solving the Mystery of the Maya Collapse*. Thames and Hudson.

21 ORIGINS OF AGRICULTURE IN EASTERN NORTH AMERICA

Ruth Osterweis Selig

This chapter details the dramatic story of Bruce D. Smith's groundbreaking research to document the eastern United States as an independent center of agricultural origins. The essay by Selig, along with Smith's update, answers such questions as what new technologies were used to document early North American plant domestication, why this domestication was important, and how the discovery of wild gourds in eastern North America proved pivotal to solving the research puzzle.

Long before the introduction of maize, farming economies and an agrarian way of life had been established in Eastern North America. . . . Documenting the origins of agriculture in North America emerged from revolutionary improvements in collecting ancient seeds combined with the application of new, sophisticated technologies—and the puzzle's missing pieces finally fell into place.

—Bruce D. Smith

Plant domestication can be defined as the human creation for human purposes of a new form of plant. Such a domesticated plant is clearly distinguishable from its wild ancestors and its wild relatives living today, and is dependent on human intervention—harvesting and planting—for survival. Today we take the domestication of plants and animals for granted, but the grains, vegetables, fruits, milk products, and meats we eat every day come from long-ago human intervention in the life cycles of wild plants and animals. Plant domestication is not simply a physical change. It is a revolutionary alteration of the relationship between human societies and plants brought under their control, enabling relatively few people to create food for large human populations, freeing most people to pursue other activities.

Many textbooks today still assert that agriculture in the New World originated in Mesoamerica, and that maize and squash spread from Mexico to eastern North America. Textbooks explain that Native Americans learned to cultivate not only maize and squash but also beans and a few indigenous seed crops such as sunflower. The growing of corn, squash, and beans thus enabled eastern North Americans to build larger settlements and more complex societies that depended on maize agriculture imported from Mesoamerica, where larger-scale societies had also developed.

New research shows that contrary to this long-held belief, eastern North America now can be unequivocally identified as an independent center of plant domestication, along with the Near East, China, Mesoamerica, and South America (Smith 1998, 2002). In fact, eastern North America provides the most detailed record of agricultural origins available anywhere in the world, providing new understanding of the processes involved in this key transformation in human history. *Turning point*

The beginning of agriculture marks a clear watershed and defines one of the major ecological changes in the history of the planet. However, revolutionary changes producing dramatic transformations may not be particularly dramatic in their origins or swift in their impact, or even easy to pinpoint and document.

PUZZLE PIECES

What were the domesticated food crops that Native American farmers grew in eastern North America? When and how did their domestication occur? Why has it taken so long to discover and recognize the contribution Native North Americans made to the origins of agriculture in the history of humankind? The understanding of Native American domestication in eastern North America is a story that can be visualized as a puzzle, with some pieces in place long before the full picture emerged.

Some pieces were discovered in the nineteenth century: Ebenezer Andrews excavated the first cache of stored indigenous seeds in Ash Cave, Ohio, in 1876. Many pieces emerged in the 1930s and 1950s, but several key pieces came together only in the late 1980s and early 1990s as new evidence—seeds and gourds—came to light and new technologies for dating and analysis were applied.

This chapter tells the story of several transformations: Native North Americans slowly changing their own way of life from foraging to farming; a new generation of archaeologists transforming their discipline with new

THE TRANSITION FROM HUNTING AND GATHERING TO DOMESTICATION

discoveries, questions, and sophisticated technologies; and one particular scientist, Smithsonian archaeologist Bruce Smith, working to put some of the final puzzle pieces in place. A scientist who relishes puzzles, theoretical challenges, and the opportunity to turn conventional wisdom on its head, Smith found the pieces in some unlikely places: in an old cigar box containing thousands of tiny ancient seeds, and along an Arkansas river valley where a bunch of small, wild, lemon-sized gourds grew.

EARLY NATIVE AMERICAN FARMERS

These facts now are indisputable. By 2000 B.C. in the eastern woodlands, Native Americans deliberately planted and harvested at least four indigenous seed plants independently of outside influences. This activity marked the beginning of their transition from foragers to farmers. Maize arrived from Mexico about 100 B.C., but for nine hundred years thereafter, corn was not a major food source. Why corn did not become widespread until after A.D. 800 remains a mystery; at first it may have been used only for religious and ceremonial purposes. After A.D. 800 intensive maize agriculture spread quickly and widely throughout the eastern woodlands as corn became a major staple of the diet.

With new tools, archaeologists have documented three major episodes in native North American domestication, as discussed below.

Phase One: 3000 to 2000 B.C.

Native Americans discovered that wild seed plants growing along river floodplains could be controlled, that plants could be harvested and used as food, with seeds stored and replanted in prepared garden plots the next year. Four indigenous plants underwent this transition to full domesticates, with clear morphological changes taking place in their seeds; three additional cultigens appear as food crops as Native Americans encouraged and harvested these previously wild sources of food. The highly nutritious seeds from these seven plants could be variously boiled into cereals, ground into flours, or eaten directly.

Each of the seven indigenous plants involved—chenopod, marsh elder, squash, sunflower, erect knotweed, little barley, and maygrass—had its own particular course of development. Most began as wild plants growing along river floodplains that Native North Americans first gathered and utilized, then gradually brought under their control as they harvested them and planted their seeds in prepared fields the following year, sometimes quite far from their original habitats. There is evidence of indigenous crop domestication occurring over a broad geographical area by 2000 B.C., on lands today known as Tennessee, Arkansas, Illinois, Kentucky, Ohio, Missouri, and Alabama. After a slow beginning for each crop, the overall shift occurred rather abruptly, and in groups, with several spring and fall crops introduced together, some high in oil and some in starch. As Bruce Smith wryly comments:

> If domestication occurred in some other part of the world, and involved grains such as wheats or barleys, such an abrupt, broad scale, and highly visible transition to an increased economic presence of seven domesticated and cultivated plants would quickly be acknowledged as marking a major shift toward farming economies. But in Eastern North America . . . where the indigenous crops in question have little name recognition, this transition is still often brushed aside as involving minor crops of little economic import, in all likelihood grown only in small garden plots. (Smith 2002:14)

Phase Two: 250 B.C. to A.D. 200

In this phase food production economies emerged. Much greater amounts of seed appear in the diet, and seed crops become the focus of more intensive cultivation, as farmers plant crops away from their original habitats. Maize first appears in small amounts.

New information pinpoints the emergence of indigenous crop economies, not maize, as parallel in time with Hopewellian cultures. Ohio, Illinois, and states farther south are dotted with the remains of farming communities that existed between 250 B.C. and A.D. 200, many of them marked by Hopewellian features such as large geometric earthworks, conical burial mounds, elaborate mortuary decorations, and beautifully molded pipes, bowls, icons, and other objects.

Members of Hopewell farming societies lived in single-household settlements of perhaps a dozen individuals. They settled in river valleys—ideal locations for small fields—and crafted hoes and other tools suited for small-scale land clearing. Studies of modern wild stands of the crop plants grown by these farmers indicate that the plants have high potential harvest rates and yields. For example, a square field, 200 feet on a side, planted equally with marsh elder and chenopod, could have been harvested by five people in little more than a week. Even more impressive, nutritional analyses indicate that a field of this size and content would have provided half the caloric requirements of a household of 10 for a period of six months.

Phase Three: A.D. 800 to 1100

Because of the earlier emergence of agriculture, which served as a preadaptation, a rapid and broad-scale shift to large-field, maize-centered agriculture emerges.

Food-producing economies based on indigenous crops flourished from about A.D. 200 until about A.D. 800, when a new, nonindigenous crop plant—maize—came to dominate the fields and diets of ancient North American farmers extending from what is now northern Florida to Ontario in Canada, from the Atlantic coast to the Great Plains. Archaeologists now know that maize appeared in Native American villages more than 2,000 years after indigenous plants were domesticated and well after the rise of Hopewell societies. Even more dramatic and interesting is the coincident emergence of a second major episode of social transformation known as the Mississippian chiefdoms. From A.D. 800 until about A.D. 1000, the river valleys of the Southeast and the Midwest became dominated by the fortified villages of Mississippian chiefdoms. These societies exhibited considerable social inequality and organizational complexity reflected in raised mounds surrounding central plazas occupied by privileged individuals who enjoyed more ceremonial burials than the general populace.

RESISTANCE TO NEW THEORIES

If Native Americans domesticated indigenous seed plants deliberately and independently between 3000 B.C. and 2000 B.C. in the eastern woodlands, why has it taken so long for their enormous contribution to be recognized? Perhaps it is because the domesticated seed crops themselves are so little known, since they did not survive as domesticates, in contrast to maize and beans. Only squash and sunflower are used today. In addition, they come from plants with difficult-to-pronounce names and obscure identities and uses. They include *Cucurbita pepo* (squash), *Iva annua* (marsh elder or sumpweed), *Helianthus annuus* (sunflower), and *Chenopodium berlandieri* (chenopod or goosefoot), as well as three cultigens whose seeds do not reflect the same distinct morphological changes that would enable archaeologists to call them full domesticates—erect knotweed, little barley, and maygrass.

The obscurity of most of these seed crops in today's world, and the rich descriptions early settlers left of Indians growing corn, beans, and squash, go far toward explaining why it is so difficult to change people's conceptions of the origins of Native American agriculture:

> School children across America learn that Indians of the East grew maize, beans, and squash . . . southeastern tribes made more than ninety different dishes from corn. More importantly, maize [or corn] is an ever-present dietary element in modern America. We consume corn oil and margarine, corn on the cob, creamed corn, popcorn, caramel corn, corn nuts, corn flakes, corn fritters, and corn. . . . We know what we eat. (Smith 2002:6)

SCIENTISTS AS DETECTIVES

In the early 1980s Smith was increasingly convinced that it was eastern Native Americans who discovered farming, and that seed crops other than maize explained the appearance of Hopewell societies. But how could he find evidence to strengthen this idea and convince those who still did not believe it, that Native North Americans independently discovered agriculture?

Smith knew the answer must lie within ancient plant remains. In the 1960s and 1970s, several investigators had documented two local domesticates—sunflower and marsh elder—and had proposed various plants as likely candidates for early domestication, among them a chenopod that was found in such abundance in archaeological sites that it seemed unlikely to have been merely gathered in the wild. To Smith, chenopod seemed a particularly good potential domesticate to study because he could compare any ancient seeds he found with seeds from the modern Mexican domesticate, *Chenopodium berlandieri,* and also compare the ancient seeds with modern wild chenopods in the eastern United States. These comparisons would show whether or not the ancient seeds carried the clear markers of domestication.

Smith reasoned he would have a chance to find the linchpin evidence if he could find one good-sized collection of whole, well-preserved chenopod seeds clearly stored by ancient farmers. The seeds had to come from an undisturbed site with good temporal context, and they had to date to a time before maize was first introduced to eastern North America. If Smith could find one such collection, and if all the seeds showed the telltale thin, somewhat rectangular coat of domestication when examined in a scanning electron microscope, then he would have added another local domesticate to the list and put one of the final key puzzle pieces in place.

RUSSELL CAVE

Smith began to search old archaeological reports for references to seeds excavated from storage contexts. One collection seemed particularly promising: Russell Cave, Alabama. Fortuitously, Russell Cave had been excavated in 1956 by Carl Miller, then with the River Basin Surveys of the Smithsonian Institution. Smith knew that the large amounts of uncataloged material from these surveys were down the hall from his office in the National Museum of Natural History and that if seeds still existed, he might have some chance of rediscovering them.

Smith read everything Miller wrote about his excavation but found only a brief paragraph describing a spectacular seed discovery:

> During the first season's work in Russell Cave, the charred remains of a small hemispherically-shaped basket were found filled with equally charred *Chenopodium* seeds. The seeds were later identified by experts in the US Department of Agriculture as belonging to this plant family. Their presence on the Early Woodland horizon, about 5,000 years ago, indicate that *these people knew the potential of these wild uncultivated seeds as a single food source,* harvested them by means of seed beaters and baskets and converted them to food. (Quoted in Smith 2002:117; emphasis added)

Could these "wild seeds" be, in fact, from domesticated plants? Could this basket be the needle in the haystack that Smith was trying to find? First, of course, he had to find the seeds. Unfortunately, there had been a tragic loss of the original storage basket during the excavation:

> At about seven feet we came across the basket . . . made of coiled strands of grass fiber . . . [the basket was] filled with small seeds, probably some wild grain the cave men gathered and ate. . . . Since it was late in the evening when we found the basket, I decided to wait until morning before trying to dig it out . . . but when we entered the cave the next morning, we were dismayed to find it gone . . . someone had vandalized the cave. (Quoted in Smith 2002:117)

Despite the basket's destruction, Smith decided to search through the 38 drawers of unaccessioned Russell Cave materials at the National Museum of Natural History. Toward the end of several days of endlessly sorting through lithic materials, Smith found an old cigar box (Tampa Nugget Sublimes) bearing the longhand inscription "Basket F.S. [field specimen] 23." He opened the box and found only an old, crumpled brown paper bag inside, but it too was labeled "F.S. 23." This bag could be the way Miller stored the seeds that had spilled out from the missing basket. With both apprehension and anticipation, Smith unfolded the paper bag and found exactly what he had hoped for: a bunch of very old, very dark, and very charred seeds. In fact, as he examined the plant remains, Smith estimated there to be perhaps 50,000 carbonized chenopod seeds. This spectacular discovery was exactly what he needed!

ARCHAEOBOTANY

Smith next turned to the new tools that were revolutionizing the field of archaeology and strengthening the subdiscipline of archaeobotany. By dating and then analyzing the size, shape, and structure of the Russell Cave chenopod seeds as well as modern domesticated chenopod and modern wild species, Smith could begin to pinpoint the exact time of chenopod domestication.

Smith's research included innovative applications of recent developments in scientific technology. Most of his discoveries, in fact, are attributable to four new technological advances, serving to underscore the important role instrumentation plays in guiding and stimulating scientific research:

1. *Water flotation technology* dramatically improves the recovery of small carbonized seeds and other plant parts from the archaeological context. The principle is simple: huge amounts of excavated soil are mixed with water, allowing seeds, charcoal, and other light materials to float to the top.
2. *Accelerator mass spectrometry (AMS)* allows radiocarbon dating of individual seeds and other tiny samples.
3. *Scanning electron microscopy (SEM)*, like AMS dating, revolutionized the field of archaeobotany in the 1980s, since SEM can magnify small objects many thousands of times more than conventional microscopes. Only with SEM can the seed coat thickness, indicating domestication, be measured.
4. *Stable carbon isotope analysis* of human bone allows scientists to document the consumption of maize. Maize, a tropical grass, has less carbon-13 than food plants of temperate North America; this deficiency in carbon-13 shows up in the bones of the people in North America who began to eat large quantities of corn after A.D. 900.

Using these new tools, Smith demonstrated without a doubt that the Russell Cave cache of *Chenopodium* was a very early collection of stored *domesticated* seeds, put aside for planting by early Native American farmers at least 2,000 years ago.

A NORTH AMERICAN SQUASH?

The diffusionists, however, still had one ace in the hole to prove their theory of Mesoamerican origins for North American agriculture. Mexico was clearly the hearth from which sprang all of today's New World pumpkins, squashes, and gourds, members of the large species *Cucurbita pepo,* which includes many cultivated varieties. In the late 1960s and early 1970s a number of archaeological discoveries of domesticated *Cucurbita pepo* seeds in Mexico were dated to nearly 8000 B.C., strengthening the belief that Mexico was the primary source of New World domestication. In addition, there were no documented wild *C. pepo* in North America at all, so it was logically assumed that all the prehistoric remains of *C. pepo* found in eastern North America, including some charred rind fragments that were dated as early as 7,000 years ago, must represent domesticated squash that had been introduced from Mexico.

Smith and his colleagues, however, were not convinced. They wondered if the 7,000-year-old fragments of burned *Cucurbita pepo* rind could have come from wild gourds. If Smith could prove that the tiny 7,000-year-old rind fragments were from wild and not domesticated gourd plants, and if he could locate closely related present-day wild gourds in eastern North America, the puzzle might at last be complete and the diffusionist theory overturned.

Smith and his colleagues raised some interesting questions. If domesticated gourds were introduced 7,000 years ago in the east, and eastern hunters and gatherers turned to farming, why was this the only crop they grew for the next 3,000 years? More important, if the gourd had been domesticated for 3,000 years, why was it morphologically identical to wild gourds—with its small size, thin rind, and small seeds? Even more curiously, why would *Cucurbita pepo* materials from eastern North America that were 4,000 years old exhibit clear morphological changes indicating domestication when materials 3,000 years older did not show such signs? Smith noted, with satisfaction, that the morphological signs of domestication for *Cucurbita* squash (larger seeds, thicker rind) appeared just at the same time that similar changes signaled the domestication of three eastern North American seed plants—sunflower, marsh elder, and chenopod.

To Smith and his colleagues, this fact suggested the real possibility that the 7,000- to 4,000-year-old *C. pepo* rinds in the East resulted not from an introduced domesticate but from an indigenous wild *C. pepo* gourd that was domesticated along with the other three eastern plants about 4,000 years ago. But if this was true, why were there no wild gourds left in eastern North America today?

At this point in time a stunning piece of evidence came out of the blue—from a 1986 doctoral dissertation written by botanist Deena Decker-

Walters—providing the first modern evolutionary and taxonomic analysis of the species *C. pepo*. Decker-Walters' research proved through isozyme chemical analysis that the *C. pepo* domesticates fall into two separate genetic groups: the orange-skinned pumpkins (known to have originated in Mexico) in one developmental lineage, and the green and yellow squashes and acorns in a genetically quite different group, suggesting two distinct developmental histories and origins. Hence it was very possible that Native Americans in eastern North America had domesticated indigenous wild gourds about 4,000 years ago. But if they did, there should be modern wild gourds still existing today.

IN SEARCH OF THE WILD EASTERN GOURD

The existence of modern wild gourds could prove once and for all that the second lineage—the summer squashes and acorns—came from indigenous plants, since the 7,000-year-old rind fragments showed no definite signs of domestication and hence easily could have come from wild plants. Not knowing much about gourds but willing to look for them, Smith and his colleague C. Wesley Cowan set out to find them in 1990. In initial response to their questions about wild gourds in eastern North America, several gourd experts told them there were none, nor had there ever been wild gourds in the region. Following the lead of earlier researchers, however, Smith and Cowan began to ask around, and much to their surprise, they heard of free-living gourds in Arkansas, Kentucky, Missouri, Alabama, Illinois, Tennessee, and Louisiana—a number-one weed problem, they were told. They went back to the gourd experts for confirmation. "Oh, *those* gourds," Smith and Cowan were told by the gourd experts. "We know all about those gourds. They are not wild but feral gourds that were derived from domesticated, ornamental gourds that escaped from cultivation and since World War II have become agricultural weeds."

Realizing they might just be on the trail of wild gourds, Cowan and Smith decided next to turn to herbaria to find out how long these "escaped" gourds had been around in the United States. To their delight, a survey of herbaria yielded reams of new data, herbaria sheets showing gourds collected from across eleven states, from Texas north into Illinois and east along the Gulf coast to Florida. Even more interesting, the history of collecting this free-living gourd extended long before World War II, well back into the nineteenth century, with a number of specimen sheets from the St. Louis area dating to the 1850s and 1860s. Smith and Cowan then questioned where these nineteenth-century gourds could have come from and were told that early settlers were growing gourds and that some had "escaped" even back in the nineteenth century. But where did the early settlers get these gourds if there were no wild gourds? The answer again came quickly: from seed catalogs.

Beltsville, Maryland, is home to the National Agricultural Library, which houses the largest collection of seed catalogs in the country. Browsing through reams of seed catalogs in search of an obscure Ozark gourd, Cowan and Smith discovered that with few exceptions *C. pepo* gourds did not begin to grace the pages of seed catalogs until well into the 1870s, several decades after gourds had been collected in St. Louis, as evidenced in the old herbaria sheets.

Smith and Cowan next turned to the Ozark River floodplains. They chose the Buffalo River, unsettled until the 1850s, never much of a farming community, and since the 1950s a national scenic river with virtually no cultivation of any kind carried out in its watershed for four decades. Much to their delight, the Ozark gourds were all over the place. As Smith explains, "In almost every stream or river we investigated, we found wild gourd vines climbing up into trees and bushes or stretching across gravel bars. These gourds had been hiding in plain sight for 150 years!"

THE PUZZLE COMPLETED

The two archaeologists found literally hundreds of wild gourds, each about the size of a hardball or even smaller, ivory-colored with occasional green stripes. Each gourd contained from 100 to 200 seeds; these were an excellent food source because they were 25 percent protein. Smith and Cowan turned their cache of gourds over to Deena Decker-Walters, an authority on *Cucurbita* taxonomy, genetics, and evolution. She and Terrence Walters compared the isozyme profile of the Ozark wild gourd with other wild gourds and with a wide range of domesticated pumpkins and squashes belonging to the species *Cucurbita pepo*. They concluded that the Ozark wild gourd exhibited a unique genetic profile, confirmed it as a wild plant and not a garden escapee, and established it as the likely wild ancestor of the eastern North American domesticated squashes, a lineage with a history quite separate from the pumpkins of Mexico!

Still surviving today in the Ozarks, it was this wild gourd that Native Americans living in eastern North America developed into different varieties of domesticated squashes about 5,000 years ago, at the same time that they domesticated sunflower, marsh elder, and chenopod. The old diffusionist theory had been toppled, and the textbooks should now read:

> Native American women and men domesticated local plants, including the
> wild gourd squash and several highly nutritious seed crops, long before any

domesticated plants were introduced from Mesoamerica. This revolutionary contribution of Native North Americans makes eastern North America one of the world's major independent centers of plant domestication, along with the Middle East, China, Mesoamerica, and South America.

UPDATE

Bruce D. Smith

In the ten years that have passed since this chapter was written, research on the origins of agriculture in eastern North America has continued at a rapid pace. Scholars are filling in missing pieces of the existing puzzle and beginning to work on a number of new puzzles. Flotation recovery and direct accelerator mass spectrometry radiocarbon dating of seeds of early eastern domesticates continues to improve our understanding of when and where different crop plants were first domesticated.

Gary Crites of the University of Tennessee, for example, has pushed back the earliest evidence of sunflower domestication in the East to 2300 B.C. following his discovery and direct AMS dating of domesticated sunflower seeds at the Hayes site in Tennessee (1993). Other researchers, including Gayle Fritz of Washington University in St. Louis and Kristin Gremillion of Ohio State University, have been investigating regional differences in pre-maize-farming economies that existed in different parts of the Midwest and Southeast (Fritz 1990; Gremillion 1997; Scarry 1993). They have found not only that the relative importance of different indigenous eastern crops varied considerably from region to region, but also that the crops themselves differed regionally, as indicated by microscopic comparison of seeds. Fritz and Gremillion, along with other scholars, also are comparing the long and sometimes quite different developmental histories of farming economies in various parts of the East. Fritz, for example, has examined why the shift to maize agriculture appears to have taken place much later in Louisiana than in other regions (Fritz and Kidder 1993).

In recent years parallel research on how and when the shift over to farming took place in other adjacent parts of North America also has intensified. Mary Adair, at the University of Kansas, has been studying the ways in which Indian societies of the eastern grasslands added crop plants into their way of life (Green 1994). Similarly, Gary Crawford of the University of Toronto, John Hart of the New York State Museum, and a number of other researchers are documenting when and why different crop plants, particularly maize, were selectively added to local economies by Indian societies in different parts of southern Ontario and across the Northeast (Hart 1999).

There is continuing interest in the relative dietary importance of indigenous eastern seed plants during the first 2,000 years after they were domesticated (2500–500 B.C.). Settlements of this time period have yielded relatively few seeds of the eastern crop plants; hence some scholars have concluded that plant cultivation played a relatively minor role in overall economies prior to about 500 B.C. Other researchers, however, have pointed to a unique archaeological collection as providing evidence that crop plants gained dietary importance much earlier in time. Deep within Mammoth and Salts Caves, Kentucky, hundreds of human paleofeces have been found scattered along the passageways, and direct AMS radiocarbon dating indicates many were deposited between 1000 and 500 B.C. by miners searching for mineral deposits. Providing direct evidence of what these early cavers were eating, the human coprolites (feces) contain large numbers of seeds of eastern crop plants. Are these paleofeces representative of the general diet of the times, and do they indicate that crop plants were important much earlier than previously thought? Or do they represent a special "trail mix" diet carried into the caves by these early miners? Although not conclusive, recent analysis of hormone traces in the coprolites by Kristen Gremillion and Kristin Sobolik indicates that they were exclusively male in origin, which adds support to the specialized trail-mix interpretation (Gremillion and Sobolik 1996).

Finally, well-preserved dung of another kind has also provided strong supporting evidence for the deep time depth of wild *Cucurbita* gourds in eastern North America. Mammoth dung deposits from the Page-Ladson site in

Florida, recently analyzed by Lee Newsom of Southern Illinois University, Carbondale, dated to 12,500 years ago, contained dozens of seeds of wild *Cucurbita* gourds, providing another key puzzle piece in proving that squash was independently domesticated in eastern North America.

Researchers, including myself, are also focusing on determining when various Mexican crop plants, including maize, amaranth, the common bean, and different squashes (e.g., Mexican pumpkins and Hubbard squashes) first arrived in the eastern woodlands of the United States through the Southwest, and why some crops, such as maize, appear to have played such a minor dietary role for such a long period of time in the East (Fritz 1992). The long period of time that separates the initial domestication of plants in the eastern United States about five thousand years ago (3000 B.C.), and the development of the first maize-centered farming societies that had a substantial reliance on domesticated crop plants as a food source, about one thousand years ago (A.D. 800–1000), clearly indicates that the developmental journey from hunting and gathering was a long one and is still a poorly understood chapter in human history (Smith 2001).

FURTHER READING

Crites, Gary. 1993. "Domesticated Sunflowers in 5th Millennium B.P. Temporal Context: New Evidence from Middle Tennessee." *American Antiquity* 58:146–48.

Decker-Walters, Deena, D. D. Staub, J. E. Chung, Nakata Sang Min, and Hector Quemada. 2002. "Diversity in Free-Living Populations of *Cucurbita pepo* (Cucurbitaceae) as Assessed by Random Amplified Polymorphic DNA." *Systematic Botany* 27(1):19–28.

Fritz, Gayle. 1990. "Multiple Pathways to Farming in Precontact Eastern North America." *Journal of World Prehistory* 4:387–435.

Fritz, Gayle. 1992. "'Newer,' 'Better' Maize and the Mississippian Emergence." In Woods 2002, pp. 19–43.

Fritz, Gayle, and T. R. Kidder. 1993. "Recent Investigations into Prehistoric Agriculture in the Lower Mississippi Valley." *Southeastern Archaeology* 12:1–14.

Green, William, ed. 1994. *Agricultural Origins and Development in the Midcontinent*. Report No. 19, Office of the State Archaeologist, University of Iowa.

Gremillion, Kristen, ed. 1997. *People, Plants, and Landscapes*. University of Alabama Press.

Gremillion, Kristen, and Kristin D. Sobolik. 1996. "Dietary Variability Among Prehistoric Forager-Farmers of Eastern North America." *Current Anthropology* 37:529–39.

Hart, John, ed. 1999. *Current Northeast Paleoethnobotany*. Bulletin 494, New York State Museum. State University of New York, State Education Department.

Scarry, Margaret, ed. 1993. *Foraging and Farming in the Eastern Woodlands*. University Press of Florida.

Smith, Bruce D. 1991. "Harvest of Prehistory." *The Sciences* 31(May/June):30–35.

Smith, Bruce D. 1998. *The Emergence of Agriculture*. W. H. Freeman.

Smith, Bruce D. 2001. "Low-Level Food Production." *Journal of Archaeological Research* 9:1–43.

Smith, Bruce D. 2002. *Rivers of Change: Essays on Early Agriculture in Eastern North America*. Smithsonian Institution Press.

Woods, William, ed. 1992. *Late Prehistoric Agriculture: Observations from the Midwest*. Studies in Illinois Archaeology No. 8. Illinois Historic Preservation Agency, Urbana, Illinois.

22 EAST MEETS WEST

New View of Arctic Peoples

William W. Fitzhugh

*This chapter illuminates the age-old question of where Eskimo culture origi-
nated, what scholars now know and do not know about its birthplace, and
how Eskimo culture has changed through time. The contrast between
reindeer-herding Eurasian peoples and North American hunters underscores
the role of the North Pacific Rim as both buffer and transmitter of culture
change. Fitzhugh's update focuses on global warming, demonstrating how
research in the Arctic helps tell the story of environmental change while
also developing powerful new tools for investigating the past and predicting
the future.*

For many years anthropologists believed that Eskimos were the isolated
descendants of Ice Age hunters, marginal refugees whose Paleolithic
cultures had been preserved for thousands of years in a kind of cultural deep freeze.

In recent years, a quite different view of Arctic cultures has emerged, challenging this "relic-of-the-past" theory with a new view of circumpolar history as a unique and dynamic adaptation to a relatively "friendly" Arctic—
if you know how to live there. The cultural similarities among native peoples
on either side of the Pacific Basin, from Siberia to Alaska and the Columbia
River and across the North American Arctic to Canada and Greenland,
demonstrate a long and complex history of culture contact, migrations, and
exchange in Arctic regions, and provide a new perspective on the question
of the "independent" history of the Americas. Seen from a global, circumpolar perspective, Arctic and Subarctic regions and their adjacent coasts are

increasingly perceived as long-standing "highways" rather than as barriers to the flow of plants and animals, peoples and cultures. Today we recognize Siberian influence in several early Alaskan cultures, and Bering Strait sources are known for many features of Eskimo cultures found across the Arctic.

FIRST CONTACT

Slightly more than 1,000 years ago Norsemen from Scandinavia crossed the North Atlantic and discovered Greenland and North America. They found these new lands cold and bleak and were surprised to discover them inhabited by "skraelings," whom they described as semihuman creatures with one leg and screeching voices [see Fitzhugh, "The Vikings: Old Views and New Findings," in this volume]. Five hundred years later the Englishman Martin Frobisher reached Greenland and Baffin Island (1576–78) while searching for the Northwest Passage. Frobisher, too, met native Inuit, but despite their skin clothes and animal-like sod house dwellings, he noted they were shrewd traders and crafty warriors, not afraid to die for their homes or their freedom. Frobisher managed to capture several Inuit, bringing them home to present to Queen Elizabeth I as "tokens of possession" of new lands claimed for England. Lacking resistance to European diseases, these people soon died, but their Asian features and metal tools suggested Frobisher had indeed discovered the threshold of the fabled Northwest Passage to Asia.

Early descriptions of Arctic peoples also were recorded in the European Arctic. According to an Old English text, Ohthere, an intrepid Norse chieftain of the late ninth century, described the Saami (Lapp) peoples of northern Scandinavia in fearsome terms. He and other travelers reported meeting Russian Arctic peoples with powerful sled dogs and boats made from the skins of seals.

Today we know these northern peoples as Inuit (Eskimos) in North America and the western side of Bering Strait; Chukchi, Yukaghir, Dolgans, and Nenets inhabiting Siberia; and Saami (Lapps) living in Scandinavia. Occupying similar Arctic lands for thousands of years, these various peoples developed similar cultures, using skin and feather clothing, harpoons, dog and reindeer sleds, oil lamps, underground houses, and skin boats. Many of these people shared shamanistic beliefs and nearly identical folktales of Raven and the aurora borealis.

Who were these Arctic peoples who so fascinated European explorers and travelers? What was their origin and history? Did they come from a single people who spread eastward from northern Europe around the northern rim of the globe, or did they undergo convergent development following independent origins in different areas of the North?

Early anthropologists explored these questions in two ways. First, they tried to connect the cultures of living Arctic peoples to the early hunting cultures of Paleolithic Europe; second, they explored similarities and differences among living Arctic peoples, in the hope of identifying living traces of the earliest "original" Arctic people.

ESKIMO ORIGINS

The search for Eskimo origins began with Martin Frobisher and Europe's introduction to Frobisher's Inuit. Northern lands were indeed hostile to inexperienced Arctic navigators such as Frobisher, and they were decidedly so for Sir John Franklin, who lost his life, his ships, and his crew exploring the Northwest Passage in Arctic Canada in the 1840s. Such events influenced how Euroamericans imagined Arctic lands—as hostile to human life—and the history of its peoples as remote from the centers of developing civilizations. Generations of scholars came to view the Arctic as a refuge, where Ice Age peoples with their cultures had migrated and then survived down to the present, in a kind of cultural and biological deep freeze.

Encouragement for this view came from the mid-nineteenth-century discovery of European Paleolithic sites containing harpoons for hunting sea mammals, throwing sticks for hurling spears, ivory figurines, pictographic art, and shaft straighteners—all nearly identical to tools known from historic Eskimo cultures and their Thule-culture archaeological ancestors in Greenland, Canada, and Alaska. It seemed logical to archaeologists that the Eskimos, for whom these similarities were most striking, were the direct descendants of European Paleolithic reindeer hunters who had retreated north, following the melting ice and the northward movement of animals at the end of the Ice Age. The discovery of cave paintings depicting Ice Age hunters whose prey included reindeer and other Arctic animals only confirmed this view. The Eskimos, it was believed, had preserved the remnants of an ancient Ice Age culture even to the modern day, hunting sea mammals, caribou, musk-ox, polar bears, and other Arctic game. But not all Arctic peoples lived this way.

The peoples of the Russian Arctic in historical times were reindeer herders, not sea mammal hunters, and they practiced a northern variant of animal domestication. Even though their reindeer were not completely tame and could easily be lost if a herder was not attentive, reindeer herding provided a margin of safety for Eurasian Arctic peoples that was missing in the North American Arctic. The implications of this new economy were enormous. A careful herding family did not need to worry where their next meal would come from, and it could devote its energies to other activities, such as trading furs for European or Chinese goods, metalworking, and exchanges with far-flung tribes. In time the reindeer-herding culture expanded from central Eurasia west into Scandinavia and east to Bering Strait, transforming cultures in its path, exterminating wild reindeer (caribou), and imposing a near monoculture economic system throughout much of the Eurasian Arctic.

Interestingly, reindeer herding reached Bering Strait about 1,000 years ago but never entered Alaska. Some Eskimo peoples on the Siberian side adopted reindeer breeding, while others continued to live as sea mammal hunters. In this instance, Bering Strait was both a geographic and ethnic barrier, for none of the American Eskimos adopted reindeer breeding. The rich maritime economy of Bering Strait offered a hearty subsistence for Eskimo peoples who lived there, and when reindeer fur was needed for clothing it could be obtained from the Siberian Chukchi. The spread of reindeer-herding peoples and the revolution of reindeer herding that spread through the Eurasian Arctic never entered the New World, and the Eskimo and northern Indian peoples there continued to hunt wild animals as they had for thousands of years. It is only in this sense that North American Arctic peoples can be said to have preserved an ancient hunting tradition and religious beliefs whose roots can indeed be traced to Ice Age times.

Today, archaeological methods have replaced ethnographic parallels in determining the history of Arctic peoples, including Eskimos. At the same time, archaeological interpretations of the evidence of extinct cultures are influenced by the description and analyses of ethnographic (both historical and modern) cultures around the world, as knowledge of known cultural systems help fill in the inevitable gaps in archaeological evidence. After nearly one hundred years, archaeologists are confident that the Bering Sea region was the birthplace of Eskimo culture. But beyond this, there is disagreement as to exactly where this culture first developed; eastern Siberia, Kodiak Island, the Alaska Peninsula, and Western Alaska are all still in the running. Resolving this question will not be easy because postglacial submergence, tidal waves, and earthquakes have destroyed much of the coastal zones inhabited by these early cultures, making archaeological investigation of many key areas impossible.

NORTH PACIFIC RIM PEOPLES

The distinction across the North Atlantic between the herding Eurasian and the hunting North American Arctic peoples stands in marked contrast to the cultural and economic similarities among the peoples living along both shores of the North Pacific Rim. The North Pacific Rim peoples, furthermore, provide a fascinating case study of culture contact and change through time. Ironically, it was along the Pacific Rim, where native peoples had been in contact for millennia before Europeans arrived, that the recent twentieth-century history of political antagonisms masked the very real and very long continuities of cultures. Early ethnographic collections made by nineteenth-century Russian exploring expeditions to Russian America (Alaska) ended up in museums in St. Petersburg, Russia, while eastern Siberian collections made by Franz Boas' Jesup Expedition of 1897–1902 ended up in New York, at the American Museum of Natural History. Fortunately, now there are few physical or political barriers to the exchange of information, peoples, and materials across the Bering Strait, and joint exhibition projects such as the Smithsonian's 1988 "Crossroads of Continents" could reassemble these collections from their places of origin.

The Smithsonian's "Crossroads" exhibition combined cultural materials from northeastern Siberia and northwestern North America into a single traveling exhibition seen by peoples on both sides of the Bering Strait. A smaller version of the "Crossroads" exhibit, with strong local education components and many miniature artifacts made originally as toys and models, toured villages throughout Alaska in 1993–95, and a Russian-language version traveled in the Russian Far East.

PEOPLING THE NEW WORLD

Archaeologists investigating the history of cultures around Bering Strait have found clear evidence of the movement of Asian peoples into northeastern Siberia and their subsequent migration into Alaska and the Americas [see Selig and Stanford, "Researching the First Americans: One Archaeologist's Journey," in this volume]. Dates from stratified cave sites along the Aldan River, a tributary of the Lena, in the Sakha Republic (formerly Yakutia) begin as early as 35,000 years ago. Comparable dates are known from sites in northern Japan. Confirmation of the northeastern movement of peoples and acquisition of Arctic adaptation is seen in the trend of archaeological dates upward toward 12,000 years ago as one approaches Bering Strait. At about this time, settled riverside fishing villages also appear on the lower Amur River and in Kamchatka. In both cases data indicate seasonally settled villages, and sites on the Amur contain some of the earliest ceramics in the world—fired clay animal figurines and grit-tempered pottery have been recovered.

Around 12,000 years ago the first well-dated stratified sites appear in Alaska on the Nenana River and in a number of other locations, both in the interior and on the coast. Almost instantaneously, sites of this age also appear at many locations in North and South America. This pattern indicates a very rapid southward movement of peoples from Alaska. Although pottery and pit-house villages have not been found in the earliest Alaskan sites, the presence of sites at both coastal and interior locations document adaptation to a wide range of environments.

The cultures of these earliest Siberian and Alaskan peoples were very similar. Although the early fluted (Clovis-like) points known from northwestern Alaska have not been found in Siberia, these early Siberian-American paleo-Arctic peoples employed similar bifacial and microblade (core and blade) technologies and clearly shared a cultural tradition. Unlike the earliest Siberian ancestors, who followed a more nomadic hunting way of life, by 12,000 years ago coastal peoples had already begun to turn their attention to the more abundant and stable resources of the sea.

By 10,000 years ago this maritime-focused economy was present along both the Siberian and American sides of the North Pacific, from Japan to Alaska and down to British Columbia and Washington State in a giant arc connecting the two continents. The northernmost section of this North Pacific culture area was occupied by the ancestors of present-day Yupik Eskimos and Aleuts in Western Alaska and of several Native nations in northeastern Siberia: Koryak, Itelmen, Chukchi, Nivkh, and Asiatic or Siberian Eskimos. Ancestral cultures leading to these ethnographic peoples have been documented throughout this region. Although details of this development are best known from North American sites, a comparable sequence is emerging as archaeological work expands in Siberia. Throughout the region, the trend in coastal regions was toward increasing sedentism and intensive exploitation of marine resources and reached its peak in the early historical period.

These North Pacific developments also appear to have stimulated adaptation of peoples to the icy coasts and Arctic interior regions north of Bering Strait. One prominent theory holds that early Eskimo-like cultures, originating as maritime-based cultures in Kodiak and the Aleutian Islands, spread north along the Alaskan coast as the land bridge was inundated after 11,000 years ago, and became adapted to Arctic regions. About 4,500 years ago the

North Alaska hunting peoples received impulses from Siberian Neolithic cultures, which gave rise to the Alaskan Denbigh and Arctic Small Tool Tradition cultures. These groups, in turn, expanded eastward into the newly ice-free Canadian Arctic, reaching Greenland and Labrador by 4,000 years ago, making this the last major area of the New World to be colonized permanently by humans.

As Igor Krupnik (1995) has noted, the historic Siberian Eskimo and Chukchi inhabitants of the Bering Strait region shared a number of cultural adaptations growing out of an economy based on hunting for sea mammals, either from boats or on ice, hunting for land mammals and birds, and fishing. They mastered the art of dogsled driving and built sophisticated boats of skin and wood propelled by paddles and sails. When they settled on the coast they gathered in permanent villages, consisting of sod houses or dugouts in winter, skin or birch-bark tents and wooden plank houses in summer. Evidence of ancient origins for their elaborate rituals and community festivals, which included decorated fur and gutskin clothing, skin drums, wooden masks, and ivory carvings, has been found in the Old Bering Sea cultures of this region dating to as early as 2,000 years ago.

In Siberia about 2,000 years ago those peoples who did not move to the coast preserved their original nomadic lifestyle of hunting and fishing and developed a distinct cultural pattern focusing on the domesticated reindeer. "Mastering reindeer herding was the second most important economic revolution for Siberian native people, after mastering the resources of the sea" (Krupnik 1993:23). As should be clear by now, cultural similarities abound on either side of the Pacific Basin. Sites from both Siberia and Alaska contain early forms of microblade technology. Sites from later times show similarities in Neolithic microblades, ceramics, and architecture. Many of these similarities, such as whalebone semisubterranean housing, can be traced eastward into Canada and Greenland. Others, such as the distinctive Old Bering Sea, Okvik, and Ipiutak art styles, remain rooted in the Bering Strait region. What is less clear is whether these similarities developed from deep cultural strata accumulated from the cultural residues of shared history before the peopling of the New World or whether they are instead the result of more recent contact and exchange.

Detailed archaeological comparisons and dating have revealed that many of these similarities resulted from historical contacts. As noted above, we can trace the eastward spread of Paleolithic core and blade technology into Alaska from Siberia about 12,000 years ago. There appears to have been a similar dispersal of Siberian Neolithic blade industry into Western Alaska, Canada, and Greenland at 4,500 years ago and of Asian ceramics into Alaska about 2,000 years ago. But are the advent of intensive maritime adaptation and the use of seasonal pit-house villages local adaptations or introduced phenomena? And what can be said of Old Bering Sea burial ritual and art? While many of these developments reflect local adaptations and trends, external impulses often had dramatic effects, as seen by dramatic Siberian shamanistic influences in Ipiutak burial ritual at Point Hope, Alaska, about A.D. 500.

GLOBAL ASPECTS OF CULTURE CONTACT AND EXCHANGE

Exploration of culture contact and exchange in Arctic regions provides a new and different perspective on the question of the "independent" history of the Americas. As new data begin to emerge from these relatively unknown northern lands (especially from Northeast Asia), evidence for a continuing history of Beringian exchange is mounting.

The circumpolar region can be seen as a natural pathway for the movement of peoples and ideas between Asia and the Americas. Before A.D. 1000–1500 it was the only conduit we can document through which Asian and American populations interacted. Whether such interaction was initiated by historical and cultural forces of evolution, technological development, population growth, or the indirect influence of climatic change or animal movements, the circumpolar region with its Bering Sea zone has been the sole point of contact and transmission between the New and Old Worlds. In this sense northern regions have played a unique role as buffer and transmitter of transcontinental historical forces. Most of these seem to have flowed from the centers of more complex cultural development in Asia into the New World. Few, if any, traces of American cultures seem to have influenced Siberian or East Asian culture history.

THE LATITUDINAL/LONGITUDINAL PERSPECTIVE

The circumpolar distribution of clothing styles, blubber lamps, harpoons, skin boats, shamanism, bear ceremonialism, and mythology are striking reminders of common elements in the ethnographic cultures of northern peoples. A comparable suite of common features has been identified in archaeological cultures of this region: persistence of early core and blade industries, ground slate technology, wrench-like shaft straighteners, hunting art employing skeletal and joint-mark art, and others. Mechanisms of culture contact and exchange are visibly recognizable; migration and diffusion in the sparsely populated expanses of northern regions are well documented in historical literature, in ethnographic and linguistic continuities, and in archaeological evidence. The Eskimo peoples and cultures rapidly expanded into the Canadian Arctic, first about 4,000 years ago and later with the whale-

hunting Thule migration at A.D. 1000. Reindeer breeding and herding occurred throughout the Eurasian Arctic and boreal regions during the past
1,500 years. Cultural features—including art styles, iron technology, glass
beads, and tobacco—moved rapidly from Siberia into North America. All of
these exemplify the existence of latitudinal global conduits and channels for
forces of culture contact and change.

Contrasting the circumpolar latitudinal homogeneity is the longitudinal,
environmental, and cultural diversity that occurs in both Eurasia and North
America on the north-south axis. Throughout history we have seen the increasing divergence in levels of cultural development and complexity between
the tropical and temperate regions, on the one hand, and boreal and Arctic
regions, on the other. State development processes and the formation of civilizations have been at work in southern Eurasia and Central America for
thousands of years, always expanding northward, transforming northern
peoples. In the north, environmental conditions and a big-game hunting tradition helped Paleolithic and Mesolithic hunting traditions and technology
persist into the twentieth century.

One of the more remarkable features of this persistence is the recent discovery that dwarf mammoths existed in some regions of the Eurasian Arctic nearly 5,000 years longer than anywhere else in the world. Paleontologi-
cal remains of a miniature type of mammoth on Wrangel Island, 100 miles
north of the Chukotka coast, demonstrate a Pleistocene "refugium" until
4,500 years ago, or even later. The discovery by Russians of archaeological
sites at Chertov Ovrag (Devil's Gorge) on Wrangel dating to 4,000 years ago
raises questions of possible human intervention in the ultimate demise of this
great Ice Age mammal.

IMPACT OF THE MODERN WORLD

Several dramatic changes have taken place in the Arctic in recent years. Indigenous populations have expanded, but while growing rapidly, they are

now a minority in their homelands in all but a few locations. Native subsistence economies have changed under the pressure of modernization, commercial exploitation, and governmental policies. A number of ethnic groups described by nineteenth-century anthropologists, including the Sadlermiut of Hudson Bay, the Eyak of southeast Alaska, and the Aliutor of Kamchatka, have become extinct. Of the eight North American Eskimo languages known historically, only three—Greenlandic, Inuktitut, and Yupik—will survive into the mid-twenty-first century. The cultural diversity and integrity of much of the region is equally threatened.

As the world approaches the end of the twentieth century and faces a new millennium, scholars and the public alike are concerned about the dramatic outcomes of the past century and the legacy it will leave to future generations. Environmental degradation, pollution, and loss of species and ecosystem integrity are issues of major concern. A similar set of concerns is expressed by both the general public and social scientists regarding human cultural diversity and the rights of indigenous people. Paternalistic governmental policies, industrialization, and the spread of consumerist values have damaged indigenous subsistence and languages and distorted their cultural continuity and ethnic diversity.

During this century thousands of Siberian, Alaskan, and Northwest Coast natives abandoned their traditional lifestyles and joined the modern workforce in increasingly industrialized urban settings. Huge numbers of outsiders immigrated into their territories, bringing demographic, social, and political change. Entrepreneurism, business interests, and military policies have made major impacts on both human and natural environments. While many groups continue to live in their homelands, most have lost their native languages, adopted imported religious beliefs, and rely on modern technology.

Equally dramatic changes have taken place in Siberia. State-controlled hierarchies have dictated policy, floods of recruited and imprisoned outsiders have arrived, and some native groups have been deprived of traditional livelihoods, while others involved in state-owned reindeer herding, pelt farming, and fishing have been artificially subsidized. Official policies of "Russification" and relocation have reduced the viability of native life and economy. State-controlled industrial development has had a devastating impact on land and resources over which native people have had little control.

Despite differences in political systems, in many respects the results of twentieth-century developments in Siberia and northwest North America have produced surprisingly similar results. In both areas native people have lost much of their ability to direct their own futures; languages have been weakened or lost; poverty has increased; subsistence economies have been weakened; and alcoholism and social disorders have become serious problems.

In both areas cultural and language survival, native rights, education policy, and economic and political issues loom as major problems for the future.

CONCLUSION

After five centuries of a dominant Atlantic perspective on world history and politics, we are entering an era in which Pacific resources and relations are assuming an ever more significant role in world affairs. Viewing the globe from a circumpolar perspective becomes more important, while understanding the lands, peoples, and cultures of the North Pacific Rim can provide immense benefits to northern peoples and to public and scientific understanding of a little known but increasingly important part of the world. As our understanding increases through scientific research and public dissemination, new perspectives on the circumpolar Arctic in general, and the North Pacific Rim specifically, should help prepare younger generations to live in an increasingly global world. Arctic regions and peoples are part of that world. In fact, they may be the most "global" of all!

UPDATE

In the six years since this article was first published, research has advanced our understanding of both the history of the circumpolar regions and global culture change among circumpolar peoples. Studies have provided new information about the history of Arctic peoples, cultures, and environments, and also have documented modern warming trends throughout much of the Arctic region. In addition, these studies illustrate new ways of thinking about how to conduct research in northern regions where native people still maintain subsistence lifestyles, continuing to adapt in a region that has always been marked by extreme environmental variability (Fitzhugh 2002).

One of the most dramatic changes in our view of the globe has come from studies of climate records and the processes driving the modern climate system. Better monitoring systems and models have enabled scientists to predict *El Niño,* the warming of the eastern Pacific, and the climatic effects resulting from it. Other features such as the North Atlantic Oscillation produce similar systemic changes in weather pattern in northern regions. Historical studies of water temperature, pack ice and iceberg abundance, and pollen extracted from lake and sea sediment cores have provided longer and more detailed climatic records. It is beginning to be possible to link these records with the modern processes driving climate change. Some of the most dramatic information for northern areas of the globe has come from the analysis of long ice cores drilled from the annually layered Greenland ice cap. These ice cores have produced continuous records of climate, temperature, pollutants, and particulate matter such as volcanic debris, sea salt, and windblown dust, extending back for 200,000 years (Mayewski and White 2002).

These types of records have begun to show that the Arctic has never been a homogeneous, uniform "refrigerator." In fact, they reveal a constantly changing Arctic where some regions warm while others cool in response to regional atmospheric and ocean current conditions. Recent record-breaking warmth in the western Russian Arctic, Alaska, and Greenland have been offset by lower temperature in eastern Siberia and eastern Canada. Even so, the general trend of the past several decades has been a significant warming that, if it continues, will have profound effects on the Arctic environment and the animals and people who live there.

A dramatic case of early climatic impact has recently been discovered from archaeological work on Zhokhov Island in the Russian high Arctic. When polar-bear- and reindeer-hunting peoples lived here in the early Holocene, 8,000 years ago, they built their houses with driftwood on a mainland cape that jutted out into a seasonally ice-free Arctic Ocean. Zhokhov's people were among the first known to have begun the transition from reindeer hunting to sea mammal hunting in the Siberian Arctic, at a time when the local climate was about 4 to 5 degrees centigrade higher than today. Their Arctic paradise did not last long. A combination of sea level rise and coastal permafrost melting was causing the coast to recede southward 16 kilometers every year. Today Zhokhov is a tiny, abandoned ice-bound island 500 kilometers north of the mainland Laptev Sea coast (Pitulko and Kasparov 1996).

Such dramatic change may not happen today, but the effects of climate and environmental change are accelerating after a period of cooling in the mid-twentieth century. Given the connectedness of the global economy, the opening of previously frozen shipping lanes, the melting of permafrost, the increase in industrial activity, and shifts in animals populations are likely to have major effects not only on Arctic residents but on the world at large.

Melting pack ice, thinning permafrost, the erosion of coastlines, earlier growing seasons, and changes in storm intensity and frequency all attest to a new phase of the climate cycle. In addition to new techniques and theories, scientists are beginning to learn from native residents who have been observing and coping with extreme variability and changes in climate and animal life for generations. One challenge facing researchers is developing ways to utilize the knowledge Arctic peoples already have of their environments. During the past few years scientists and native peoples have begun experimenting with ways to combine these two streams of knowledge—Western science and Native science—for the first time, providing powerful new tools for investigating the past, understanding the present, and predicting the future (Krupnik and Jolly 2002).

FURTHER READING

Chaussonnet, Valerie, ed. 1995. *Crossroads Alaska: Native Cultures of Alaska and Siberia*. Arctic Studies Center, National Museum of Natural History, Smithsonian Institution.

Fitzhugh, William W. 2002. "Yamal to Greenland: Global Connections in Circumpolar Archaeology." In Barry Cunliffe, ed., *Archaeology: The Widening Debate*. Oxford University Press.

Fitzhugh, William W., and Valerie Chaussonnet, eds. 1994. *Anthropology of the North Pacific Rim*. Smithsonian Institution Press.

Fitzhugh, William W., and Aron Crowell, eds. 1988. *Crossroads of Continents: Cultures of Siberia and Alaska*. Smithsonian Institution Press.

Fitzhugh, William W., and Susan A. Kaplan. 1982. *Inua: Spirit World of the Bering Sea Eskimo*. Smithsonian Institution Press.

Krupnik, Igor I. 1993. *Arctic Adaptations: Native Whalers and Reindeer Herders of Northern Eurasia*. University Press of New England.

Krupnik, Igor I. 1995. "Native Peoples of the Russian Far East." In Valerie Chaussonnet, ed., *Crossroads Alaska: Native Cultures of Alaska and Siberia*. Arctic Studies Center, National Museum of Natural History, Smithsonian Institution.

Krupnik, Igor, and Dyanna Jolly, eds. 2002. *The Earth Is Faster Now: Indigenous Observations of Arctic Environmental Change*. Frontiers in Polar Social Science. Arctic Research Consortium of the United States in cooperation with the Arctic Studies Center, Smithsonian Institution.

Mayewski, Paul Andrew, and Frank White. 2002. *The Ice Chronicles: the Quest to Understand Global Climate Change*. University Press of New England.

Pitulko, Vladimir V., and Aleksei K. Kasparov. 1996. "Ancient Arctic Hunters: Material Culture and Survival Strategy." *Arctic Anthropology* 33(1):1–31.

23 THE ARCHAEOLOGY OF AFRICAN AMERICAN LIFE

Theresa A. Singleton

African American archaeology (now also referred to as the archaeology of the African diaspora) is a rapidly changing area of research, as described by one of its leading specialists, Theresa Singleton. This chapter demonstrates the challenges of interpreting, through artifacts, the lives of enslaved African Americans who themselves left few written documents, and determining what these artifacts suggest about the African heritage of this transplanted population. In her update, Singleton describes how African American archaeology has broadened its geographic scope to the global community, has introduced new areas of inquiry such as cultural identity, and has impacted other areas of anthropology and archaeology by focusing on new subjects such as social inequality and resistance outside of the Americas.

Excavations of slave cabins in the late 1960s marked the beginning of a new and important field known as African American archaeology. African American archaeology studies the daily lives of past African American communities through the analysis of the tangible material remains recovered from the places where members of these communities once lived and worked. From the careful study of broken pottery, mortar, food bone, tools, buttons, beads, and other objects, archaeologists are able to piece together information on the ways African Americans built their houses, prepared their food, and crafted household equipment and personal possessions.

Archaeologists engaged in this research are ultimately seeking answers to questions such as: How was an African heritage transplanted, replaced, or reinterpreted in America? In what ways are the recovered artifacts from

African American sites the reflection of cultural patterns or of social conditions such as poverty and restricted access to material goods? What are the differences in the material lives of slaves, free blacks, and tenant farmers and of African Americans living in urban versus rural communities? How did African Americans survive the rigors of everyday life?

Archaeologists first began to study African Americans as part of a growing scholarly interest emphasizing the history of people who created or left behind few written documents. Enslaved African Americans were generally denied the opportunity to learn reading and writing skills. Even after emancipation, many former slaves, lacking other alternatives, were forced to return to plantations as wage laborers and land renters, where they remained poor and illiterate. Thus most of the written records used to examine the five-hundred-year history of African Americans are the products of European Americans, whose understanding of African American culture was often flawed. In addition, these records are one-sided in that they contain only information of interest to the author. For example, slave owners and plantation managers generally recorded information on a slave's health, his or her capacity to perform work, and behavior considered deviant. These documents rarely contain descriptions of objects slaves made and used or of other cultural expressions.

The archaeological record is also biased. The archaeologist can only interpret abandoned, discarded, or lost objects preserved in buried deposits. This leaves out any object that may have been kept through the years and handed down from generation to generation or any object made of materials that do not preserve well underground. Moreover, artifacts provide the basis for inferences about particular aspects of behavior, not direct evidence of behavior. Therefore, the interpretation of the material record requires archaeologists to incorporate historical and ethnographic descriptions of behavior derived from written sources and oral tradition.

THE SEARCH FOR AN AFRICAN HERITAGE: CERAMICS, MUD HOUSES, AND RITUAL ITEMS

In the archaeological study of African American sites, archaeologists are particularly interested in artifacts suggestive of either an African heritage or newly created African American traditions. Although the evidence thus far uncovered is fragmentary and interpretations are tentative, these finds supply empirical data for the widely held view that enslaved Africans and their descendants nurtured and sustained cultural traditions in spite of the oppressive, dehumanizing conditions of slavery. Some of the most convincing evidence that supports the persistence of African heritage includes slave-made

ceramics recovered from plantations in South Carolina and Virginia, the building of African-style mud-wall houses on eighteenth-century plantations in South Carolina, and ritual paraphernalia of a traditional healer recovered from a cabin in Texas occupied during and after slavery.

The most frequently recovered artifacts produced by African Americans are ceramics used for preparing, serving, and storing food. So far, ceramics produced by African Americans have been recovered from numerous sites in South Carolina, Virginia, and several islands in the Caribbean. In the southern United States, these ceramics, called "colonoware," are low-fired, unglazed earthenware that resembles traditional pottery produced by Native Americans. Until the past decade, archaeologists thought that only Native Americans had produced colonoware, and it still seems likely that Indians created certain European-style vessels such as shallow plates and bowls with ring feet that English settlers would have valued. But now most scholars agree that African slaves produced a special variety of this hand-built pottery, particularly the rounded forms, because much of it has been found at sites that date long after the demise of local Indians.

In South Carolina, the first real clue that African Americans made their own pottery came when fragments turned up that appeared to have been fired on the premises of Drayton Hall, a plantation located west of Charleston, South Carolina. Colonoware often makes up 80 to 90 percent of the ceramics found at sites occupied by slaves in the 1700s. Further research by Leland Ferguson, a historical archaeologist at the University of South Carolina, has shown that some of the South Carolina forms resemble pottery still made in parts of West Africa today. More recently, he has identified markings on some pottery fragments that are similar to the cosmograms used in the traditional rituals of peoples in the Congo-Angolan region of Africa. Cosmograms symbolize the way a society perceives the universe. The markings consist of a cross enclosed in a circle, which represents the daily course of the sun and the continuity of life: birth, death, and rebirth.

Why is evidence of pottery making among enslaved African Americans important? The use of this pottery suggests that enslaved African Americans prepared food to suit their own taste, perhaps incorporating aspects of traditional African cuisines. In addition, slaves also used these ceramics to prepare food for their masters, as colonoware accounts for a significant portion—sometimes more than half—of the ceramics used in planter households. This suggests that culinary techniques used by slaves influenced local southern white cuisine as well.

Excavations at the sites of Curriboo and Yaughan, two former indigo plantations in Berkeley County, South Carolina, revealed what may have been rectangular African-style houses designed and built by slaves. These slave quarters consisted of mud walls, presumably covered with thatched palmetto leaves, similar to thatched-roof houses in many parts of Africa. Although no standing walls exist, archaeologists have found wall trenches containing a mortarlike clay. The presence of numerous pits, apparently used to extract clay, found throughout the sites further suggests the use of clay as the primary construction material.

Since this discovery, a careful examination of written records has revealed several scattered references to slave-built, mud-walled structures. Indeed, previously unnoticed written descriptions seem to suggest that these African-style houses may have been commonplace. W. E. B. Du Bois offered a description of palmetto-leaf construction in his 1908 survey of African and African American houses: "The dwellings of slaves were palmetto huts built by themselves of stakes and poles, with the palmetto leaf. The door, when they had any, was generally of the same materials, sometimes boards found on the beach. They had no floors, no separate apartments" (Du Bois 1969 [1908]:49).

The mud houses at Curriboo and Yaughan plantation were built and occupied between 1740 and 1790. They were abandoned and replaced with European American–style framed dwellings in the early 1800s. This change in housing styles coincided with a period when many European Americans came to view anything African as backward, inferior, and, in the case of housing, unhealthy. As a result, many slaveholders began to impose their standards of appropriate housing upon slaves.

At the Jordan Plantation, approximately 60 miles south of the modern city of Houston, Texas, archaeologist Kenneth Brown uncovered an assemblage of artifacts apparently used in healing and divination rituals. The Jordan plantation operated as a slave-worked plantation from 1848 until emancipation and continued with wage laborers, many of whom were former slaves of the plantation, until 1890. Nine cabins were excavated and the materials from several individual cabins revealed evidence of the specialized activities of a carpenter, seamstress, cattle herder (cowboy), and shaman/healer. The materials from the shaman's cabin consisted of the bases from cast-iron kettles, pieces of utilized chalk, fragments of a small scale, bird skulls, an animal's paw, medicine bottles, ocean shells, doll parts, spoons, nails, knives, and chert scrapers. Many of these objects could have functioned in other activities and most likely did at various points in their lives. But when the artifacts are taken together, they suggest some form of ritual use. Support for this thesis comes from abundant ethnographic studies conducted in the Caribbean and parts of Africa that describe the use of wooden or metal trays, white chalk or powder, metal staffs, bird symbolism, and other objects used in healing rituals.

The assemblage of artifacts from the Jordan Plantation presents an excellent example of African Americans using mass-produced and reworked objects for a special African American meaning. Another example of the special use of manufactured objects is the occurrence of colored glass beads, particularly blue beads, that are found on slave sites throughout the South from Virginia to Texas. William Adams, an archaeologist at Oregon State University, recently suggested that blue beads may be related to a widespread belief in the Moslem world, including parts of Africa, that a single blue bead worn or shown on clothing protected the wearer against the Evil Eye. Undoubtedly, other artifacts uncovered from African American sites have been ignored by archaeologists who have been unable to decipher the special function certain objects occupied in African American culture.

ARCHAEOLOGICAL EVIDENCE OF FREE AND FREED AFRICAN AMERICAN COMMUNITIES

Slave sites, the primary focus of African American archaeology, sometimes contain deposits that date after emancipation. Plantation sites containing deposits dating from before and after emancipation often reflect continuity from slave to free labor, as was the case at the Jordan Plantation. However, a wide variety of African American sites have been studied; in fact, archaeological investigations at African American sites have been undertaken in at least thirty states, Canada, and several Caribbean islands. These investigations range from the home sites of well-known, often prominent individuals such as Benjamin Banneker, Frederick Douglass, and W. E. B. Du Bois to entire towns such as Allensworth, California, and Buxton, Iowa. Archaeologists have also examined African American neighborhoods in several cities and isolated rural settlements. For many of these sites, archaeology is the only source of information that describes the everyday lives of people who once lived at these locations.

Studies of free and freed African American communities have addressed questions similar to those of slave sites: What were the living conditions and basic material culture of these communities? Which aspects of the archaeological record related to ethnic behavior and which to economic and social conditions? Unlike the growing evidence at slave sites for ethnic behavior in ceramic production and use, architecture, and ritual objects, archaeological evidence of ethnicity at nonslave sites varies from site to site and is much more subtle. In some cases—for example, at Benjamin Banneker's home site—no evidence of Banneker's ethnicity is revealed from the archaeological record. The assemblage from his eighteenth-century farmstead in rural Maryland was found to be identical to those recovered from sites of European American settlers of similar social and economic status living at the same time as Banneker. This degree of assimilation may characterize many other free African Americans living during the time of slavery who owned property and enjoyed a material life beyond bare necessities. However, bound by race, free blacks occupied a tenuous position, where they were constantly at the mercy of whites, regardless of their material wealth.

A comparison of poor African Americans and poor European Americans suggests a similar pattern. Archaeology at Millwood, a plantation worked by tenant farmers and wage laborers from 1865 to 1925, revealed that the quality of material life was not based upon ethnicity or race but upon one's position in the plantation hierarchy. Archaeologist Charles Orser identified five classes of occupants living on the plantation (landlord, millwright, tenant, servant, and wage laborer) and observed that blacks and whites of the same class experienced similar material conditions (1990).

Archaeological studies of African American neighborhoods in Alexandria, Virginia, and Washington, D.C., suggest that ethnic behavior is most evident in food preferences. In both studies, the archaeological records of the African Americans were compared with those of European Americans of similar economic status. Although subtle differences were evident in purchased ceramics and other artifacts, the most striking difference was found in foodways (encompassing everything from food procurement and preparation to consumption habits), an aspect of culture that frequently indicates ethnic preferences. The African Americans at both sites consumed much more pork than European Americans and displayed a particular preference for pigs' feet. Floral and faunal analyses indicated that an African American community in Washington also consumed collard greens and opossum.

Archaeology can also be used to examine material conditions associated with special circumstances experienced by African Americans. For example, preliminary work I conducted on sites associated with recently emancipated slaves suggest that former slaves living along the Georgia coast were, in some cases, materially worse off in the first years of freedom than they were as slaves. Structural remains from the cabins of freed men and women indicated that the chimney was constructed of reused brick, haphazardly built on a bed of oyster shell. Tools were used until they were completely worn, and occupants of the site subsisted almost entirely upon wild game: turtle, fish, and small mammals. A recent excavation of another refugee camp of former slaves should provide additional information of the immediate material effects of emancipation.

THE DIET AND HEALTH OF SLAVES AND FREE BLACKS

Archaeological studies of nutrition are particularly important to discussions of slave nutrition, a realm of slave life that has been greatly debated by students of slavery. One school of thought suggests that a typical slave diet was nutritious and that caloric intake often exceeded modern recommended levels of chief nutrients. The more accepted view is that slave diet was typically inadequate and malnutrition was a frequent problem, reflected in high child mortality and in the prevalence of diseases resulting from nutritional deficiencies. The analysis of food remains can contribute to this discussion by documenting the kinds of foods slaves consumed. Studies conducted by zooarchaeologists (archaeologists who analyze nonhuman bones) indicate that slaves supplemented their mundane plantation rations of cornmeal and fatback with small mammals they hunted and fish they collected in nets. Several studies of faunal remains collected from sites in the southeastern United States suggest that food collection activities of slaves accounted for 35 to 40 percent of the meat in the slave diet.

Analyses of human remains provide a wide range of information on nutrition, pathological conditions, and occupational stresses. One of the largest skeletal samples of African Americans was unearthed from an abandoned cemetery of Philadelphia's First African Baptist Church (FABC), which served as a burial ground for free African Americans between 1823 and 1843. More than 140 adult and child skeletons were analyzed and reburied. Analyses revealed that the quality of life and the health status of free black Philadelphians and various slave populations were similar. These conditions were particularly evident in the analysis of dental enamel undertaken by Michael Blakey, a physical anthropologist at Howard University. Blakey introduced a new method that gives a record of fetal and childhood health by measuring defects in the dental enamel of adult skeletons. Results show that their lives were particularly harsh, especially as fetuses (linked to maternal health) and as children. This finding came as a surprise to Blakey, who had thought that free African American children would have had somewhat better health than did slave children.

Occupational stress in the FABC population was particularly evident among females, many of whom were laundresses. The stress of laundering is evident in their well-developed triceps and pectoral muscles and fingers. One individual displayed evidence of breakdown of the cervical vertebrae, perhaps from carrying the laundry as a head load, and of bending stress on lower vertebrae. Tuberculosis, iron deficiency anemia, arthritis, and cholera are among the diseases the cemetery population suffered.

The healing paraphernalia uncovered from the Jordan Plantation in Texas suggest the kinds of folk medicine sought by African Americans, but excavations of slave cabins and plantation infirmaries give indications of the kinds of medications slave owners administered to the slaves. Excavations of slave cabins along the Georgia coast indicate that slaves regularly consumed patent medicines with high alcohol content and brewed alcoholic beverages. While some of this consumption was perhaps recreational in nature, the plantation records of a slave site I excavated indicated that patent medicines and homemade rum regularly were dispensed to the slaves as a preventative for rheumatic diseases. Future excavations of plantation infirmaries will possibly turn up medical instruments and other objects used to treat slaves.

From this brief overview of African American archaeology, it should be apparent that this research presents new and provocative information on the lives of African Americans. Critics of historical archaeology often claim that all this information is in the written record; I challenge them to find it.

UPDATE

This research area continues to grow both inside and outside the United States. It is now most often referred to as the archaeology of the African diaspora to encompass its broad geographic scope. In archaeological practice, the term refers specifically to the study of people of African descent whose forebears were captives in the transatlantic slave trade. Archaeological studies of the African diaspora have been undertaken throughout the Americas, quite literally from Canada to Argentina. Studies of plantation slavery still dominate this research, but increasingly more work is being conducted on diverse topics. Studies of maroons—black freedom fighters who successfully escaped enslavement and formed their own autonomous communities—have been conducted in Brazil, Cuba, the Dominican Republic, Florida, Jamaica, and Suriname. Most of these investigations are still in preliminary stages of locating and identifying sites, which were almost always in remote areas such as mountainous terrains or dense tropical forests. To be viable, maroon communities had to be located in places that were inaccessible to the penetration of militias or patrols that could attack and re-enslave them. Archaeological research on maroon communities is expected to provide clues on how maroons overcame these hostile environments and established social, political, and economic systems. Maroon communities still exist in Jamaica and Suriname (Agorsah 1994).

Other studies counter the erasure or silencing of the black presence in local histories. In Buenos Aires, Argentina, archaeological investigations yielded information on everyday life, religious practices, and pottery production of Afro-Argentines, who comprised 35 percent of the city's population in the early nineteenth century. Today, the number of Afro-Argentines is near zero, due in part to "whitening" Buenos Aires' population through falsifying racial data in official city records. Afro-Argentines "disappeared" in census records but also in the writing of the country's history. Daniel Schávelzon's recent book on black Buenos Aires, analyzing the historical archaeology of a city made silent, uses archaeology and documentary sources to restore Afro-Argentine history and culture (2003). Similarly, excavations of a black-owned saloon that black Nevadans frequented not only establish an African American presence in nineteenth-century Nevada but, more importantly, reaffirm the roles African Americans played as settlers in many western states (Kelly Dixon, pers. comm., 2000).

The emphasis on identifying African elements and describing material possessions, food habits, or health status illustrated by the original *AnthroNotes* article has given way in recent years to archaeological analyses of race, class, gender, and identity formation. Archaeologists are increasingly attempting to understand how artifacts shed light on the ways in which African Americans actively shaped their material world, constructed their own cultural identity, and negotiated racism and other forms of oppression. For example, Paul Mullins examines African Americans' participation in the consumer society of Annapolis, Maryland, from the 1850s to the 1930s in order to understand African American perceptions of consumption (Mullins 1999). Using the black scholar W. E. B. Du Bois' concept of double-consciousness, Mullins probes the meanings behind the acquisition and use of certain objects such as bric-a-brac, bottled and canned goods, political knickknacks, and mass-produced foods. Du Bois coined the term *double-consciousness* to characterize the internal struggle within African Americans to live and operate in two worlds, one black and the other white, during the period of legal segregation from 1896 to 1964. Mullins suggests that African American consumption was ideologically driven toward achieving socioeconomic self-determination. His study fully integrates archaeological findings with the analysis of written sources, producing a seamless narrative of African American life.

Studies of the African diaspora are slowly making an impact in other areas of archaeology. Archaeologists pursuing investigations focusing on subjects such as social inequality, resistance, or slavery outside the Americas are beginning to utilize approaches or ideas from work being undertaken on the African diaspora. For example, the concept of double-consciousness has been used to analyze oppressed people in other contexts. The archaeology of the African diaspora is also playing a leading role in discussions concerning the ethical responsibilities of archaeologists to descendant communities and to the public in general. Some archaeologists engaged in research on the African diaspora have formed partnerships with descendant communities, involving them in various aspects of research, from the formulation of research questions to the development of public programs (see studies in McDavid and Babson 1997). Although some archaeologists believe they should avoid getting entangled in the political agendas of descendant communities, more and more archaeologists are working with these communities. Linking people today with their pasts has become an integral part of the archaeological study of the African diaspora.

FURTHER READING

Agorsah, E. Kofi, ed. 1994. *Maroon Heritage: Archaeological, Ethnographic and Historical Perspectives*. Canoe.

Delle, James A. 1998. *An Archaeology of Social Space: Analyzing Coffee Plantations in Jamaica's Blue Mountains*. Plenum.

Du Bois, W. E. B. 1969 [1908]. *The Negro American Family*. Negro Universities Press.

Farnsworth, Paul, ed. 2001. *Island Lives: Historical Archaeologies of the Caribbean*. University of Alabama Press.

Ferguson, Leland G. 1992. *Uncommon Ground: Archaeology and Early African America, 1650–1800*. Smithsonian Institution Press.

Haviser, Jay B., ed. 1999. *African Sites Archaeology in the Caribbean*. Markus Wiener.

Heath, Barbara J. 1999. *Hidden Lives: The Archaeology of Slave Life at Thomas Jefferson's Poplar Forest*. University Press of Virginia.

McDavid, C., and D. W. Babson, eds. 1997. "In the Realm of Politics: Prospects for Public Participation in African-American and Plantation Archaeology." Special issue. *Historical Archaeology* 31(3).

Mullins, Paul R. 1999. *Race and Affluence: An Archaeology of African America and Consumer Culture*. Kluwer Academic/Plenum.

Orser, Charles E. 1990. "Historical Archaeology on Southern Plantations and Farms." *Historical Archaeology* 24(4):1–6.

Schávelzon, Daniel. 2003. *Buenos Aires Negra: Arqueología histórica de una ciudad silenciada* [Black Buenos Aires: Historical archaeology of a city made silent]. Foreword by Theresa Singleton. Emece.

Singleton, Theresa A. 1995. "The Archaeology of Slavery in North America." *Annual Review of Anthropology* 24:119–40.

Singleton, Theresa A., ed. 1999. *I, Too, Am America*: *Archaeological Studies of African-American Life*. University Press of Virginia.

Singleton, Theresa A., and Mark D. Bograd. 1995. "The Archaeology of the African Diaspora in the Americas." *Guides to the Archaeological Literature of the Immigrant Experience in America*, no. 2. Society for Historical Archaeology.

Wilkie, Laurie A. 2000. *Creating Freedom: Material Culture and African American Identity at Oakley Plantation, Louisiana, 1840–1950*. Louisiana State University Press.

Yentsch, Anne E. 1994. *A Chesapeake Family and Their Slaves: A Study in Historical Archaeology*. Cambridge University Press.

EXPLORING OUR MANY CULTURES

Why do we live in such diverse cultures?

How have cultures changed over time?

How do anthropologists study other cultures?

How does culture help us adapt and survive?

24 CULTURAL RELATIVISM AND UNIVERSAL HUMAN RIGHTS

Carolyn Fluehr-Lobban

One of the most controversial issues within anthropology today concerns the sensitive intersection and potential contradiction between cultural relativism and universal human rights. Fluehr-Lobban's article helps define the issue, details specific illustrative cases from both abroad and in the United States, and suggests how anthropologists can be helpful in cases dealing with universal rights, including the right to "avoid harm" in societies that sanction abuse in various forms.

What members of one culture might view as strange and bizarre in another culture (for example, polygamy, body tattooing, or strict dietary laws) can be understood best within that culture's context—or so cultural relativists believe. Cultural relativism, a hallmark of anthropology from its beginnings, asserts that cultural traits are best understood within the context of the cultural system of which they are a part and should not be judged by external or absolute standards. Cultural relativists believe further that since each culture has its own inherent integrity, with unique values and practices, value judgments should be withheld or suspended until cultural context is taken into account. Theoretically, anthropologists always should be observers and recorders, not evaluators of other people's customs and values.

While some anthropologists still agree with this view, others, both inside the field and outside, especially in the arena of human rights, are challenging this concept. Today, cultural relativism is experiencing a period of critical self-examination within the field of anthropology. But it is important to state at the outset that universal human rights and cultural relativism are not philosophically or morally opposed to one another; the terrain between them is fluid and rich. Human rights, defined as the rights to which one is entitled simply by virtue of being human, are universal by definition. So although human behavior is necessarily culturally relative, human rights are universal entitlements that are grounded in cross-culturally recognized moral values.

ANTHROPOLOGY'S ROLE IN HUMAN RIGHTS

Historically, anthropology as a discipline declined to participate in the international dialogues that produced conventions regarding human rights, mainly due to philosophical constraints stemming from cultural relativism. In 1947 the Executive Board of the American Anthropological Association decided not to take part in the discussions that produced the Universal Declaration of Human Rights (1948), used subsequently as a foundation for opposition to authoritarian and politically repressive regimes. Nor was anthropology's voice included in the drafting of human rights statements such as the United Nations' Convention on the Elimination of All Forms of Discrimination Against Women (1979) or the Convention on the Rights of the Child (1989). Despite this, some anthropologists have been active in cultural survival and human rights of threatened groups.

As I explained in a 1995 article, anthropologists "are in a unique position to lend knowledge and expertise to the international debate regarding human rights." And, in fact, anthropologists have spoken out against reprehensible practices such as genocide. They have testified in U.S. courts against government rules that impinge on the religious traditions or sacred lands of Native Americans. But there are other human rights issues, from domestic abuse to female circumcision to culturally based forms of homicide, about which anthropologists have remained silent. Thus, anthropologists have not built up accumulated experience in the area of human rights informed by cultural relativist considerations.

This chapter is an attempt to lay out some of the basic issues and considerations in this arena, looking at the intersection of cultural relativism and the human rights issues that have gained more public awareness than ever before.

THE LIMITS OF CULTURAL RELATIVISM

Cultural relativism may be taken to extremes. Some argue that since cultures vary and each culture has its own unique moral system, we cannot make judgments about "right" and "wrong" in comparing one culture to another.

Thus, one cannot reject any form of culturally acceptable homicide—for example, infanticide, senilicide, or "honor" killing of women in Mediterranean and Middle Eastern societies for alleged sexual misconduct—on moral grounds because cultural acceptance or condemnation is equally valid. This extreme relativist position is actually a form of absolutism with which few anthropologists would agree. Anthropologists did not defend Nazi genocide or South African apartheid with cultural relativist arguments, and many have been critical of relativist defenses especially of Western practices they see as harmful, such as cultural institutions emphasizing violence.

The truth about our complex world of cultural difference is that moral perplexity abounds. The ability to accept that another person's or culture's position with which one disagrees is nevertheless rational or intelligible lays the basis for discussion of differences.

Relativism can be used as a way of living in society with others. An egalitarian relativist sees all human beings as moral agents with equal potential for making ethical judgments. Though moral judgments in and of themselves are not scientific, they can be socially analyzed. That is, relativism and universalism in cultural values or practices (including international standards of human rights) need not be opposed morally, but they can be discussed, debated, and assessed by the social sciences, including anthropology.

RELATIVIST CHALLENGE TO UNIVERSAL RIGHTS: ISLAMIC SOCIETIES AND THE WEST

In the conflict between cultural relativism and universal rights, one area where there is a seeming clash between cultures and a war of words is where the West meets the Islamic world. The highly politicized context of this discourse and occasional real warfare reminds us of another kind of cold war between the United States and the Soviet Union. The subjective perceptions of morality and immorality, of right and wrong, on both sides can be so powerful that objective discourse and cultural negotiation may seem impossible.

Islamic governments from Iran to Afghanistan to the Sudan have claimed cultural and religious immunity from international human rights standards. For example, the perceived Islamic responsibility to protect women by restricting their activities has been asserted in defense of public morality. This stand has been criticized in the context of Western human rights and feminism. Some Islamic theologians and political activists deny that a woman can be head of a family or head of state. Their position violates international standards of women's rights and human rights, particularly as outlined in the United Nations' 1979 Convention on the Elimination of All Forms of Discrimination Against Women. Muslims in several states, however, have disregarded such advice, making Benazir Bhutto prime minister of the Islamic Republic of Pakistan and Tansu Cillar and Sheikh Hasina the heads of state in Turkey and Bangladesh, respectively. Western nations actually have proportionately fewer female heads of state and may be accused of hypocrisy in their finger-pointing at the Islamic world.

During the Fourth World Conference on Women, held in Beijing in 1995, positions on women's rights expressed by some Muslim activists diverged from the majority feminist view. Debates over sexual and reproductive health and sexual orientation in terms of universal rights met with opposition not only from Muslim nations such as Iran and Egypt but also from the Vatican and other Catholic representatives at the conference. In the end, the disagreements proved not to be destructive, and there was frank acknowledgment that reasonable persons (and by extension, cultures) could disagree. This is a relativist solution to different views about the "universal rights" of women. But consensus was achieved on a host of other issues, including opposing all forms of violence against women, opposing female genital mutilation, and identifying rape during armed conflict as a war crime and in certain cases a crime against humanity. Relativism expressed with respect to the religious sentiments of some delegates eased the negotiated terrain and permitted dialogue that achieved consensus on many other points while allowing reasonable difference to be asserted on other matters. Recently, the application in the Sudan and northern Nigeria of the Islamic *hudud* ("to the limit") punishment of stoning for the crime of adultery has raised fresh questions about violence and discrimination against women as well as the limits of cultural relativism.

UNIVERSAL RIGHTS CHALLENGE RELATIVISM: FEMALE CIRCUMCISION

One of the most culturally and emotionally charged battlegrounds where the cultural relativist confronts the advocate of universal human rights is the issue of female circumcision or female genital mutilation (FGM). Female circumcision is the removal of all or part of the clitoris and/or labia. The issue of female circumcision has set Western feminism against African cultural traditions and Islam, and has pitted Muslim against Muslim and African against African. Despite female circumcision's prevalence in African Islamic societies, it is also found in some non-Islamic African contexts and is rare in Islamic contexts outside Africa. There is no consensus among Muslim scholars or among African Muslims about whether female circumcision is mandated by religion. Religious interpretation in the Sudan as early as 1939 determined that female circumcision is only "desirable" (*manduh*), not compulsory (Fluehr-Lobban 1987:96), while in 1994 the late grand sheikh of Al-Azhar University in

Cairo, Gad al-Haq Ali Gad al-Haq, called female circumcision "a noble practice which does honor to women." His chief rival, the grand mufti of the Egyptian Republic, said that female circumcision is not part of Islamic teaching and is a matter best evaluated by medical professionals (Sipress 1995).

I have previously written about confronting my own personal struggle between cultural relativism and universal rights regarding female circumcision in the Sudan (Fluehr-Lobban 1995):

> For nearly 25 years, I have conducted research in the Sudan, one of the African countries where the practice of female circumcision is widespread, affecting the vast majority of females in the northern Sudan. Chronic infections are a common result, and sexual intercourse and childbirth are rendered difficult and painful. However, cultural ideology in the Sudan holds that an uncircumcised woman is not respectable, and few families would risk their daughter's chances of marrying by not having her circumcised. British colonial officials outlawed the practice in 1946, but this served only to make it surreptitious and thus more dangerous. Women found it harder to get treatment for mistakes or for side effects of the illegal surgery.

For a long time I felt trapped between my anthropological understanding of the custom and of the sensitivities about it among the people with whom I was working, on one side, and the largely feminist campaign in the West to eradicate what critics see as a "barbaric" custom, on the other side. To ally myself with Western feminists and condemn female circumcision seemed to me a betrayal of the value system and culture of the Sudan, which I had come to understand. But as I was asked over the years to comment on female circumcision because of my expertise in the Sudan, I came to realize how deeply I felt that the practice was harmful and wrong. In 1993, female circumcision was one of the practices deemed harmful by delegates at the International Human Rights Conference in Vienna. During their discussions, they came to view circumcision as a violation of the rights of children as well as of the women who suffer its consequences throughout life. Those discussions made me realize that there was a moral agenda larger than myself, larger than Western culture or the culture of the northern Sudan, or of my discipline. I decided to join colleagues from other disciplines and cultures in speaking out against the practice.

THE ANTHROPOLOGIST'S DILEMMA

The sense of paralysis that kept me from directly opposing female circumcision for decades was largely attributable to my anthropological training in cultural relativism. From a fieldworker's standpoint, my neutralist position stemmed from the anthropologist's firsthand knowledge of the local sensitivities about the practice, along with the fact that dialogue was actively under way in the Sudan leading in the direction of changes ameliorating the practice. While I would not hesitate to criticize breast implants or other Western surgical adjustments of the female body, I withheld judgment of female circumcision as though the moral considerations were fundamentally different.

My socialization as an anthropology undergraduate and graduate student, along with years of anthropology teaching, conditioned a relativist reflex to almost any challenge to cultural practice on moral or philosophical grounds, especially ones that appeared to privilege the West. However, I realized that a double standard had crept into my teaching. For example, I would readily criticize rampant domestic violence in the United States and then attempt to rationalize the killing of wives and sisters from the Middle East to Latin America by men whose "honor" had been violated by their female relation's alleged misdeeds, from flirtation to adultery. Of course, cultural context is critical and the reading of cultural difference our stock in trade. One may lament the rising divorce rate and destruction of family life in the United States while applauding increasing rights for judicial divorce for Middle Eastern women. At times relativism may frame and enlighten the debate, but, in the end, moral judgment and human rights take precedence and choices must be made.

What shifted my view away from the conditioned relativist response was the international, cross-cultural, interdisciplinary dialogue that placed female circumcision on a level of such harm that whatever social good it represents (in terms of sexual propriety and marriage norms), the harm to the more basic rights of women and girls outweighed the culturally understandable good. Moreover, active feminist agitation against female circumcision within the Sudan has fostered the kind of indigenous response that anthropologists like, so as not to appear to join the ranks of the Western feminists who had patronizingly tried to dictate the "correct" agenda to women most directly affected by the practice. Women's and human rights associations in the Ivory Coast and Egypt, as well as the Sudan, have also called for an end to female circumcision, while the Cairo Institute for Human Rights reported in 1995 the first publicly acknowledged marriage of an uncircumcised woman. In other words, a broad spectrum of the human community has come to an agreement that genital mutilation of girls and women is wrong.

THE CHANGING U.S. LEGAL CONTEXT

Beyond these cultural and moral considerations is a changed legal environment in the United States and elsewhere. The granting of political asylum by the U.S. government in 1996 to Fauziya Kasinga, a Togolese woman who argued that her return to her country would result in the forcible circumcision of her daughter and thus violate her human rights, was a turning point. Prior to this decision, articles had appeared in American law journals arguing for the United States to follow the examples of France and Canada and legally protect women and girls at risk by criminalizing female circumcision and by extending political asylum. Authors also argued against the cultural relativist or traditionalist justification for female circumcision.

Typical customary cultural arguments in defense of female circumcision are that it is a deeply rooted practice, that it prevents promiscuity and promotes cleanliness and aesthetics, and that it enhances fertility. Defenders of the practice, female and male, African and Western, inevitably invoke cultural relativism and ethnocentrism. For nonanthropologists, especially moral philosophers and legal practitioners, evocation of relativist arguments as a "defense" of or excuse for violence, injustice, or other social ills is patently offensive. "Cultural values and cultural practice are as legitimately subject to criticism from a human rights perspective as a structural aspect of a society. African 'culture' may not be used as a defense of human rights abuses" (Howard 1986:16).

There is nothing particularly African, Sudanese, or Nigerian about violence or injustice. This is true of violations of human rights whether they are in the form of arbitrary arrest, detention, and torture inflicted by the state or in the form of female circumcision imposed by custom. Moreover, many African progressives have taken an active role in evaluating the contemporary legitimacy and relevance of cultural practices arguing for the retention of useful traditions and the abandonment of practices that inflict harm or injury. Ethnic scarification has all but disappeared among peoples for whom this practice was routine only a few generations removed from the present day. And the fact that female circumcision is an ancient custom found in many diverse cultures does not legitimate its continued persistence (Lawrence 1993:1944).

Beyond the standard of harm evoked in this argument, it is increasingly evident that attempts to justify the control of female sexuality—whether using aesthetics, cleanliness, respectability, or religious ideology—increasingly are being questioned and rebuked in different cultures and cannot be sustained as a justification for the continuation of a harmful practice.

AN ANTHROPOLOGIST'S EXPERT TESTIMONY

I had the opportunity to offer expert testimony in an Immigration and Naturalization Service (INS) case involving application for asylum and withholding of deportation for a Nigerian family. The case revolved around the issues of Muslim persecution of Christians and the fear of female circumcision for the two young daughters of the parents, the wife having already undergone circumcision. My testimony involved responding to questions about female circumcision from the attorney for the Nigerian family and the judge. I was examined and cross-examined especially on the issue of the probability that the girls would be circumcised in their home community in northern Nigeria even if the father and mother opposed this.

Interestingly, after the 1996 Kasinga case, described above, the U.S. State Department issued guidelines to the INS and its courts suggesting that uncircumcised girls would not be at risk if their fathers opposed the practice. I explained that on the basis of my knowledge of the practice in a comparable African Muslim context, female circumcision is the province of female kin. There is no assurance, given the influence of extended family ties, that the girls would be protected on the strength of their parents', or just their father's, opposition. The matter of the state protecting the girls was moot given its lack of interest in regulating matters of "custom" and Nigeria's poor human rights record. Even in the Sudan, where female circumcision has been illegal since 1946, there has been little or no enforcement of the law. I was not asked if I believed that female circumcision is a violation of human rights, women's rights, or the rights of children. At a subsequent hearing, the mother, who had been circumcised as a child, testified about her fears of her daughters' forcible circumcision or, if no circumcision was performed, of their inability to be married in Nigeria, as they would be socially unacceptable women. These arguments persuaded the judge in 1997 to suspend deportation and to consider a positive case for asylum for this family.

"AVOIDANCE OF HARM" AS A KEY STANDARD

Harm may be considered to take place when there is death, pain, disability, loss of freedom or pleasure that results from an act by one human upon another (Gert 1988:47–49). It is the notion of harm done to individuals or groups that can be used to explore the terrain between universal rights and cultural relativism. When reasonable persons from different cultural backgrounds agree that certain institutions or cultural practices cause harm, then the moral neutrality of cultural relativism must be suspended. The concept of "harm" has been a driving force behind the medical, psychological, feminist, and cultural opposition to FGM.

Avoidance of harm has been the key concept in the development of ethical guidelines in medical and biological research and also in federal regulations regulating research in the behavioral sciences (Fluehr-Lobban 1994:3).

Philosophers have also refined concepts of harm and benefit; however, the discussion more frequently occurs around the prevention of harm rather than the promotion of benefit.

Even the most experienced anthropological fieldworker must negotiate the terrain between universal rights and cultural relativism with caution, to avoid the pitfalls of claiming scientific or disciplinary superiority. The anthropologist is capable of hearing, recording, and incorporating the multiple voices that speak to issues of cultural specificity and universal human rights, as some have done admirably (Dwyer 1991). But even when various perspectives are taken into consideration, in the end a judgment may have to be made when harm is a factor.

CASE STUDY: DOMESTIC ABUSE

The concept of *darar* in the Arabic language and in Islamic family law translates as "harm" or "abuse" and is broadly applied in Islamic law (shari'a) and specifically in three different cultural settings I have studied, in the Sudan, Egypt, and Tunisia (Fluehr-Lobban 1987). *Darar* comes from the same root as the term used to describe a strike or a physical blow. However, *darar* in Muslim family law as a ground for divorce has been interpreted to include both physical harm and emotional harm, the latter usually described as insulting words or behavior. The distinction between human rights and cultural practice is probably clearest when physical harm or abuse is taking place, such as physical abuse of women within marriage. Indeed, Western ideas of physical and mental cruelty as grounds for divorce mesh well with the concept of harm as reflected in *talaq al-darar*, divorce due to harm or abuse. A woman who comes to court, alleges harm, proves it with her own testimony or that of witnesses, and is granted a divorce is probably a woman who has experienced the abuse for some time and is using the court, as women often do in Muslim settings, as a last resort.

The divorced husband often does not acknowledge the harm, as is frequently the case with abusive husbands in other countries where the "right" of a husband to discipline a wife is a cultural norm. A relativist position might attempt to split the difference here between the cultural "right" of the husband to discipline a wife and the wife's right to resist. Moreover, the relativist's position would be upheld by cultural institutions and persons in authority—judges, for example—with the legitimate right to enforce the norm of "obedience" of wives. My own research shows that wives have often "disobeyed" their husbands and repeatedly fled from abusive domestic cohabitation (Fluehr-Lobban 1987:120–25). Historically, the frequency of such

cases in the Islamic courts led to practical reform favorable to abused wives whereby "obedience" orders to return to their husbands were issued a maximum of three times only. Ultimately, in the Sudan and in Egypt the "house obedience" (*bayt al-ta'a*) law was abolished, largely due to feminist agitation and reformist political pressure.

The cultural "right" of a man to discipline, slap, hit, or beat his wife (and often by extension his children) is widely recognized across a myriad of different cultures throughout the world where male dominance is an accepted fact of life. Indeed, the issue of domestic violence has only recently been added to the international human rights agenda, but it is firmly in place since the Vienna Conference of 1993 and the United Nations Beijing Women's Conference in 1995. The various strands of this relatively new dialogue intersect at a point where the individual rights of the woman clash with a potential cultural defense of a man practicing harm, and is a dialogue that anthropologists could inform and enrich tremendously by their firsthand knowledge of community and family life. Violence against women and children—against people—is not acceptable on moral grounds, nor is it defensible on cultural grounds, although an examination of its many expressions and facets is useful knowledge for both social science and public policy. The future development of a cross-cultural framework analyzing domestic violence would serve both scientific and human rights work.

STONING FOR ADULTERY IN THE SUDAN AND NIGERIA

Few Muslim states apply the *hudud* penalty of stoning for the crime of adultery, and when it does occur, often there is a larger political agenda. The Sudan made shari'a (Islamic law) state law in 1983 as an instrument of its dominance over the insurgent non-Muslim southern region that has been in resistance and civil war against the north since independence in 1956. Shortly after this political Islamization of its law, the Sudan began applying the harsh punishment of amputation for theft and threatened the use of the penalty of stoning for adultery. In predominantly Muslim northern Nigeria, a comparable trend toward Islamization has occurred in the past decade, with twelve of its northern states making shari'a provincial law. In both cases these moves exacerbated poor Muslim-Christian relations, intensifying the civil war in the Sudan and resulting in widespread and deadly rioting in Nigeria.

Shari'a courts in both countries have sentenced women to be stoned to death for convictions of adultery or fornication. In each of these cases national and international women's and human rights groups condemned the stoning sentences as cruel and inappropriate by international human rights standards. In one case a young Christian woman from the largest southern ethnic group in the Sudan, the Dinka, was sentenced to be stoned for being pregnant and unwed at the time of her trial in one of the "emergency" courts in Darfur. Despite the widely held view that Christians should not be judged by Islamic law, the Sudanese justice minister argued that Christians living in predominantly Muslim areas (such as Darfur) are subject to the majority law; however, he did criticize the ruling as "excessive and cruel" (Associated Press 2002). In Nigeria, two women were convicted of adultery and sentenced to stoning; protests arose, and the sentences were overturned. Nigerian president Olusegun Obasanjo declared the *hudud* punishments of stoning, beheadings, and amputations unconstitutional (McKenzie 2002), thus potentially setting the stage for a constitutional confrontation between secular Nigerian national law and shari'a in the powerful north.

Human rights, cultural relativism, and the standard of harm all intersect in this example. A minority of Muslim leaders connected to political agendas associated with the strict application of shari'a *hudud* penalties defend these punishments, but a wide range of constituencies from advocacy groups to national political leaders have not supported their application. Anthropologists would test the limits of their relativism to defend stoning and other *hudud* sanctions. Harm clearly occurs, as pain is inflicted in any potential application of the sentence; harm also occurs particularly to women, as they and not their partners are penalized. The fact that the penalty of stoning has not been carried out in either country suggests that the severity of potential harm that the punishment inflicts, combined with human rights activism, has restrained those authorities empowered to apply it.

CONCLUSION

The terrain between universal rights and cultural relativism can be puzzling and difficult to negotiate, but the use of the idea of "avoidance of harm" can help anthropologists and others map out a course of thinking and action. We are coming to the recognition that violence against women should be an acknowledged wrong, a violation of the basic human right to be free from harm that cannot be excused or justified on cultural grounds. Likewise, children in every culture have the right to be free from harm and to be nurtured under secure and adequate conditions. Understanding the diverse cultural contexts where harm or violence may take place is valuable and important, but suspending or withholding judgment because of cultural relativism is intellectually and morally irresponsible. Anthropologists cannot be bystanders when they witness harm being practiced upon any people they study.

Anthropologists can aid the international dialogue enormously by developing approaches to universal human rights that are respectful of cultural considerations but are morally responsible. For anthropologists a proactive interest and participation in human rights is desirable. Areas of human rights that might come to our attention in our work include cultural survival, rights of indigenous peoples, defense against "ethnic cleansing," or interest in the rights of women, children, and other persons in danger of harm. Instead of the more usual negative reaction to public disclosure of gross violations of human rights, anthropologists could position themselves to play an early-warning role that might prevent or ameliorate harm to human beings. Simplistic notions of cultural relativism no longer need impede the engagement of anthropologists in international human rights discourse.

In this spirit, anthropologists could be among the best brokers for intercultural dialogue regarding human rights. We have moved beyond the idea of a value-free social science to the task of developing a moral system at the level of our shared humanity that must at certain times supersede cultural relativism. Reassessing the value of cultural relativism does not diminish the continued value of studying and valuing diversity around the globe.

Anthropologists can lend their knowledge and expertise to the international discussion and debates regarding human rights by playing a brokering role between indigenous or local peoples they know firsthand and the international governmental and nongovernmental agencies whose policies affect the lives of people they study. Anthropologists also can write or speak out about human rights issues in public media where their expertise might inform positions taken by human rights advocacy groups, or decisions made by governments or other bodies that affect the well-being of people they study. If they choose, they can provide professional advice or offer expert testimony where culturally sensitive matters intersect with human rights issues, such as with female circumcision or with a cultural defense or justification of domestic violence. In these and other ways anthropologists can engage with human rights issues without the limitations that cultural relativism may impose.

FURTHER READING

Associated Press. 2002. "Sudan's Justice Minister Says Islamic Punishments Shall Be Correctly Implemented." March 27. Available at www.ap.org.

Bashir, L. M. 1996. "Female Genital Mutilation in the United States: An Examination of Criminal and Asylum Law." *The American University Journal of Gender and the Law* 4 (spring): 415–54.

Dwyer, Kevin. 1991. *Arab Voices: The Human Rights Debate in the Middle East.* University of California Press.

Fluehr-Lobban, Carolyn. 1987. *Islamic Law and Society in the Sudan.* Frank Cass.

Fluehr-Lobban, Carolyn. 1994. "Informed Consent in Anthropological Research: We Are Not Exempt." *Human Organization* 53(1):1–10.

Fluehr-Lobban, Carolyn. 1995. "Anthropologists, Cultural Relativism, and Universal Rights." *The Chronicle of Higher Education* (June 9):B1–2.

Gert, Bernard. 1988. *Morality: A New Justification of the Moral Rules.* Oxford University Press.

Gruenbaum, Ellen. 2001. *The Female Circumcision Controversy: An Anthropological Perspective.* University of Pennsylvania Press.

Howard, R. E. 1986. *Human Rights in Commonwealth Africa.* Rowman and Littlefield.

Lawrence, Harriet. 1993. "What's Culture Got to Do with It? Excising the Harmful Tradition of Female Circumcision." *Harvard Law Review* (June):1944–61.

McKenzie, Glenn. 2002. "Nigerian Woman Acquitted." Associated Press, March 26.

Sipress, Alan. 1995. "Egyptian Rights Group Sues Sheikh on Support of Female Circumcision." *The Philadelphia Inquirer,* April 13, p. A3.

Toubia, Nahid. 1995. *Female Genital Mutilation: A Call for Global Action.* 2nd ed. Women, Ink.

UNICEF/UNIFEM. n.d. "Convention on the Elimination of All Forms of Discrimination Against Women." UNICEF and UNIFEM.

25 ANDEAN WOMEN

United We Sit

Catherine J. Allen

This chapter with its update describes changing women's roles in the traditional highland Peruvian community of Sonqo that the author visited in 1975 and again in 1995 and 2000. As Allen explains, "Women support and anchor the life of the community and household, and it is in this that their power resides." However, it is the dual organization of men and women and the changes taking place in gender roles and relationships that raise the central two questions of the chapter: What is the role and influence of women in a traditional Andean society? How can women be so influential and powerful if they are almost invisible in community politics?

During my first month of fieldwork in Sonqo, a Quechua-speaking community in the highlands of southern Peru, I found myself extremely irritated by the apparently secondary status of women. They seemed to me like a flock of morose and timid crows—all dressed alike, hanging back at public assemblies, allowing themselves to be greeted and served last, and watching their menfolk eat at fiestas while they themselves went hungry. Frequently I had to choke back an urge to jump up and start lecturing them with evangelical zeal. None of these facts has changed, but my perception of them has. Sonqo's women no longer seem subordinate to their menfolk; indeed, one might argue, also erroneously, that the opposite is true.

TRADITIONAL GENDER ROLES

Traditional Andean ideology, which is very strong in rural communities such as Sonqo, is based on a principle of dual organization that structures the whole of society and the cosmos. In this dualistic mode of thought, the two parts of any given entity are related in a dialectical fashion, often expressed in the word *tinkuy,* the encounter that creates unity out of opposition. *Tinkuy* refers, for example, to the turbulent convergence of two streams, as well as to ritual battles between the two halves or moieties of a community.

Obviously, this way of thinking affects the way the sexes are conceptualized and how they are expected to behave toward each other. The household, as a functioning production unit, is built around the married couple, called *warmiqhari,* literally "woman-man," the fusion of two different but interdependent kinds of human being, with separate but complementary knowledge, interest and abilities. This relationship is summed up in various ways:

- "Women know how to work with their hands; men know how to work with their feet." So women spin, weave, and cook in or near their homes, while men plow the earth and travel.
- "Women are horizontal, their place is the *pampa,* the flat ground; men are vertical, they perform their activities standing or sitting on seats." So the vertical upright loom with foot pedals is suitable for males, while the horizontal loom is suitable for females. The great extensive earth is female, Pachamama or Mother Earth, while the high snow-capped mountains are male, called Apus (lords) or Taytakuna (fathers).
- "Men don't know how to take care of growing things." On the other hand, "Men know how to talk in the assembly; women don't know how." So women bear and tend children and look after the animals. Men pass through a hierarchy of community offices. At public functions men sit on seats in a line, roughly in order of seniority, while women sit in a crowd on the ground.

The image of woman evoked by these dichotomies is characterized by immobility. While the men are coming and going, building and talking, and passing vertically through a civil-religious hierarchy of offices, the women are sitting on the ground covered by layers of heavy skirts, their hands busily reaching in all directions. How beautifully this idea is expressed in dancing, as the women bend over their full skirts and twirl around in place, while the men go stamping and leaping around them! It is also well expressed in the different expressions of respect suitable for men and women: a prosperous influential man is called *qhapac,* which can be translated as "noble" or "mighty." The comparable term for women is *wira*, which means "fat" or "substantial."

Although a woman may not have a man's mobility, she is neither inactive nor passive. On the contrary, she has a female way of asserting herself. Women support and anchor the life of the community and household, and it is in this that their power resides.

THE ALL-MALE ASSEMBLY

Turning to the realms of community politics, this sexual ideology would seem to (and in certain respects does) put women at a distinct disadvantage in relation to men. The central governing body of Sonqo is the assembly, considered the voice of the *ayllu runa*, the people of the community. The constitutive units of the assembly are households, not individuals. Each of Sonqo's eighty-four households is represented by its senior male member. The women in attendance seldom number more than four or five, widows and women whose husbands are ill or absent. These women sit in a group apart from the men, sometimes at such a distance that it is difficult to hear the proceedings, much less take part in them.

The president of administration presides over the assembly, accompanied by a vice president and secretary, and often by the *alcalde* (mayor) with his staff of office. Often they are "assisted" by a schoolteacher or government agent. The presiding officers are elected by the assembly and serve for a term of two years. As the president represents the community to the national government and its agents, his position provides opportunities for self-aggrandizement and exercise of personal power. Sonqueños are keenly aware of this danger and repeatedly emphasized to me that it is the assembly, not the president or other officers, that makes decisions. On one occasion the president was nearly impeached for having accepted a government loan of eucalyptus trees without consulting the assembly. So the individuals who hold political office are not supposed to wield political power; they simply proclaim and carry out the collective will. The *alcalde,* in particular, with his staff of office, is a validator and by his presence makes the *ayllu*'s decisions official.

But what *is* the *ayllu*? Is it the group of men and few silent women who meet at intervals to argue and vote? Initially this seems to be the case; watching the assembly gives the impression that decision making is vested in a group of young and middle-aged males, with females and old men excluded from the political process. But this is a mistaken impression, similar to that created by a play, which fixes our attention on the actors on the stage and makes us forget that the observable action is produced and directed from behind the scenes. In Sonqo, while vigorous men play out the public drama of

political life, the women and old men are the invisible production crew. While we focus our attention on the public stage, we miss half the action, and inevitably must fail to understand how community politics function.

Although during my fieldwork I lived in the president's house and attended the assemblies, I usually had the feeling that the way things were "really" getting done was eluding me. I wondered whether there was a council of elders, but eventually I realized that no such council exists. Decision making goes on through seemingly casual visiting, as influential men and women (the *qhapac* and the *wira*) call on each other in the evening or before breakfast to chat and chew coca, or talk soberly during communal work parties while younger men work noisily at heavy tasks.

In this elusive process of sub rosa decision making, the opinions of the substantial women (*wira warmi*) carry a great deal of weight. In assemblies, the *mamakuna* (mothers, mature women) and *kuraq taytakuna* (elder fathers) are a significant, albeit invisible, presence. The men in the assembly do not represent themselves as individuals, but represent their households, including their wives and aged parents, and are accountable to them. This makes the decision-making process difficult to understand for the government agent, schoolteacher, or anthropologist who watches only the public drama.

THE POWER OF WOMEN

But what about situations in which women have to enter the public arena to achieve a goal that cannot be achieved otherwise? Clearly a woman without a husband for a mouthpiece, or who is seriously at odds with her husband, is at a great disadvantage. The most unpleasant incidents I witnessed in Sonqo were those in which women tried to address the assembly as individuals, inevitably without success. In one case, a woman who had married into Sonqo but returned to her natal community after her husband's death showed up in the assembly to demand her widow's rights of seed potatoes and labor. She was rejected without hesitation, and her gift of *trago* (cane alcohol) was returned unopened by the president.

Having failed to press her case as a single woman in a male forum, the widow changed her tactics. She did have a certain amount of sympathy from other women who had married into Sonqo. At the next communal work party these women appeared among the kinswomen of the hosting officials, bringing food and *chicha* (corn beer) for the laboring menfolk. After the work was finished, the gathering divided into the usual male and female groupings, who sat around chatting and chewing coca. At this point the widow appeared again and was loudly welcomed by the women who sympathized with her. Sonqueños consider it impossibly rude to turn away a guest who has been invited by even one member of a party, so while most of the men and many of the women were quietly displeased, the widow settled down and was offered coca and *chicha*. After a few minutes she presented the president with two bottles of *trago*. To my surprise, he accepted them and had them served to the gatherings. The husband of another woman, who had also married in, rose to argue the widow's case. Even before he began it was clear that she had already won, and the ensuing debate centered not on whether she would be helped, but on how much she would be helped.

Later I asked the president why he accepted the *trago* when it committed the *ayllu* to an unwelcome contract it had previously refused. "The *mamakuna* accepted her," he answered, "so we had to accept her too."

The widow achieved her goal by confronting the men not on their own terms but on a woman's terms. She recruited a collective base of female support at a gathering properly attended by both sexes. This group of women cleverly maneuvered the men into risking a serious breach of etiquette. Finally, they exploited a male representative. This collective female support with a male mouthpiece won the day before a word was spoken.

In another incident a woman proved able to enforce the *ayllu*'s will when the men were unsuccessful. In 1975 the *alcalde*-elect announced that he would not accept his office. In spite of his public election and unremitting pressure from his elders and peers, he stubbornly held out into December, only a few weeks before his inauguration. Backed by a group of women, his mother coerced him into serving, exploiting a religious feast day, another occasion on which both men and women gather to eat and drink together. Seated next to a big jar of *chicha,* surrounded by a crowd of women, she began to scream at her son, "What are you? Are you a Quechua person?" continuing with a long stream of condemnations. Although most of the men agreed with her, in a subdued chorus they begged her to be quiet. Eventually she subsided, and the feast continued. The next day the word was out that the *alcalde*-elect had agreed to accept his office.

To summarize, female power is exerted collectively and consists essentially in the power of veto and commentary. Those who have spent time in Quechua households will find this familiar—recalling how as a man of the house prepares his family offering to Pachamama and Apus, his wife sits at his side selecting the ingredients and correcting his invocation; how as a man tells traditional stories, his wife coaches him and he accepts her corrections. The political sphere is not essentially different; in assemblies the *mamakuna* are not physically at their husbands' side, but their invisible presence weighs heavily nonetheless. When, in extreme cases, women as a group decide to "go public," they cause a kind of social earthquake—an upheaval of the private substream of public life.

This way of operating does not sit well with a modern professional woman, eager to meet men on her own terms in a public forum. But there is much to be learned from it: that this is not a simple matter of female subordination but something much more subtle and complex; and that the powers as well as the limitations of Sonqo women are inherent in the total sociocultural system, a system whose resilience and strength resides to a great extent in the invisible, elusive—and potentially violent—character of female power.

UPDATE

Many changes have taken place since I first went to Sonqo in 1975. I returned there in both 1995 and 2000 and found that two-story tile-roofed houses, some with TV antennas, were replacing the one-room thatched houses. The road now is passable year-round, and Sonqueños have more opportunities to participate directly in urban markets. They have abandoned their coordinated community-wide system of crop rotation in favor of more intensive, individualized cultivation of cash crops. About half of the community's inhabitants have found in evangelical Protestantism an alternative to the old nativistic faith in their Inca ancestry. Protestant and Catholic/Andean alike are looking away from their local landscape to more distant, expanding horizons of opportunity.

Women's Mobility

Wira warmi, the old feminine ideal, was embodied in the way a woman hunkered down by her low earthen stove, her hands moving busily as she cooked food and nurtured children. It was embodied in a woman's heavy conical form and her rocking, swishing gait. During Carnival, *sargento* dancers asked the *alcalde*'s permission—*"Lisinciayki, taytáy!"*—to dance in couples, with the men ducking and bobbing and the women, bent slightly over their many skirts, turning in place. Today, in cities and towns, female dance troupes do not express this horizontal/vertical gender complementarity. They dance in rows, bobbing up and down, as they move forward down the street. *Wira warmi*—a fat, substantial woman, loaded with ponderous skirts and a heavy bundle—is an outmoded ideal from their grandmothers' time. As public performers, these women display a new kind of female assertiveness and mobility.

This new mobility characterizes rural wives as well as city-bred girls, as I learned vividly in 2000. Although I did not have an opportunity to observe communal assemblies during this visit, I was able to attend a *faena* (work party) in a sector of Sonqo called Mama Samana. Its purpose was to build a communal kitchen adjoining the neighborhood meeting house. Only seven men from Mama Samana's fourteen households attended. Three women showed up to represent their absent husbands (families who were not represented had to pay a fine). The women went off to gather firewood while the men set to work treading straw into a big mud puddle and then plopping the straw-mud into wooden forms to shape adobe bricks. By noon they were hungry and ready to eat.

Fortunately, three more women arrived to help with the cooking. Inside the community house these *mamakuna*—members of the Mothers Club—were hurriedly preparing a meal. A big pot of water was boiling on a fire near one end of the room. My old friend Josefa explained that they were preparing only hot drink, for there had been no time to cook soup. They all had too much to do that morning. The latecomers had only just arrived back from a trip to Cuzco, and two other women were attending a meeting at their children's school in Colquepata. Nevertheless, they lost no time worrying about the lack of soup. Out came a big bundle of greens from their solar garden. Quickly they washed the salad in a bucket, tossed it in a big plastic basin with some salt, and—presto!—lunch was ready.

Salad and Soccer

The men came in and sat down in a line along one wall. Two of the younger women sat on a bench along the opposite wall, while the others sat on the ground near the fireplace or around the salad bowl. Josefa doled out plates of salad, and the men accepted with the familiar gracious thanks. Although later that evening I was to hear some grumbling about the unsatisfying food, the men expressed no discontent as they ate their meal. They seemed proud of the home-grown greens and helped themselves to seconds, urging me to do the same. Soon there was not a scrap of lettuce left in the basin. The mothers then produced a big bag of sweetened powdered oatmeal donated to the Mothers Club by a Peruvian aid program. They mixed it with the hot water and served it up in metal mugs. The men finished their oatmeal, excused themselves, and went out to chew coca in the warm sunshine. The women stayed inside to wash up the mugs, in very high spirits. Outside, the neighborhood president had very little coca to distribute, and three of the younger men had brought none of their own. After a brief and subdued interlude they went back to work.

Inside, I was feeling confused. The mothers were trying to decide whether to play soccer or take me to see their garden. Finally they decided that they could do both. As we climbed up the hillside to see the garden, I felt sure that I had misunderstood something. Maybe their children were going to play soccer. I pondered the question while they showed me their remarkable solar greenhouse, an adobe enclosure roofed with translucent plastic. It seemed like Shangri-la hidden in Sonqo's dry and barren terrain. But the biggest surprise was yet in store—for it was indeed the mothers who played soccer. They had a wonderful, boisterous time, and played remarkably well. There was no doubt that these women knew how to use their feet!

After a while I moseyed over the hillside to see how the men were taking it. They were busy, studiously ignoring the game, their attention focused on a new mold for adobe bricks that wasn't quite the right size. Bemused, I went back to watch the darting, kicking, laughing women. *Well, wonders will never cease,* I thought. *These* mamakuna *fed their men salad and then ran off to play soccer. And the men put up with it!*

Mother House/Mother Earth

Wira warmi, fat, substantial woman, was embodied in the house itself. A *wasitira* (house-earth) was a living female, a localized version of Pachamama (Mother Earth). A house should be warm and protective—"like a mother hen who keeps her chicks under her wings," Luis once told me, his face lighting up as he spoke. His sister used a similar metaphor, describing the house as a nest. The warmth and closeness of the small one-room houses, their comfortable disorder of cloth and crockery, the crowding together of their inhabitants—these fostered a nestlike experience. If the interior of the house was rather smothering, it was also comfortable and secure. It was a place for rest, safety and nourishment; all other activities were carried on outdoors.

The old nestlike houses are rapidly being relegated to the "olden days" by new two-story tile-roofed houses, financed by an development program called Plan International. These more open, multiroom structures—with glass-pane windows and six-foot-high doors—restructure their inhabitants' relationship to their activities and environment. The low doors in the old-style houses force you to bend over as you cross the threshold, whereas you enter the new ones standing upright. Entering the old house produced a qualitative change in consciousness every time you crossed the threshold, straightened up, and readjusted your senses to different light, temperature, smells and spatial dimensions. The perceptual contrast was strong and definite. The change in housing—one aspect of a complex process of cultural transformation—will transform Sonqueños' lives in manifold ways. It will affect the rhythm of their daily activities, their bodily habits, and their use of personal space.

The old houses are stuffier and smokier while the new ones are colder. They have more interior space to heat; the windows and doors that let in light and fresh air also let in the cold wind. The new houses are also more spacious and can accommodate activities such as weaving and potato sorting that were previously done outdoors. In years past the European tradition of furniture never caught on with native Andeans, but this too is changing. If (as Sonqueños expect) Plan International provides tables and chairs, household activities will be conducted away from the ground, placing distance between a family and its *wasitira*. If electricity ever comes to Sonqo (as it eventually is likely to), families will be able to stay up at night doing chores, watching TV, reading, doing homework.

But not everything is changing. Inside their homes most women prefer to maintain the hearth and to cook as their mothers did. The new houses could easily accommodate waist-high wood-burning stoves with adjoining counter space. This would move food preparation off the dirt floors and allow the cook more mobility. Women know that this is the "modern" way to cook, yet they continue to build their low clay *q'uncha*s (which look rather like small kilns with a round opening on top for the soup pot). They explained that they find it more comfortable and natural to work sitting down, with ingredients and cookware on the floor within arm's reach. In the city of Cuzco, my friend Emilia expressed the same sentiments. Although she is an up-and-coming urban migrant, she proudly showed me the *q'uncha* in her new kitchen. Food cooked there was healthier and tasted better than food prepared on a kerosene or gas stove, she insisted. And she felt more comfortable cooking that way.

So it is that *wira warmi* and her warm round stove abide at the center of the new houses just as they did in the old ones. Many things are changing, but some stay the same.

FURTHER READING

Allen, Catherine J. 2002. *The Hold Life Has: Coca and Cultural Identity in an Andean Community*. 2nd ed. Smithsonian Institution Press. (The second edition includes a new chapter describing Sonqo as it was in 1995 and 2000. Allen's *Anthropology Explored* update is an excerpt, with some adaptation, from this chapter.)

Allen, Catherine J., and Nathan Garner. 1997. *Condor Qatay: Anthropology in Performance*. Waveland Press.

Bastien, Joseph W. 1985. *Mountain of the Condor: Metaphor and Ritual in an Andean Ayllu*. Waveland Press.

Behar, Ruth. 1993. *Translated Woman: Crossing the Border with Esperanza's Story*. Beacon Press.

Bolin, Inge. 1998. *Rituals of Respect: The Secret of Survival in the High Peruvian Andes*. University of Texas Press.

De la Cadena, Marisol. 2000. *Indigenous Mestizos: The Politics of Race and Culture in Cuzco, Peru, 1919–1991*. Duke University Press.

Condori Mamani, Gregorio. 1996. *Andean Lives: Gregorio Condori Mamani and Asunta Quispe Huamán*. Ed. R. Valderrama and Carmen Escalante; translated from the Quechua with introduction and annotations by P. Gelles and G. Martínez. University of Texas Press.

Isbell, Billie Jean. 1985. *To Defend Ourselves: Ecology and Ritual in an Andean Village*. Waveland Press.

Meyerson, Julia. 1990. *Tambo: Life in an Andean Village*. University of Texas Press.

Rosaldo, Michelle Z., and Louise Lamphere, eds. 1974. *Woman, Culture, and Society*. Stanford University Press.

Weismantel, Mary J. 1998. *Food, Gender, and Poverty in the Ecuadorean Andes*. Waveland Press.

26 IDENTITY IN COLONIAL NORTHERN MEXICO

William L. Merrill

Despite the transformations that have taken place since European contact, many Indian societies in northern Mexico have been able to maintain their distinctive Indian identity. Merrill's chapter addresses two major questions: What effect did colonization have in transforming Indian identity in northern Mexico, and what role did language play in forming and retaining identity for indigenous Mexican cultures during Spanish colonization?

Con gran facilidad mudarán a semejanza de los mulatos y mestizos su traje, dejando crecer el cabello, trocando la tilma por un capote; pues con esta transformación se llaman gente de razon, y se eximen de pagar tributo.

—Jesuit priest, 1754

In 1754 Spanish officials and Catholic missionaries in the province of Sinaloa, located in northwestern Mexico, debated the wisdom of requiring local Indians to pay tribute to the king of Spain while exempting certain non-Indian settlers from such payments. A Jesuit missionary, whose opinion but not his name is preserved in the historical record, as shown above, argued against the measure, indicating that the Indians would simply change their identity: "With great ease they will come to resemble mulattos and mestizos in their dress, letting their hair grow and exchanging their capes for cloaks, and with this transformation they call themselves people of reason and are exempted from paying tribute."

HISTORICAL BACKGROUND

During the century following the Spanish Conquest of the Aztec capital of Tenochtitlán in 1521, Spanish settlers spread from central Mexico as far north as what is now the southwestern United States. Drawn especially by major strikes of silver and gold in the modern state of Chihuahua, miners were joined by missionaries, ranchers, farmers, and merchants in an effort to establish firm Spanish control over the northern frontier.

At the time of European contact, Chihuahua was populated by a number of distinct Indian groups speaking mutually unintelligible languages. Nomadic, hunting-gathering bands lived in eastern and northern Chihuahua, while in central and western Chihuahua sedentary societies supplemented their agriculture with extensive collecting of wild resources. All these societies were egalitarian and locally autonomous. At the time of contact, there were no native conquest states in this region (such as the Aztec and Inca farther south), and while local groups probably formed alliances during times of conflict, no political organization existed that encompassed more than a few small bands or contiguous rancherías.

Franciscan and Jesuit missionaries first contacted the Indians of Chihuahua in the second half of the sixteenth century, but they did not begin to create a network of permanent missions until the early decades of the seventeenth century. Indian revolts throughout the second half of the seventeenth century disrupted their efforts, but by the early eighteenth century this mission system covered most of central and western Chihuahua. In 1767 King Charles III of Spain expelled the Jesuits from all of his New World empire, and Franciscan missionaries and diocesan priests divided the responsibility for their missions in northern Mexico.

CONCEPT OF IDENTITY

The expansion of the Spanish colonial system and particularly the Catholic mission system in the region brought about important changes in local Indian identity. Identity is one of the few concepts to have made the transition from the social sciences to popular culture with its technical definitions largely intact. Academic and popular views of the concept of identity agree that identity is, in essence, who I think I am and who others think I am, or, on a more sociological level, who we think we are and who others think we are. These views also concur that identity is the product of the interplay between these insider and outsider perspectives, and that it is subject to change as the circumstances change within which an individual or group operates.

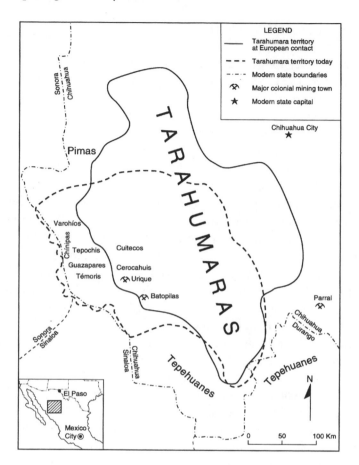

Tarahumara Territories (courtesy Marcia Bakry)

Although the concept of identity is relatively uncomplicated—we might even say self-evident—this fact does not diminish its importance as a central feature of human existence. Moreover, although we may have a clear idea of what identity is, we still have much to learn about how identities are created, maintained, and transformed.

Colonial contexts offer an excellent opportunity to examine these processes. The expansion of colonialism usually involves the formation of new kinds of social, economic, and political relations among the members of societies and between societies that have had limited previous contact with one another. In such settings, existing schemes of identity classification must be revised and the significance and implications of these classifications defined. Seldom do the colonized passively accept the classifications that their colonizers intend to impose on them, for important political and economic and psychological interests are at stake. More frequently, identities and the relations of inequality typically assigned to them are openly contested.

Here I explore processes of identity formation, maintenance, and transformation during the colonial and immediate postcolonial periods in the Tarahumara region of central and western Chihuahua. At the time of European contact, the Tarahumara, who today call themselves Ralámuli, farmed, hunted, and gathered in a territory that covered about 50,000 square kilometers in central and western Chihuahua (see map). During the past four hundred years, they have been displaced from much of their original territory and are found today in the foothills, mountains, and canyons of western Chihuahua. They speak a language that is related to the languages spoken by their neighbors in northern Mexico—the Guarijío, Tepehuan, Pima, Yaqui, and Mayo—as well as more distant Indian societies such as the Comanche, Hopi, and Aztec, all of which belong to the Uto-Aztecan language family.

ETHNIC CLASSIFICATIONS

When the Spanish arrived in northern Mexico, they brought with them a scheme of ethnic classification derived ultimately from Iberian and European concepts of ethnicity and modified during the previous century on the basis of their experience in other parts of the New World. The basic distinction in this scheme was that between "Spaniards" and "Indians." The category of "Spaniard," itself a subcategory of "European," was divided into two principal subcategories, the first encompassing Spaniards born in Spain (*peninsulares*) and the second Spaniards born in the New World (*criollos*). The category of "Indians" also was subdivided. Distinct Indian groups were labeled according to tribal identities, which were crosscut by several general categories. For example, Indians were classified as being "civilized" or "barbaric"—a distinction that reflected the prejudices not only of Europeans but also of central Mexican Indians—depending primarily on the complexity of their societies. Those Indians who converted to Christianity were called "Christians" (*cristianos*), "baptized people" (*bautizados*), or "converts" (*conversos*), and were distinguished from those who did not, who usually were referred to as "gentiles."

Christian Indians were further distinguished according to their inclination to accept the conditions of colonial existence that their colonizers attempted to impose upon them. There were "good Christians," who tended to accept these conditions, and "bad Christians," who did not. Those "bad Christians" who abandoned their mission pueblos and the Spanish economic centers to live in areas beyond Spanish control were in addition characterized as "apostates," "fugitives," or "cimarrones." The term *cimarrones* originally meant

"runaways" and is the source of the name "Seminoles," which labeled Indians and African slaves who sought refuge from European colonialism in remote areas of Florida.

Apostate and fugitive Indians often moved into established communities of gentile Indians. In fact, people in Chihuahua today use the terms "gentiles" and "cimarrones" interchangeably to designate the descendants of those Indians who remained outside the colonial system. However, not all gentiles rejected baptism and incorporation into the mission pueblos. Many remained outside the mission system simply because the opportunity to join had not presented itself or because they did not want to abandon their rancherías, which frequently were located long distances from the mission pueblos. As the mission system expanded into their areas, they often accepted baptism. Thus, over the course of the colonial period, the number of Indians identified as "gentiles" tended to decrease and to include primarily those Indians who intentionally rejected an affiliation with the Catholic mission system.

Joining the categories of "Spaniards" and "Indians" in the Spanish ethnic classification was a third division composed of a complicated set of categories that labeled individuals of mixed European, Indian, and African genetic heritage. These categories, theoretically infinite in number, were collapsed under the general term of "castes" (castas). The people so classified also were categorized collectively as *gente de razón,* a term that literally means "people of reason" but was originally used to designate non-Spaniards and especially people of mixed genetic heritage who were able to speak the Spanish language. Today non-Indians in Chihuahua sometimes refer to all local non-Indians as *gente de razón* regardless of their genetic heritage. However, colonial documents reveal that many Spaniards carefully distinguished themselves from the ethnically mixed *gente de razón,* whom they tended to consider of inferior status.

The Indians of Chihuahua maintained their own schemes of ethnic classification, but it is impossible to determine with any confidence what these schemes might have been because all of our information is filtered through documents produced by Europeans. From the evidence that is available, it appears that the Indians emphasized language as the principal marker of ethnicity, further distinguishing among speakers of the same language on the basis of locality. There was some blurring of identity along the borders of different language groups, where speakers of distinct languages intermarried, lived in the same or adjacent rancherías, and occasionally shared political leaders. Yet even in such border areas, where bilingualism was the rule, a person's first or preferred language appears to have been the key element in determining his or her ethnic identity.

The Spanish and Indian schemes of ethnic classification probably differed primarily in the degree to which the categories they included were ranked. In the Spanish scheme, Spaniards and other Europeans were located at the top, *castas* in the middle, and Indians at the bottom. In specific areas, however, Indians and in particular "good Christian Indians" were considered by Europeans to be morally if not socially superior to certain people of mixed heritage whose libertine ways were felt to jeopardize the progress of "civilization" on the frontier.

Given the egalitarianism of the Indian societies in northern Mexico, it is unlikely that their schemes of ethnic classification were as hierarchical as that of the Spaniards, although they may have thought of themselves as superior to the Spaniards. Today the Tarahumara Indians classify all non-Indians as "whiskered ones" (*chabochi*) and say that they are the children of the Devil, while considering themselves and all other Indians to be equals and the children of God.

FEWER INDIAN IDENTITIES

One of the most notable features of the history of identity formation in colonial northern Mexico is the decline in the number of distinct Indian groups noted in the documentary record between the seventeenth and eighteenth centuries. In some cases, especially among nomadic Indian societies in eastern Chihuahua, entire groups disappeared because the majority of their members died in epidemics or conflicts with the Spanish, the survivors joining other Indian groups or assimilating into the emerging mestizo population. Epidemics and military conflicts also had an important impact on the more sedentary Indian populations in central and western Chihuahua. In these areas, however, the reduction in the number of distinct Indian identities appears to have been due primarily to the emergence of more inclusive categories of ethnicity and a better understanding of the linguistic and cultural relationships among the Indians on the part of missionaries and colonial officials.

At the time of European contact, the greatest ethnic diversity in the region was reported from the mountains and rugged canyon country of western Chihuahua. The first missionaries to visit and work in this area identified these Indians as comprising a number of distinct "nations" (*naciones*): Chínipas, Varohíos, Guazapares, Témoris, Tepochis, Cuitecos, Cerocahuis, and so on. However, their perspectives on local ethnic diversity was strongly affected by their previous experience in the Sinaloan missions to the south, where the Indians belonged to a number of politically autonomous groups and spoke many distinct languages. When they arrived in western Chihuahua, these missionaries failed to realize that the various politically autonomous groups that they encountered probably were subdivisions of but two ethnic groups: the Varohío (known today as Guarijío) and the Guazapar, who probably spoke a dialect of Tarahumara rather than a distinct language.

In 1632 the Varohíos and Guazapares expelled the missionaries and other outsiders from their territories. It was not until the late seventeenth century that the Spanish had an opportunity to acquire a more profound understanding of the cultural and linguistic affiliations of these groups. From that point on, the missionaries began using fewer terms to distinguish among the Indians in the region.

It is also likely that the influx of Tarahumaras and Indians from other areas into western Chihuahua resulted in some cultural and linguistic homogenization across the region. Large numbers of Tarahumaras began migrating into this area during the major revolts in the mid- and late seventeenth century, and the immigrants probably included both rebels fleeing from the Spanish military and other Tarahumaras who sought to avoid the violence altogether.

Where the number of Tarahumara immigrants was small, they were absorbed by the local communities, eventually substituting local Indian identities for their own. A similar loss of identity may also have occurred where the number of Tarahumara immigrants was more substantial, but the outcome for ethnic identity was not always the same. The large numbers of

Tarahumara immigrants who entered the Varohío area of western Chihuahua apparently were assimilated into the Varohío communities: the Varohíos continue to live today as a distinct ethnic group in roughly the same area as they did in the seventeenth century. In contrast, the Tarahumaras who migrated to the neighboring Guazapares region did not lose their identity but instead, by the eighteenth century, the Guazapares became known as Tarahumaras and apparently identified themselves as such.

If comparable numbers of Tarahumaras migrated into the Guazapar and Varohío areas, how can we explain the fact that the Varohíos retained their distinct identity while the Guazapares lost theirs? I believe that the key lies in differences in the degree to which the languages spoken by the Varohíos and Guazapares were similar to the Tarahumara language spoken by immigrants into their communities. Although closely related to Tarahumara, Varohío is nonetheless a distinct language. The Guazapar language, on the other hand, probably was a mutually intelligible variant of Tarahumara. Assuming an identity as "Tarahumaras" thus would have been simpler for the Guazapares than for the Varohíos. Indeed, given the linguistic and cultural similarities between the Guazapares and the Tarahumaras, it is possible that the Guazapares identified themselves as Tarahumaras before the arrival of the Spanish, who might have concluded incorrectly that "Guazapares" labeled a separate ethnic group rather than a subdivision of the Tarahumaras.

In the eighteenth and nineteenth centuries the Spanish expanded the semantic scope of the term *Tarahumara* to label both Tarahumaras and other Indians who closely resembled them. They did this even in the case of Indians who did not identify themselves as Tarahumaras. This reformulation of the category "Tarahumaras" by the Spanish may have paralleled and even contributed to the adoption of the term as a more encompassing ethnic label by the Indians in the region. During the colonial period, Indian groups from widely separated areas came into contact with one another in Spanish mines, haciendas, and other population centers. It is reasonable to assume that this increased interaction, combined with the growing presence of non-Indians with whom to contrast themselves, encouraged the emergence of a sense of common identity among the Indians, an identity that came to be labeled as "Tarahumara."

Today the Tarahumaras consider the term *Tarahumara* to be a Spanish word, and they refer to themselves as Ralámuli. The term *Ralámuli* has meanings on four increasingly specific levels of significance. At the most general level, it designates "human beings" in contrast to "nonhumans." At the second level, it labels "Indians" in contrast to "non-Indians." At the third level, it refers only to Ralámuli Indians in contrast to the members of other Indian groups. Finally, at the most specific level, it designates Ralámuli men in contrast to Ralámuli women. A recognition of these different senses clearly indicates that the term *Ralámuli,* semantically one of the most complex words in the Ralámuli language today, was adjusted, if not created, to accommodate the distinction between Indians and non-Indians that impinged itself upon the Ralámuli and other Indian people in the colonial period.

The word *Ralámuli* first appears in the historical literature in 1826 in a sermon prepared in the Tarahumara language by the Franciscan missionary Miguel Tellechea. Given its late appearance, I am inclined to conclude that the Tarahumaras adopted the term during the course of the colonial period to label the more inclusive ethnic identity that was being forged out of the multiple and often very localized identities of the precontact period. Because the term *Tarahumar* was used by the Spanish from the time of their arrival in Chihuahua, the Tarahumaras later on in the colonial period might have identified it as a Spanish rather than native word, as they do today. If so, they may have rejected it as an inappropriate label with which to distinguish themselves from non-Indians.

THE SPATIALIZATION OF IDENTITY

The Tarahumaras responded to the Spanish colonial system in a variety of ways, ranging from enthusiastic acceptance to near total rejection. Through time these differences in attitude became increasingly associated with communities located in different areas rather than being replicated within each Tarahumara community.

By 1767, when the Jesuits were expelled, the Tarahumaras who rejected most aspects of the Spanish colonial system lived in the remoter reaches of western and southern Tarahumara country, far from major Spanish settlements and economic centers. There they were little affected by labor drafts, Spanish encroachment on their lands, and the programs of directed culture change administered by the Catholic missionaries.

These isolated communities of Tarahumaras contrast with those located in and around the missions and Spanish economic centers of east-central Chihuahua and northern Durango. Here the Indians participated extensively in the regional colonial economy and were described by the missionaries and Spanish colonial officials as having accepted much of Spanish colonial society and culture. Between these two groups were the Tarahumaras who lived within the mission system but some distance from major Spanish economic centers. These Indians created a synthetic culture that combined both indigenous and introduced ideas and practices. They also retained their distinct Indian identity, which they modified to reflect their affiliation with the Catholic mission system.

SUMMARY

In this essay I have discussed three basic processes related to the formation and transformation of Indian identity in colonial northern Mexico. All three processes took place simultaneously and were inextricably linked to more general processes of the colonial endeavor.

The first process involved modifications in the Indian schemes of ethnic classification. Unlike the Spanish, who employed essentially the same scheme in northern Mexico as the one they had developed earlier in central Mexico, the local Indians modified their preexisting schemes rather extensively. They created new terms to label non-Indians, as well as new or modified terms to label the emerging category of "Indian." They also adopted ethnic labels from the Spanish to designate subgroups of Indians who varied from one another in their responses to the colonial system.

The second process was the reduction in the number of terms used to label local groups. In other areas of the New World, the emergence of more inclusive ethnic categories often resulted from the consolidation of remnant groups into new ethnic units. In central and western Chihuahua, in contrast, most Indian groups were sufficiently large to sustain their biological reproduction and avoid reduction to the status of remnant societies, at least until the twentieth century. The Spanish began using fewer terms to label these groups because they gradually came to recognize the cultural and linguistic affinities among them. In northern Mexico, as in other areas of the New World, they sometimes carried this process too far, lumping together Indians who probably were sufficiently different to warrant designation as distinct groups. During the same period, the Indians in the region also apparently began employing broader ethnic labels to designate themselves, in part because the Spanish were using these terms in a more inclusive sense, in part because of the cultural and linguistic homogenization that resulted from population movements, but most importantly because they were forging a sense of common Indian identity to contrast with that of non-Indians.

The third process was the spatialization of identity, in which internal divisions within the more inclusive Indian identities became associated with distinct geographical areas. These divisions were defined in terms of the different stances that different Indian people and groups took with respect to the Spanish colonial and mission enterprise and, on a superficial level at least, the Spanish and Indians agreed on what the distinctions were.

The interplay of both external and internal factors is evident in all three of these interconnected processes. Colonial categories and policies forced people to be "Indians" as well as specific kinds of "Indians," but at the same time they motivated Indian people to create a common identity as "Indians" that at different times and places served as the basis for political solidarity against the Spanish. Yet while the Spanish presence engendered solidarity at one level, it produced internal divisions and conflicts at another. At no time during the colonial period did all the Tarahumaras unite to support or oppose the Spanish.

The Spanish presence also stimulated the movement of Indians out of their home communities, either to avoid contact with the Spanish or to trade with and work for them. People from many different ethnic groups, often including both Indians and non-Indians, came together in refuge areas, in missions near Spanish settlements, and in Spanish economic centers, where identities were both reinforced and revised. One result was the transformation of large numbers of Indians into mestizos, either because of their assimilation into the emerging mestizo society or because of the creation of offspring of mixed ethnic and genetic heritage through interethnic marriage or sexual relations.

Although less frequent, the transformation of non-Indians into Indians also occurred. Non-Indian criminals and other fugitives from Spanish society sometimes joined communities of fugitive and gentile Indians, many of whom themselves came from distinct Indian societies. The emergence of a common identity within these communities depended upon overcoming the ethnic diversity of their members, a process no doubt facilitated by the physical isolation of the communities and their marginal and often oppositional stance with respect to the Spanish.

Despite the transformations that have taken place in their lives since European contact, many Indian societies in northern Mexico have succeeded in maintaining their distinctive identities. During the past century, several developments in Mexico—including the *indigenista* movement, the organization of Indian communities into collective landholding and economic units called *ejidos,* and changes to the Mexican constitution, which now acknowledges that Mexico is a multiethnic and multicultural society—have promoted the persistence of separate Indian identities. However, Indian people have never depended on external structures and forces for the maintenance of their identities. Instead they have produced and reproduced their identities as part of their pursuit of the goals and interests that they have defined as fundamental to their survival.

UPDATE

Historical anthropological studies such as the one presented here rely on data gleaned from documents that have survived from the time period under consideration and are found today for the most part in public or private archives.

Although the documentary materials that are preserved seldom represent more than a small percentage of those originally produced, they often are sufficiently extensive to require years to review. This process proceeds slowly because the number of scholars dedicated to exploring a particular topic tends to be rather limited and most prefer to consult the original documents rather than depending upon secondary accounts of them. New data emerge when previously unknown documents are discovered or known documents are reanalyzed in terms of new perspectives. Such new perspectives themselves emerge as the practitioners of a discipline confront the limitations of the perspectives they have inherited from their predecessors and begin addressing different kinds of questions. This is a process typically repeated at least once with each new generation of scholars.

Archival research that I have conducted since 1997, when "Identity Transformation in Colonial Northern Mexico" was originally published, has not yielded any new data that would require my interpretations to be revised, nor have new perspectives on identity, either in Spanish colonial Mexico or other times and places, been developed that would challenge earlier conclusions. An expanded version of this study was published in 2001, in Spanish, in a collection of essays organized around the theme of identity and culture in the Sierra Tarahumara (Molinari and Porras 2001). The authors of these essays examine diverse aspects of identity among the Ralámuli (Tarahumara) as well as other, neighboring indigenous societies from before the arrival of the Spanish to today, providing a broader context within which to interpret transformations in identity in the region during the Spanish colonial period. Particularly relevant is an essay by Professor Susan Deeds of Northern Arizona University, who explores both the persistence and loss of cultural identities among five indigenous societies in colonial northern Mexico, including the Ralámuli (Deeds 2001). A recently published book (Deeds 2003) explores these themes in depth.

In a separate publication, Professor Jon Olson of California State University, Los Angeles provides an intriguing comparison between the processes of identity transformation proposed for the Sierra Tarahumara and those that occurred during and following the Spanish colonial period in Nuevo León, an adjacent area of northern Mexico (Olson 2000). Reconstructing these processes on the basis of both historical and contemporary ethnographic data, Olson concludes that while Spanish colonialism developed in a parallel fashion in the two areas, demographic and cultural differences produced significantly different outcomes in local indigenous identities. Indigenous people in Nuevo León adopted the colonial identity of "*indio*" (Indian) that the Spanish assigned to them, and this new identity eventually came to replace entirely their preexisting and more specific cultural group identities.

His research documents the diversity and complex interplay of the factors that must be taken into consideration to understand processes of identity formation not only in northern Mexico but, as a number of studies have demonstrated (for example, Hill 1996; Proschan 1997), around the world.

FURTHER READING

Barth, Fredrik, ed. 1969. *Ethnic Groups and Boundaries: The Social Organization of Culture Difference*. Little, Brown.

Cohen, Ronald. 1978. "Ethnicity: Problem and Focus in Anthropology." *Annual Review of Anthropology* 7:379–403.

Deeds, Susan M. 2001. "Resistencia indígena y vida cotidiana en la Nueva Vizcaya. Trastornos y cambios étnico-culturales en la época colonial." In Molinari and Porras, eds., pp. 55–69.

Deeds, Susan M. 2003. *Defiance and Deference in Mexico's Colonial North: Indians under Spanish Rule in Nueva Vizcaya*. University of Texas Press.

Eriksen, Thomas H. 1991. "The Cultural Contexts of Ethnic Differences." *Man* 26:127–44.

Hill, Jonathan D., ed. 1996. *History, Power, and Identity: Ethnogenesis in the Americas, 1492–1992*. University of Iowa Press.

Merrill, William L. 1988. *Raramuri Souls: Knowledge and Social Process in Northern Mexico*. Smithsonian Institution Press.

Merrill, William L. 1993. "Conversion and Colonialism in Northern Mexico: The Tarahumara Response to the Jesuit Mission Program, 1601–1767," in Robert W. Hefner, ed., *Conversion to Christianity: Historical and Anthropological Perspectives on a Great Transformation*, pp. 129–63. University of California Press.

Merrill, William L. 2001. "La identidad ralámuli, una perspectiva histórica." In Molinari and Porras, eds., pp. 71–103.

Molinari, Claudia, and Eugeni Porras, eds. 2001. *Identidad y cultura en la Sierra Tarahumara*. Instituto Nacional de Antropología e Historia and Congreso del Gobierno del Estado de Chihuahua.

Olson, Jon L. 2000. "Some Thoughts on Race and Ethnicity in Northeastern Mexico." *California Anthropologist* 27:17–23.

Proschan, Frank. 1997. "'We Are All Kmhmu, Just the Same': Ethnonyms, Ethnic Identities, and Ethnic Groups." *American Ethnologist* 24:91–113.

Spicer, Edward H. 1971. "Persistent Cultural Systems." *Science* 174:795–800.

27 WHOSE PAST IS IT ANYWAY?

Plains Indian History

Loretta Fowler

One of the country's leading specialists in Plains Indian history offers a summary of her life's work, the study of three different but closely related tribes—the Gros Ventres of Montana, the Northern Arapahoes of Wyoming, and the Southern Arapahoes of Oklahoma. Intent to understand the particular ways these groups developed over time, Fowler combined three methodologies to examine each culture: ethnohistory, cohort analysis, and folk history. The chapter answers many questions, such as: What types of information does each methodology offer? What are the benefits of comparing closely related but separate cultures? What are the ways Native American cultures have changed in the twentieth century?

My work with Plains Indians began in Wyoming, where I studied the way of life of the Arapahoes on the Wind River Reservation. I went to Fort Belknap, Montana, because the Gros Ventres there are a related people. In fact the Gros Ventres and the Arapahoes used to be one people. They speak the same language, though different dialects. But when I got to Fort Belknap, I was amazed to find the Gros Ventres so different culturally from the Arapahoes.

Fort Belknap proved to be a very complicated community, with two tribal groups—the Gros Ventres and the Assiniboines—sharing a single reservation. Between these two groups there was a lack of agreement about the meaning of shared cultural symbols and about the interpretation of their common past. In addition, there was a pronounced generation gap between the views of Gros Ventre elders and youths concerning culture and history.

The cultural complexity within a small, "face-to-face" reservation community forced me to ask some very difficult questions. Should I treat this complexity as factionalism, as many anthropologists have done in their work on the Plains? Should I adopt one particular interpretation, such as one age group's views, and ignore the others? Should I concentrate exclusively on the Gros Ventres, even though they literally live side by side, interact intensively, and intermarry with the Assiniboines?

My decision to confront the cultural complexity at Fort Belknap led me to some new ways of doing Plains anthropology. I decided to use a variety of methodologies to understand this contemporary Indian society. The three methodologies I used in examining the relationship between past and present were ethnohistory, cohort analysis, and the analysis of folk history.

ETHNOHISTORY

Ethnohistory is a term used differently by many people. I use it to mean interpreting documents from an anthropological perspective. For example, one aspect of the anthropological approach is to try to see interconnections between different aspects of life: how politics is affected by economics, how artwork is tied to world view, or how religion is related to economics. For example, in my first Arapahoe study I obtained important information about politics from looking at museum files on art. These documents became, in a sense, my informants, enabling me to learn something about the whole culture from one aspect of it.

For my Gros Ventre work, the first thing I did was study every document written over the past two hundred years that I could find about these people. I looked at records of traders in Canada and Montana. I also consulted anthropologists' field notes, including those of Regina Flannery, who did an excellent study on the Gros Ventres in the late 1930s and 1940s. Her unpublished notes were a wonderful source of information about people born in the 1850s. She had recorded their conversations—what they thought of life, of each other, of particular families and events. Several women, for example, had lived in polygynous households, where they had been one among several wives. They had tanned buffalo robes and forded the Missouri River to trade their robes at Fort Benton and elsewhere.

In doing ethnohistory, you have to play detective. You try to put yourself back in time and figure out where people would have left a trace of what they were doing and then try to find that trace. This ethnohistorical approach taught me a lot about Fort Belknap. For one thing, it demonstrated quite clearly that, contrary to what other writers have reported, there were real continuities in Gros Ventre culture, in what Clifford Geertz has called

ETHNOHISTORY

FOLK HISTORY

COHORT ANALYSIS

"ethos," the kinds of motivations and perceptions people have about things, the style they have in coping with life (1993).

ENEMY-FRIEND RELATIONSHIP

One of the continuities was that the Gros Ventres at Fort Belknap, as far back as the late eighteenth century, were very competitive with other Gros Ventres and with other peoples. For example, in the late eighteenth century through the early twentieth century, Gros Ventres had an institution called the enemy-friend relationship. A man would pick another Gros Ventre, and when he went to battle and captured a trophy, perhaps a shield, he would bring it back as a gift to his enemy-friend. The gift meant that the enemy-friend was obligated to do something just as brave and generous in return. Sometimes an enemy-friend would feast widows and orphans and then his enemy-friend would be obligated to do something equally generous. Competition reinforced sharing, establishing a system in which goods, food, and property circulated through the society. In this way people who could not go out and hunt would still eat, and people who could not obtain hides would be able to clothe themselves. Competition for war honors became more intense, escalating intertribal fighting, after the introduction of guns by European traders.

There are recurrent references to the Gros Ventres as the most competitive of the northern Plains people in the accounts of traders in the late eighteenth century and early nineteenth century. Traders noted that the Gros Ventres always brought in the best-prepared robes, and that they took pride in getting a higher price for their robes than other tribes. The Gros Ventres' emphasis on competitiveness and on the pursuit of public recognition of prominence through generosity (as in large public giveaways of property) is evident. It can still be observed today. By looking at a culture over a long time span, by studying documents as well as living people, I can see continuities that other researchers have missed by looking at only one particular era. I can correct other kinds of misinterpretations as well. Gros Ventre cultural identity was not anchored in particular ceremonies or customs. Rather, it hinged on the Gros Ventres' interpretations of change. The giveaway held at powwows (intertribal celebrations, including dancing)—although a twentieth-century phenomenon—expresses the same value on competitive generosity as the enemy-friend relationship and thus is viewed by the Gros Ventres as "traditional."

COHORT ANALYSIS

The method of cohort analysis comes from the sociologist Karl Mannheim, who developed this approach to better understand the relationships between generations. Mannheim argued that people who are born within a particular time span often have shared experiences that significantly distinguish them from other cohorts in their society (1997 [1952]).

The first step is to identify cohorts and to determine what distinguishes them from one another. I found two cohorts at Fort Belknap, one I called the elder cohort, the other the youth cohort. Members of the elder cohort, today ages fifty-six to ninety, were born between 1895 and 1929. They were all children when Gros Ventre ceremonial life was in its heyday. As children or young adults, they were not considered mature enough to hold positions of ritual responsibility, but they attended the ceremonies. They attended secular dances in which they saw elderly warriors acting out what they had done in battles.

The elder cohort's parents encouraged them to speak English, and their schoolteachers threatened with severe punishment those who continued to speak their native language. Although they spoke English in the schools, they spoke Gros Ventre with their grandparents.

Their elders did not encourage them to pursue an interest in native religion. They were told that Gros Ventre religion would not be of use to them in the future. Elders insisted that it was more important for them to learn skills that would enable them to compete successfully with non-Indians. Gros Ventre adults in the early twentieth century wanted their children, those born between 1895 and 1929, to compete successfully with non-Indians so that they would not be exploited or abused. When elders told one young boy (now seventy years old) that he was not going to be a warrior like his grand-father, but that instead he must get an education to learn to compete suc-cessfully with the non-Indian, the boy saw schooling as a kind of warfare. He would not ride into battle against the Piegan or the Sioux, but instead he would compete against non-Indians. As a child, the elder cohort of today was strongly motivated to go to school, get an education, and find a trade. Nothing was too difficult for the Gros Ventre child who was reared by the old warriors and medicine men.

Members of the youth cohort, today ages thirty to fifty-five, were born be-tween 1930 and 1955. What sets this group apart is that they were too young to have experienced Gros Ventre ceremonial life in its heyday. They never saw a medicine man cure a patient, nor did they attend a religious ritual. They never went to a dance in which warriors acted out their battle exploits. Youths did not speak the Gros Ventre language as children. Many of them had grown up off the reservation with only occasional contact with Fort Belknap.

On the other hand, they were the right age to take full advantage of new opportunities in the late 1960s and 1970s—the affirmative action programs, the educational grants for Vietnam veterans, and self-determination legisla-tion affecting tribal governments. New jobs opened up to them through mi-nority recruitment. And many moved back to the reservation to accept the new jobs. In school they were exposed to a positive view of Indian culture and history through Native American studies programs. The youth cohort, then, experienced the 1960s and 1970s differently from the elders who could not take advantage of college or job opportunities to the extent that youths did.

THE GENERATION UNIT

In my cohort analysis I also found Mannheim's concept of a generation unit useful. Within a single cohort or generation, there are people who experience life differently, who make different choices. At Fort Belknap there were two generation units that I called the education clique and the militants. The ed-ucation clique were people who went to college in Montana. Their concept of Indianness developed or was embellished on Montana campuses, at Mis-soula, Bozeman, or Billings. Even though as children they had not been in-volved with Gros Ventre religion, at college many of them had roommates from other tribes where native religion was more important. The college campuses also had Indian clubs that put on powwows to which they invited singers and dancers from other tribes. This was the first ceremonial experience of this kind for many of the Gros Ventres. They became part of a network of powwow people and made contacts throughout Montana. They also got involved in politics by going to the state legislature and persuading the legislators to make college tuition free for Indians on Montana campuses. This group of Gros Ventres became aware of their potential and, with the encouragement of their parents, set high goals for themselves. They returned to Fort Belknap and set out to achieve greater self-determination for the Indian people and to revive ceremonial life.

The militants were people who developed or embellished their concept of Indianness outside of Montana, where they lived in urban areas. Many of them attended colleges such as the University of Washington in Seattle, the University of California at Los Angeles, and Harvard. They took jobs in urban poverty programs and became involved in social protest movements that were much more active than those in Montana. Many took part in confrontations such as sit-ins or marches.

POWWOWING

What insights were obtained by comparing interpretations of culture and history in elders and youths? It is clear that the contrasting experiences of these cohorts, and of the education clique and the militants, have shaped the way Fort Belknap culture and society are changing today. We sometimes tend to think that change in Indian communities comes only from ideas and customs introduced by non-Indians. But a great deal of change and the way change is made culturally acceptable comes from the interplay and exchange of different interpretations held by cohorts. To youths, reviving Indian ceremonies such as the powwow is an important goal. Thus they have organized and expanded these dances.

In the powwow sponsored by the education clique, one major theme is hospitality to visiting tribes. Much effort is exerted to raise money for dance contest prizes and to purchase groceries to distribute to visitors. Moreover, the veteran plays a prominent role in the powwow. There are flag-raising ceremonies and special dances done by veterans. But to the militants the U.S. military represents an oppressor, and so they deemphasize flag symbolism or veteran participation in the powwow they sponsor, the Chief Joseph powwow. An aspect of this powwow is the laying of wreaths or other kinds of grave offerings at the site of the Nez Perce's battle with the U.S. military. The battle site is twenty miles west of Fort Belknap. There Nez Perce people were killed by the army while trying to cross the border into Canada. For the militants, Chief Joseph symbolizes resistance to an unjust U.S. government.

Both elders and youths participate in powwows to varying degrees. But the powwow has come to symbolize different things to elders and youths and to the education clique and the militants. For the education clique, for example, the powwow is a vehicle for expressing Gros Ventre competitive drive. One of their goals is to attract bigger crowds than do powwows on other reservations. Militant youths interpret the powwow as a vehicle for the expression of protest against the U.S. government. These interpretations reflect the youths' contrasting involvements in the Native American pride movements of the 1970s.

FOLK HISTORY

The third method I used was the analysis of the stories that people tell about their past. Gros Ventres and Assiniboines have shared a reservation since 1878, and they have participated in the same events. Their ancestors sat together at the same councils and attended many of the same ceremonies. Although they were participants in the same events, they perceived them very differently. I was interested in looking at folk history as an entry to contemporary symbols and their meanings, not in looking at the stories in terms of whether or not they were accurate or compatible with the documentary record.

Gros Ventre and Assiniboine versions of the history of the U.S. government's relations with the Fort Belknap peoples are quite different. In stories about events from the late nineteenth century to the present, the Gros Ventres portray themselves as fully capable of managing their community by themselves and capable of competing successfully with whites if given a fair chance. Gros Ventres attribute reservation problems to the failure of Assiniboines—Assiniboines are not assertive enough with federal officials. Assiniboines portray themselves as expert in living harmoniously with others. In their stories, reservation problems are attributed to the obstinate nature of Gros Ventres. Folk history serves to orient social action. The contrast in Gros Ventre and Assiniboine interpretations of history works to stimulate flexibility, maneuverability, and creativity. Individuals have a wider range of potential strategies and choices. Variant interpretations encourage intertribal competition, as well. Each tribe presents the other somewhat negatively. The competitive component of symbols of identity fosters a sense of cultural distinctiveness that is important to Indian people today. As one youth told me, "When the new Indian awareness came, it wasn't enough just to realize you were Indian; it was what kind of Indian [that mattered]."

Each of the three ways of interpreting the past contributed to my understanding of Fort Belknap. Ethnohistory made clear that long-term cultural continuities were possible even though the Gros Ventres had to change their way of life to cope with their changing environment. Cohort analysis revealed that age groups differed in their interpretations of their past. Folk history was a good way to learn how images of the past contribute to cultural identity, and how these same images motivate behavior.

By combining the three approaches, I was able to reach an understanding of the dynamics of culture change: how change actually occurs, and how people accept it or initiate it. At Fort Belknap, innovation has come about as generations and tribes, Indians and whites, continually adjust and reformulate their notions of the past and the present in order to cope with the conflicting interpretations of one another. By influencing one another, they influence the way in which their society changes. The anthropologist, by confronting the complexities of culture, can see things about a society that would not be seen by focusing on one group's perspective or on one point in time.

UPDATE

My research on the culture and history of the Gros Ventre people at Fort Belknap Reservation spanned 1979–85 and culminated in the publication of a book in 1987. In the book, I draw some conclusions about why life was changing in a particular direction for the Gros Ventres during 1979–85 and about why the Gros Ventres have been able to maintain a distinct cultural identity despite extensive changes in their circumstances during the past two hundred years and despite the fact that intermarriage has taken place between Gros Ventres and other peoples. The conclusions I reached had their basis in the research theory and method described in "Whose Past Is It Anyway?"

The different and conflicting views of elders and youths, Gros Ventres and Assiniboines, led to ritual and political innovations in the 1980s and gave shape to more recent developments. By 1997 the youths of my study had become middle-aged or elderly.

Ritual activity and symbolism at Fort Belknap was changing at a very fast pace when I was there. Gros Ventres were sponsoring ceremonies associated with the late nineteenth and early twentieth centuries, that is, reviving traditional rituals. The clash in views between elders and youths led to an emphasis on secular rituals, such as naming ceremonies, memorial rituals, and the powwow, rather than religious ones. In this way, youths reached an accommodation with the elders, who believed that the youths were not qualified to attempt the religious rituals they had experienced in the early twentieth century. Youths drew on knowledge and recollections of elderly Assiniboines to organize powwows, reinterpreting the meanings of various phases of powwow ritual to fit Gros Ventre perspectives. And gradually they interpreted some of the powwow features as sacred. By the 1990s the youths in my study began to introduce religious ceremonies based on nineteenth-century rituals, this time without opposition, for the elders of the early 1980s were deceased.

The innovations in the 1980s not only were a result of the youths' relations with Gros Ventre elders but also were made possible by the influence that Assiniboine ideas about ritual innovations had on Gros Ventre youths. From the Assiniboine perspective, dreams gave supernatural validation to innovation, and favorable response to the requests of others for help brought a supernatural blessing. Thus Assiniboines, acting on their own interpretation of the history of their relations with the Gros Ventres, helped Gros Ventre youths sponsor powwows and other rituals. The new ritual activity could be viewed as traditionally Gros Ventre in large part because a competitive element had been introduced by the youths; that is, as the Gros Ventres had done for generations, they competed with the Assiniboines and others—in this case, to make the Gros Ventre powwow more elaborate or larger than others. This emphasis on the quest for primacy has been viewed by the Gros Ventres as a "natural" outgrowth of their tenacious nature and an important element of Gros Ventre identity, at least since the early nineteenth century. In the 1980s, competition in the ritual sphere was one means of expressing Gros Ventre identity.

Another arena for innovation at Fort Belknap was tribal government. The War on Poverty programs and the opportunities posed by the Self-Determination Act of 1975 (which allowed tribes to contract for programs previously administered by federal agencies) worked to draw back to Fort Belknap many individuals who had moved to towns and cities in the 1950s to find employment in the aftermath of the collapse of an agricultural economy on Fort Belknap Reservation. Many of the Gros Ventre youths had acquired skills, as well as a commitment to reviving Native American traditions, in universities or urban areas in the 1960s and early 1970s. They began to return to Fort Belknap and assume managerial positions in the new programs or the local federal bureaucracy. At the same time, housing projects and other new services attracted Gros Ventre elders in their retirement years. The youths had political contacts with young people on other reservations whom they had known at universities or people who had been members of national Native American advocacy groups. The reservation government was a joint Gros Ventre–Assiniboine "business committee" in the 1970s. By the mid-1990s, youths had established separate tribal governments. The movement for separation from the Assiniboines also resulted in the creation of new criteria for legal enrollment in the Gros Ventre tribe. To Gros Ventres, these political developments expressed their "traditional" commitment to establishing Gros Ventre primacy at Fort Belknap.

Anthropologists proceed from detailed case studies to comparative studies in order to make broader generalizations about sociocultural change. I was able to compare my earlier study of the Arapahoes with my Gros Ventres research, placing the history of both these peoples in regional context. The Gros Ventres were situated on the Northwestern Plains, where they had an advantageous position in the fur and robe trade. Traders courted individuals and promoted interpersonal rivalry among the Gros Ventres. Also wealthy in horses, because of their easy access to groups that could obtain large numbers of horses from the Southwest, the Gros Ventres used their wealth in horses and trade goods in competitive rituals. Lavish and generous distribution of property bought prestige and leadership positions to individuals and allowed the Gros Ventres leverage against neighboring groups. On the Northwestern Plains, groups were spared the large-scale intrusions of settlers and troops in the 1850s and 1860s. The Gros Ventres never had a hostile encounter with troops and, in fact, were military allies with troops and traders against more hostile peoples, such as the Sioux groups who moved into Montana. After the Gros Ventres moved onto their reservation, settlers began to pressure the federal government to move them. Not viewed as a military threat, the Gros Ventres were thought to be vulnerable to dislocation. In this context, then, the Gros Ventres allied with Catholic missionaries and the powerful Catholic lobby in Washington, D.C., to persuade the government to honor their title to the reservation. In 1896 they could not prevent the cession of a southern portion of their reservation that was rich in mineral resources. This left them unable to develop the reservation economy after the collapse of agriculture in the 1930s and led to the exodus of young people from the reservation in the 1940s and 1950s.

The Arapahoes are a good comparison to the Gros Ventres, for at one time these two peoples were one. They settled in different regions and their histories took different turns. The Arapahoes occupied the Central Plains. There, all the groups had easy access to horses but the volume of trade was less than on the Northwestern Plains. Arapahoe ceremonial life did not place as much emphasis on lavish generosity or on competition. When settlers began moving west, they crossed through the best hunting territories of the Central Plains, and they and American troops came into conflict with the native peoples there. The Arapahoes fought the army for several years. Even after the Northern Arapahoes settled on a reservation in 1878, they were regarded as a potential threat to the settlement of the Western United States. They, in turn, were suspicious of officials and missionaries. They gave the appearance of being accommodating, in allowing Catholic missionaries to live on the reservation, but retained their commitment to their own religious rituals. The Northern Arapahoes' reservation in Wyoming had rich oil deposits and was too arid for profitable agriculture. They retained their land base with its mineral resources and, in the 1940s, Arapahoe leaders persuaded Congress to allow them to collect the royalties from the oil production. With a monthly per capita payment from the tribe's oil royalties, Arapahoe young people continued to live on the reservation and elders continued to preside over Arapahoe ritual life, giving direction to the lives of their juniors and schooling young people in ritual leadership during the florescence of Indian identity in the 1970s.

The Southern Arapahoe split off from their northern kinsmen after the massacre at Sand Creek, Colorado, in November 1864. Here Colorado volunteer militia attacked a friendly camp of Arapahoe and Cheyenne without warning, killing over five hundred men, women, and children. While the Northern Arapahoe stayed north of Colorado in Wyoming and Montana over the next few years, the Southern Arapahoe remained on their hunting grounds on the plains of Kansas and Oklahoma and acquired by treaty a reservation where they believed they would be safe from attack. The two Arapahoe divisions did stay in contact with each other even though they settled on different reservations. In 1892, in spite of protests by Arapahoe leaders, the federal government dismantled the reservation in Oklahoma and subsequently gave most of the land to settlers. The Southern Arapahoe then did not have a land base that could produce income. In large part, they dealt with the deprivation that followed by accepting peyote ritual from other tribes in Oklahoma. Peyote ritual (the Native American Church) combined traditional and Christian precepts and offered comfort and guidance to individuals trying to cope with poverty and other problems. Without local resources, many Arapahoes joined the military in the 1940s and took jobs in nearby cities. Ritual life in Oklahoma flourished from the elaboration of secular dancing and men's societies in the context of the powwow. The many different tribes in Oklahoma stimulated new developments in each other's ritual life. In short, elders were not able to transfer Arapahoe ritual knowledge as they had in Wyoming. Thus, today the Southern Arapahoe travel to Wyoming to participate in Araphaoe religious ceremonies, and they have introduced new styles of dancing and singing to the Northern Arapahoe.

By comparing the Gros Ventre with the Northern and Southern Arapahoes (and comparing other groups in the various Plains region), anthropologists can better understand why native peoples' cultures and histories developed in particular ways over time.

FURTHER READING

Cooper, John M. 1957. *The Gros Ventres of Montana. Part II: Religion and Ritual,* ed. Regina Flannery. Catholic University of America Press.

Flannery, Regina. 1953. *The Gros Ventres of Montana. Part I: Social Life.* Catholic University of America Press.

Fowler, Loretta. 1982. *Arapahoe Politics, 1851–1978: Symbols in Crises of Authority.* University of Nebraska Press.

Fowler, Loretta. 1987. *Shared Symbols, Contested Meanings: Gros Ventre Culture and History, 1778–1984.* Cornell University Press.

Fowler, Loretta. 1994. "The Civilization Strategy: Gros Ventres, Northern and Southern Arapahos Compared." In Raymond J. DeMallie and Alfonso Ortiz, eds., *North American Indian Anthropology: Essays on Society and Culture,* pp. 220–57. University of Oklahoma Press.

Fowler, Loretta. 2002. *Tribal Sovereignty and the Historical Imagination: Cheyenne-Arapaho Politics.* University of Nebraska Press.

Geertz, Clifford. 1993. *The Interpretation of Cultures: Selected Essays.* Fontana Press.

Mannheim, Karl. 1997. "The Problem of Generations." In Paul Kecskemeti, ed., *Essays on the Sociology of Knowledge.* Collected Works of Karl Mannheim, vol. 5. Routledge. (1952 edition published by Oxford University Press.)

Stewart, Omer C. 1987. *Peyote Religion: A History.* University of Oklahoma Press.

28 NATIVE AMERICANS AND SMITHSONIAN RESEARCH

JoAllyn Archambault and William C. Sturtevant

From the Smithsonian's nineteenth-century beginnings, Native Americans have held a special place at the Institution, both as a focus of research and also as contributors and users of knowledge, collections, and archival materials. The Smithsonian's research staff nearly always has included Native American scholars, including one of the authors of this article. Readers will learn how anthropology has contributed to the preservation of Indian cultures, languages, and history, but also how the study of native peoples has changed as different approaches have been used through the years.

Preserving the past for the future has always been an important mission of the Smithsonian Institution. From the beginning, Native Americans have held a special place in this endeavor, as contributors and users of knowledge. The Smithsonian, a great repository of cultural, social, and biological information, has often assisted tribal groups in preserving, strengthening, and renewing knowledge of their own culture and history. In turn, native people have been actively involved in major contributions to the research goals of the Institution. We present here a short overview of the Department of Anthropology's ethnological and archaeological research on the peoples and cultures of the Americas and native participation in this work.

BACKGROUND

The Smithsonian Institution was founded by legislation signed August 10, 1846. Almost immediately it became the leading supporter of anthropological research in America. The first secretary, Joseph Henry, instituted a series of publications called Smithsonian Contributions to Knowledge to record "new discoveries in science." Among the earliest volumes was a report on Indian mounds in the eastern United States, which demonstrated that they had been built by prehistoric Indian societies, not by some unknown non-Indian civilization as many scholars thought. Other reports based on investigations of prehistoric and living Indian societies soon followed. The U.S. National Museum served as the repository for contemporary and archaeological Native American collections and works of art. These are now kept in the successor museum, the National Museum of Natural History. Many of these collections were gathered by Smithsonian staff members and other people, including Native Americans, and are preserved for exhibition and especially for study to benefit all peoples.

Native American research at the Smithsonian grew rapidly, especially after the founding in 1879 of the Smithsonian's Bureau of American Ethnology (BAE), a Smithsonian research unit (independent of the U.S. National Museum) that specialized in Native American studies, particularly in ethnology and linguistics. The research of the BAE was preserved and disseminated in several ways. The BAE had a publication series that issued more than 250 volumes describing Native American cultures, languages, prehistory, and history. In addition, the BAE maintained a large archive of manuscript and photographic results of research. The objects collected by the BAE as documents of both living and prehistoric Indian cultures were preserved by the museum and are now in the National Museum of Natural History. Much of the information recorded in the published volumes and a great deal of the data preserved in manuscripts and photographs archived by the BAE are documented nowhere else. Without active collecting, much of this material would have been lost forever as Indian cultures, societies, and languages underwent rapid changes.

In 1965 the staff and archives of the BAE were merged with the Department of Anthropology in the National Museum of Natural History, whose primary emphasis was then on archaeology and physical anthropology. Today, the department continues to focus on Native American studies alongside interests in the peoples and cultures of Asia, Africa, Oceania, and South America and involves all subdisciplines of anthropology (ethnology, linguistics, archaeology, physical/biological anthropology, and applied anthropology).

INDIAN PARTICIPATION

Research and publication on American Indian languages, literatures, history, and social relations depend on contributions by the people who are the bearers of the cultures. To record, analyze, and describe a language, a literature, a traditional history, a religion, or a system of social relations requires the cooperation and the active assistance of those who speak the language and possess the knowledge and beliefs that are recorded. In some cases, Native Americans write the information and organize it for publication. In other cases, they explain to others who serve as recorders and analysts. Archaeology and physical anthropology are less dependent on the active participation of Native Americans, although their insight has proven beneficial. The Smithsonian anthropological staff, from its early days, has included distinguished Indian scholars, such as Francis LaFlesche (Omaha) and J. N. B. Hewitt (Tuscarora). Many other Indians were important correspondents and contributors, although not staff members. Among these were Andrew John (Seneca), Phoebe Maddux (Karok), James Murie (Pawnee), Whewa (Zuni), George Bushotter (Sioux), George Washington Grayson (Creek), George Hunt (Tlingit-Kwakiutl), John Squint Eyes (Cheyenne), George Sword (Lakota), Alfred Kiyana (Mesquakie), Henry Tate (Tsimshian), William Jones (Fox), Isabel Meadows (Costanoan), and Seth Newhouse (Mohawk). Scores of individual members of tribes in all parts of North America have contributed knowledge and information that was recorded by Smithsonian staff members and other contributors to the Smithsonian archives and publications. The Department of Anthropology's staff currently includes two archaeologists of Indian ancestry, and the ethnologist director of its American Indian Program is an enrolled member of the Standing Rock Sioux tribe.

One current project of the department is the twenty-volume *Handbook of North American Indians,* an encyclopedia summarizing knowledge of the cultures, history, and human biology of all the tribes of the continent. Indians have been active in planning this reference work and in writing many chapters; three of the volumes have Indian editors. Since 1978 twelve volumes have been published, and the rest are in active preparation.

PAST AND PRESENT RESEARCH

Smithsonian anthropologists were prominent pioneers advocating Indian rights and respect for Indian cultures and languages and have remained so. "Anthropologists were among the few who felt that Indian cultures had any value in the late nineteenth century," says JoAllyn Archambault (Standing Rock Sioux), who directs the American Indian Program of the Department of Anthropology. "They felt that Indian lives and culture had meaning. That is why they wanted to document and save the information and images of our people. And they saved them for future generations of every race."

Anthropologists learned from Indian people and tried, quite successfully, to pass on to others what they learned about the richness and variety of

Indian cultures, the complexity and sophistication of Indian thought and belief, the great antiquity of Indian settlement of the Americas, and the thousands of years of inventions and adjustments to the environment. They have continually reminded those who came later how much is owed to their Indian predecessors, and how much was unjustly taken from them.

One of the first Smithsonian anthropologists was Frank Hamilton Cushing, who lived at Zuni Pueblo in New Mexico for four years in the early 1880s. Learning the language, he was adopted by Palowahtiwa, the Zuni governor, and given a ritual position in the Pueblo. Cushing pioneered the anthropological method of participant observation that was reinvented elsewhere in the twentieth century. After he had compiled a valuable record of Zuni culture, he was recalled to Washington because he had defended the Pueblo against the illegal taking of its lands by a politically well-connected outsider.

About the same time another Smithsonian anthropologist, James Mooney, began long-term study of the Eastern Cherokee, recording their historical struggle to remain in their homeland. He collected native curing formulas written in Sequoyah's syllabary and studied ball games and other features of Cherokee culture. In the 1890s he conducted a firsthand study of the new Ghost Dance in the West, interviewing Wovoka, the founding prophet. Mooney demonstrated the religious nature of the movement in an attempt to convince the U.S. government that it posed no military threat. He then began an extensive study of Kiowa heraldry (manifested in designs on shields and tipis) in Indian Territory (present-day Oklahoma), which he soon was forced to give up as a result of his activities defending participants in the Native American Church.

Working in Washington, D.C., in the latter half of the nineteenth century, C. C. Royce compiled a detailed study of Indian lands lost throughout the country. The maps he prepared, published by the Smithsonian, served some fifty years later as the fundamental evidence by which Indian tribes were recompensed via hearings held by the Indian Claims Commission.

The first scientifically based and accepted classification of the historical relationships of North American native languages was published in 1891 under the direction of John Wesley Powell, the founder and first chief of the Bureau of American Ethnology. Much of the evidence for that classification is preserved in the department's archives; some of it is irreplaceable data on languages that have ceased to be spoken.

In the mid-twentieth century, Smithsonian ethnologist John C. Ewers wrote the standard text used in Blackfeet Indian schools to teach Blackfeet history. Ewers attributed the success of his research to the Blackfeet elders, born in the middle of the last century, who passed on their knowledge to him.

Today, many Tzotzil Indians in Chiapas, Mexico, are producing a literature in their own language, thanks to the literacy program of the Chiapas

Writers' Cooperative encouraged and assisted by Smithsonian anthropologist Robert M. Laughlin. Laughlin has devoted thirty years to research in Chiapas, publishing two massive dictionaries of the Tzotzil language. These provide important evidence used in the decipherment of ancient Maya inscriptions that is revealing the history of this Native American civilization. He has also published several volumes of native literature in Tzotzil as well as in English translation.

Ives Goddard, linguist at the Smithsonian, published with Kathleen Bragdon, *Native Writings in Massachusett,* two large volumes that contain all known writings in the Massachusett language by its speakers, together with new translations into English and annotations on the grammar and vocabulary. This language, extinct since about 1826, was spoken by the ancestors of the present-day Wampanoag Indians of Mashpee and Gay Head, Massachusetts.

William C. Sturtevant, general editor of the *Handbook of North American Indians,* researched the cultures and history of the Florida Seminoles and New York Senecas and over the years has provided expert testimony in defense of Indian land rights and in support of federal recognition of Indian tribes. The testimony of Smithsonian anthropologists, behind the scenes and in formal hearings before the courts and congressional committees, often has proven helpful to Indian communities. Smithsonian anthropologists, known as objective, knowledgeable authorities on Indian history and Indian cultures, have frequently been called on.

The Arctic Studies Center, established in the department in 1988 by William Fitzhugh, is an extension of research begun in the 1860s in Alaska and the western part of Arctic and Subarctic Canada. Other early Smithsonian research, both ethnological and archaeological, was carried out among Indians and Inuit in the eastern Arctic. The new center is involved in research, education, and training of native peoples and the coordination of activities with other government agencies. Fellowships and internships in Arctic and Subarctic studies are available to native individuals. Before and after the establishment of the center, Fitzhugh organized major exhibitions of Arctic native cultures at the Smithsonian, which then traveled to other locations, including cities in Alaska. Special versions were sent to rural locations in Alaska and Siberia making available to native peoples aspects of their own history. Assistance to native museums is a continuing interest of the Arctic Studies Center [see Fitzhugh, "East Meets West: New View of Arctic Peoples," in this volume].

The Archives Program administers both the National Anthropological Archives (NAA) and the Human Studies Film Archives (HSFA). The NAA is the repository for manuscript records on Native American and other cultures and languages, for many thousands of historical photographs of American Indian subjects, and for the papers of Indian and anthropological organizations. The papers of the National Congress of American Indians, the National Tribal Chairmen's Association, and the Native American anthropologists Beatrice Medicine (Standing Rock Sioux) and Helen Peterson (Pine Ridge Oglala) are deposited in the NAA. The core of the NAA are the records and photographs collected by the former Bureau of American Ethnology and the museum department since its beginnings. The HSFA collects and documents ethnographic film and video records (Homiak 1998). It also serves as a clearinghouse for Native American films and videos produced by other organizations and makes films and videos available to Indian communities.

THE AMERICAN INDIAN PROGRAM

The American Indian Program of the Department of Anthropology was founded in 1986 to coordinate and increase Native American involvement with the department. The program provides outreach to Indian communities and individuals, making the department more accessible to native people. It encourages research, collection of contemporary Indian objects, exhibitions, and public programming by and about native people. It has initiated numerous programs with reservation-based community colleges, tribal museums, tribal education departments, and elder groups. Fellows in the American Indian Program are diverse in age, experience, background, and interest. Their projects have been equally diverse, ranging from film research to object collection research by artists to inform their art making. The results of their projects are now used in various community activities in urban and reservation areas. Most recently a group from the Coquille reservation in Oregon found thousands of pages of relevant materials in Washington, had them copied, and deposited the copies in a local archives where they can be used by tribal members for their own personal research. Several tribes have obtained language materials from the National Anthropological Archives for use in their language programs. Others have used historical photographs to enhance exhibits created for their tribal museums. The program provides technical assistance to tribal museums and cultural programs upon request.

UPDATE

Since the original publication of this article, the Anthropology Department in the Smithsonian's Natural Museum of Natural History has continued to strengthen collegial relationships with Indian people at the community level and with professional Indian scholars and to make contributions to the scholarship about native history and culture.

The Paleoindian Program regularly holds hands-on educational opportunities for community members to work alongside professional archaeologists on organized expeditions, provides field training for individuals who are earning certifications as archaeological paraprofessionals, and organizes public workshops and lectures to showcase the collaborative nature of community-based, cooperative research. American Indian archaeologists have participated in some of the Smithsonian-sponsored summer excavations, and Ute community elders have visited sites and consulted with the staff.

The Arctic Studies Center has produced two exhibits about native peoples of Alaska and Japan: *Looking Both Ways: Heritage and Identity of the Alutiiq People* opened in Kodiak, Alaska, in 2001; *Ainu: Spirit of a Northern People* opened in Washington in 1999. These exhibits involved extensive consultation and collaboration with the Alutiiq in Alaska and the Ainu communities in Japan. Cultural experts from both visited the museum and discussed collections and interpretive strategies for the exhibitions. Community archaeology programs with the Innu and Inuit in Labrador, which involve local elders serving as interpreters to younger community members and the archaeological team, have been a great success. The 2002–3 Alaska Collections Project, funded by the Rasmussen Foundation, involves group visits of elders to Washington, D.C., to study and to assist museum staff in the documentation and interpretation of their cultural and archival materials. The information gleaned is shared with the museum, native communities, and wider audiences by electronic media.

Curator Robert Laughlin has facilitated the publication and presentation of plays and stories by Mayan writers and playwrights. His virtual exhibit, *Unmasking the Maya: The Story of Sna Jtz'ibajom* (www.mnh.si.edu/anthro/maya), relates the experiences of a Tzotzil-Tzeltal Maya cultural cooperative, including its visits to Maya farm workers in the United States, and appears also in Spanish, Tzotzil, and Tzeltal [see Laughlin, "Linguistic Survival Among the Maya," in this volume].

The American Indian Program has sponsored public workshops given by master craftswomen in Alaska and Oklahoma. In Alaska, the Sealaska Heritage Foundation organized a public workshop for native weavers interested in Tlingit basket weaving. In Oklahoma, the National Heritage Award winner, Vanessa Jennings, a Kiowa traditional artist, gave several public workshops to the local community on making cradles and clothing. The American Indian Program also has been instrumental in the organization of the first professional American Indian Anthropologist Association (AINAAN). Members of AINAAN organize all-Indian panels for paper presentations at the annual meeting of the national organization, the American Anthropological Association. The American Indian Program facilitated the creation of the Ella Deloria Award, which is given to Indian graduate students in anthropology degree programs. Currently there are ninety-two professional anthropologists of Indian heritage; the Program works to involve them in a variety of professional activities at the Smithsonian.

Recently, the American Indian Program gave support to SWORP (Southwest Oregon Research Project), which utilized the resources of the Smithsonian's National Anthropological Archives in the Department of Anthropology. Copies of collected archival materials were deposited at the University of Oregon, and, copied in duplicate, were presented at a potlatch ceremony to representatives from all the tribes in Oregon and Washington. The knowledge gathered by SWORP was shared with all the tribes in these region in a gesture of traditional generosity.

FURTHER READING

Archambault, JoAllyn. 1993. "American Indians and American museums." *Zeitschrift für Ethnologie* 118:7–22.

Archambault, JoAllyn. 2001a. "Sun Dance." In Raymond J. DeMallie, ed., *Handbook of North American Indians,* vol. 13, part 2, *Plains,* pp. 983–95. Smithsonian Institution.

Archambault, JoAllyn. 2001b. "Art Since 1900." In Raymond J. DeMallie, ed., *Handbook of North American Indians,* vol. 13, part 2, *Plains,* pp. 1055–61. Smithsonian Institution.

Hinsley, Curtis M. 1994. *The Smithsonian and the American Indian: Making a Moral Anthropology in Victorian America.* Smithsonian Institution Press.

Homiak, John P. 1998. "Ethnographic Film: Then and Now." In Ruth Osterweis Selig and Marilyn R. London, eds., *Anthropology Explored: The Best of Smithsonian AnthroNotes,* 298–307. Smithsonian Institution Press.

Medicine, Beatrice. 2001. *Learning to Be an Anthropologist and Remaining "Native": Selected Writings.* University of Illinois Press.

Sturtevant, William C., ed. 1978–. *Handbook of North American Indians.* Smithsonian Institution.

National Anthropological Archives, Smithsonian Institution: www.nmnh.si.edu/naa
"Unmasking the Maya: The Story of Sna Jta'ibajom": www.mnh.si.edu/anthro/maya
Arctic Studies Center, Smithsonian Institution: www.nmnh.si.edu/arctic

29 THE SILK ROAD

A Global Cultural Economy

Richard Kurin

In the summer of 2002, the Smithsonian Folklife Festival, working with famed cellist Yo-Yo Ma and his Silk Road Project, brought more than four hundred artists, musicians, and scholars from twenty-eight nations to the National Mall to demonstrate Silk Road cultural traditions. Kurin's chapter details the history of this ancient complex of trade routes, offering answers to questions such as: What is the origin of the Silk Road and silk production? What are the major periods of Silk Road exchange? What were the roles of Marco Polo, Genghis Khan, and Kublai Khan? What is the Silk Road's current influence?

The Silk Road spanned the Asian continent and represented a form of global economy when the known world was smaller but more difficult to traverse than it is nowadays. The network of trading routes known as the Silk Road stretched from China to Japan in the East and to Turkey and Italy in the West, encompassing Afghanistan, India, Pakistan, and the other lands of Central Asia, and linking the ancient Mediterranean world to the empires of China. For thousands of years, highly valued silk, cotton, wool, glass, jade, lapis lazuli, metals, salt, spices, tea, herbal medicines, fruits, flowers, horses, and musical instruments moved back and forth along various portions of the Silk Road. Each item has a history, and many of these histories are connected to contemporary life.

Consider, for example, stringed musical instruments. In Central Asia, *faqīrs* or Muslim mystics still play a one-stringed instrument called quite simply the *ektār*. *Tār* means "string," and *ek*, "one," is taken metaphorically to

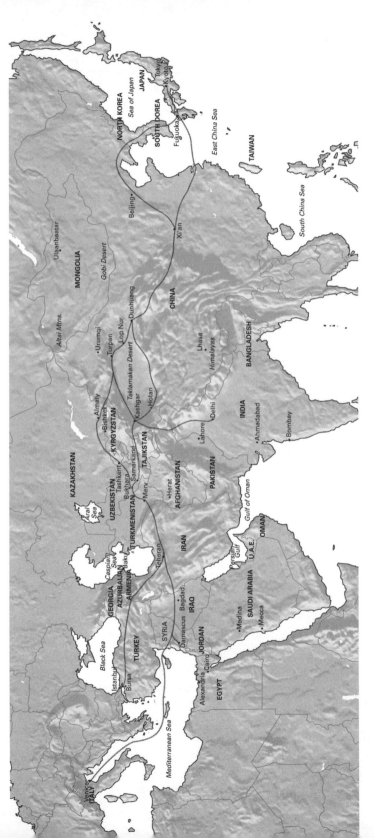

The Silk Road Network of Ancient Trade Routes (courtesy Richard Kurin)

refer to one God. In Iran there is the *dutār* (literally "two strings") and in India the multi-stringed *sitār*. The terminology is linguistically related to the Greek term *cithara*, the Arabic term *quitara*, and our English term *zither*, all referring to stringed instruments. A short lute with four pairs of strings developed in fifteenth-century Spain and was called the *guitara*. By the nineteenth century, it had been transformed into a six-stringed instrument with other modifications and came to America as the guitar, the key instrument of folk and country music and, in electrified form, of rock and roll.

The Silk Road provides us with a symbol for complex cultural exchange. For contemporary cellist Yo-Yo Ma, the Silk Road answers this question: What happens when strangers meet? Historically along the Silk Road when strangers met in bazaars, courts, oases, and caravanserai (caravan rest houses), they shared and exchanged their goods and ideas. They traded the finest goods produced by their respective native master artisans and created new things—instruments, songs, food, clothing, and philosophies. The historical Silk Road teaches us the importance of connecting different peoples and cultures as a way of encouraging human creativity. "Now, more than ever," Yo-Yo Ma observes, "we cannot afford not to know the thoughts, the habits, the ways of life of other people." The famed musician has illustrated this lesson by forming a Silk Road Ensemble including artists from Central Asia, East Asia, the Middle East, the United States, and Europe. The ensemble uses a variety of musical instruments from Europe and Asia to bridge different musical languages and cultures. "Our goal is to make innovation and tradition sit down together," explains Ma (quoted in Kennicott 2001).

WHERE WAS THE SILK ROAD?

The Silk Road was actually a network of thousands of miles of land and sea trade routes traversing regions of Asia, connecting markets and centers of cultural production in China, India, Central Asia, Iran, and the Middle East, and extending to those in Europe, Japan, Southeast Asia, and Africa. Specifically, the roads were those taken by caravans and extended out from the old city of Chang'an, which was the capital of China until 1215, when Genghis Khan established a new capital in Beijing. Chang'an (also called Xi'an since the nineteenth century) was the world's largest city in the year A.D. 1000. Silk Road routes beginning in Chang'an extended to the Buddhist center of Dunhuang, diverging both to the north and to the south of the Taklamakan Desert, running through the Central Asian market towns of Kashgar, Samarkand, Bukhara, and Tashkent, crossing the Persian plateau into Baghdad, and ending at the eastern shores of the Mediterranean Sea in the Levantine towns of Antioch and Tyre and in Anatolian ports such as Constantinople (Istanbul). Extending from these roads were many terrestrial and maritime extensions, eastward from China to Korea and across the East China Sea to Japan and its old capital, Nara. Routes turned northward from China to Mongolia; southward from China into Burma and then into what is now Bengal; southward from Central Asia through Afghanistan, the Buddhist site of Bamiyan, and the mountain passes into Kashmir, Pakistan, and India; and northward from the Persian plateau through the Caucasus mountain regions of Armenia, Azerbaijan, and Georgia. Silk routes also ran alternatively southward along the Persian Gulf, north to Basra, and west into the Arabian Peninsula, then north through Turkey to Istanbul, and across the Mediterranean into the Balkans, or to Venice. From these points, the network extended still further, to the coastal towns of south India and along the east coast of Africa past Zanzibar and across North Africa and the Mediterranean to Morocco and Spain, and north through the Balkans to Romania and Western Europe. Most (but not all) of these routes are shown on the map.

The Silk Road developed because the goods traded were quite valuable and useful, worth the trouble of transporting them great distances. Roads were generally in disrepair. Caravans had to brave bleak deserts, high mountains, extreme heat and cold. They had to face bandits and raiders, imprisonment, starvation, and other forms of deprivation. Those going by sea braved the uncertainties of weather, poorly constructed ships, and pirates. Yet luxury goods traveled in both directions along the Silk Road and included silk, spices, tea, precious metals, fine artwork, and crafts—goods that were in demand and commanded high prices and often courtly rewards. While many items were traded along the Silk Road, it was silk that had an exceedingly long history and was among the most valuable of goods traded.

SILK PRODUCTION

Silk cultivation and production is such an extraordinary process that it is easy to see why its earliest invention is unknown, and its discovery eluded many who sought to learn its secrets. Silk is made from the secretions of certain kinds of caterpillars conventionally called silkworms. These secretions dry into a filament that forms a cocoon. The origins of silk making as well as the methods for unraveling the cocoons and reeling the silk filament are shrouded in legend and mystery. In the Yangzi Valley in south China, silk cloth fragments and a cup carved with a silkworm design have been dated to between six thousand and seven thousand years ago, suggesting that silk was cultivated from the time of the first Chinese farming villages. Dated fragments of silk fabric have been found in the southern coastal region (Zhejiang

Province) from 3000 B.C., and a silkworm cocoon found in the Yellow River valley of North China was dated to ca. 2500 B.C.

There are several types of silkworms in Asia. One of the native Chinese varieties has the scientific name *Bombyx mori*. It is a blind, flightless moth that lays about four hundred eggs in four to six days and then dies. The eggs must be kept at a warm temperature. The caterpillars hatch and feast on chopped leaves of the white mulberry tree twenty-four hours a day for about five weeks, growing to be about ten thousand times their original weight. When large enough, the worms produce, through their glands, a liquid gel that dries into a threadlike filament, which wraps around itself and forms a cocoon. The amazing feature of *Bombyx mori* is that its filament, generally between six hundred and twelve hundred yards long, can be unwrapped. If seen in cross-section, its filament is round (others are flat) and very strong. To "unwind" the filament in the silk production process, the cocoons are boiled. This kills the pupae inside and dissolves the gum resin (seracin) that holds the cocoon together. The cocoons may then be soaked in warm water and unwound, or be dried for storage, sale, and shipment. To make silk, the cocoon filament is unwrapped by hand and then wrapped onto reels. Several filaments are combined to form a silk thread. An ounce of eggs produces worms that require a ton of leaves to eat, resulting in thirty thousand cocoons, which produce about twelve pounds of raw silk. The silk threads may then be woven together, often with other yarn, and dyed to make all sorts of products. The Chinese traditionally incubated the eggs during the spring, timing their hatching as the mulberry trees were coming to leaf. Typically, silk production was women's work, intensive, difficult, and time-consuming.

Silk has long been considered a special type of cloth. It keeps one cool in the summer and warm in the winter. It is good at holding color dyes and drapes the body particularly well. It is very strong and resistant to rot and to fire. Early in Chinese history, silk was used for clothing the emperor, but its use eventually extended widely throughout the society. Silk proved to have other valuable uses—for making fishing lines, paper, and musical instrument strings.

NAMING THE SILK ROAD

The term "Silk Road" in modern usage grows out of the fascination with cultural diffusion, particularly in nineteenth-century Germany and England. The term was first used by the German geologist, traveler, and economic historian Baron Ferdinand von Richthofen. In a paper published in 1877 he coined the term *Seidenstrassen* or "Silk Roads" in referring to the Central Asian land bridge between China and Europe. Richthofen conceived of Central Asia as a subcontinent—a region that not only connected distant civilizations but also provided a source of cultural creativity in its own right.

Richthofen's formulation paralleled those of others who were discovering and articulating a variety of trade, migration, and cultural diffusion routes connecting Asia and Europe. European scholarly explorations of the region and debates over its connections to other lands and civilizations were quite lively, coinciding with important empirical findings in linguistics, archaeology, and biology.

THREE SILK ROAD PERIODS

The Silk Roads were used continuously for millennia, promoting not only the exchange of goods but also exchanges of culture, including poetry, literature, art, and music. Conventionally historians refer to three particularly intensified periods of exchange.

The first period (206 B.C. to A.D. 220) involved trade between the ancient Chinese Han Dynasty and Central Asia, extending all the way to Rome and Egypt.

The second period (A.D. 618 to 907) involved trade between China during the Tang Dynasty and Central Asia, Byzantium, the Arab Umayyad and Abbasid empires, the Sassanian Persian empire, and India, coinciding with the spread of Buddhism and later the expansion of Islam as well as Nestorian Christianity into Central Asia.

The third period (thirteenth and fourteenth centuries) involved trade between China, Central Asia, Persia, India, and early modern Europe, facilitated by Mongol control of most of the Silk Road region.

Some add a pre–Silk Road period during which silks from China and India made their way to ancient Greece and perhaps Egypt. For example, near the Valley of the Kings in Egypt a female mummy was buried with silk in 1070 B.C. Others add a modern Silk Road period, beginning in the nineteenth century with the "Great Game"—the competition between Britain and Russia for influence over Central Asia—and extending through today.

From Han China to Rome

Under the Han dynasty (206 B.C. to A.D. 220) silk became a great trade item, used for royal gifts and tribute. It also became a generalized medium of exchange, like gold or money. Civil servants were paid in silk. Chinese farmers could pay their taxes in silk.

The Chinese traded silk widely but closely guarded the method of silk production from outsiders. Sericulture (the raising of silkworms) traveled eastward, first with Chinese immigrants to Korea in about 200 B.C. and then to Japan in the third century A.D.

By the first century B.C., silk had traveled to Egypt and Rome, though the Romans did not know how it was made. Coinciding with the development of ruling elites and the beginnings of empire, silk became associated with wealth and power—Julius Caesar entered Rome in triumph under silk canopies. Regarded as "delicate" material, silk was associated with female apparel; in 14 B.C. the Roman Senate forbade males from wearing it, to no avail. Over the next three centuries, silk imports increased, especially with the Pax Romana of the early emperors, which opened up trade routes in Asia Minor and the Middle East. Roman glass made its way back to China, as did asbestos, amber, and red coral. The Romans increasingly spent wealth on silk, leading to a drain of precious metals; several warned of the deleterious consequences of this practice. Yet silk became a medium of exchange and tribute, and when in A.D. 408 Alaric the Visigoth besieged Rome, he demanded and received as ransom five thousand pounds of gold and four thousand tunics of silk.

Tang Silk Road: Connecting Cultures

Silk continued to be popular in the Mediterranean even as Rome declined. In Byzantium, the eastern successor of the Roman state, silk purchases accounted for a large drain on the treasury. How silk making came to the West is unclear, although legend has it that silkworms were smuggled out of China by two Nestorain monks and brought to Constantinople (Istanbul). Under Byzantine emperor Justinian I, Constantinople became a center of silk production, its cloth used throughout Europe for religious vestments and aristocratic dress. The Persians too acquired the knowledge of silk production.

A second Silk Road developed under the Tang dynasty in China (A.D. 618 to 907). Though Central Asians had learned silk cultivation, Chinese silks were still in demand, given their exceptional quality. The Tang rulers, like their Han ancestors, needed horses for their military. The best horses were in the west, held by nomads of the steppes and the people of the Ferghana Valley, in what is now Uzbekistan, Kyrgyzstan, and Tajikistan. The Tang traded silk for horses, forty bolts for each pony in the eighth century.

The growth of silk as a trade item both stimulated and characterized other types of exchanges during this era. Caravans and ships carried silk, but also gemstones, precious metals, and other goods. Not only did materials move, but also designs and motifs, as well as techniques for weaving and embroidering silk. Chinese silk weaving was influenced by Central Asian, Persian Sassanian, and Indian patterns and styles. For example, Chinese weavers adapted patterns such as the Assyrian tree of life and bearded horsemen on winged horses from the Sassanians, along with the use of beaded roundels.

From the Indians they adapted the use of gold-wrapped thread and a variety of knot styles, as well as conch shell and lotus designs. During the Tang dynasty, cultural exchange based upon silk reached its apex.

Cultural exchange went beyond silks. Curative herbs, ideas of astronomy, and even religion moved along the Silk Road network. Arabs traveled to India and China; Chinese traveled to Central Asia, India, and Persia. Buddhism was carried along these roads from India to Tibet and into China. Islam was carried by Sufi teachers and by armies moving across the continent from Western Asia into Persia and Central Asia and into China and India. Martial arts, calligraphy, tile making, and painting also traversed these roads. The Tang capital of Chang'an became a cosmopolitan city, peopled with traders from all along the Silk Road, as well as monks, missionaries, and emissaries from across the continent.

Mongol Silk Road (Marco Polo)

The transcontinental exchange diminished in the later Middle Ages, and in Europe knowledge of the East receded in memory, as did the connection of European history to its own ancient Greek and Roman roots. The Christian Crusades to the Middle East and the Holy Land, from 1096 to the mid-1200s, brought many Europeans and Muslims into contact, and the Moorish influence in Spain rekindled European interest in Asia. The Moors brought silk production to Spain and Sicily in the eleventh century. Through Arab scholars, Europeans gained access to Indian and Chinese advances in medicine, chemistry, and mathematics, and also access to ancient Greek and Roman written works that had survived in Arabic translations and commentaries. The availability of this knowledge helped fuel the Renaissance in Europe, with the growth of trade and cities, guilds, arts, and scholarship. Mediterranean city-states, including Venice, Genoa, and Barcelona, prospered creatively and commercially.

One Venetian, Marco Polo, traveled across Asia by land and sea over a period of twenty-four years beginning in 1271. The tales of his travels spurred broad European interest. He told of the Mongols who under Genghis Khan and his successor Kublai Khan had taken over China and expanded their dominion across Asia, into Central Asia, India, Persia, and Asia Minor. Marco Polo narrated fantastic tales of the lands he had visited, the great sites he had seen, and the vast treasures of Asia. He was one of several European travelers of the time; others included emissaries of the Pope seeking alliances with the Mongols.

The thirteenth and fourteenth centuries were characterized by considerable political, commercial, and religious competition between kingdoms, markets, and sects across Eurasia. The Mongols, whose empire extended from the Pacific to the Black Sea, were, through a mixture of hegemony and brutality, able to ensure a measure of peace within their domains, a Pax Mongolica. They were also quite tolerant of diversity in the arts and religion. Their ancient Mongolian capital, Qaraqorum, was home to a dozen Buddhist temples, two mosques, and one church. Kublai Khan hosted European, Chinese, Persian, and Arab astronomers and established the Institute of Muslim Astronomy. He also established the Imperial Academy of Medicine, including Indian, Middle Eastern, Muslim, and Chinese physicians. European, Persian, Chinese, Arab, Armenian, and Russian traders and missionaries traveled the Silk Road, and in 1335 a Mongol mission to the Pope at Avignon reflected increased trade and cultural contacts.

While silk was still a highly valued Chinese export, it was not the primary commodity of this "third" Silk Road. Silk production was known in the Arab world and had spread to southern Europe. Silk weavers, relocated from Constantinople to northern Italy, energized the development of silk tapestry as Renaissance art.

Commercial trade and competition was of great importance by the fifteenth century with the growth of European cities, guilds, and royal states. Europeans wanted pearls and precious gems, spices, precious metals and medicines, ceramics, carpets, other fabrics, and lacquerware. All kingdoms needed horses, weapons, and armaments. The trade in silk and these other goods helped fuel the commercial transformation of Western Europe. King Charles VII of France and the dukes of Burgundy participated heavily in the silk and luxuries trade. Markets were established in Bruges, Amsterdam, and Lyon. But trading overland with China, Persia, and India was neither the most reliable nor most economical means for European rulers to acquire silk and other luxury goods.

With the decline of Mongol power and the rise of the Ottomans, control over trade routes was vital. Indeed, the motivation behind Portuguese explorations of a sea route to India and East Asia was to ensure safer and cheaper passage of trade goods than could be secured by depending upon land caravans subject to exorbitant protection fees or raiding by bandits. The Ottoman Empire, which held sway over much of Central Asia, controlled the land routes and prevented direct European trade with the East. Indeed, it was the search for a sea route to the East that led Columbus westward to the New World. After Vasco de Gama found the sea route to India, other European explorers opened up direct shipping links with China. Overland contact between Western Europe and Central Asia decreased dramatically.

From Japan to Jersey

European rulers wanted to control their own trade in silk through its direct production. Italian silk production was emulated by the French, whose own silk industry was centered in Lyon in the 1500s. The English developed a silk industry as well, trying silk cultivation in Ireland and even in the New World. King James I was a silk enthusiast. Mulberry trees and silkworms went with settlers to Jamestown, Virginia, in the early 1600s. Refugee French Huguenot artisans were encouraged to inhabit the new colony. Silk cultivation was successful, but only for a time, and was followed with other attempts later in Georgia, among the nineteenth-century Harmonists in Pennsylvania, and even among the Shakers in Kentucky. Still, imported silks showed the long reach of international trade. Silk kerchiefs were imported from India and worn by cowboys in the American West, who called them bandannas, a variant of the Bengali term *bandhānī* (binding).

By the mid-1800s silk weaving was industrialized, with the invention of new looms and synthetic dyeing processes that allowed for mass-produced lines of silk clothing and furnishings. Raw silk was shipped from cultivation centers to design and production factories to meet the demand of the period. This extended to the United States, as raw silk was imported from Japan, dyed in the soft waters of the Passaic River, and distributed through companies headquartered in Paterson, New Jersey—dubbed "America's Silk City." Silk as a valuable traded commodity both epitomized and played a major role in the early development of what we now characterize as a global economy.

SILK ROAD STORIES

Just as there was not one Silk Road, nor one historical period or product, there also is not one story that conveys the essence of the Silk Road. Scholars working on the Silk Road have found a variety of stories to tell.

J. Mark Kenoyer, an archaeologist at the University of Wisconsin, digs every year in Harappa, the ancient Indus Valley site. He has found seashells, lapis lazuli, carnelian, and other beads that indicate contact with other major urban centers in Arabia, Mesopotamia, Baluchistan, Central Asia, and possibly even China. For him, the Silk Road reaches far back, to somewhere around 2500 to 3000 B.C. The same land and sea routes that may have carried ancient silk also carried beads as trade items. Following the beads is a way of ascertaining cultural contact and of understanding the growth of various centers of civilization.

The global stretch of the Silk Road is well illustrated by the story of porcelain. Many Americans keep their china in cabinets, attesting to its value. But how many think of it as Chinese? Chinese porcelain made its way around the world. Yankee clipper ships brought it to New England. Europeans imitated it and still do, as with delftware from the Netherlands. Calling fine ceramics "china" is something Americans share with Turks. Indiana University folklorist Henry Glassie has done extensive studies of porcelain and *çini* in Turkey. One type, the ubiquitous blue and white ware, originated in Jiangdezhen, China. Jiangdezhen was an important center of ceramics manufacture; it was located in south China just north of Guangdong (Canton). Under the Song Dynasty (A.D. 960–1279), some seven hundred artisans turned the rich kaolin clay into vases, plates, and other types of ceramics for the emperor. (The blue color, however, came from cobalt mined in Persia.) When the first Mongols invaded China in A.D. 1126, the Song rulers fled their northern capital and went south to Hangzhou in Jiangxi Province; the royal potters fled to nearby Jiangdezhen.

Under the Mongol Yuan Dynasty (A.D. 1271–1368), the fine blue and white porcelain was traded along the Silk Road to Turkey. The Turks found their own way of imitating and producing the porcelain. Interestingly, Chinese designs were replaced with new visual elements. Plates featured Islamic calligraphy with phrases of the Koran crafted in elaborate styles. Arrangements of fruits, flowers, and leaves encoded images of spiritual significance. The tradition is still vital. Glassie, conducting field research in the major Turkish center of Kutahya, reports thousands of potters at work. Their art is visionary, as the resulting plates become objects of meditation and reflection.

For Ted Levin, a Dartmouth ethnomusicologist, the Silk Road tells a tale of musical invention, diffusion, and continual transformation. Levin and his colleague Jean During of the Aga Khan Trust for Culture have studied *maqam,* a classical musical tradition that spread through Islamic Azerbaijan, Persia, Transoxania, and western China, influencing the music of the Indian subcontinent. This is a tradition as complex and sophisticated as the Western classical tradition, but predating it by hundreds of years. While it continues as an art or courtly music, it also adapts to new settings. Levin has found this music in the United States among Bukharan Jewish immigrant musicians from Uzbekistan playing at community functions in New Jersey and restaurants in Queens, New York. Here the musical tradition is imbued with a new vitality, symbolizing the identity of a people in a new home.

Similarly rich stories can be told of a variety of Silk Road commodities. Richard Kennedy, Smithsonian cultural historian, notes how paper, first made by the Chinese, was picked up by the Arabs and eventually brought to Europe in the 1400s, enabling the revolution in printing, one of the key innovations of the modern era. Rajeev Sethi, a designer from India, is enamored with the movement of design motifs—trees of life, supernatural winged beings, vines, and stars—that traverse the Silk Road expanse.

Polo

My favorite Silk Road story is that of polo. Scholars trace its origins to some-where in Central Asia around 600 B.C. There are many variations, including a rather sophisticated version played by Chinese women during the Tang dynasty. American polo is derived from the game viewed by British soldiers on the northwestern frontier of nineteenth-century colonial India. There another version of the game, known as *bushkashi,* is still a raucous, physical exercise of competitive horsemanship. Two large teams play against each other. The field might be a large meadow, with an area or pit designated as the goal. A goat or calf carcass is the "ball." Horsemen from one side must scoop up the carcass, ride around a pole or designated marker, reverse course, and drop it into the goal. Players use their skill as horsemen and a repertoire of hand-held armaments to either aid or attack the carcass carrier. This is a wild, rough-and-tumble game in which injuries are common. The social purpose may be sport, but the game teaches and encourages excellent horsemanship skills, precisely those needed to attack caravans, raid towns, and rout opposing forces. Watching the players, you can easily visualize the horsemen descending upon a Silk Road caravan loaded with luxury goods intended for far-off rulers and capitals. In 2002, Afghans celebrated their liberation from the Taliban regime with games of *bushkashi.*

While polo also evolved as a sport in central Asia, it was Victorian Englishmen who turned it into the game that Americans know today. We think of polo as a sophisticated game requiring upper-class connections and money to maintain special ponies and stables. Interestingly enough, the story continues. Today, Afghan immigrants to the United States play a form of "macho polo," which combines the structure of the formal game with the attitude and style of its rougher cousin. Polo is a fine example of how meanings and practices can be transformed as they move across cultures and time periods—certainly a wonderful Silk Road story.

THE SILK ROAD TODAY

Today, the Silk Road region, particularly Central Asia, is of immense interest to political and civic leaders, religious figures, corporate entrepreneurs, and a broad international public. The Silk Road skirts the southern edge of the old Soviet Union—Georgia, Armenia, Azerbaijan, Kazakhstan, Turkmenistan, Uzbekistan, Tajikistan, and Kyrgyzstan were part of that Russian empire, and other states such as Afghanistan and Mongolia were closely related to it. The collapse of the Soviet Union brought new, often competing political and economic systems into the region. These nations, home to ancient cultures, face tough questions: Should they reform the communist polity and economy they inherited? Should they embrace a Western, capitalistic democracy? Or should they develop new forms of the national state adapting Western and Soviet practices to those of local significance?

Today ideal visions collide with rancorous political factions, rebel movements, the lack of strong civic institutions, and the intransigence of old power holders to keep the region in flux. Even long-established nations such as China face internal challenges, with changing political realities and ethnic minorities including Muslim Uighurs and Buddhist Tibetans seeking autonomy. The civil war in Afghanistan between the Taliban and its opponents, the Northern Alliance and various Pushtun tribes, brought some of these conflicts into American consciousness. The future of national stability and viability in the region is unknown.

So too is the issue of how to deal with religion in Central Asia. Should the Muslim-majority states of Central Asia incorporate religious law into civil practice? Should they be theocratic? How much diversity, both within Islam and among other groups, should they accommodate? Parties from Turkey, Iran, Saudi Arabia, and Pakistan have offered competing visions of the relationship between Islam and the state. These questions emerged dramatically in Afghanistan. When the Taliban blew up the Buddhist statues of Bamiyan, the whole world cringed. These statues represented a truly ancient symbol of the Silk Road. In their contemporary state, they stood for an appreciation of a commonly shared though diverse cultural heritage of humanity. These statues' destruction turned out to be an eerie prelude to the 2001 attack on the World Trade Center, a thoroughly modern symbol of a world joined in a network of commercial relations. In the aftermath of these events, Central Asians grapple with the question of the proper relationship between religion, society, and the state.

Economic uncertainty has also followed independence from the Soviet Union. Nations struggling to build their own economies must develop local markets, industries, and infrastructures while at the same time participating in an increasingly globalized world economy. Some local entrepreneurs seek to rebuild economies based upon a traditional repertoire of deeply ingrained Silk Road commercial skills. In Pakistan, for example, instead of caravans of decorated camels, beautifully painted trucks in caravan ply the Karakoram Highway, moving trade goods between that nation and China. Transnational corporations seek the development of natural resources, particularly oil, in Azerbaijan, Kazakhstan, and western China. The Silk Road of old will become a sort of high-tech pipeline—a Slick Road, moving the valuable commodity of oil across the region to the rest of the world.

Some leaders such as the Aga Khan, an international humanitarian, philanthropist, and leader of the Muslim Ismaili community, see the rebirth of these societies in terms of building an infrastructure that allows for civic and economic development. The Aga Khan and his organization are developing new institutions—universities, hospitals, medical schools, and financial organizations. At the same time, they are encouraging a contemporary revival of traditional knowledge, architecture, and artistry embedded in Central Asian history. Their goal is for an educated and skilled citizenry to thrive in healthy economies throughout the region.

FURTHER READING

Chambers, James. 1999. *Genghis Khan*. Sutton Publishing.

Elisseeff, Vadime, ed. 2000. *The Silk Roads: Highways of Culture and Commerce*. Berghahn Books.

Gilchrist, Cherry. 1999. *Stories From the Silk Road*. Illustrated by Nilesh Mistry. Barefoot Books.

Glassie, Henry. 2000. *The Potter's Art*. Indiana University Press.

Hopkirk, Peter. 2001. *Foreign Devils on the Silk Road: The Search for the Lost Cities and Treasures of Chinese Central Asia*. Oxford University Press.

Kennicott, Phillip. 2001. "Harmony of Cultures: Yo-Yo Ma's Silk Road Project Seeks Key to Appreciating Others." *Washington Post* (October 18): C1, 8.

Kurin, Richard. 1997. *Reflections of a Culture Broker: A View from the Smithsonian*. Smithsonian Institution Press.

Levin, Theodore. 1996. *The Hundred Thousand Fools of God: Musical Travels in Central Asia*. Indiana University Press.

Liu, Xinru. 1998. *The Silk Road: Overland Trade and Cultural Interactions in Eurasia*. American Historical Association.

Macdonald, Fiona. 1998. *Marco Polo: A Journey Through China*. Illustrated by Mark Bergin. Franklin Watts.

Major, John. 1995. *The Silk Route: 7000 Miles of History*. HarperCollins.

Scott, Philippa. 1993. *The Book of Silk*. Thames and Hudson.

The Silk Road: A Musical Caravan. 2002. Smithsonian Folkways.

Smithsonian Folklife Festival Program Book. 2002. Smithsonian Center for Folklife and Cultural Heritage.

ten Grotenhuis, Elizabeth, ed. 2001. *Along the Silk Road*. Asian Art & Culture Series. Arthur M. Sackler Gallery, in association with the University of Washington Press and the Silk Road Project, Inc.

When Strangers Meet: Silk Road Journeys. Yo-Yo Ma and the Silk Road Ensemble. 2002. Sony Classical.Whitefield, Susan. 1999. *Life Along the Silk Road*. University of California Press.

Wood, Frances. 1996. *Did Marco Polo Go to China?* Westview Press.

Wriggins, Sally Hovey. 1996. *Xuanzang: A Buddhist Pilgrim on the Silk Road*. Westview Press.

The Silk Road Project: www.silkroadproject.org

30 REFUGEES

Worldwide Displacement and International Response

Stephen C. Lubkemann

This article offers an anthropological perspective on one of the international community's most pressing moral and ethical dilemmas today: the massive forced displacement of large numbers of people to escape war, persecution, and natural disasters. The article offers definitions, analyses of causes and effects, case studies, and a discussion of international policies and dilemmas.

Throughout history people have been forced to flee their homes in order to escape war, persecution, and natural disasters. The twentieth century has witnessed massive forced migrations. Political conflicts have been motivated by the widespread growth of ethnonationalism, resistance to colonial rule, and the Cold War confrontation between capitalism and communism. Economic processes such as impoverishment due to development policies and global environmental degradation also have resulted in widespread population displacement.

Forced migration has been particularly affected by the emergence of "total warfare" in which noncombatants have increasingly borne the brunt of wartime violence. According to the Independent Commission on International Humanitarian Issues, 95 percent of the casualties suffered in World War I were combatants and only 5 percent were civilians, whereas in most current conflicts civilians often account for 90 percent or more of wartime casualties. Technology has also greatly increased the destructiveness of armed conflict, thus causing greater displacement.

REFUGEES AND INTERNALLY DISPLACED PERSONS

While attempts to assist uprooted people occurred throughout history, only in the twentieth century did international standards and institutions for protecting displaced people emerge. The 1951 United Nations Refugee Convention defines refugees as "individuals who are outside their own country and are unable to return as a result of a well-founded fear of persecution on grounds of race, religion, nationality, political opinion, or membership of a social group." Refugees are entitled to asylum, education, and medical care, and to not be repatriated against their will. The rights of refugees also include freedom of thought, freedom of movement, and freedom from torture or degrading treatment. The convention defines the duties of states to include upholding these rights as a matter of international law. It also requires refugees to uphold the laws of their host countries and to be noncombatants.

It is important to understand that displacement is a process that includes but is not limited to those who meet the legal criteria for refugee status (often called "Convention Refugees"). In fact, the vast majority of those who are forcibly uprooted from their homes do not fit the criteria that would allow them to be categorized as Convention Refugees. Some are internally displaced persons (IDPs) within their own countries. Others have been forced to move for reasons other than those specified in the convention, such as natural disasters, environmental degradation, or extreme economic duress. The number of those who are displaced worldwide is thus three or four times larger than the number of those who are officially designated as Convention Refugees. Those without Convention Refugee status are not entitled to the legal protections that the convention affords.

Moreover, those adversely affected by displacement often include people other than forced migrants themselves—such as the host populations in the impoverished third world nations where most uprooted people are resettled. Thus the majority of those who suffer as a result of displacement do not benefit from the legal rights and entitlements afforded to Convention Refugees by international law.

COMPLEX CAUSES AND EFFECTS

Displacement is one of humanity's harshest and most traumatizing conditions and thus constitutes one of the international community's most pressing moral and ethical dilemmas for the twenty-first century. Armed conflict has persisted, sometimes for decades, in many places throughout the world, such as Angola, Somalia, Sri Lanka, Kurdistan, Colombia, Rwanda, Afghanistan, Palestine, and Kashmir. In such contexts, displacement is not an exceptional interruption in the flow of "normal" life. Instead it has become an integral feature of social life that shapes all aspects of everyday routine. Anthropologists who strive to understand how social and cultural life are organized in these societies must examine how displacement affects many different dimensions of social life, including subsistence strategies, household formation, gender relations, and national identity.

In my own work with Mozambicans who fled their country's civil war, fifteen years of displacement resulted in radical changes in the way residence and marriage were organized. While leaving their wives and children in safe areas within Mozambique, many men migrated to South Africa to avoid being conscripted by the military. Because the war persisted for so long, many of these men eventually constituted second households by also marrying South African women. Although polygyny (men having multiple wives) was already a feature of these men's society, it had never before been transnationalized in this way. In this case long-term displacement created a new form of transnational community in which households, kinship networks, and economic strategies spanned international borders. This form of social organization had not existed before the war but persisted after it.

Over the last three decades social scientists and policy makers have begun to recognize refugees as more than simply the unfortunate by-products of conflict. They have started to study how displacement and forced migration affect broader processes of social change and international security. Some of the issues and phenomena that affect displacement and are, in turn, influenced by refugees are development, demographic change, immigration, ethnonationalism, public health, the environment, and conflict resolution. In the social sciences anthropologists have played a leading role in investigating the causes, organization, and effects of displacement and have focused, in particular, on how displacement affects social relations, organizations, and identities.

Causes of Displacement

Typically those fleeing wars and political violence have been designated "involuntary migrants" as distinguished from "voluntary migrants," a term reserved for those who migrate primarily to improve their economic situation. Increasingly anthropologists have questioned the sharpness of the distinction between political and economic motives for migration by showing that political conflict and economic well-being are often closely related. Researchers have pointed out that people who migrate because their economies or subsistence environment have been devastated by war are also involuntary migrants, even if they have not been directly targeted by military violence. ·
In places such as Sudan or Ethiopia, governments have forbidden the

distribution of food aid in insurgent areas in an effort to starve populations thought to be harboring enemy troops.

Wars also can produce forced migration constricting the options that people have for coping with adverse environmental conditions. During times of famine in Mozambique, rural peasants traditionally coped with food shortages by temporarily moving to urban centers where they could find short-term work, enabling them to purchase food. However, during the Mozambican civil war, the fact that the government held most of the urban areas while the insurgency held rural areas made it virtually impossible to safely transit back and forth between the two. Intense drought conditions resulted in massive forced migration across international borders because the political conditions of the war impeded traditional mechanisms for coping with environmental hardship. Such examples demonstrate how economic, environmental, and political processes can be complexly interrelated in ways that make it difficult to reasonably distinguish political from economic motives, or migration as either voluntary or involuntary.

Political processes such as nationalism and state-building can result in different forms of displacement. The Indonesian government has pursued a policy of forcibly relocating many of its citizens of the dominant ethnic group on the main island of Java to outlying islands in an attempt to influence the ethnic balance of power and cultural practices of ethnic minorities. This policy of transmigration is a deliberate attempt to build a unified national identity by "Javanizing" ethnic minorities. Unsurprisingly, this policy has aggravated ethnic tensions and resulted in violent conflict that has produced displacement in its own right.

Development initiatives are another major cause of displacement. Colonial development projects often displaced tens or even hundreds of thousands of people to make room for settlers (as in South Africa, Zimbabwe, Mexico, and the United States) or to complete projects such as building massive dams. American anthropologist Elizabeth Colson has conducted one of the most important studies of the long-term social effects of development-induced displacement in her fifty years of research on the Gwembe Tonga in Zambia. The Tonga were displaced as the result of a dam project. The ongoing construction of the massive Three Gorges Dam on China's Yellow River provides a contemporary example of a major development project that will eventually displace up to 10 million people.

Economic and applied anthropologists also have shown how prevailing macroeconomic policies such as structural adjustment can affect social and political environments in ways that produce forced relocation. Structural adjustment economic policies generally oblige governments to reduce their public expenditures, often resulting in the loss of jobs and public services. These

APPLYING ANTHROPOLOGY

policies also can produce cost-of-living increases as governments stop sub-sidizing the cost of food or other basic amenities. Anthropologist James Fer-guson demonstrates the consequences of such policies in Zambia, where people who have worked their entire lives in urban areas have been forced to relocate to less expensive rural areas and to pursue unfamiliar agricultural subsistence strategies.

More recently, environmental degradation also has been identified as a major cause of forced migration. Researchers working in Bangladesh and Africa coined the term "environmental refugees" to refer to those displaced because of environmental degradation or natural disasters such as earth-quakes, floods, and volcanic eruptions. Although it is caused by natural events such as these, environmental displacement also is influenced by social, political, and economic factors. People who are economically and politically marginalized are more likely to have to live in areas vulnerable to cata-strophic events and are thus more likely to become environmental refugees. Research is just beginning to consider the potential effects of worldwide en-vironmental trends such as global warming on the potential future displace-ment of such marginal populations as those bordering the Sahel in Africa.

Effects of Displacement

Displacement has a broad range of political, economic, social, and psychological effects, which anthropologists and other social scientists have begun to focus their research attention on. The experience of displacement, particularly when it is prolonged, often leads to the forging of sociopolitical consciousness and national political identity. Millions of Palestinians, Rwandese, and Afghanis have been living in camps or other forms of exile for decades. In such cases, multiple generations actually have been born and grown up in conditions of displacement. Contrary to prevalent media depictions of refugees as merely passive victims of larger circumstances, anthropologists working with these populations have demonstrated how the experience of prolonged displacement can motivate people to politically organize and react against the perceived causes of their displacement. Not surprisingly, refugee camps in Palestine and Afghanistan have proven to be fertile recruiting grounds for military groups fighting against Israel and in successive conflicts in Afghanistan. Both the Taliban and the earlier anti-Soviet mujaheddin movements, which the Taliban ousted, originated within Afghan refugee communities in Pakistan.

Anthropologists working with refugees in Kenya, the Democratic Republic of the Congo, Uganda, Macedonia, Turkey, Rwanda, and Burundi also have examined how national political stability can be affected when massive population movements influence ethnic composition and balances of power within host countries. For example, during the international coalition's war against Iraq in 1990, Turkey feared that a massive influx of ethnic Kurds from Iraq would further strengthen the Kurdish resistance movement within its own borders. Turkey, therefore, refused entry to displaced Kurds attempting to flee the regime of Saddam Hussein.

The rapid arrival of large numbers of destitute and desperate refugees usually has significant, though often contradictory and socially differentiated, economic impacts on host populations. Researchers in East Africa have demonstrated how the arrival of large numbers of refugees may drive down the price of labor in host areas. This may provide a boon to wealthier segments of the host population who are in a position to hire labor. However, it may also drive down wages and increase competition for jobs with other poorer locals who also subsist by providing labor. Similarly massive population influxes may increase pressure on scarce resources such as land or fuel. The influx of Mozambican refugees into Zimbabwe during the 1980s eventually produced a popular backlash because there was already stiff competition for land within Zimbabwe, and Mozambicans were occupying more and more of it. Such effects can increase socioeconomic differentiation (i.e., increasing the gap between the rich and poor) within host populations, creating new forms of social tension and conflict. These socioeconomic impacts are particularly pronounced in many of the third world countries that bear the brunt of the world's refugee burden and in which poverty may already be widespread.

These impacts are likely to be further pronounced if displaced populations do not settle in visible refugee camps or receive official assistance but rather "self-settle" in the midst of host populations. Anthropologists working in Africa and Latin America have provided most of the few in-depth examinations of these so-called self-settled refugees. Throughout the 1970s and into the 1980s, there was evidence that many self-settled refugees were able to successfully integrate into local host communities in rural border areas, usually by drawing on extended kinship or ethnic ties that spanned these borders. Recent work by anthropologists points to the fact that an increasing number of the self-settled seem to be establishing themselves in major urban centers rather than in rural areas bordering their countries of origin. While it is clear that the self-settled comprise a majority of the displaced (some estimates range as high as 80 percent of all displaced), exact estimates are hard to come by. Since the majority of these individuals are technically illegal immigrants, they have a vested interest in concealing their national origins in order to avoid deportation.

Anthropologists have been particularly successful and pioneering in working with self-settled refugees because their fieldwork methods allow them better access to these populations. Through long-term interaction with their subjects, anthropologists are able to build stronger, more trusting relationships than are possible through other methods. This rapport also provides for a deeper and more holistic understanding of the complex social effects of displacement. Many anthropologists have consequently become strong advocates for the refugee populations with whom they work. The precarious legal status of many displaced people and their traumatic histories force anthropologists to grapple with difficult ethical dilemmas and with the challenge of how best to protect their research collaborators.

Anthropologists have increasingly examined how displacement is a highly gendered process that reorganizes social relations and identities. In many refugee situations women and children account for more than 80 percent of the refugee population. There is also evidence that wartime violence and displacement often have more negative economic and social effects on women than on men. For example, refugee women are usually more vulnerable to predatory sexual violence than refugee men. A great deal of policy research has attempted to identify the most vulnerable groups within displaced populations, such as women-headed households, children, the elderly, and those with disabilities, in order to identify ways to provide greater assistance and protection.

Anthropologists have shown that culturally specific social systems play an important role in constituting vulnerability. Vulnerability is not merely a function of biological factors such as age or sex. It is primarily related to the ways in which social roles bind people to certain obligations and entitle them to certain rights. Social roles vary widely across different cultures. In my own work in Mozambique, I was able to show organizations assisting refugees that their assumptions that elderly widows were more vulnerable than elderly widowers was incorrect because it did not account for the way the local kinship system worked. In this particular social context, elderly women almost always were supported not by their husbands but by their sons and their wives. Elderly men, on the other hand, depended on their wives for support. The loss of a spouse was therefore much more consequential for elderly men than for elderly women.

Displacement also may have profound effects on the gendered distribution of labor, on the way gendered relationships such as marriage or parentage are organized, and on how gendered and other social roles change in terms of the obligations and rights these imply. Thus, for example, in rural Mozambique, displacement had profoundly disempowering effects for women. It reconfigured gender relations and the social institution of marriage in very detrimental ways for many women. Displaced women who resettled in refugee camps were unable to engage in subsistence agriculture, which was their primary economic activity and the basis of their social influence within their households. On the other hand, many men were able to continue their primary economic activity—labor migration. The fact that many of these migrant men took additional wives in their migration destinations also disempowered their Mozambican wives. These wives who remained behind in refugee camps found it difficult to claim their share of their husbands' earnings. Conversely, in other contexts, such as among Eritrean refugees settled in Canada, women have been able to assume new social roles previously unavailable to them, resulting in their relative empowerment vis-à-vis Eritrean men.

The experience of having to adapt to an unfamiliar social and cultural environment can make forced migration and resettlement particularly difficult experiences. It is important to realize that displaced people arrive in new societies with their own sets of values and aspirations. The maintenance of particular cultural differences may become crucial to refugee constructions of meaningful identities and life strategies in novel social environments. For example, several anthropologists who have worked with Hmong refugees from Cambodia in the United States have noted the critical role that religion has continued to play in organizing these refugee communities and in constituting a sense of social identity.

Differences between the cultural norms of refugees and those of host societies concerning appropriate codes of social behavior sometimes create tensions between refugees and the communities in which they have resettled. Exposure to new value systems and cultural norms can also generate conflict within refugee communities and households themselves. Men and women, or different generations, often have divergent views about which features of their own original culture should be maintained and which from the new host society should be adapted as their own. Anthropologists working with Afghani and Laotian refugees in the United States and with the Palestinians in Germany have taken particular note of intergenerational differences in how parental authority is regarded. For example, anthropologist Dima Abdulrahim has documented the disputes that arise within Palestinian refugee households in Germany over whether or not fathers should have the right to dictate whom their daughters marry.

Those studying other groups such as Sudanese or Ethiopians in the United States, Mozambicans in South Africa, or Burundians in Tanzania have noted how internal tensions and arguments often emerge over changing norms in the way gender roles and relationships are defined. In my own work I found that Mozambican women who joined their husbands in South Africa often observed that there was a greater sharing of domestic tasks by men in South African households. They consequently began to question the gendered division of labor within their own households. Mozambican men resisted the erosion of their privileges. In many cases they eventually went out of their way to avoid having their Mozambican wives join them in South Africa in order to prevent them from exposure to new norms.

Effects on Health

The psychological effects of exposure to violence and displacement are attracting increased attention from mental health experts, including medical and psychological anthropologists. The trauma of displacement can make adaptation to new and unfamiliar social and cultural environments particularly difficult. Anthropologists have demonstrated how different cultural beliefs play a central role in the way individuals interpret and cope with traumatic experiences such as displacement. The challenges of adaptation may be further intensified by the uncertainty and insecurity of temporary status or a sense of being highly constrained in a refugee camp environment. Prolonged dependence on aid in long-term refugee camp situations can lead to diminished self-esteem and a sense of dependency and disempowerment.

One of the most fruitful recent areas of collaboration between researchers and organizations assisting refugees has been in understanding and improving humanitarian reactions to the health problems faced in complex emergencies. The catastrophic mortality rates in the Rwandan refugee camps in eastern Zaire (now the Democratic Republic of the Congo) sounded a wake-up call within the humanitarian community that has since sparked greater collaboration with the Centers for Disease Control and Prevention (CDC), as well as research and training programs on refugee health at leading schools of public health such as Johns Hopkins and Columbia University.

In 1999 the National Research Council Committee on Population created a Roundtable on Forced Migration to assess and encourage research on the demographic effects of displacement. Research on refugee mortality and morbidity represents only the first step in a much needed examination of the broader demographic effects of forced migration. It is worth noting that Africa is the continent with the greatest number of IDPs, the world's highest fertility rates, fastest urban growth, and highest rates of HIV. Remarkably, however, the relationship of forced migration to these important demographic processes has scarcely been examined to date.

THE ANTHROPOLOGY OF HUMANITARIAN ACTION

Anthropologists working on refugees have focused largely on how displacement affects and is affected by social organization. Increasingly many of us see the necessity of also focusing on the larger political-economic systems and organizations that intervene in the lives of the displaced. The humanitarian regime consists of those organizations that assist or interact with displaced populations, the systemic relationships among these organizations, and their institutionalized set of practices. The anthropology of humanitarian action focuses on the social, cultural, economic, and political factors that shape those practices and the relationships of power among those organizations.

The office of the United Nations High Commissioner for Refugees (UNHCR), created in 1950 following post–World War II reconstruction in Europe, continues to play the leading role in international efforts to assist and protect refugees and displaced people worldwide. Throughout the last decade of the twentieth century, the number of "persons of concern" to the UNHCR rose from 14.92 million to 22.26 million.

Regional international bodies such as the Organization of African Unity (OAU) and the Organization of American States (OAS) extended the definition of refugee to include individuals and groups forced to flee their countries because of conditions of generalized violence and insecurity rather than because of individual-specific persecution. At best these criteria only have been applied within these regions. Unfortunately, countries throughout the world increasingly have followed the lead of Western European and North American governments in pursuing more restrictive asylum-granting policies that limit the number of refugees allowed to settle within their borders.

Such policies are a reaction by the governments of industrialized nations to two decades of rapid growth in immigration. This flow has been caused by people fleeing deteriorating political and economic conditions in developing countries such as Haiti, Mexico, and Nigeria and former communist-bloc countries such as Romania and Nicaragua. Such people come seeking greater opportunity. The globalization of mass communication has increased awareness of the opportunities available in many industrialized nations. The development of international transportation systems has facilitated transcontinental travel. These aspects of globalization have played an important role in motivating international migration.

The UNHCR can only advise individual states on how to interpret the Refugee Convention's criteria when applying them to individuals seeking asylum within their own borders. Consequently, governments always have been able to restrict whom they accept as refugees in ways that serve their political and economic interests. Fears of the negative economic effects of excessive immigration have led industrialized nations to interpret the convention's criteria in ever more restrictive terms. Thus, for example, in several cases in North America during the 1990s, courts recognized that asylum seekers fled their countries of origin because of a legitimate fear of violence but still denied them refugee status, because it was determined that they were being persecuted for "nonpolitical" reasons (such as sexual orientation or gender).

Governments also have developed ways to provide temporary relief for those fleeing insecurity without incurring the legal obligations implied in granting Convention Refugee status. Throughout Europe and North America, different forms of temporary protection status (TPS) have emerged that provide an interim solution to populations fleeing generalized violence until it is safe for them to return. Initially put forth as a short-term measure, TPS does not usually provide the social benefits to which refugees are entitled, such as education and employment or the possibility of seeking asylum or permanent resettlement. However, the prolonged insecurity and challenging conditions in countries such as Liberia and Guatemala have led to annual renewals of TPS status in the United States for displaced populations from these countries for up to a decade.

My work with Liberian refugees in the United States has shown how the TPS status has had mixed effects. On the one hand, it has constrained people's economic mobility and social integration into American society. The constant uncertainty over whether TPS will be renewed serves as a disincentive for longer-term social investment in their host communities. On the other hand, the threat of TPS termination has mobilized Liberian community members around a common cause as they lobby for permanent residence status. This has allowed them to transcend longstanding ethnic and socioeconomic divisions that played a significant role in causing the Liberian civil war in the first place.

In the most extreme cases, industrialized nations have resorted to more severe measures to prevent the influx of forced migrants. European Union states have refused entry to asylum seekers on the grounds that they already had passed through "safe countries" en route from their countries of origin. Heavy fines have been imposed on airlines that transport asylum seekers who do not already have visas. Even more draconian and legally dubious measures have involved intercepting refugees before they arrive on host country shores and turning them back without asylum hearings. This was the U.S. government's policy toward thousands of Haitian boat people who sought to land on American shores during the 1990s. This package of increasingly restrictive measures represent a policy of "containment," often described as an attempt to create "fortress" regions that make access to forced and other migrants more difficult.

Such policies have not stemmed the rising tide of forced migrants. Instead they have produced greater levels of clandestine immigration into industrialized nations. Moreover, they have placed the economic burden of displacement on other less-industrialized countries, which are even more adversely affected by massive refugee influxes. Meanwhile, the levels of financial assistance that industrialized nations provide to international organizations and developing nations to assist refugees also has diminished. Unsurprisingly, the willingness of governments everywhere to host refugees has eroded. In this environment refugees throughout the world have experienced rising levels of violence and hostility from host populations and governments. Even governments that have long proven to be generous hosts to large refugee populations, such as Iran and Tanzania, undertook large-scale forced repatriations during the late 1990s and closed off their borders against further refugee flows.

The restriction of asylum also increasingly reduces the options for the displaced in ways that subject them to greater risk of violence. One example is the creation of so-called safe zones within conflict areas as an alternative to allowing refugees to cross international borders. European Union countries already overwhelmed by massive population influxes that resulted from the fall of the Berlin Wall urged the creation of "safe zones" in Bosnia-Herzegovina because of their reluctance to receive refugees from the former Yugoslavia. However, insufficient military means for ensuring their safety led to notorious calamities in 1995 when the safe zones in Srebrenica and Žepa were overrun and thousands of Bosnian civilians were massacred.

Restrictive immigration policies do not prevent forced migration because they fail to address the root causes of migration—namely, the precarious political and economic conditions that compel people to move. The growing worldwide reluctance to accept refugee resettlement and the increasing trend toward civil (as opposed to interstate) warfare has resulted in a dramatic increase in the number of IDPs worldwide. The appointment in 1992 of the first UN Special Representative on Internally Displaced Persons represented a critical step in institutionalizing international concern for this issue.

The nature of post–Cold War conflicts presents considerable new challenges to organizations that want to assist the displaced. Many civil wars—such as those in the former Yugoslavia and Rwanda—have been driven by ethnonationalist sentiments aiming to create ethnically homogeneous countries. In these conflicts military forces have directly targeted civilian populations in an effort to eliminate or forcibly uproot minorities—a process called "ethnic cleansing." In such cases humanitarian efforts to assist the displaced do not serve the interest of warring parties and are often hindered. Long-term solutions to the displacement produced by ethnically driven violence may be particularly difficult to find. Repatriation attempts that bring ethnic groups back into contact often spark further violence, revenge killings, and new displacement—as was most recently the case in Kosovo.

In other situations warring parties have developed an interest in the persistence of conflict. The "blood diamond" trade in Sierra Leone and narco-trafficking in Colombia are cases in which the targeting of populations and ongoing displacement help perpetuate the conditions of violence, instability, and insecurity upon which illegal profitable activities thrive. Finally, in places such as Somalia, humanitarian aid itself has been increasingly appropriated by combatants. In these cases, ironically, assistance is transformed into a means for supporting the conflict that is producing displacement in the first place.

The problems of IDPs and the fact that fortress policies do not successfully contain forced migrations have led the international community to consider how to prevent displacement in the first place, by addressing its root causes. In the 1990s the international community took unprecedented steps by intervening in the internal affairs of Iraq and Serbia (Kosovo) in order to protect displaced people but also to prevent forced migration flows across international borders.

Ultimately, however, there is still reluctance on the part of most states and international organizations to challenge the principle of national sovereignty by interfering in the internal affairs of other countries. In conflicts that have produced large numbers of IDPs, such as in Sierra Leone, Iraq, Chechnya, Colombia, and Bosnia-Herzegovina, assisting displaced populations has presented new challenges to policy makers. The UN is an organization premised on the sovereignty of its members. Moreover, the UNHCR can act only at the request and with the permission of sovereign governments. These realities have made it difficult for the UNHCR to provide assistance in some of these cases. International nongovernmental organizations (NGOs) remain divided on this issue. Some organizations have taken positions in cases such as the Sudan and Sierra Leone that clearly prioritize assistance at the expense of considerations of national sovereignty.

THE ROLE OF NGOs

Over the last three decades international NGOs, including CARE, Oxfam, the International Rescue Committee, Doctors Without Borders, Catholic Relief Services, and Save the Children, have come to play a pivotal role in organizing and providing assistance to displaced and war-affected people worldwide. Many of these organizations work with UNHCR, doing much of the operational work on the ground. Increasingly they have influenced policy makers and national governments by bringing the plight of displaced people to the attention of the global media, as in the recent cases of Rwanda and Kosovo.

Policy makers and humanitarian organizations have increasingly moved beyond merely providing assistance to protecting those assisted and those assisting from violence. Some organizations in the international humanitarian community have started to place a greater emphasis on promoting the human rights of the displaced. Thus the NGO Doctors Without Borders—recipient of the 2000 Nobel peace prize—publicly denounces human rights violations, even if this insults a government and thereby prevents them from carrying out assistance activities. In some situations in which assistance has been diverted to serve the interests of combatants (such as in the Rwandan refugee camps in eastern Zaire) or where human rights violations have been particularly grave (such as the Taliban's mistreatment of women in Afghanistan), some NGOs have ceased their assistance activity altogether. Other organizations such as the International Red Cross have chosen not to comment on human rights violations and remain politically neutral in order to continue providing assistance, even if it is diverted or has unintended and undesired consequences.

HUMANITARIAN ACTION

Anthropologists have increasingly examined the activities of the organizations that provide assistance to refugees. Barbara Harrell-Bond's landmark study *Imposing Aid* (1986), confronted humanitarian organizations with research demonstrating that their activities were often more responsive to external pressures such as funding and interorganizational rivalry than to the needs of the refugees themselves. My own work with the Humanitarianism and War Project showed how NGOs in Mozambique are primarily accountable to the interests of the government agencies that fund them rather than to the people who receive their services. As a result, decisions are often made that do not create sustainable solutions to the problems that are most important to locals. Instead assistance often serves to promote the international visibility or political agendas of donors.

Anthropologists also have shown that humanitarian assistance that does not create sustainable solutions or use local capacities causes considerable harm rather than helping refugee or other war-affected populations. In Mozambique my work demonstrated that the unwillingness of modern medical doctors to work with traditional medical practitioners created local suspicion and hostility that proved detrimental to public health. Locals tended to visit traditional medical practitioners first because they were less expensive. Since these practitioners had been alienated by the hospital doctors, they rarely referred sick patients to hospitals but instead would refer them only to other traditional medical practitioners. Consequently, patients often would arrive at hospitals only after a disease had progressed so far that the costs for curing it were exceedingly high.

Recently there have been important collaborative attempts to improve humanitarian action and advocacy. The establishment in the mid-1990s of InterAction—a coalition of over 165 associations involved in humanitarian work—and the Sphere initiative, to establish a voluntary charter with standards and ethical principles for humanitarian action, represent important developments in this direction.

Refugees and displacement are increasingly recognized as only one aspect of a set of interrelated political, economic, and military problems constituting what have come to be called "complex emergencies." Humanitarian assistance is only one component necessary for the solution of these challenges; by itself it cannot solve the problems that displaced people face. International humanitarian assistance continues to gradually expand in scope to provide assistance to all populations affected by displacement (including IDPs, hosts, and even those left behind by forced migrants in devastated war zones—the "displaced in place"). However, it has become increasingly evident that humanitarian action can be effective only if the more fundamental political and economic roots of displacement and conflict are addressed. Anthropologists will continue to play an important role in studying the experiences of the displaced and the effects of displacement. However, they also have an important role to play in understanding the international political systems within which displacement occurs and in identifying the social factors that constrain and shape responses to displacement.

FURTHER READING

Ahearn, Frederick L. ed. 2000. *Psychosocial Wellness of Refugees: Issues in Qualitative and Quantitative Research*. Berghahn.

Bascom, Jonathan. 1998. *Losing Place: Refugees and Rural Transformations in East Africa*. Berghahn.

Black, Richard. 1998. *Refugees, Environment, and Development*. Longman.

Black, Richard, and Khalid Koser, eds. 1999. *The End of the Refugee Cycle? Refugee Repatriation and Reconstruction*. Berghahn.

Cernea, Michael, and Christopher McDowell. 2000. *Risks and Reconstruction: Experiences of Resettlers and Refugees*. World Bank.

Cohen, Roberta, and Francis Deng. 1998. *Masses in Flight: The Global Crisis of Internal Displacement*. Brookings Institution.

Colson, Elizabeth. 1971. *The Social Consequences of Resettlement*. Manchester University Press.

Daniel, E. V., and J. Knudsen, eds. *Mistrusting Refugees*. 1995. University of California Press.

Giles, Wenona, Helene Moussa, and Penny Van Esterlik, eds. 1996. *Development and Diaspora: Gender and the Refugee Experience*. Artemis.

Godziak, Elzbieta M., and Dianne J. Shandy, eds. 2000. *Rethinking Refuge and Displacement: Selected Papers on Refugees and Immigrants*, volume 8. American Anthropological Association.

Hanes, David W., ed. 1996. *Refugees in America in the 1990s: A Reference Handbook*. Greenwood.

Harrell-Bond, Barbara. 1986. *Imposing Aid: Emergency Assistance to Refugees*. Oxford University Press.

Indra, Doreen, ed. 1999. *Engendering Forced Migration: Theory and Practice*. Berghahn.

Krufeld, Ruth M., and Jeffrey L. MacDonald. 1998. *Power, Ethics, and Human Rights: Anthropological Studies of Refugee Research and Action*. Rowman and Littlefield.

Kushner, Tony, and Katharine Knox. 1999. *Refugees in an Age of Genocide: Global, National, and Local Perspectives During the Twentieth Century*. Frank Cass.

Loescher, Gil. 1993. *Beyond Charity*. Oxford University Press.

Lubkemann, Stephen C. 2002. "Refugees." In *World at Risk: A Global Issues Sourcebook*, pp. 522–44. CQ Press. (This chapter of *Anthropology Explored* is an extensive adaptation of this much longer article.)

Malkki, Lisa H. 1995. *Purity and Exile: Violence, Memory, and National Cosmology Among Hutu Refugees in Tanzania*. University of Chicago Press.

Minear, Larry. 2002. *The Humanitarian Enterprise*. Kumarian.

United Nations High Commission for Refugees. 1997. *The State of the World's Refugees: A Humanitarian Agenda*. Oxford University Press.

Van Hear, Nicholas. 1998. *New Diasporas: The Mass Exodus, Dispersal and Regrouping of Migrant Communities*. University College London Press.

31 LINGUISTIC SURVIVAL AMONG THE MAYA

Robert M. Laughlin

This chapter tells the inspiring story of Robert Laughlin, whose research among the descendants of the Maya Indians led to his commitment to bringing Maya literacy to these modern inhabitants of Chiapas, Mexico. In 1975 Laughlin published the first Tzotzil dictionary; by 1982 he had helped create a writers' cooperative and a bilingual publication program. In more recent years, a puppet theater, a live theater, a radio program, and a full-scale literacy project have developed, with over five thousand graduates, while the theater performances have been seen in Mexico, Central America, the United States, and Canada.

My work with the Maya Indians of Chiapas in southern Mexico began in 1959. I was a member of the Harvard Chiapas Project, the goal of which was to document culture change in a Maya community. There I met Romin Teratol, a Tzotzil Maya Indian who was employed as a puppeteer at the National Indian Institute (INI). My wife and I moved briefly into his mother's second house and began learning his language. My predecessor in the project, Lore Colby, had typed up a provisional dictionary, but it was just a start. Soon I was collecting folktales and thereby adding vocabulary to the dictionary. Then I collected dreams. When I suggested the possibility of publishing those dreams, however, I was advised that I should be able to analyze them according to Freud, Jung, and who knows who else. So I decided it would be easier and more useful to compile a thorough dictionary. This process took the next fourteen years! In 1975 *The Great Tzotzil Dictionary of San Lorenzo Zinacantán* was published. In 1980

I published *Of Shoes and Ships and Sealing Wax: Sundries from Zinacantán,* based on the journals of Romin and his neighbor, Antzelmo Peres, who had become my collaborators. They had twice traveled to the United States to finish our opus and offer a description of life in another world.

Eventually the collections of folktales and dreams were published in Tzotzil and English: *Of Cabbages and Kings: Tales from Zinacantán* (1977) and *Of Wonders Wild and New: Dreams from Zinacantán* (1976). Selections from these were published in *The People of the Bat: Mayan Tales and Dreams from Zinacantán* (1988; 1996, paperback ed.). My publication *The Great Tzotzil Dictionary of Santo Domingo Zinacantán* (1988) is a translation and reordering of a sixteenth-century Spanish-Tzotzil dictionary that I found in my hometown of Princeton in 1974. Heart metaphors from this dictionary create a Mayan romance of the heart (2002).

In 1982, aided by the Maya poet Jaime Sabines, brother to the governor of Chiapas, Mexico, a group of Tzotzil Maya Indians who had worked with me or with anthropology colleagues over many years secured funding for a writers' cooperative and published two bilingual booklets. However, the governor's term was ending and, lacking further support, this line was permanently cut. I was then approached by the late Romin's son, Xun, by Antzelmo Peres, and by Maryan Lopis Mentes of neighboring Chamula, whom I had known for many years. I had hoped, during the years of my anthropological and linguistic research, that somehow my work might return to Zinacantán. I saw this as an opportunity—an opportunity to help bring Maya literacy to Chiapas.

By chance, a conference that same year celebrating forty years of anthropological research in Chiapas was scheduled to begin. I urged my Maya friends to address the many assembled anthropologists and linguists. This they did, explaining, "You have awakened our interest in our own culture, you have published many studies, but always in other countries, where we never see the results. Our young people are now literate in Spanish and think they are very smart, but they don't know a quarter of what their fathers know. We would like, at least, to put on paper our customs for the sake of our children and grandchildren."

The next few years, aided by Cultural Survival, a human rights nonprofit organization, we founded Sna Jtz'ibajom (House of the Writer), a Tzotzil-Tzeltal writers' cooperative. Currently the cooperative publishes bilingual booklets in two Maya languages; these booklets cover history, oral history, and customs. The cooperative has also established a puppet theater, a live theater, and a weekly Tzotzil-Tzeltal radio program. The puppet theater draws on folktales but also presents didactic skits on alcoholism, medicine, and bilingual education. The live theater has dramatized a folktale and created a family-planning play.

The cooperative also has started a Tzotzil literacy project. Initially I contacted two religious scribes and a secretary of the school committee of Zinacantán to teach. Currently the teachers give two-hour classes in Tzotzil twice a week in their own homes for ten to twelve of their neighbors. The interest in the project was so great that one teacher requested to teach overtime.

Those eligible to participate in the literacy program must already be minimally literate in Spanish. Initially there was some discussion as to whether women should be allowed to take classes. The idea of women and men spending time together in the evening at first made many feel uncomfortable. One prospective student thought that learning Tzotzil would enable him and his girlfriend to write secret messages to each other since his father knew only Spanish. In two years, the project has awarded five hundred diplomas to men, women, and children in two communities. At present we have two directors, fourteen teachers, and 144 students enrolled each semester. Although Tzotzil is not the government or official language, that has not discouraged the Mayas' enrollment in the evening language classes. Students are encouraged to record personal and family histories as well as to produce creative

writing. Stories are reviewed and edited by Sna Jtz'ibajom. The federal publisher has agreed to print three thousand copies of each work submitted by
the cooperative. Students give the following reasons for learning Tzotzil: to
improve their Spanish by working with translations, to learn, to become
smarter, and to appreciate their own tradition. Besides the personal enrichment the students receive from learning to read and write their native language, Maya society also benefits through the national and international
recognition the cooperative is receiving. The cooperative's success has been
due in part to the talent of its members as writers, actors, artists, and teachers, and also to the great pride that the people have in their culture and their
new desire to be literate in their mother tongue, to "become smart."

We have already come a long way since our beginning eight years ago. We
next would like to see the establishment of culture centers in each community, linked to a Maya Academy of Letters based in San Cristóbal, where
teachers could be trained to spread our activities throughout the Maya areas
of the state.

My first responsibility to the cooperative as an anthropological linguist has
been to train its members to write their language correctly. While spelling is
quickly learned, the decision as to where words begin and end is a problem
even for linguists. For example, when the particles *to* (indicating an incom-
plete or future action) and *ox* (a completed or future action) occur together
to mean "used to [do something]," should they be kept separate or merged?

Second, the economic crisis in Mexico, severely restricting government
funding, combined with the lack of a tradition of charitable giving in
Mexico, forces the cooperative to look outside for support. Very few foundations grant internationally, and of those a very small number support cultural projects. Even then, support is limited to two to three years, so it is difficult to plan for the future. I have been able thus far to steer the cooperative
to appropriate foundations. For a weaving cooperative, self-sufficiency may
be possible, but for writers?

As a member of Sna Jtz'ibajom, I see the significance of the project as
strengthening the Maya culture for the Mayas themselves and offering an alternative to the non-Maya media barrage. Just as important, the cooperative
is awakening an interest among non-Indian Mexicans in their Indian heritage
and informing the outside world that Maya culture is alive and flourishing.

UPDATE

The House of the Writer has achieved international renown. The Spanish versions of two of its folktales have been published by the Mexican Department
of Education in two editions totaling 71,500 copies. The first three volumes

of *Colección de Letras Mayas Contemporáneas Chiapas* (Collection of Maya Writings from Chiapas), edited by Carlos Montemayor, are dedicated to six of our plays in Spanish and Tzotzil. Recently acquired computer equipment gives us a desktop publishing capability.

Our theater, El Teatro Lo'il Maxil (Monkey Business Theater), with its dozen plays created under the direction of Ralph Lee and more recently, Michael Garcés of New York City, has given over five hundred performances in Chiapas. It has toured in southern Mexico, Mexico City, Monterrey, Guatemala, Honduras, Canada, and the United States, where it has visited a dozen universities as well as museums, schools, and community centers. This theater gave rise to Mexico's first two Indian women playwrights, who have won several state and national prizes and participated in women playwrights' conferences in Canada and Australia. They separated from our cooperative to create Fomma, an association dedicated to the Indian women and children now living in the city, providing them with a day care center and training in native literacy and theater. One of its founders, Petrona de la Cruz Cruz, is the first Indian member of the state's human rights commission. Diego Méndez Guzmán is Mexico's first Maya novelist, author of a bilingual epic re-creation of the birth of his town, *El Kajkanantik, los dioses del bien y el mal: Luchas de liberación de un pueblo tzeltal.* He took an active role in the dialogue between the Mexican government and the Zapatista rebels, demanding that Indian culture be given new respect and support in his country. Under our guidance, *casas de cultura,* centers for celebrating local culture, have been established in many of the Indian towns.

As the members have gained confidence and a new awareness of social forces, the subjects of our plays have combined the dramatization of traditional folktales with the discovery of ancient Mayan history and an exploration of recent and current social, economic, and political problems. The performance of a play in Immokalee, Florida, inspired the audience of Guatemalan and Mexican field hands, who are paid miserable wages, to hold its first strike. In 2001 Ralph Lee revised our play *When Corn Was Born* for the La Jolla Playhouse Outreach Program so that it could be presented in local southern California schools in English and Spanglish.

Our literacy project now teaches Tzeltal as well as Tzotzil. It is in such demand among the Tzeltal people that teachers are accepting students who are totally illiterate and who, nevertheless, are able to complete their training. Over 5,500 men, women, and children have received diplomas.

The Chiapas Photography Project, directed by Carlota Duarte, provided our members with darkroom experience, leading to the production of photo comic books and exhibits in Mexico City and the United States. The photographs of Maruch Sántiz Gómez, Mexico's first recognized Indian woman photographer, have also been on exhibit in Johannesburg, South Africa.

Sna Jtz'ibajom has contributed actors and film to the production of video documentaries by Mexican and foreign studios. Four of Sna's actors starred in John Sayles' award-winning movie *Men with Guns.*

FURTHER READING

Breedlove, Dennis E., and Robert M. Laughlin. 1993. *The Flowering of Man: A Tzotzil Botany of Zinacantán.* Smithsonian Institution Press.

Collier, George Allen, and Elizabeth Lowery Quaratiello. 1999. *Basta! Land and the Zapatista Rebellion in Chiapas.* Food First Books.

Frischmann, Donald H. 1994. "New Mayan Theatre in Chiapas: Anthropology, Literacy and Social Drama." In Diana Taylor and Juan Villegas, eds., *Negotiating Performance: Gender, Sexuality and Theatricality in Latin/o America*, pp. 212–38. Duke University Press.

Laughlin, Robert M. 1975. *The Great Tzotzil Dictionary of San Lorenzo Zinacantán.* Smithsonian Institution Press.

Laughlin, Robert M. 1976. *Of Wonders Wild and New: Dreams from Zinacantán.* Smithsonian Institution Press.

Laughlin, Robert M. 1977. *Of Cabbages and Kings: Tales from Zinacantán.* Smithsonian Institution Press.

Laughlin, Robert M. 1980. *Of Shoes and Ships and Sealing Wax: Sundries from Zinacantán.* Smithsonian Institution Press.

Laughlin, Robert M. 1995. "From All for All: A Tzotzil-Tzeltal Tragicomedy." *American Anthropologist* 97(3):528–42.

Laughlin, Robert M. 2001. "Beware the Great Horned Serpent: Insurgencies in Chiapa in 1812 and Chiapas, 1994." *Estudios de Cultura Maya* 21:181–94.

Laughlin, Robert M. 2002. *Mayan Hearts.* Taller Leñateros.

Laughlin, Robert M. 2003. *Beware the Great Horned Serpent: Chiapas Under the Threat of Napoleon.* Institute of Mesoamerican Studies.

Laughlin, Robert M., coll. and trans., and Carol Karasik, ed. 1988. *The People of the Bat: Mayan Tales and Dreams from Zinacantán.* Smithsonian Institution Press. (Paperback ed., 1996, *Mayan Tales from Zinacantán: Dreams and Stories from the People of the Bat.*)

Laughlin, Robert M., with John B. Haviland. 1988. *The Great Tzotzil Dictionary of Santo Domingo Zinacantán: With Grammatical Analyses and Historical Commentary.* Smithsonian Institution Press.

Montemayor, Carlos, ed. 1994. *Colección Letras Mayas Contemporáneas, Chiapas.* 3 vols. Instituto Nacional Indigenista.

Wilson, Carter. 1974. *Crazy February: Death and Life in the Mayan Highlands of Mexico.* University of California Press.

Wilson, Carter. 1995. *A Green Tree and a Dry Tree: A Novel of Chiapas.* University of New Mexico Press.

"Unmasking the Maya: The Story of Sna Jtz'ibajom":
www.mnh.si.edu/anthro/maya

32 FROM TATTOO TO PIERCING

Body Art as Visual Language

Enid Schildkrout and Adrienne L. Kaeppler

For thousands of years and in all cultures, people have adorned their bodies to show status, convey symbolic messages, signal cultural identity or individuality, and display artistic ability. This chapter, consisting of two parts by two different authors, addresses some fascinating questions: How does body art function as a form of communication? What is the relationship of the modern tattoo to various practices throughout the Pacific? How may a form of body art lose its original meaning as it makes the transition across cultural boundaries? The chapter and its associated Web sites detail and illustrate the many techniques and types of body art that humans have used throughout history.

BODY ART AS VISUAL LANGUAGE

Enid Schildkrout

Body art is an ancient and almost universal practice and can be seen today in cultures around the world, including our own in the United States. Body art is not just the latest fashion. In fact, if the impulse to create art is one of the defining signs of humanity, the body may well have been the first canvas. Alongside paintings on cave walls created by early humans over 30,000 years ago, we find handprints and ochre deposits suggesting body painting [see cover illustration, this volume]. People were buried with ornaments that would have been worn through body piercings, and remains of others show intentionally elongated or flattened skulls. Head shaping was practiced 5,000 years ago in Chile and until the eighteenth century in France. Stone and ceramic figurines found in ancient graves depict people with every kind of body art known today. People have always marked their bodies with signs of individuality, social status, and cultural identity.

THE LANGUAGE OF BODY ART

There is no culture in which people do not, or did not, paint, pierce, tattoo, reshape, or simply adorn their bodies. Fashions change and forms of body art come and go, but people everywhere do something or other to "package" their appearance. No sane or civilized person goes out in the raw; everyone grooms, dresses, or adorns some part of their body to present to the world. Body art communicates a person's status in society; displays accomplishments; and encodes memories, desires, and life histories. [Consult Web sites listed at the end of this chapter for illustrations.]

Body art is a visual language. To understand it one needs to know the vocabulary, including the shared symbols, myths, and social values that are written on the body. From tattoos to top hats, body art makes a statement about the person who wears it. But body art is often misunderstood and misinterpreted because its messages do not necessarily translate across cultures. Elaborately pictorial Japanese tattooing started among men in certain occupational groups and depicts the exploits of a gangster hero drawn from a Chinese epic. The tattoos have more meaning to those who know the stories underlying the images than they do to people unfamiliar with the tales. Traditional Polynesian tattooing is mainly geometric and denotes rank and political status but more recently has been used to define ethnic identity within Pacific island societies [see figures 3–5, this chapter].

In an increasingly global world, designs, motifs, even techniques of body modification move across cultural boundaries, but in the process their original meanings are often lost. An animal crest worn as a tattoo, carved into a totem pole, or woven into a blanket may signify membership in a particular clan among Indians on the Northwest Coast of North America, but when worn by people outside these cultures, the designs may simply refer to the wearer's identification with an alternative way of life. Polynesian or Indonesian tattoo designs worn by Westerners are admired for the beauty of their graphic qualities, but their original cultural meanings are rarely understood. A tattoo from Borneo was once worn to light the path of a person's soul after death, but in New York or Berlin it becomes a sign of rebellion from "coat-and-tie" culture.

Because body art is such an obvious way of signaling cultural differences, people often use it to identify, exoticize, and ostracize others. Tattoos, scarification, or head shaping may be a sign of high status in one culture and low status in another, but to a total outsider these practices may appear to be simply "mutilation." From the earliest voyages of discovery to contemporary tourism, travelers of all sorts—explorers and missionaries, soldiers and sailors, traders and tourists—have brought back images of the people they meet. These depictions sometimes reveal as much about the people looking at the body art as about the people making and wearing it. Some early images of Europeans and Americans by non-Westerners emphasized elaborate clothing and facial hair. Alternatively, Western images of Africans, Polynesians, and Native Americans focused on the absence of clothes and the presence of tattoos, body paint, and patterns of scars. Representations of body art in engravings, paintings, photographs, and film are powerful visual metaphors that have been used both to record cultural differences and to proclaim one group's supposed superiority over another.

BODY ART: PERMANENT AND EPHEMERAL

Most people think that permanent modification of the skin, muscles, and bones is what body art is all about. But if one looks at body art as a form of communication, there is no logical reason to separate permanent forms of body art, like tattoos, scarification, piercing, or plastic surgery, from temporary forms, such as makeup, clothing, or hairstyles. Punks and sideshow artists may have what appears to be extreme body art, but everyone does it in one way or another. All of these modifications convey information about a person's identity.

Nonetheless, some forms of body art are undeniably more permanent than others. The decision to display a tattoo is obviously different from the decision to change the color of one's lipstick or to dye one's hair. Tattooing, piercing, and scarification are more likely to be ways of signaling one's place in society, or an irreversible life passage like the change from childhood to adulthood. Temporary forms of body art, like clothing, ornaments, and painting, more often mark a moment or simply follow a fashion. But these dichotomies don't stand up to close scrutiny across cultures: tattoos and scarification marks are often done to celebrate an event, and dyeing or cutting one's hair, while temporary, may signal a life-changing event, such as a wedding or a funeral.

BODY ART TECHNIQUES

Body Painting

Body painting, the most ephemeral and flexible of all body art, has the greatest potential for transforming a person into something else—a spirit, a work of art, another gender, even a map to a sacred place including the afterlife. It can be simply a way of emphasizing a person's visual appeal, a serious statement of allegiance, or a protective and empowering coating.

Natural clays and pigments made from a great variety of plants and minerals are often mixed with vegetable oils and animal fat to make body paint. These include red and yellow ochre (iron-rich clay), red cam wood, cinnabar, gold dust, roots, fruits, flowers, cedar bark, white kaolin, chalk, and temporary skin dyes made from indigo and henna leaves. People all over the world adorn the living and also treat the dead with body paint.

The colors of body paint often have symbolic significance, varying from culture to culture. Some clays and body paints are felt to have protective and auspicious properties, making them ideal for use in initiation rituals, for weddings, and for funerals—all occasions of transition from one life stage to another.

Makeup

Makeup consists of removable substances—paint, powders, and dyes—applied to enhance or transform appearance. For vanity and social acceptance, or for medicinal or ritual purposes, people regularly transform every visible part of their body. They have tanned or whitened skin; changed the color of their lips, eyes, teeth, and hair; and added or removed "beauty" spots.

From the tenth to the nineteenth century Japanese married women and courtesans blackened their teeth with a paste made from a mixture of tea and sake soaked in iron scraps; black teeth were considered beautiful and sexually appealing.

Makeup can accentuate the contrast between men and women, camouflage perceived imperfections, or signify a special occasion or ritual state. Makeup, like clothing and hairstyles, allows people to reinvent themselves in everyday life.

Rituals and ceremonies often require people to wear certain kinds of makeup, clothing, or hairstyles to indicate that a person is taking on a new identity (representing an ancestor or a spirit in a masquerade, for example) or transforming his or her social identity as in an initiation ceremony, wedding, graduation, or naming ceremony. Male Japanese actors in Kabuki theater represent women by using strictly codified paints and motifs, and the designs and motifs of Chinese theatrical makeup indicate the identity of a character.

Hair

Hair is one the easiest and most obvious parts of the body subject to change, and combing and washing hair is part of everyday grooming in most cultures.

Styles of combing, braiding, parting, and wrapping hair can signify status and gender, age, and ritual status, or membership in a certain group.

Hair often has powerful symbolic significance. Covering the head can be a sign of piety and respect, whether in a place of worship or all the time. Orthodox Jewish women shave their heads but also cover them with wigs or scarves. Muslim women in many parts of the world cover their heads, and sometimes their faces too, with scarves or veils. Sikh men in India never cut their hair and cover their heads with turbans; the Queen of England is rarely seen without a hat.

Cutting hair is a ritual act in some cultures and heads are often shaved during rituals that signify the passage from one life stage to another. Hair itself, once cut, can be used as a symbolic substance. Being part, and yet not part, of a person, living or dead, hair can take on the symbolic power of the person. Some Native Americans formerly attached hair from enemies to war shirts, while warriors in Borneo formerly attached hair from captured enemies to war shields.

Reversing the normal treatment of hair, whatever that is in a particular culture, can be a sign of rebellion or of special status. Adopting the uncombed hair of the Rastafarians can be a sign of rebellion among some people, while for Rastafarians it is a sign of membership in a particular religious group. In many cultures people in mourning deliberately do not comb or wash their hair for a period of time, thereby showing that they are temporarily not part of normal everyday life.

What we do with our hair is a way of expressing our identity, and it is easy to look around and see how hair color, cut, style, and its very presence or absence tell others much about how we want to be seen.

Body Shaping

The shape of the human body changes throughout life, but in many cultures people have found ways to permanently or temporarily sculpt the body. To conform to culturally defined ideals of male and female beauty, people have bound the soft bones of babies' skulls or children's feet, stretched their necks with rings, removed ribs to achieve tiny waists, and sculpted the body through plastic surgery.

Becoming fat is a sign of health, wealth, and fertility in some societies, and fattening is sometimes part of a girl's coming of age ceremony. Tiny waists, small feet, and large or small breasts and buttocks have been prized or scorned as ideals of female beauty. Less common are ways of shaping men's bodies, but developing muscles, shaping the head, or gaining weight are ways in which cultural ideals of male beauty and power have been expressed.

Head shaping is still done in parts of South America. For the Inca of South

America and the Maya of Central America and Mexico, a specially shaped head once signified nobility. Because the skull bones of infants and children are not completely fused, the application of pressure with pads, boards, bindings, or massage results in a gently shaped head that can be a mark of high status or local identity.

While Western plastic surgery developed first as a way of correcting the injuries of war, particularly after World War II, today people use plastic surgery to smooth their skin, remove unwanted fat, and reshape parts of their bodies.

Scarification

Permanent patterns of scars on the skin, inscribed onto the body through scarification, can be signs of beauty and indicators of status. In some cultures, a smooth, unmarked skin represents an ideal of beauty, but people in many other cultures see smooth skin as a naked, unattractive surface. Scarification, also called cicatrisation, alters skin texture by cutting the skin and controlling the body's healing process. The cuts are treated to prevent infection and to enhance the scars' visibility. Deep cuts leave visible incisions after the skin heals, while inserting substances such as clay or ash in the cuts results in permanently raised wheals or bumps, known as keloids. Substances inserted into the wounds may result in changes in skin color, creating marks similar to tattoos. Cutting elaborate and extensive decorative patterns into the skin usually indicates a permanent change in a person's status. Because scarification is painful, the richly scarred person is often honored for endurance and courage. Branding is a form of scarification that creates a scar after the surface of the skin has been burned. Branding was done in some societies as a part of a rite of passage, but in western Europe and elsewhere branding, as well as some forms of tattoo, were widely used to mark captives, enslaved peoples, and criminals. Recently, some individuals and members of fraternities on U.S. college campuses have adopted branding as a radical form of decoration and self-identification.

Tattooing

Tattoo is the insertion of ink or some other pigment through the outer covering of the body, the epidermis, into the dermis, the second layer of skin. Tattooists use a sharp implement to puncture the skin and thus make an indelible mark, design, or picture on the body. The resulting patterns or figures vary according to the purpose of the tattoo and the materials available for its coloration.

Different groups and cultures have used a variety of techniques in this process. Traditional Polynesian tattooists punctured the skin by tapping a needle with a small hammer. The Japanese work by hand but with bundles of needles set in wooden handles. Since the late nineteenth century the electric tattoo machine and related technological advances in equipment have revolutionized tattoo in the West, expanding the range of possible designs, the colors available, and the ease with which a tattoo can be applied to the body. Prisoners have used materials as disparate as guitar strings and reconstructed electric shavers to create tattoos. Tattoos are usually intended as permanent markings, and it is only recently through the use of expensive laser techniques that they can be removed.

While often decorative, tattoos send important cultural messages. The "text" on the skin can be read as a commitment to some group, an emblem of a rite of passage, a personal or a fashion statement. In fact, cosmetic tattooing of eyebrows and eyeliner is one of the fastest-growing of all tattoo enterprises. Tattoos can also signify bravery and commitment to a long, painful process—as is the case with Japanese full-body tattooing or Māori body and facial patterns. Though there have been numerous religious and social injunctions against tattooing, marking the body in this way has been one of the most persistent and universal forms of body art.

Piercing

Body piercing, which allows ornaments to be worn in the body, has been a widespread practice since ancient times. Piercing involves long-term insertion of an object through the skin in a way that permits healing around the opening. Most commonly pierced are the soft tissues of the face, but many peoples, past and present, have also pierced the genitals and the chest. Ear, nose, and lip ornaments, as well as pierced figurines, have been found in ancient burials of the Inca and Moche of Peru, the Aztecs and Maya of ancient Mexico, and in graves of central Asian, European, and Mediterranean peoples.

The act of piercing is often part of a ritual change of status. Bleeding that occurs during piercing is sometimes thought of as an offering to gods, spirits, or ancestors. Particular ornaments may be restricted to certain groups—men or women, rulers or priests—or may be inserted as part of a ceremony marking a change in status. Because ornaments can be made of precious and rare materials, they may signal privilege and wealth.

CULTURAL IDEALS OF BEAUTY

Ideas of beauty vary from one culture to another. The beautiful body is often associated with the healthy body, but this does not mean that beauty is defined the same way in all cultures: some see fat as an indication of health and wealth, while others feel quite the opposite. People in some cultures admire and respect signs of aging, while others do all they can to hide gray hair and wrinkles.

Notwithstanding the fact that parents often make decisions for their children, like whether or not to pierce the ears of infants, in general, to be considered art and not just a marking, body art has to have some measure of freedom and intentionality in its creation. The brands put on enslaved people, the numbers tattooed on concentration camp victims, or the scars left from an unwanted injury are body markings, not body art.

CULTURAL SIGNIFICANCE OF BODY ART

Body art is always changing, and in some form or another always engaging: it allows people to reinvent themselves—to rebel, to follow fashion, or to play and experiment with new identities. Like performance artists and actors, people in everyday life use body art to cross boundaries of gender, national identity, and cultural stereotypes.

Body art can be an expression of individuality, but it can also be an expression of group identity. Body art is about conformity and rebellion, freedom and authority. Its messages and meanings make sense only in the context of culture, but because it is such a personal art form, it continually challenges cultural assumptions about the ideal, the desirable, and the appropriately presented body.

Body art takes on specific meanings in different cultures. It can serve as a link with ancestors, deities, or spirits. Besides being decorative, tattoos, paint, and scars can mediate the relationships between people and the supernatural world. The decorated body can serve as a shield to repel evil or as a means of attracting good fortune. Tattoos in central Borneo had the same designs as objects of everyday use and shielded people from dangerous spirits. Selk'nam men in Tierra del Fuego painted their bodies to transform themselves into spirits for initiation ceremonies. Australian Aborigines painted similar designs on cave walls and their bodies to indicate the location of sacred places revealed in dreams.

Transitions in status and identity, for example the transition between childhood and adulthood, are often seen as times of danger. Body art protects a vulnerable person, whether an initiate, a bride, or a deceased person, in this transitional phase. To ensure her good fortune, an Indian bride's hands and feet are covered in henna designs that also emphasize her beauty. For protection during initiation, a central African Chokwe girl's body is covered in white kaolin. In many societies, both the dead and those who mourn them are covered with paints and powders for decoration and protection.

Worldwide travel, large-scale migrations, and increasing access to global networks of communication mean that body art today is a kaleidoscopic mix of traditional practices and new inventions. Materials, designs, and practices move from one cultural context to another. Traditional body art practices are given new meanings as they move across cultural and social boundaries.

TATTOOED BEAUTY: A PACIFIC CASE STUDY

Adrienne L. Kaeppler

Recent feature articles in prominent newspapers and in other popular media such as television suggest that tattoo has become high fashion. Entire novels are built around tattoo, such as Akimitsu Takagi's *The Tattoo Murder Case*. The back cover reads: "The human canvas for a famous tattoo is destroyed, the tattoo stolen, along with the torso."

When Westerners first came into contact with Pacific Islanders, they were amazed at the widespread use and complexity of tattoo. In the novel *Moby Dick*, Melville describes Ishmael's initial meeting in a New Bedford inn with Queequeg, the harpooner, "a native of Kokovoko, an island far away to the West and South, where he was the son of a King" (Melville 1851:150).

> Meanwhile he continued the business of undressing, and at last showed his chest and arms. As I live, these covered parts of him were checkered with the same squares as his face, his back, too, was all over the same dark squares. . . . Still more, his very legs were marked, as if a parcel of dark green frogs were running up the trunks of young palms. It was now quite plain that he must be some abominable savage or other shipped aboard of a whaleman in the South Seas, and so landed in this Christian country. (Ibid.:115)

In the West, tattoo became the domain of sailors, adventurers, and prison inmates. In Japan, it carried an association with the criminal element known as yakuza (McCallum 1988:128–29). Today, not only have the wearers of tattoo changed, but tattooers, once considered craftsmen, are now considered artists.

One of the seminal events that helped make tattoo "respectable" in the academic world was a symposium in 1983 held at the University of California, Los Angeles, entitled "Art of the Body." Arnold Rubin's edited book *Marks of Civilization,* based on this symposium, included papers on topics ranging from tattoo in ancient Egypt to historic and contemporary tattoo in Asia, North America, and the Pacific Islands, as well as the tattoo renaissance in the United States. This volume remains the best academic book for serious study of the history and social significance of tattoo cross-culturally.

To the wearer, tattoo not only enhances the beauty of the human body but

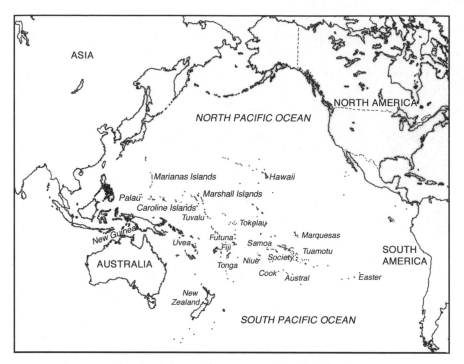

Islands of the Pacific (courtesy Marcia Bakry)

marks social status, conveys symbolic hidden meanings, and proclaims its maker's artistic ability. Contemporary tattoo in Western culture is often an individualized statement of revolution or modernity, but this was not the background for traditional tattoo in Polynesia and Micronesia, where tattoo signified group identity and conformity with the norms of a widely accepted or even high-status group.

The Polynesian term *tatu* is the origin of the English word *tattoo*. It was carried to its high points among the New Zealand Māori, and in the Marquesas, where high-status men were completely tattooed. Considerable portions of the body were also tattooed in Sāmoa, Tahiti, Hawai'i, Easter Island, and elsewhere. Many Polynesian tattoo designs are derived from designs found on Lapita pottery found in Polynesian archaeological sites dating at least two thousand years ago (Green 1979). The antiquity of tattoo in Polynesia is unquestioned.

POLYNESIAN TATTOOING

Polynesian tattoo was done by dipping a prepared tattooing implement— made of bone, turtleshell, or seashell hafted to a handle—into a black dye.

The tattoo artist placed the instrument on the skin, striking it with a mallet or other hammer-like implement. This broke the skin and implanted the dye. It also drew blood and caused considerable pain.

Marquesas Tattooing

In the Marquesas, tattoo seems to have been intimately associated with gender, wealth, and status, but not necessarily chiefly rank. It marked one's association with a particular group of warriors, graded associations, "chief's banqueting societies," or groups of entertainers called *ka'ioi,* as well as the ability to pay the tattooer's fees and the capacity to endure pain. Acquisition of tattoo in honor of special events such as chiefly rites of passage, victories in battle, or participation in feasts commemorated the event and symbolically represented it.

In organizing the tattoo designs, the body was divided into zones, which were then divided into smaller spaces (figure 1). Patterns, often named, were fitted into these spaces. There was an overall symmetry in the zoned composition on each side of the body, but within the zones the designs were often asymmetrical. Women were tattooed on the hands, arms, wrists, feet, ears and lips.

Although it is possible that design models were used, such as the decorated wooden legs and arms found today in museum collections, there is no firsthand evidence that these objects were tattooing models (figure 2). Marquesan tattoo-related designs also appear on barkcloth skull wrappers and on wooden plaques covered with barkcloth. A scholar of tattoo, Carol Ivory (1990), relates the fish designs on the barkcloth skull wrappers to fish designs worked into tattoo and with warriors—fishers of men.

Māori Tattooing

Māori tattoo (*moko*) has fascinated outsiders since the voyages of Captain James Cook, when Cook's artists depicted several tattooed individuals (figure 3). Māori facial designs were carved into the skin with adze-like implements, much like wood carving, to which it can be related both in design and technique. The technique used for female tattoo and men's body tattoo was similar to tattoo techniques elsewhere in Polynesia. Women's tattoo was limited to the lips and the chin (figure 4), while men's body tattoo was between the waist and the knees (figure 5). Facial tattoo was especially important for high-born men of chiefly rank. These individuals were *tabu* (sacred) during the operation and thus could not eat in the normal way. They were fed with carved feeding funnels decorated with tattoo designs.

Rather than designs that associated men together in groups, as in the Marquesas, Māori designs were individualized. Māori chiefs drew their facial

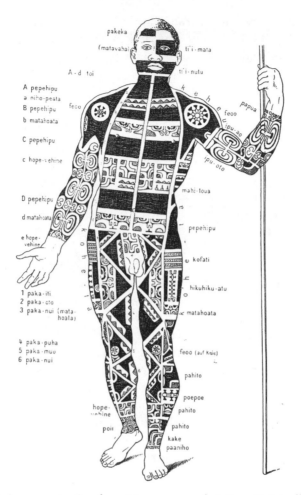

Figure 1. Design organization for a Marquesan male tattoo. Originally published in Karl von den Steinen's *Die Marquesaner und ihre Kunst*, Germany, 1925. In Mark Blackburn, *Tattoos from Paradise: Traditional Polynesian Patterns* (Schiffer, 1999), p. 129.

tattoos as signatures to sign documents during the nineteenth century. As in Marquesan tattoo, Māori designs were divided into zones and these were further divided, giving an overall symmetry. Jackson (1972:70) and Gathercole (1988:175) see this symmetry as the pairing of life with death, or of *tapu* (sacred) with *noa* (not sacred), elements of Māori culture that together expressed the unity of nature and culture. The design elements and their organization within the zones, however, were often asymmetrical, giving it the autographic quality noted above. Tattooing styles varied from tribe to tribe and region to region, as well as over time. Although the classical curvilinear

Figure 2. (above left) Wooden arm from the Marquesas Islands collected by Robert Louis Stevenson, 1890–1894, decorated with tattoo designs. Artifact at the Peabody and Essex Museum, Salem, Massachusetts. Drawing by Marcia Bakry, after photo in Adrienne Kaeppler, Christian Kaufmann, and Douglas Newton, *L'Art Océanien* (Citadelles et Mazenod, 1993), p. 115.

Figure 3. (above right) Tattooed Māori, drawn by Sydney Parkinson during the first voyage of Captain James Cook, 1769–1770. Drawing adapted by Marcia Bakry from photograph of original engraving in Mark Blackburn, *Tattoos from Paradise: Traditional Polynesian Patterns* (Schiffer, 1999), p. 49.

style of tattoo predominated during the nineteenth century, both vertical and horizontal parallel lines were also found, sometimes overlaid with curvilinear designs (such as on figure 3).

The association of Māori tattoo with carved figures is also seen in the carved houseposts of meeting houses, where the buttocks of the ancestral figures have tattoo designs, echoing the tattooed buttocks of important men. The tattoo of this area of men's bodies is also found in Sāmoa, where tattoo generally extends from above the waist to the thighs. Tattoo is publicly exhibited when a man accompanies a high-ranking female dancer. He tucks up his wraparound skirt to show his waist tattoo and the thigh tattoo below. In Tahiti, tattoo was applied to the buttocks of both men and women, sometimes blackening the buttocks completely. This emphasized the underarching crescent shape of the lower buttocks; other crescent designs were placed above the blackened areas. In both Sāmoa and Tahiti tattooing was

Figure 4. Watercolor of a Māori woman by General Horatio Gordon Robley, 1860s. Drawing adapted by Marcia Bakry from photograph in Mark Blackburn, *Tattoos from Paradise: Traditional Polynesian Patterns* (Schiffer, 1999), p. 28.

associated with puberty; it was universal in Tahiti, but in Sāmoa apparently only men of certain status required it.

Hawaiian Tattooing

In Hawai'i, in contrast to most other Polynesian areas, tattooing was decidedly asymmetrical (figure 6). The term for the technique was *kakau i ka uhi*, literally, "to strike on the black," but the organization of the designs had names. For example, a tattoo that made the right side of the body solid black was *pahupahu*. The Maui chief Kahekili, descendant of the thunder god Kanehekili, had this tattoo, as did his warrior chiefs and household companions. In addition, Kahekili's head was shaved on both sides of the central hair crest and tattooed with *hoaka*, crescent designs. Overarching and underarching crescents are tattooed asymmetrically on the left shoulder of the Hawaiian man depicted by John Webber on Cook's third voyage. Elaborate tattoos were applied to one arm or one leg (figure 7). Women were tattooed on the back of the hands, sometimes on an arm or leg, and occasionally the

Figure 5. Watercolor of tattooed Māori men by Joseph Jenner Merrett (1816–1854). Drawing adapted by Marcia Bakry from photograph in Mark Blackburn, *Tattoos from Paradise: Traditional Polynesian Patterns* (Schiffer, 1999), p. 33.

chest. Tattooing the most tender parts of the body, for example the tongue, was practiced to commemorate the death of an important chief. It is likely that Hawaiian tattooing was a protective device, applied in conjunction with chanted prayers, capturing the prayer in the tattoo, thus offering permanent protection. The right arm especially needed sacred protection and help, as it was this bare arm—raised in a crescent—that threw the spear. Likewise, tattooing a row of dots around an ankle was a charm against sharks. In pre-European times, tattoos were protective and informative genealogical devices, usually applied asymmetrically (Kaeppler 1988). In post-European times, at least some of them became decorative and symmetrical, and included exotic motifs of European origin—hunting horns, goats, and lettering.

Figure 6. Colored engraving of a Hawaiian chief by Jacques Arago in 1819. Adapted by Marcia Bakry from original lithograph in a private collection. See Adrienne L. Kaeppler, "Hawaiian Tattoo: A Conjunction of Genealogy and Aesthetics," in Arnold Rubin, ed., *Marks of Civilization: Artistic Transformation of the Human Body* (Museum of Cultural History, University of California, 1988), p. 163.

MICRONESIAN TATTOOING

In the Marshall Islands in Micronesia, people believed that the gods of tattoo gave tattoo art to the Marshall Islanders especially to make them beautiful, and gave them the following message:

> You should be tattooed so that you become beautiful and so your skin does not shrink with age. The fishes in the water are striped and have lines; therefore, also human beings should have stripes and lines. Everything disappears after death, only the tattoo continues to exist; it will surpass you. The human being leaves everything behind on earth, all his possessions, only the tattooing he takes with him into the grave. (Krämer 1904)

A tattooer's inspiration was regarded as a gift from the gods, and he required complete silence while he drew the preliminary design. Offerings of food and mats were presented a week before the tattooing took place. The gods were called upon the night before and if an audible sound in agreement was not heard, the operation was not undertaken; if the gods were not heeded, the ocean would flood the island and the land would disappear. The Marshallese

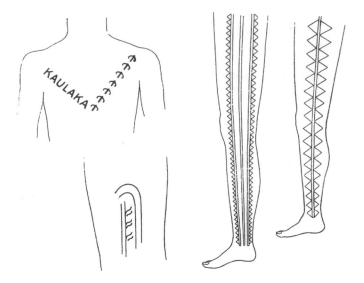

Figure 7. Drawing of Hawaiian tattoo motifs by Augustin Krämer, 1897. In Mark Blackburn, *Tattoos from Paradise: Traditional Polynesian Patterns* (Schiffer, 1999), p. 104.

believed that tattoo did not change or disfigure forms; rather, it harmonized with the form in decorative designs and brought out beauty (Krämer 1906).

Tattoo enhanced the body as an object to be admired and evaluated apart from its temporary ornaments and clothing. Besides being a decorative device urged and sanctioned by the gods, tattooing was embedded in social and economic life. Marking a boy's elevation to manhood, the beauty of his tattoo attracted women to his manliness, demonstrated by his ability to endure pain. Parts of the tattoo are usually covered by clothing and can be seen only at intimate times. The great chiefs had the finest ornamentation, and face tattooing to cover the wrinkles of age was a prerogative of the chiefs. Chiefs' wives had the fingers and backs of their hands tattooed. Wealth was also necessary and the extent and beauty of the designs were dependent on offerings to the gods and the necessary payments to the tattooer in food, mats, and a feast.

Tattooing began with a great chief and then moved on to the commoners. A drawing implement made of the tail feather of a tropicbird or the midrib of a coconut leaf was used for the preliminary drawing. The tattooing chisels, made of fish or bird bones, were of two sizes (depending on the desired fineness of the lines), dipped in dye made of burned coconut sheaths mixed with water, placed on the skin, and struck with a mallet of the midstem of a coconut leaf or other piece of wood. The blackness of the sea swallow (noddy tern) was emulated for color, and the lines of a butterfly fish were the model for the design. The Marshallese word for tattoo (*ao*) means "to

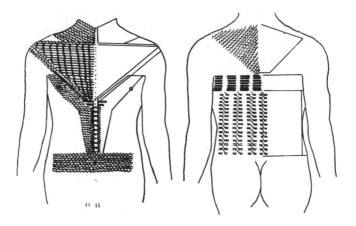

Figure 8. Drawing of breast and back tattoos from the Marshall Islands by Augustin Krämer. From *Archiv für Anthropologie* 30 (1904). In E. H. Bryan Jr., *Life in the Marshall Islands* (Bernice P. Bishop Museum, 1972), p. 182.

draw lines," and straight and zigzag lines were the basic elements. As described and illustrated by Krämer (1906), a breast and back tattoo took about one month and was very painful (figure 8). The body swelled, and the tattoo was rubbed with coconut juice medicine and covered with healing leaves. When the preliminary drawing of the design was finished, songs accompanied by drumming and hand clapping were performed to overcome pain, and the face of a tattooed man was covered with a special mat. A man's tattooing ornamented the chest, back, arms, shoulders, neck, face, thighs, and genitals, depending on preference, rank, and wealth, while a woman's tattoo ornamented her shoulders, arms, and hands.

CONTEMPORARY TATTOO

In the past, tattoo in the Pacific Islands located a major aesthetic form in the body itself, one that revealed the importance of an individual's social status. In contemporary global society, tattoo is more likely to indicate a person's individuality while drawing on traditions from around the world.

As tattoo has become more accepted in Western culture, it has been used in remarkable ways. After the adoption of Christianity by the New Zealand Māori, a Māori artist enlivened a sculpture of the Madonna and Child with the most beautiful decoration, that is, with tattoo. And on April 29, 2000, the Victoria and Albert Museum in London held "Tattoo: A Day of Record." The advertisement depicting Māori tattoo invited the public to "come to the V & A and have your tattoos photographed for inclusion in the Museum

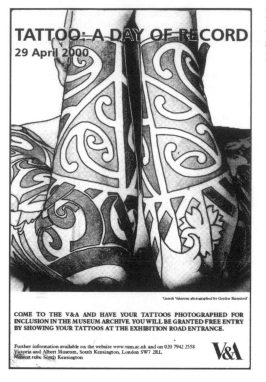

Figure 9. Postcard illustrating Māori tattooed arms. The Victoria and Albert Museum, London. Reprinted with permission.

archive. You will be granted free entry by showing your tattoos at the Exhibition Road entrance" (figure 9). The twentieth century in the West has witnessed an evolution of tattoo from its use as identifying marks by prison inmates to adornment for film stars as well as a revolution from declassé to high art. Who knows where the twenty-first century will lead?

FURTHER READING

Blackburn, Mark. 1999. *Tattoos from Paradise: Traditional Polynesian Patterns*. Schiffer.

Caplan, Jane, ed. 2000. *Written on the Body: The Tattoo in European and American History*. Princeton University Press.

Cook, James, and James King. 1784. *A Voyage Round the World . . . 1776–1780*. London.

DeMello, Margo. 2000. *Bodies of Inscription: A Cultural History of the Modern Tattoo Community*. Duke University Press.

Faces. 1994. Special issue (10[9]): "Hair."

Faces. 1995. Special issue (12[4]): "Ornaments."

Gathercole, Peter. 1988. "Contexts of Maori Moko." In Rubin 1988, pp. 171–77.

Green, Roger C. 1979. "Early Lapita Art from Polynesia and Island Melanesia:

Continuities in Ceramic, Barkcloth, and Tattoo Decorations." In Sidney M. Mead, ed., *Exploring the Visual Art of Oceania: Australia, Melanesia, Micronesia, and Polynesia.* University Press of Hawai'i.

Ivory, Carol Susan. 1990. "Marquesan Art in the Early Contact Period 1774–1821." Ph.D. dissertation, University of Washington.

Jackson, Michael. 1972. "Aspects of Symbolism and Composition in Māori Art." *Bijdragen tot de taal-, Land-en Volkenkunde* 128(14):33–80.

Kaeppler, Adrienne L. 1988. "Hawaiian Tattoo: A Conjunction of Genealogy and Aesthetics." In Rubin 1988, pp.157–70.

Krämer, Augustin. 1904. "The Ornamentation of Dress Mats and Tattooing in the Marshall Islands." Translated by Ilse Grimm. *Archiv für Anthropologie* 30:1–28.

Krämer, Augustin. 1906. *Hawaii, Ostmikronesien, und Samoa.* Schweizerbartische.

Mayor, Adrienne. 1999. "People Illustrated: In Antiquity Tattoos Could Beautify, Shock, or Humiliate." *Archaeology* 52(2):54–57.

McCallum, Donald. 1988. "Historical and Cultural Dimensions of the Tattoo in Japan." In Rubin 1988, pp. 128–29.

Melville, Herman. 1851. *Moby-Dick; or, The Whale.* 1986. Edited and with an introduction and commentary by Harold Beaver. Penguin Classics.

Mifflin, Margo. 2001. *Bodies of Subversion: A Secret History of Women and Tattoo.* 2nd ed. Juno.

Robley, Horatio Gordon. 1896. *Moko; or Maori Tattooing.* Chapman and Hall.

Rubin, Arnold, ed. 1988. *Marks of Civilization: Artistic Transformations of the Human Body.* Museum of Cultural History, University of California.

Takagi, Akimitsu. 1998. *The Tattoo Murder Case.* Translated by Deborah Bolivar. Boehm Soho.

AnthroNotes, winter 2001 issue, includes original publication of this chapter, with illustrations throughout: www.nmnh.si.edu/anthro/outreach/anthnote/Winter01/anthnote.html

Body Art: Marks of Identity, an American Museum of Natural History exhibit, curated by Enid Schildkrout: www.amnh.org/exhibitions/bodyart

Tattoos.com: http://tattoos.com/jane/steve/toc.htm

33   MEDICINE, LAW, AND EDUCATION

Applied Linguistics

P. Ann Kaupp

Doctors, lawyers, and educators all work within a distinct social context and often must communicate highly technical information to members of the general public. Traditionally, applied linguistics referred almost exclusively to the teaching and learning of language. This article by P. Ann Kaupp, along with an update by linguist Roger Shuy, demonstrates how linguists today often assist highly specialized practitioners in medicine, law, and education, as well as help all of us better understand that our everyday use of language affects our relationships, both at work and at home.

What do medicine, law, and education have in common? Each involves specialized communication between a practitioner and members of the general public, within a distinct social context. Each is, further, the subject of a new area of study: applied linguistic analysis.

In recent years the role of linguistics in anthropology has focused increasingly on the study of communication behavior and its relationship to the culture as a whole. This approach can be used not only to further the research interests of anthropologists but also to address and possibly resolve common, everyday problems in communication. New subfields in linguistic behavior have arisen, such as *sociolinguistics,* the study of the structure and use of language as it relates to its social setting, and *psycholinguistics,* the study of the structure and use of language behavior, how it is learned, produced, and understood. The application of studies of linguistics to real-life problems is the concern of *applied linguistics.* Traditionally, applied linguistics has dealt almost exclusively with language learning and teaching. Recently, however, its

focus has been expanded to other issues such as those described here, reflected in publications by Georgetown University linguistics professor Roger Shuy. Some of the latest applied psycho- and sociolinguistic communication research is taking place in the fields of medicine, law, and education.

LANGUAGE AND MEDICINE

Shuy points out that linguistic work on medical communication assumes that talk between patients and doctors has "deep clinical significance" (Shuy 1984:422). This research involves the analysis of "the speech event itself rather than the physician's interpretation of the patient's responses" (Shuy 1984:422–23).

The medical profession claims that 95 percent of treatment success depends on the physician's ability to elicit accurate information from the medical interview. Physicians' use of tenses, hedges, euphemisms, ambiguous adjectives, intensifiers, tag questions (questions that almost invariably influence the respondent to agree with the speaker's proposition, whether or not one wants to agree), and question-answering avoidance techniques influences patient behavior and can lead to misunderstandings between the doctor and patient that grow out of "differences in experience, needs, goals, and world knowledge" (Shuy 1984:424).

Shuy and his colleagues conducted research on cross-cultural communication problems of black inner-city patients and their physicians, analyzing their attitudes toward medical delivery service and the communication breakdowns that occurred in the tape-recorded interviews. They discovered that patients speaking vernacular English "worked very hard at learning the vocabulary, question response routines, and perspectives of their physicians during the interview, but that there was little, if any, reciprocal learning attempted or evidenced by their physicians" (Shuy 1984:423). In addition, the doctors' categories of questions "severely limited the patients' opportunities for providing adequate and even accurate information" (Shuy 1987:423). From more than one hundred taped interviews, they concluded that the tremendous asymmetry in such communication almost ensured misunderstanding and miscommunication.

According to Shuy, the impact of this recent linguistic research on medical communication has been meager. One reason may be that the field of medicine has not felt a particularly strong need for it (1984).

LANGUAGE AND THE LAW

Language in the Courtroom

The study of courtroom language ranges from the perceptions and evaluations of jurors to the actual language used by witnesses, judges, attorneys, and defendants, to the language of question asking, jury instructions, defendants' constitutional rights, and interpreter competence. One example of jurors' perceptions in the courtroom setting is an experiment carried out by a Duke University research team.

When a witness was permitted to respond at length with considerable freedom, that testimony (called "narrative testimony") elicited more favorable responses from jurors than did the more common courtroom style of highly controlled, brief answer testimony (called "fragmented testimony"). Interestingly, male responders believed that the attorneys who interrupted and talked over the witnesses the most were the most skillful and competent, while the female subjects disagreed, ranking such attorneys as less competent and less likeable (Shuy 1984:429).

One group of researchers studying witnesses' responses to the wording of an attorney's courtroom question found that answers to the question "About how fast were the cars going when they smashed into each other?" more consistently mentioned higher speeds than answers to the question, "About how fast were the cars going when they hit each other?" A week later, the subjects were asked whether they had seen any broken glass in the filmed accident

WITNESS RESPONDING AT LENGTH WITH "NARRATIVE TESTIMONY"

stimulus used in the experiment. Those who had been asked the question with "smashed" in it responded "yes" twice as often as those who had been asked the question with "hit" in it, even though the film showed no broken glass at all. This kind of research on the psychology of eyewitness testimony and memory is of great significance to both linguists and legal practice. It demonstrates, for one thing, that language form and content affect mental processes such as situation and memory of important details, and it strongly suggests that attorneys need to take into account lexicon, syntax, semantics, pragmatics, and social context in their litigation efforts (Shuy 1984:427).

Language as Evidence

Another area of linguistic study concerns the use of language as evidence. Secondary evidence from witnesses becomes less useful when jurors are able to hear tape-recorded, or primary, evidence, which is thought to speak for itself. The applied linguist, however, knows that a tape-recorded event is not the real event. Audiotape tells a great deal, but it tells little about how far away from each other the speakers were or, in fact, who was actually talking with whom. Although videotapes may give better evidence of speakers and distances, they may also provide misleading appearances (Shuy 1984:431).

For example, the many Abscam conversations videotaped in the rooms of the Marriott Hotel in Arlington, Virginia, were in black and white, which made the expensive rooms look "grimy, run-down, and dark" and thus gave support to the appearance of sleaziness that was advantageous to the prosecution.

Linguists assist attorneys in preparing their cases for trial and, in some cases, appear as expert witnesses in criminal and civil court cases. In one instance, a man accused of making a bomb threat during a telephone call to an international airline was acquitted when a linguist compared the speech on the tape-recorded call with that of the defendant and showed it to be a quite different dialect.

Indeed, when tape-recorded evidence is available, linguists play an important role in helping the jury understand the case. Linguists can help the jury determine who said what to whom, discern speakers' intentions from available clues in the tapes, and identify the conversational strategies of the speakers (Shuy 1984:432).

LANGUAGE AND EDUCATION

As a composition teacher for nine years at both the secondary and college levels, Roger Shuy realized that it was easier to edit student papers with such remarks as "monot." or "awk." than to explain why the papers read that way. Our educational preoccupation is with language forms (phonology, morphology, vocabulary, syntax) rather than with language functions (using language effectively in life functions such as requesting, denying, asserting). How people use language to get things done turns out to be a higher-order skill or competence than the simple mastery of grammatical forms.

As Shuy explains, our tradition of teaching reading, writing, and foreign languages has developed not holistically (taking into account both linguistic environment and social context) but in the opposite direction, from surface to deep, from form to function, from part to whole. We teach language, then expect people to use it. Recent studies on teaching English as a second language to adult foreign students demonstrates that learning improves when form follows function, when language is taught within the context of its practical use. An experiment consisted of control classes using traditional form-oriented teaching and experimental classes using the functional approach, in which students were involved in typical life situations. At the end of the year, the latter group was considerably ahead of the control group "not only on how to use the language to get things done (such as to complain, to request, to deny, to clarify), but also in sheer fluency and, most surprisingly of all, on skill in English forms (past tense, etc.) even though such forms were not directly instructed" (Shuy 1981:108–9).

Holistic language training also considers social contexts. For instance, the British Council's English for Special Purposes teaches adults in a work context. "Turkish mechanics are taught English through a curriculum which has as its content the topic of mechanics. Such an approach contextualizes the learning into the learner's world and frame of reference" (Shuy 1981:107).

Dialogue Journals

Large classes and the traditional emphasis on paying quiet attention and on taking turns can thwart the improvement of oral language ability. Classroom talk usually consists of question-answer sequences. Dialogue, on the other hand, is a natural learning device for language acquisition, which begins with the dialogue between parents and child. Efforts are being made to bring dialogue back into the classroom by way of dialogue journals between teacher and student. Dialogue journals are conversational in style and allow the teacher and student to discuss important topics. Unlike the classroom setting, dialogue journals enable the student to generate the topics for discussion.

Oral language research has shown that teachers in elementary classrooms talk about 95 percent of the time; this talk is divided about equally between asking questions, giving directions, and evaluating. In dialogue journal writing, however, Shuy found that these forms of teacher communication were cut almost in half. "The big difference, though, was in the type of questions asked. In the classroom, teachers ask test-type questions—ones that the teacher already knows the answer to. In their journals, teachers' questions were new, information-type questions, genuine requests for knowledge of something that only the students had" (Shuy 1987:894).

The following is an example from the dialogue journal of a second-grader having difficulty learning to read and to write in the classroom but eager to write to her teacher and to receive her responses:

> *Kelly:* I have problems some times well I have this problim it is I am not very god on my writeing.
>
> *Teacher:* I think you *are* a good writer. Keep on trying your best. I like the Little Red Hen, too, Kelly. Keep on writing!
>
> *Kelly:* Oh kay. Do you have a problem. if you do I will help you and what are going to be for Halloween.
>
> *Teacher:* I am going to be a farmer. . . . Everybody has problems, Kelly. Some problems are big and some are small. One of my small problems is I can't stop eating chocolate when I see it!

Language functions of predicting, evaluating, and complaining, which take more thinking and reasoning skills, increased from 3 percent in classroom talk to 23 percent in journal writing. In journal writing, students also increased by 50 percent the number of information questions they asked of the teacher (Shuy 1987:895).

Effective Complaints

Another important aspect of dialogue journal writing is that it provides the student an opportunity to complain, which is an important language function (Staton et al. 1988:143). Student complaining can be instructive for the teacher, providing important information about how students perceive what is going on, which in turn enables the teacher to determine what to reinforce, repeat, stop, supplement, or avoid. More important, says Shuy, complaining is a thinking process. Complaints can be true or false. But to be felicitous (or effective), they must be uttered sincerely, or rather the speaker must *believe* that the complaint is true.

In examining six sixth-grade student journals consisting of student-teacher exchanges for one school year, Shuy tallied 365 student complaints in three basic areas: academic concerns (134), student and teacher relationships (198), and personal matters (33) (Staton et al. 1988:149). Of the 365 complaints given, 167 were structurally felicitous ("with stated conflict, an account given and new information provided" [Staton et al. 1988:153]) and were convincing. The most felicitous complaints were those relating to student-teacher relations and personal matters. Although the students were at different stages of developing communicative competence in complaining, over the year they all found that their ability to produce a felicitous complaint had improved, and most even reduced the number of complaints (Staton et al. 1988:156).

Willy is an example of an effective complainer, one who mitigates his directness with positive evaluation. He has learned how to use the social skills of language effectively, with the aid of the following strategies: direct discontent, mitigation, indirect discontent, and positive evaluation. An excerpt from his journal reveals some of these characteristics.

> Feb. 29: I hope we don't keep studying about India to the end of the semester because truthfully I'm getting tired of studying about India every morning. I like studying about it and all but I think we are spending too much time on India and its getting kind of boring although I like making maps. (Staton et al. 1988:145)

Other Studies

Sex differences in classroom response are just beginning to attract the attention of researchers. As part of a linguistic study of a high school class, led by former U.S. Secretary of Education William Bennett, Shuy looked at male-female responses. He found male students responded more frequently than female students to the teacher's (Bennett's) questions and that males answering the teacher's questions were interrupted less (19 percent) by the teacher than were the females (27 percent) (Shuy 1986b:319).

Also noted were Bennett's responses to the student's answers. He gave four types of evaluative responses to their answers: negative, challenge, neutral, and positive. Of particular interest were his neutral and challenge evaluations:

> Neutral evaluations neither praised nor condemned. They usually took the form of "Okay" or "Alright," spoken with flat intonation. Bennett's challenges usually repeated the words of the student in a question intonation . . . indicating that part of the answer was right but not all of it, or he asked the student to say the answer in another way. (Shuy 1986b:322)

In fact, Bennett offered challenges only to male students and neutral evaluations only to females. Although aware that this is a limited study, Shuy asks if teachers do tend to challenge males more than females and if male teachers challenge males, while female teachers challenge females. These are questions that teachers as well as linguists ought to consider.

CONCLUSION

As Shuy (1984:439) states: "What is glaringly omitted in all three professions [medicine, law, and education] is the use of functional, interactive, self-generated language performance data as the major source of diagnosis and evaluation for medical service, legal evidence, and learning/teaching." As is clear from Shuy's update, however, some progress has occurred in more recent years.

The fact that there are common research methods that cut across as well as emerge from these linguistic studies may have encouraged a more widespread use of linguistic approaches in other professions, such as law, medicine, and teaching. These similar methods include: (1) a reliance on *direct observation* of the communicative event, (2) analysis of the *interactions* themselves, (3) discovery of the *structure* of the communicative event to obtain a holistic, contextualized perspective, (4) inclusion of the *perspective* of the patient, defendant, plaintiff, and learner as well, (5) use of *technology* (audio- and videotaping, for example) to capture and freeze the event, and (6) *construction* of meaning, referential and inferential, by the interaction of conversing participants (Shuy 1984:440). Shuy's research strongly suggests that if lawyers, doctors, and teachers would use linguistic studies more widely, they would better serve not only their professions but also their own clients.

UPDATE

Roger Shuy

The journey of linguists into related fields such as medicine, law, and education continues to be healthy some sixteen years after the preceding essay first appeared. New linguistic subfields and analytical routines have grown, such as discourse analysis and pragmatics, aiding the relationships greatly. But contemporary linguistic theory continues to be split between the generativist's focus on forms, universals, and the mind and the functionalist's focus on studying language holistically in context, accounting for its variability, its conveyed meaning, and its discourse structure.

This theoretical division has implications for education, since functionalists advocate immersion of language learners into environments with such approaches as "whole language," "dialogue journals," and "the writing process." Advocates of this holistic approach claim that learners should be immersed in natural communicative settings, noting that humans learn best when their learning is functional, self-motivated, and self-directed, not when it is imposed on them by out-of-context, direct instruction. They often cite the way infants learn language in context as a model for later instruction in literacy activities.

In contrast, generativists claim that humans have innate, built-in language-learning capabilities and that the role of biology in first-language acquisition tells us nothing about how literacy, second-language learning, or content are learned. In educational settings, this theoretical split has led some Massachusetts generative linguists to sign a petition against that state's standards embracing the whole-language approach to teaching reading, arguing instead for direct instruction in the phonics approach. But it is the federally mandated Education Act of 2001, more than the split between linguists, that has spearheaded the current move toward direct teaching and phonics instruction and away from such approaches as whole language. This battleground should be watched carefully (Gee 2001).

Other than this recent controversy, linguistic impact in the field of education in the 1960s and 1970s has abated considerably, perhaps because so few linguists have shown interest in native-speaker problems with reading and writing. They have turned their attention more to first-language learning, language teaching, testing, and English as a Second Language (ESL). Dialogue journals are now used commonly in ESL classes more than with native speakers. Attention is still strong on gender issues in education as well as in other areas, including medical communication and courtroom language.

In 1988 the impact of linguistic knowledge on medical communication seemed meager. Today, however, scholars who have endured the unenthusiastic responses of the field of medicine are beginning to see hopeful gains. Some medical training programs, such as the Rochester Medical School, now train future physicians in effective communication strategies. Schools of nursing, as might be expected, have shown much more interest in this issue. In addition, growing interest in the elderly and terminally ill has spawned ethnographic research in more effective communication across age groups (Hamilton 1994; Roberts 1999; Staton, Shuy, and Byock 2001).

The relationship between language and law has also grown considerably. The International Association of Forensic Linguistics was founded in 1994, producing a journal called *Forensic Linguistics*. There are now many books on various aspects of this field (see "Further Reading"). Criminal attorneys for both the defendant and the prosecution, as well as civil attorneys for both plaintiff and defendant, now commonly call on linguists to assist them with the language issues in their cases. It is clear that this area of applied linguistics is maturing nicely.

The area of applied sociolinguistics that seems to attract the most attention today, however, is gender-related studies, thanks mostly to the pioneering and effectively communicated contributions of scholars such as Deborah Tannen and Robin Lakoff. This field transcends the more particularized areas of medical communication, law, and education and has created renewed interest in issues such as language in the workplace, therapy, gender relationships, and the socialization of both men and women.

Other areas of applied sociolinguistics have also emerged in recent years. Geis has produced a useful book on the language of advertising and another on the language of politics. These areas appear to be emerging as important thrusts of the work of linguists and bear watching in the near future.

It has been said that there are two types of scholars: those who work on minute, theoretical issues and those who expose their work, like missionaries, to allied fields. In my opinion, it is unfortunate that the label "applied linguistics" has been limited only to first- and second-language learning and teaching. Although this is an important focus, there is far, far more territory to cover.

FURTHER READING

Berk-Seligson, Susan. 1990. *The Bilingual Courtroom: Court Interpreters in the Judicial Process*. University of Chicago Press.

Conley, John, and William O'Barr. 1998. *Just Words: Law, Language, and Power*. University of Chicago Press.

Gee, James P. 2001. "Educational Linguistics." In Mark Aronoff and Janie Rees-Miller, eds., *The Handbook of Linguistics*, pp. 647–63. Blackwell.

Geis, Michael L. 1987. *The Language of Politics*. Springer-Verlag.

Geis, Michael L. 1995. *Speech Acts and Conversational Interaction.* Cambridge University Press.

Hamilton, Heidi. 1994. *Conversations with an Alzheimer's Patient: An Interactional Sociolinguistic Study.* Cambridge University Press.

Hollien, Harry. 1990. *The Acoustics of Crime: The New Science of Forensic Phonetics.* Plenum.

Lakoff, Robin. 1990. *Talking Power.* Basic Books.

McMenamin, Gerald R. 1993. *Forensic Stylistics.* Elsevier.

Roberts, Felicia. 1999. *Talking About Treatment: Recommendations for Breast Cancer Adjuvant Therapy.* Oxford University Press.

Shuy, Roger W. 1981. "A Holistic View of Language Training." *Research in the Teaching of English* 15(2):101–11.

Shuy, Roger W. 1984. "Linguistics in Other Professions." *Annual Review of Anthropology* 13:419–45.

Shuy, Roger W. 1986a. "Language and the Law." *Annual Review of Applied Linguistics.* 7:50–63.

Shuy, Roger W. 1986b. "Secretary Bennett's Teaching: An Argument for Responsive Teaching." *Teacher and Teacher Education* 4:315–23.

Shuy, Roger W. 1987. "Dialogue as the Heart of Learning." *Language Arts* 64(8):890–97.

Shuy, Roger W. 1993. *Language Crimes.* Blackwell.

Shuy, Roger W. 1998a. *The Language of Confession, Interrogation and Deception.* Sage Publications.

Shuy, Roger W. 1998b. *Bureaucratic Language in Government and Business.* Georgetown University Press.

Shuy, Roger W. 2002. *Linguistic Battles in Trademark Disputes.* Palgrave.

Solan, Lawrence. 1993. *The Language of Judges.* University of Chicago Press.

Staton, Jana, Roger Shuy, and Ira Byock. 2001. *A Few Months to Live: Different Paths to Life's End.* Georgetown University Press.

Staton, Jana, Roger Shuy, Joy Kreeft, and Leslie Reed. 1988. *Dialogue Journal Communication: Classroom Linguistic Social and Cognitive Views.* Ablex.

Stygall, Gail. 1994. *Trial Language: Differential Discourse Processing and Discursive Formation.* J. Benjamins.

Tannen, Deborah. 1992. *You Just Don't Understand: Women and Men in Conversation.* Virago.

Tiersma, Peter. 1999. *Legal Language.* University of Chicago Press.

34 THE REPATRIATION MANDATE

A Clash of World Views

Tamara L. Bray

As archaeologist Tamara Bray explains in this article, "The central issue in the debate over repatriation revolves around the question of whether Native American interests in reburying ancestral skeletal remains should take precedence over the interests of archaeologists and physical anthropologists in studying and preserving them." The article offers a concise summary of the various arguments, issues, and perspectives highlighted by the repatriation debate. It also demonstrates why this debate might best be understood as a clash between competing value systems and world views of Native Americans and professional archaeologists and physical anthropologists.

More than a decade after legislation first thrust the requirement of repatriation upon the museum world, the issue continues to be of considerable importance in public and academic institutions across the United States. The term *repatriation,* as used here, refers to the legislatively mandated return of human remains and specific categories of cultural items housed in museums and other institutions to culturally affiliated Native American groups. The point of returning materials in most instances is for purposes of reburial, though with regard to sacred items, a concern with the cultural revitalization of specific groups is often involved. Categories of cultural items encompassed within the repatriation mandate include funerary articles, sacred objects, and items of cultural patrimony. *Funerary objects* are defined as items believed to have been intentionally placed with an individual at the time of death as part of a death rite or cultural ceremony. *Sacred objects* are defined as specific ceremonial articles that are needed by traditional Native American religious leaders for the practice of traditional Native American religions. *Cultural patrimony* is defined as communally owned cultural property that has an ongoing historical, traditional, or cultural importance central to a Native American group. Objects of cultural patrimony, by definition, could not have been legally alienated, appropriated or conveyed by any individual, regardless of whether or not that person is a member of a Native American tribe or Native Hawaiian organization (P.L. 101-601).

The repatriation mandate has frequently been described as the result of a clash of world views, the outcome of a head-on collision between diametrically opposed belief systems. It is worth noting, however, that the two belief systems involved are not equally weighted in contemporary society, since one pertains to a minority group, and that it took an act of Congress to move the scientific community to address the repatriation concerns raised by Native peoples. In the context of museums, repatriation has created a space where varied currents of history, science, and politics converge, and where the interests of museums, Native peoples, archaeologists, and physical anthropologists intersect. As such, repatriation constitutes a highly charged site where old relationships are being shattered and new ones forged.

For all parties involved, repatriation is an issue of considerable importance. In Indian country, there has been a groundswell of interest in and commitment to seeing the mandate for repatriation carried out. In the academic community, repatriation has had a profound impact on the way archaeologists and anthropologists go about their work in the United States. Within the museum world, repatriation has caused concern about the loss of collections and their accessibility. For both Native and non-Native people, human remains possess meaning. For many, if not all, Indian people, ancestral bones hold spiritual significance and power. For scientists, skeletal remains are meaningful sources of data that are highly relevant for biomedical research, for studies of the evolution of human disease, and for solving forensic cases. The physical anthropologists who study human remains have tended to treat them as depersonalized and desanctified, though they are nonetheless highly meaningful. The fundamental differences in these two approaches to human skeletal remains relate to differences in world view and value systems.

Repatriation may best be understood within the broader historical context of global decolonization (Bray 1996). It parallels and is on a continuum with other indigenous movements around the world in which Native rights are asserted. Among the concerns pressed are the right of control over one's own cultural heritage and the right to sanctity of the grave. Embedded within the repatriation movement are a number of fundamental issues that challenge our views of Native American peoples, call into question the "absolute" values of science, and force us to take a critical look at the role of museums in Western society.

HISTORY OF THE REPATRIATION MOVEMENT IN THE UNITED STATES

The roots of repatriation can be found in the historical context of the civil rights movements of the 1960s. During this period Native Americans, like other minority groups within the United States, gained newfound political influence and recognition. It was during the activist climate of this era that some Native people began to openly express strong opposition to archaeological excavations, the public display of American Indian burials, and the maintenance of permanent collections of Native American remains in museums.

The differential treatment of Native burials and the seeming disregard displayed by archaeologists toward them were seen by some in the Native community as powerful symbols of oppression and the pervasiveness of racist practices. In 1974, an activist group known as American Indians Against Desecration (AIAD) formed with the explicit intent of bringing political pressure to bear on the question of the return and reburial of Native American remains. The group argued that all Indians, past and present, are spiritually linked and, consequently, that modern Native peoples are responsible for the security of their ancestors' remains. They also argued that the removal and collection of human remains caused spiritual disturbances that could have a potential negative impact on the well-being of modern Indian peoples.

REPATRIATION LEGISLATION

Through the efforts of the AIAD and the widespread media attention that followed, the repatriation issue slowly bubbled to the surface of public consciousness and eventually captured the attention of several sympathetic lawmakers in the U.S. Congress. The first piece of legislation to treat this issue was the National Museum of the American Indian (NMAI) Act, passed by Congress in 1989 to establish a new museum. This act authorized the transfer of the Heye Foundation's Museum of the American Indian collections in New York City to the Smithsonian Institution. This incomparable collection of Native American ethnographic material was to become the core of the Smithsonian's new National Museum of the American Indian. The NMAI Act also mandated that all other Smithsonian museums inventory their collections of Native American human remains and funerary objects and make these items available for return to culturally affiliated groups. The idea that there must be a demonstrable relationship of cultural affiliation between the remains or objects in question and the tribal group to whom they would be offered for return was the cornerstone of this landmark legislation.

The Native American Graves Protection and Repatriation Act (NAGPRA) was passed a short time later, in 1990. This law expanded the repatriation mandate beyond human remains and funerary objects to include the categories of sacred objects and cultural patrimony. The act also extended the applicability of this mandate to all federally funded museums, institutions, and agencies. Because the Smithsonian Institution was already covered by the NMAI Act, it was exempted from NAGPRA. However, in 1996, Congress amended the NMAI Act, broadening the Smithsonian's repatriation mandate to include sacred objects and cultural patrimony and thus bringing it fully into alignment with NAGPRA.

The NAGPRA legislation had four provisions: (1) increasing protection for Native American graves and providing for the disposition of cultural remains inadvertently discovered on tribal and federal lands; (2) prohibiting traffic in Native American human remains; (3) requiring federal museums and institutions to inventory their collections of Native American human remains and funerary objects within five years of passage of the act and repatriate them to culturally affiliated tribes upon request; and (4) requiring museums to provide summaries of collections of Native American sacred objects and cultural patrimony within three years of passage and repatriate them if demonstrated that the institution did not have right of possession.

The Native American Graves Protection and Repatriation Act, like the National Museum of the American Indian Act, has been considered by many an important piece of human rights legislation for Native Americans. These acts also represent landmark legislation for museums insofar as they acknowledge that scientific rights do not automatically take precedence over religious and cultural beliefs in the United States. The passage of these laws represent the culmination of years of struggle for Native American groups and arduous negotiations with institutions holding collections of human remains and cultural objects. In essence, these two acts legislate respect for the dead. The acts serve to establish a new ethical outlook for museums in their relationships with Native peoples and other minority groups and provide a framework within which museums and Native peoples are developing new kinds of partnerships and collaborative relations.

ISSUES IN REPATRIATION

The central issue in the debate over repatriation revolves around the question of whether Native American interests in reburying ancestral skeletal remains should take precedence over the interests of archaeologists and physical anthropologists in studying and preserving them. From the outset, repatriation was portrayed as a controversy between museums, archaeologists, and anthropologists, on one side, and Native peoples, on the other. Discussion between the various parties affected was initially very polarized and often characterized in terms of science versus religion. Portraying the repatriation issue in this way had the effect of casting Native peoples as anti-science or anti-intellectual, playing upon and promoting existing stereotypes of Native peoples as "backward" or "primitive." To escape this kind of simplistic analysis, it is helpful to think of the controversy over repatriation as a clash between competing value systems rather than as a clash between science and religion. This requires a recognition of the fact that science is legitimately subject to criticism on the level of values as well as facts. Anthropology, archaeology, and science in general have their own agendas and their own particular politics, including a commitment to the notion of scientific and technological progress.

To better understand the positions and world views of the protagonists in the repatriation debate, it is important to consider the arguments and issues from various points of view. From the perspective of Native Americans, the main issues in repatriation revolve around the differential treatment of the dead, the lack of respect for Native beliefs and feelings, the treatment of people as objects of study, and the evidence of racist attitudes, as reflected in the disproportionate number of Native American remains given over to scientific study. From the professional community's point of view, the notion of repatriating collections for purposes of reburial is contrary to the most fundamental principles of museum preservation and academic scholarship. The loss of collections is seen as an irreplaceable loss of data for scientific and educational purposes. The different issues embedded in these two world views are discussed below.

NATIVE CONCERNS

1. Many museums, the popular media, and school texts present stereotypes of Indian peoples as foreign, vanishing members of a different race, distinct and apart from the rest of society. The generally held belief that Native cultures eventually would become extinct in North America was one of the original justifications for the collecting practices of museums and the work of anthropologists in the nineteenth century. Reburial is an important political issue on the Indian rights agenda in part because, by asserting their rights to protect the sanctity of their ancestors, Indian people assert that

they have not vanished, and that their beliefs and feelings are entitled to the same respect as those of other Americans.

2. Native Americans view the collections of Indian human remains housed in museums as disrespectful, racist, and colonialist. To many, the collecting of their ancestors' bones by museums is a source of pain and humiliation, the last stage of a conquest that had already robbed them of their lands and their way of life. As evidence, they cite museums' institutionalized treatment of Native Americans as objects of natural history, in which elements of their traditional lifeways are collected as "specimens" and the remains of their ancestors are treated like fossils. Native peoples ask what critical knowledge has been produced through the study of these remains. They also ask why museums need so many skeletal remains to study.

3. There is a question of differential respect for the sanctity of the grave. Native peoples ask why Euro-American burials that are accidentally exposed or uncovered are immediately reburied, while Native American burials are sent to museums or universities for further study. Indian arguments for the sanctity of the grave tend to be based on beliefs in the sacred nature of burials and a concern for the spiritual well-being of the deceased. Their concept of ancestry is a communal one that compels respect for the dead even in the absence of direct familial relations. The differences in attitudes between Euro-Americans and Native Americans may be seen to revolve around constructs of secular versus sacred with respect to the sanctity of the grave and to individual versus community responsibility to one's forebears.

4. There is the question of who controls the past and who has the right to interpret and inscribe history. Native peoples have, for the most part, been denied the ability to present their own past. There has been a general reluctance among scientists to accept different ways of knowing, understanding, or interpreting the past in any ways other than those offered by historians and archaeologists. This is related to the elevation of science as the supreme epistemology and the corresponding devaluation of other ways of knowing the world, such as through oral history, legend, and myth.

MUSEUM AND SCIENTIFIC CONCERNS

1. For many in the museum world, the notion of repatriating collections for purposes of reburial runs contrary to the most fundamental

principles of the preservation and increase of knowledge. It has been viewed as tantamount to the purposeful destruction of information. Museums are seen, by those who value them, as storehouses of knowledge and data preserved for study by future generations. Physical anthropologists note that the materials now in collections provide information on the history and descent of the people represented. They believe that new developments in the areas of DNA research, genetics, and chemical analysis may hold the key to such questions as the peopling of the New World, human origins, and the evolution of disease.

2. Scholars argue that archaeological finds constitute a part of the national heritage and hence do not belong to one special-interest group. Since all humans are members of a single species, and ancient skeletons are the remnants of nonduplicable evolutionary events, all living and future peoples have a right to know about and study these human remains. That is, ancient human skeletons belong to everyone.

3. Anthropologists argue that it was museums and museum personnel who were, in large part, responsible for the preservation of knowledge of Native American lifeways when Native cultures were on the wane or in the process of being systematically destroyed during the late nineteenth and early twentieth centuries. Museum people note, with no little irony, that in cultural revitalization movements, Native peoples have often recovered information on their heritage and traditions from the collections, archival records, and photographs of the very institutions they now criticize and oppose.

4. It has also been argued that it might be considered racist *not* to have collections of Native American remains in New World museums since such collections include non-Native American human remains from most other parts of the world. Such a situation would imply a lack of interest in the history of Native peoples of this continent.

POSITIVE OUTCOMES OF REPATRIATION

It is clear from the decade following legislation that laws cannot fully settle the issues surrounding repatriation. The murky language employed by the authors of the federal acts leaves a number of technical and philosophical questions unreconciled. These may prove to be intractable unless we are able to understand the repatriation issue within the broader social, political, and historical context of global decolonization. In the context of decolonization, the past forms a critical locus in the struggle to reconstitute cultural identities and culture histories that have been severely impacted by the relentless drive and destructive policies of the nation state. What we are witnessing today with the repatriation movement is a struggle for self-determination and control over cultural heritage. This struggle represents an effort on the part of indigenous peoples to reconstitute a collective cultural identity in the aftermath of severe colonial policies and practices.

While having a direct and profound impact on Native communities in this country, repatriation also can be construed as a step in the right direction toward improving relations among Native peoples, anthropologists, and museums. Repatriation legislation provides a framework within which to develop better lines of communication and foster greater understanding and dialogue between the different parties affected. The change in attitudes and values developing out of encounters based on the repatriation mandate has begun to lay a foundation for museums, anthropologists, and Native peoples to work together in a spirit of mutual cooperation and collaboration. Such a sea change in the manner of interaction between Indian people and museum personnel can be clearly documented in the decade-long history of the Repatriation Office at the National Museum of National History [see Billeck, "Museums and Repatriation: One Case Study," in this volume].

FURTHER READING

Bray, Tamara L. 1996. "Repatriation, Power Relations, and the Politics of the Past." *Antiquity* 70:440–44.

Bray, Tamara L., ed. 2001. *The Future of the Past: Archaeologists, Native Americans, and Repatriation.* Garland.

Bray, Tamara L., and Thomas W. Killion, eds. 1994. *Reckoning with the Dead: The Larsen Bay Repatriation and the Smithsonian Institution.* Smithsonian Institution Press.

Goldstein, Lynne. 1992. "The Potential for Future Relationships Between Archaeologists and Native Americans." In LuAnn Wandsnider, ed., *Quandaries and Quests: Visions of Archaeology's Future*, pp. 59–71. Center for Archaeological Investigations, Southern Illinois University, Occasional Paper no. 20.

Killion, Thomas W. 2001. "On the Course of Repatriation: Process, Practice, and Progress at the National Museum of Natural History." In Bray 2001, pp. 149–68.

Klesert, Anthony L., and Shirley Powell. 1993. "A Perspective on Ethics and the Reburial Controversy." *American Antiquity* 58(2):348–54.

Meighan, Clement. 1992. "Some Scholars' Views on Reburial." *American Antiquity* 57(4):704–10.

Ubelaker, Douglas H., and Lauryn Guttenplan Grant. 1989. "Human Skeletal Remains: Preservation or Reburial?" *Yearbook of Physical Anthropology* 32:249–87.

Zimmerman, Larry. 1994. "Sharing Control of the Past." *Archaeology* 47(6):65–68.

35 MUSEUMS AND REPATRIATION

One Case Study

William T. Billeck

Archaeologist William Billeck's article describing repatriation efforts at the Smithsonian's National Museum of Natural History since 1991 offers a case study of one of the most active repatriation programs in the country. How the museum has handled difficult and sensitive cases is detailed, along with the inspiring repatriation involvement of Connie Hart Yellowman, former Cheyenne-Arapaho Tribes Supreme Court judge and deputy director of the Cheyenne Cultural Center.

In August 1868, at Walnut Creek near Fort Larned, Kansas, a Cheyenne child died and was placed on a traditional burial scaffold near a recently abandoned Cheyenne Sun Dance lodge, together with a variety of offerings and remembrances. Soon after, U.S. Army soldiers tracking the Cheyenne came upon the site. They took the child's remains and accompanying burial objects and sent them to the Army Medical Museum in Washington, D.C., a practice encouraged by the Army Surgeon General of the time. The burial frame and grave objects were subsequently transferred to the National Museum of Natural History (NMNH). The child's remains have long since been lost. The 36 objects in the funerary assemblage accessioned into the NMNH included the burial frame, buffalo hides, beaded cradle covers, trade blankets and cloth, beaded bags, and several articles of clothing. (NMNH 1996:18)

Under the federal repatriation laws enacted in 1989 and 1990, museums throughout the United States must return Native American remains and burial objects in their collections to tribal groups with which they are culturally linked. In July 1993 the remains of over thirty

Cheyenne were returned by the National Museum of Natural History (NMNH) to the tribe and reinterred according to traditional burial practices. The Cheyenne repatriation and the reburial of the remains received widespread media coverage. Many other tribal representatives who have visited the NMNH Repatriation Office have seen the film coverage and newspaper accounts that documented the repatriation and consider it a model.

The story, however, did not end there. In August 1996, Cheyenne elders and repatriation representatives called a meeting of traditional and ceremonial leaders and tribal members to voice their concerns about repatriating the thirty-six burial objects from Fort Larned, Kansas, including the heavy trade blankets and several buffalo calf robes and hides. The items deposited with the child would have undoubtedly been highly prized given the circumstances of the times, with the Cheyenne tribe facing extreme hardship, deprivation, and the coming winter cold. The modern Cheyenne representatives knew these objects would be reburied or burned upon their repatriation to the tribe. Therefore, they questioned whether this act would be the best way to uphold their people's values and pass them on to the next generation. Connie Hart Yellowman, former Cheyenne-Arapaho Tribes Supreme Court judge and deputy director of the Cultural Center, expressed her sentiment this way:

> Think of the sacrifice that [the child's] burial represents . . . the Cheyenne couldn't go out and buy new blankets. Those things show how much our people loved that child. There's nothing I could do today to equal what they did for her. . . . I do not want to be part of the generation that is part of the destruction of these objects. For nearly 130 years, no Cheyenne saw [these objects]. And I've learned so much from them. A hundred and thirty years from now, this Cheyenne child's burial collection will continue to educate our people. (NMNH 1996:19)

On December 5, 1996, in a quiet, moving ceremony, Gordon Yellowman, on behalf of the Cheyenne and Arapaho tribes of Oklahoma, and museum director Robert W. Fri signed an unprecedented document stating that the "36 burial objects of Cheyenne origin in the Museum's collections are to be retained by the Museum for preservation, and for research and education to be conducted by scholars and the Cheyenne people." The agreement further stated that any publication of photographs or exhibition of the objects required the written consent of the designated Cheyenne representatives (see Bray 2001:245). The museum is currently working with tribal representatives on a proposed exhibit of the objects.

The Cheyenne story recounted at the beginning of this chapter is an unusual one, but each of the Smithsonian repatriations that have taken place in the last twelve years has had its own unique story. In 1991, soon after the first repatriation law was passed, the Smithsonian Institution established a

Repatriation Office at the National Museum of Natural History. Today the NMNH has the most active repatriation program in the nation. Of the museum's original count of approximately 32,000 sets of human skeletal remains, about half were Native American.

In the last several years, extensive information regarding these collections has been provided to the approximately five hundred federally recognized Tribes in the lower forty-eight states, three hundred Alaska Native villages and corporations, and Native Hawaiian organizations. Information on the human remains and archaeological objects were organized by state, county, and site location and consisted of object name, count, collector, date acquired by the museum, and tribal affiliation, when noted in the museum records. Information on the ethnological objects was organized by tribe and included object name, location, collector name, a brief background on the collector, and date acquired by the museum.

As outlined in legislation passed by the U.S. Congress, a tribe must submit a claim to the museum in order to initiate a repatriation. The Repatriation Office staff then conducts research using multiple lines of evidence, including biological, geographical, historical (both written and oral), genealogical, archaeological, linguistic, folkloric, ethnological, and archival. Expert opinion or any other relevant information can be used to evaluate the claim, and all the evidence is then summarized in a report. In order for the human remains to be recommended for repatriation, they must be culturally affiliated with the requesting tribe. Objects must also be affiliated with the requesting tribe and must fit the definitions of funerary object, sacred object, or object of cultural patrimony. The report that documents the repatriation assessment is sent to the tribal representatives and becomes part of the museum's permanent record.

REPATRIATIONS 1991–2003

To date, the human remains of approximately 3,600 individuals and thousands of objects have been offered for repatriation to eighty-four tribes. Forty-eight repatriations have been completed, resulting in the return of the remains of approximately 3,300 individuals to forty-eight different tribes. In addition, 87,000 archaeological objects have been returned to twenty tribes during thirteen repatriations, and 159 ethnological objects were returned to ten tribes in ten repatriations.

The remains of approximately three hundred additional individuals have been offered for repatriation to thirty-one tribes, and we await decisions by the tribes on how they wish to proceed. The museum currently has eighteen pending claims from thirty tribes to address. In the next year the museum will complete the reports that respond to seven of these claims, in which the repatriation status of 1,500 individuals and 20,000 archaeological objects are evaluated. As new claims arrive at the museum, they will be addressed in the order in which they have been received. The tribes have no deadlines to make repatriation claims; repatriation will continue into the future.

The Repatriation Office has hosted more than 250 visits by tribal representatives to the museum to discuss repatriation, to examine collections and records, and to repatriate human remains and objects. Sixty-four of the visits have been supported by grants sponsored by the outside Repatriation Review Committee. This review committee is an independent, congressionally mandated outside group of seven members (including two Native traditional religious leaders), which is advisory to the Secretary of the Institution, and monitors the repatriation activities of the Smithsonian, primarily at the National Museum of Natural History. The Committee also reviews repatriation disputes.

During the course of their visits to the collections, several tribal representatives expressed concern about the ways in which some sacred, religious, and ceremonial objects were stored by the museum. In response to these concerns, the museum now incorporates traditional care in the storage of objects. This may be as simple as changing the orientation of the object or rearranging the storage location so that associated objects are stored together and objects that should not be near each other are separated. Sometimes objects are smudged (traditional cleansing with smoke) and tobacco offerings placed with them.

THE ARMY MEDICAL MUSEUM COLLECTION

Most of the repatriation claims to date have been for the return of human remains, a large majority obtained during archaeological excavations. However, there are remains of individuals whose names are known; some of these remains come from a group of one hundred individuals killed during the Indian Wars, between the 1860s and 1880s. They were collected by army medical staff for the Army Medical Museum and transferred to the Smithsonian in about 1900. The Army Medical Museum collection continues to be one of great sensitivity. The collection contains about 2,300 sets of remains, many of which date to historical periods and are explicitly identified with regard to cultural origins. The Army Medical Museum was founded in 1862 to perform biomedical and pathological studies on the Civil War dead. At the close of the Civil War, the Army Medical Museum began collecting Native American skeletal remains. By the late 1890s, the museum stopped collecting Native American remains.

Because the Army Medical Museum collection has been of special concern and has special significance to some tribes, return of the remains from this collection has been made a priority. Museum policy prior to the repatriation law was that named individuals would be returned to lineal descendants, but in many cases, no lineal relatives were known. Lineal descendants still have first standing under the repatriation laws.

ISHI

One of the most prominent repatriations for a named individual at the Smithsonian involved Ishi, a Yana Indian from northern California, who was the last member of his tribe to come into direct contact with Euro-Americans in 1911. Ishi lived at the University of California's Anthropology Museum for a few years until his death in 1916. After his death, Ishi's brain was removed during an autopsy. Alfred Kroeber, an anthropologist who had worked with Ishi, considered him a valued friend and had wanted his remains cremated following Yana tradition. However, Ishi died while Kroeber was away on travel. When he returned, Kroeber found that Ishi had died and had been cremated, but his brain had been saved. Not knowing what to do in this unusual situation, Kroeber sent Ishi's brain to the Smithsonian in 1917.

Ishi was often referred to as the last Yana because many in California believed that with his death, the Yana ceased to exist. No family members who would have been able to make a claim for his remains as a lineal descendant are known. The affiliation study by the Repatriation Office found that, contrary to general opinion, the Yana had not ceased to exist with the death of Ishi. While Ishi was the last of the Yana to come into contact with Euro-Americans, there were many Yana who had come into contact with the outside world before Ishi, and these individuals had been placed by the United States government on nearby reservations. Today the Yana descendants live among the Pit River Tribe and on the Redding Rancheria in California. Ishi's remains were repatriated to these groups in 1999.

THE CHEYENNE CASE STUDY

The repatriation of Ishi is but one example of the thousands of human remains that have been repatriated by the museum, and all of them have their own histories. It is impossible to present them all here or even to summarize them. The repatriation experience of the Cheyenne, described at the beginning of this chapter, illustrates some of the potential of repatriation and the new ways in which museums are working with Native Americans. The

Cheyenne have been leaders in the repatriation process and are by no means typical in their repatriation experiences. Their tribal representatives are very interested in what museum collections reveal of their history and are concerned about the preservation of their heritage. The Cheyenne interactions with the museum have resulted in the repatriation of many human remains. But the positive relationships also have brought about changes in the storage conditions of significant cultural objects and development of alternatives to repatriation and reburial of objects.

For example, a buffalo skull used by the Southern Cheyenne in the 1903 Sun Dance ceremony in Oklahoma fits the definition of a sacred object and could have been returned to the tribe if they wished. Instead, because of its ceremonial significance, the skull was removed from exhibit upon the request of the Cheyenne Sun Dance priests. The Cheyenne representatives then elected to leave the skull at the museum because it is so fragile but asked that it be specially stored in an upside-down position. In consultation with Cheyenne tribal representatives, a special base was constructed by the conservation staff to support the skull. To cover the buffalo skull, a twelve-sided box with twelve painted panels that symbolizes the shape of the Sun Dance lodge is being designed by Cheyenne artist Gordon Yellowman, in consultation with the repatriation and museum staff. The buffalo skull now will be stored in the museum collections in a way that the Cheyenne representatives and Sun Dance priests have deemed appropriate.

FURTHER CONSULTATION

The Repatriation Office staff has become a source of expertise for tribal representatives to consult about the repatriation process beyond the Smithsonian. Often this may involve discussion of the law or the identification of the sources of archival records and expert opinion. The staff of the Repatriation Office has become very knowledgeable in assessing affiliation through the study of the skeletal remains. This expertise is available on a limited basis to tribal representatives if they wish an assessment of human remains that are not part of the Smithsonian collections. For example, Cheyenne tribal representatives have asked the Repatriation Office staff to examine for their cultural affiliation the skeletal remains of one individual believed to have been killed during the Fort Robinson outbreak in 1879 and two individuals from burials in Montana. These studies are ongoing, and the results will be used by tribal representatives in making decisions on how to proceed in the repatriation process.

Tribes have been considering the proper approaches to repatriation, and many only now are beginning to act. To date, nearly all of the repatriations have resulted in the reburial of human remains and associated funerary objects. From the museum perspective, repatriation has led to the loss of scientifically and historically significant collections, but it also has increased the positive interaction between Native Americans and the museum. Native Americans have shared their knowledge about the objects in the collections, particularly ethnological objects, and this knowledge has been added to the museum's records.

Repatriation now is a major contact point between tribes and the museum. It is an opportunity for both the museum and tribes not only to complete repatriations but to find common interests that can result in increased knowledge and educational opportunities. Museums also hold many Native American collections that will not be subject to repatriation. With much to learn about these collections, it would be a major loss to all if the interactions between museums and tribes ended at repatriation. Dialogues begun during the repatriation process should be the starting point for future positive relationships.

FURTHER READING

Bieder, Robert E. 1986 *Science Encounters the Indian: A Study of the Early Years of American Ethnology, 1820–1880.* University of Oklahoma Press.

Bray, Tamara L., ed. 2001. *The Future of the Past: Archaeologists, Native Americans, and Repatriation.* Garland.

Bray, Tamara, and Thomas W. Killion, eds. 1994. *Reckoning with the Dead: The Larsen Bay Repatriation and the Smithsonian Institution.* Smithsonian Institution Press.

Flynn, Gillian, and Deborah Hull-Walski. 2001. "Merging Traditional Indigenous Curation Methods with Modern Museum Standards of Care." *Museum Anthropology* 25(1):31–40.

Gould, Stephen Jay. 1996. *The Mismeasure of Man.* Rev. and expanded edition. W. W. Norton.

Killion, Thomas W. 2001. "On the Course of Repatriation: Process, Practice, and Progress at the National Museum of Natural History." In Bray 2001, pp. 149–68.

Loring, Stephen. 2001. "Repatriation and Community Anthropology: The Smithsonian Institution's Arctic Studies Center." In Bray 2001, pp. 185–200.

National Museum of Natural History. 1996. "Preserving Cultural Values: Respect for What the Past Can Teach Leads the Cheyenne and Arapaho Tribes of Oklahoma to Seek an Alternative to Repatriation." *Annual Report,* National Museum of Natural History. Smithsonian Institution.

Watkins, Joe. 2000. *Indigenous Archaeology: American Indian Values and Scientific Practice.* Altamira.

Yellowman, Connie Hart. 1996. "'Naevahoo'ohtseme'—We Are Going Back Home: The Cheyenne Repatriation of Human Remains—A Woman's Perspective." *St. Thomas Law Review* 9:103–16.

36 AGING

An Anthropological Perspective

Alison S. Brooks and Patricia Draper

In today's society, aging is an increasingly important topic, for researchers and the general population alike. This chapter reports on a long-term study of aging in several different societies, comparing the living conditions, concerns, and even the definition of the elderly—all of which are strongly conditioned by cultural values and societal variables. Both authors have done fieldwork over several decades among the !Kung (the Ju/'hoansi San) in Botswana and are able to bring the chapter up-to-date from their own personal experiences in a country that has long fascinated anthropologists.

Patricia Draper, anthropologist: What is one of the good things about being an old person?

!Kung informant, western Botswana: There is nothing good about being old. An old person can just sit and think about death. If you have a child who takes care of you and feeds you, you have a life.

Old age is often considered to be a unique biological characteristic of modern humans. Physical anthropologists tell us that, like most other mammals, our distant ancestors rarely if ever lived beyond their reproductive years. One evolutionary explanation for old age holds that females who lived longer but whose fertility was curtailed in later adult life were more successful at rearing their last-born children and may have contributed to the reproductive success of their earlier children.

Today, however, many of us live in societies that are grappling with the problems of the elderly and in which the elderly seem increasingly divorced from the productivity and success of everyday life. What are the similarities and differences between the lives of elders in modern, complex society and the lives of elders in more traditional, simple societies? Are there more elderly in our society than in others? Are the elderly in other societies happier or better cared for than in America? How old is "old"? What defines an old person? A middle-aged person? Is old age a good time of life? Are elders respected or given special status, and why or why not? What kinds of circumstances make for a happy old age or an unhappy one? These and other questions have given rise to a cross-cultural study of aging in seven locations.

THE CROSS-CULTURAL STUDY

Central to anthropology is a cross-cultural perspective that asks the question "How does the human experience differ from one society or cultural tradition to another?" As many times as this comparative question has been asked, researchers have had to grapple with the problem of which aspects of experience to compare across societies. In the United States, for example, older people value independence. They and their younger kin go to great lengths to arrange for the financial and residential independence of older people from younger kin. In many traditional societies, however, independence of the generations is neither valued nor a practical goal. Therefore, a cross-cultural study of how elders achieve independence in old age would be ill advised. Project A.G.E. (age, generation, and experience), described more fully below, attempted to avoid such pitfalls by investigating the meanings attached to old age by members of several selected communities.

Project A.G.E. is a long-term cross-cultural study of aging funded by the National Institutes of Health, through the National Institute on Aging, and directed by Christine Fry (Loyola University, Chicago) and Jennie Keith (Swarthmore College). This research project was designed to minimize the opportunity for Western or American assumptions about successful aging to be imposed on respondents in other culturally distinct communities. The study involves seven anthropologists and locations in five cultures: !Kung villages of northwestern Botswana (Patricia Draper); Herero agropastoralist villages of Botswana (Henry Harpending); four neighborhoods in Hong Kong (Charlotte Ikels); Blessington, Ireland, a suburb of Dublin (Jeanette Dickerson-Putman); Clifden, Ireland, an isolated seaside town in County Galway, Ireland (Anthony Glascock); Swarthmore, Pennsylvania, a suburb of Philadelphia (Jennie Keith); and Momence, Illinois, a small rural community a two-hour drive from Chicago (Christine Fry).

The seven communities were deliberately chosen to maximize diversity in the sociocultural variables of size, social complexity, economy, mobility,

scale, and technology, all thought to influence both the sense of well-being of the elderly and their participation in society.

The focus of the project is not simply to study aging but to understand how culture shapes the structuring of social roles across the life span. All researchers but one had previously carried out fieldwork as participant observers in the culture under study. Each researcher spent at least one year at the research site. Before any formal interviewing was done for Project A.G.E., each researcher spent several weeks in the community eliciting information about the vocabulary and semantics of age terminology so that the basic interview questions could be framed in terms comprehensible to the respondents. The plan called for 200 interviews at each location: 150 subjects evenly divided by sex and (adult) age category, and an additional 50 from the two oldest age groups. Questions about aging were phrased in such a way that differences in people's attitudes about aging (both within and between cultures) could emerge. Questions fell into five categories:

1. Terminology and differentiation: What do you call people of different ages, and how are they different? What are the best and worst aspects of each? What age group are you in?
2. Transitions between age groups: What happened to you to change you from your former age group to your present one? How will you know when you have moved into the next age group?
3. Feelings about age transitions: Do you like your present age? How do you feel about entering the next age group?
4. Evaluative questions about the age groups: In what age groups do you know the most or least people? What age group are you most comfortable with? What are the best and worst ages to be?
5. Past and future questions: Are you better off now than you were ten years ago? What do you imagine about your life five years from now?

PROBLEMS OF RESEARCH AMONG THE !KUNG

These and related questions were readily answered and yielded abundant interesting data in two American sites, in Hong Kong, in the urbanized Irish community (Blessington), and among the Herero. In contrast, the more rural Irish (Clifden) and the !Kung were alternately puzzled, irritated, and amused by the age questions. Many grew visibly anxious at not being able to provide answers. Since both the Irish and the !Kung are famous (at least in anthropological circles) for their talkativeness, this result in two independent communities was puzzling. The informants knew the researchers well and appeared comfortable with them, and great care had been taken to phrase the questions in the local idiom. Moreover, aging and senescence were familiar to every informant. What, then, accounts for the relative failure of this approach in these two sites?

What informants in these two communities share is a low salience of aging categories. That is, although age terminology may exist, people do not categorize or identify particular people by their age, nor do they readily generalize on the basis of age. For example, a !Kung informant was asked, "What do you call people of different ages?"

Respondent: Oh, they have all kinds of names. There's John, Sue, Jane, George . . .

Pat Draper: No, I mean, when people have different ages, how do you distinguish among them?

Respondent: Well, that's easy. Come on over here and I'll point them out to you. See, there's Jane, and Sue is over there. John isn't here now, but George . . .

In this society, personality, residence, sex, and health are more important than age in distinguishing individuals. From start to finish, interviews with the !Kung were like pulling teeth.

> *Pat Draper:* So, you say that for women you would use four age terms . . . young . . . middle-aged . . . elder . . . and aged. . . . For example, let's start with the young women. What is it about the young women that makes them alike? What do they have in common?
>
> *Respondent:* What do you mean alike? They're nothing alike! I've already told you that. Some of them are hard workers, others are lazy; some of them have children, others have no children. What makes you think they are alike? They are all different.

Throughout the study, informants failed to identify age as the key part of the questions.

> *Pat Draper:* If you were at your village one day, and there wasn't anyone to talk to, and you were sort of lonely, wishing for conversation, what age person would you most like/not like to have visit you?
>
> *Respondent 1:* Why would I be alone at the village? If I were alone, I wouldn't want anyone to visit me.
>
> *Respondent 2:* Well, I would prefer that someone I knew would visit me.
>
> *Respondent 3:* I don't like to be visited by a Herero.
>
> *Respondent 4:* Anyone who visits me is welcome. I don't refuse anyone! Children, old people, young adults, they are all welcome. If I have tobacco, we will sit together and smoke and talk.

Questions about how many acquaintances an informant had in each age group were unanswerable by !Kung informants, who have no indigenous system of counting above three and rarely use "foreign" number systems except for counting cows. The questions about past and future were defeated by the strong theme of empiricism and practicality in the !Kung world view.

> *Pat Draper:* If you could be any age you wanted to be, what age would you be?
>
> *Respondent:* It is not possible to change your age. How would that happen?

Questions designed to elicit cultural norms or individual feelings about moving from one age to another were also unsuccessful.

> *Pat Draper:* What happens, for example, in a woman's life to move her along?
>
> *Respondent:* Age, just age.
>
> *Pat Draper:* Is there nothing else you can tell me about what happens that makes the difference between, say, a middle-aged woman and an elder woman?

Respondent: Well, you see, it is the seasons. First it is winter and dry, then the rains come and then that season is past and then the winter comes along again. That is how it happens that you get older. Now do you understand?

In addition to these problems, the short question-and-answer format of individual interviews violated the normal rules of discourse among the !Kung. In their conversational style several people participate in turn, each speaking for several minutes. Nevertheless, a small number of informants (far below the target sample of 200) did become interested in the issues and provided interesting and informative data on this topic (see below).

PROBLEMS OF RESEARCH IN RURAL IRELAND

Like many communities in rural Ireland, the population of Clifden has been dramatically affected by emigration. If children are excluded, more than 25 percent of the population is over sixty, in contrast to 19.1 percent of the adult population of Swarthmore, another study site. In addition to questions of the type posed to the !Kung, residents of Clifden were asked to sort a series of cards on which were written a brief description: for example, "a widow who lives in a nursing home, with married children and grandchildren." Age was not mentioned on the cards, and respondents were asked to sort the cards into age categories and were asked questions about their categories. Over half of the respondents could not complete this task, since, as in the !Kung example, people rarely think of one another in age categories, and generalization based on age has a low salience. One Irish woman began to ask questions about a card that described a hypothetical person as "a married woman, daughter takes care of her and her husband, has great-grandchildren."

Respondent: Ah, about what age was she when she married? If she married quite young, she wouldn't be that old.

A. Glascock: I can't say; you have to use what is on the card.

Respondent: Well then, was her first child a daughter?

A. Glascock: I don't know; she is not a real person.

Respondent: How old was her daughter when she married?

A. Glascock: I can't say; all I know about her is what is on the card.

Respondent: Ah now, it wouldn't be possible for me to say who this person is without knowing something about her.

Respondents had little trouble naming "women living on Bridge Street" but experienced considerable difficulty in naming "older women living in Clifden." Questions such as "How does your health compare to other people of your age?" were answered in many cases by responses such as "I couldn't say, really. Everyone's different and there's no way to say just one thing." In addition, as among the !Kung, the standard questionnaire format violated the normal rules of discourse, which among the rural Irish is indirect and allusive. For example, the local people communicated in various behavioral ways the irritation they felt with the probing nature of the card sort: they moved away from the table, looked away, crossed their arms, or changed the tone of their voice. All these behaviors disappeared when the card sort and the interview were finished.

Despite methodological problems, such as the evident absence of a universal age category of "old" and the difficulty people in many societies experience in being asked to categorize people into age classes, the study has yielded interesting results.

AMERICA'S ELDERLY ARE NOT UNIQUE

In the United States, society's treatment of the elderly and the problems of elder care are prominent issues for politicians, community organizers, public health workers, authors, television producers, religious leaders, and even the courts. We often imagine that the problems of our society are unique: that we have more elders than ever before and that they are lonelier, more childless, more single, and therefore more dependent on strangers than in other societies. The study suggests, however, that the proportion of individuals over sixty (19 percent in Swarthmore, 30 percent in Momence) in the American study sites is not greater than in some of the other sites. In Clifden, Ireland, for example, more than a quarter of the adult population is over 65, and the proportion of elderly among !Kung and Herero adults is slightly larger than in Swarthmore.

Nor are Americans less likely to have children. In America we often hear that declining birth rates coupled with greater longevity have produced increasing numbers of old people with only one or no surviving child to provide care in their parents' old age. Yet here as well, Americans are not extreme. About 90 percent of the elderly men in the Swarthmore study and 82 percent of the elderly women had at least one child, in sharp contrast to the !Kung, among whom about 30 percent of the elderly were childless, although in the latter case, a number of parents had outlived their children—only 12–13 percent had never had a child. A similar pattern was observed among the Herero: 25 percent of elderly women were childless, but about half of these women had borne children who later died. In rural Ireland, more children survive but fewer adults have children. While only about 12 percent of elderly women were childless, fully 63 percent of elderly men had no offspring.

Americans also tend to think that the feminization of old age and the tendency for older women, in particular, to be unmarried or widowed is an artifact of demography and is universal. The A.G.E. study suggests that customs and values surrounding marriage have a greater effect than demography on the household composition of the elderly. Elderly people of both sexes in Swarthmore were as likely to be married as were the !Kung. For example, about one-quarter of the women and a smaller percentage of the men in each group were widowed. The !Kung value companionship in marriage and will remarry after the death of a spouse. Among the Herero, on the other hand, while three-quarters of the elderly *men* are married, three-quarters of the elderly *women* are single, widowed, or separated. In this society, marriage sanctified by the exchange of cattle is generally contracted between young girls and older men, who have the most cattle. Only 6 percent of the women never married, but widows do not remarry, and in any case, women do not look to their husbands for care or companionship. In Clifden, Ireland, in contrast, only about a quarter of elderly men *and* women are married. While over half of the elderly women are widowed, almost half of the elderly men (44 percent) in this community have *never* married. This phenomenon has been variously attributed to emigration and the absence of economic opportunity in a culture where men are expected to support wives and children. Unemployment among men is currently 35 percent and about three out of every five adults have lived overseas for at least one year.

It has been argued that the United States is such a mobile society that even if older people do have children, they rarely live close enough to be helpful. Among the !Kung, the Herero, and in Clifden, a large proportion (77 to 85 percent) of the elderly who had children had at least one living nearby. This proportion was somewhat smaller in Swarthmore, but of the Swarthmore elderly with children, about 60 percent had at least one child living in Swarthmore or within one hour's travel time. While child mobility is greater in the American sample than among the !Kung or Herero, it is even greater in the Irish sample. Many of the children of Clifden residents have emigrated and live abroad. The study found that 90 percent of the older people with children had at least one child overseas.

WHO CARES FOR THE ELDERLY?

In all the study sites, families, loosely defined, provide the majority of elder care, whether this is limited to economic assistance (provisioning) or extends to help with daily tasks. Yet both the definition of responsibility for elder care and the type of care expected differ markedly from site to site. In the United

States, elders expect to be financially independent, even when they need help with daily tasks. In rural Ireland, where so many of the elderly, particularly men, are unmarried or childless or whose children live far away, and where economic assistance is provided by the state, daily or occasional help with living tasks is often provided by collateral relatives such as siblings, nieces, and nephews, or simply by close neighbors. About one-quarter of the Clifden elderly have no close relatives at all in Clifden, and about a third of older men have only one close relative in the community, usually an older sibling. A third of the elderly in this community live alone. Among the !Kung, who have no government help or stored capital, food and other economic assistance, as well as help with daily tasks, are expected from adult children but may also be provided by other close relatives living together in a small village. The presence of two or more adult children was correlated with an increase in the life expectancy of elderly mothers but not of elderly fathers. Young children are not expected to care for the elderly on a regular basis. Because of remarriage, spouses are more available for care among the !Kung than among the Herero or Irish.

If demography accounts for all the differences in elder care, why are the elderly Herero, with their high rate of childlessness and large number of old unmarried women, not in trouble? Instead, the proportion of elderly Herero in the adult population, in general, and among women, in particular, is slightly higher than among the !Kung. Each Herero belongs to a cattle-holding lineage group, whose members are responsible for the economic well-being of its members. In addition, much as Americans and other societies derive great self-esteem from the care given to their children, a Herero draws more of his or her self-esteem from the care given to parents and older relatives. Since many elders are childless or have children away at school, young children are loaned or even fostered out to elders for the express purpose of providing care. Approximately 40 percent of all Herero children are reared by foster parents.

What happens when an elderly individual becomes frail and unable to care for himself or herself? In rural Ireland, behaviors that would signal an end of independent living in America—leaving the stove on, forgetting to turn on the heat, inability to drive, falling down the stairs, not recognizing friends and family—do not endanger the person or others to the same extent as in America. Houses do not have second stories, most older people do not drive in any case, and shopping can be done on foot. Neighbors and the community's visiting nurses make sure that the chimney has smoke coming out of it on a cold day. An old man who does not really recognize his surroundings might be escorted to and from the pub, where he will spend the day in a warm corner. Inappropriate behavior is explained as "He's a bit mental, you know."

ARE THE ELDERLY HAPPY?

One of the striking contrasts is the degree to which elderly Americans described themselves as happy, whereas the younger members of the American population were more negative in their self-evaluations. Americans place great emphasis on economic independence, and the elderly have this to a greater extent than the young and middle-aged. The elderly Irish of Clifden were also very happy with their lives, in part because they have a degree of economic security in the government dole, in part because they have access to good, almost free, low-tech health care. Two doctors and several visiting nurses make sure that every sick or frail individual is seen on a daily basis if necessary. The Clifden elderly also remember that life was much harder in this community forty to sixty years ago, when they were young. The !Kung elderly, in contrast, rated their quality of life low, but only slightly less than the self-ratings of the middle-aged. Old Herero were at the opposite end of the scale in describing their age in the most pessimistic terms of any age group, despite what an outsider might see as a very high level of social support. In a somewhat rosy view of an imagined past in which old age was happily spent in the bosom of one's family, we tend to forget that modern society has mitigated many of the real discomforts of the elderly. The good to excellent level of social support routinely available in the two African sites cannot begin to compensate for the absence of furniture, mattresses, running water, central heat, antibiotics, eyeglasses, Tylenol, and false teeth.

A source of unhappiness in the American communities, but less so in Ireland or among the Herero or !Kung, was the degree to which American elderhood is marked by abrupt transitions, such as retirement or change of residence in order to be in a more manageable house or nearer to a child. Elders in the other societies more often continued their adult patterns of work, residence, and social interaction into elderhood. The abrupt transitions that mark elderhood in America, and which are less pronounced in a rural community such as Momence, are in part a corollary of the economic independence and wealth of elders. If private housing were uncommon and economic interdependence the norm, elders would find it easier to get help without compromising their cultural values.

THE A.G.E. PROJECT

The comparison of aging in seven locations has demonstrated that the living conditions and concerns of the elderly, and even the definition of the category "elderly," are strongly conditioned by cultural values and societal variables. Very different networks have been developed for caregiving in each society. The relatively high status of elderhood in some societies (e.g., in China, or among the Herero, where the elders nominally control the ownership and disposition of lineage cattle) does not appear to be correlated with happiness among the elderly. Though elders in more traditional societies are more likely to remain situated in supportive families and familiar communities, they feel keenly the physical losses of aging under circumstances in which there are few cushions or prostheses to ease their discomforts. Indeed, there is a fine irony in the finding that traditional and modern societies satisfy different and mutually exclusive goals of the elderly: social connectedness in traditional societies and freedom from physical discomfort in more modern societies.

UPDATE

Much of this chapter reported on Project A.G.E., a long-term cross-cultural study of aging directed by anthropologists Christine Fry and Jennie Keith. The study involved multiple anthropologists and multiple sites in four different countries: Botswana (including both the !Kung and Herero cultures), Hong Kong, Ireland, and the United States. The article focused on findings primarily among the !Kung, in rural Irish communities, and among Americans in several United States communities. Since this article first appeared in *AnthroNotes*, Project A.G.E. and its associated studies have generated many publications, now reflected in the updated bibliography (see in particular Dickerson-Putman 1997; Dickerson-Putman and Brown 1998; Draper and Keith 1992; Draper and Hames 2000; Howell 2000; and Keith, Fry, and Glascock 1994). The citations to Dickerson-Putman are about Ireland and are derivative of her work there; the citation to Draper and Hames is about the importance of sibling ties among !Kung middle-aged and elderly adults.

In Ireland, membership in the European Union brought about a vibrant new economy that is keeping young people at home rather than their emigrating abroad, as they had since the 1840s. If this trend continues, in time it will dramatically increase the number of grandchildren potentially caring for an elderly parent.

The !Kung of Botswana and Namibia are doing reasonably well. Eastern Namibia continues to be plagued by frequent and severe drought. Government supplied medical services provide infant immunizations, maternal care, and basic treatment for communicable diseases. Malaria can be a serious health threat in the rare years of heavy rains. However, in Botswana, the local health clinic personnel distribute antimalarials and also provide follow-up treatment for tuberculosis patients when they return to the region after having completed intensive treatment in hospitals in the distant regional administrative center of Maun.

The Botswana government also provides for periodic distribution of drought relief foods, ensuring that the health of the population is not severely threatened. Deep borehole wells now are more common in the area, and this means that more people have access to clean drinking water. During the 2000–01 cattle lung disease epidemic, the Botswana government slaughtered all the cattle in the north to contain the disease, so there are very few cattle there today. In mid-July 2002, a formal border crossing between Namibia and Botswana was opened in the north at Dobe. This change will bring greatly increased traffic—commercial, tourist, and administrative—into the remote parts of Botswana that previously were visited by relatively small numbers of outsiders. While many adults died in the TB epidemics of the 1970s and 1980s, settlements continue to include a healthy mix of elderly grandparents, parents, and children.

The !Kung are coping with rapid change on many fronts, social as well as economic [see Fisher, "Ethnoarchaeology Among the Efe: African Hunter-Gatherers," in this volume]. There are encouraging signs of ethnic resilience in the face of these challenges. The !Kung are forming interest groups for the purpose of lobbying both governmental and nongovernmental organizations to secure better representation and better understandings of the problems faced by people of their unique historical and cultural background. Both Namibia and Botswana are representative democracies, and there is some reason to hope that the spirit and well-being of the !Kung will be preserved, even as their lifestyle and subsistence practices change.

The most serious threat of all to the future of the !Kung is the high rate of HIV infection existing along the edges of the Kalahari. In the urban areas of Botswana, where most people live, the HIV infection rate in women was almost 50 percent in 2002. Many young women and their children die every day, leaving old people to look after the babies with no one to take care of them as they age. Only education and massive international efforts can stem the tide of this horrendous epidemic.

FURTHER READING

Biesele, Megan. 1995. "Human Rights and Democratization in Namibia: Some Grassroots Political Perspectives." *African Rural and Urban Studies* 1(2):49–72.

Biesele, Megan, and Robert K. Hitchcock. 2000. "The Ju/'hoansi San Under Two States: Impacts of the South West African Administration and the Government of the Republic of Namibia." In Peter P. Schweitzer, Megan Biesele, and Robert Hitchcock, eds., *Hunters and Gatherers in the Modern World: Conflict, Resistance, and Self-Determination*, pp. 305–26. Berghahn.

Blurton Jones, N. G., K. Hawkes, and P. Draper. 1994. "Differences Between Hadza and !Kung Children's Work: Original Affluence or Practical Reason?" In E. S. Burch, ed., *Key Issues in Hunter Gatherer Research*, pp. 189–215. Berg.

Blurton Jones, Nicholas G., Kristen Hawkes, and Patricia Draper. 1994. "Foraging Returns of !Kung Adults and Children: Why Didn't !Kung Children Forage?" *Journal of Anthropological Research* 50:217–48.

Dickerson-Putman, Jeannette. 1997. "History, Community Context and the Perception of Old Age in a Rural Irish Community." In Sokolovsky 1997, pp. 364–73. 2nd ed. Bergin and Garvey.

Dickerson-Putman, Jeannette, and Judith K. Brown, eds. 1998. *Women Among Women: Anthropological Perspectives on Female Age Hierarchies*. University of Illinois Press.

Draper, Patricia. 1997. "Institutional, Evolutionary, and Demographic Contexts of Gender Roles: A Case Study of !Kung Bushmen." In M. E. Morbeck, A. Galloway, and A. Zihlman, eds., *The Evolving Female*, pp. 220–31. Princeton University Press.

Draper, Patricia. 1999. "Room to Maneuver: !Kung Women Cope with Men." In D. A. Counts, J. K. Brown, and J. C. Campbell, eds., *To Have and to Hit: Cultural Perspectives on Wife Beating*, pp. 53–72. University of Illinois Press.

Draper, Patricia, and Anne Buchanan. 1992. "If You Have a Child You Have a Life: Demographic and Cultural Perspectives on Fathering in Old Age in !Kung Society." In Barry S. Hewlett, ed., *Father-Child Relations: Cultural and Biosocial Contexts*, pp. 131–52. Aldine de Gruyter.

Draper, Patricia, and Henry C. Harpending. 1994. "Work and Aging in Two African Societies: !Kung and Herero." In Bette R. Bonder and Marilyn B. Wagner, eds., *Functional Performance in Older Adults*, pp. 15–27. F. A. Davis.

Draper, Patricia, and Raymond Hames. 2000. "Birth Order, Sibling Investment and Fertility Among the Ju/'hoansi (!Kung)." *Human Nature* 11(2):117–56.

Draper, Patricia, and Jennie Keith. 1992. "Cultural Context of Care: Family Caregiving for Elderly in America and Africa." *Journal of Aging Studies* 6(2):113–33.

Fry, Christine L., and Jennie Keith, eds. 1986. *New Methods for Old-Age Research: Strategies for Studying Diversity*. Bergin and Garvey.

Howell, Nancy. 2000. *Demography of the Dobe !Kung*. 2nd ed. Aldine de Gruyter.

Keith, Jennie, Christine L. Fry, and Anthony P. Glascock. 1994. *The Aging Experience: Diversity and Commonality Across Cultures*. Sage.

Sokolovsky, Jay, ed. 1997. *The Cultural Context of Aging: Worldwide Perspectives*. 2nd ed. Bergin and Garvey.

CONTRIBUTORS

Catherine J. Allen is professor of anthropology at the George Washington University, specializing in art, symbolism, and religion, as well as South American cultures. She received her Ph.D. at the University of Illinois, Urbana, in 1978. She is coauthor of a research-based play, teaches Anthropology in Performance, and is writing a book on expressive strategies in Andean storytelling.

JoAllyn Archambault (Standing Rock Sioux) is the director of the American Indian Program in the Department of Anthropology at the Smithsonian's National Museum of Natural History. She received her Ph.D. from the University of California, Berkeley, in 1984. She has conducted research on American Indian art, Indian women, the Plains Sun Dance, and Indian-white relations.

George J. Armelagos is professor of anthropology at Emory University and former president of the American Association of Physical Anthropologists. He received his Ph.D. from the University of Colorado in 1968. His research has focused on diet and disease in human adaptation.

Kathleen C. Barnes is an instructor at the Johns Hopkins Center for Asthma and Allergy in Baltimore, Maryland. She received her Ph.D. in anthropology from the University of Florida, Gainesville, in 1992. Her interests include health and disease in the Caribbean.

William T. Billeck is the program manager of the Repatriation Office of the National Museum of Natural History, Smithsonian Institution, where he has worked since 1994. He received his Ph.D. at the University of Missouri in 1993. His research interest is in North American archaeology, with specific concentrations on seventeenth- through nineteenth-century Native American and European fur trade archaeological sites in the Plains area of the United States and glass trade bead studies.

Tamara L. Bray is associate professor of anthropology at Wayne State University in Detroit, Michigan. She received her Ph.D. from the State University of New York, Binghamton, in 1991 and served as a case officer for the National Museum of Natural History's Repatriation Office from 1991 to 1995. She is the editor of two books and author of several articles on the subject of repatriation. Her research interests include Andean archaeology, the politics of the past, and contemporary Native American issues.

Alison S. Brooks is Distinguished Columbian Professor at the George Washington University, where she serves as chair of its Anthropology Department. She also is a research associate at the Smithsonian Institution. She received her Ph.D. in anthropology from Harvard University in 1979. She has published on topics in palaeoanthropology as well as the ethnoarchaeology of Botswana's San people. She has conducted field research in the Middle East, Scandinavia, France, China, and Africa. She was principal investigator of the George Washington University/Smithsonian Institution Anthropology for Teachers Program funded by the National Science Foundation and is an *AnthroNotes* editor.

Mark N. Cohen is a Distinguished Teaching Professor in the Department of Anthropology at the State University of New York, Plattsburgh, and a recipient of the SUNY Chancellor's Award for excellence in scholarship. He received his Ph.D. in anthropology from Columbia University in 1971. He has conducted field research in South America, Central America, Europe, and North America and has written about human populations and ecology.

Tom D. Dillehay is the T. Marshall Hahn Jr. Professor of Anthropology at the University of Kentucky, Lexington. He received his Ph.D. at the University of Texas, Austin, in 1976. He has taught at several universities in Europe, the United States, and South America; his current research interests include complex societies and prehistoric urbanization.

Patricia Draper is professor of anthropology in the Department of Anthropology and Geography at the University of Nebraska, Lincoln. She received her Ph.D. in anthropology from Harvard University in 1972. Her academic interests include cultural anthropology, cross-cultural studies of aging and adult development, evolutionary ecology, hunter-gatherers, and Africa.

John W. Fisher Jr. is associate professor of anthropology in the Department of Sociology and Anthropology at Montana State University, Bozeman. He received his Ph.D. in anthropology in 1987 from the University of California, Berkeley. In addition to teaching, Fisher conducts archaeological research in Montana and ethnoarchaeological research in Africa, and he is involved in public archaeology throughout Montana.

William W. Fitzhugh is currently chair of the Department of Anthropology as well as curator of Arctic archaeology and director of the Arctic Studies Center at the Smithsonian Institution's National Museum of Natural History. He received his Ph.D. from Harvard in 1970. A specialist in circumpolar anthropology and archaeology, he has spent more than thirty years conducting fieldwork and organizing large exhibitions focused on Arctic peoples and cultures in Canada, Alaska, and Siberia.

Carolyn Fluehr-Lobban is professor of anthropology and the director of general education at Rhode Island College, Providence. During spring 2003 she was NEH Professor of the Humanities at Colgate University. She received her Ph.D. from Northwestern University in 1973. She has conducted research in three different North African Muslim countries—Sudan, Egypt, and Tunisia—and specializes in Islamic law, women's rights, and movements against extremism in Islam.

Loretta Fowler is professor of anthropology at the University of Oklahoma. She received her Ph.D. from the University of Illinois in 1970. Her research interests include sociocultural anthropology, historical anthropology, politics, aging, and gender, as well as Plains Indian history and culture change.

Diane Gifford-Gonzalez is professor of anthropology at the University of California, Santa Cruz. She received her Ph.D. in anthropology in 1977 from the University of California, Berkeley. For three decades she has worked as a zooarchaeologist in Kenya and Tanzania, investigating early African pastoralists. In the last ten years, she also has developed research interests in colonial New Mexico.

Kathleen D. Gordon is a physical anthropologist employed by the Smithsonian Institution's National Museum of Natural History as an exhibit developer. She received her Ph.D. from Yale University in 1980. Her research interests and publications focus on paleoanthropology, primate and early hominid feeding behavior, and prehistoric human subsistence and nutrition.

Roy Richard Grinker is professor of anthropology and international affairs at the George Washington University. He received his Ph.D. from Harvard in 1989. He has conducted fieldwork in and published books about the cultural history of the Democratic Republic of the Congo and Korea. He also wrote a biography of the ethnologist Colin Turnbull, author of *The Forest People*.

Thomas D. Holland is the scientific director of the U.S. Army Central Identification Laboratory, Hawai'i (CILHI), where he has worked since 1992. He obtained his Ph.D. from the University of Missouri in 1991. He is a board-certified forensic anthropologist with research interests in evolutionary archaeology and site taphonomy and serves on several international advisory boards.

Robert L. Humphrey provided all cartoon illustrations for *AnthroNotes* from 1979 until his untimely death in 2002. He received his B.A. in art history from American University, Washington, D.C., and his Ph.D. in anthropology from the University of New Mexico in 1970. He conducted archaeological research in northern Alaska, the American Southwest, Mexico and Central America, and the Potomac Valley. In 1967 he began teaching anthropology at the George Washington University and directed the University Summer Field Programs in Mesoamerican archaeology, ecology, and history. He founded the Museum Studies Program at the university and was its first director as well as chair of the Anthropology Department for twelve years. In 1990 he published a book of cartoons, *The Last Elephant,* with the Smithsonian's National Zoological Park. He began cartooning in the 1950s, and his work appeared in *Zoogoer, Faces,* and *Politics,* as well as *AnthroNotes.* He also had several one-person art shows exhibiting the range of his multimedia work.

Fatimah L. C. Jackson is professor of anthropology and Distinguished Scholar-Teacher at the University of Maryland. She received her Ph.D. in biological anthropology from Cornell University in 1981. Her areas of research include metabolic and genomic effects of exposure to plant phytochemicals, biological diversity in contemporary and ancient African peoples, and bioanthropological perspectives on human disease.

Adrienne L. Kaeppler is curator of oceanic ethnology in the Smithsonian's Department of Anthropology, National Museum of Natural History. She received her Ph.D. from the University of Hawai'i in 1967. She has carried out fieldwork in Tonga, Hawai'i, Easter Island, and other parts of the Pacific, with a research focus on the interrelationships between social structure and the arts, especially dance, music, and the visual arts.

P. Ann Kaupp is head of the Smithsonian Institution's Anthropology Outreach Office and managing editor of *AnthroNotes.* She received a B.A. in anthropology from the George Washington University, where she did graduate studies in anthropology. She has worked in the Smithsonian's Department of Anthropology since 1978 and has organized teacher workshops on American Indians and archaeology, attended by educators from throughout the country.

Richard Kurin is director of the Smithsonian Center for Folklife and Cultural Heritage where he oversees the Smithsonian Folklife Festival and Smithsonian Folkways Recordings. He received his Ph.D. in anthropology in 1981 from the University of Chicago. He has conducted most of his fieldwork in India and Pakistan.

JoAnne Lanouette is chair of the English Department at the Sidwell Friends School, Washington, D.C., where she has taught since 1984. She received her B.S. in English and education from the University of Minnesota and an M.A. in anthropology from the George Washington University. She was the principal faculty member of the George Washington University/Smithsonian Institution Anthropology for Teachers Program from 1978 to 1983 and has been an editor of *AnthroNotes* since its inception, along with Alison S. Brooks, P. Ann Kaupp, and Ruth O. Selig.

Robert M. Laughlin is curator of Mesoamerican ethnology in the Department of Anthropology at the Smithsonian's National Museum of Natural History. He received his Ph.D. in anthropology from Harvard University in 1963. His research focuses on the ethnology, history, and linguistics of the Tzotzil and Tzeltal Maya of Chiapas, Mexico.

James Lin majored in anthropology and human biology at Emory University and is interested in health policy research.

Marilyn R. London is a research collaborator in physical anthropology in the Smithsonian's Department of Anthropology. She received a B.A. in anthropology at the George Washington University and an M.A. in biological anthropology at the University of New Mexico. She is the forensic anthropology consultant for the State of Rhode Island's Office of Medical Examiners. During 1994–95, with Ann Kaupp on leave, she ran the Department of Anthropology's Outreach Office and served as an editor of *AnthroNotes*.

Stephen C. Lubkemann is assistant professor of anthropology at the George Washington University and adjunct assistant professor of research at the Watson Institute for International Studies at Brown University. He received his Ph.D. in anthropology from Brown University in 2000. He has worked with the Humanitarianism and War Project and served as a member of the first National Academy of Sciences Roundtable on Forced Migration. His current research focuses on the social and demographic effects of displacement.

Robert W. Mann has spent the last ten years at the U.S. Army Central Identification Laboratory, Hawai'i (CILHI), where he is the senior forensic anthropologist. Prior to this work, he spent several years working in the Smithsonian's Division of Physical Anthropology. He received his Ph.D. in anthropology from the University of Hawai'i in 2001. His research interests include skeletal trauma, bone disease, and human skeletal variation.

David W. McCurdy is a professor emeritus of anthropology at Macalester College in St. Paul, Minnesota, where he served as chair of his department for more than a decade. He received his Ph.D. from Cornell University in 1964. He is coeditor of the widely used *Conformity and Conflict: Readings in Cultural Anthropology* and served as treasurer and president of the General Anthropology Division within the American Anthropological Association. He continues to serve as coeditor of the American Anthropological Association publication *General Anthropology.*

William L. Merrill is curator of North American ethnology in the Smithsonian's Department of Anthropology, National Museum of Natural History. He received his Ph.D. in anthropology in 1981 from the University of Michigan. Merrill's principal interests are religion, historical anthropology, ideology, social organization, and material culture of Native American societies, particularly in northern Mexico and the southwestern United States. Since 1977 his research has focused on the culture and history of the Ralámuli people of Chihuahua, Mexico.

Rick Potts is curator of physical anthropology and director of the Human Origins Program in the Department of Anthropology at the Smithsonian's National Museum of Natural History. He received his Ph.D. from Harvard University in 1982. An internationally recognized authority on human evolution, Potts has conducted long-term excavations in East Africa and more recently in China.

Boyce Rensberger directs the Knight Science Journalism Fellowship program at the Massachusetts Institute of Technology. This program allows journalists to spend a sabbatical year studying science. Before going to MIT, Rensberger was for thirty-two years a science writer or science editor, mainly for newspapers, including the *New York Times* and the *Washington Post*. He has written four books, most recently *Life Itself: Exploring the Realm of the Living Cell.*

Jeremy A. Sabloff is Williams Director of the University of Pennsylvania Museum of Archaeology and Anthropology. He received his Ph.D. from Harvard University in 1969. His research and writings have focused on ancient

Maya civilization, settlement pattern studies, preindustrial urbanism, the history of archaeology, and archaeological theory and method.

Enid Schildkrout is curator in the Division of Anthropology, American Museum of Natural History, New York, and adjunct professor at Columbia University. She received her Ph.D. from Cambridge University in 1970. Her work focuses on ethnicity, women and children in West Africa, and African art. At the American Museum of Natural History, she curated the 1999–2000 exhibition *Body Art: Marks of Identity*.

Ruth Osterweis Selig, editor of *AnthroNotes,* has held several senior administrative positions at the Smithsonian Institution, where she is currently the special assistant to the director of the National Museum of Natural History. After her formal eduction in history (Wellesley B.A.), social science teaching (Harvard M.A.T.), and anthropology (George Washington M.A.), she taught English and anthropology to high school and college students before coming to the Smithsonian to develop an anthropology outreach office and direct joint university/museum NSF- and NEH-funded anthropology teacher training programs in Washington (with Alison S. Brooks) and Wyoming.

Roger W. Shuy is Distinguished Research Professor of Linguistics Emeritus at Georgetown University, where he created the Sociolinguistics Program in 1970. He received his Ph.D. from Case Western Reserve University in 1962. His research and publications span a broad area of applied linguistics, including regional and social dialects, classroom language, literacy, medical communication, and forensic linguistics.

Theresa A. Singleton is associate professor of anthropology at Syracuse University. She received her Ph.D. in anthropology from the University of Florida in 1980. Her research focuses on historical archaeology, with an emphasis on the archaeology of the African diaspora. She is presently undertaking an archaeological study of slavery on coffee plantations in Cuba.

Bruce D. Smith is the director of the Archaeobiology Program in the Department of Anthropology at the Smithsonian's National Museum of Natural History. He received his Ph.D. from the University of Michigan in 1973. A recently elected member of the National Academy of Sciences, Smith continues to do research on the origins of agriculture in the Americas.

Dennis J. Stanford is head of the PaleoIndian Program in the Department of Anthropology at the Smithsonian's National Museum of Natural History and past chair of the department. He received his Ph.D. in anthropology from the University of New Mexico in 1972. He has done extensive field research in Colorado, Wyoming, and Alaska.

William C. Sturtevant is curator of North American ethnology in the Department of Anthropology at the Smithsonian's National Museum of Natural History and general editor for the encyclopedic *Handbook of North American Indians*. He received his Ph.D. in anthropology from Yale University in 1955. His research interests include the ethnography and ethnohistory of eastern North American Indians (especially the Seminole and Seneca), the history of stereotypes of North American Indians, and European and Euro-American visual depictions of Native Americans before 1860.

Robert W. Sussman is professor of anthropology at Washington University, St. Louis, and former editor-in-chief of *American Anthropologist*, the journal of the American Anthropological Association. He received his Ph.D. in anthropology from Duke University in 1972. His research focuses on the behavior, ecology, evolution, and conservation of human and nonhuman primates, and he has conducted research in Madagascar, Mauritius, Central America, and South America.

John W. Verano is associate professor of anthropology at Tulane University. He received his Ph.D. in anthropology from the University of California, Los Angeles, in 1987 and since 1983 has twice served as a Fulbright Lecturer in Peru. A physical anthropologist, he has conducted field and museum research focusing on the health, demography, and mortuary practices of prehistoric Peruvian populations.

Stephen Williams is Peabody Professor of American Archaeology Emeritus in the Department of Anthropology, Harvard University, and honorary curator of North American archaeology and ethnology at Harvard's Peabody Museum. He received his Ph.D. in anthropology from Yale University in 1954. His archaeological research has focused on the southeastern United States, and he is currently researching and writing about the history of North American archaeology.

Melinda A. Zeder is curator of Old World archaeology and zooarchaeology and a member of the Smithsonian Institution's Archaeobiology Program in the Department of Anthropology. She received her Ph.D. from the University of Michigan in 1985. Her research interests include the domestication of animals and the social and environmental consequences of early agriculture in the ancient Near East.

INDEX